The Conquest of Ruins

The Conquest of Ruins

The Third Reich and the Fall of Rome

JULIA HELL

The University of Chicago Press   Chicago and London

The University of Chicago Press, Chicago 60637
The University of Chicago Press, Ltd., London

Published 2019
Printed in the United States of America

28 27 26 25 24 23 22 21 20 19   1 2 3 4 5

ISBN-13: 978-0-226-58805-6 (cloth)
ISBN-13: 978-0-226-58819-3 (paper)
ISBN-13: 978-0-226-58822-3 (e-book)
DOI: https://doi.org/10.7208/chicago/9780226588223.001.0001

Library of Congress Cataloging-in-Publication Data
Names: Hell, Julia, author.
Title: The conquest of ruins : The Third Reich and the fall of Rome / Julia Hell.
Description: Chicago : The University of Chicago Press, 2018. | Includes bibliographical references and index.
Identifiers: LCCN 2018010427 | ISBN 9780226588056 (cloth : alk. paper) | ISBN 9780226588193 (pbk. : alk. paper) | ISBN 9780226588223 (e-book)
Subjects: LCSH: National socialism and archaeology. | Germany—Civilization—20th century—Roman influences. | Europe—Civilization—Roman influences. | Excavations (Archaeology)—Political aspects—Germany—History—20th century. | Imitation—Political aspects—Germany. | Germany—History—1933–1945. | Imperialism—History.
Classification: LCC DD256.6 .H45 2018 | DDC 937/.09—dc23
LC record available at https://lccn.loc.gov/2018010427

♾ This paper meets the requirements of ANSI/NISO Z39.48-1992 (Permanence of Paper).

To George, as always

and

Franz Hell (1930–2010)

and Waltraut Hell-Scherschlicht (1932–2012),

in memoriam

Contents

Acknowledgments

After having written about ruins in the twentieth-century German context, I decided in 2009 to write a book on the connection of ruins to empire that would take me back to ancient Rome. In the years I spent researching and writing this book, many colleagues and friends shared their expertise and knowledge. For this generosity I would like to thank Vanessa Agnew, Kerstin Barndt, Duncan Bell, Matthew Biro, Kathleen Coleman, Derek Collins, Basil Dufallo, Geoff Eley, Andreas Gailus, Danny Herwitz, Alan Itkin, Kader Konuk, Amy Kulper, Gina Morantz-Sanchez, Dirk Moses, David Potter, Helmut Puff, Rick Rentschler, Anton Shamas, and Johannes von Moltke. I also relied on two very skilled research assistants, Kathryn Sederberg and Naomi Vaughan, who helped me greatly at various stages of the research.

There are friends and colleagues without whose thoughts and encouragement it would have been much harder and much less exciting to write this book. In the course of the seminar I taught with my former colleague, Andreas Schönle, and the conference on the *Ruins of Modernity* that we organized together, I realized I was a ruinologist at heart. I was extraordinarily lucky to meet François Hartog during my year at the Michigan Institute for the Humanities at a time when I was starting to rethink my book as a project crossing the antiquity/modernity divide. Finally, I wish to express my deep gratitude to Susan Siegfried and Alex Potts for their many helpful suggestions, and patience in dealing with the questions of an outsider snooping around on their turf.

The University of Chicago Press turned out to be the right home for my baroque postclassicist book. Without Doug

Mitchell's enthusiasm and unwavering support over many years, I would not have conquered my ruins. I am also grateful to Kyle Wagner and Michael Koplow for their expert, often last-minute help. If I still had one of the Stakhanov medals I bought in Berlin in 1989, I would gladly give it to Marianne Tatom. For her editing, Marianne has my eternal gratitude. And so does my other editor, Dr. Lena Theodorou Ehrlich, for all of her hard archeological labor.

George Steinmetz, my dear companion and fearless colleague, accompanied me through the writing and rewriting of the book, encouraging me to stick to my project and ideas and adding books and articles to the piles accumulating around us. That and our long conversation about empires and imperialism, colonialism and the state, culture and politics, political and cultural theory, and a thousand other things made writing this book immensely enjoyable. And I am still not bored.

Parts of the book build on previously published materials. Chapter 22 draws on my contribution for *Ruins of Modernity* (Duke University Press, 2009), entitled "Imperial Ruin Gazers, or Why Did Scipio Weep?" In chapter 24, I worked with material from "*Katechon*: Carl Schmitt's Imperial Theology and the Ruins of the Future," *Germanic Review: Literature, Culture, Theory*, volume 84.4 (Fall 2009): 283–326. The book's epilogue relies on "The Twin Towers of Anselm Kiefer and the Trope of Imperial Decline," *Germanic Review: Literature, Culture, Theory* 84.1 (Winter 2009): 84–93.

Abbreviations

AFa: Virgil, *The Aeneid,* translated by Robert Fagles
AFi: Virgil, *The Aeneid,* translated by Robert Fitzgerald
AGI, AGII: Friedrich Ratzel, *Anthropo-Geographie,* 2 vols.
BC: Martin Heidegger, *Basic Concepts*
BWW: Carl Schmitt, "Beschleuniger wider Willen"
C: Augustine, *Concerning the City of God against the Pagans*
CW: Lucan, *The Pharsalia* (also *The Civil War*)
DFI, DFII, DFIII: Edward Gibbon, *The History of the Decline and Fall of the Roman Empire,* 3 vols.
DI, DII: Oswald Spengler, *The Decline of the West,* 2 vols.
DW: Gottfried Benn, "Dorische Welt: Eine Untersuchung über die Beziehung von Kunst und Macht"
FE: Georg Forster, *A Voyage Round the World,* 2 vols.
FG: Georg Forster, *Reise um die Welt*
FP: Jean-Baptiste-Joseph Fourier, "Préface historique" to *Description de L'Égypte*
G1, G2: Pausanias, *Guide to Greece,* 2 vols.
GO: Carl Schmitt, "Völkerrechtliche Großraumordnung"
GRA: Wilhelm Jensen, *Gradiva: A Pompeiian Fancy*
GV: Werner Best, "Grundfragen einer deutschen Grossraum-Verwaltung"
H: Oswald Spengler, *The Hour of Decision*
HS: Anonymous (Werner Best), "Herrenschicht oder Führungsvolk?"
I: Johann Gottfried Herder, *Ideen zur Philosophie der Geschichte der Menschheit*
J: Flavius Josephus, *The Jewish War* (*Bellum Judaicum*)
KM: Gottfried Benn, "Kunst und Macht"
L: Carl Schmitt, *Land und Meer* (1942)
MK: Adolf Hitler, *Mein Kampf* (1942)
MKe: Adolf Hitler, *Mein Kampf,* translated by Ralph Manheim

OU: Friedrich Nietzsche, "On the Uses and Disadvantages of History for Life"
PR: Heinrich Himmler, "Rede des Reichsführers SS bei der SS-Gruppenführertagung in Posen am 4. Oktober 1943"
R: Polybios, *The Rise of the Roman Empire*
RE: Constantin-François de Volney, *The Ruins, or, Meditations on the Revolutions of Empire*
RI: Carl Schmitt, "Raumrevolution: vom Geist des Abendlandes" (1942)
RII: Carl Schmitt, "Die Raumrevolution: durch den totalen Krieg zu einem totalen Frieden" (1940)
RR: Joseph Vogt, *Vom Reichsgedanken der Römer*
SD: Albert Speer, *Spandau: The Secret Diaries*
SM: Albert Speer, *Inside the Third Reich: Memoirs*
ST: Albert Speer, *Spandauer Tagebücher*
T: Giorgio Agamben, *The Time That Remains*
U: Oswald Spengler, *Der Untergang des Abendlandes: Umrisse einer Morphologie der Weltgeschichte*
UL: Friedrich Nietzsche, "The Utility and Liability of History for Life"
ÜVII: Martin Heidegger, *Überlegungen VII–XI (Schwarze Hefte 1939–1941)*
ÜXII: Martin Heidegger, *Überlegungen XII–XV (Schwarze Hefte 1939–1941)*

Introduction: Neo-Roman Mimesis and the Law of Ruin

The danger of imitation is terrible. FRANÇOIS-RENÉ DE CHATEAUBRIAND (1797)[1]

One thought alone preoccupies the submerged mind of Empire: how not to end, how not to die, how to prolong its era. By day it pursues its enemies . . . By night it feeds on images of disaster: the sack of cities, the rape of populations, pyramids of bones, acres of desolation.
J. M. COETZEE, *WAITING FOR THE BARBARIANS* (1997)

"Ancient Rome is important." With this wry statement, Mary Beard opens her history of the city.[2] That French revolutionaries masqueraded as Romans was Marx's famous claim in *The Eighteenth Brumaire* (1852). Marx knew that Saint-Just had called on his fellow-revolutionaries to "be Romans,"[3] declaring: "The world has been empty since the Romans, and only their memory fills it."[4] Distinguishing between the French and American revolutions, between "founding 'Rome anew'" versus "founding a 'new Rome,'" Hannah Arendt too quoted Saint-Just's statement.[5] Establishing *a new Rome* was the project of the American revolutionaries, who came to understand that "the thread of continuity" tying Western politics to Rome's founding was irrevocably "broken."[6]

Privileging the American over the French Revolution, Arendt was blind to the imperial project that was part of the

American republic's foundation.[7] As an imperial power, the United States joined its European predecessors in the imitation of Rome. In recent years modernists started debating whether the United States had become a world empire.[8] With this question in mind, political theorists and historians quickly turned to the comparison with the Roman Empire. Charles Maier put it this way: "Might the United States become an empire? We shall have to return to Rome."[9] Among modernists, these debates also led to a renewed focus on the rewriting of world history in terms of empire.[10] Once more "Rome's empire," as the classicist Catharine Edwards noted, "continues to be irresistible."[11] Other classicists contributed to these debates and the renewed interest in the history and theory of empires by publishing political and cultural histories of the Roman Empire, reflecting on how the Roman model was used "into more recent times."[12]

In this context, Sheldon Pollock argued that it is in the nature of empires to imitate.[13] That the West imitated Rome, thus creating the ancient empire as "the supreme expression of imperial power," is the basic premise of this book.[14] My admittedly imprudent goal is to reconstruct and analyze the long afterlife of the Roman Empire as Western Europe's history of neo-Roman mimesis.[15] I trace this cultural history of political acts and the wide array of aesthetic, performative, and architectural practices of imitation that emerge around these acts by singling out specific cases of neo-Roman empire-making, starting with the Tunisian Campaign of Charles V in 1535 and ending with the Nazi empire's eastward expansion.

Each particular moment in the long European history of imitating Rome generated its own mimetic practices as well as a vast body of texts reflecting on the history and theory of Roman and neo-Roman empires. My central claim, however, is that all these acts of neo-Roman mimesis and the imperial imaginaries that they engendered have one thing in common: they revolved around what I call the scenario of imperial ruin gazing, a scopic scenario visualizing the end of the Roman Empire.[16] The reason for this obsession with Rome's ruins is obvious: if we think of European empires as neo-Roman empires, then mimetic desire—the desire to make the self in the image of the other—becomes problematic, because this desire confronts a lack, a failure, a death—the fall of the Roman Empire.

This obsession with the empire's end did not begin with Rome's imitators. On the contrary, the idea of the empire's inevitable end arose at the very moment when the Roman Empire established its hegemony in the Mediterranean. Ruin gazer scenarios, we will find, kept alive the haunting story of imperial rise and fall, empire-building and ruination—in the Roman past and in the neo-Roman present. Centered on empire's ruined theo-political stage, they also relentlessly conjured the threat of the barbarian enemy, scanning the ruins of the post-Roman future. There is no Western empire without ruins, there are no ruins without "barbarians,"[17] and there is no imperial imaginary without ruin gazer scenarios.

Moreover, imperial leaders and theorists of empire kept reflecting on the meaning of Rome's ruinous end. In the imagination of Western Europe's political and intellectual elites, this model empire, whose history of permanent warfare is all too often left unmentioned,[18] is thus at once triumphantly powerful *and* a remarkably fragile fabrication, a monumental memory-fortress *and* a vast ruinscape that continues to exert pressure on our ways of thinking about empire.[19]

Writing the first and, by necessity, fragmentary history of neo-Roman mimesis in the West, I will reconstruct and analyze the many different ways in which Europeans connected empire to ruins. More specifically, I trace neo-Roman mimesis across multiple levels by always returning to the ruin scenarios circling through these practices and discourses. Operating in the endzone, political leaders, theorists, and artists went in search of strategies that would fortify their post-Roman empires. The Romans' monumentalizing empire-making—their imperial architecture and arts, performances, and political, literary, and theoretical texts—prestructured the processes of imitation. From this ancient world-making, Rome emerged as the empire's ruined stage, Augustus as imperial sovereign demanding to be imitated, the barbarian as the political enemy, realism as the aesthetic mode of mimesis and the imperial imaginary—and, ultimately, ruin gazer scenarios as power structures in need of constant fortification.

"Empire is born and shows itself as crisis."[20] Exploring the works of imperial theorists who reflected on the meaning of Rome's ruinous end for the post-Roman present is one of the major strands of my analytical narrative. Unraveling this intellectual history as the intertwined story of political theory and ruin gazer scenarios, I begin with the Roman Empire and one of the empire's first theorists, Polybios, the Greco-Roman historian who was present at the demolition of Carthage in 146 BCE, and end with the Nazi empire and one of its main theorists, Carl Schmitt.[21] One of my overarching goals is to analyze the specificity of both the Third Reich, an empire of "horrible originality,"[22] and Schmitt's *katechontic* theory of empire, a theory developed in hindsight in the ruins of the Third Reich.

The Conquest of Ruins thus connects *imperium studies* (as the analysis of Rome's afterlife) to *ruin studies* (as the analysis of the concept, politics, and aesthetics of Roman ruins).[23] By approaching the study of empire through the dual lens of *imperium-cum-*ruin studies, we understand how the West's model empire functioned as a ruined stage, how the West's mimetic conquest of this ruined stage worked, and what exactly this stage-in-ruins meant for theories of empire and neo-Roman imaginaries. Moreover, this perspective allows me to excavate the proper genealogy for the ruin-obsession that characterized the neo-Roman Nazi empire.[24] And finally, it sheds light on two characteristics of Europe's theorists of empire, their obsession with empire's time and sympathies for the politics of the so-called conservative revolution.

Instead of using this introduction to present the overall structure of the book, I will discuss the claims that I made above in more depth by explaining my understanding of the key concepts—mimesis, scopic scenario, imaginary, resurrectional realism—and introducing my methodological and theoretical approach. Outlining the overall structure of *The Conquest of Ruins*, the prefaces to each part substitute for chapter summaries. The book is organized chronologically, moving from imperial Rome to Spanish, British, French, and then German cases of neo-Roman mimesis.[25] Given the length of the book and its nature as a sustained argument, I opted for a style that contains considerable signposting. While this inevitably produces a certain amount of repetition, it also allows for a selective reading of the book.[26]

The Law of Ruin

By engaging in the analytical reconstruction of a deep history of imitations and the scenarios that constitute its hard, resistant core, I propose to analyze a particular history of *ruinography*. I want to begin my reflections on the dangers of neo-Roman mimesis by turning to the immediate aftermath of the Third Reich and a cursory glance at the work of three thinkers: Albert Speer, Hitler's architect and armaments minister; Hannah Arendt, the exiled political philosopher; and Rose Macaulay, the author of *Pleasure of Ruins* (1953). What unites these very different people is a preoccupation not only with ruinous endings but with the very *law of ruin*, which each of them defines in their own more or less idiosyncratic way.

In August 1948, Albert Speer revisited *Germania*, the Third Reich's new metropole whose construction began in 1938 and was supposed to be completed by 1950. More precisely, Speer spent an entire month as an inmate in the Spandau prison working on a drawing showing the Great Hall, which his plans had located at one end of the north-south axis opposite Berlin's new Arch of Triumph. Speer's and Hitler's plans were inspired by Rome: the avenue was a *via triumphalis* lined with military objects captured from the *Reich*'s enemies, and their Great Hall, designed for mass meetings, was a version of the Pantheon.[27] As "an architectural stage set of imperial majesty," *Germania* was built with the proportions of the future empire in mind.[28] The metropolis was also built to last: the triumphal arch would be made of granite, and the Great Hall paved in granite. Yet what Speer drew in minutest detail was not the Great Hall as it had been shown in numerous models starting in 1940, but a ruined structure adjacent to a massive fortress-like building (figure 0.1). In the caption to the drawing, Speer mentioned that the columns of the Great Hall's portico measured thirty meters and added: "I thus imagined it as a ruin."[29]

The drawing's affinity to Piranesi's depictions of ruins in his *Le Antichità Romane* (1756) is hard to miss. Piranesi often combined two things: scenes of Roman ruins "viewed at an angle" and from a vanishing point that heightens the effect of their monumentality.[30] Speer echoes this staging of ruins. The drawing shows Speer and his wife, sitting in the foreground with their backs turned to the beholder, their heads covered with black shrouds.[31] Their gaze is directed at the ruins of the Great Hall (the structure at the far right of the image, to the right of the columns), not the so-called *Führerbau*. Towering slightly to their left, the Roman-style fortress of the *Führerbau* is drawn at an angle and set behind the massive columns of the Great Hall. Like Piranesi, Speer thus emphasized the monumentality of the barely damaged *Führerbau* and the columns of the Great Hall, and he reinforced the stagelike quality of the artist's views of ruined Rome by introducing surrogate spectators.

Speer's amateurish take on Piranesi is both fascinating and repellant. Repellant, because here is Hitler's armaments minister, mourning the end of the Nazi empire and his own fall from power. Fascinating, because we see an architect contemplating ruins who is known not only for his neo-Roman architecture but also for his "law of ruins."[32] This "law" meant that the ruins of Speer's buildings would one day resemble those of ancient Rome, and that future generations of Germans would be gazing at these ruins.

Speer's image thus realized the neo-Roman future that he and Hitler had anticipated—a Great Hall and an entire imperial metropolis in ruins that were as awe-inspiring as those left by Rome. Yet, as we know, this hall had never been built, and the Nazis' neo-Roman empire had disappeared from the face of the earth much faster than Hitler, Speer, or any other Nazi had anticipated. Still participating in the Nazis' project of Roman mimesis, Speer thus represents an anticipated future—the empire's end in ruins—as the recent past.[33] In his later memoirs, Speer analyzed the Third Reich as a decaying Roman Empire.[34]

While Speer spent his time reproducing ruins and commonplaces

0.1 Albert Speer. Ruin drawing (1948).

about Nazis and Romans, Hannah Arendt, the exiled philosopher, embarked on her project to understand the Third Reich, which she thought of as an "unexpected" event.[35] Arendt made three points, all having to do with her understanding of what constitutes the singularity of historical events. First, the true meaning of historical events cannot be understood if we explain them with insights won from the study of past events. Like totalitarianism, imperialism was one such unprecedented event. Comparing modern imperialism to Roman "empire-building" and Cecil Rhodes to Caesar would lead one to misunderstand the motives driving nineteenth-century imperialism as a Roman "lust for conquest."[36] Arendt's second thesis was that every historical event "illuminates its own past" and "can never be deduced from it."[37]

Understanding an event like National Socialism is the very precondition of politics, the "conscious beginning of something new," and that is what really mattered to Arendt.[38] Augustine, the Carthaginian theologian, "discovered" how important new beginnings are, while living in a moment which "resembled our own more than any other in recorded history."[39] Comparing the end of the Roman Empire to the end of the Third Reich, Arendt thus risked returning to the Roman past. Quoting Augustine on natality, she observed that the Carthaginian Roman "wrote under the full impact of a catastrophic end" (that is, the sacking of Rome in 410).[40]

This end, Arendt continued with some caution, "perhaps resembles the end to which we have come."[41]

Arendt thus engaged in the very practice that she had criticized, that is, the comparison between new and old events, modern imperialism and the Roman Empire.[42] She believed that the Third Reich was not an *imperium* driven by the desire for conquest but a new form of political rule, whose iron ideology was organized around a single idea, race.[43] Deducing all politics from one single idea was the ultimate form of determinism. And determinism as the anticipation of the future, deduced from the past, is Arendt's version of the "law of ruin":

> In so far as life is decline which ultimately leads to death, it can be foretold. In a dissolving society which blindly follows *the natural course of ruin*, catastrophe can be foreseen. Only salvation, not ruin, comes unexpectedly, for salvation and not ruin, depends upon the liberty and will of men.[44]

These reflections on *the course of ruin* were part of an essay on Kafka, in which Arendt praised the writer for having analyzed the "underlying structures which today have come into the open."[45] With an eye toward her analysis of totalitarian forms of rule, Arendt wrote: "These ruinous structures were supported, and the process of ruin itself accelerated, by the belief, almost universal in his time, in a necessary and automatic process to which man must submit."[46] As "functionar[ies] of necessity," Nazis and their collaborators were "agent[s] of the *natural law of ruin*."[47]

Elaborating on this analysis of the logic of determinism, Arendt took her ruin imagery further, using an analogy of man-made building to man-made world:[48] "Just as a house which has been abandoned by men to its natural fate will slowly follow *the course of ruin* which somehow is *inherent in all human work*, so surely the world, fabricated by men and constituted according to human and not natural laws, will become again part of nature and will follow the *law of ruin* when man decides to become himself a part of nature."[49] That is, "renouncing his supreme faculty of creating laws himself and even prescribing them to nature."[50] There is thus a law of ruin—or "Ruinanz," in Heidegger's early terminology—and a law of new beginnings, foundational acts that break with nature's cycle of decay.[51] In *The Origins of Totalitarianism*, Arendt specifically addressed the trope of "rise and fall" as the defining feature of fascist "ideology," a "historical" way of thinking "concerned with becoming and perishing" that is "never interested in the miracle of being."[52]

While Arendt fled from Paris to New York, thinking and writing about her present, Rose Macaulay lived in wartime London, thinking and writing about the ruins of the European past. Writing what she called her "perverse" book, Macaulay formulated her own law of ruins.[53] Or, more precisely, her ruin laws, the first of which—that ruins are symbols of all "things 'going to earth'"—was rather conventional.[54] The second law combines the familiar and the new: the pleasure we experience at the sight of ruins, Macaulay wrote, is rooted in nostalgia *and* in our "destruction seeking souls."[55] "Ruinenlust" is thus a problematic pleasure—the pleasure associated with what Arendt called the lust of conquest.[56] Universalizing human destructiveness, Macaulay developed something akin to a religious anthropology of ruin gazing. Surrounded by the ruins and rubble of London, she also reaffirmed neoclassicist aesthetics, anchoring her version in the theology not of Augustine, but of St. Thomas Aquinas.

Concluding her history of ruin gazing with the "new ruins" of World War II, Macaulay wrote that the pleasure in ruins "has come full circle: we have had our fill."[57] Ruin gazing was always linked to a particular kind of nostalgia: the desire to see the ancient cities intact as they once were, but "broken beauty is all we have" and these fragments from the past are what "we cherish."[58] In 1945, there is no broken beauty. Europe's bombed cathedrals leave only "resentful sadness."[59] Paradoxically these new ruins remind us, she argued, what beauty is truly about: the un-destroyed, the unharmed—objects that are whole. Like Arendt, Macaulay was invested in new beginnings but to her, new beginnings required the revival of neoclassicist aesthetics with a theological grounding. What her experience with the Nazis' unfettered *Ruinenlust* taught her was that "[r]uin pleasure must be at one remove, softened by art" and the passing of time.[60] London's ruins taught her that St. Thomas Aquinas was correct in writing "that, in beauty, wholeness is all."[61] Beauty resides in wholeness, not the ruinous fragment.

Macaulay's book on the aesthetics of ruins is thus a political book, but perhaps more political and differently enmeshed in politics than she intended. *Pleasure of Ruins* is a history of ruin aesthetics *and* a survey of the world's ruins from Rome, Egypt, and Greece to wartime England. With this survey Macaulay made Europe's noble ruins once more visible against the background of the jagged, burned-out ruinscapes of the war.[62] It is above all Rome's imperial ruins that attract her attention. This is less a nostalgic gesture than a defiant one. Tracing the ruin-strewn borders of the Roman Mediterranean, Macaulay rescued the remnants of European Greco-Roman culture at a moment when "everything seemed to have come to an end,"[63] wresting European Greco-Roman civilization and its "shattered heritage" from the new barbarians, from men like Speer in Germany and Mussolini in Italy.[64]

Like Speer's memoirs or Arendt's *Origins* or Macaulay's *Pleasure*, *The Conquest of Ruins* is a book about the law of ruin.[65] Or, more precisely, it is a book about imperial administrators, theorists, and artists who seem to return again and again to the question of whether there is a law of ruin at work in all imperial projects—Roman and neo-Roman. Is the act of imitating Rome lethal, they wonder, or is there a possibility of repetition-with-a-difference—a form of mimesis that breaks the cycle, a modern form of building, thinking, and imagining empire that is stable and enduring?

The Greek historian and theorist of empire who posed this question about the course of empire was Polybios. Writing about the rise of Rome, the Punic Wars, and the destruction of Carthage, Polybios reflected in his *Histories* on the natural law of ruin and visualized it in the ruin gazer scenario, with which he concluded his text (see chapter 1).[66] I consider this text and this scenario as a kind of *ur-text* and *ur-scene* of the European discourse, theory, and critique of neo-Roman mimesis. Freud taught us to be suspicious of *ur-scenes*, and I use the word in Arendt's sense, that is, her claim that historical events *create* their past, their points of origin. What I mean by this is the following: with each act of Roman mimesis, neo-Roman conquerors, theorists, and artists will obsessively return to Polybios's scene and frequently to his text, thus *creating* the *ur-scene* of Western imperialism. Yet, as I wrote above, neo-Romans were not the first ones to do so. Augustan authors like Virgil had already reflected on Polybios's scene and its meaning for understanding the logic of empire.

Polybios's *natural law* is the law that Arendt and Macaulay wrote about in the wake of the Third Reich: that all things eventually perish—including the Roman Empire.[67] And Polybios was able to grasp the history and something about the essence of this empire, looking back from the vantage point of Carthage, that is, the moment that constituted the end of Rome's ascendancy to hegemony in the Mediterranean. What Polybios understood, he condensed in his scenario, depicting Scipio the Younger overlooking the burning rubble of Carthage and wondering whether he was witness to Rome's future. Staging the Roman conqueror, the general given *imperium* or command, this Carthaginian scenario is about the relentlessness and violence of imperial expansion; it is about the barbarian and the barbarian's revenge, and it is about inexorable imperial endings.[68] Most crucially, what Polybios inscribed in this scenario is his understanding of imperial time as the time before the end—*the time that remains*.[69]

Scipio at Carthage is a scenario that *visualizes* imperial endtime and the violence of conquest. In Polybios's scenario, there are no ruins yet, only Carthage's rubble, signifiers of imperial violence. It will be the work of Roman authors and architects to create this object of awed contemplation, the majestic ruins of the Roman Empire. As I will discuss in part 1, the architectural remodeling of imperial Rome in the age of Augustus coincided with the invention of its ruins. In other words, I dispute the claim that the concept of Rome's sublime imperial ruins arose only with the Renaissance's "re-discovery" of the city.

Neo-Roman Mimesis: A Model

The Conquest of Ruins is a cultural and intellectual history of neo-Roman mimesis, a study of a particular history of *ruinography*. In this section I will elaborate on my concept of imperial mimesis and the ways in which my model is closely linked to the concept of the (neo)Roman imaginary centered on scenes of ruin gazing. In *The Conquest of Ruins, I e*xplore the nexus between the production of Roman and neo-Roman imperial imaginaries *and* a particular *topos*: the end of the Roman Empire in ruins—an end located, for the Romans, in the future, and for the neo-Romans, in the future past. Ruin gazer scenarios visually crystallized this *topos*. Roman and neo-Roman imperial imaginaries are thus always already *ruinous* imaginaries, and like ruin gazer scenarios they have a scenographic structure. This theatrical structure has its roots in the Romans' imperial politics as spectacle.

In *Roman Social Imaginaries: Language and Thought in Contexts of Empire* (2015), Clifford Ando starts his investigation into the legal and political language of the Roman Empire with an interesting thesis: "the realities created by imperial political and juridical action raced ahead of linguistic-cognitive apparatus and assumptions of homeomorphy between the geographic extension of political communities and territorial reach of their jurisdictions began to break down."[70] In other words, as Rome expanded into the Mediterranean, a whole new language and vocabulary had to be created, a process that resulted among other things in the gradual change of the meaning of *imperium* or notions of Roman citizenship. Drawing on Charles Taylor's *Modern Social Imaginaries*, Ando summarizes the latter's project as an inquiry into the common "background understanding behind practice" in order to arrive at a fuller depiction of the "thought-world" of Western modernity.[71] Ando shares with Taylor the project of exploring this background to propositional statements but diverges methodologically by exploring the "birth, development, and naturalization (or death, if you will) of specific figures, or changes in the metonymic reach of certain clusters."[72]

Neo-Roman empires seem to invert Ando's thesis about the relationship between imperial expansion and the conceptual apparatus of empire. Here, instead of the political reality speeding ahead of the linguistic-cognitive apparatus, the political reality of conquest comes with a look backward at the Roman model. But even this picture is a bit too simple. Empires are not founded by one single military-political act; rather, empires take shape retroactively as an accumulation of conquests.[73] Yet each one of these conquests, involving the military invasion of hitherto unoccupied territory, marks a "beginning," in the sense that Arendt used this word.[74] Distinguishing the French from the American Revolution, Arendt argued that the latter event constituted a genuine beginning because the American revolutionaries understood that "what saves the act of beginning from its own arbitrariness is that it carries its own principle within itself."[75] As she defines this identity of beginning and principle, Arendt first reaches back to the Latin word *principium* as meaning both source and principle, and then quotes Polybios: "the beginning is not merely half of the whole but reaches out towards the end."[76]

I use Arendt's idea of beginning to describe the nature of *neo-Roman* imperial conquests, a revisionist use that Arendt might have resisted.[77] That is, acts of neo-Roman conquest are moments when neo-Roman rulers and their theorists, historians, and artists looked back at Rome to find the *principle* of their imperial beginnings. Struggling with "the perplexities of beginning as they appear in the very act of foundation," these neo-Roman conquerors and their theorists all converged on the same principle or "absolute from which the beginning is to derive its validity": the Roman idea of *humanitas* or the West's civilizing mission.[78] They also discovered the actors in this story, the Roman conqueror/sovereign and the conquered "barbarian." And, turning their eyes to the distant and not-so-distant past, neo-Roman rulers and imperial theorists deciphered two Roman laws. The first was the imperative to expand relentlessly, first formulated by Virgil in his Augustan epic as *imperium sine fine*. The second law these neo-Roman conquerors and intellectuals discovered was Polybios's law of ruin. The Roman Empire developed its imaginaries catching up with its own military conquests and bursts of empire-building. In the case of neo-Roman empires, this logic is reversed. Creating something new, they looked back in time as they set out to conquer—and in the course of conquest they developed imaginaries centered on Rome's ruins as signifiers of the empire's power and its death.

The Conquest of Ruins begins with the Romans' conquest of Carthage in 146 BCE and ends with the Nazi empire's failed expansion into Eastern Europe. Clearly, there is no way *The Conquest of Ruins* could cover the entire history of Western European neo-Roman mimesis. I selected a number of salient cases of neo-Roman conquest, all but one concentrating on the Mediterranean space.[79] So let me revise the above claim: beginning with Rome's rise to hegemony in the wake of the Punic Wars, and the creation of the Augustan Empire, I organize the reconstruction of European imperialism's imitation of ancient Rome and Europe's ruinous imaginary around particular moments of conquest: Charles V and the conquest of Tunis in 1535;[80] Cook's exploratory voyages to the South Pacific; the French invasion of Egypt in 1798 and conquest of Algeria in 1830; the *Kaiserreich*'s brief period of colonial ventures at the end of the nineteenth century, Italy's conquest of North African territory in the 1930s, and finally, the frenzied rush of the Third Reich's eastward expansion.[81]

I thus reconstruct the European history of neo-Roman mimesis as a series of historical snapshots, a trajectory that meanders across national boundaries.[82] Each of the six cases of neo-Roman mimesis is an act of conquest and, thus, a new beginning. For instance, while Spain had already conquered territory in the New World and elsewhere, the military campaign in North Africa was a new venture. In the case of the French Empire, I will argue, Napoleon's failed conquest of Egypt was stage one of modern French empire-building, followed by the successful military conquest of Algeria. Or, to add a final example, the German *Kaiserreich* was the era when Germany acquired its colonies in rapid bursts of conquests.[83]

I propose a model of neo-Roman mimesis as a political and aesthetic practice that essentially consists of five parts.[84] This practice involves first acts of imitation that are imperial in nature, for instance, Napoleon's Egyptian Campaign in 1798 as a repetition of Augustus's conquest of Egypt. Second, mimesis as the imitation of Rome refers to the neo-Roman ruler's mimicry of the Roman model as a *public* act, either in the form of public declaration or as a performance on the Roman stage. This latter act of imitation brings me to my third point: moments of neo-Roman conquests come with the refashioning of an entire culture as neo-Roman. That is, they initiate the elaborate imitation of the ancient empire's imperial culture, its texts and images, its architecture and imperial spectacles. Neo-Roman mimesis thus covers both the political act of mimicry and the aesthetic practices and techniques of mimesis, the first impossible without the second.

On the one hand, these mimetic practices and discourses constructed the ancient empire as all-powerful. On the other hand, the rulers, theorists, and artists also invent their own stories about Rome's end—stories about its decline, or sudden fall, and so forth. The imitation of the Roman model—and I will repeat this throughout the book—always eventually becomes an encounter with Rome's death. In chapter 6, I analyze the conqueror's act of imitation of the Roman model as a series of (symbolic) identifications analogous to the Roman custom of actors wearing death masks at aristocratic funerals. This performative mimetic act responds to the desire of the past, a desire for recognition *and* imitation that the realist texts and visual arts of the Augustan era articulated. This encounter with the Roman model, and this is my fourth point, produced the West's ruin gazer scenarios. Fifth, in the encounter with Rome's end, imperial rulers, administrators, theorists, and artists developed strategies of postponing the empire's end.

Ruin gazer scenarios not only shadow these acts of conquests as imperial rulers, administrators, political theorists, and artists reflect on them; they are also frequently inscribed into public performances of mimesis. Representing in condensed form what is at the core of the practices and representations of neo-Roman mimesis—the staging of the Roman ruler/conqueror looking at the ruined Roman stage—they crystallize the tensions at the heart of the imitation of Rome.

Scopic Scenarios: The Politics of Spectacle and the Roman Stage

I want to begin the discussion of the key concepts involved in this model of neo-Roman mimesis—mimesis, imaginary, and the ruin gazer scenario—with an explanation of my concept of the *scopic scenario*. The word *scene* refers us to theater and the conceptual apparatus of psychoanalysis, spectacle, and the *mise-en-scène* of desire, in which acts of looking/being looked at play a crucial role. *Scopic scenario* is a concept that brings these two aspects together. Scenarios are visual "scripts" consisting of "organized scenes which are capable of dramatization."[85] *Scopic* refers to Freud's reflections on the "scopophilic drive" and (post)Freudian discussions of scopic mastery, or the urgent desire to see and the equally urgent desire for mastery over what is seen and the act of seeing itself.[86]

Polybios's Carthaginian scene does not only visualize endtime. This scopic scenario also hinted at the barbarian enemy *and* it structures acts of looking. This structuring in turn visualizes imperial power relations. In Polybios's scenario and the many variations of it that we will encounter, one of the main things at stake is *scopic mastery*: a constellation that keeps the (neo)Roman sovereign, the imperial subject, not the subjected barbarian, in the position of the one who is looking at the ruins of empire—or in the position of the one who is looking at the barbarian, looking.[87]

Ruins are odd objects, since they are both present and absent, provoking us to complete them by intuiting their former shape. More than any other object, ruins push scopic desire into overdrive, "a kind of scopic rush," as the subject's eyes scrutinize the contours of the visible and are obsessively drawn to the almost-visible.[88] With ruins something always threatens to escape the subject's gaze, and because of this threat, ruins lend a particular urgency to the desire for scopic mastery. I refer to the attainment of scopic mastery as *fortification* of the gaze. Ruin gazer scenarios stage the fortified imperial gaze, the gaze that masters the elusive object of the ruin and what it signifies: the end of empire, empire as endtime.

Ruin gazer scenarios are thus first scopic regimes in miniature, staging and ordering acts of looking, scopic desire, and power.[89] Second, they are part of a political imaginary that is grounded in the performance space of Greek and Roman theaters. On the most basic level, *scene* (or *scaena* in Latin) refers to performance space. The word is derived from the Greek word *skene*, the scene-building representing the house of death and the house of the sovereign on the stages of imperial Athens. Greco-Roman culture is ocularcentric, a culture based in an empiricist epistemology that asserts the nexus of seeing and knowing and is committed to a form of aesthetics that renders the world visible. The subject of this culture is a self that is invested in seeing and aware of being seen, of existing under the gaze of the gods.[90]

So what does it mean to claim that ruin gazer scenarios are part of a politics of spectacle? These scenarios belong to an imperial culture in which metropolitan Rome with its theo-political architecture functioned as a stage. Moreover, Polybios wrote the scenario as if it were a scene taking place on the Greco-Roman stage where the scene-building functioned as a site of sovereignty. The theatrical *mise-en-scène* of Polybios's Carthaginian scenario and the later Roman ruin gazer scenarios reference this Roman stage metonymically as the scene-building. Later manifestations of the scenario, Roman and neo-Roman, preserved this connection to the Greco-Roman stage architecture. Scopic regimes visualizing time and thematizing mastery, they are also scenographic in nature.

Polybios not only put his Carthaginian scenario onstage, however; he also operated with the metaphor of history as spectacle. This historical spectacle was Rome's spectacular rise to hegemony, a rise resulting in the creation of Rome as the empire's monumental stage at the time of Augustus. This extensive remodeling program *visibly* articulated the imperial order around Augustan Rome as the empire's sacred center from which this new, ever-expanding imperial world was ruled—a center whose monumentality was meant to signify the unlimited duration of Rome's rule. Representing the locus of imperial sovereignty, the Augustan stage was the site where the theatrical *mise-en-scène* of imperial power was performed. Rome's emperors and the empire's aristocratic elite saw themselves as actors on this stage, performing "'in *scaena*,'" for the eyes of "all the citizens" and all of the empire's "nations."[91] All of this—the architectural remodeling under Augustus, the political ceremonies, the triumphs, and so on—I will discuss in chapter 2. At the very center of this stage stood Augustus's Mausoleum, its entrance decorated with the *Res Gestae Divi Augusti*, the script for European empire-making that will be rewritten again and again.

To think of history as drama and of Rome as the empire's stage also means to think of the world in empiricist terms—if we understand empiricism as that epistemology which makes us conceive of the world as visible and understandable through observation.[92] These scenographic Roman practices thus produced a spatio-temporal imaginary that mobilized the desire to see, making great men, their deeds and their enemies, and the world in which they acted visible. With an eye on this scenographic architecture of power and the main actors of this new imperial spectacle, Virgil had the audacity to ask his readers to imagine the Roman stage in ruins. In other words, I will argue that Virgil invented the glorious ruins of imperial Rome (see chapter 3). Or, put differently, the creation of Rome as the empire's stage—a stage on which the Roman emperor performed as the sovereign with *imperium*, military and political command—went hand in hand with the invention of Rome as a stage filled with awe-inspiring ruins.

Virgil's provocative gesture, his demand that his readers imagine the Roman world in ruins, drives imperial imaginaries of the Roman and neo-Roman kind. With his Taylorian concept of the social imaginary, Ando embraces "the necessary and essential role of figurative language" and resituates the emerging ways of speaking, caused by the gap between the traditional Roman concept of *civitas* and the nascent empire's territorial expansion in their changing historical-political contexts.[93] However, imaginaries are discursive formations involving more than propositional statements, and more than the mental images evoked by metonymies or metaphors. Imaginaries are scopic regimes obeying their own visual grammar.[94] Connected to the empiricist epistemology informing Roman scenographic architecture and theatrical politics, imperial imaginaries render the world visible. This making visible exceeds the mental images evoked by the use of metonymies or metaphors.

Carl Schmitt emphasized the scopic and scenographic dimension proper to the Roman and neo-Roman imperial imaginary. Based on Oswald Spengler's reflections on the West's scopic regime, Schmitt theorized the nexus of conquest and spatial imagination in 1942 as a spatial revolution (chapter 24). Schmitt later theorized *Landnahme* or "land-appropriation" as the founding act of imperial power, beginning with conquest and inaugurating the political order.[95] On the most basic level, sovereignty for Schmitt means being master of territory or "the territorial sovereign."[96] Taking Aristotle's *Politics* as his point of departure, Schmitt argued that the effect of land-appropriation was a "spatially concrete" order.[97] Schmitt called this articulation of order and territorialization *nomos*. Involving specific forms of theo-politics, this nomotic space is always oriented toward a symbolic center, a site like Rome.[98] The Schmittian imaginary connects this orientation toward a theo-political center to the making visible of the nomotic order. Every land-appropriation, Schmitt argued, generated its own images of the world and its political spaces, a form of *Bildnahme* or *taking-of-a-picture* that postcolonial scholars later theorized as the symbolic gestures of scopic mastery inscribed in imperial imaginaries. *Nomos* is a "spatially visible" order.[99]

Theatricality and imperial visuality are inseparable, and Schmitt's thinking remained informed by the Greco-Roman metaphor of history as grand spectacle, the world as stage.[100] Later acts of empire-building inherited this idea of history and politics of spectacle centered on Rome's monumental architectural stage where imperial expansions and the Roman sovereign as ruler-conqueror were ritually celebrated. Indeed, the symbolic conquest of Rome's ruined architectural stage is a core feature of neo-Roman mimesis. First, the acts of conquest I explore in this book were always connected to the Roman stage. In the case of Algeria, for instance, archeologists uncovered the ruins of the Roman Empire almost simultaneously with the conquest in 1830, turning the territory into a Roman stage set. Second, these conquests always involved mimetic performances on the Roman stage. Or, more precisely, the architectural stage on which these performances took place was always symbolically related to the ancient imperial metropolis whether the act of imitation happened in Rome's ruin-center or elsewhere. Practices of neo-Roman mimesis thus involved different ways in which neo-Roman rulers, intellectuals, and artists related the imperial metropolis of their present to that of the ancient past.

Experts in mimesis prepared the actual performances in Rome by rearranging the ancient architectural stage. For instance, after the occupation of Rome, French engineers and archeologists re-created their version of the ruined stage after declaring Rome the Napoleonic Empire's Second City (chapter 10). These experts in mimesis executed their program of urban restructuring with Napoleon's future triumph in mind. Mussolini's demolition-reconstruction experts would reopen the triumphal entryway into Rome's ruined core, claiming to have re-created the route taken by

Charles V on his triumphal return from North Africa (chapter 17).[101] These restorations always involved a set of key buildings. For instance, Mussolini's urban planners integrated Augustus's Mausoleum into their "urban scenography."[102]

The performance of Charles V on the ruined Roman stage framed the conquest as an act of mimesis, the identification with the Roman model. Practices of neo-Roman mimesis thus include the imperial ruler's public performance and the elaborate mimetic practices surrounding these events. In addition, these acts of conquest were framed by contemporary theoretical or historical reflections on the Roman model, on empire, and on the concept of mimesis itself. All of this generated a voluminous intermedial archive about the Roman past, accumulated re-creations of imperial Rome, its metropolitan stage, actors, and ritual events.

Resurrectional Realism: The Desire for the Roman and the Aesthetics of Ruins

Acts of neo-Roman mimesis, I claimed, are acts of resurrection with their own practices and representational form. One of the purposes of these performances and their mimetic practices was the resurrection of the Roman past in the service of the neo-Roman present. Imagination as the production of vivid mental images is at the heart of the Aristotelian concept of poetic mimesis. It is also at the heart of neo-Roman mimesis as a project of re-creating a Roman world that no longer exists. European conquerors and their mimetic experts worked hard to mobilize the powers of the imagination in the service of their neo-Roman projects.

Analyzing the practices of this mimetic resurrection, I will emphasize three things: first and foremost, imitating Rome involves a continual *creation* of the ancient Roman world, a production of that which is being imitated. I mentioned the architectural restoration and restructuring of the Roman stage above. This ancient imperial stage was also continually reassembled for the eyes of the European public in other media, with reassemblies ranging from Edward Gibbon's textual reconstruction (chapter 8) to the scale models exhibited in fascist Rome at the occasion of Augustus's bimillenary in 1937–1938 (chapter 17).[103] Finally, Europe's capitals were remade in the image of Rome, with Berlin/*Germania* the most extreme example of this monumentalizing imperial architecture.

Second, Romans also provided the model for the mode of representation involved in these re-creations. I am referring to the realism of their art, a mimetic realism producing the effect of recognition of the original in the reader/spectator, indeed asking for recognition and, as I will argue, imitation. Acts of mimesis thus respond to the desire of the past. I will refer to the mode of representation involved in these re-creations of the Roman past as resurrectional realism.[104] While I ground my analysis in the mimetic realism of Augustan Rome, I do not define this mode of representation strictly in terms of a conventional realist epistemology but primarily as a mode driven by the desire for the Roman original. What matters is thus a specific desire at work in the techniques of neo-Roman mimesis striving to re-present the Roman past, the desire to "get hold of an object at very close range by way of its likeness, its reproduction."[105] This desire to hold, indeed to conquer the image of the past, I will argue, responds to the Roman desire to be imitated and, thus, to the desire of the past (chapter 6).

The third aspect of these mimetic practices concerns resurrectional realism with its empiricist epistemology as a form of *ruinography*. One of the characteristic features of this resurrectional mode of representation is the mobilization of the register of dense descriptions, mimicking visual perception, across a wide variety of media, both textual and visual. In other words, there is a form of representation at work here wedded to the *desire* to seize the past that strives to make the Roman world fully visible by relying heavily on the empiricism proper to the descriptive mode and the act of looking that is proper to it: the scrutinizing, inventorying gaze.[106] I propose to understand this resurrectional aesthetic of neo-Roman mimesis as a particular kind of ruin aesthetic. First, ruins are visible remnants, and "detailed description seems to suit [their] representation."[107] Second, like all ruin sites, *Rome*'s *imperial ruins* asked their beholders to cross the threshold from "visual perception" to "imagination."[108] Peter Geimer explains why this is the case. "As remnants of antiquity," ruin sites constitute a peculiar kind of "void."[109] These sites stimulate creativity by giving "free rein to the (power of) the imagination."[110] All meditations on ruins, it seems, thus veer "away from this austere minimalism [of close description]."[111]

Ontologically, ruins thus defy realism as the empiricist representation of the visually observable detail. However, in the case of the political-aesthetic projects of the imitation of Rome, this connection between *imperial* ruins, imagination, and representation works in a specific way. Here, Rome's ruin sites do not primarily function as voids giving free rein to the imagination. On the contrary, in this imperial context, the imagination is reined in, made to operate under the constraints of the resurrectional imperative. That is, Rome's imperial ruin sites awaken first and foremost the empiricist desire to restore the original object by privileging the descriptive register. Thus Louis-François Cassas, who visited Palmyra in 1785, restored the former Roman colony's ruins in his drawings. While some of his drawings veer into Orientalism, they nevertheless retained this empiricist commitment to meticulous description. The multi-medial neo-Roman practices of mimesis thus tended to subject their representations of Rome's ruined world to the resurrectional imperative of their political project and the desire for the original that drives it.

The connection of *imperium* to ruin studies that I propose on the level of aesthetic practices also involves the unique nature of ruin sites as a kind of "time machine," carrying the beholder back to the past.[112] Wilhelm von Humboldt described the power of Rome's ruins as a kind of irresistible "violence" that "pulls us [into the past]."[113] My study of this particular aspect of neo-Roman mimesis includes what I refer to as resurrectional exercises, exercises in the resurrectional aesthetics of immersion that transport their readers and viewers back into the Roman past. In this context, I read Wilhelm Jensen's *Gradiva: A Pompeiian Fancy*, for instance, as a post-Nietzschean text about the perfect act of mimesis (chapter 15).[114]

The resurrectional ruin aesthetics and exercises in immersion are one of the strands that I explore throughout this book. Some theorists also reflected on the proper ways of imitating and the concept of mimesis itself, while others argue against Roman mimesis. This is another analytical thread running through the book. Writing at the dawn of Europe's second wave of imperialism and in the context of Cook's voyages, Johann Gottfried Herder, for instance, combined his critique of the imitation of Rome with a radically anticolonial stance (chapter 7). Another example is Nietzsche's classic essay on monumental history, a reflection on neo-Roman mimesis in the modernist mode (chapter 15).

Roman versus Neo-Roman Imaginary

Let me summarize the argument regarding the concept and processes of imitation so far. Neo-Roman mimesis is the conqueror's performance on the Roman stage, the moment when the neo-Roman actor selects his death masks. But it is also much more: it is the *creation* of the Roman world of the past for the neo-Roman present, through multi-medial re-presentations, in the resurrectional mode. Each act of neo-Roman mimesis thus engendered a whole archive of texts and images, "making present what [was] actually absent," to use Arendt's paraphrase of the Aristotelian concept of mimesis as re-presentation.[115] Let me remind you of St. Just's statement:

"The world has been empty since the Romans, and only their memory fills it." Experts in neo-Roman mimesis, authors and artists, "filled" the world with simulacra of ancient Rome, re-creating the Roman model at each step. There is not one model, there are many.[116]

The concept of mimesis thus covers everything from the political and very public performance of identification on the part of individual rulers to the imitation of an entire culture by the neo-Roman present.[117] In the wake of these discrete moments of empire-building, a specific way of thinking about and imagining the world of Western Europe's neo-Roman empires emerged. Or, put more precisely, from the mimetic politics and intellectual and aesthetic labors of mimesis emerged the West's ruinous neo-Roman imaginary. Discussing Augustan Rome's ocularcentric regime and scenographic architecture, I introduced a Schmittian version of this scenographic imperial imaginary: the making visible and being visible of the imperial world, seen from the position of the imperial subject and centered on the metropolitan stage.

The *neo-Roman* imaginary is different from this spatio-temporal imaginary. Rendering the Roman past newly visible, this specific kind of spatio-temporal imaginary produced a neo-Roman time-space, a kind of shadowy twilight zone in which the world of imperial Rome is brought into close proximity to the imperial present. The past is kept alive, or rather, brought back to life, in the present. Generating their own scopic regimes, imperial imaginaries are also always discursive formations with a thick layer of images.[118] In the case of neo-Roman imaginaries, these images are vividly evoked by the resurrectional strategies not only of texts, but of the visual arts and other mimetic media and performative practices mobilized in the acts of neo-Roman mimesis. In these imaginary Roman zones, the difference between past and present is thus destabilized if not erased in favor of their similarity. Ruins as material remnants of a vanished past function as central signifiers of these zones. Moreover, as a part of a scenographic imaginary dedicated to rendering the world visible, what is absent in the ruin does not signify the irretrievability or undecipherability of the past but, rather, its invisibility. Here, the past can be retrieved from its ruins and it can be made visible.

This analysis of the (neo)Roman imaginary as a specific scopic regime centered on scenographic ruin gazer scenarios and involving the creation of an imaginary twilight zone that in turn involves *the creation of a neo-Roman gaze at the past* constitutes a first intersection between my study and postcolonial theory as visual studies. I am referring here to *Imperial Eyes: Travel Writing and Transculturation* (2003), Mary Louise Pratt's classic exploration of the imperial gaze as constitutive of a visual order attempting to establish mastery over newly conquered territory.[119] To Pratt's theory of the imperial gaze, I add the neo-Roman gaze at the Roman past. In a twist on Svetlana Alpers's study of the exhaustive descriptive practices characteristic of Dutch colonialism's visual culture as a form of "attention to the surface of the world," I add the importance of the meticulous description not only of what is seen but of what is absent—the Roman Empire itself, its rulers and barbarians, and always, the Roman stage and Rome's ruins.[120]

I began this discussion of my model of neo-Roman mimesis with an inversion of the temporal trajectory in Ando's model of the Roman imaginary, presenting neo-Roman conquests as political acts looking back at the Roman model. Discussing resurrectional practices, I arrived at the notion of a neo-Roman gaze, acts of looking for and at the past inscribed in the imaginary Roman zones generated by these practices. Throughout this discussion, I repeatedly thematized the desire to see at work in ruin gazer scenarios, in a theo-political order centered on the Roman stage, and in the modes of representation re-creating the Roman past. Reading Polybios's Carthaginian scene as a scopic scenario, I referenced Freud's scopophilic drive.[121] Here, I will introduce an early text by Freud that connects the empiricist desire to see at work in neo-Roman mimesis to the idea of a *stage-in-ruins*.[122] In the scenographic Roman and neo-Roman imperial imaginaries and their ruin gazer scenarios, the Roman performance space functions as this kind of broken, ruined stage: a stage that while attracting intense empiricist desires to scrutinize, resurrect, and reconstruct, ultimately defies them.

Freud: The Secret of Empire and the Ruined Stage

In his dream book, Freud takes his readers to Rome, analyzing his *cathexis* of "the Semitic Hannibal," the kernel of this fantasy being a scene from Polybios's *Histories*.[123] However, for a concept of the *ruined stage* we need to turn toward Freud's earlier texts on the hysteric's "theater" of the self.[124] Here, Freud for the first time explained the work of the analyst with the model of archeology. In his "Fragment of an Analysis of a Case of Hysteria" (1905), he described his "model" in the following way: "those discoverers whose good fortune it is to bring to the light of the day after their long burial the priceless though mutilated relics [*Reste*] of antiquity."[125] The goal of this exploration is to "trace a hysterical symptom back to a traumatic scene [*Szene*]."[126] At the heart of this search for knowledge among the rubble of the past is a relentless *empiricist desire*, or scopic drive, longing to witness the events of a remote age enacted on a stage that lies now in ruins.

Let's trace Freud's "analogy" of analyst and archeologist and the search for the stage on which this traumatic scene took place in more depth. Here is the opening sentence: "Imagine that an explorer arrives in a little known region where his interest is aroused by an expanse of rubble [*Trümmerfeld*], with remains of walls, fragments of columns, and tablets with half-effaced and unreadable inscriptions."[127] We are thus dealing with an archeologist-explorer, a ruin traveler in non-European territory surrounded by "semi-barbaric people."[128] This archeologist-explorer has the choice between two procedures: "*He may content himself with inspecting what lies exposed to view*, with questioning the inhabitants—perhaps semi-barbaric people—who live in the vicinity, about what tradition tells them about the history and meaning of these archeological remains, and with noting down what they tell him—and he may then proceed on his journey."[129] What is the alternative? ". . . he may act differently," Freud writes.[130] "He may have brought spicks, shovels and spades with him, and he may set the inhabitants to work with these implements."[131] With the help of these men, "he may start upon the expanse of rubble [*Trümmerfeld*], clear away the rubbish, and, *beginning from the visible remains, uncover what is buried*."[132]

Let us keep in mind that Freud has not yet used the word ruin [*Ruine*] in this passage.[133] And let us keep in mind the visual register of Freud's language: his "explorer" either contents himself with *inspecting what lies exposed to view*—that is, he studies what is visible: the "*Trümmerfeld*," or field of rubble, or rubbish, with its remains and fragments.[134] Or he uncovers visible objects that are not yet visible: *beginning from the visible remains, uncover what is buried*. Once the archeologist starts to clear away the debris, again two options emerge:

> If his work is crowned with success, *the discoveries explain themselves*: the remnants of the walls [*Mauerreste*] are parts of the ramparts of a palace, or a treasure-house; from the fragments of columns a temple complements itself [*von den Säulentrümmern ergänzt sich ein Tempel*]; the numerous inscriptions . . . reveal an alphabet and a language, and, when they have been deciphered and translated, yield undreamed-of-information about *the events of the remote past, to commemorate which the monuments were built* [*Ereignisse der Vorzeit, zu deren Gedächtnis jene Monumente erbaut worden sind*]. *Saxa loquuntur!*[135]

Once this labor is accomplished, the stones will speak; they speak as stones that commemorate events of the remote past.

In this text, ruins come into being under the archeologist's intense scrutiny; they take shape as the effects of a visual trajectory, discrete acts of looking: *beginning from the visible remains, uncover what is buried* and *the fragments of columns can be filled out into a temple.* All Freud's archeologist needs to do is look, look and read, since the "discoveries are self-explanatory."[136] Despite his emphasis on the archeologist's acts of looking and reading, however, the passage is written in the passive voice, in an odd stylistic choice that we should not erase as the standard edition does. Freud does not write that "the explorer" reassembles the temple from "the fragments of the columns" but "*von den Säulentrümmern ergänzt sich ein Tempel*," picturing the process of reconstruction step by step in his mind.[137] What Freud emphasizes here is the fact that these *saxa/stones* are covered with inscriptions *and* that they are ruins: objects, whose outline lets us intuit their former shape by supplying the missing elements. Ruins are stones that speak: because we can *see* what is missing. It is this "self-explanatory" nature that the passive voice underscores.

In other words, the essence of this analogy between psychoanalysis and archeology is empiricism, the unmediated apprehension and comprehension of the world through vision. Freud will complicate this picture, both in later sections of *The Aetiology of Hysteria* and in his later writings—a point I will come back to later. Let us first continue the search for the original stage and ask what it is that the archeologist uncovers. He lays bare a space, a ruined urban space where stones and their inscriptions tell the story of events that once happened in *this* space. What is important is the following: this space is *a stage-in-ruins*. This stage-in-ruins in turn was built to *commemorate* another stage, one on which the events took place that caused the symptoms: "the scene . . . in which and through which that symptom arose."[138] At the "deepest" level, Freud's explorer hopes to uncover a scene that can be observed—a plot performed by actors, a visible world of visible events, witnessed by a spectator from a different time. Taking place on a stage, of which nothing remains but its ruins.

Freud finishes the analogy between psychoanalytic process and archeological discovery and recovery by comparing stones and symptoms. Like the stones that the archeologist works with, the hysteric's symptoms need to start speaking, and they will do so when the patient's attention is redirected from the symptoms or "mnemic symbols [*Erinnerungssymbole*]" to the original stage and the scene "in which and through which that symptom arose":[139]

> If we try, in an approximately similar way, to induce the symptoms of a hysteria to make themselves heard as witnesses of the origin of the illness, we must take our start from Josef Breuer's momentous discovery: *the symptoms of hysteria . . . are determined*

> *by certain experiences of the patient's which have operated in a traumatic fashion and which are being reproduced in his psychical life in the form of mnemic symbols*. What we have to do is to apply Breuer's method . . . so as to lead the patient's attention back from his symptom to the scene in which and through which the symptom arose.[140]

Or, put differently, like stones, symptoms need to start speaking, need to start telling the story that once took place on a stage now in ruins.

On the most basic level, the archeological model involves three different layers: first, the field of rubble; second, the ruins of a stage laid bare once the rubble is removed; and third, the original site *in memory of which this ruined stage was built* and *which no longer exists*, not even in ruins. And we have at least two sets of actors and two plots: the events enacted on the ruined stage that mimicked in some way the events enacted on the original site. We tend to think of this hermeneutic depth model that the archeology-analysis analogy proposes as the idea of the layering of time—the depth model of conscious and unconscious as *Zeit* and *Vorzeit*—the latter the layer of "truth" that we need to reach by penetrating the first. At the risk of repetition, this passage complicates the scheme, since what we find are *the ruins of a stage* that commemorates a scene having taken place on *a prior stage* that no longer exists—not even in its ruins. For as we have seen, the ruins—or symptoms—are part of a stage erected to commemorate the earlier one.

Of course, the stones, with which the memory-stage (the stage in ruins) was built, could have been *spoliae*, that is, rubble left by the original stage. All of this leads us into the heart of the epistemological debates surrounding Freud's "scene" (and his concept of psychic reality), that is, the question of its realism, or the realist status of the "trace"; in other words, do we assume the existence of an original scene?[141] The fact that *the stage is ruined*, I think, indicates that even in his early text Freud already touches on the impossibility of ever fully restoring the primal scene.

When Freud finally introduced the concept of the "*ur-scene*," in a 1914 text on the Wolf Man, we again come across the idea of the ruined stage.[142] In this story, the primal scene is a "scene of observing" and the event taking place on its stage is understood as an "act of violence" that the Wolf Man watches with "strained attention."[143] Now Freud explicitly thematizes the "constructed" nature of this *ur-scene*. Nothing, he explains, is left of this event, and thus of the stage on which it took place, other than fragments or "*Bruchstücke*"—literally, pieces that have broken apart.[144]

Let us return to Freud's archeological dig. Here, Freud tells a story about history and the *ruined stage* of this history; he also tells a story about empiricism. The core of empiricism is its visual epistemology: what we are looking for are *visible* objects that will "tell" us something about the "mechanism" that produced the symptom—in other words, visible events taking place in a visible universe. If we successfully remove rubble, we will find ruins—and then a whole world to be surveyed by the explorer's inquisitive gaze, a gaze whose intensity mirrors the "strained attention" of the Wolf Man staring at his *ur-scene*. In other words, with Freud's empiricist explorer, his visual epistemology, and above all, his urgent desire to see, we have returned to the West's neo-Roman imperial imaginaries, the intense empiricist desires that animate these scenographic imaginaries and their *ur-scene*: a Roman model of which nothing remains but a *stage-in-ruins*.

From the Freudian Stage to the Lessons of Empire, or How to Delay the End

In the age of modern empires, we are stuck with ruins, odd objects both present and absent, provoking us to complete them by intuiting their former shape. Every neo-Roman ruin gazer is in the position of Freud's archeologist-analyst, trying to find the solution to an enigma: Why did Rome fall? What was the story enacted on this ruined stage? What was the middle; what was the beginning of this plot of which nothing but the end remains? Who were the actors in this drama, who were the barbarians, who were the non-barbarians? Where did this drama take place? And, of course, the question: What does it mean for us? Were there decisive moments in this drama, moments when the decline or the fall could have been prevented? Would *we* be able to stop it? And if not, would we at least be able to postpone it?

Like Freud's explorer, the neo-Roman conquerors (and their theorists and artists) kept staring at the Roman stage, thinking of their acts as a repetition of the story that had taken place on this stage—an improved story, a repetition-with-a-difference. The intellectual history that I trace in this book is the long history of thinking about the causes of Rome's end, the lessons to be derived from these causes. Above all, it is the history of imperial theorists reflecting on how to delay the end—and on forms of imperial sovereignty that would do so.[145] Ranging from Polybios to Schmitt, this long intellectual history shows that neo-Roman thinkers are as invested in duration as were the theorists of the Roman Empire.

In the *Aeneid*, Virgil captured the problematic of imitation as difference and sameness. On his journey to Carthage, Aeneas and his crew stop at a place where some of their fellow-Trojans had built "a little Troy, a miniature, mimicking our great Trojan towers."[146] Unconvinced by this all too "concrete attempt at commemoration," Aeneas leaves and founds his Rome—a majestic, monumental metropolis.[147] Empire, Charles Maier writes, "strives to be its own monument."[148] This concern with the empire's duration spills over into other cultural and aesthetic practices. The desire for duration manifests itself for instance in the case of the lethally literal-minded Nazi leadership as an obsession with the fortification of their empire—and of the Third Reich's imperial imaginary. But this is not unique to the Nazi empire. Romans were also invested in the fortification of imperial space, time, gaze, and ruins. The Nazis merely took this to an extreme. In *The Conquest of Ruins*, I draw attention to theories and practices of fortification that concern architecture, for instance, and the peculiar way in which this desire for duration operates with respect to ruin gazer scenarios, the nature of their scopic regimes and performances.

"Why does an empire break apart?" the East German playwright Heiner Müller asked in 1993, and added: "Die Trümmer antworten nicht"—*saxa non loquuntur*.[149] The imperial leaders and theorists engaged in neo-Roman mimesis thought otherwise, producing a wave of texts about causes and lessons drawn from these endless acts of ruin gazing. What could be done to prevent the repetition of Rome's fall? Principal among these texts inquiring into the causes of Rome's decline or fall in the modern age is Edward Gibbon's *The Decline and Fall of Rome*, a multivolume story of Rome that famously attributes the collapse to barbarism, Christianity, and unrestrained expansion. Not surprisingly, by the time we get to the imperial theorists and would-be theorists of the Third Reich, the causes of Rome's fall have been reduced to race.[150]

In the course of the process of imitating Rome, lessons drawn very often combined with assertions of superiority. Conquerors like Cortes, for instance, bragged about their superior military skills. In a similar gesture, Lord Cromer, the British governor of Egypt, professed attachment to the Roman model while claiming superiority.[151] By 1909, the lessons and warnings of the Roman Empire had been debated at great length.[152] Cromer was above all concerned with the question of whether the British imitation of one of the main strategies of Roman rule (that is, the "hazardous experiment" of employing subjects from the colonies) would bring the British Empire down as it had Rome.[153] Believing in "the value of repetition," his answer was a hesitant no.[154]

Much of *The Conquest of Ruins* is concerned with the work of Roman and neo-Roman theorists writing about this question of repetition trying to figure out whether there is a law of ruin at work in the imitation of Rome. I trace this vast body of texts that was shaped by and contributed to the West's ruinous imperial imaginaries from Polybios's *Histories* to

C. F. Volney's *The Ruins, or, Meditation on the Revolutions of Empires* (1791), Edward Gibbon's *The Decline and Fall of the Roman Empire* (1776–1789), Oswald Spengler's *The Decline of the West* (1916 and 1922), Carl Schmitt's Nazi-era texts on *nomos*/empire, and finally Martin Heidegger's so-called *Black Notebooks*. This strand of reflections on empire, imperialism, and the end of Rome also includes Heinrich Himmler's infamous speech about empire-building, held in Poznań in 1943.

What is at stake in the writings of these imperial theorists? They reflected at length on ancient and modern barbarians and created an endless series of their own ruin gazer scenarios. Most importantly, they addressed Polybios's thesis that imperial time is the time before the end of empire. Some of these imperial theorists argued for interrupting the imperial cycle of rise and fall. Volney, the French Jacobin and later supporter of Napoleon's invasion of Egypt, argued that a new sovereign—the people of a new world republic based on natural law— would be able to break the law of ruin (chapter 7).

Others thought about the many ways that their imperial present might be made to endure. Central to the Roman and neo-Roman imperial imagination was thus the idea of postponing the inevitable end in ruins. I reconstruct a deep history running from Polybios's and Virgil's strategies of *fortifying time*, to Paul's concept of the *katechontic* sovereign, to Spengler's redefinition of the *katechontic* sovereign as Caesarism, and finally to Carl Schmitt's retheorizing of the *katechon*.

The Conquest of Ruins concludes with a chapter on Martin Heidegger, like Schmitt a radical conservative critic of modernity and modern imperialism. As one of the Nazis' leading theorists of neo-Roman imperial mimesis, Schmitt returned to Paul's *Letters to the Thessalonians* from which he derived the theo-political concept of the Roman Empire/emperor as *katechon* as delayer of the end. When Heidegger thought about the idea of *Reich*, he turned to the antagonistic Greek city-states. Hitler, Himmler, and Speer proposed a thousand-year *Reich* and thousands of years of glorious ruins. Carl Schmitt devoted himself to the problem of how to prolong the time before the fall. Privileging ancient Greek readiness to face the end, Heidegger analyzed and criticized this Roman desire to endure.

Interventions 1: At the Intersection of Classical Studies and Postcolonial Theory

For quite some time classicists have imported the concerns if not theoretical models of postcolonial theory and visual studies into the study of

Greco-Roman antiquity, often revising the assumptions of modernists.[155] In the process they have initiated a much-needed debate about the short memory of postcolonial studies, the "length and intricacy of the history of [their topics and categories]."[156] Reconstructing and analyzing the longer *durée* of neo-Roman imitation contributes new insights to postcolonial theory and scholarship, insights that go beyond the mere historicizing of postcolonial categories. Let me return to the performances on the Roman stage as paradigmatic *acts of imitation* of the Roman model to make my case. These performative acts, I wrote above, respond to the desires of the past to be recognized and emulated. Imperial Rome also provided the cultural practices, such as the display of death masks, for these public acts of mimesis. More importantly, studying the longer *durée* of this cultural process of imitation involves examining these neo-Roman acts of recognition and identification from a diachronic angle.

This specific intervention thus concerns the axes along which postcolonial theory has analyzed the relations of imitation. Homi Bhabha's classic essays on colonial subject formation and mimicry describe the power relation between colonizers and colonized as the unsettling effects of the colonized's mimicry (or partial identification with, and imitation of, the colonizer) as a process that then lays bare the *lack* at the core of the colonizer's subjectivity. In *Mimesis and Alterity* (1993), Michael Taussig explored the ways in which "the West itself [is] mirrored in the eyes and handiwork [images and goods] of its Others."[157] Both Bhabha's essays and Taussig's book stimulated scholarship tracing mimesis as a two-way praxis across the borders of empires, from metropole to periphery and back.[158] Analyzing the desires and practices at work in neo-Roman mimesis, I introduce a new *historical* axis into the study of European imperialisms, their cultures and imaginaries. More precisely, I propose to think of imperial power relations in terms of a triangulation between imperial subject and "barbarian," on the one hand, and imperial subject and Roman model, on the other.[159]

According to Gayatri Spivak, postcolonial theory ought to theorize "the itinerary of the consolidation of Europe as sovereign subject."[160] At stake in this study of neo-Roman mimesis is the European subject as the imperial ruler. Classicists and modernists have explained the reasons for the imitation of the Roman Empire largely in terms of political legitimacy.[161] I would like to emphasize that the (public) performances of identification with the Roman model created the neo-Roman sovereign embodying centralized imperial power. That is, these acts symbolically consolidated neo-Roman sovereignty drawing on the politics of spectacle surrounding the Roman emperor-conqueror and the semantics of the Latin word *imperium*.[162] Originally *imperium* signified the Roman magistrates' power "to command and expect obedience."[163] Over time, the word came to mean "the power of the Roman people as a whole" and later "that of the emperor."[164]

Neo-Roman acts of imitation sought this particular conception of the imperial sovereign's power, the combination of executive political-military power and "performative" power.[165] But there is more at stake in these performative acts of identification with the Roman model. Galinsky's definition of Augustus's power (the power of the office combined with the ruler's personal qualities) leaves out the theatrical *mise-en-scène* of sovereignty as divinely sanctioned.[166] Donning the mask of the Roman model, neo-Roman conquerors, intellectuals, and mimetic artists kept this theatrical Roman theo-politics alive.

European neo-Roman mimesis thus enacts a kind of consolidation, fortification even, of imperial sovereignty over time.[167] My central claim in this book, however, is that these processes of imitation were always haunted by the specter of Rome's end and its ruins. Exploring the history of neo-Roman mimesis, I argue that imperial sovereignty is a form of sovereignty that, while claiming the mantle of the Roman model, is also haunted by the shadow of Rome's end. Rethinking Bhabha's concept of mimicry, I argue that the public acts of imitation of the Roman model are always encounters with death—not encounters with the ontological lack at the core of subjectivity, but with a simple empirical fact: Rome fell. Neo-Roman rulers did not merely borrow the "clothes of the *roman maiores*," to use the metaphor that Arendt employed with respect to the American revolutionaries' imitation of Rome.[168] In the triangulation of the neo-Roman sovereign with the Roman model and the conquered barbarian that I am tracing through Europe's mimetic *ruinography*, neo-Roman sovereigns were wearing Augustus's death mask.[169]

There is an additional intersection with the postcolonial having to do with conceptions of time. I touched on this topic when I discussed the neo-Roman imaginary as a particular time-space. There are several issues at stake here, the first of them having to do with being at odds with conceptualizations of the temporality of Western modernity, of the way in which time is conceived and lived as linear and open-ended. Here, my first point relates to the following: as I will insist throughout this book, the temporal consciousness of neo-Roman empires involves a different way of conceiving and living time: the time of empire as the time before the end, as *imperial endtime*. This is the conception of time inscribed in ruin gazer scenarios, the scenarios at the heart of the ruinous imperial imaginaries. My second point relates to the twilight zone of neo-Roman mimesis. Neo-Roman imaginaries create an imaginary zone in which the Roman past is made to exist in the present—a space of simultaneity or synchronicity.

Both of these temporal imaginaries are at odds with the idea of Europe's modernity as involving an open-ended and hyper-linear temporality. Postcolonial theorists have described this contrast between Western and non-Western, or modern and traditional, understandings of time as an aspect of colonial domination.[170] On the one hand, there is the premodern regime of cyclical time; on the other, there is the Hegelian teleology of modernity, stadial theories of civilizational progress, and Darwinian evolutionary paradigms. In an inversion of this model, I find that imperial Europeans were themselves living in premodern time, to the extent that they operated within neo-Roman imaginaries. That is, European modernity as imperial modernity conceives and lives historical temporality not just as linear but also as cyclical, as the story of imperial rise and fall.

The third intersection with postcolonial theory as *visual studies* concerns my claim regarding the longer *durée* of Western imperialism's ruinous imperial imaginaries. Arguing against Heidegger's thesis of one dominant visual culture of modernity, Martin Jay proposed to think of (Western) modernity as consisting of different scopic regimes.[171] By proposing a concept of the (neo-Roman) imperial imaginary whose scopic regime is structured by and centered on the ruined Roman stage, I assert that there is a specific form of imperial imaginary that crosses the antiquity-modernity divide.[172]

As I wrote above, this scopic regime of Western imperialism becomes a neo-Roman regime whose visual field orients the gaze toward the Roman past and its ruins. Crucially, this also involves a gaze seeking to master the barbarian. The core of the book's argument involves the stabilization and fortification of ruin gazer scenarios across centuries. These scopic scenarios dramatize their versions of the (post)Roman script of imperial politics as spectacle. Centered on the ruined site of Roman sovereignty, the scenarios staged power relations between sovereign imperial subjects and conquered barbarians, inscribing their own visual regimes, deeply invested in maintaining scopic mastery. I read the interminable circulation of ruin gazer scenarios across centuries as political, theoretical, and aesthetic labor producing a hardened *topos* in the form of a scenario whose scopic regime is fortified.[173] That is, the imperial sovereign is kept in a position of scopic mastery and his gaze is fortified.

On the level of these neo-Roman imaginaries, nothing remains more constant than the figure of the "barbarian." Barbarians exist as long as there are empires.[174] "It is Rome above all," Morley writes, "that leads us to view those outside of our culture as barbarians."[175] I reconstruct the story of the neo-Roman barbarian as the political *enemy* of empire. That is, in this neo-Roman context, the barbarian is not primarily a racial concept but the effect of the friend-enemy constellations that define empires.[176]

Both classicists and modernists agree that empire is a political formation in permanent readiness to conquer and suppress rebellions. "The scale of Rome's martial effort and colonial violence," Mattingly writes, "was unprecedented in antiquity."[177] Empires, Jürgen Osterhammel writes, "rest on the permanent latent threat of violence."[178] In other words, *imperia* always exist in a state of exception, an insight Schmitt articulated in the ruins of the Third Reich (chapter 25). And this permanent state of exception involves the permanent construction of the barbarian enemy.[179]

Let me briefly recapitulate what we know about the concept of barbarity. By the fourth century BCE, "*barbaros*" had come to mean someone who babbled, someone who did not speak Greek, implying cultural and mental inferiority.[180] Lacking Greek, the language of reason, meant two things: that barbarians lacked "the ability to form civil societies" and did not share the values of the "Hellenic community."[181] Ultimately, the Greeks' refusal to recognize the "*barbaroi*" meant that they were closer to animals than humans, exhibiting signs of ferocious "unrestraint."[182] Romans knew about Greek "primitivism" and the many portraits of "excitable barbarians," and liked the irony of referring to themselves as barbarians.[183] Nevertheless, they too applied the concept of "'barbarians'" to their subjects or those "unaccustomed to our ways."[184] In the modern period, the Greco-Roman conception remained part of the imperial texts about the inferiority of the colonized, not least because modern colonizers tried to figure out whether the unfamiliar people they were sent to identify and classify were the same as the familiar barbarians of antiquity.[185]

In the Roman and neo-Roman imperial imaginaries, the barbarian primarily functions as a political figure. Caesar defined the enemy or those who resisted conquest as barbarians.[186] Louis Bertrand, the public intellectual of Algerian settlers, formulated this concept most clearly. In the context of his bellicose theories about African Latinity and Muslims as Europe's most dangerous enemy, Bertrand wrote in *Le Sens de L'Ennemi* (*The Meaning of the Enemy*; 1917): "I use the word Barbarian in the widest sense, ranging from foreigner to savage and enemy of civilization."[187] With this statement, he captured the essence of the modern concept of the barbarian.

There is no empire without ruins and barbarians. The West's idealization of Rome, Mattingly observes, merely elided the "ideological necessity for a negative image of the barbarian."[188] This ideological necessity is not a thing of the deep past. On the contrary, the figure of the barbarian and the strategies aimed at mastering this figure remain a feature of the neo-Roman imaginaries. I will reconstruct part of this story, examining the reconfiguration of ancient barbarians as enemies of empire, by tracing an arc from Carthage to New Zealand: from Polybios and Virgil's Hannibal to Gibbon's and Forster's reinvention of the modern barbarian as South Sea Islander or Maori, to Thomas Macaulay's iconic New Zealander overlooking the ruins of London, to Hitler's idiosyncratic rediscovery of the Maori as Poles. Chapter 12 is devoted to a more detailed analysis of these scenarios and the efforts to maintain the scopic power constellation. In the book's epilogue about Anselm Kiefer's concrete towers at the 2006 *Monumenta* exhibit devoted to the artist's work, I will discuss an example of deconstructing scopic mastery, indeed the very armature of the ruin gazer scenario.

These scenographic ruin gazer scenarios connect *imperium* to ruin studies, and here we find yet another point of contact with postcolonial studies. Edward Said famously analyzed the imperial representations of the countries of the Ottoman Empire as "a dead world" covered in "suggestive ruins."[189] Postcolonial scholars explored how Western powers justified colonial rule portraying themselves as restorers of the present and curators of the past. From the moment of conquest, colonial powers set out to remove what they deemed the worthless debris of the present and to guard the valued ancient ruins.[190] In their eyes Europe's colonies were characterized by the "absence of ruins."[191] As I wrote above, I trace this contrast between worthless rubble and valorized ruins back to the Punic Wars. Out of this context, two discrete ideas emerge: of Rome's noble ruins and of the ignoble rubble of the conquered. While devaluing the enemy, the latter here signifies first and foremost defeat and the swift violence of the act of conquest.

Examining the literal and aesthetic appropriation of ruins in colonial/imperial contexts, most postcolonial scholars tacitly accept one of European ruin studies' dominant paradigms. That is, the idea that the concept of ruins emerged in the early modern period, signifying the epochal rupture between the modern and the premodern, between religion and secular order, eschatology and history, and ultimately, leading to modernism's aesthetics of fragmentation. Walter Benjamin, with his reflections on the Baroque's mourning-plays, is of course the example that most readily comes to mind.[192] Likewise, Oswald Spengler claimed that before the Renaissance, people did not think of the "rubble-like" as ruins.[193] Spengler theorizes ruins, their particular epistemology and aesthetics, when writing about the West's unique fascination with infinite space. Only the Faustian soul reveres "the timeworn witnesses," remnants of a past that is at once visible and invisible.[194] No ancient Greek, Spengler writes, would have thought to preserve ruins.[195]

Andreas Schönle and I essentially subscribed to this paradigm in which the Renaissance functions as the watershed moment in the intellectual history of Europe's fascination with ancient ruins.[196] At the same time, we argued in *Ruins of Modernity* (2010) that European modernity created its own ruin consciousness and its own ruins, signs of European modernity's dialectic of creation and destruction. In my own contribution to the volume, I wrote about the Third Reich's ruin scenarios, working with Macaulay's *Pleasure of Ruins* (1953). In contrast to Benjamin and Spengler, Macaulay's presumption of an anthropological constant locates *Ruinenlust* as *Zerstörungslust* (destruction-lust) in classical antiquity.[197] Like the ruins in Pompeiian frescoes, Corinth's ruins are Greek, the conquered city having been razed by the Romans in 146 BCE. By the time Romans decorated their Pompeiian villas with Hellenistic wall paintings, Macaulay writes, we had "arrived at an age of ruin-sentiment."[198]

Macaulay traces this "poetry of ruins" from Pompeii to Lucan's civil war epic, *Pharsalia* (61–65 CE). Obsessing about ruins, Macaulay demonstrated, was not restricted to European modernity. Deeply committed to the British Empire, Macaulay trained her attention on the ruins of the Roman Empire lining the shores of the Mediterranean. In a move anticipating postcolonial ideas, she observed that some of the Pompeiian murals depict ruins painted by "melancholy" Greeks who have seen their country ruined by their Roman masters.[199] I follow Macaulay's lead back to ancient Rome, replacing her nostalgic imperialist perspective with a critical postimperial lens, analyzing the Roman Empire's production of the idea of noble imperial ruins and the ignoble rubble of the conquered.[200]

Interventions 2: At the Intersection of Classics as Reception Studies, the Historiography of Empires, and the Third Reich

The practice of postcolonial studies is no longer the exclusive purview of modernists. On the contrary, classicists in the fields of history, archeology, and literary and cultural studies have imported and revised postcolonial theory for quite some time now. In the process, they initiated a much-needed debate about the "short memory" of postcolonial studies. In addition, classicists have contributed to visual studies, analyzing the scopic regimes of antiquity.[201] Simultaneously, the field of classics moved toward reception studies. Relying heavily on this body of work, I add what James I. Porter calls "longitudinal" studies, that is, a study of the role of the Roman Empire and its ruins across chronological boundaries.[202] With this longitudinal approach crossing the antiquity/modernity divide, *The Conquest of Ruins* revises empire studies as *imperium* studies or as an exploration of the long-term effects of late republican and imperial Rome and of the thick texture produced by mimesis as political, aesthetic, and theoretical praxis. In *The Conquest of Ruins*, I experiment with *imperium* studies in the longer *durée*.[203]

Let me return to what I called one of the overarching goals of this book: to further elucidate the phenomenon of the Third Reich. By situating the Third Reich in this particular transnational and transhistorical trajectory, I rewrite its historiography. But let me be clear: *The Conquest of Ruins* is not an exhaustive explanation of the Nazi experiment in empire-building. Rather, it is an attempt to trace one of the strands that were mobilized for this deadly experiment.[204] As I wrote above, Arendt argued that every historical event "illuminates its own past."[205] Two insights are condensed in this claim: first, the Hegelian claim that only owls can truly understand historical events—that events can only be fully comprehended once they have come to their conclusion.[206] And second, that the event's past "comes into being only with the event itself."[207] Events are crystallizations, the results of dense articulations of multiple, hitherto hidden causes.[208] Arendt thus conceptualized historical events in terms of overdetermination, as a beginning that never was a single cause.[209] In my analysis of the Third Reich as neo-Roman Empire, I follow Arendt's lead. The Nazi leadership and many of the conservative Nazi collaborators thought and wrote much more extensively about Rome as a model than we have been aware of.[210] More importantly, I argue that the Third Reich takes neo-Roman mimesis to its extreme.[211]

Finally, I would like to return to a topic that I briefly discussed above, that is, the topic of Western modernity's "regimes of historicity."[212] Working toward a more complex model of living and thinking time and temporalities in modernity, Reinhard Koselleck introduced the idea of layers of time, temporal regimes as palimpsests. He also argued that the cyclical model of rise and decline remained part of modernity's regime of historicity.[213] I argue that in the ruinous historical imaginary of Western imperialism, this model of thinking and imagining time was far more than a relic of the past surfacing occasionally. On the contrary, rise and decline and the terror of imperial endtime remained vividly alive.[214] Their gaze captured by Rome's ruins, imperial theorists kept wondering whether there are two temporal logics at work in (pre)modernity, one being progress, the other the endless repetition of imperial rise and fall.

Conclusion

A question that I have neglected to address so far is how ideas, images, and scenarios traveled across several centuries. One of the answers to this question has to do with the transmission of knowledge about Greco-Roman antiquity, its authors and their texts, its artists and their works—what Beard calls "our long conversation with them."[215] The political leaders, authors, and artists I discuss in this book were members of Europe's educated elite. The classical canon was part of their background—in the cases of Gottfried Benn and Carl Schmitt as much as Garcilaso de la Vega, a Spanish nobleman and poet who accompanied Charles V on his North African campaign, or Georg Forster and William Hodges, who took part in Captain James Cook's second journey to the South Pacific.[216] This also applies to some members of the Nazi leadership, like Heinrich Himmler, whose father was a classicist.[217]

Neo-Roman mimesis is a long and contested process. As I wrote above, Europe's long mimetic practice saw writers critical of the very concept of neo-Roman mimesis. Others asserted the difference between ancient and modern empires combined with appeals "not to reason too much from precedent."[218] In addition, as Gibbon demonstrated with his episode about the Ottoman conquest of Constantinople in 1453, there is also no rigid division into Eastern and Western traditions of ruin gazing (see chapter 13). In his anecdote involving Mehmed II, Gibbon hints at a hybrid ruin gazer scenario drawing on a non-Western literary tradition.[219] On the other hand, the sultan was celebrated as an expert in the art of the neo-Roman ruin gaze. Touring the Acropolis in 1438, he "reconstructed mentally [from the ruins and remains] the ancient buildings," which was considered a sign of being "a wise man" and a "great king."[220]

I need to address one last point of a more pragmatic nature. While I present the chronological sweep of the book as essentially linear, the trajectory of *The Conquest of Ruins* deviates at one point from a strictly chronological order. Thus, the reconstruction of the French case in part 3 proceeds from the invasion of Egypt to Louis Bertrand's essays about North African *Latinité* in the mid-1930s. At the beginning of part 4, I will then backtrack to the era of the anti-Napoleonic movement, and the theme of anti-Roman barbarians. Devoted to the German case, part 4 will end with a chapter on Oswald Spengler's *The Decline of the West.* With my analysis of Spengler's *Decline,* I will reconnect with Bertrand's radical conservative politics.

As I mentioned above, Schmitt was a conservative revolutionary like Heidegger. Far from being a marginal phenomenon, the conservative-revolutionary way of thinking and imagining empire constituted a strong (post)Roman tradition. This discursive formation includes Oswald Spengler and Friedrich Ratzel, the imperial theorists of the *Kaiserreich* (discussed in chapter 17), and the conservative Catholics Chateaubriand and Louis Bertrand (discussed in chapter 11)—all of them authors who develop their theories of empire and critique of imperialist modernity with an eye on the Roman Empire.[221]

Reconstructing European mimesis, I unravel this vast intermedial formation by privileging various strands of this fabric. The history of ruin gazer scenarios is one of those threads; the intellectual history concerned with the theorizing of empire and the strategies to delay the end is another one. This book thus traces the long history of the enduring efforts of Western imperialism's leaders, theorists, and artists to interrogate, and, ultimately, to conquer, the ruins of what became in the process the West's "archetypal empire."[222] The history of neo-Roman mimesis is the history of an ever-more-panicked attempt to conquer Rome's ruins.

PART ONE

After Carthage: The Roman Empire and Its Ruins

Preface

In this part, I will analyze the emergence of the Roman ruin gazer scenarios out of Polybios's *rubble gazer scenario*. I will trace the genesis of this scopic scenario between Polybios's pre-Augustan eyewitness report about the capture of Carthage in the last Punic War in 146 BCE and Pausanias's post-Augustan *Guide to Greece*. Roman propaganda portrayed Carthage as a city in which nothing remained standing after Scipio's victory—not even ruins. Having theorized the rise and fall of empires, Polybios's *Histories* conclude with a scene that connects rubble, the barbarian, and the idea of imperial time as endtime. The genesis of the ruin gazer scenario at Carthage thus involves the transformation of rubble into ruins, worthless Carthaginian debris into noble Roman ruins. The topic stays the same: the visualization of the end of one empire and the premonition of the fall of another. The scenario's power constellation also remains in place: the conquering subject looking at the conquered, and imagining the reversal of this relationship between imperial subject and subject of empire. But one of the core components of the scenario changes: ruin, not rubble, becomes the object of the conqueror's gaze. With Josephus's *Jewish War* and Pausanias's *Periegesis Hellados*, the scenarios change, taking us into the territory of the colonized and the concept of their ruins (chapter 4).

In chapter 1, I focus on the content and form of Polybios's rubble scenario, analyzing the latter in the context of Greek and Roman ocularcentric cultures, focused on the Greco-Roman theater and the scene-building as the site of imperial sovereignty. In the following chapters, I analyze the emergence of the concept of Roman ruins and ruin consciousness as the nexus between the Augustan building program, a manifestation of political theology in stone, and Virgil's work in his *Aeneid* and Lucan's in his *Pharsalia* (chapters 2 and 3).

This ruin consciousness and its representation in the various scenarios draw on the Augustan creation of Rome the city as the empire's stage. Polybios frames Scipio's rubble gazing as a scene from the theater of history, set in front of the Carthaginian *skene*. Later authors continue to use this framing. Briefly recapitulating my ideas about the distinction between rubble scenarios and ruin scenarios, chapter 5 then concentrates on Paul's letters to the Thessalonians, connecting early Christian eschatology and the concept of the *katechon* to the Roman problematic of imperial endtime.

ONE

In the Rubble of Carthage: Polybios's *Histories* and the Time That Remains

Introduction

Historians of Republican imperialism point to the year 146 BCE as a decisive turning point. After the victory over the Achaean League and the Carthaginians, "a conquest state" emerged that was "geared toward constant expansion."[1] Carthage, on the other hand, is reduced from naval "world power to a minor state."[2] In the three Punic Wars, the Romans fought against their present rival and "the future empire they feared or professed to fear."[3] At stake in the victory over Carthage was the expansion of Rome into Northern Africa (Carthaginian territory became *Africa Proconsularis*), Sicily, and the newly created Phoenician empire in Spain.[4] This expansion together with the conquest of Greece meant that a new imperial formation was emerging in the Mediterranean.

The obliteration of Corinth and Carthage is testimony to the ruthlessness of the emerging world power and its aggressive "drive to conquer."[5] The Third Punic War began with an ultimatum demanding that the Carthaginians resettle miles from the sea. The city would be razed, the Roman ambassadors suggested, but shrines and cemeteries would be left intact.[6] When Carthage rejected this demand, the war began. When it was won, the republican elite reveled in its victory.

Pliny the Elder mentions the public exhibition of a painting depicting the final assault on Carthage in the Forum. The event was organized by one of the commanders of the Roman fleet, who "standing near the picture" explained "details of the siege."[7] Appian, a first-century Greek historian, described the arrival of the news about the conquest of Carthage as a moment when Romans were "delivered from some great fear" and "confirmed in their world-wide supremacy."[8] Talking all night about the assault on Byrsa, Carthage's innermost fortress, they "pictured to each other the whole war, as though it were just taking place under their own eyes," and "seemed to see Scipio on the ladders, on shipboard, on the gates, in the battles."[9]

The memory of Scipio the Younger, who leveled Carthage at the end of the Third Punic War, and Hannibal (whom Scipio the Elder defeated in 202 BCE at Zama, thus ending the second Punic War) will play a central role in my analysis of (post)Roman ruin gazing. The conqueror of Carthage and Rome's most notorious enemy also loom large in Polybios's multivolume *Histories* (parts of which were published by 150 BCE).[10] For Rome's imperial ruin gazer scenario originates with Scipio overlooking Carthage at the moment of its destruction. The Carthaginian general who invaded Italy in the Second Punic War is also part of this scenario, a shadowy but no less powerful presence.

The Punic city would continue to haunt the Romans' imagination long after the Punic Wars ended. To the Romans, Ellen O'Gorman writes, the "loss of world rule" that Carthage represented meant "symbolic death."[11] Linking the "struggle for empire" to the "struggle against death and annihilation," Carthage functioned as the "undead city."[12] Polybios's scenario of Scipio weeping at Carthage would transmit the knowledge of Carthage's death and the meaning that many Roman and neo-Roman intellectuals attributed to this death, across the centuries. It is the content *and* the form of this scenario in its many later versions that is the subject of this book.

What do we know about Polybios? Born in the Arcadian city of Megalopolis, Polybios came to Rome as a hostage. A military man by training, he befriended Scipio the Younger, becoming the young aristocrat's mentor, doubting initially whether Scipio possessed "the typical Roman urge to action."[13] Accompanying Scipio on his African campaign, Polybios participated in the final assault on Carthage. This chapter will conclude with a close reading of the Greco-Roman historian's famous passage concluding his account of the conquest of Carthage in *The Histories*.[14] This rubble gazer scenario, connecting the Roman to the barbarian and the imperial present to the future, is embedded in an Aristotelian narrative of Rome's rise to hegemony in the Mediterranean. Avoiding the addition of parts in favor of picturing a whole, Polybios captures the Roman Empire and its ever-expanding space. Second, Polybios's scenario is tied to a general theory of imperial rise and fall.

Not only did Polybios invent this rubble gazer scenario, he was also one of the first theorists of imperial rise and decline, concluding his celebratory narrative of Rome's imperial ascendancy with a scenario predicting the empire's eventual end. Yet this scopic scenario does not merely articulate a theory of history as repetition, as a succession of rising and declining empires, of which Rome is the most recent, the strongest, and the longest-lasting. It also connects this logic of inevitable decline with the unexpected historical event—the revenge of the barbarian—which makes the narrative of rise and fall into a story of triumph and terror. Finally, Polybios writes this concluding scene of his account of Rome's rise as if it were performed on a Greek stage. Polybios's scene is a scopic scenario that is scenographic in nature.

Rome's Rise, or Narrating the Event without Precedent

In the eyes of this Greek intellectual, Rome's unprecedented expansion made it an empire different from all previous empires. In particular, the "grand spectacle" of Rome's rise surpassed that of Macedonia. While Alexander ruled Asia and conquered Europe from the Adriatic to the Danube, the Macedonian Empire "still left the greater part of the inhabited world in the hands of others" (R, 42). The Romans, he writes, have succeeded in bringing "almost the whole of the world under their rule," thus establishing an empire that is far greater than "any that exists today or is likely to succeed it" (R, 42).[15] Polybios's *Histories* would, he promised, explain the "element of the unexpected in the events" (R, 41).[16] Having explained this "event completely without precedent," Polybios takes leave of his readers, announcing: "I returned home from Rome." The Greek historian has accomplished his Roman "task" (R, 541 and 540).

Polybios authorized his story by emphasizing that he "[made] himself an eye-witness" (R, 230), following in the footsteps of Herodotus, who invented the historian as traveler.[17] Discussing the historian's reliance on previous eyewitness reports and the need for "reliable description" of the world's known regions, Polybios presents himself as a traveler who has "seen" the world, having crossed "Africa, Spain and Gaul" and sailed the sea to the west of these countries (R, 231). Even when they reached "the furthest confines of the world," ancient travelers often were unable to "observe phenomena at first hand" because these parts of the world were too "barbarous" or "desolate" for firsthand observation (R, 230). With the age of empire, things had changed. Travelers now had access to almost all "regions" because Alexander had established his empire in Asia "and the Romans in other parts of the world" (R, 231).

Seeing the new world through Greek and Roman eyes, Polybios, the colonial subject, thus praised Rome's achievements, but salvaged the legacy of the erstwhile Greek hegemon. Moreover, claiming the vantage point of the colonial intellectual living in the empire's metropolis, Polybios asserted an epistemological privilege. Having been colonized, Greek men "have been released from the pressures of political or military ambition" and are now devoting themselves to "research," producing a far "more accurate picture" of the previously unknown parts of the world (R, 231). Romans act and Greeks think: the Roman general creates imperial space and the Greek subject surveys it, writing the first universal history or history under "one synoptical view," while remaining anchored in his imperial Macedonian legacy (R, 44).[18]

Writing the history of empire as "drive toward synchronization," Polybios takes the concept of plot (or the proper relation of parts to whole) from Aristotle's definition of epic poetry but abandons poetry's philosophical truth claim.[19] Replacing the concept of the particular with the idea of the partial as local and the concept of the general with the global, Polybios invented history as universal "in the spatial sense."[20] Polybios thus moved from Aristotle's philosophical to a spatialized paradigm. Put differently, at the beginning of imperial historiography, geographical replaced philosophical totality.[21] Polybios imagines the new entity that he proposes to analyze—a universal empire and its dizzying expansion—in analogy to a living body.[22] Synopsis is autopsy that creates the history of Rome and its empire as a complete living being; it will conjure this whole being before the reader's eyes, inscribing its spatio-temporal coordinates in their imaginations. To do so, Polybios knows, required a particular "vividness of presentation" (R, 444) or Aristotelian *energeia* achieved through "graphic clarity."[23]

Having "consciously become the eye of Rome,"[24] Polybios followed in the footsteps of Fortune, who had abandoned Greece for Rome: "Just as Fortune has steered almost all of the affairs of the world in one direction and forced them to converge upon one and the same goal, so it is the task of the historian to present to his readers under one synoptical view the process by which she has accomplished this general design" (R, 44). The Greco-Roman historian ends his account of the rise of imperial power at Carthage, having followed both Fortune and Scipio, the "annihilator of Carthage."[25]

It is at Carthage that the historian invents what Johann Gottfried Herder will later describe so vividly as the *scenario of retaliation*.[26] We can thus trace this scenario visualizing the end of empire back to 146 BCE, to the moment when Rome destroyed Phoenician Carthage and inherited the Carthaginians' maritime empire in the Mediterranean. Before analyzing Polybios's famous scene in detail, however, let us first become acquainted with his reflections on the rise and fall of empires.

Fortune Taking Off Her Wings: Theorizing Imperial Rise and Fall

Inventing imperial historiography as a world power's "general history," not an accumulation of unrelated parts, Polybios wanted to understand the causes of Rome's sudden rise (R, 44). Living in Rome, Polybios benefited from the Romans' "historical consciousness," that is, their sense of continuity with the past and of history as both national and world history.[27] Polybios's plot is "the unification of the world" under Roman leadership.[28] This synoptical view included the idea of non-synchronicity, an idea that we will again encounter in the context of Oswald Spengler's morphological history. The cause of Rome's victory over Carthage, Polybios maintains, had to do with uneven development of the two empires. Rome, he argued, was expanding, while the state of Carthage was already in decline (R, 345).

So how exactly did Polybios theorize the cycle of rise and fall? Comparing the Roman Empire to "the empires of the past" (R, 42), Polybios touched on the theorem of "four successive empires."[29] Polybios's reflections deal specifically with the Roman Empire as the last stage in this sequence. Roughly covering the period of the Second and Third Punic Wars, Polybios was very specific about his effort to "understand the formation and growth of the Roman Empire" in a period of "less than fifty-three years" (R, 112, 41). Declaring that "[a]ll existing things are subject to decay" (R, 350), Polybios linked this "inevitable law of nature" (R, 310) to three successive forms of government: monarchy, aristocracy, and democracy. Decay rules the entire sequence and each specific "constitution," because each form "possesses its own inherent and inseparable vice" (R, 310). Thus, each constitution will degenerate "into the debased form of itself" (R, 310).

This degeneration can be controlled by a mixed form of government such as that of Lycurgus at Sparta.[30] Unlike the rulers of previous empires, the Romans, Polybios claimed, had adopted this felicitous form of mixed rule, thus creating a stable empire. The effect of this form of government is to *postpone* decline; it is a "device for slowing down the movement of the anacyclosis."[31] Nevertheless, decline is inevitable, and the cycle of birth and death will begin anew. Yet if you want to rule the world, Polybios writes, you must opt for the Roman way, that is, a single-minded focus on expansion—knowing that the empire will eventually end in ruins (see R, 310–311).

At the core of Polybios's theory of imperial rise and fall, we again find traces of Aristotle's philosophy. "[N]othing," Aristotle wrote, "will be eternal or unmovable; for all perceptible things perish and are in movement."[32] His example is the *house* which, like all things, "perish[es] by being resolved into the elements of which they consist."[33] This is what Polybios calls the "law of nature" or the "inexorable course of nature" that turns everything—bodies, houses, and empires—into ruins, rubble, and dust (R, 310 and 350).

However, we ought to keep in mind that in this text Polybios entangles two logics: the time of empire is *the time before the end*, that is, before its inevitable (natural) death and before Fortune's decision to favor another people. Fortune or *Tyche*, Polybios writes, "is forever producing something new" (R, 44). Polybios uses *Tyche* in at least two senses: as contingency or "pure chance" and as providence. Even when he uses Tyche in the sense of "providential plan,"[34] the goddess ultimately signifies contingency and mutability. Polybios's source for the concept is a treatise entitled "On Fortune" by Demetrius of Phalerum, a commentary on the destruction of the Persian Empire by Alexander the Great. Demetrius argued that "Fortune, the incalculable power which enters into no compact with mortal men, had merely granted the Macedonians the wealth of Persia to enjoy *for a time*—until she decided to deal differently with them."[35]

Whether as a cipher for a providential plan or as the break with this plan, Fortune is the goddess who embodies the unexpected. The logic of Polybios's text about the Romans' rise to power in less than fifty-three years is thus a double logic. One is the natural logic of inevitability, the other a logic of pure contingency—no one knows the mind of Fortune. All that can be known about her is what she has done and is likely to do again.

History as Spectacle: Toward an Analysis of Polybios's Carthaginian Scenario

Against Aristotle's claim that tragedy was "'more philosophical'" than history, Polybios "insisted on the superiority of history to poetry because its subject-matter is true."[36] And yet, demythologizing history and using Fortune to think contingency, the Greek writer nevertheless liked the metaphor of history as spectacle. Fortune, Polybios writes, is "forever enacting a drama in the lives of men, yet she has never before in a single instance created such a composition or put on such a show-piece as that which we have witnessed in our time" (R, 44). Concluding with the scene of Scipio at Carthage, the historian-as-eyewitness does the work of Fortune. Putting on a "show-piece," he sets up a Carthaginian stage, on which he exhibits the Carthaginian remains of empire and writes Scipio's moment of triumph as a scene of contemplation.

With this theatrical staging, Polybios writes himself into a Greek tradition. Ancient Greek historians and poets thought of history as a spectacle of "great and wonderful deeds" performed for the gods and, sometimes, by the gods.[37] This conception is part of what Martin Jay calls "ocularcentrism of Greek thought."[38] Privileging sight, the Greek philosophers, historians, and poets asserted and explored the nexus of seeing and knowing; they were deeply invested in acts of looking at the world and acts of making their world visible. The subject of this culture is a self at once invested in seeing and being aware of being seen, of existing under the gaze of the gods. Polybios's scenario partakes in this ocularcentric culture. Arresting the flow of his narrative of conquest, he has Scipio reflect on its meaning for Rome. I will explore both the content and the particular form this contemplative moment takes. Putting Scipio onstage, Polybios engages his readers in a *mise-en-scène* of acts of looking that involves Scipio and the barbarian enemy as well as Polybios and his Roman readers.

"A Day Will Come": Polybios at Carthage

Polybios's pivotal scene is the culmination of days of slaughter. His account of the actual conquest of Carthage's citadel is lost. Based on *The Histories*, Appian (ca. 95–165 CE) reports in his *Punic Wars* how Scipio and his men entered the city through the narrow streets leading to the citadel. The street fighting turned into "scenes of horror" when the soldiers set fire to the houses. Appian writes, "the crashing grew louder, and many corpses fell with the stones in the midst."[39] Then the "street cleaners" used the mass of falling debris and human bodies—some dead, others still dying—to make a level road, across which the army entered the town, the horses "crushing their faces and skulls."[40] After six days and nights of fighting, Scipio "sat down on a high place where he could overlook the work."[41] "Much remained to be ravaged," Appian continued, but then Scipio relented.[42]

Appian's scene of Scipio overlooking his army's "work" is based on Polybios's "eyewitness account."[43] This is also the case with Appian's version of Polybios's scene of the weeping Scipio. Reading the *Punic Wars* as "literature of anti-imperialism," Pocock points out that Appian portrays "Polybius' hero" in a critical light.[44] In contrast, Polybios portrays Scipio as a "great and perfect man, a man in short worthy to be remembered."[45] No ruthless conqueror, the Roman general felt deeply ambivalent about the Senate's order to raze the city. In Appian's transmission of the Carthaginian scenario, Scipio famously retains this compassionate character.

Let me quote the passage in its entirety:

> Scipio, when he looked upon the city as it was utterly perishing and in the last throes of its complete destruction, is said to have shed tears and wept openly for his enemies. After being wrapped in thought for long, and realizing that all cities, nations, and authorities must, like men, meet their doom; that this happened to Ilium, once a prosperous city, to the empires of Assyria, Media, and Persia, the greatest of their time, and to Macedonia itself, the brilliance of which was so recent, either deliberately or the verses escaping him, he said:
>
> *A day will come* when sacred Troy shall perish,
> And Priam and his people will be slain.[46]
>
> And when Polybius speaking with freedom to him, for he was his teacher, asked him what he meant by the words, they say that without any attempt at concealment he named his own country, for which he feared when he reflected on the fate of all things human.[47]

A day will come—this Homeric quote constitutes the heart of the passage, which Appian concludes by invoking again the authority of Polybios's autopsy: "Polybius actually heard him and recalls it in his history."[48]

Framed as an incident of eyewitnessing, the text invites the reader to "see" a man who stands above the city in a contemplative pose. This effect of "imaginative eyewitnessing" is an aspect of mimesis that Aristotle defines as the pursuit of "vividness" or *energeia*.[49] As the tempo of the narrative slows down, setting and protagonist suddenly seem to come closer, and the narrator appears to take a step back, foregrounding the protagonists.[50] Beginning to display affinities with another medium, drama, Polybios's historical narrative spatializes, creating its own performance space and staging a scene, in this case a particularly vivid scene of quiet contemplation that is Aristotelian in nature. For political life, Aristotle thought, is characterized by "un-quiet," contemplative activity by "an almost breathless abstention from external physical movement and activity of every kind."[51]

Having narrated the un-quiet of military conquest, Polybios thus staged an incident of action arrested, a moment of *contemplative activity*.[52] This contemplative thought, Aristotle believed, always required images: "when the mind is actively aware of anything it is necessarily aware of it along with an image."[53] As I will argue in more depth later, representing the perishing Carthaginian "house," this scenario of Scipio gazing at Carthage references the performance space of ancient Greece, in particular, the Greek scene-building. It also references the way in which this visual order, inextricably linking theater, religion, and politics, positioned subjects as looking and being looked at. Finally, like this performance space, the Polybian scenario privileges sight, tightly interweaving multiple acts of looking and their temporal trajectory.

Dense intertextuality is the second aspect of this scene that matters for my reading. The historian, Momigliano writes, "knows he has a literary tradition behind him."[54] With Scipio's Homeric quote, Polybios references a specific *teichoscopic* moment or incident of watching from the city walls: standing on Troy's rampart, Andromache implores Hector to limit the fighting to the defense of Troy as she points out the fortress's weak spots from her elevated vantage point. Hector's response is heroic posturing, promising to fight while knowing "in [his] heart and soul" that "the day will come when sacred Troy must die."[55] Greek tragedies restaged this "privileged scene of viewing."[56] In Euripides's *Trojan Women*, for instance, Hecuba witnesses the destruction of Troy, the play asking its audience to imagine the fire "as burning in the background"; the tragedy ends with the chorus reporting "the sound of the citadel crashing."[57]

The theorem of the four successive world empires is the second intertext. *The Histories* share this intertext familiar to Polybios from Demetrius's "On Fortune" with the Book of Daniel (written around 164–163 BCE).[58] A kind of *chronosophy*, mixing prophecy and periodization, the latter text focuses on Daniel's interpretation of a dream haunting Antiochus IV.[59] Like the Homeric quote, it thus references a text based on the nexus of seeing and knowing. Bringing together two ancient ways of thinking about time, the "metallic schema" and the succession of empires, the text adds an "apocalyptic perspective."[60] In this dream, the king sees a statue made of gold, silver, copper, iron, and clay being smashed by a stone. This vision, Daniel explains, signifies a succession of four empires leading from Antiochus's golden empire to a fourth iron kingdom. Daniel's prophecy of things to come then opens onto an eschatological horizon, the eternal kingdom. Having destroyed all previous empires, this empire "will itself endure forever."[61] Versions of this *chronosophy* began circulating as Greeks and "Orientals" witnessed "Romans taking over everywhere," expressing their hopes that history would be reversed, "giv[ing] back to Greece or to the East the world-rule they had lost."[62]

Like the Homeric quote, this chronosophic text does two things: it registers the triumph of conquest—Rome is now one of the empires. And it thematizes imperial time as limited. There is thus more at stake in this scene than Polybios, the embedded historian, paying homage to Scipio. Speaking at the moment of glory, the Roman general's foreboding also signifies more than a mere awareness of the mutability of Fate or the possible reversal of circumstances. What Scipio understands at this moment is *the inevitability of the end of empire*. And what Scipio voices at this moment (quoting Homer and alluding to the texts about the succession of empires) is Polybios's "inevitable law of nature"—that all things are destined to perish (R, 310).

This tension between imperial triumphalism and the terror of the end will accompany all of Western imperialism. But let us return to the actual scene that Polybios so skillfully puts before his readers' eyes. The temporal dimension of the text's scopic trajectory is clear. As readers, we are looking with the narrator at Scipio in the act of looking at both present and past. In the present, we are told that his tear-filled eyes are resting on Carthage, a city in the process of being destroyed. Polybios does not detail what precisely Scipio and Polybios saw at that moment, watching the city *in the last throes of its complete destruction*—there is no mention of collapsing houses or crumbling walls, no tale of conquest in Appian's manner. Then affect and gaze change, as Scipio, emerging from a long moment of silent reflection, stares into the past, his inner eye fixed on images of a long series of wrecked imperial cities. That is, Carthage's debris deflects Scipio's gaze into the recent and not-so-recent past: before Carthage perished, other empires and their cities also perished—most recently Macedonia, now occupied by the Romans, and Corinth brutally razed to the ground like Carthage.

The image of Carthage burning is thus part of a series of (mental) images of destroyed cities. Scipio's backward look is of course doubly mediated: we are talking about a (realist) text and, as I already pointed out, the Roman general's eyes seize upon mental images: images of ravaged Troy remembered from another text, Homer's *Iliad* and its staged versions, images of the dead cities of previous empires. This scene makes readers participate—however indirectly—in Scipio's gaze at the present and the past, makes them participate in his production of mental images.

After turning from present to past, the text at the end then opens toward the future and Scipio's fear for his own country. Yet when it comes to the future, the text's visual layer fades away. What we are not given to see, and what Polybios wants us to think Scipio might have seen, is the wreckage of Rome and the barbarian enemy watching Rome perish. In this passage, the future enemy, the one who might be looking at Rome "as it was utterly perishing and in the last throes of its complete destruction," is thus not given shape, yet the shadowy presence of the barbarian avenger is palpably present.

Scipio's enemy is Hasdrubal, but in the mind of Roman commanders it is the image of Hannibal that lingers. Polybios's *Histories* contributed to this phenomenon, singling out two particular features of Hannibal: first, Polybios repeatedly returns to Hannibal's "hatred of Rome" (R, 189) and, second, he locates this enemy at the very borderline between civilization and barbarism.[63] In a "scene" that Freud analyzed as the *ur-scene* of his identification with Rome's Semitic enemy, Polybios explains how Hannibal's fierce hatred originated with his father's demand to swear eternal enmity to Rome.[64] Narrating the battle of Zama, Polybios writes a scene of enmity beyond reconciliation. Here, Hannibal reminds his Roman enemy who he was: "I am that Hannibal who after the battle of Cannae became master of almost the whole of Italy, who later advanced up to Rome itself, pitched camp within five miles of her walls" (R, 470).[65]

Polybios never uses the word "barbarian" for the general in command of the "barbarians," a mercenary army whose "strange babble of shouts and yells" is a sign that they are lacking the unity that characterized Rome's legions (R, 476).[66] And yet in the *Histories*, Rome's fiercest enemy is both noble general *and* barbarian. Contrasting Hannibal with Hannibal Monomachus, a gladiator, Polybios reports that the latter proposed that they "teach the army to eat human flesh and accustom themselves to this" (R, 401). Hannibal refuses the monstrous proposal, and yet the shadow of Hannibal-Monomachus lingers. Moreover, Hannibal's "acts of cruelty" (R, 401) were as legendary as those of his successor, Hasdrubal. The latter made himself "an *object of terror*" to the Romans and his fellow-citizens alike by having his Roman prisoners tortured on the walls of Byrsa "in full sight of their comrades," having their eyes and tongues torn out, and flaying them alive.[67] In Polybios's end-of-empire scenario, the image of the barbarian enemy is present as the afterimage of Hasdrubal's dead predecessor. Or, put more precisely, the afterimage of Hannibal hovers at the periphery of Scipio's and the reader's vision as the shadow of Hannibal-Monomachus is falling on the Roman victor at the moment of his triumph.

So what exactly does Polybios capture in this "funereal vision," his scenario of gazing at the wreckage of a conquered city?[68] First, this

Carthaginian scenario inscribes a specific understanding of *imperial time* as *endtime* into the Roman imagination. "Empire," Charles Maier writes, "is a project to dominate time as well as space."[69] The scenario refers us back once more to the text's double logic, the tension between the Aristotelian law of nature and Fortune's law of pure contingency. Scipio at Carthage stages a moment of "full understanding of the basic causal principles that govern the operations of the universe," Polybios's insight into the natural law of ruin at work at the heart of empire-building.[70]

Polybios thus came to understand that like all other living things *in the long term*, empires will perish.[71] This is his Aristotelian law of ruin. We need to understand Polybios's barbarian enemy with this temporal logic in mind. In his scenario, Polybios makes the barbarian enemy the figure of contingency, that is, of the possibility of the end—*in the short term*. This metonymy, the figure of contingency as barbarian, introduces the idea of the conquest of time. In the same way as barbarians and *barbaricum*, their territory, need to be conquered and the empire needs to be fortified against their incursions from the outside, so imperial endtime needs to be conquered and fortified. *Imperial time*, Polybios thus teaches his readers, from the very beginning of the empire's foundation in violence, is a time suspended between the *Romans' military disciplining of time into imperial duration* and *the barbarians' irruption into the space of disciplined time*, between the stasis of duration and the explosion of the unpredictable—the unpredictable that needs to be conquered again and again. Scipio at Carthage is thus not an apocalyptic scenario of impending doom; it is a scenario that conceives of imperial time as *the time before the end*—a time to be counted in decades, if not centuries, not in weeks, days, or hours.

Second, Scipio at Carthage is a *rubble gazer scenario*. Scipio is not looking at the ruins of a former empire, signaling its power by the splendor of buildings whose remnants still allow the beholder to imagine former perfection. What Polybios makes him see, albeit in a mediated way, is a burning, "falling" city—the wreckage, the "fallen" objects—houses, walls, towers—of conquest. And what will be left of the great merchant empire that the Romans fought for two centuries will be broken things, objects smashed and burned. Signifying defeat, this debris indexes power and the end of a "noble empire," but not the kind of *sublime* power that will be associated with the Roman Empire, the first to have established "sovereignty of the world" (R, 469 and 472). Such sublimity the Romans reserved for themselves. Carthage's remains lack the political-aesthetic value of former grandeur that ruins index. And unlike ruins, they do not evoke the combined affect of pleasure and horror, but sheer naked terror.

Is Scipio at Carthage about the "natural cycle" of birth and death thus a scenario of "imperial melancholia," to use Charles Maier's phrase (R, 345)?[72] Not exactly. The affect that this scenario captures is of a stronger, more violent type. Johann Gottfried Herder (1744–1803), the German philosopher and theologian, read a different law into Polybios's scenario, and I think correctly so. The scene of Scipio weeping, Herder wrote, exemplified "an eternal natural order," the "law of retaliation" and "revenge."[73] What Polybios captures is a moment of imperial terror—the conqueror standing in the wreckage of Carthage overcome with terror born of the idea of *retaliation* and the inevitable *end of empire*. The scenario hints at the possibility that the vanquished—the people Romans still called "barbarians"—might be the same ones who in some indeterminate future will scan the "fallen" things left after their assault on Rome. The end will come—regardless of Fortune's whims—because the end of all things is a law of nature. And at the end there will be the barbarian.

On the Carthaginian Stage

Polybios, I argue, constructed his scene as if it were staged and watched. This theatrical aspect of his multilayered image-text requires a brief excursus, concerning the performance space of archaic Greek theater. Vividly depicting a moment of Aristotelian contemplation, Polybios's scene traces the production of images in the "activity of reason."[74] What matters to us is the following: Plato's and Aristotle's "conception of philosophical 'vision,'" Andrea Nightingale argues, was modeled on the viewing of "the sacred images and spectacles."[75] *Theoria* first designated the journey of a man called the "*theoros,*" whom Greek cities sent to sacred sites or religious festivals, events like the City Dionysia held in imperial Athens to honor the god.[76] Combining "theos (god)" and "thea ('sight,' 'spectacle')," philosophical *theoria* turns the theo-aesthetic mode of the Dionysia into the metaphysical gaze.[77]

As I mentioned above, Polybios's reference to Homer concerns a teichoscopic moment in the Trojan epic and on the stages of Greece. Greek playwrights used the *skene* or scene-building as a means to stage *teichoscopy*, the act of viewing from the city's walls, having messengers standing on the building's roof. It is this building that is of particular interest here. By the fifth century BCE, the City Dionysia (a kind of "Empire festival" uniting all 400 communities subject to Athens) included a permanent performance space.[78] Initially, the theater's basic features consisted of the banked *theatron* or "watching-place" on the slope of the Acropolis, and the *orchestra* (the space of the *chorus* and the actors, all of whom were wearing masks).[79] Imperial citizens and colonial "*theoroi*" sent to attend the pan-Hellenic spectacles were not the only and perhaps not even the most avid spectators.[80] The playing space of the Dionysus theater was a sacred space (located between the god's temple and the altar) where plays were staged for the god, who was present "in the person of the priest and his statue."[81]

Aeschylus added the *skene* as the third element of the sacred performance space of ancient Greek theater. What do we know about this background-building? First, in Greek tragedy, killing and dying happened inside the *skene*. Second, Aeschylus's plays defined the stage-building as a palace or house. From wooden hut, the *skene* developed into a solid stone building and stage sets began to include what Aristotle called *skenographia*, which literally means "'painting of/on a *skene*.'"[82] In *The Persians*, the *skene* is still missing and the barbarian locale is signified by the Persian chorus itself; the *Oresteia* then names the *skene* as Agamemnon's palace.[83] In the *Bacchae*, Euripides juxtaposed *skene* and "memorial," a second palace whose "burnt ruins" are visible onstage next to the scene-building.[84] In contrast to Euripides's juxtaposition of *skene* and smoldering ruin, in *Agamemnon* Aeschylus used only one building onstage, calling on the audience to visualize in quick succession first an intact palace (the *skene* onstage) and then the ruin of Paris's palace in faraway Troy, described by the returning herald.[85]

In Greek tragedy the *skene* thus stands for the House of Death and the House of the Sovereign; it appears onstage and offstage, intact and ruined. Needless to say, Polybios was intimately familiar with the way in which the performance spaces of imperial Athens embodied the site of sovereignty. After all, the agora of Megalopolis, Polybios's place of birth, included one of the largest Greek theaters.[86] Rome, on the other hand, did not have a permanent theater until 55 BCE. Nevertheless, theatrical production exploded in the wake of the Punic Wars and plays with titles like *The Trojan Horse* introduced the Romans to the "events of the Trojan War."[87] These plays, staged on temporary wooden stages, were performed during the *Ludi Romani* or other theo-political games, held with increasing frequency "during the dark days of the Second Punic War, when Hannibal was regularly ravaging the countryside."[88]

The temporary stages became part of the "theatricality" of the aristocracy's self-presentation in public life.[89] On these wooden stages, "*trompe-l'oeil* elements" replaced the *skene*, feigning the architecture of power with ever more elaborate perspectival scenes painted on wooden panels, in some cases entire cityscapes.[90] In the case of permanent stone theaters outside Rome, this remodeling of the "Hellenistic stages into the Roman type" included a basic scene-building with three openings.[91] The playwright Plautus uses the word *scaena* for the scene-building, its scenic façade, *and* the stage itself.[92]

As I discussed in the introduction, my concept of *scopic scene* or *scenario* refers to Freud's reflections on scopophilia and the performance space of Greek and Roman theaters. What Polybios wants his readers to *see* is a great man on the stage of world history, but there is more at stake in his passage about Carthage's rubble. I propose to read the narrative performance space of Polybios's scene as a text that relies on its readers' familiarity with the stage architecture of Greek and Roman theater and the use of the *skene*.[93] This involves two things: first, Polybios stages the fall of the Carthaginian Empire as the ruination of the scene-house. Second, in the space of this scenario, the Aristotelian "house" (the philosopher's example of the cycle of life and death) reemerges in the form of the *skene* as the site of Carthaginian sovereignty. Seated in the watching-space of Dionysus's theater, the spectators were straining to see the people and objects on the stage. In Polybios's scenario, we stare with Scipio at the Carthaginian *skene*. This *skene* is smashed to pieces in an orgy of destructiveness. And this shattered Carthaginian stage threatens to become the ruined stage of Rome.

This strong affinity to the stage as one of the core institutions of the ocularcentric culture of ancient Greece and Rome is one important aspect of Polybios's rubble scenario. In the introduction, I discussed the inquisitive gaze of Freud's explorer in the ruins of his theater, and I now want to work out in more detail one last aspect of Polybios's densely visual text, its *mise-en-scène* of different acts of looking. Aristotle thought that looking was best suited to define pleasure because in this activity, the passage of time is completely absent: "Seeing seems to be *at any moment complete*, for it does not lack anything which coming into being later will complete its form."[94] Freud theorized this "Schaulust" as "the scopophilic drive";[95] and he emphasized the particularly "pressing" nature of this drive.[96] This pressing desire to see is more directly linked to primary narcissism than other drives.

This hunger for images, or what Goldhill calls "the desiring eye," is also at work in Polybios's scenario.[97] In this scenario, Freud's "narcissistic subject" of scopophilia is the imperial subject:[98] the conqueror, who saw, seized, and demolished the Carthaginian Byrsa/*skene*, still chasing images, pursuing them into the interior spaces of his imagination and groping in the twilight zone of his memories for the image of the barbarian hovering at the periphery of his vision. And Polybios wants his readers to capture all of this at one glance. A *scopic scenario*, this scene about imperial endtime also enacts a craving for visual mastery, putting into place a basic power constellation: it is the Roman, the imperial subject, who is looking at the conquered city and holds the image of the enemy in his mind, however fleetingly. Or, put differently, visualizing the possible death of his own empire, Scipio is capturing the image of the barbarian he imagines looking at Roman rubble in some remote future. With this constellation of imperial subject looking and barbarian subject being looked at, Polybios's scene lays the groundwork for ruin gazer scenarios visualizing *the imperial subject in a position of scopic mastery*, a *sovereign* subject taking hold of the image of the barbarian it has conquered.

Conclusion: The Memory of Scipio and the Specter of Hannibal

After Carthage, the memory of Scipio was kept alive. "Memory," Karl Galinsky writes, "defined Roman civilization."[99] The Roman triumph was one of the techniques of this memorial image-making, creating the cultural memory of Roman history as "the deeds of Roman people" and staging the empire—its geography and subject peoples—for all to see.[100] Eventually earned for "adding to the Empire," triumphs were state rituals whose "documentary realism" exhibiting "living images" made generals and exotic prisoners part of the Romans' culture of spectacle.[101] Both Scipios held triumphs after the victory over Hannibal at Zama and the capture of Carthage. After their death, they continued to live as images. Scipio the Younger was honored by having his *imago* or wax mask stored in Jupiter's temple on the Capitoline Hill.[102] The gallery of great men or "summi viri" in the Augustan Forum most likely included his statue.[103] Romans "walked under a kind of city in the sky, where roof sculptures, honorific column portraits, and arch groups" honored "the highly placed."[104] The decorative arch installed by Scipio on the Capitoline was among the more "demonstrative" displays.[105]

Living on as images, they also continued living in texts. In *De Republica*, for instance, Cicero immortalized grandfather and grandson, and he celebrated their patriotism in his *"Dream of Scipio."*[106] Finally, Tacitus reported that Scipio was the object of a particular act of imitation on the part of Germanicus. After having put down the string of German rebellions that began with the battle in the Teutoburg Forest (in 9 CE), Germanicus was reassigned to Syria. Going on a grand tour of Roman Egypt, the future Syrian governor emulated Scipio Africanus walking around in "Greek clothes."[107]

The friend-enemy imaginary that Polybios's *Histories* narrated also kept the memory of Hannibal alive. Repeatedly eluding capture, Hannibal died at his own hand in 183 BCE, but for centuries he remained a powerful spectral presence in the Roman imagination. Sallust (ca. 86–35 BCE), the theorist of Roman decadence, discovered the Carthaginians as a remedy against Rome's decay and the destructive effects of the "acquisition of empire."[108] Before the seizure of Carthage, Sallust believed, "the dread of an enemy maintained the community in its good practices."[109] Once this *metus hostilis* or "source of alarm" was gone, politics degenerated into looting and the republic "split into two parties."[110] Hannibal embodied this *metus hostilis*, and he did not disappear with the victory over Carthage. On the contrary, the threat of the external enemy remained alive.

Mary Beard argues that triumphs sometimes hinted at the "ambivalent power struggle" between conquerors and conquered.[111] Scipio the Younger displayed objects "that the Carthaginians had brought to Africa from all over the world."[112] One empire thus ended up displaying the spoils of another, thereby hinting at the "fragility" of imperial power.[113] Scipio the Elder supposedly paraded a Numidian prince and ally of the Carthaginians through the streets of Rome, a spectacle that might have drawn attention to Hannibal's absent presence. Polybios's scenario also merely gestured at the figure of the barbarian avenger, leaving a void to be filled in the reader's imagination by their image of Hannibal. Likewise, Virgil construed his readers as imperial ruin gazers with a firm grasp of the barbarian enemy as their eyes were scanning ruins—objects whose peculiar articulation of absence and presence defies any attempt at full scopic mastery. In the wake of Virgil's attempt to fortify the imperial Roman subject's gaze and stabilize its scopic mastery over the barbarian avenger, Silius Italicus (ca. 28–103 CE), Roman consul and poet, will create a remarkably different scenario, anticipating Herder's postcolonial revision.

TWO

Building the Roman Stage: The Scenographic Architecture of the Augustan Era

Introduction

With this chapter, the focus of analysis will move from the imperialism of the Roman Republic and Polybios, the first theorist of empire, to the Augustan Principate and Augustus himself. In this era, the official consensus was that Fortune would abide in the metropole forever and ever. It was Virgil who expressed this consciousness most memorably in book 1 of the *Aeneid*, where Jupiter, speaking from the deep Trojan past of the Romans, utters his famous prophecy that Romulus "will inherit the line and build the walls of Mars / and after his own name, call his people Romans. / On them I set no limits, space or time: / I have granted them power, empire without end [*imperium sine fine*]" (AFa, 56). Rome, the *Aeneid* asserted again and again, will be built, and it will exercise its empire unlimited by space and time.

The focus of this chapter is the Augustan-era renovation of Rome and the creation of an imperial imaginary, a spatio-temporal imagination centered on Rome as the empire's stage.[1] One of the questions I will address in part 1 is the following: If Polybios depicts Scipio staring at Carthage's *rubble*, how does Virgil then succeed in getting his readers to conjure a mental image of (Hannibal contemplating) Rome's *ruins*? Or, put differently, how did the Romans themselves think about ruins? That is, did they develop a way of thinking that lent meaning to fragmented remains? And did they strive to render their own ruins—past, present, and future—visible? My answer to this question is affirmative. Ruins, I will argue, refer to a theo-political order, rubble does not; imperial ruins belong to the conquerors, meaningless rubble to the conquered.

On the most basic level, this means that in order to perceive, for instance, the falling structure of Jupiter's golden-roofed temple in the *Punica* of Silius Italicus (ca. 28–103 CE) as ruination—as the production of a ruined structure signifying imperial glory—it had to be part of imperial architecture in the first place. The temple belonged to a monumental imperial architecture that, on the one hand, created Rome as the sacred center and stage of the empire and, on the other, made this order visible at Rome and across the empire. This theo-political order made of stone inscribed an eschatological temporality, Rome's infinite duration, into the Roman imaginary, thus providing a visible ground plan on which the new imperial imaginary about disciplined Roman space and time rested.

Augustus: Performing the Principate

In his *Res Gestae Divi Augusti*, a manifesto of heroic conquest and benign imperial rule written near the end of his life, Augustus portrayed himself as empire-builder as well as builder and restorer of Rome.[2] Octavian was named "Imperator Augustus Caesar D(ivi) F(ilius) Augustus" in 28–27 BCE after his victory at Actium, a battle ending the "excruciating period of civil wars."[3] The title *imperator* means commander, while *Augustus* combines multiple meanings deriving from *augere* (to augment or increase), *auctoritas* and, finally, *augury* (connecting political rule to Roman theology).[4] Claiming to restore the republic, Augustus and his allies announced a program of "moral rearmament, and recovery, sponsored by the gods."[5] Central values were *pietas* (as respect for the customs of the ancestors) and a glorification of the warrior-farmer.

Augustus added the titles *pater patriae* and *princeps*. An experiment, the *principate* never "abolished the institutional apparatus of the republic."[6] Augustus developed "the role of the emperor" gradually.[7] He then initiated a period of conquest (with campaigns against the Parthians that secured the east and military forays across the Rhine and along the Danube).[8] Since Augustus's *Pax Romana* tends to be seen through a rather enchanted lens, it is worth remembering one of the instruments of imperial rule, mass crucifixions, the most spectacular happening before and after Augustus's rule: six thousand of Spartacus's followers in 71 BCE (one year before Virgil's birth) and five hundred rebels whom Titus crucified every day during the siege of Jerusalem in 70 CE until "there was not enough room for the crosses."[9] "Civilization of terror" adequately describes the other side of imperial Rome's culture of spectacle.[10]

Having produced a culture replete with "images of world conquest," the Augustan era came to a close with the emperor's deification.[11] Following Augustus's own script, the spectacular funeral pageant put on show a wax effigy of the emperor clad in triumphal garb and one made of gold seated on a triumphal chariot. A cortege of ancestors that included the mythic Aeneas and consisted of actors wearing masks advanced to the Campus Martius, where the body was burned. The emperor's ashes were later placed in the Augustan mausoleum, completed in 28 BCE at Augustus's behest. This dynastic house of death was originally flanked by two bronze tablets displaying the text of the *Res Gestae Divi Augusti*. Written in 13 BCE, the *Res Gestae* were introduced as "a copy of the achievements of the deified Augustus, by which he made the world subject to the rule of the Roman people."[12]

Bookended by the triple triumph and the ritual of the apotheosis, the Augustan Principate instituted a theo-political order based on the Romans' culture of the spectacle. This post-republican order was centered on a new kind of leader who was fond of theater and acting. Augustus's performances served to create the office of the emperor for this new political regime. As he was dying, Augustus famously demanded a mirror, asking his entourage "whether he had played his part well in the mime of life."[13] One of Suetonius's "scenarii" recalls Augustus masquerading as Apollo, the god who intervened in the battle of Actium on the emperor's side.[14] This marriage of politics and theatricality was not Augustus's individual style but that of the Roman aristocracy;[15] it was not a new phenomenon but one that the Augustan regime kept perfecting.[16]

Making Rome Visible: Scenographic Architecture and the Imperial Stage

"I found Rome a city of clay; I left it a city of marble" is the other famous sentence that Augustus pronounced on his deathbed.[17] Augustus's *Res Gestae* expressed a new "ecumenical conception of the Roman Empire" surfacing at this time.[18] "Imperial Rome" now meant "the Rome of the empire" in a territorial sense, and "the Rome of the emperor (who governs), absorb[ing] in its fate the fate of mankind."[19] Augustus's report shows that the empire was "almost a new world which had been discovered, explored and mastered."[20] By publicly exhibiting a text that drew the boundaries of the new *imperium* by recounting his conquests with topographic precision, Augustus inscribed the image of this new world into the imagination of Rome's citizens and the visitors who came to the city from all corners of the empire.[21] Providing the backdrop for the spectacles of power, Augustus's ambitious program of urban preservation and transformation turned the city's fora and public buildings into "monument[s] to imperial power."[22]

The man who wrote the architectural treatise theorizing Roman classicism was Vitruvius, a military engineer. He dedicated *De Architectura* (ca. 15 BCE) to Augustus as empire-builder, comparing him to Alexander the Great and modeling himself on the latter's architect. Vitruvius emphasizes the "principle of soundness" in the laying of firm foundations and choice of durable materials.[23] With an eye on the Greek past, the Roman architect explained to Augustus that civic architecture has to represent the "greatness" [*maiestas]* and "authority" [*auctoritas]* of the imperial state.[24] According to Vitruvius, this monumental Greco-Roman style married durability to beauty following nature's design of the human body and adjusting for our deceptive eyes.

It seems that it was also a response to the haunting presence of Carthage. Trauma, Eric Santner writes, is an event that has not yet happened.[25] Roman intellectuals and politicians kept returning to the era of the Punic Wars, belatedly producing and reproducing the meaning of this event by repeating Polybios's scenario and by searching for answers to the question of why the rival empire fell. This cultural work on the event of Carthage penetrated their architectural imagination. Cicero, for instance, argued that the ideal city needed to be located at a distance to the sea. Carthage's location, Cicero had Scipio explain, "already holds the potential for its own destruction."[26] Two aspects of maritime trading cities accounted for the "mercantile decadence" of the old Carthaginian enemy: first, by mixing "languages and practices," trade led to the undermining of tradition; second, the cities' cosmopolitan inhabitants abandoned "agriculture and warfare," following their "indolent desires."[27] In contrast to Carthage, Rome's location provided "safety on solid ground."[28]

Roman civic architecture consisted of "tall, highly visible structures."[29] Its deliberate neoclassicism was meant as a contrast to the supposed Orientalism of Anthony, Augustus's former adversary. Manifesting the power of the new empire, this neoclassicist monumentality with its "robust objects" also meant heightened visibility.[30] With these architectural changes and the apotheosis of Julius Caesar (in 44 BCE) and Augustus in 14 CE (leading to a conception of Roman emperors as guarantors of earthly and divine order), the city of Rome became the world's *stage*, the building process *visibly* articulating imperial *Ordnung* and *Ortung*, or order and territorialization, around Augustan Rome as the empire's sacred center and the "theater of the world."[31]

Drawing on the vast literature on the "significance of the gaze in the economy of the Roman imagination," Richard Jenkyns's study of the ways in which Romans experienced and represented their city emphasizes this spectacular dimension.[32] Jenkyns quotes a piece of fictional advice to Augustus—"You will live, [Maecenas] says, in a sort of theater of the whole world"—and then explains that the author wrote in Greek, "and so the root meaning of 'theater' is fully alive in his text: 'a looking on.'"[33]

Let me begin this discussion of the restructuring of Rome as world stage with the topic of restorations. What do we know about them? Varro's appeal "for the rescue of the temples fallen in ruins" was heeded at the end of the republic.[34] During the Augustan age, preservation became state policy.[35] Looking back at this reconfiguration of Rome, Ovid wrote: "Crude simplicity is a thing of the past," adding: "Now Rome is golden [*aurea Roma est*] and possesses the vast wealth of the conquered world."[36] Put more bluntly, the city was now expensively, and probably also garishly, renovated, and it was filled with the spoils of war—temple façades from Greece, obelisks from Egypt, and later, cult objects from the temple in Jerusalem.

The literature on this urban renewal program is vast, and I will limit myself to the sites and buildings that will be the object of later renovations and restructurings. Like Caesar, Augustus lived in a residential compound on the Palatine, right next to the new newly built sanctuary of Apollo, thereby blurring the distinction between "human and divine."[37] The complex was located in the "heart of the ancient city of Romulus," close to the casa Romuli, the archaic hut of Rome's founder.[38] A "holy relic" connecting the present to Rome's distant Latin past, the archaic hut was constantly restored.[39] The practice signaled the emperor's veneration for the city's Latin past, the "mores maiorum," or customs of the ancestors, and the simpler values of the soldier-farmer.[40]

To Vitruvius, the archaic hut represented a "barbarian style" still alive in the less developed parts of the empire.[41] The colossal mausoleum, on the other hand, represented the power of the empire's core. Completed by 28 BCE, the monument reaffirmed Octavian's victory over Antony at Actium, ending the civil wars, and the fall of Alexandria in 31 BCE.[42] Flanked by two Egyptian obelisks, the mausoleum signified the might of the newly restored empire, founded on the emperor's "triumph over the so-called

2.1 Altar of Augustan Peace, frontal view. Museum of the *Ara Pacis*, Rome. Photograph by George Steinmetz.

eastern barbarian," referencing east and west in complex ways.[43] On the one hand, it clearly echoed Alexander's tomb at Alexandria, claiming the imperial legacy of the Macedonian *hegemon* who had Hellenized the East, Persia and India.[44] On the other hand, it located the Roman emperor's body in the West. While the body of his rival remained in the East, buried next to the Ptolemaic kings and queens, Augustus would be interred at Rome.[45]

Between 13 and 9 BCE, the mausoleum was made the "reference point" in a "new colossal complex" formed by the *Ara Pacis* (Altar of Peace), and the *Horologium* or sundial with an Egyptian obelisk removed from Heliopolis.[46] One of the most famous monuments of the Augustan period, the *Ara Pacis* was erected by order of the Senate after Augustus pacified the western regions of the empire, Hispania and Gallia, and its "official inauguration took place on 30 January 9 BC."[47] According to Zanker, two of the figural reliefs, *Pax* and *Roma*, on the altar's back side combine bucolic depictions of a golden age with a "warlike" Roma, representing Augustus's peaceful reign (figure 2.1).[48] With these two panels, the altar made the connection between "imperial victories over barbarian enemies" and the *Pax Augusta*, establishing a golden age for the Empire and the entire known inhabited world or *oikumene*.[49] The procession panels on the north and south side of the altar realistically represent Augustus together with other historical figures, Rome's political-religious elite.

A piece of Augustan propaganda, the altar connects Augustus to Aeneas in one of the panels depicting Aeneas sacrificing to the Penates. The lines linking the mausoleum, altar, and *horologium* (sundial) inscribed the birth, death, and horoscope of Augustus into the topography of the imperial city.[50] Augustan architects also remodeled the landscape of the city's fora, among them the Roman Forum, which was one of the stages in the ritual of the triumphal processions. The renovations included one of the many newly built "billboards for propaganda," an honorific arch whose narrative panels glorified Augustus's victory over the Parthians.[51] In addition, the *princeps* commissioned a *Forum Augustum* next to Caesar's forum that included a temple to Mars Ultor, or Mars the Avenger.

Not surprisingly, the Forum's gallery of great men included a statue of Scipio, since Rome's every "corner reflected the Roman culture of triumph."[52] Theaters and the grandiose new Roman-style scene-buildings, the *scaenae frons*, were an integral part of this scenographic cityscape. Pompey ordered the first permanent theater built in 55 BCE, and Augustus's urban renewal administration restored the ostentatious building. With his theater legislation, Augustus re-emphasized the boundary between the stage and the civic space of the state, and added two new permanent theaters.[53]

The Roman Stage

The Roman invention of the *scaenae frons* was part of this transformation of Rome into a "performative stage."[54] This new kind of scene-building introduced the imperial grandeur of Augustan architecture into the performance space of Roman theaters. Replacing the Greek *skene*, this ornate three-storied "stage facade" was made of stone and arranged around three evenly spaced doors, with all of its niches filled with statues of emperors and gods (figure 2.2).[55] Vitruvius prescribed that the "royal door" or *regia* at the center "ought to be decorated in a manner befitting a palace."[56] The Theater of Marcellus, one of the two theaters built under Augustus, directed the audience's gaze at such a massive *scaenae frons*, representing imperial sovereignty.

These new stage-buildings had their precursors on the temporary stages. While the *scaenae frons* in Augustus's theater was not quite as ornate as the three-story-high "theatrical extravaganza" decorating one of the temporary stages, it was an imposing, solid stone structure representing imperial power.[57] This imperial *scaenae frons* architecture asserts the end

2.2 *Scaenae frons*, Roman Theater, Merida, Spain. Photograph by Håkan Svensson, CC BY-SA 3.0.

2.3 Room of Masks, Villa of Augustus. Photograph by George Steinmetz.

of history with its immutable decor, establishing the image of "a stable and hierarchical cosmos."[58] Moreover, the combination of royal door and enormous exedra symbolizes the reconciliation of earth and heaven around the *princeps*. Virgil relies on the existence of an image of this new scene-building in the mind of his Roman contemporaries, when he re-creates Polybios's imperial endtime scenario as a staged scene.

Policing the city's stages, the emperor reserved the stage as a space of political action for himself. Augustus's house on the Palatine, located next to the Temple of Apollo, contained rooms whose walls were covered with frescoes modeled on stage fronts.[59] In the Room of the Masks, for instance, all four walls of the room were painted as stage sets. Modeled on the *scaenae frons*, the niches between central door and side doors are decorated with images of intricately drawn theater masks; the central door opens onto an idyllic landscape with an archaic cult-object set, the artists' perspectival technique lending depth to the proscenium (figure 2.3). Theater masks also appear to the left and right of the central stage structure. Like the combination of temple and residence, the presence of this theatrical architecture points to "Augustus' integration of the public and private spheres of his life."[60] Channeling the Late Republic's "theatricality . . . into a subtle embellishment of centralized authority," Augustus "laid the metaphorical foundation for the future self-dramatization of imperial office."[61] The juxtaposition of religious still-life and masks expresses the tension between pacified empire and the continuing violence of imperial conquest involving the emperor as heroic actor on the world stage.

Rebuilt under Augustus, Rome was then endlessly described. Affirming the reality of the city as the empire's stage, these descriptions often elaborated on the theater metaphor.[62] Strabo, for instance, ends his Rome visit in his *Geography* (ca. 7 BCE) with a walk that takes him past the Augustan Mausoleum, pointing to the fora and "temples," or "the Capitolium and the works of art there."[63] Underlining the *spectacular* aspect of the city, Strabo concludes that these renovations turned Rome into a mesmerizing "spectacle": all of this "presents to the eye the appearance of a stage-painting."[64] With his metaphor, Strabo hints at the fact that Rome's core now functioned as an architectural stage on which monumental buildings represented the site of sovereignty in the same way the *skene* or, rather, the Roman *scaenae frons*, did in Roman theaters. This stage metaphor will remain one of the central elements of the language of geopolitics.

Under the reign of Augustus, Rome became a metropolis signifying sovereignty: it was here that imperial policy was decided. With its new monumental architecture as backdrop, the metropolis now functioned as a stage where imperial power was performed. Dominating the city was the massive Temple of Jupiter on the Capitoline Hill, its roof made of gilded tiles, a "half-barbarous adaptation of a Greek model."[65] From this hill, the god looked down at the Roman stage much like Dionysus did in his Athenian theater.

Representing a theo-imperial sovereignty written in stone, this Augustan stage was the site where the rituals of empire were performed. To the Romans, "'spectacle'" meant "visible glory" or "grandeur," and "'theatricality'" carried connotations of solemnity and magnificence.[66] These elaborate spectacles staged the great men and heroic events of Roman history—events like the *Ludi Scaenici*, the theatrical performances that were part of the public games, or the extravagant aristocratic funeral processions, and rituals of deifications. The triumphal processions with their aesthetic of "'documentary realism'" advanced toward the Temple of Jupiter on the Capitol Hill, their "imperial geography" staging empire for all to *see*.[67] These rituals displayed exotic barbarians, living captives or their effigies, alongside spoils of war, panels of battle scenes, and models of captured towns. Visually demonstrating the idea of Rome's "conquest of the globe," they forced captives into "the role of actors, miming their moment of defeat."[68]

Many of these theo-political rituals included actual theatrical performances with temporary stages, and all of this—the architectural remodeling, the rituals, the plays—created an imperial culture that mobilized the desire to see, making great men and their deeds and the world, in which they acted, its space and its people, visible.[69] And let us not forget the other spectacles, the crucifixion of slaves or rebels on the Campus Esquilinus, the ritual execution of captives at the end of the triumphs, and "the ritualized terror of gladiatorial games."[70]

The City and the Empire

Augustan Rome was the center of this brutal world rendered visible by Roman experts with the help of so many different media. Yet what the Roman god saw from his perch was more than Rome: "when Jupiter gazes [spectat] from his Capitol over the whole globe, he has nothing to look upon [quod tueatur] which is not Roman."[71] Exhibited across the empire, maps like Agrippa's map in the Campus Martius added a global dimension to this picture. Pliny described the map's effect as "[setting the world] before the eyes so it can be seen"—showing not just the *orbis Romanum* and its provinces, but the entire "*orbis terrarum*."[72]

Other media besides maps and geographical texts made the empire (the articulation of *urbis* and *orbis*) visible in Pliny's sense—set before the eyes, so it can be seen. As I mentioned before, honorific arches multiplied, and with their decorative relief panels incorporated the "theme of the universal empire" into the new layout of the city. Trajan's Column with the sculptors' rendition of the Dacian Wars as expedition into "deep barbaricum" and encounters with new peoples is only one example, albeit from a later period.[73] The paean to the Romans' civilizing mission by Aristides of Smyrna, entitled *To Rome* (144 or 156 CE), sketched the empire as a global space opened up by Roman engineers and as *a space open to be seen* by all. And Tacitus reports that "barbarians" visited the city marveling at Rome's might as they toured "the sights," their tour often ending at Pompey's theater.[74]

Thus texts, maps, and monuments *set empire before the eyes*, and so did the global architecture with its new imperial style. "In architecture, as in so much else," William MacDonald writes, "the Romans overcame: their buildings quickly arose in distant places that knew Rome's power and its agents."[75] With the Augustan age, permanent theaters began to appear across the entire empire, the founding of *coloniae* often including large theaters from the very beginning. We find, for instance, remnants of theaters and *scaenae frons* in France, Spain, Turkey, or Palmyra. After being razed, parts of Corinth's theater were shipped to Rome and Carthage's theater suffered the same fate. However, the re-foundation of the city as Roman Carthage at the time of Augustus included a massive theater representing Roman sovereignty in the African colony.[76]

Throughout the eastern and western parts of the empire—across Roman Syria, Greece, Spain, and Africa—temples and altars to Augustus and Rome were built, often filled with statues of the emperor. Heliopolis, now known as Lebanon's Baalbek, was built up into one of the largest sanctuaries in the empire. Local aristocracies also erected imitations of Roman monuments. Cities on the periphery that were conquered and rebuilt—Carthaginian Cordoba in the Third Punic War, Palmyra in the third century CE—all came to exhibit this standardized visual language of Roman imperial art and architecture.

The effect of this construction and representation of imperial space through architecture, maps, and texts was an imperial imaginary, a spatio-political imagination centered on Rome. The imaginary's spatial dimension was firmly in place by the end of the third century when a Gallic rhetor spoke in the forum of Augustodunum (present-day Autun) about a map displayed on the porticus of a school. By "studying the map of the world," he explained, "we see that no country is foreign."[77] Making Romans *see that no country is foreign*: this is the pleasure and power of Roman maps—to create a mental image of politically mastered imperial space.

What about the temporal dimension of this architectural imaginary? Romans were building and rebuilding for their own glory, the monumentality of their stone buildings promising durability and duration. By turning Rome from a "city of brick to more durable marble," Augustus stated that "[t]he future of Rome is secure."[78] Inscribed into the empire's geopolitical space in hard, everlasting stone, the time of Augustan Empire is eschatological. Like its space, the empire's future was infinite.[79] And yet, Polybios's scenario of imperial endtime was so indelibly imprinted on the Roman elite's memory that even at the time when Romans tended to think *their* empire might last forever, the scenario remained insistently present.

At the time of Augustus, Rome was thus reconfigured as the sacred center of the world, based on a political theology organized around the Divine Augustus, proclaiming that secular history had come to an end and divine order had been realized.[80] This eschatology in stone needed to be maintained as such. One of the last major restorations of the city was undertaken by Theodoric, who asked architects in 500 CE to restore the damage inflicted by time and "barbarian" attacks. Stating that Rome's buildings were witnesses to the empire's "power" and "grandeur," Theodoric asked the architects to safeguard "all that is ancient."[81] The purpose of this preservation program sounds uncannily modern: "To leave to future generations," Theodoric wrote, "monuments that will fill them with admiration."[82]

Conclusion

Architectural designs and foundations have a strange affinity to ruins, Louis Marin writes, because foundations are the only traces left once a building has gone to dust.[83] The Roman Empire, whose capital was built on solid ground, with solid stones, remained visible in its equally solid ruins. In 1945, Macaulay calls it "an imposing revenant," tracing the line of ruined cities along the North African shore where "the Roman ruins stand like outposts of a ghostly world, forming the frontier of a crumbled empire whose legions march the paved streets through the arches of triumph, whose colonists murmur in the stone theatres."[84] Proud of her own empire and disdainful of the Nazis' attempt to build one, Macaulay surveys this North African ruin belt, finding "grace and civility" in these African-Roman ruins and the "pioneering empire's" firm and "proud domination of the ruling race in savage lands."[85] Algerian Timgad still "has a firm masculine beauty," expressing a kind of imperial vigor, Macaulay implies, that the Nazis aspired to but ultimately lacked.[86] "Rome in Africa," Macaulay writes, possibly with an eye toward the British reoccupation of their colonies, "may yet resurrect."[87]

Roman Carthage belonged to Macauley's ghostly ruin belt. At the time of Virgil's writing of the *Aeneid*, the city of the ruin gazer scenario was a construction site, the city's Roman aristocracy imitating the monumental architecture of the capital city.[88] Virgil celebrated Augustus's Rome of marble and gold and invented the golden ruins of its deep past. As Catharine Edwards writes, "Rome's ruined past is part of the city even before its foundation."[89] On the site of this new Roman Carthage, Virgil then confronted his readers with the sight of the Roman *scaenae frons* in pieces.

THREE

Virgil's Imperial Epic and Lucan's *Pharsalia*, or the Specter of Hannibal and the Ruins of Rome

Introduction

"The stage," T. P. Wiseman writes, was Rome's "mass medium."[1] Virgil (70–19 BCE) was known to his contemporaries because he recited his early epic poems in Roman theaters to large audiences. He also read excerpts of *The Aeneid* (29–19 BCE) to Augustus on four consecutive days in 23 BCE. The first public reading of the West's most famous epic of empire thus coincided with the refashioning of the empire's metropolis into a monumental stage. Virgil then had the audacity to ask his readers to imagine this splendid stage in ruins.

Dido, David Quint argued, "embodies a monstrosity that characterized Carthage itself, the great barbarian foe of Rome."[2] As they sacked, rebuilt, and sacked again the Phoenician city, the victors began to think that this "cyclical repetition of Carthage's rise and fall" was "demonic."[3] Centuries later, J. M. W. Turner captured the Romans' obsession with the Punic city in *Regulus* (1828), titled after one of the Roman generals of the Second Punic War tortured at Carthage by having his eyelids removed. The spatial composition echoes Turner's allegorical Carthage pictures set in the city's harbor (figure 3.1). Positioning the spectator in that same harbor, *Regulus* takes her right into the scene, staring into the glaring

3.1 J. M. W. Turner, *Regulus* (1828).

sun. Its white-yellow center holds the spectator's gaze captive at the same time as it erases everything located in the far distance of the scene, making the horizon vanish and leaving only the faintest trace of the buildings at the end of the harbor. Only when we manage to detach our eyes from this blinding core do we notice the left side of the harbor with its churning water and warships and the right side with its monumental architecture drenched in the same whitish-yellow light.[4] There is pleasure involved in the act of viewing and an intimation of terror at the sight of the world dissolving into a glaring void.

Turner transmitted some of the meaning of the Polybian scenario, and so did Virgil. In the epic's most melodramatic scene, Dido, queen of Carthage, cries out for revenge, conjuring Hannibal from a future that is already the past for Virgil's audience—Hannibal, to whom Virgil's friend Horace referred to as "an abomination to our parents," and about whom Augustine will write that he set out to "liberate" the world from the Romans.[5] Having read Polybios's *Histories* with their scenario of imperial endings, Virgil gives Scipio's inchoate fears a firmer shape. Inventing his own scenario of the end of empire and imperial retaliation, like so many of his fellow Romans Virgil returned to Polybios's Carthaginian scene and its theatrical aesthetics. As his audience listens to Dido's curse, they "see"

Augustan Rome crumble into imperial ruins while Carthage turns into rubble one more time.

Virgil's Epic of Rise and Fall

The *Aeneid* is an epic of political eschatology celebrating Augustus's reign as the new golden age, divinely ordained and restoring the ancient Latin values. Hannibal's name is absent from Virgil's epic, a text that insistently foregrounds acts of looking within its scenes and invites its implied viewers to stop and stare, but both Regulus and Scipio make an appearance and the story of the century-long war "constantly shadow[s]" the journey of Aeneas and his men.[6] Narrating the ancient prehistory of Romans as Trojans, whose mission is the founding of their city on Italian soil, Carthage's destruction is an event in the story's future that is never told. But it is known by Virgil's Augustan audience, just as they know that Rome is no longer the archaic Trojan settlement of their own founding legend but the bright gilded center of the world—and they know too that Polybios made Scipio face a blinding truth about the newly risen Rome.

Eschatological in nature, the West's most famous imperial epic is marked by anxieties about the repetition of decline *and* the empire's eventual fall. Creating a palimpsest of ravaged cities, Virgil portrayed not only Dido, Carthage's founder and its queen, but also Aeneas, the heroic founder of Rome, as imperial ruin gazers. "There was an ancient city (colonists from Tyre possessed it): Carthage, far opposite to Italy and the mouths of the Tiber, rich in wealth and most fierce in zeal for war."[7] These lines about the "rich new town" are part of the *Aeneid*'s opening section, written more than a century after Roman armies sacked the "savage city" on the shores of today's Tunisia.[8] In the wake of Octavian's acceptance of the title Augustus in 27 BCE, the Roman author thus celebrated the new age by narrating a mythical re-foundation, that of "Asian" Troy as Rome.

In this tale, the conflict with Carthage and memories of the city's destruction play a central role. In the epic's opening section, the struggle over hegemony is presented as a struggle between Juno on one side, Jupiter (and Venus) on the other. "Juno, we are told, cared more for Carthage / Than for any other walled city of the earth," Virgil writes, "and fate permitting, / Carthage would be the ruler of the world" (AFi, 3, 4). However, Juno "had heard long since / That generations born of Trojan blood / Would one day overthrow her Tyrian walls" (AFi, 4). Anxious to prevent Carthage's fall, Juno "buffeted on the waste of sea those Trojans / Left by the Greeks and pitiless Achilles / Keeping them from Latium, holding in memory /

The old war she had carried at Troy" (AFi, 4). The Trojans thus "wandered [for years] as their destiny drove them on / From one sea to the next: so hard and huge / A task it was to found the Roman people" (AFi, 4).

This "task" is Aeneas's, a task for which he is prepared by Virgil's divine machinery acting under Jupiter's gaze.[9] Escaping from burning Troy, carrying his father on his back, Aeneas promises his men: "We hold our course for Latium, where the Fates / Hold our settlement and rest for us / Troy's kingdom there shall rise again" (AFi, 10). We are thus again told a story about a rising city and a story of resurrection: the resurrection of Scipio and his enemy, Hannibal.

Virgil's Palimpsest of Fallen Cities

As Virgil had promised in his *Georgics*, Octavian/Augustus is at the center of the epic poem both in the guise of his Trojan ancestor, Aeneas, and as the emperor whose reign establishing Rome's universal dominion the poem celebrates as the *telos* of Roman history.[10] The epic tells this story as the fulfillment of Jupiter's prophecy of Rome's "empire without end"—of time and space (AFi, 13).[11] But the *Aeneid* is not a story about the glorious Augustan present. Instead, as Duncan Kennedy observes, "rather than looking back from the age of Augustus to Troy, the poem takes as its narrative 'present' events in the aftermath of the fall of Troy and insistently looks 'forward' from there to the age of Augustus."[12] Moreover, Virgil has his readers see beyond "the events of the poet's own time," because Jupiter's prophecy extends Rome's time: "empire without end"—*imperium sine fine* (AFi, 13).[13]

On one level, the story Virgil tells is a simple travel narrative involving a group of wandering Trojans and a series of imperial cities: Aeneas and his men leave Troy, a city that no longer exists; they spend time in Carthage, a city that is being built by Phoenician colonists; they then alight on the shores of Italy, where they found Rome, a city—such is Jupiter's promise—that will last forever, and become the center of an empire without limits. The city that these travelers will found will then destroy its rival, Carthage. Within the foundational logic of this imperial epic, Aeneas's sojourn in Carthage (and his love affair with Dido, the "Oriental" queen) is a detour, albeit a necessary one, since it helps Virgil establish Roman-ness as distinct from its "Oriental" enemy (AFa, 64).[14]

When Aeneas lands on Libyan shores, he discovers a temple to Juno that Dido is building. Standing "spellbound" in front of a frieze narrating the Trojan War and the city's ruination, "Trojan Aeneas" stared "in awe at all the scenes of Troy."[15] The fall of Troy—the city Aeneas is called upon to re-found as Rome—is the epic's "traumatic kernel," and its image in the vicinity of Carthage, a city equally doomed to fall, captures the anxiety at the core of imperial mimesis.[16] But let us return to the epic's opening. What makes this beginning so intriguing is the odd temporality it sets in place: as I already mentioned above, Virgil's contemporary readers knew that Scipio had ruined Punic Carthage. That is, embarking on their adventure of reading (or listening to) Virgil's epic, they knew of the impending fall of the ancient city and its "hostile race" (AFi, 104). With this peculiar temporal structure, a kind of "hindsight-in-foresight," Virgil made the Punic Wars, the epic battle between Trojans-become-Romans and their "Oriental" other, the most important event in Roman history.[17]

The prolepsis also created a particular subject position: while Virgil first called Carthage an "ancient city," he later had the readers/listeners gaze at a "new city," a city in the process of being built, as they wandered its streets in the company of Aeneas. Furthermore, Virgil writes about the founding of Punic Carthage at the very moment when Roman Carthage is being rebuilt a third time under the aegis of Augustus.[18] Yet regardless of whether Virgil called the city ancient or new, he drew on his readers' imagination to provide images of this same city in ruins—events vividly depicted by Polybios's and Appian's texts and the many Roman paintings or frescoes similar to the one in Dido's imaginary temple. Familiar with vivid accounts of Carthage's fall, the audience also knew about the fall of Carthage's predecessor, Tyre.

Augustan Rome, the imperial city that does not yet exist, is present throughout the epic. In book 8, Aeneas and his men finally arrive in Italy and the site of the ancient city, and Virgil compares past and present, what the Trojan immigrants saw (a small settlement) and what his listeners see in the present: "[D]istant still they saw / Wall, citadel, a few house tops—the town / Built heavenward by Roman power now" (AFi, 232). In the first lines of book 1, we find a reference to the newly restored metropolis and its "high walls" (AFi, 3).[19] As Jenkyns points out, Virgil's technique here amounts to "indirections" of "paradoxical vividness."[20] This ekphrastic image of the city in its imperial splendor is haunted by images of splendor in ruins.

Telling his famous story about Rome's long-distant past, Virgil thus used his readers' knowledge of the future to come—the fall of Carthage and the rise of Rome, Scipio's destruction of Carthage and Augustus's architectural reconstruction of Rome as the imperial center of the Roman world. The ways in which Virgil created this implied ruin gazer are worth analyzing in more detail. His construction involved Carthage and Troy,

Aeneas and Dido. We first encounter Carthage at the moment of its founding. Yet after the Carthaginian queen kills herself out of love for faithless Aeneas and curses Rome, the lines that follow evoke the future sacking of her "noble city" (AFa, 150): "[F]or all the world *as if* enemies stormed the walls / and all of Carthage or old Tyre were toppling down / and flames in their fury, wave on mounting wave / were billowing over the roofs of men and gods" (AFa, 150–151; emphasis mine). Virgil's simile describing the Phoenician city's reaction to the death of their queen was meant to recall to his listeners' minds the event that established Rome's dominion in the Mediterranean—and it revived images of the aftermath of the battle, images of Carthage in ruins.

In the case of Aeneas's gaze at his ruined Troy, Virgil uses a narrative technique that is similarly based on a temporal gap: Aeneas's scenes of ruin gazing constitute brief interludes in the hero's account of the battles that raged during Troy's last hours, switching between vivid descriptions that bring the ancient battle back to life and contemplative moments in the present of the storyteller. Classicists refer to these scenes as belonging to a particular genre, the *lament for the fallen city*; I would propose to understand them as a form of imperial ruin gazing.[21] Thus Aeneas tells his audience what he saw standing on the roof of his father's palace: "Already there the grand house of Deiphobus stormed by fire, crashing in ruins" (AFa, 85).

This moment of teichoscopic viewing is familiar to Virgil's audience from Roman plays about the Trojan War. It also references a viewpoint located in the past-as-present, that is, in the middle of the raging battle. But when Aeneas arrives at the most dramatic moment of his tale, Virgil interrupts the story with a lament that transforms his epic hero into a contemplative ruin gazer. "An ancient city is falling," Aeneas tells his audience, "a power that ruled for ages, now in ruins" (AFa, 87). The rubble, the things that had fallen, should be ruins because Troy was an empire.

At the onset of book three, Aeneas again draws the audience's attention to the ruined city, as he begins to tell the Carthaginians about the "exiles'" journey and their decision to leave the "plains where Troy once stood" (AFa, 103). This shift in narrative mode between vivid tableaux of battles and urban laments involves two aspects: on the one hand, the text describes moments of the fall (*urbs antiqua ruit*, i.e., the ancient city is falling), and on the other, it elegiacally surveys the desolate time after the fall: the time not of ruination, but of the ruins themselves (*ruina urbis*, the fallen or ruined city). Virgil emphasized the first, and this emphasis fits with the heroic drive of the imperial narrative that foregrounds the moment of battle, not its aftermath. And yet the sight of the aftermath of empire lingers: Troy was "razed from the earth" and Aeneas—as well as Virgil's readers—remained transfixed by this sight (AFa, 97).

Virgil's palimpsest of fallen cities—from Tyre to Troy to Carthage—opens multiple possibilities for our reading. Does the *Aeneid* unconditionally celebrate Augustus's *pax romana*? Virgil might imply that Rome will be durable and eternal, a contrast to other ancient imperial cities. Tyre, Troy, and Carthage vanished, but Jupiter granted Rome "empire without end": "On them I set no limits, space or time: / I have granted them power, empire without end"—*imperium sine fine* (AFa, 56).[22] Or, alternately, we might read the images of destroyed cities that hover over his epic's first lines and accumulate in the course of time as signs of Virgilian "melancholy," as "an acknowledgment of ambivalence about the triumph of Rome," of the "costs of Aeneas' mission."[23] Or, a third possibility: we could read Jupiter's "empire without end" as mere promise or wish, not as a guarantee.[24] And thus imperial Rome might indeed fall—as did Tyre, as did Troy, as did Carthage.

"Something Terrible Was Born":[25] Dido's Curse and the Specter of Hannibal

The sections of the text dealing with the Carthaginian queen Dido are crucial to this overall construction of the reader as ruin gazer. In my discussion of Polybios's rubble gazer scenario, I argued that Hannibal, the barbarian ruin gazer, maintained a shadowy presence. With Dido's story, Virgil revives that threatening shadow and the terror it still has the power to spread at the height of the Augustan Empire.[26]

I began the discussion of Virgil with his description of Carthage at the moment of Dido's death *as if* enemy troops were raging through the city. In the following, I will trace the ways in which Virgil rewrites Polybios's rubble gazer scenario around the figure of Carthage's queen. My reflections on Virgil's rewritings of Polybios's rubble gazer scenario will focus on the ways in which he engages his listeners' knowledge of this scenario. The scene of Dido driven mad by love and killing herself with Aeneas's sword is part of Virgil's rewriting of Scipio's moment of terror or "dread foreboding" at Carthage.

Let us first follow how Virgil evokes a particular affect, *terror*. Dido's scene evokes "terror" in the hearts of Carthage's citizens (AFi, 120). Mad fury and terror are also the affects that dominate in the passages leading up to this seminal scene. On the one hand, this anxiety is articulated around the city of Carthage. Enraged by Dido's condition, Juno assaults Venus, the goddess who sides with Jove in his attempts to make Aeneas leave the city: "Your fear of our new walls has not escaped me, / Fear and distrust of Carthage at her height" (AFi, 99). This *topos* of dangerous Carthage at the height of power is embedded in a story about a city's rise and fall, revolving around the metaphor of a construction site. When Jupiter finds Aeneas at work "lay[ing] the stones for Carthage's high walls," he summons Mercury to remind the Trojan of his task to rule "Italy, / Potential empire" (AFi, 105, 103). When Dido realizes that Aeneas is preparing to leave, she appeals to her lover: "Have pity now on a declining house!" (AFi, 107). The picture of this decline is an empty construction site of "half-built" towers on which all work has stopped: "Projects were broken off, / Laid over, and the menacing huge walls / With cranes unmoving stood against the sky" (AFi, 98). Barely built, the city is already dying—as is its queen.

The queen's fall is a story about revenge, and this is the *Aeneid*'s second connection to Polybios's story. "I die unavenged," Dido exclaims at the moment of her death (AFi, 120). But as she watches the Trojans leave from her tower, she calls upon the "avenging furies" to "overshadow" her "hell" with their "power" (AFi, 118). What then follows is her famous *cri de coeur*, invoking the specter of Hannibal:

> Then, O my Tyrians, besiege with hate / His [Aeneas] progeny and all his race to come: / Make this your offerings to my dust. No love / No pact must be between our peoples; No, / But rise up from my bones, avenging spirit! / Harry with fire and sword the Dardan countrymen / Now, or hereafter, at whatever time / The strength will be afforded. (AFi, 118–119)

Spoken before she climbs her pyre, "roll[ing] her bloodshot eyes" (AFi, 119), these words articulate the terror Scipio experienced at Carthage by evoking the shadowy image of his barbarian enemy lingering at the margins of his field of vision.

Scipio was haunted by his enemy, and Dido promises her "enemy" (AFi, 116) that she will haunt him. Imagining Aeneas's death "on some grinding reef / Midway at sea," she cries out: "I shall be everywhere / A shade to haunt you" (AFi, 109). At the moment when her "desolation" grows into "terror," she relives the fate of her avenger, hunted from one place of exile to the other (AFi, 112). Dreaming as "the night owl / Seemed to lament, in melancholy notes," she "thrill[s] with fear" and identifies with Hannibal, seeing herself "hunted down / By pitiless Aeneas," a fugitive "[d]eserted always, unaccompanied always," searching "for her Tyrians / In desolate landscapes" (AFi, 112). She then compares herself to Orestes, "hounded on the stage" by his "mother armed with burning brands" while "in the doorway squat the Avenging Ones" (AFi, 113). This was Hannibal's fate at the hands of his Roman avengers: to be hunted, isolated, killed. Merging Dido with Rome's most feared enemy, Virgil thus portrays the barbarian ruin gazer, envisioned by Scipio at Carthage, as Dido-Hannibal.

On the Carthaginian Stage 1

Virgil stages Dido's scene of ruin gazing in ways that provoke his audience to imagine the Roman site of sovereignty in ruins. Much has been written about the theatricality of Dido's scene.[27] The strongest hint at "the theatricality of [Dido's] story" is the nightmare discussed above, in which Virgil references the *Oresteia*, the play in which Aeschylus introduced the *skene* (see chapter 1).[28] I propose to understand Virgil's *mise-en-scène* of Dido's death with the stagelike aesthetics of Polybios's endtime scenario in mind. Dido erects her pyre "deep in the heart of her house" (AFa, 145). That is, in the courtyard of her palace located in the Byrsa, the Carthaginian capitol and site of sovereignty.

The queen first stands on "her high tower" (AFa, 148), hurling her curse at Aeneas and his line. After this prologue, Virgil narrates the scene taking place in the palace's "inner courtyard" (AFa, 150). Making his audience witness Dido "clamber[ing] in frenzy up the soaring pyre," Virgil shows her on the couple's bed installed on the pyre, next to Aeneas's sword and his "effigy" (AFa, 150, 145). The scene culminates in her death, witnessed by a chorus of women who "see her, doubled over her sword, the blood / foaming over the blade, her hands splattered red" (AFa, 150). Transgressing the boundaries of Greco-Roman civilization, Dido joins the savage women of Athenian tragedy. Ultimately, she resembles Hannibal as Polybios portrayed him: a barbarian.

Blurring the boundaries between Greek theater and epic, Polybios arranged his scene in a manner that let his readers imagine the Byrsa, the Carthaginian site of sovereignty, as a smashed *skene*. Trusting in his audience's theatrical imagination and their familiarity with Polybios's scenario, Virgil takes his listeners back to the same setting, where he confronts his readers with a scene in which Dido calls on Hannibal to destroy the city that Aeneas will found. But while Polybios engaged his audience's knowledge of the performance space of Greek theater centered on the Greek scene-building, the *skene* of Virgil pointed them in a different direction.

Virgil's audience knew that the Augustan re-foundation of Carthage included the building of a theater, and in the scene narrating Aeneas's arrival at Carthage, Virgil does two things: he foregrounds the spectacular dimension of his epic, and he reminds his readers of this newly constructed theater. Catching his first glimpse of the city, "Aeneas marvels at the immensity, formerly huts."[29] This striking hexameter, Elizabeth Young writes, "prompt[s] the reader to stop and stare."[30] Standing on a steep hill, Aeneas sees a construction site, describing one part of this site, Carthage's theater, in more detail than the others. Workers are "lay[ing] foundations / deep for the theater, quarrying out of rock great columns / to form a fitting scene for stages still to come" (AFa, 62). Roman Carthage's theater contained one of the most ornate *scaenae frons*, the new kind of Roman scene-building dominating the performance space by its massive stone architecture.[31] Virgil, I would venture, asked his audience to replace in their mind's eye the smashing of the Carthaginian *skene* with the demolition of the Roman *scaenae frons*, and the rubble of conquest with the ruins of empire.[32]

The second aspect of Virgil's staging of Dido has to do with the scopic dimensions of power inscribed into his ruin gazer scenario. J. D. Reed analyzes the uncommonly strong visual quality of Virgil's writing, with its frequent emphasis on what "we see." Exploring the gaze of the "implied viewer of Virgil's scenes," Reed comes to the conclusion that "Virgil's gaze is imperial."[33] Let me briefly return to Aristotle's thoughts on poetic image-making. The power to vividly imagine the event described by the epic poet or staged by the playwright, Aristotle believed, belongs to both the authors and their audience: if the poet "put the actual scenes as far as possible before *his* eyes," then the audience will experience the scene "as if [it were] present."[34]

Virgil acts as the master of image production. Like Polybios, he mobilizes the readers' scopophilia, the pressing desire to see, while keeping a tight rein on what is seen. More than in any other scene, Virgil mobilizes the desire to seize the image in Dido's death scene. Here Dido is both seer and seen, Virgil's formal strategies making the reader see her world and death from her point of view but at the same time, always through the eyes of the implied Roman viewer.[35] Offering a meticulously scripted scene on the Carthaginian stage, Virgil stages a moment of scopic conquest, one in which the text creates the conditions for his Roman readers to seize the image of the queen—and through her burning angry eyes the specter of Hannibal.[36]

Virgil thus did not merely remind the Romans of their glorious victory over Carthage; he also called back to mind Scipio's dread foreboding: that a time might come when the barbarian ruin gazer might look upon the ruins of Rome. Virgil alludes to the issue of time in Dido's curse: "But rise up from my bones, avenging spirit! / Harry with fire and sword the Dardan countrymen / *Now, or hereafter, at whatever time / The strength will be afforded*" (AFi, 119). The time of empire is the indefinite time that remains—*not* now, but hereafter. Dido kills herself, as Hannibal did long ago. On the one hand, the *Aeneid* affirms that Rome's enemies are dead. Augustus resides over Rome's golden age—the eternal present of empire restored. On the other hand, Virgil keeps Polybios's scenario of imperial endings alive, leaving it to his readers to find reassurance in his text.[37]

Book 6, or the Future of Rome

Virgil's listeners might have found this reassurance in book 6, where Virgil narrates Aeneas's descent to the underworld.[38] Having left Carthage for Italy, Aeneas undergoes a kind of re-education in the form of this *katabasis*, eventually encountering his father, Anchises, who prophesies Aeneas's future and the future of Rome as imperial power. What follows then is the "odd device of the parade of heroes who have not yet been born."[39] Inviting Aeneas to take a look at "your own Romans," Anchises begins by praising Julius Caesar and Augustus, who "shall bring once again an Age of Gold" and "extend his power" far to the "north and south" (AFi, 187, 188). Toward the end of his story of Rome's inexorable rise, Anchises dwells on Rome's victory over Carthage. By having Anchises refer to the Scipios and other heroes of the Punic Wars, Virgil might have intended to exorcize Dido's curse—but the very need for this "exorcism" testifies to the raw power of the curse.[40] And just in case Virgil's listeners may have been reassured that the time of empire is infinite, Anchises mentions the untimely death of Aeneas's son, Marcellus, hinting at the gods' desire to punish the Romans for their imperial hubris.

The intertextual entanglement of book 6 and Cicero's *Dream of Scipio* or *Somnium Scipionis* with its conversation among the dead heroes of the Punic Wars also reinforces the tension between Virgil's glorification of the Augustan restoration and the idea of empire's fragility. This dialogue between Scipio the Elder and Scipio the Younger and its cosmic setting (the conversation takes place in the Milky Way) relativizes *imperium*—the "futility" of the glory of political and military command—and the Roman Empire.[41] Looking down at Carthage, Rome, and its world empire, Scipio the Younger is surprised by the empire's small size, a sharp contrast with Virgil's obsessive descriptions of its ever-expanding space. Virgil ends book 6 with Aeneas's departure for Latium and the site of the future Rome, once again certain of his "destiny" (AFi, 186).[42] Yet neither Dido's curse nor the memory of Polybios's scenario of imperial endings is exorcized by book 6. On the contrary, Scipio's dread foreboding is kept very much alive: there will be a time when a barbarian conqueror will overlook the ruins of Rome.

Ruina derives from the Latin verb *ruere*—to fall means that something has fallen. "The Greek words for ruin, *olethros* and *ereipion*," Robert Ginsberg explains, "designate torn down, fallen, wreck, destruction, death," and "[s]imilarly, the Latin ruina . . . signifies something fallen, often said of walls, and by extension, of disaster generally."[43] Virgil's epic is characterized by the tension between the eschatological narrative of Rome's rise to hegemony under Augustus and a narrative of imperial endings that keeps the Polybian scenario a living memory. This scenario connected the sight of a *falling* city and its *fallen* structures, that is, the rubble of conquest, with Hannibal, the figure of the barbarian avenger, and the end of empire. In Virgil's text, *ruinae* are not simply fallen things, bits and pieces of a structure—a tower or a wall—destroyed by war (and further ruined by neglect). Reanimating Hannibal, Virgil replaced the rubble of the conquered with Rome's imperial ruins.

Hannibal's Vision

Inspired by Virgil, Silius Italicus (ca. 28–103 CE), Roman consul and poet, wrote the history of the Second Punic War, in which Hannibal functions as "a sort of anti-Aeneas."[44] Like Virgil's *Aeneid*, the *Punica* (ca. 83–103 CE) is a text that incites its readers to create a particular mental image, the image of Rome in ruins. Silius brings his *Punica* to a close by calling up a picture of Hannibal, escaping after the battle: "But no sight attracted the eyes and minds of the people more than the picture of Hannibal in retreat over the plains."[45]

This picture of Rome's "fiercest enemy" concludes a history of the nascent empire's struggle with Carthage that contains a remarkable scene of Hannibal imagining the future ruin of Rome. More precisely, he imagines a frieze similar to the one about the end of the Trojan War that Aeneas contemplates in Juno's temple at Carthage. This frieze installed at Carthage, Hannibal imagines, would narrate the Carthaginians' capture of Saguntum (in Spain), and in a reversal of the Romans' painting it would show Scipio "tak[ing] flight and be[ing] carried to his comrades," wounded.[46]

Hannibal's scanning of the imaginary Carthaginian frieze culminates in the fantasy of a Punic conquest of Rome. Having Hannibal address his troops, Silius writes:

Show these sights to the people, Carthage; and greater sights shall be forthcoming in the future: *you shall display Rome blazing with Libyan firebrands and the Thunderer cast down from the Tarpeian rock.* For the present, ye soldiers, by whose valour my great deeds are accomplished, make haste to do what is right to be done: throw these pictures into the fire and wrap them in flames. (emphasis mine)[47]

Hannibal's revenge fantasy of Rome in flames and its sacred center, Jupiter's golden-roofed temple on the Tarpeian rock, smashed to pieces, is his response to the sight of a series of panels in an (imaginary) temple at Liternum in book 6 of the *Punica*. These panels, representing the end of the First Punic War from the Romans' perspective, provoke Hannibal's rage:[48]

All these pictures Hannibal surveyed with a face of anger and contempt, and then cried out with rising passion: "Deeds as great as these, the work of my own right arm, shall Carthage yet display [inscribed] upon her walls."[49]

Hannibal's act of reading the Romans' representation of the Punic War repeats Aeneas's surveying of the frieze about Troy's end in Juno's temple at Carthage. Whereas Aeneas saw the city of Troy falling, Hannibal makes his soldiers imagine Rome falling. Or rather, the frieze that does not yet exist will make them see in their mind's eye the picture of Rome's downfall at some point in the future; they *will be* rubble gazers after Rome will have fallen. Hannibal's gesture in the *futur antérieur*—we *will display* pictures of Jupiter's temple crumbling into pieces at Carthage after Rome *will have fallen*—gives form to the vision that Polybios conjured when Scipio averted his eyes from burning Carthage: the barbarian victor celebrating the ruin of Rome.

Inventing the Ancient Ruins of Rome: Aeneas's Arrival in Arcadia

I argued that the *Aeneid* provokes its readers to imagine the heart of the Roman Empire as a ruined *scaenae frons*, and I made the same claim about Silius's Hannibalian scenario. Let me now explain why I think book 8 of the epic justifies using the term *ruin gazers* in the Augustan era and its aftermath. After all, Polybios's scenario, which remained so present in Virgil's epic, was a rubble gazer scenario, and the same applies to Aeneas's sight of Troy—"in reality," and as he contemplates the falling city standing in front of Dido's frieze. Central to my argument is the moment when the Arcadian king Evander takes Aeneas and his men through his modest settlement, Pallanteum, the future site of Rome.

Having landed on Italian shores and about to enter the terrain of these ancient Greek colonists, Aeneas has a vision of this future city in all its glory. From a distance, "they saw / Wall, citadel, a few house tops—the town / Built heavenward by Roman power now / But meager then, and poor, held by Evander" (AFi, 232). Evander, whom Virgil calls "founder unaware / Of Rome's great citadel" (AFi, 240), acts as tour guide, pointing out the major sites of the Arcadian settlement, and Virgil complements the guide's topography, superimposing the map of present-day Rome: "he showed the altar and the gate the Romans call / Carmental" (AFi, 241).[50] The tour takes them to the site of the Capitol, the same site Silius's Hannibal imagines in ruins. Evander, Virgil writes, led Aeneas "to our Tarpeian site and Capitol, / All golden now, in those days tangled, wild / With underbrush—but *awesome even then*" (AFi, 241). They stop at Evander's "austere house," surrounded by grazing cattle and located on "what is now / Rome's Forum and her fashionable quarter" (AFi, 242).

Between the site of the future Capitol and the Forum, they come upon ancient "[m]onuments": "Here too, in these walls, / Long fallen down, you see what were two towns, / Monuments of the ancients. Father Janus founded one stronghold, Saturn the other" (AFi, 241–42). The Latin text uses two words to signify these relics: *reliquias* and *monimenta*.[51] Fagles translates: "you can [here] see relics, monuments of the men of old" (AFa, 253). It is these ruins that interest me, fortifications that have long fallen down but whose outlines are still discernible: "in these walls . . . you see what were two towns" (AFi, 241); and perhaps like the wild underbrush of what one day will be the Capitol, *awesome even then*.[52]

Evander, the Arcadian "exile" (AFi, 241) and "amateur antiquary,"[53] explains that this site, the Pallanteum, was once the home of people living in a state of nature. Fleeing Jove, Saturn arrived on their terrain, united these primitive nomads and hunters, giving them laws, Evander explains, naming the area Latium, and inaugurating "the golden centuries" (AFi, 240).[54] Saturnia, the ruined town, dates from this deep pre-Trojan past, and Virgil makes us understand that Augustan Rome was built on the ancient ruins of Latium's first savage inhabitants.

As Catharine Edwards writes, "Rome's ruined past is part of the city even before its foundation."[55] My point is not merely that Augustan Rome will—or might—fall back into ruins, that Jupiter's golden-roofed temple might one day be nothing more than a *reliquia* in the wilderness.[56] Rather, as I mentioned above, I want to use these ancient barbarian ruins to make a point about Virgil's invention of the concept of imperial ruins in this epic.[57] Crucial to this invention is the concept of a first and second golden age, the age of Saturn and the age of Augustus.[58]

In Evander's view, the ancient monuments of Latium were the worthy destination for his guided tour because they are remnants testifying to Latium's golden age. Connecting this first golden age to Rome's second golden age under Augustus, book 8 also connects the remains of the ancients with the imperial architecture of the moderns. This latter move, I will argue, provides the basis for Virgil's invention of the concept of Rome's glorious imperial ruins.[59] Let me argue this in more detail. Book 8 ends with a famous ekphrastic evocation of Rome's second golden age under Augustus, Virgil's description of Aeneas's shield, seen through the latter's eyes. As Virgil's listeners knew, Augustus had restored Jupiter's golden-roofed temple on the Capitoline Hill and this temple is depicted on the shield.

Once more, Virgil's listeners are told the Romans' future history and "triumphs," but in a different medium (AFi, 252). The shield's ekphrastic narrative of Rome's rise to Augustus's golden age is a cornerstone of all readings, raising the question whether this epic is pure Augustan propaganda. In this "account of the rise of Rome virtually *ex nihilo* to a position of world-empire,"[60] we visit and revisit the city of Rome, from the time of its founding to Augustus's triple triumph in 29 BCE.

Evander's site of ancient monuments is now the sacred urban center of Rome, the city of the Tarpeian Rock, of temples and the Capitoline Hill. Describing Augustus's triumph, Virgil depicts the emperor "enthroned" at his triumph, watching the "long procession" of "[c]onquered races" (AFi, 254). This moment, Virgil wants his audience to understand, is the advent of the second golden age.[61] Virgil's apotheosis of Augustus with the triumphal marches of books 6 and 8 is simultaneously a celebration of the city of Rome at the height of its splendor. However, more significant is this: sketching an arc in book 8 from the first to the second golden age, from the monuments of the ancients to the recently restored and remodeled center of the world, Virgil provides the foundations for his ruin gazer scenario.[62]

All of these awe-inspiring buildings of the Augustan age—the restored Temple of Jupiter, the new Forum, Augustus's own house—might one day too become ruins, revered by the heirs of Augustus.[63] Or they might be the objects of a barbarian conqueror's gaze. Regardless of who will contemplate these ruins, they will not be meaningless rubble. Like Evander's fallen "monuments," they will be noble remnants of a golden age. It is thus Virgil who invents imperial ruins by connecting imperial Rome's prehistory and the history of its future, Evander's archaic ruins and Augustus's monumental stage.

Let me summarize my discussion of Virgil's imperial ruins. Continuing a line of argument exploring the tensions within Virgil's imperial epic, I argued that Virgil rewrote Polybios's rubble gazer scenario. The essence of the argument is the following: that the mental image of glorious Rome in ruins that Virgil invites but never represents is based on two things: first, the image of the metropolis as the theo-political center of the empire—as it was being built and rebuilt more splendidly than ever at the very moment of the epic's writing, and then written in numerous texts;[64] and second, the invention of the concept and the representation of imperial ruins: the foundational ruins of Rome's deep past and the noble ruins of Rome's remote future. The making visible of Rome as the empire's stage achieved by Roman architects and authors working under Augustus coincided with the making visible of its ruins. Virgil began this cultural work in his epic, and Lucan continued it.

Virgil *in extremis*: Lucan's *Ruinas*, or the Vestiges of Venerable Things

Virgil read his epic to Augustus, Lucan (39–65 CE) his *Civil War* or *Pharsalia* (ca. 62–65 CE) to Nero. Having naming Lucan *quaestor* and *augur*, Nero later "compelled" the Spanish-born poet who participated in a conspiracy against the emperor to commit suicide.[65] Lucan's post-Virgilian epic pits Pompey, the defender of the republic, against Caesar, the despot. Focusing on the bloody price paid for Augustus's restoration, the poet's lament accentuates the devastation wrought by the civil wars. The battle at Pharsalus is "the death scene of the Roman Republic"[66] and the republic's glorious empire.[67]

Ruination and its representation is Lucan's focus. The public reading's "heard images"[68] paint the dwellings in Italian cities as "half-ruined" with "huge blocks of stones" from battered ramparts lying about the streets [saxa iacent].[69] "[S]axa iacent"—this expression and the image it evokes return again and again. And so does the idea that "no great power can escape" its end (CW, 9). Lucan expresses the idea of the end in the language of "falling": "Great things come crashing down [ruunt] upon themselves—such is the limit of growth ordained by heaven for success" (CW, 9, 8). Like houses or ramparts, empires crash and fall: "*ruunt*" (CW, 8).

Lucan raises the stakes. That is, at stake is not only the vanishing Roman republic or the entire empire, but the end of the world. When "the final hour, closing so many ages," arrives, everything "reverts to primeval chaos" (CW, 9). Lucan echoes Virgil's apocalyptic depiction of the civil wars in the *Georgics* as "the hour of darkness" raging from the Euphrates to Germany.[70] With Lucan's *Pharsalia*, we enter the terrain of the complexly layered "regime of historicity" (or articulation of past-present-future) in the first century where Roman, Jewish, and Christian conceptions of time and temporalities coexist.[71] I will discuss the Book of Daniel and Paul's eschatological *Letters to the Thessalonians* in the next chapter.[72] Stoic philosophy's "founding myth" of conflagration or recurrence of the world's birth and death in fire is the other context for Lucan's apocalyptic tenor.[73] My reading foregrounds the text's entanglement in the Carthaginian scenarios of imperial endtime.

Lucan links his hyperbolic representation of the conflict between Caesar and Pompeii to Carthage. "The Carthaginian" did not cause as much damage as these fratricidal wars (CW, 5). This "carnage" is, Lucan writes, Hannibal's revenge, his ghost feeding on the Roman dead (CW, 5). In the *Pharsalia*, the memory of Carthage is ever present. Lucan recalls Scipio appeasing the ghosts of Carthage with his blood and has two generals refight the battle of Carthage. Not much is left of the powerful Phoenician empire but the "half-ruined [semirutas] citadels" of Carthage, whose shades haunt the Roman warriors as they slaughter each other (CW, 217, 216).

Filled with patriotic despair, Lucan thus returned to Virgil, to Carthage and, as we will see below, to Troy. He thematizes the end of imperial time—and the end of all time—connecting the trope to Carthage (i.e., Dido's curse), to imperial overreach (i.e., politics), and to Fortune (i.e., Greco-Roman theo-philosophy of history). Prophesying Caesar's death, Lucan also invokes his Stoic version of the law of nature in a passage about the great conflagration and "Mother Earth" receiving the "bones" of all men (CW, 429).

No epic is as replete with images of imperial ruination as the *Pharsalia*, which details the destruction of Italy, its capital—and the entire Roman Empire. After this battle, Lucan writes, "all the Latin race will be a legend" and in Italy's cities "dust-covered ruins [ruinas] will scarce be able to indicate the site of Gabii and Veii and Cora" (CW, 399, 398). And the lament continues: Rome, deserted by Romans, "swarms with the refuse of mankind" (CW, 399).[74]

This lament about the ruination of a country and its capital is followed by an elegiac passage decrying the end of an entire empire. "Fortune," Lucan writes, "wished to show to collapsing Rome, what greatness fell with her" (CW, 401). No "city ever possessed a wider empire," war after war having expanded its reign into the east, but the "fatal day of Pharsalia reversed her destiny" (CW, 401). After Caesar's victory on the Thessalian plains, Rome lay deserted amid a landscape of ruins, and the republic's glorious empire that once reached from the shores of Britain to the African coast died, suffering the fate of Troy and Carthage.

Unlike Virgil's *Aeneid*, Lucan's lament speaks explicitly of *ruins*. That is, like Virgil, Lucan writes about famous "monuments," signifiers of things *ancient* and *venerable*, now destroyed. Drawing attention to Italy's "ghost towns,"[75] he observes that "the memorials [monimenta] of the past" were not ruined by nature or time but war (CW, 399). He also makes ruins/*ruinae* the center of one of the epic's most famous passages: Caesar, erring across the site of Troy after his victory over Pompey, "searched for the mighty remains" of the city's walls (CW, 577). Here, Lucan combines the word *memorable*—"nomen memorabile Troiae"—with "*vestigia*" and "*ruinae*" (CW, 576, 578). There is nothing at all left to see: lying about stones lost their "sacred" shape and Assaracus's "palace" is buried under moldering trunks (CW, 579, 577). Troy's "very ruins have been destroyed"—"*etiam periere ruinae*" (CW, 577, 576).

Lucan explicitly contrasts the ruined ruins of Troy with Caesar's desire to conquer the world. Filled by the desolate sight of "venerable antiquity," Caesar addresses the gods keeping watch over Troy's "ruins [*ruinas*]," asking for "prosperity to the end" to his campaign, promising in exchange that "a Roman Troy shall rise" (CW, 579, 578). Reasserting the power of empire, Caesar thus counters the threat of imperial endings with the command to build a Roman colony. This scene of the total erasure of Troy—and Caesar's insistence on new imperial beginnings—is as famous as Erichtho's resurrection of the fallen Roman soldiers who voice the fear that Lucan's epic repeats incessantly: that this war might spell the end of Rome's vast empire. After Rome conquered Europe, Asia, and Libya, Lucan writes addressing Caesar, "Fortune" is preparing his "graves" in these "lands" (CW, 365).

Lucan, one might argue, takes the *Aeneid* to an extreme.[76] Making the end of empire a central topic, the first-century poet asks his readers to imagine the end of the world. Transforming Virgil's heroic epic into Roman Gothic, Lucan alludes to Carthage, Scipio, and the revenge of Carthage's ghosts. Most importantly for our context, Lucan elaborates on Virgil's invention of imperial ruins, writing about the ruination of Italy and the world, of Troy and Rome—and about the ruination of ruins.

FOUR

The Ruins of the Conquered: Josephus's *Jewish War* and Pausanias's *Periegesis*

History is not always controlled by the victors.

SIMON GOLDHILL, *JERUSALEM: CITY OF LONGING*, 67

Introduction

When discussing the origin of Europe's ruin consciousness, ruin studies, I wrote in the introduction, is stuck in the Renaissance. Rose Macaulay disputed the claim that Romans considered ruins as useless debris and not yet as objects venerable in their own right (see introduction). In the spirit of Macaulay, I proposed that Romans invented the very concept of *imperial ruins*. More precisely, the Romans had a political concept of their own ruins and the ruins of those they conquered. By the Romans' own ruins of empire, I mean two things: first, ruins as signifiers of Roman foundations or beginnings, such as the *crumbled fortifications on the site of prehistoric Rome* that Evander points out to Aeneas upon the latter's arrival on Italian shores in Virgil's *Aeneid*.

Second, the ruined ruins of Troy (represented in the *Aeneid* and *Pharsalia*), referring to the end of King Priam's empire and Troy's *resurrection* or re-foundation as Rome, signified the beginning of a *new* empire, the onset of a whole new historical era in Roman history, if not the history of the entire world. Virgil, I argued, invented the concept—and textualized image—of Rome's *imperial* ruins. In the *Aeneid*, the Roman Empire begins with ruins, and Lucan seized on this invention in his Gothic epic, summoning image after image of ruined Rome.

These are then Rome's ruins of empire. But there is a second ruinscape: the ruins of the countries conquered by Rome. To the Romans these *ruinae* were mere rubble, signifiers of their triumphs and conquering prowess. As we have seen, the rubble of Carthage played a central role in Polybios's history of the Punic Wars. In the *Aeneid*, Virgil reinvented the Polybian scene on the site of the Punic city, asking his readers to imagine the ruined Rome not as a site of rubble but as a stage filled with splendid Augustan ruins. With the advent of the Augustan age, we thus moved from the representation of the enemy's *rubble* in Polybios's *Histories* to the representations of Rome's *imperial ruins*, in the Roman past and in the future.

The Western concept of imperial ruins thus originated together with the concept of the meaningless, worthless rubble of the conquered. That is, the idea of Roman ruins arises out of Carthage's rubble. Or, put differently, empire begins in rubble and ends in ruins. In addition, the concept required the imagination of an imperial space tied to a specific symbolic order, Augustan theo-politics: Rome as a layered space, consisting of the venerated ruins of the archaic Roman past and the imposing architectural structures of the present. Moreover, Roman ruin consciousness involved the concept of imperial endtime. Finally, ruin consciousness as consciousness of imperial endtime is tied to the concept of the barbarian as enemy. In sum, the imperial imaginary as ruinous imaginary organized around ruin gazer scenarios emerges in the culture of Augustan Rome.

The discussion of Josephus's *Jewish War* and the travelogue about Roman Greece by Pausanias, the Greek colonial intellectual, takes us to the beginning of the second century. Josephus (37–ca. 100 CE) and Pausanias (ca. 115–180 CE) are two authors, writing about the empire by taking their readers to the colonies. Appropriating the culture of their colony, the Romans painted Greek ruins on the walls of their villas.[1] In Pausanias's *Periegesis Hellados* or *Guide to Greece*, the Greek traveler's obsession with ruins has a different origin: to remember all that was lost with the conquest of his native country. By the time of Pausanias's loving description of all of Greece's ravaged, ruined sites, and Josephus's lament about Jerusalem, the concept of *ruinae* in Diderot's sense as noble remnants of "palaces, sumptuous tombs, or public monuments" already exists.[2]

Reading Francesco Colonna's *Dream of Poliphilus* (1447), Michel Makarius draws attention to the author's tarrying with the scopic pleasures of ruin gazing as the alert, precise tracking of the remnants leading to the imagination of their original shape. Stumbling through a Roman landscape of stones, rubble, and ruins, the main character voices "wondrous pleasure," his eyes never "[getting] enough."[3] Similarly, Rose Macaulay locates the pleasure of "ruin-gazing" in the "guessing" as the production of an endless chain of (visual) associations.[4] The ruin constitutes the vacant space or "void" in which the imagination's power is set in motion.[5] No classical author was more invested in this guessing and more haunted by ruins than Pausanias.

Appropriating the Roman concept of ruins, Josephus and Pausanias created their own ruins, while participating in the project of expanding the time of empire as endtime. They also worked with the friend-enemy constellation so important to Roman writers since Polybios, albeit making it more complex. Finally, their appropriation included the theatrical staging of the ruin gazer scenario that positions subjects as viewers, organizes the scopic relations of power among them, and visualizes the ruination of the Roman stage: Pausanias writes his ruin gazer scenario in Megalopolis, the capital of Greek Arcadia, with its enormous theater that functioned as a political site and as a performance space linking theater and temple. Josephus explores the spectacle of Titus's triumphal procession with its temporary stages as the mirror image of the ruin gazer scenario.

Bellum Judaicum: Roman Rubble and the Ruins of the Conquered

In his *Res Gestae*, Augustus wrote: "When foreign peoples could safely be pardoned, I preferred to preserve rather than to exterminate them."[6] Going back in time to the civil wars, Lucan's ruin aesthetics laid bare the violence at the heart of Roman imperialism. He was not the only one. Flavius Josephus, who had fought in the Jewish uprising against the Romans (66–70 CE) as commander of Judean forces, became the chronicler of the Romans' war against the Roman province of Judaea.[7] Writing his *Bellum Judaicum* or *Jewish War* (publication date between 75 and 79 CE) in Rome after having defected to the Romans, Josephus narrated the empire's enduring power. He tells the story of the Jewish War as a crisis produced by the uprising in Judaea and subsequent rebellions by Germania's "barbarian hordes" who took advantage of the empire's weakness.[8] With his famous depiction of the returning general's triumph, Josephus demonstrates to his readers "the greatness of the Roman Empire" (J, 384).

Vespasian's and Titus's victory over the Jewish rebels restores imperial order, but the price is high. Josephus blames inter-Jewish fighting for the revolt, but he mentions the daily crucifixions and chronicles the extent of the destruction. By the end of the fighting, the Temple is no more; the only thing left is "the . . . spot where the Temple once stood" (J, 376). His chapter on the siege ends with a description of the Temple and its history before its destruction. With this elaborate description of the Temple's exterior and interior, Josephus creates a lasting monument. And as his depiction saves the Temple from the rubble, he inscribes it into the Polybian scenario as a ruin.

Polybios's story about Rome's rise functions as an active intertext for Josephus's *Jewish War*, generating themes and structuring the plots of his story. In the middle of his dramatic report about the soldiers' advance into the city, Josephus, emphasizing their brutality, mentions the Temple's sublime majesty. And in the midst of this carnage, Titus, the general in charge of the siege, reminds Jerusalem's inhabitants of Carthage's fate. In Josephus's eyes, the destruction of Jerusalem thus repeats the destruction of Carthage. Like Polybios before him, Josephus stands at a Roman general's side as the latter orders the city's annihilation. When there was no one left to kill, the Jewish-Roman historian writes, Titus gave the order "to raze the whole City and Sanctuary to the ground" (J, 374). To this, Josephus, the observer, adds that no future visitor will believe that people once lived on this site.

Tersely formulated, the Scipionian scenario appears in Josephus's "grim account"[9] when Titus surveys what is left of the city upon returning from his tour through defeated Judaea. Titus, Josephus had written in the preface, did everything to save the city and Temple. Here, he blames the rebels for the Romans' act of retribution. Like Polybios, Josephus shows us the Roman general at a moment of contemplation, contrasting in his mind the sight of the desolate city in the present with his memory of the magnificence of the city in the past. Before he writes this scenario of Titus gazing at the ruins of Jerusalem, Josephus again singles out the Temple. Remembering the former beauty of the city's imposing buildings, Josephus writes, Titus compared them to "*the mighty structures in ruins now*" (J, 383). Like weeping Scipio, Titus is moved. Like so much of Josephus's text, this passage produces a doubled vision. Jerusalem is the site of Roman rubble *and* Judaean ruins. Josephus attributes a deep appreciation for the ruins of the conquered to the Roman victor standing amid the rubble of conquest. In other words, Josephus appropriates the aesthetics of Roman ruins developed by Virgil and Lucan, and reconceives Polybios's rubble scenario by inscribing the magnificent ruins of the defeated into his scenario. These ruins are now the object of the conqueror's greedy desire.

Titus's and Vespasian's triumph exhibited the conquest's brutality and its world-destroying effects, staging their "imperium and auspicium," the "divine and human bases" of Roman power.[10] On this occasion, Babylonian artists turned the rubble of conquest into Roman art. One of the moving stages consisted of a multistory *skene* decorated with *tableaux* whose vividness made every spectator see the siege "as clearly as if they had been there," and every stage exhibited "the commander of a captured town" (J, 385). Exorcizing the memory of the Polybian scenario, this imperial *mise-en-scène* reproduced the scopic relations of domination structuring Polybios's *ur-scene*: the conqueror's hungry gaze at the remains of the city, the desire to take hold of the image of the barbarian enemy.

At the Temple of Jupiter, Vespasian and Titus—clothed in purple togas, their faces painted red—awaited the news of the rebel leader's execution. To Josephus, this demonstration of imperial power and the Roman arts of *energeia* proved that "the Roman empire was now most firmly established" (J, 386). Scipio imagined the revenge of the conquered, and Josephus tells the story of their rebellion. They lost, and the empire endures. In his later *Jewish Antiquities* (93–94 CE), Josephus relates Daniel's interpretation of Nebuchadnezzar's dream, dwelling on the power of the iron empire.[11] After the suppression of the Jewish revolt, Josephus came to the conclusion that God "had granted sovereignty currently to Rome," thus reaffirming the empire's duration.[12] He might evoke Daniel's eschatological prophecy about the rise and fall of empires, but he did not think the Roman Empire's end imminent.

"Getting as Far as Arcadia": The Ruins of Roman Greece

Pausanias too reaffirmed Rome's duration, its power to extend its present into the future. Let us move to Rome's Greek territory, to Pausanias's anti-imperial archeology and aesthetics of Greek ruins. Tacitus famously gave voice to the British chieftain Calgacus, who called Britannia's conquerors "[r]obbers of the world."[13] Pausanias does not hurl accusations, he quietly points to the scars of conquest, thoroughly undermining the Augustan fiction of benevolent empire. In the wake of Virgil and Lucan, Josephus found a way to use their ruin concept for the colonized in his text about "the very spot where the Temple had once stood" (J, 376). Pausanias, resigned to the idea that Rome will endure, develops a fully elaborated ruin aesthetic in the Greek colony.

Fortune had left Carthage—and at the same time it abandoned Corinth. If Polybios—intentionally or not—wrote an elegy to the rubble of Carthage, Pausanias composed a lament to the cities of conquered Greece, his *Periegesis*.[14] It is likely that Pausanias traveled in the footsteps of Hadrian, whose many tours of the empire took him to Athens, the Peloponnese, and central Greece.[15] What I am interested in is Pausanias's discovery of Greek ruins in the desolate rubble left behind by the conquerors. Second, I will explore Pausanias's description of Arcadia as Greece's most ancient and most devastated part, and his in-depth look at Megalopolis, the Arcadian capital—an area where there is "nothing but ruins to admire."[16]

Polybios expressed his ambivalence toward the empire he admired by concluding his narrative of Rome's rise with a text that gestures toward the colonial subject as ruin gazer. Pausanias shared Polybios's ambiguity, renouncing the older historian's double vision in favor of a nostalgic resurrection of an idealized ancient Greece. The very first sentence of the *Guide to Greece* raises the issue of colonization, the contrast between Greek city and Roman colony. For the first monument Pausanias singles out as worth visiting, the Temple of Athene of Sounian, was looted, its façade transported to Rome.

Undertaking a kind of "commemorative archeology of Greece,"[17] Pausanias never lets the reader forget the presence of the Roman conquerors. Written during the Antonine period, his project of a general description of Greece does not tarry in the present but instead "heads back in time, seeking a Greece long gone which . . . virtually never was."[18] Touring the ruined sites of present-day Greece, Pausanias strives to restore the memory of a Greece united and free. This pan-Hellenic "historical myth of a total Greece" is the text that emerges with the obsessive description of Greece's decrepit *monumenta*, empty ruinscapes, cities that are now villages or no longer exist at all.[19] A utopia of autonomy, Pausanias's "nationalist response" to Roman domination is a narrative of decline that lists the glories of ancient Greece and assigns blame:[20] had the Greeks been united, Rome would not have won. Rome having won, Pausanias is now in the position of evoking the memories of a Greece that never was, "yet which, nevertheless, was Greece."[21] Thus, Pausanias's mythical Greece paradoxically comes into existence as the effect of Greece being a province of Rome.[22]

The story of Rome frames Pausanias's archeology. Like the rest of the world, Greece is now subject to Rome and "resettled by colonists from the Roman empire."[23] Yet, in contrast to Livy, Strabo, or Appian, Pausanias deliberately foregoes a universal framework, focusing instead on one part of the empire, Greece; within that framework, he ends with Arcadia, geographically the colony's heart on the Peloponnese and chronologically its most ancient territory. Or so it functions within Greek discourse, where Arcadia meant "above all an extremely ancient land" characterized by unstable boundaries between civilization and "[s]avagery."[24] According to Polybios, who was a native of Arcadia, "the Arcadian nation as a whole enjoys a high reputation for virtue" and "humanity" (R, 280), but he also wrote about the savage inhabitants living on the edge of Arcadian civilization.

In the Augustan age, the Romans appropriated Arcadia for their fantasies, fashioning the picture of a simple pastoral society in harmony with nature and the cosmos. Painters decorating villas were fond of bucolic scenes, painting shepherds and their flock, gathering shrines and statues of goddesses.[25] Augustan Rome celebrated the city, and so did Virgil in the *Aeneid* with his proleptic image of Rome, the gleaming marble city that does not yet exist but Aeneas is made to see in a dream. But Virgil was also the poet of the pastoral idyll, extolling simple country life and hard work over the excesses of the city.[26] In his *Georgics*, Virgil wrote a eulogy to "unglamorous" country life on Italian soil, with men belonging to Saturn's golden age (which, as Evander explains to Aeneas in the *Aeneid*, preceded the arrival of the Arcadian settlers on Italian soil).[27] In the *Aeneid*, Virgil again appropriates the memory of virtuous Greek Arcadia, making *Pallanteum*, the new Arcadia on Italian soil, the site of founding Roman ruins.

With paintings like *The Arrival of Aeneas at Pallanteum* (1675), Claude Lorrain translated this Arcadian imagery in the seventeenth century into Italianate landscapes, sending "the imagination back into antiquity" in the same way Roman artists did in the Augustan age.[28] Long after Romans subjected Greece to their rule, Pausanias too takes his readers' imagination back into the Arcadian past, symbolically reappropriating this savage land, "now a minor province in someone else's empire," for his own fantasy: the "grandeur still living in the forgotten shrines and half-ruined statues of the present."[29] In the aftermath of Roman conquest, the landscapes of Greece are palimpsests bearing the disfiguring traces of the Romans. The statue of Athena from the Tegean Sanctuary of Alean Athena now graces the *Forum Augustum* in Rome (G2, 485). Observing an "established ancient tradition observed both by Greeks and barbarians" (G2, 485), Pausanias writes, Augustus, the Roman barbarian, added this Greek statue to the loot with which he filled his new *Forum*.

The way in which Pausanias discusses the restoration of the city of Pallantion by Antoninus (138–161 CE), an example of Roman appropriation through restoration, goes right to the heart of Virgil's symbolic recolonization of Arcadia in the *Aeneid*. Antoninus "made a city out of a village"

(G2, 479), thus reversing the course of Pausanias's Herodotian narrative about the collapse of Greece's cities into villages. In Pausanias's eyes, this Roman restoration of the city expropriates Greece's ancient heartland for the myth of Rome's Greek foundation:

> They say the most intelligent Arkadian and best soldier was Euander . . . He was sent to found a colony with an Arkadian expeditionary force from Pallantion, and founded a city on the river Tiber: and part of the city of Rome today, which was founded by Euander and his Arkadian followers, was called Pallantion in memory of the city in Arkadia. (G2, 479)

Pausanias opens this section rather laconically: "From here the discussion takes us to Pallantion, supposing there is anything there to be recorded" (G2, 479).

Restored Pallantion, the colonial city, is not worth describing. What is worth taking note of is paradoxically something that can no longer be seen, but whose existence can be inferred. Polybios recorded what he saw and heard; Pausanias combines autopsy with hearsay, the stories he is told and has read about the remnants of the Greece that he has lost. These stories often help render visible what is no longer there. The passage that has acquired some notoriety among Pausanias scholars is the story about a work of art that no longer exists. Right before arriving at Pallantion, Pausanias stops at the cave and reports that "the oldest man we met told us there had been a fall of rocks from the roof that hit the statue three generations before his time." From this man, he learns that "the statue was smashed and had completely disappeared," and concludes with the observation that "you could still see in the roof of the cave how the rocks had broken off" (G2, 478–479).

This is a story about utter loss. There are no ruins here, only traces left of falling stones that smashed the work of art. Pausanias's remnants thus range from the invisible to the barely visible: from the non-existing statue to the surviving "foundations" of buildings (G2, 452), "pillars still surviv[ing] in the ruins [of a temple]" (G2, 435), columns of sanctuaries "still standing" (G2, 481), "deserted cities" (G2, 439), sanctuaries "of which only the ruins survive" (G2, 428), and towns "that in our times lie in ruins and there is not a lot you can make out even of the ruins" (G2, 414). Lucan's *etiam periere ruinas* might well serve as Pausanias's motto.

Virgil, you will recall, made Arcadia the site of Rome's venerable foundational ruins. Pausanias's narrator scans the rubble left by Roman imperialism, turning this rubble into ruins by visualizing the precolonial past as if it were present.[30] This imaginary resurrection of the past is undertaken on the site of ancient Arcadia, wresting its "trace-objects" or "sublime ruins" away from Virgil's epic grip.[31] This gesture is complex: on the one hand, Pausanias's ruin gazing is part of Augustan classicism and the Romans' mimesis of Greece. On the other hand, it points to the "chasm that unites and separates the Roman-dominated present from the (idealized) Greek past"—and widens it.[32]

Roman conquest comes with rubble. This rubble surrounds and sometimes covers Greece's ancient ruins, ruins that Pausanias makes visible and reappropriates. The most remarkable example of this reappropriation is Hadrian's Temple to Poseidon. "It was built in our time by Hadrian," Pausanias writes, "who put inspectors over the workmen to see that no one looked inside the ancient sanctuary or shifted a stone of its ruins: he ordered them to build the new temple all round it" (G2, 394).

Rome has taken possession of Greece's ruins. Pausanias's descriptive register ("That is what there is" [G2, 444]) has a flat tonality, but we should not be deceived by this subdued affect. Pausanias completely omits any description of this Roman temple and instead returns to the moment of the original temple's construction and the ancient stories about it. Establishing the object as steeped in Greek history, this genealogical approach renders the broken-down object meaningful. That, and the visitor's awestruck stance toward the ancient vestiges, invites us to read Pausanias's representation of the temple ruin as a gesture of nationalist reappropriation *and* ruin construction on occupied territory—the re-signification of a material remnant as an object both sacred *and* beautiful.

Pausanias at Megalopolis

Let us rejoin Pausanias in Arcadia. All this destruction, all these fallen stones—the result of war and the neglect that follows upon wars of conquest—culminates in Pausanias's description of Arcadia's once marvelous capital, Megalopolis. This new city housed the largest theater in Greece (see chapter 1). The Arcadian federation used the performance space as a theater and for political assemblies. When the Arcadians used the space for political purposes, the audience faced the "grand front porch of the [city's] assembly hall," or what Pausanias mentions as "the foundations that have survived from the Council-House" (G2, 452). The theater was equipped with a "stage building," and when the space was used for plays, "a wooden façade" was brought in as a backdrop.[33] A sacred route linked the theater to Dionysus's shrine, which Pausanias visits—but again: "in my day there was not much left of the ruins" (G2, 453).

Pausanias thus takes his readers to what once was the theo-political stage of ancient Megalopolis but is now a Roman theater in a Roman colony. After having described this particular site, Pausanias concludes this part of his travelogue with a powerful narrative of rise and decline:

> I am not astounded that the Great City which the Arkadians founded . . . should have lost all its beauty and ancient prosperity, or that most of it should be ruins nowadays, because . . . I know that fortune alters everything, strong and weak, things at their beginning and things at their ending. (G2, 454)

Fortune thus makes her appearance again, Fortune who now resides in Rome. And Pausanias continues with his breathtaking view of this "spectacle of changing fortunes,"[34] listing all the cities and imperial metropolises that were once powerful and are now destroyed: Mycenae and Nineveh, Boiotian Thebes, and other wealthy cities of antiquity, like Thebes in Egypt. To these he adds Delos and Babylon. Then the story changes: "Alexander's city in Egypt and Seleukos's city on the Orontes were built yesterday and the day before, and have risen to such greatness and prosperity because Fortune is favoring them" (G2, 455). With this story of "the tragedies and the happiness of cities," Fortune demonstrates her power once again (G2, 455). "That is how temporary and completely insecure human things are" is the sentence with which Pausanias sums up the meaning of Fortune's grand drama (G2, 455).[35]

Virgil's epic was haunted by Polybios's law of ruin, and so was Lucan's. Pausanias, in contrast, stages Polybios's theoric scene, with a difference: he is not astounded that Megalopolis is ruined like so many cities before because, Pausanias writes, he knows how "the daemonic powers" work (G2, 454). The colonized Greek intellectual does not recall the Carthaginian scenario to remind Romans of Polybios's law of ruin. And why should he? Between 146 BCE and now, the second half of the second century, the Romans have been warned about Scipio's premonition often enough. With his gaze turned away from the Roman metropolis, Pausanias restages the scenario in Megalopolis against the Romans' myth of their benevolent empire, reminding the conquered of the effects of Rome's historic victory at Carthage and Corinth: Megalopolis's site of sovereignty, the councilhouse, is reduced to its foundations, and the greatest theater in Greece has become a Roman stage. Perhaps Pausanias knew about Calgacus's furious indictment of the Romans: "they make a desert and call it peace."[36]

Standing in the rubble left by Roman armies, surrounded by the portraits and statues of their emperors, Pausanias knows about the annihilating power of Roman imperialism. Entering the city's marketplace, Pausanias had come across a relief of Polybios, and provided a synopsis of the inscription: "he was an ally of Rome, and he ended the Roman anger with Greece" (G2, 449; emphasis mine). He then instructs his readers that "Polybios wrote a Roman history," narrating Rome's war with Carthage. "Scipio, whom they call the Carthaginian," he continued, "put an end to the war and destroyed Carthage *to its foundations"* (G2, 449). The Romans' anger at their enemies, Pausanias reminds his readers, leads to the destruction of cities—*to their foundations*.

In this version of Polybios's account of the end of Carthage in rubble and dust, there is no mention of Roman compassion or Scipio weeping. One of Alexander's successors, Seleukos, Pausanias had written earlier, "let stand the walls of Babylon, and let stand the temple of Bel with the Chaldaeans living around it" when he founded his new city.[37] Scipio, we know, did not let anything *stand*. Neither did the "Roman king," who destroyed Jerusalem "*to its foundations*" in 70 CE (G2, 412; emphasis mine), and neither did the Roman troops who sacked Corinth. To the Romans, victory meant that everything had to *fall*.

In the *Periegesis*'s restaged Polybian scene, Pausanias writes as Greek Polybios without the latter's ambivalent admiration for the new imperialists. And Scipio's barbarians are now the Romans. They are not barbarians of the future; they are already here, on the shattered Greek stage, and to Pausanias's great dismay, they can't stop staring at the ruins that are not theirs. According to Porter, the "workings of fortune" are Pausanias's "true subject."[38] Writing about Fortune, Pausanias has lost faith in the power of Polybios's law. As he restages the Carthaginian scene about imperial endtime, Pausanias takes a swipe at the new barbarians: Alexandria and Seleucia/Antioch are now the Roman capitals of colonized Syria and Egypt, two of the empire's cities that were rebuilt and restored under Augustus. But the founders of these great cities were Macedonians, who brought civilization to the barbarous East long before Pompey made Syria a Roman province and Augustus occupied Egypt. The gesture is important as another example of Pausanias's resistance to the present and to the Romans' "lust for power" or *libido dominandi*.[39] But if Pausanias's text conveys a single message, then it is the same as Virgil's: Rome is here to stay.

Conclusion

Virgil symbolically seized Arcadia and made it the site of the archaic ruins of Rome, objects from a glorious past made visible to the eyes of modern

Romans, and made so to be venerated. Unlike Josephus, who ceded Judaea to the Romans, Pausanias reconquered the Greek heartland, making it the site of postcolonial ruins, beautiful objects in a landscape of rubble left by plundering Roman legions. This makes Pausanias one of the coauthors of the discourse on the ruins of the Roman Empire.

FIVE

Rubble, Ruins, and the Time before the End: Paul, Tertullian, and the Roman Empire as *Katechon*

Introduction: From Rubble Gazing to Ruin Gazer Scenarios

The tension between conquest and fall, the empire's triumph and its end, I maintained in the previous chapters, was characteristic of Roman imperialism. One of my goals was to clarify the distinction between scenarios of rubble and ruin gazing. The transition I traced from rubble to ruin is on one level the transition from falling or fallen walls to ruins, from speaking about the damage caused by warfare and the rubble that results, to speaking about the symbolic value acquired by these vestiges. On the one hand, this transition is a diachronic process from Polybios's Republican to Virgil's imperial Rome; on the other, the opposition of rubble versus ruin remains operative in the consciousness of Roman imperialism as signifying the worthless rubble of the enemy versus the noble ruins of the conqueror, the time of conquest and the time of empire.

Polybios's scenario of imperial endings at Carthage is the beginning of a series of scenarios that thematize the murderous violence of empire-building. The Romans' conquest of their new imperial world began with the devastation of the old Mediterranean, and out of the rubble of Carthage the theorists and artists of the emerging empire fashioned the concept of Rome's imperial ruins. At some point in the far future, Rome will become Carthage, it will be destroyed, but its ruins will be nobler than the rubble of its enemies. It was Virgil who narrated this story, by inventing this new object, Rome's imperial ruins, and by giving the space of Polybios's scenario a new form.

With Virgil, empire begins and ends in ruins. Discussing imperial *space* and its imagination, centered on Rome's theo-political stage, I extended my analysis to the performance space of Virgil's ruin gazer scenario. In the *Aeneid*, Aeneas dutifully pursues his destiny to lay the foundations of Rome and Virgil represents the ruined fortifications at Pallanteum as part of these foundations. As they listen to Dido's curse, Virgil's listeners "see" their Rome crumbling into imperial ruins while Carthage once more turns into rubble. More precisely, restaging the theatrical space of Polybios's scenario, Virgil invites them to "see" the crumbling of the *scaenae frons*. He does so by mobilizing his readers' theatrical imagination and familiarity with the Roman stages' new architecture of spectatorship, replacing the Polybian *skene* with the Roman *scaenae frons*.

In the Augustan era, rubble and ruins thus become different objects; they signify different processes but also different temporalities. While both of these objects metonymically signify the undisciplined violence at the heart of the imperial project, in the new ruin consciousness of (post)Augustan imperialism, rubble belongs to the conquered, and ruins are the property of the empire. In terms of temporality, Roman ruins paradoxically signify the end of empire *and* the *longue durée* of empire, whereas rubble signifies the beginning of empire in a brief rush of violence, the very moment of victorious conquest and triumph.

Like Virgil's story, Lucan's later epic remains entangled in Polybios's endtime scenario, unfolding under the shadow of Carthage and obsessively working on Virgil's new object, the ruins of Rome. With an eye toward anti-imperial insurgencies, Josephus and Pausanias then mapped this opposition between rubble and ruin onto the colonized landscapes of Judaea and Greece as the rubble left by the conquerors and the ruins of the conquered.

Finally, Roman rubble and ruin gazer scenarios organize power relations between conqueror and conquered, imperial subject and subjected, along the lines of sight. Polybios, for instance, puts Scipio (and his Roman readers) into the position of scopic mastery and hints at a scenario set in the remote future, in which conqueror and conquered will have traded places, the Carthaginian enemy looking at Rome's monumental structures crumbling—a scenario that Silius then spells out by having Hannibal imagine the fall of Rome. These scopic scenarios thus dramatize power relations, bringing into play the issue of scopic mastery. They also *visualize time*, the empire's time as it relates to the future.

Before I conclude this study of the emergence of the Roman ruin gazer scenarios out of the Polybian rubble gazer scenario, I want to explore in more depth the complex issue of the conceptualization of *imperial time*, this disciplined border zone of *the time before the end*, inscribed in these scenarios. I began this inquiry into the concept of the time of empire as the time before the end with Polybios's text. The medium of architecture inscribed Augustan eschatology, the advent of the golden age, as one of the temporalities of the Romans' imperial imaginary. Virgil and Lucan, the authors of Roman imperialism, maintained the tension between Rome's *duration* and the empire's end in ruins. Reinscribing Polybios's scenario in the wake of Virgil and Lucan, Josephus and Pausanias also narrated this tension. Witnesses to the fate of anti-Roman rebellions, they reaffirmed the empire's duration.

Empire, Time, and the Pauline *Katechon*

Paul's *Letters to the Thessalonians* (ca. 52 and 55 CE) and Tertullian's *Apologeticus* or *Apology* (ca. 197 CE) are two texts entangled in this particular aspect of the Roman imperial imaginary, the problematic of imperial endtime.[1] In both texts, Paul's *katechon* as the instance or ruler that postpones the empire's end becomes a central concept. In his letters, Paul first ratchets up the tension between duration and end, and then translates what Hans Blumenberg calls the "great eschatological disappointment" into a radical version of the Roman ruin gazer scenario, locating the end in an indeterminate future.[2] In contrast, Tertullian's reading of Paul's *katechon* puts the emphasis back on the durability of the Roman world. I will conclude with a brief discussion of Augustine's reflections about the Visigoths' sacking of Rome in 410, his thoughts on Paul's *katechon* and the empire's end.

The Augustan age, Koselleck argues, was a moment when a "relative model of progress" existed.[3] However, Koselleck also cautions us that "[w]hat eternal Rome's world domination could promise was duration and security but no progress leading to a better future."[4] This Roman concept of *the present as duration*, we should also keep in mind, refers to the present as a seamless continuation of a past construed as monumental, that is, as a sequence of heroic deeds imitated in the present, lacking modernity's sense of rupture between past and present.

But how does *imperial time* figure in this Roman regime of historicity centered on stasis and *duration*? With Polybios's writing of imperial history as a combination of rise and fall and the retarding mixture of constitutions, we can argue that something new comes into being: a way of thinking about the course of imperial time that emphasizes duration as the effect of deferral. Analyzing the inscription of imperial time in the Polybian scenario, I shifted the focus from the idea of duration to the idea of the *arrest of time*—a standing-still of time before the end that Polybios/Scipio knows will come, because the end is natural and because the barbarian will seek revenge. The imperial time inscribed and reinscribed in rubble and ruin gazer scenarios is thus the tension between the empire's present as eternal duration, on the one hand, *and* its present as duration before the end, on the other; between Augustan eschatology, where the present is seen as the end of history (i.e., the realization of a political order in correspondence with the order of the cosmos), and Polybios's concept of the present as *stalled time* or *the time that remains*. This tension inherent to imperial time between Rome's eternity and Rome's end, between "normal" time and time derailed, requires that the idea of imperial duration be reaffirmed again and again. In the texts discussed here, imperial time thus emerges as a spatialized border zone or *eschaton*.

Tertullian's *Apologeticus* and Paul's letters operate within two time frames, the temporal regime of the Roman Empire[5] and that of early Christianity. Blumenberg characterizes the latter's temporality as an "eschatological 'state of emergency,'" where the present is "the last moment of the decision for the approaching kingdom of God."[6] Living in the *eschaton* is the topic of Paul's letters. Paul wrote the *First Letter to the Thessalonians* around 52 CE and the Letter to the Romans in 55 CE; that is, one year after the Senate decreed Claudius's "consecratio," an event reenacting Roman political theology.[7] Paul's letters thus "arose in and addressed an imperial situation."[8] In the *First Letter to the Thessalonians*, Paul told his followers that "the day of [the] Lord" comes like "a thief in the night": "Whenever they will say: peace and security, then suddenly for them comes destruction."[9] Paul's language here "echoes" that of "Roman imperialism."[10] A challenge to Augustus's *Res Gestae*, these letters offer an alternative to the Roman order "with its promise of universal reconciliation and peace."[11] In the *Second Letter to the Thessalonians*, Paul then modified his earlier eschatological timetable. Rethinking messianic time as *the time that remains*, Paul insisted on the Roman world's duration against his followers' desire for the imminent end.[12] It is in the context of this problematic of *Nah- und Fernerwartung* (or the expectation that the end is near or remote) that Paul introduces the concept of the *katechon*.

Since Tertullian's *Apologeticus*, the *katechon* has been identified with the Roman Empire as the instance that "delays or maintains the end of time" (T, 109). *Imperial time* means living with a mixture of hope and terror, knowing that the end will eventually come and hoping that it will not come now. The new time of Christian eschatology is a time of urgency, an excited expectation of an imminent end. Believing in "the Christian teaching of the *interim time* between creation and the end of the world," the early Christians experienced themselves "since the coming of Christ" as living "within the last time period."[13] Christianity reinvented time, Hartog argues, by breaking it in two. The "decisive event of the incarnation" opened "a new time"; this *new* time "was to end with a second and last event" that is Christ's return.[14] This "in-between time," Hartog writes, "was a time of anticipation" and hoping for the end.[15]

Writing in ca. 197 CE in Carthage, Tertullian, who was probably the son of a Roman centurion, transforms the early eschatological "state of exception," extending the interim and turning eschatological fervor into "fear of the judgment and the collapse of the world."[16] Tertulllian indicts the Romans for disregarding the laws and religion of their ancestors, unfavorably comparing the moderns with Scipio and Augustus, who declined the title of "Lord."[17] Christians did not yet exist, he reminds the critics of the new religion, but their god did when Hannibal killed Romans. This *defense of Christians against the heathens* turned anti-Christian accusations into Christian *Kulturkritik*, painting the Roman Empire as decadent modernity, singling out the theaters as one of the many symptoms of decay. Explaining the *Book of Daniel*, Tertullian saw time and the history of the world as creations of the Christian God. He assaulted Roman state religion as precisely that: a religion in the service of the state and the empire, with Virgil's *Aeneid* as its founding text.

But then Tertullian paradoxically assured the Roman emperor that Christians were the empire's most loyal subjects, invested in the duration of "the last stages of time."[18] They support emperor and empire because they understand that a power exists that threatens the existence of the world. This power "is being kept back by the respite that the Roman empire means to us."[19] Tertullian then comes to the following conclusion: "We pray for the permanence of the world [*pro statu seaculi*], for peace in things, for the delay of the end [*pro mora finis*]."[20] The desire to delay the "horrors of the end" is not the only reason for these prayers.[21] Emperors are there by God's will, and prayers are thereby "state- and world-preserving," pushing the end of time into some indeterminate future.[22] The Roman emperor thus postpones the end by keeping back the force threatening the existence of the world.[23]

Living in the *eschaton* is also the topic of Paul's letters. Christianity's eschatological conception of time reinvented history as "a clearly arranged sequence of events in a finite period of time, in which the moment of the present had to be determined with precision."[24] Paul precisely determines the moment of the present, but he does so in a specific way, with his own understanding of messianic time or "the time that is left us" (T, 68). In Paul's letters, the messianic present as transition from the old to the new, from the pagan era to the era of Christ, emerges as a "tension between *an already* and a *not yet*"—between the messianic event and "an additional time" (T, 69).[25] This additional time is not about deferral but involves a layering or doubling of time: "The Messiah has already arrived, the messianic event has already happened," Agamben writes (T, 71). However, the "presence" of this messianic event "contains within itself another time" (T, 71). Agamben uses the term *parousia* (traditionally used to mean the second coming of Christ) for this other time within messianic time which, he argues, "stretches its *parousia* [presence], not in order to defer it, but, on the contrary, to make it graspable" (T, 71).[26] For we need to have a way of understanding the ending of time. In other words, there is a difference between "the end of time" and "the time of the end" or "the time that is left between time and its ending."[27]

"The Time That Is Left": Paul's Concept of the *Katechon*

Katechon is a concept from Paul's *Second Letter to the Thessalonians*. As I mentioned above, Paul preached earlier that "Sudden destruction was about to come upon the 'peace and security' of the Roman imperial order."[28] In his Second Letter, Paul does not merely correct this prophecy (warning his followers against the consequences of eschatological indifference toward the world), he also reflects on the nature of imperial power. These reflections lead to a *katechontic* scenario that unveils imperial power as a power in ruins (or, rather, falling into ruins) and reintroduces the concept of delaying the course of time.

My argument rests on the logic of Agamben's exegesis of Paul's concept of imperial sovereignty and its inherent illegitimacy. Agamben introduces the concept of the state of exception into this discussion of sovereignty. For Paul, the messianic present involved the concept of a "state of tendential lawlessness" that "radicalizes the state of exception" (where law operates by its suspension), rendering the law "inoperative" (T, 111, 106, and 110).[29] It is a mistake, Agamben argues, to read Paul's *katechon* and *anomos* (or "the one outside the law") as two "separate figures" when they are "one single power" functioning differently at two different moments (T, 110 and 111).

Let us take a closer look at Paul's passage on the *katechon* and *anomos*. The passage follows upon his warning not to expect the imminent arrival of the Messiah: "it will not be unless the apostasy shall come first, and the man of lawlessness, the son of destruction, is revealed."

Paul then interrupts, exhorting his followers to recall what he had told them in his First Letter:

> You know *what it is that is now holding him back* [*ho katechon*], so that he will be revealed when his time comes. For the mystery of anomy [*anomia*] is already at work, but only until the person now holding him back [*ho katechon*] is removed. Then the lawless one [*anomos*] will be revealed, whom the Lord will abolish with the breath of his mouth, rendering him inoperative by the manifestation of his presence [*parousia*]. The presence [*parousia*] of the former is according to the working of Satan in every power. (T, 109)

As Agamben points out, *the lawless one* is typically identified with the Antimessiah or antichrist.

Tertullian identifies the *katechon* (first used by Paul in the impersonal, then the personal form) as the Roman Empire (T, 109). Based on his reading of messianic time as a radicalized state of exception, Agamben arrives at a different conclusion. The *katechon as* "the Roman Empire as well as every constituted authority" is the power "that clashes with and hides . . . the state of tendential lawlessness that characterizes the messianic, and in this sense delays unveiling 'the mystery of lawlessness'" (T, 111). The act of "unveiling of this mystery" means laying bare "the inoperativity of the law and *the substantial illegitimacy of each and every power in messianic time*" (T, 111; emphasis mine).

Part of a larger literature debating Paul's "counter-imperial theology,"[30] Agamben's reading is directed against theorists who, identifying the *katechon* with the Roman Empire (or any state), theorize it as a *positive* concept, a form of political sovereignty founding a theological politics or political theology.[31] Tertullian argued that Rome is here to stay and its power is legitimate, ordained by the Christian god.[32] Paul reaffirms the staying power of the empire, yet he does so without affirming its legitimacy. On the contrary, he subverts its legitimacy and that of any worldly power.

The Second Letter to the Thessalonians is thus a reflection on the illegitimacy at the core of all (imperial) sovereignty. Paul, the converted Jew, Roman citizen, and former servant of the imperial state, emerges as the most radical ruin gazer. In his text, the *katechon* as imperial sovereign delays the unveiling of the illegitimacy of power—*a power in ruins*, a power ruined at its very core.[33] Unlike Tertullian, who translates Augustan into Christian political theology, Paul does indeed "declar[e] the empire dead."[34]

Rome did die, but it did not "fall"; it had many endings.[35] One of these was the Visigoths' ransacking of Rome, their demolition of the Mausoleum and scattering of Augustus's ashes in 410 CE. Another ending was the Vandals' capture of Carthage, by then "the second greatest city of the Roman west."[36] By 450 CE, the Western empire had shrunk to Italy and bits of France, existing next to "a new world of barbarian kingdoms" run by people who had been exposed to Roman culture for centuries.[37] When "half the Roman Empire" consisted of these "kingdoms," Zosimus wrote "a matching narrative" to Polybios's *Histories*, explaining that Rome fell because it ignored its pagan gods.[38] "Roman civilization continued," Woolf writes, "[b]ut the empire was gone."[39]

Educated at Carthage, Augustine wrote *City of God* in the wake of the Visigoths' sacking of Rome in order to explain the reasons for the victory of the "savage barbarians" to the Roman refugees, flooding the Roman African coast.[40] God, not pagan divinities, Augustine argued, helped the Romans achieve the "immense expansion and the long duration of their Empire" (C, 137–138). The causes of the empire's looming collapse were the Romans' "lust for power" and their decadence (C, 42). Like Tertullian before him, he ranted against Roman theaters and the emperors' theatrical politics, concluding that "theology of the city" and "theology of the theater" were inextricably intertwined (C, 247).[41]

In this state of emergency, he returned to the Carthaginian moment. Scipio knew, Augustine told the Roman exiles, that "this calamity might come upon you" (C, 42). Scipio's warnings against the Romans' lack of restraint in the wake of their victory over Carthage were in vain, and the empire became "a city which aims at domination" while being "dominated by that very lust of domination" (C, 5). Augustine also addressed Paul's eschatology and the question of the time that remains. We cannot know, he wrote, echoing Paul, how many years "remain for this world" (C, 838). Referring to Paul's passage on the *katechon*, he mentioned the common supposition "that those [obscure] words refer to the Roman imperial power" (C, 933). While he accepts this interpretation, Augustine leaves the answer to the question of when exactly the empire will end deliberately vague, merely reiterating Paul's sentences: "'Let him who now reigns, reign until he is removed from the scene,' that is, until taken away" (C, 933).

Conclusion

In part 1, I discussed the imagination of imperial space and time, keeping their articulation in the various rubble/ruin gazer scenarios in mind. The *Book of Daniel* thematized the succession of empires, the end of the world, and the coming of the messiah. Polybios theorized duration or standstill in *tension* between rise and fall; the Augustan period then centered on this suspension of time while the tension between ascent and fall was pushed into the background. But Virgil kept this tension alive. Augustan imperial ideology maintained that the emperor had received power from the hands of "Jupiter and the gods," and it was theirs to keep.[42] Yet, in the wake of Polybios, imperial time becomes one of the fortified border zones or *eschatia*. The time of empire is the time that remains, endtime militarily disciplined like all border zones of the ever-expanding empire. In this understanding of imperial time, the universal historian-geographer's primary category, space, overpowers time, colonizing it into fortified territory.

Josephus's history and Pausanias's journey reaffirmed the empire's staying power. Theorizing eschatology in the context of this tension between fortified endtime and ruinous end, Paul introduced the idea of the *katechon* into the empire's fortified border zone. In the discussion of the Pauline and Tertullianian *katechon*, I foregrounded the latter's investment in reaffirming the empire's duration. The Roman elite kept holding on to this idea. Around 350 CE, a Roman officer expressed his belief in the "a-historical endtime," describing the present as a continuation of the Augustan past.[43] Until late antiquity, authors signaled the Augustan *topos* of *Roma aeterna* or Rome's eternal present by the shorthand expression of *Roma stat*, from *stare*: to stand (still). However, while Augustan political theology rested on the core belief that the *imperium*'s eternity was divinely guaranteed, the ghosts of Carthage never died: "the fear that things might change remained as a dark background setting"—as did the image of *Roma ruina*.[44] Acts and discourses of neo-Roman mimesis would symbolically prolong the life of the empire all the way into the twentieth century. The question of the *katechon* or the strategies of preventing, or at least postponing, the end in ruins would remain a core problematic.

PART TWO

Neo-Roman Mimesis: Charles V at Tunis, 1535

Preface

In this part, I will discuss neo-Roman mimesis as a political and aesthetic practice responding to the desire of the (Augustan) past to be imitated. I will use the example of the 1535 Tunis campaign of Charles V, the successor to Isabella and Ferdinand elected Holy Roman Emperor in 1519, and his triumphal entry to Rome in 1536. Charles's advisers compared the Spanish Habsburg's imperial aspirations to Augustan imperialism. Like the neo-Roman imperial theorists that followed them, Charles's councilors were steeped in the classical canon, drawing their legitimating arguments from Augustus's *Res Gestae Divi Augusti*, Augustine's *City of God*, and centuries of interpretations of the *Book of Daniel*.

My exploration into the processes of neo Roman imitation as a response to the desire of the past starts with Freud's concept of identification as *Besetzung*, or act of conquest; I then examine the classical concept of mimesis, and analyze the demand for imitation articulated by Augustus's *Res Gestae Divi Augusti*, his retrospective account of his achievements. Neo-Roman mimesis as acts of imitation connecting Roman emperor and neo-Roman sovereign responds to this desire of the past. Moreover, the neo-Roman situation translates the problematic of ontological lack and the fetish at the center of Homi Bhabha's theory of mimicry in the colonial situation, into the problematic of Rome's fall and imperial ruins as signs of the power and death of the Roman Empire.

Part 2 ends with a Freudian proposal to think of the spatio-temporal imaginary created by these mimetic practices as a Roman zone in which the distance between Roman and neo-Roman time-space seems to contract. The artists belonging to Charles's entourage commemorated the battle as taking place among the ruins of (Roman) Carthage. Participating in the fabrication of this early modern ruinous imaginary, they revived the memory of victorious Romans and their barbarian enemies.

SIX

"The Imagoes They Leave Behind":[1] Charles's Death Masks and the Desire of the Past

Introduction

Using the Tunis expedition of Charles V in 1535 as a paradigmatic example, I will analyze imperial mimesis in this chapter as an act of imitation, an act of producing the very past that is being imitated, and the creation of an imaginary space in which the distance of Roman past and neo-Roman present collapses. Among other things, I am interested in the peculiar nature of desire at work in the imitation of the Roman past. Like later performances of (neo)Roman mimesis, the triumphant remaking of Charles V as Roman conqueror produced ruin gazer scenarios. Exploring the tension at the heart of (neo)Roman mimesis, I will thus return to the phenomenon at the center of my inquiry: that acts of imitating the Roman Empire generate imperial imaginaries structured around scenarios of ruin gazing.

Neo-Roman mimesis is a political and a cultural or aesthetic practice. Political acts of imitation mean two things: *acts of conquests* framed as repetition of a previous event, in this case Charles V's Tunisian Campaign in 1535 as a repetition of Scipio's conquest of Carthage, and *public acts of identification* with Roman models, in this case Charles V's triumphal procession through Rome. These moments of political conquests come with the imitation of Rome's entire imperial culture, a stream of texts and images, rituals and architectural (re)constructions. Chief among these neo-Roman practices framing these mimetic acts is the symbolic conquest of the ruined Roman stage.

Together, these political and artistic practices constituted an early modern act of imperial mimesis that kept the Roman past alive. Or, put more precisely, they conquered the Roman past by reanimating it. Freud theorized identity formation in terms of the act of *Besetzung* or psychic *occupation* of an object (i.e., libidinal *cathexis) and* the subsequent act of (partial or total) identification with that object, a process that resonates intriguingly with performances of imperial mimesis and their founding act, conquest as physical occupation or Schmittian land-appropriation.[2] Let me point out here that the primary meaning of the German word *Besetzung* is military, referring to the occupation of a city or country following upon its conquest. As the case of Charles V intimates, becoming Roman *begins* with *occupation*; it is based on an act of mimesis that is violent *and* accompanied by the resurrection of the past in a flood of representations of the ancient Roman model. In other words, there is no imitation without conquest and none without resurrections.

This process of imitation at work between Roman and neo-Roman empires articulates power and desire. As I mentioned above, I am interested in the specific nature of the desire at work in these acts of imitation across centuries. With respect to this aspect, my theoretical intervention is twofold. First, taking the classical concept of mimesis as imitation of great men and their deeds developed by Plato, Aristotle, and their Roman interpreters as my point of departure, I will argue that neo-Roman mimesis responds to the desires of the present *and* the past.[3] Constantly re-creating the model in the present, imperial mimesis is always also re-presentation, the copy of an "original" in realist texts and images—or, more precisely, in texts and images provoking the desire for the real, the desire to recognize the copy's original. Realist texts, images, and other cultural practices of the Roman past, I will argue, hold *cathexis* ready in anticipation of future imitators. My prime examples will be drawn from three different representational media: Augustus's *Res Gestae Divi Augusti*, a kind of imperial manifesto in the first person, the so-called procession panels of the *Altar of Peace*, and the aristocratic practice of using ancestor masks in funeral processions.

My second theoretical intervention concerns Homi Bhabha's scenes of colonial subject formation. While Bhabha's scopic scenarios of mimicry analyze the synchronic constellation of colonizer and colonized, the concept of imperial mimesis that I propose traces the processes at work in the diachronic constellation of Roman model and neo-Roman imitator.[4] Like acts of mimicry in the colonial situation, the mimetic acts involving imperial rulers/cultures of the neo-Roman present and the Roman past crystallize around a lack.

As I argued in part 1, scenarios of imperial ruin gazing articulate the constellation of imperial subject and object, conqueror and conquered. In this respect, they function in ways similar to Bhabha's colonial scenes of subject formation with their analysis of the processes of power and desire involved in the constellation of colonizer and colonized. In the trans-imperial context, these scenarios may take the form of actual performances, scripted journeys through Rome's ruins. More often they emerge as (textual and visual) representations.

As performances, these scopic scenarios are based on the (partial) identity of the conqueror of the past and neo-Roman conqueror of the present. Articulating sameness and difference, they visualize the lack at the core of the Roman model. While I will privilege the analysis of Charles's performance on Rome's ruined stage, I will also discuss the textualized and visualized form of the scenario. Unfolding the key facets of the practices and discourses of neo-Roman mimesis, I will concentrate at the end of part 2 on a particular feature of the neo-Roman imaginary: as a practice of dealing with the dead, of repeating their actions while wearing their masks, acts of imperial mimesis create a twilight zone, an imaginary time-space in which the Roman dead and their past exist in the present.

Repeat: Scipio at Tunis, 1535

With the Spanish-Portuguese conquest of America, we find ourselves on well-known terrain, the reign of Augustus, with Iberian mimesis involving the imitation of imperial politics and culture, literature and historiography. "Spaniards in the New World," David Lupher writes, "found Romans 'good to think with.'"[5] Thus, Gaspar Perez de Villagra drew on Virgil's *Aeneid* in his epic *Historia de la Nueva Mexico (1610)*. Contemplating the leveling of Acoma in 1599, one of the protagonists exclaims: *"A qui fue Troia."*[6] Other *conquistadors* compared their victories to the Romans' conquest of Carthage and reconquest of Jerusalem.[7] The sixteenth-century *conquistadors* justified their *Landnahme*, or taking-of-land in the New World, by inventing analogies between the first century CE and their own time. While this praxis of imitation primarily involved comparisons between the Spanish-Portuguese kings and Rome's emperors, it also led to analogies between the history and paganism of Rome and the New World. Bernardino de Sahagun, for instance, compared Aztec to Roman gods, and Aztec cities to Troy and Carthage.[8]

Soon there was fierce competition between Spain and England to depict themselves as "the true inheritors of Rome, assuming the epic mantle of empire."[9] Claiming Rome as their model, the Spanish kings perfected their performance of imperial mimesis over two hundred years. When the emperor Charles V conquered Tunis in 1535, he allowed the Spanish soldiers to sack the city located close to Carthage, and left a defensive emplacement in nearby Goleta.[10] A few years earlier, Charles had razed Toledo to the ground, sowing its soil with salt the way the Romans were supposed to have done at Carthage.

In Wallerstein's analysis, Charles V occupies a threshold position in the emergence of the capitalist world-system. Elected Holy Roman Emperor in 1520, Charles's legitimacy rested on the theory of *translatio imperii*.[11] Combining the territories of the Holy Roman Empire and the Spanish Empire, his reign was soon defined as a universal monarchy by sixteenth-century scholars who recovered the "maxim of Roman law" that made the imperial sovereign "legally lord of the whole world."[12] With Charles's abdication in 1556 and his dismantling of the empire, this "historical" system of "world-empire" ended.[13]

Drawn into "imperial commitments," costly military campaigns financed by debt, the aspiration to construct a world empire encompassing Europe and the Americas, Wallerstein argues, was incompatible with the logic of the emerging "capitalist world-economy" and Spain lost "the competition to be at the center of a capitalist world-economy."[14] By 1559, Spain was bankrupt and, having neglected to develop a manufacturing economy, never joined the core zone of the capitalist world-system. With the Dutch as the first hegemonic power, a new world-system of sovereign European nation-states set on dividing the non-European world among them was born.[15] The alternative to the *imperium mundi* of Charles V, this world order was codified in the 1648 Peace of Westphalia.

Charles's imperial aspirations thus ultimately failed. At the zenith of his reign, this early modern empire stretched from the Habsburg territories in Central Europe to the Americas. Let me remind you that Charles V was in power when Cortés conquered the Aztec empire in 1521 and Pizarro the empire of the Incas in 1532. Charles V was also the grandson and successor to Ferdinand and Isabella, who "liberated" Spain from the Moors, conducting their *Reconquista* on the model of the Roman conquest of *Hispania*. Designed by an architect upon his return from Rome, Charles's Palace in Granada is a neoclassical structure erected on Nasrid foundations. A "dramatic contrast with the Islamic architecture of the neighboring

Alhambra," the Palace was meant to replicate "the atmosphere of Imperial Rome."[16]

In this early modern case, neo-Roman mimesis thus involves both Spain's overseas and "domestic *imperium*."[17] Defending "Christendom from Turks," fighting at Tunis against Arab raiders and near Vienna against Suleiman the Magnificent in 1532, Charles V financed his campaigns with the tribute and labor extracted from "the Indies" and then increasingly with debt.[18] Reigning from 1519 to 1556, Charles V relinquished the crown of the Holy Roman Emperor, giving a formal account of his reign, a version of the Augustan *Res Gestae*, in which he portrayed himself as ruler seeking "peace and harmony" for his realm, a mission that had him traverse the empire fighting "Turks" and other enemies.[19] In a contemporary image, Daniel explains to Charles the messianic nature of his rule.[20] Charles's councilors also connected his reign to "the final prophetic *translatio imperii* of the Book of Daniel," presenting the Spanish Habsburgs as Augustus's "heirs," neo-Roman rulers chosen by god "to be the agents of the final unification of the world."[21] The Roman Empire, one of the court's historians boasted, "[was] still alive today."[22]

But let us return to the Tunis expedition and its mimetic practices. "The Tunis campaign," Burke writes, "was long expected."[23] First Gattinara, his chancellor, and then Sepulveda, his spiritual adviser, exhorted Charles to take up the fight against Suleiman II.[24] More importantly, this military expedition was made into a key event in the history of Charles's reign, frequently referenced by his mimetic experts as an event testifying to the emperor's imperial drive and his role as defender against Islam.[25]

Charles V left for Tunis with a large "commemorative entourage," including artists, poets, historians, and mathematicians.[26] These propagandists turned the entire campaign into a "statement about the very nature of his imperial rule," with the king writing public letters and reporting about the campaign in person to his court historian.[27] Driven by the desire to portray this Spanish Empire spanning old and New World as the new Rome, Charles V commissioned an epic on the model of the *Aeneid*, and a collection of tapestries.[28] Jan Cornelisz Vermeyen, the artist, traveled with Charles's armada to Tunis, where he sketched the drawings on which the tapestries were then based, depicting a "moment-by-moment representation of the Tunis expedition" in classicizing style.[29]

The third tapestry depicts the landing of the fleet at Tunis and includes all of the Cape of Carthage with the ruins of the Roman aqueduct (figure 6.1). The tapestry's text presumes a "viewpoint within the scene" and starts with a sentence about ancient Carthage: "Here they enter the port of Utica. Ancient Carthage receives them in her ruins [*ruinis Carthago* in

6.1 Jan Cornelisz Vermeyen, *The Landing Off the Cape of Carthage* (1548–1554).

the original Latin text]."[30] The text concludes with Carthage's ruins: "He [Charles] pitched camp beside the walls of Carthage once illustrious, today again a village of small cottages."[31]

In tapestry 3, Charles V becomes "Caesar" attacking the retreating "enemy."[32] Tapestry 6, depicting the fight against the Muslim enemy, also situates this scene in front of the ancient ruins (figure 6.2). On the far left, two pillars of the aqueduct frame the scene; farther into the background a wall-like remnant of the aqueduct serves again as a framing device, crumbling, so to speak, into several individual pillars again, with the top of the last one touching on the line of the horizon in the back.[33]

In these tapestries, the ruins of Carthage function as scenographic elements, background for the scenes from the theater of (neo)Roman history. While they draw the viewer's eyes to the ruins, the center of attention is the drama of conquest: in the "Landing," it is the dynamic constellation of ship, stylized, billowing sail, and warriors, in "Salida," the focus on the fleeing warrior on horseback, in the foreground. Charles's act of imperial mimesis thus takes place on the ruined stage of ancient Carthage, his battle with the Muslim enemy and his Moors leading to the same result as Scipio's fight against Hannibal and his Numidians: leaving the enemy city in ruins. The victory at Tunis was celebrated by a triumphal tour through Italy, during which Charles V was transformed into the "new Scipio."[34] On his journey Charles passed statues of Scipio bearing inscriptions like "Charles, you will be divine, you will be Africanus."[35]

As conqueror fighting in the ruins of Carthage, Charles V was "Africanus."[36] This identification with Scipio coexisted alongside Charles's identification with various Roman emperors. The coronation ceremony at Bologna, organized by Italian artists, included a statue of Scipio on horseback as well as medallions of Caesar, Augustus, Vespasian, and Trajan. Later, poets connected Charles to Augustus using book 6 of the *Aeneid* and the prophecy of a new "golden age."[37] At the time of the Tunis expedition, the historical analogies thus multiplied. As the Holy Roman Emperor, Charles was already heir to Augustus, bearing the title "King of the Romans, elected emperor, always august," long before he had taken Tunis.[38] But empire demands expansion. The conquest of Tunis was another repeat performance of imperial mimesis.

Charles V on the Roman Stage

Upon his return to Italy, the Habsburg stage managers organized a triumphal cavalcade through Italian cities in 1536. Beginning in Palermo and

6.2 Jan Cornelisz Vermeyen, *Sortie of Enemy from Goleta* (ca. 1500–1559).

ending in Lucca, this mimetic event "took on an even more triumphal quality than usual," and every city entry represented the capture of Tunis in one medium or other.[39] In Rome, Manetti, the papal commissioner of antiquity, arranged a triumphal parade through the ancient city (acting at the behest of Paul III). Large-scale demolitions prepared the itinerary that let Charles V "retrace the route by which the victorious processions of classical antiquity wound their way into the Roman Forum."[40] Hermann Posthumus, the painter of *Landscape with Antique Ruins*, was one of the many artists working on the *mise-en-scène* of Charles's triumph.[41]

Fighting and winning on the sacred ground of the *Aeneid*, Charles thus entered the Roman stage. Starting at the southern gate of the Porta San Sebastiano, the triumphal procession proceeded to the Roman Forum. The gateway bore the inscription "To the Destroyer of the Turks."[42] Excavating, clearing, and displaying the remains of ancient Rome, the Italian experts in mimesis re-created the ancient Roman stage as a *ruined stage*. For instance, Charles's route led through the newly isolated Arch of Constantine, which the procession approached on the Via Triumphalis.[43] The "bedraggled [and] often unintelligible landscape of jumbled ruins," Karmon writes, was transformed "into a panorama of preserved monuments standing in splendid isolation."[44] To this, the Italian stage managers added a temporary triumphal arch adorned with several "paintings of the 'Triumph of Africa,' including the battle of La Goleta, and the capture of Tunis."[45]

Paul III wanted to put Charles's power into "perspective" by making him experience the "immense symbolic weight" of ancient Rome.[46] Deploying his military force across the city, the emperor demonstrated his power and appropriated the event for his own purposes. Traversing the ruined Roman stage in the wake of his North African triumph, Charles V thus performed the role of the sovereign as neo-Roman ruin gazer. This was the Spanish Habsburgs' symbolic conquest of ruins, a ritual act of scopic mastery over the ruins of the ancient empire, signifying both the empire's power and its death. Vermeyen's tapestries echoed this act by foregrounding the drama of Charles's military conquest against the backdrop of Carthage's ruined stage. A political act of mimesis, Charles V's conquest of Tunis thus entailed the imitation of an entire culture by mimetic experts who re-created the model in all its facets, mobilizing a wide array of resurrectional techniques.

The Pleasure of Mimesis

If early modern empires engaged in the imitation of Rome, modern empires continued to do so, generating their own versions of imperial mimesis and its imaginaries. European nation-states were born on Roman territory, and they still took Rome as their model as they expanded their territories into empires in the nineteenth and twentieth centuries. As late as the 1920s, Frederick Lord Lugard, one of Great Britain's most famous imperial administrators, evoked the Roman model as the common heritage of modern European empires: "As Roman imperialism laid the foundations of modern civilization, and led the wild barbarians of these islands along the path of progress, so in Africa to-day we are repaying the debt, and bringing to the dark places of the earth, the abode of barbarism and cruelty, the torch of culture and progress, while ministering to the material needs of our own civilization."[47] Entering and taming these "dark places" was a European project, "a solemn covenant" among its rulers.

Like in the case of Charles V, the modern imitations of the ancient empire were accompanied by wave after wave of resurrecting it in texts and images. I want to single out one such act of resurrection in the twentieth century, the opening of Joseph Conrad's *Heart of Darkness* (1902). Here Marlow, Conrad's protagonist, reimagines the Roman legions' arrival in barbarian England, as the crew of the *Nellie* is waiting in the misty, gloomy landscape at the mouth of the Thames before setting out for the Congo:

> And this also, said Marlow suddenly, has been one of the dark places of the earth . . . I was thinking of very old times, when the Romans first came here . . . Imagine the feelings of a *commander . . . Imagine him here*—the very end of the world, the sea the color of lead, a sky the color of smoke . . . Here and there a military camp lost in the wilderness . . . Land in a swamp, march through the woods, and in some inland post, feel the savagery, the utter savagery, that closed around him. (emphasis mine)[48]

Working with Stanley's well-known comparison of pre-Roman England to barbarian Africa, Conrad reawakens the Roman commander as a British colonizer—as Kurtz, *feeling the savagery closing around him.*

In the passage that I quoted above, Conrad made us read the process of the British commander's identification with the Roman invader. The topic and praxis of imitation is of course not foreign to Roman politics and culture. Long before the advent of the Augustan era and its neoclassicist style, art meant the imitation and copying of Greek art. And in the eyes of some Roman authors, Alexander and his Macedonian Empire served as the model to Caesar and Augustus. Despite these analogies, however, Romans believed their "imperium" to be without "precedent."[49] And thus Romans turned themselves into models, conceiving of their past as a series of heroic deeds by great men that the present ought to imitate. Still more crucial is the fact that this view of the relation between past and present as exemplary repetition also applied to the future: politicians and intellectuals of the Augustan era thought of themselves as models that their successors would be imitating. Neo-Roman mimesis is not only a process—or performance—that obeys desires of the present; it also responds to the desires of the past inscribed in Roman texts and works of art and readily reawakened.

Imitation or *mimesis* is a concept from Plato's *The Republic* (around 380 BCE), referring to the education of future political leaders and the arts of the polis. In education, the imitation of proper models is crucial. Plato, responding to the question of whether children ought to play as many different roles as possible, recommends that they should not. However, should they act, they ought to "choose appropriate models to imitate -- people who are brave, self-disciplined, god-fearing, free."[50] If they were "good at imitating" behavior that is "illiberal," Plato fears that the "enjoyment of imitation" might "give rise to the enjoyment of the reality."[51] Mimetic practice—impersonation through repetition—thus carries considerable risks. Acts of imitation, "if long continued from an early age, become "part of a person's nature, turns into habits of body, speech and mind."[52] Yet, however risky a mechanism imitation is, it is a necessary part of being human. And there is *pleasure* involved in watching an "individual utterly versatile, able to imitate anything."[53]

It is common knowledge that Plato's view of artists and their deceptive form of mimesis was negative. Like a mirror, the artist creates but semblances of things, a world of appearances, and if the poet had a real understanding of the actions "he imitates," the poet would "be much keener on action than on the imitation of it."[54] And thus Plato returns to political imitation: "He'd try to leave many fine actions as memorials to himself, and be more eager to be the hero whom the poet honors than be the poet who praises heroes"[55]—and, we should add, more eager to be the hero whose noble deeds will be imitated in the future. This is the very foundation of the Ciceronian concept of *historia magistra vitae*, with its archive of exemplary men and deeds.[56]

Aristotle made heroes and their noble deeds the subject of poetic and historiographic mimesis. Considerably less wary of aesthetic pleasure than Plato, Aristotle writes about the pleasure in mimetic representation. Like Plato, he views imitation as an instinct and claims that poetry stems from two causes, "each of them lying deep in our nature," one being the "instinct of imitation," the other the *pleasure in seeing imitations*: "[Man] is the most imitative of living creatures, and through imitation learns his earliest lessons; and no less is the *pleasure* felt in things imitated" (emphasis mine).[57] The delight that we experience does not only stem from the precision of description that produces "fidelity" to the original.[58] It also stems from our "liveliest pleasure," the pleasure in learning: "Thus the reason why *men enjoy seeing a likeness* is, that in contemplating it they find themselves learning or inferring, and saying perhaps, 'Ah, *that is he*!'"[59]

The *pleasure of mimesis*—of seeing a well-made copy—is thus the process of "gathering the meaning of things" leading to recognition of the one who is represented, the recognition of the original in the copy: *that is he!* All genres, tragedy, epic (and historiography), work with this pleasure. While they do involve "persons acting," plot is more important than heroes: "Tragedy is an imitation, not of men, but of an action and of life, and *life consists in action*, and its end is a mode of action, not a quality" (emphasis mine).[60]

Res Gestae Divi Augusti: The Desire of the Past

Life consists in action—Aristotle's statement might well have been written a few centuries later as a summary of the *Res Gestae*. As I mentioned before, Augustus portrayed himself not only as politician and general, but as builder and religious leader, that is, restorer of the Roman republic and empire, of the city, and of the traditions of the ancestors. Inscriptions in Rome and other sites where the *Res Gestae* were displayed announced the text's subjects, "the achievements of the deified Augustus," and specifying their nature: deeds "by which he made the world subject to the rule of the Roman people."[61] Each of the thirty-five paragraphs is written in the first person; for instance: "I have often conducted war by land and sea, civil and foreign."[62]

This is history, the account of what has happened, as a long list of deeds that portrays Augustus's life as a life of actions. It aspires to the universal; since this is the story of a universal empire, the deeds discussed are of universal import, and they are taken from the life of a divine leader. With this text, Augustus asks his readers to recall the events he lists from hearsay or as eyewitness: his victory at Actium, his military expeditions and extension of the empire's borders, the founding of colonial cities, the many triumphs in which "kings or kings' children have been led in front of my chariot," his popular spectacles like the restaging of a naval battle

6.3 *Altar of Augustan Peace,* procession panel with Augustus. Photograph by George Steinmetz.

and his "building projects."[63] More importantly, with this representation of a glorious life constituted by great deeds, Augustus asks the readers to affirm: yes, *that is he!*

The *Ara Pacis Augustae*, or Altar of Peace, whose richly decorated panels serve as the background to this narrative (and whose erection Augustus mentions in paragraph 12 of his *Res Gestae*), incites the same mimetic pleasure in its beholders. Here, Augustus is depicted on two relief panels as part of a procession led by priests. Preceded by a lictor, Augustus seems to be involved in the ongoing ceremony (figure 6.3).[64] In this representation of a ritual that links historical moment and eternal order, Augustus and "the most important men have portrait features," that is, they are recognizable to the viewer.[65]

Analyzing classical visuality and the various ways in which it voyeuristically mobilizes and relies on the viewer's scopic desires, Jaś Elsner emphasizes the "naturalism" of Roman art, a style trained in the craft of copying Greek art.[66] The sculpted relief panels of the altar are one example of this *Roman realism*, which "deluded" its viewers into "thinking that the figures were not painted but . . . real beings."[67] But Augustus knew he did not want sculpted images or statues; he needed text. In the *Res Gestae*, Augustus mentions that he had the approximately "eighty statues of [himself]" removed.[68] Is this a gesture of humility on the part of the emperor who celebrated the warrior-farmer, or is more at stake? Consistent with the Aristotelian logic that informs this Augustan mimesis, the empire-builder chooses the epic text over the statue, as if he had been familiar with Lessing's reflections in his *Laocoon* on medial specificity, that is, the stasis of the visual arts versus the movement of the epic. Let us read one of the key passages:

> I extended the territories of all those provinces of the Roman people which had neighbouring people who were not subject to our rule. I brought under control the Gallic and Spanish provinces, and similarly Germany where Ocean forms a boundary from Cadiz to the mouth of the river Elbe. I brought the Alps under control from the region which is nearest to the Adriatic Sea as far as the Tyrrhenian Sea . . . My fleet navigated through Ocean from the mouth of the Rhine to the east region of the rising sun as far as the territory of the Cimbri; no Roman before this time had ever approached this area either by land or sea, and the Cimbri and Charydes and Semnones and other German peoples of the same region sent envoys to request my friendship and that of the Roman people. Under my command and auspices two armies were led at almost the same time into Aethiopia and the Arabia which is called Fortunate, and substantial enemy forces of both peoples were slaughtered in battle and many towns captured. The army reached into Aethiopia as far as the town of Nabata, to which Meroe is nearest. The army advanced into Arabia as far as the territory of the Sabaei to the town of Mariba.[69]

And then the opening sentence of the next paragraph: "I added Egypt to the rule of the Roman people."[70]

This passage of the *Res Gestae* represents action on a large stage, representing the relentless imperial drive, or what Thucydides thought of as the natural tendency of all empires. In contrast to the silver statues of the emperor, representing the glory of Roman power embodied in the divine emperor, this Augustan text mimetically renders the process of conquest and ever-greater expansion. Like all realist texts, the *Res Gestae* "has built into it the search for and desire for a prior reality, a referent more real and other" than the represented object itself—in this case the search and desire for the "real" Augustus.[71] Pursuing the subjection of the conquered, the imperial subject of the *Res Gestae* also aims for the subjection of the reader to the rule of mimetic pleasure, the narrative adding more and more pressure to perform the act of mimetic recognition: "*that is he!*"

The text concludes with the emperor's death. "When I wrote this, I was in my seventy-sixth year" is the *Res Gestae*'s last sentence.[72] Augustus's testament thus also longs for the author's immortality, prompting the reader's "learning": *that was he!* Writing in the spirit of the *historia magistra vitae* (Cicero's concept of history as an archive of *exempla* that will guide future generations), with this last will in the form of an imperial manifesto Augustus deliberately offered himself as one of the examples to be imitated. The ultimate desire expressed in the *Res Gestae* is to have the reader respond to the model, to have the reader exclaim: *that is I!*

As I wrote above, neo-Roman imperial mimesis responds to this desire of the past. Both Charles V and his imperial artists were responding to the past, to Augustus's commanding desire to be imitated, Charles by his imperial ventures in Northern Africa and the imperial artists by erecting statues of Scipio and the emperors or organizing Charles's triumph. Together, these political and artistic practices constituted an act of imperial mimesis that kept the Roman past alive. Or, put more precisely, they kept it alive by reanimating it. To recognize the self in the Augustan other across the chasm of several centuries thus involves an aesthetic act of resurrection. I propose to think about this act of resurrection in the more literal and visual terms of the imaginary: imperial mimesis needs to resurrect, to reanimate that with which it identifies. All neo-Roman mimesis needs lifelike representations of the other, and this cultural production is part of all performances of imperial mimesis.

I use the term "resurrection" deliberately. My use is based on one of the central passages in Virgil's *Aeneid*, thematizing the relation between original and copy. In the *Aeneid*, the founding of Rome is a repetition of the founding of Troy. Having Aeneas lay the foundations of Rome means "to resurrect the kingdom of Troy."[73] The Latin original reads as follows: *illic fas regna resurgere Troiae*.[74] Virgil stages this act of resurrection by having Aeneas bring Troy back to life before the Trojan hero's own eyes as he stands in front of the fresco at Carthage, and before the eyes of his Carthaginian audience as he narrates the city's fall. Granted, this is a bringing-back-to-life at the very moment of the city's annihilation; nevertheless, it is an act that resurrects Troy and its fallen heroes, as Aeneas and his audience reimagine them in a brief flash of ekphrastic visualization.

Bringing the Dead Back to Life: Historical Mimesis and Ancestor Masks

Rome's aristocratic elite invented a ritual spectacle, the display of ancestor masks or *imagines* at funeral processions, which performed this kind of resurrection. It is a ritual that again articulates the relationship between the desires of the past and the present so characteristic of Roman imperial culture, and it does so in the realist mode. For these masks were not merely displayed, they were worn by professional actors assuming the identity of the dead. According to Polybios, this kind of *imago* was "fashioned with extraordinary fidelity both in its modeling and in its complexion to represent the features of the dead man" (R, 347). The men who wore the masks were those "considered to bear the closest resemblance" to the deceased in height and general appearance (R, 347); the actors wore costumes corresponding to the office held by the ancestor, and the dead man himself was represented by an *imago*.[75]

These funerals, Polybios wrote, were "spectacles," where the dead seemed to come together "*as if alive and breathing*" (R, 347; emphasis mine). *Imagines* glorified both the individual and the Roman system of rule, and their "*raison d'être* was to allow the ancestors to be represented as living breathing Roman magistrates at the height of their careers, who had reappeared in the city to accompany their newly-dead descendant on his last journey."[76] This realistic mimesis of the subject's famous ancestors was again designed to elicit the response desired by Augustus: *it is he—he, come back to life!* And the performer of imperial mimesis—in the sands of Egypt or at the gates of Tunis—then donned the mask or *imago* of the ancestor come back to life in a gesture that declared: *it is I!*

There is a peculiar desire at work in the imitation of the Roman past, and Freud's ideas about identification further our comprehension of this desire. As I wrote above, Freud thinks of *cathexis* as *Besetzung*. He also theorizes acts of identification from the standpoint of the present as acts based on "libidinal anticipatory ideas," or "cathexis which is held ready in anticipation."[77] I think about these performances of neo-Roman imitation from not only the standpoint of the desiring present but also that of the past and its *anticipating* desires, readable in ancient texts as well as friezes, paintings, and so on. Roman realist texts, images, and other cultural practices of the Roman past hold this *cathexis* ready in anticipation of future imitators.

Was it the cultural practice of funeral masks that Karl Marx had in mind when he wrote his famous lines on historical mimesis? Writing in the wake of Napoleon's neo-Roman performances, Karl Marx reflected on the French revolutionaries' practice of "resurrect[ing] Romans."[78] "[J]ust when they seem engaged in revolutionising themselves and things, in *creating something entirely new*," Marx wrote, "precisely in such periods of revolutionary crisis they anxiously conjure up *the spirits of the past* to their service and borrow from them names, battle slogans and costumes in order to present the new scene of world history in this time-honoured disguise and this borrowed language" (emphasis mine).[79]

All of this is known—the spectral presence of the past and its theatrical appropriation, the revolutionary anxiety at the heart of historical mimesis. This mimesis, the donning of the ancestral masks, Marx argues, is a necessary stage, but one that has to be overcome. Heroic action brings the heroic "ghosts from the days of Rome"[80] back to life, but there comes a moment when the French revolutionary in Roman guise becomes a revolutionary subject. As if the living and breathing actors had shed their death masks, *their imagines*. Discussing historical mimesis, Marx collapses republican and imperial mimesis, repetition as revolution and repetition as repetition. In imperial mimesis, the *imagines* are not left behind, but kept alive in representation.

Repetition with a Difference

As the *Res Gestae*'s last sentence reminded its readers, *he*, Augustus, is dead, and the empire *he* created is in ruins. Impersonating the dead emperors and reenacting their storied conquests always runs up against this haunting fact. The neo-Roman mimics' answer to this seems to have been consistent: the assertion to be *almost the same, but better*. As Ellen O'Gorman argues in her study of Roman exemplarity, Romans were inspired to imitate by their "competitiveness and drive for glory."[81] And so were their modern successors. In his study of the many different ways in which the Spanish translated the classics into their conquest of Mexico, David Lupher highlighted the conquistadors' challenge to the "prestige of the Romans": while Charles V claimed Caesar, Scipio, and Augustus as his ancestors, Hernan Cortés (and his chroniclers) presented Roman "generals and conquerors" as the modern heroes' rivals, sounding a "note of defiance."[82] Cortés, informing Charles that he had given the name *Nueva Espana* to the territory he had just seized, justified this decision by the unprecedented nature of the event: "A new fact elicits a new opinion."[83]

Thus, while Charles operated on the "principle of attachment" to the Roman past, Cortés was not only invested in proving his military skills to be above those of the ancient generals, but also inclined to think in terms of "adaptation and innovation."[84] Driven to think of themselves as fiercely independent of the past, Cortés and his men invented an "anticlassical tradition," taking an agonistic stance toward the classical model advanced by other contemporary historians and theorists.[85] As I mentioned in the introduction, Lord Cromer, the British governor of Egypt, repeated the gesture, professing attachment to the Roman model while claiming superiority. It would be wrong to think that this meant the classical model was dead; on the contrary, "only a still numinous model could attract such passionate emulous hostility."[86] Claiming the uniqueness of empire is a very Roman gesture. This tension between on the one hand the claim to be heir to the Romans' imperial spirit and on the other the assertion of superiority is another characteristic feature of all neo-Roman imperial discourses.

Neo-Roman imperial mimesis and empire-building means repetition: what began with the Spanish-Portuguese response to Augustus's mimetic desire (to be recognized and imitated) continued with British, French, German, and Italian empire-building as neo-Roman mimesis. As acts of repetition, all imperial mimesis focused on strategies that would address the obstinate specter of decline and devise ways of preventing—or at least delaying—the end. Cromer was not the only colonial administrator haunted by Rome's fate. Reconstructing the role Roman and Greek models played in the discourse and practices of British colonizers, Phiroze Vasunia added the perspective of the colonized. Gandhi, having read Gibbon, contrasted India's longevity with the "pitiable condition" of the empires of the West:

> Rome went . . . but India is still, somehow or other, sound at the foundation . . . In trying to learn their lessons [from the writings of the men of Greece and Rome], the Europeans imagine they will avoid the mistakes of Greece and Rome . . . In the midst of all this, India remains immovable, and that is her glory.[87]

Critics of empire echoed Gandhi's thoughts about the death of Rome; proponents kept arguing against it, debating again and again the lessons to be found in the past. The renowned British historian of Augustan Rome, Robert Syme, argued in 1958 against the law of ruin, mobilizing Polybian contingency against Polybian determinism: "[T]here is this to be said—that almost anything can happen in history. Let us refuse to be intimidated by 'the inevitable,' or discouraged by the elaborate constructions of Spengler and Toynbee, the laws they devise and impose."[88]

These are examples from the British case, but as I will argue throughout this book, all neo-Roman imperial mimesis focuses on strategies addressing the obstinate specter of the end and devising ways of preventing—or at least delaying—the end, strategies that are narrowly political and broadly symbolic or aesthetic in nature. Among the *political* strategies, two stand out. One involved avoiding what in contemporary parlance is called imperial overreach, and in the quaint vocabulary of the eighteenth century was known as immodesty. The second strategy focused on native policies, or the question of the barbarian.[89] Thus Rome was a model, as powerful as it was problematic. Neo-Roman imperial mimesis had to be a repetition with a difference, and imperial imaginaries were the product of this mimesis, signifying sameness *and* difference: *the same, but not quite*—to use Bhabha's famous phrase.

Of Mimicry and Empire

So far I have approached neo-Roman mimesis as a practice that responds to the desire of the past. In this section, I will shift the focus of analysis, exploring acts of imperial mimesis as acts that crystallize around a lack at the core of the Roman model. The neo-Roman conqueror's performance of ruin gazing on the Roman stage will be the focus of this analysis. In part 1, I traced Roman imperial imaginaries as staging imperial space (centered on the Roman stage) and time (endtime), and as articulations of imperial subject and object. Roman ruin gazer scenarios in particular, I argued, dramatized this articulation of imperial subject and conquered barbarian. *Neo-Roman* imaginaries dramatize not only articulations of conqueror and barbarian, but also Roman and neo-Roman imperial sovereign. The ruin gazer scenarios that acts of imitation endlessly generate cannot be separated from the dramatization of imperial mimesis *per se*; rather, they are particular manifestations of these mimetic scenarios.

How does mimetic desire work if we move beyond Bhabha's model of colonial mimicry to the context of the longer *durée* of empire and the problematic of Rome's fall? Colonial culture is a world in search of "a particularly appropriate form of colonial subjectivity,"[90] Bhabha argues, theorizing colonial subject formation (meaning the subject produced in and subjected to colonial discourses and practices) as mimicry. The partial imitation of the colonizer, mimicry means assuming a specific subject position: in Bhabha's well-known phrase, "*a subject of a difference that is almost the same but not quite.*"[91] In Bhabha's scopic scene of power and desire, mimicry also means wearing a mask, the mask of the European colonizer.[92] Unlike mimesis, Bhabha argues, mimicry "*repeats* rather than re-presents," a partial imitation that performs subjectivity by wearing a "mask."[93] Both desired *and* perceived as a menace, this act of repetition is terrifying, because it has the potential to unmask the original—or the subject of the colonizer—as being as inauthentic as the imitation.[94] Mimicry—the mask the colonized is asked to wear to "facilitate" rule *and* the mask the colonized decides to wear to become part of the system of rule—is thus (a potentially political) act that "mimes" like the fetish.[95] That is, it stages its own forms of disavowal and acknowledgment of lack. By doing so, it alienates the colonizer's (and colonized's) identity or what is lived in the imaginary register as essence.

Neo-Roman Mimesis: "A Subject of a Difference That Is Almost the Same but Not Quite"

Bhabha's model of synchronous colonial subject formation and the act of mimicry as its most overtly politicized form is, I think, also valid for the premodern Roman context of Roman and Romanized subject, Roman and non-Romanized barbarian. The Roman subject does not recognize itself in the barbarian; it does recognize itself in the partial reflection of the Romanized barbarian. In contrast, neo-Roman mimesis poses the question of imperial identity formation diachronically, that is, as an articulation of past and present identities, of Roman model and neo-Roman imitator. What Bhabha lets us understand (via Fanon's Hegelian existentialism [and its dialectic of recognition arrested by racism] and Lacan's reading of this dialectic [in terms of the ontological non-identity of the subject]) is the following: first, imperial mimesis is a form of mimicry, producing *a subject of a difference that is almost the same but not quite*. Neo-Roman imitators stage their identity as imperial sovereigns by *publicly performing* their neo-Roman identity, deliberately wearing the masks of their Roman ancestors.[96]

I use *masks* here in the widest sense, referring to the whole archive of representations of the Roman past. As I argued earlier, in using these masks, the imitator responds to the desire of the Roman past to be imitated, to be kept alive in images, words, and deeds. As I wrote above, Charles V and his imperial artists were responding to the past, to Augustus's commanding desire to be imitated, by the *political* event of the campaign and the *cultural* performances that followed in its wake. These performances of imperial mimesis, partial imitations of the Roman model, take place on the level of the symbolic, within a symbolic order that relentlessly produces representations of Rome. Observing one of the Spanish rituals of Roman-ness, a spectator described Charles as "immovable as an icon," surrounded by stage accessories "like Augustus before him."[97] Having acted his part in these spectacles by wearing the mask of the dead, Charles knew that he too had become an image.

Second, this partial identification with the models of the past is also an act of self-alienation in the *imago* of the other, an act of being "I" by being "he/Roman." Involving the register of the imaginary, this particular form of miming is arguably sustained by imaginary identifications with the heroes of the past, identifications unknown to the sovereign subject, the emperor, or his administrators. As is the case with all forms of imaginary identifications, this self-alienation would then be an encounter with difference, non-identity, lack—in short, a confrontation with the real that in registers of the imaginary and the symbolic is a form of death.[98] What matters in the neo-Roman situation is the following: taking on the mask of the Roman, repeating Rome, means encountering death on the level of the symbolic: the Roman Empire ended, and it ended in ruins.[99] Acts of imperial mimesis are thus encounters with death, possibly ontologically as the encounter with non-identity, and definitely symbolically as the assumption of the identity of the dead, the dead and their ruined empire.

Let me summarize: in the trans-imperial context of neo-Roman mimesis, Bhabha's scenes of colonial identity formation and mimicry, staging the workings of desire, lack, and the scopic drive, emerge as only one aspect of the articulations of imperial power and desire. While Bhabha's scopic scenarios explain the synchronic constellation of colonizer and colonized, the concept of imperial mimesis that I propose explains the processes at work in the diachronic constellation of Roman model and neo-Roman imitator.[100] This is as valid in Charles's case as it is in the case of his successors. The (early) modern imperial subject's recognition of itself as Roman is also an act in which this subject encounters historical lack—however powerful and triumphant the images of Rome are that this modern subject produces for the performance of imperial mimesis. A process of self-alienation, the performance makes the neo-Roman subject a sovereign who assumes the Roman other's historical lack—assumes it in a triumphant gesture of omnipotence.

Discussing Charles's performance on the Roman stage, I drew attention to the triumphant quality of the ruin gazer scenario at the heart of this neo Roman performance. Maintaining the neo Roman subject, the subject wearing the mask of the Roman conqueror, in the position of the one who is looking (at the ruins, at the barbarian enemy), is one of the symbolic strategies involved in neo-Roman mimesis as a repetition-with-a-difference. Moreover, public acts of symbolic identification are accompanied by statements (and practices) asserting difference. Here, the ruin gazer scenario as performance on the stage-in-ruins visualizes sameness as difference.

And yet, being Roman or, rather, becoming Roman on the public stage involves an acknowledgment and disavowal of lack. In these particular scenarios, spectacular performances on the Roman stage-in-ruins, the ruins become the most visible fetish of empire—denying the historical lack around which neo-Roman mimesis revolves and acknowledging it. Analyzing Vermeyen's tapestries, ruin gazer scenarios in a different medium, I pointed to the theatrical composition of the battle scenes as scenes taking place on the ruined Carthaginian stage. Referring to "Carthage's ruins," the explanatory text leaves us with a telling ambiguity: Are these the ruins of Punic or Roman Carthage? If they are the former, they fit into the triumphalist narrative of the Tunis expedition. If they are the latter, they raise again the specter of Rome's fall.

A "Closet of Masks"[101]

Death lurks at the heart of every act of imitation. With this insight in mind, let us return to the events of 1535. The Roman ritual of ruin gazing completed Charles's neo-Roman conquest of Tunis. Charles's African campaign produced a ruin gazer scenario in another medium, poetry, thematizing the violence of conquest. Garcilaso de la Vega, a Spanish nobleman who accompanied Charles on his North African campaign, wrote a sonnet in 1535 entitled *Sonnet to Boscan from Goleta*. Figuring the Spanish troops as Roman warriors, this poem celebrates the ancient and modern empires' strength while recalling their founding violence.

> Boscan, arms and the fury of Mars, which watering the African soil with its own strength, make the Roman Empire *flourish once again* in this region, / Have led back to memory the art and ancient Italian valor by whose strength and valorous hand Africa was leveled from end to end. / Here, where the Roman conflagration, where fire and licentious flame left only the name of Carthage, / love turns and turns again my thought, wounds and inflames my fearful soul, and in tears and ashes I am undone.[102]

As Helgerson points out, the poem begins with an allusion to the opening lines of Virgil's *Aeneid*—"Wars and a man I sing" (AFa, 47). The text then deepens this intertextual link by alluding not only to the moment of Dido's death at the end of book 4 but also to the opening lines, in which Virgil tells us about Dido's "pain of love," her "wound," the "fire burning in her heart" (AFa, 127). In Garcilaso's sonnet, the poet becomes Dido, burning on the pyre.[103]

Like Vermeyen's tapestries, this sonnet where *only the name of Carthage* is left raises the question: Who will be undone? Helgerson reads de Vega's poem, early modern imperial culture, and the Spanish king's mimesis of Rome as forms of "cultural self-alienation," a practice of making the familiar strange, the self-other.[104] In his reading of Garcilaso's lines, this self-alienation in the service of imperial power leads to the poet's death in an act of identification with the victim of imperial violence, Dido, the queen of Carthage.[105] Donning the *imago* of the dead, he is dying.

I ask you to read Garcilaso's mimetic act—I am undone—with his double function as poet and military commander in mind. Garcilaso is both, Dido and Scipio, conqueror and conquered. This play with the masks of the dead restages the tension of the Polybian scenario on the Carthaginian scene. Like Garcilaso the poet wearing Dido's mask, so Garcilaso, the imperial servant and military commander wearing the mask of Scipio, will be undone.[106] Garcilaso thus at once asserts the triumphant reawakening of empire and restages Polybios's prophecy of death to come in the rubble of Carthage. The poet and colonial servant of Charles V knew that he could rely on his readers' recall of the relevant details from the Virgilian original: the classical author's prophetic violent simile of Carthage crumbling, Dido's passionate invocation of Hannibal and the vision of Rome in ruins that Virgil sought to bring before his listeners' "fearful" eyes.[107]

In his ruin gazer scenario, Garcilaso does not put the barbarian enemy in the place of the imperial subject. Instead, the Spanish poet performs the victor's identification with both the conqueror and the vanquished enemy. Or, put differently, by opening up a "closet of masks," the poet-conqueror creates a new permutation of the scenario and thereby a new exploration of the tension between triumph and death that it thematizes.[108] *Imperial* mimesis is thus an act responding to the desire of the past. It is an act of symbolic identification with an object of the past—a hero, his conquests, his empire, and imperial culture—that is kept alive in representations, so many masks fashioned by the neo-Roman subject and culture. And it is an act that forgets the future past of this Roman object while remaining haunted by the knowledge of this ruination. Reenacting past events of conquest and colonization, this act of identification with the imperial object is a performance that takes place on a stage, one littered with the ruins of the past. Napoleon engaged in this mimetic performance in Egypt among Roman ruins, Charles V in Tunis among the ruins of Carthage.

Freud and the Impossible Time-Space of Imperial Mimesis

At his abdication ceremony in 1556, Charles spoke of the "need to lay down the burden of office," affirming albeit unintentionally the "burial of world-empire as a mode of organizing the world-system."[109] This early modern spectacle of Roman-ness with its steady accumulation of texts and images devoted to the fabrication of Charles's neo-Roman sovereignty has an excessive quality to it, and by the end, the universal monarch appears to falter under the weight of this excess. According to Burke, this overproduction of Charles's mimetic machinery signifies the "myth of imperial agency."[110] With Wallerstein, we might argue that it testifies to the failure of the Spanish Habsburgs' imperial project.

With an eye toward later European projects of mimesis, this symptomatic excess ought to attract our attention for different reasons. The Romans' ritual practices and arts constituted an archive, emitting a "powerful stimulus to emulation."[111] At the beginning of the modern age, Charles's image-producers left behind an equally vast archive of refashioned Roman practices and materials that later imitators will use for their own purposes. We will encounter, for instance, the re-creation and symbolic appropriation of Rome's ruined architectural stage in later centuries. We will also encounter other instances of the performance of sovereign ruin gazing in the city of Rome at the moment of conquest.

With this wealth of political and aesthetic practices of resurrection at their disposal, modern experts in mimesis will create their empires' imaginary Roman zone. Garcilaso's *Sonnet to Boscan from Goleta* intriguingly gestures at this imaginary zone. When the poem's "I" becomes Dido, it creates a space, in which the past exists in the present. Like the other mimetic practices I discussed in this chapter, the poem's mimetic imitation of classical texts creates an imaginary twilight zone where the past is a more or less shadowy part of the present. Ruins are material remnants of a vanished past, and as such are central signifiers of all such acts of mimesis.

Freud's famous passage on the ruins of Rome in his *Unbehagen in der Kultur* (1931) invites us to further reflect on the nature of this twilight zone of neo-Roman imperial imaginaries, its temporality, and the gaze that it inscribes. How do we grasp the fact that no "memory-trace" is ever destroyed, Freud asks as he returns to the Roman stage?[112] To understand this, we need to imagine the unconscious as a space in which past and present coexist. Taking the reader on an imaginary tour of contemporary Rome, Freud explains to us what we would discover about the way in which "the past is preserved in historical sites like Rome."[113] The traveler would "see" remnants of the oldest wall but not the buildings that once filled this frame, because they are either completely gone, or they are "ruins" that are vestiges of later restorations.[114] Moreover, a lot of remnants are still entirely buried under the modern metropolis.

Much of ancient Rome has thus perished. If we want to imagine a space in which nothing has ever perished, only a "flight of imagination" would help us: What would Rome look like today if all of these "phases of development" coexisted?[115] That is, if, for instance, "the palaces of the Caesars and the Septizonium of Septimius Severus would still be rising to their old height on the Palatine."[116] In this imaginary Rome, "we should find not only the Pantheon of to-day, as it was bequeathed to us by Hadrian, but, on the same site, the original edifice erected by Agrippa; indeed the same piece of ground would be supporting the church of Santa Maria sopra Minerva and the ancient temple over which it was built."[117] Freud's effort to make us imagine the unconscious produces an impossible imaginary space in which everything that ever existed is preserved intact. And this space is connected to a form of scopic mastery that allows a simultaneous view of past and present: "[T]he observer would perhaps only have to change the direction of his glance or his position in order to call up the one view or the other."[118]

Here the concept of time—concepts of past, present, or future—does not exist, only the simultaneous presence of things or events. But this is not the main point I want to make. My point is that this describes the *imaginary space* of imperial mimesis: the coexistence or close proximity of Roman past and neo-Roman present. The distance that political and aesthetic acts of imperial mimesis establish in this twilight zone between past and present will vary, and sometimes attempts will be made to completely collapse the distance.

PART THREE

Neo-Roman Mimesis in the Modern Age: Cook's Second Voyage to the South Pacific and the French Conquest of Egypt and Algeria

Preface

The Conquest of Ruins treats the theories and practices of neo-Roman mimesis as a Western European phenomenon that crosses chronological and national boundaries. In part 1, I discussed the emergence of the Roman ruin gazer scenario in the context of Augustan empire-building. In part 2, using Charles's conquest of Tunis in 1535, I focused on the concept of imperial mimesis, addressing the processes at work in the diachronic constellation of Roman model and neo-Roman imitator/imitation. Part 3 will move us from the sixteenth century to the end of the eighteenth century, and thus to the moment when European states embarked on the second, modern wave of empire-building. These modern empires obeyed the same imperative to expand as their Roman and Spanish-Roman predecessors. "[T]o cease to acquire," one of Britain's colonial politicians wrote with Roman urgency in 1808, "is to begin to lose."[1]

Two cases of modern imperial mimesis are at the heart of part 3: first, the brief but significant episode of Cook's voyages and the British conquest of the South Pacific at the end of the eighteenth century; and second, the drawn-out process of the French case of neo-Roman mimesis, starting with the invasion of Egypt in 1798. The theorists, artists, and mimetic experts whom I will study in part 3 differ with respect to their direct engagement in these British and French projects of neo-Roman empire-building. Some of them were outspoken critics of the modern projects of imitating Rome; others theorized the form this imitation ought to take. Yet, regardless of their actual involvement or ideological position toward these imperial ventures, all of them remained haunted by Rome's fall and its causes. Some of them came up with ways to break the cycle of imperial rise and fall, but most continued to think of ways to prolong the time of empire—the time that remains before the inescapable fall. And regardless of their role or stance, they contributed to the resurrection of the Roman past and thus to the creation of the new age's imperial imaginaries.

Part 3 deals therefore with modern acts of neo-Roman mimesis that defied the risks and dangers inherent in the act of repetition, undeterred gestures of repetition generating their own imaginaries centered on their own ruin gazer scenarios. In terms of political chronology, part 3 spans this second phase of imperial expansion from its onset in the late eighteenth century to its zenith around 1900. That is, it begins with the American Revolution, Captain Cook's voyages to the South Pacific, and the French Army's invasion of Egypt in 1798. From there it moves to the conquest of Algeria in 1830, and concludes with a quick foray into the late nineteenth century and the Roman ruins of Tipasa in French Algeria.

For the British and French empires, the period between 1780 and 1820 is a moment of triumphant expansion in the wake of crisis: the British loss of the American colonies and its turn to its possessions in the East; the French loss of Haiti and the Napoleonic Campaign in Egypt. The texts I will discuss in chapters 7 and 8 reflect on this new wave of imperialism, on neo-Roman mimesis, the meaning of Rome's fall for their present, and the barbarians of the modern age. In chapter 7, I examine Johann Gottfried Herder's writings on world history, published between 1774 and 1791, and François de Volney's *Ruins or Meditations on Empire* (1791). Chapter 8 looks at Edward Gibbon's *The Decline and Fall of the Roman Empire* (1776–1789).

Cook's voyages to the South Pacific played a crucial role in Gibbon's revival of Polybios's endtime scenario and reflections on ways of delaying this end. In chapter 9, I explore the ways in which two men who accompanied Cook on board the *Resolution*, the German naturalist and author Georg Forster and the neoclassical painter William Hodges, framed this voyage in neo-Roman terms. I will read Forster's *Voyage Round the World* (1777) as a Virgilian fragment, and analyze Hodges's painting *A View of the*

Monuments of Easter Island (1775) as a similarly intermedial work of art. Together, Forster and Hodges created the South Pacific at the moment of conquest as a neo-Roman space.

Chapters 10 and 11 will then concentrate on the French case of neo-Roman empire-building. In chapter 10, I will present this case as a series of conquests surrounded by a drawn-out performance of imperial mimesis. I begin the analysis of the French state's performance of becoming Roman with the Egyptian Campaign, the remaking of Napoleon as Roman emperor, and the framing of Egypt as ruined Roman stage. I then analyze the literal and symbolic conquest of the Roman stage during the occupation of the city of Rome (1808–1814). Chapter 10 concludes with Joseph Fourier's introduction to the *Description de L'Égypte* (1809–1828) and the way that Fourier translated the failure of the Egyptian adventure into the future success of French conquests in North Africa and elsewhere. By the time of the conquest of Algeria in 1830, the French state's neo-Roman mimesis is in place. Chapter 11 will focus on the role of the Roman Empire and its ruins in the conquest of North Africa, concluding with Louis Bertrand's *fin-de-siècle* concept of *African Latinité* and his resurrectional theo-politics.

Hegel, theorizing modernity in his lectures on world history as teleological process (held in 1822–1823), declared the Roman Empire dead. In the modern world, nothing remained of the rotting corpse of Rome but its ruins. Entangling the new linear narrative in stories about cyclical history, the modern projects of neo-Roman mimesis labored hard to keep the Roman Empire alive, whether we find ourselves with Georg Forster and William Hodges in the South Pacific, with Napoleon's generals, scientists, and artists in Egypt, or with Louis Bertrand and his companion, the archeologist Stéphane Gsell, in Algeria and Tunisia.

Louis Bertrand advocated the complete reconstitution of Carthage's ruined Roman stage as the theo-political center of the French Empire in North Africa. The work on Rome's ruined stage thus continued in the modern era, work both literal—as in the case of the reconstruction of Rome in the Napoleonic era—and aesthetic in nature. Piranesi's eighteenth-century engravings resurrected the power of Roman ruins, rendering them newly visible as a monumental stage set at a time when Europe entered the second wave of empire-building and colonialism. Gibbon and Fourier, among others, undertook this labor of restoration with the help of their own medium, fine-grained empiricist descriptions of great visual power.

These modern acts of imperial mimesis and their ruinous imaginaries, centered on the Roman stage, thus continued to thematize and visualize the tensions at the heart of neo-Roman imperial mimesis. Polybios's scenario introduced the barbarian as a sign of contingency (potentially disrupting the course of time subject to the natural law of ruin) and as part of a scopic constellation visualizing power relations. Devoting his life to uncovering the Roman ruins in French Algeria and Tunisia, the archeologist Stéphane Gsell rewrote the history of Rome's fall in Northern Africa, and like Volney before him, introduced the Muslim barbarian into his ruin gazer scenarios. Bertrand, the organic intellectual of settlers in Algeria, theorized this barbarian as the Enemy. Muslims—Ottomans, Mamelukes, North Africans—thus emerged as one of the modern era's ciphers for the neo-Roman barbarian.

At the same time, in the texts by Volney, Gibbon, Forster, and Diderot, and the many visual materials produced during and in the wake of Cook's voyages, the tattooed inhabitants of the South Pacific became the other iconic image embodying the barbarian of the modern age. I conclude with a chapter on one of Gustave Doré's engravings, *The New Zealander* (1872). I take this iconic image as the point of departure to continue my inquiry into the scenario's relations of scopic mastery.

In part 3, I thus pursue the topic of neo-Roman mimesis from the beginning of Europe's second wave of imperial ventures to Bertrand's epiphany in 1895, organized around specific instances of conquest. With Marx, we can understand the onset of this second wave as a process that, for the non-European world, entailed "moments of primitive accumulation" of extraordinary violence.[2] Marx made this point by paraphrasing Virgil: "So great was the effort required [to found the Roman race]—to unleash the 'eternal natural laws' of the capitalist mode of production."[3] With chapter 11, I begin to explore the emergence of a particular strand in the large fabric of neo-Roman mimesis, the critique of modernity by members of the so-called conservative revolution. Reflecting on the corroding effects of capitalist imperialism on the state and the primacy of the political in general, conservative intellectuals like Louis Bertrand, Oswald Spengler, many of the Third Reich's classicists and geopoliticians, and, finally, Carl Schmitt link their views of decaying European culture to visions of neo-Roman empire-building and a new form of sovereignty with the power to delay the empire's end.

SEVEN

Against Neo-Roman Mimesis: Johann Gottfried Herder at Carthage and François de Volney at Palmyra

Introduction: Piranesi's Ruined Stage

With his eyes riveted on the crumbling, neglected remnants of ancient Rome, Piranesi coined the term "speaking ruins," ruins that spoke to him of Rome's former grandeur.[1] In ways similar to the Renaissance scholars who entered the wilderness that was Rome in the early sixteenth century, Piranesi made the imperial Roman stage *visible* once again.[2] Establishing himself as the premier ruin gazer of the modern age, Piranesi endowed Rome's ruins with new vitality. By the time Piranesi was selling his mass-produced *vedute* in Britain, Charles's conquistadors had performed their bloody imperial mimesis in the New World, reading Virgil and boasting that they were better colonizers than the Romans. Now Britain was about to follow suit, turning from its Western to its Eastern empire.

The era that saw the American Revolution, the revolutions in France and Haiti, and their Napoleonic aftermath was an era that reinvented imperial mimesis in theory and practice. This process helped center the era's imperial imagination on the metropolitan cities of Paris or London as well as Rome's ruined stage. In this context, late eighteenth- and early nineteenth-century European philosophers and historians continued to puzzle over the riddle of why Rome fell, none more obsessively than Edward Gibbon, whose *The Decline and Fall of the Roman Empire* (published between 1776 and 1788) I will discuss in chapter 8. Gibbon—and other metropolitan intellectuals before and after him—saw the shadows looming over this act of repetition. For they had read their classics, chief among them Polybios's *Histories* and Virgil's *Aeneid*.

They were also well acquainted with the trope of the world as the theater of grand politics and the idea of Rome as the empire's stage; or, rather, they rendered the latter newly operative. The fall of Rome, Gibbon wrote, was "the greatest, perhaps, and most awful scene in the history of mankind."[3] Piranesi shared Gibbon's sense of history as grand spectacle and portrayed the city as a stage filled with majestic remnants. Piranesi's *Le Antichità Romane* (1756) contained 250 plates, surveying the remains of the Eternal City.[4] Opening with a reconstructed map, the plates showed the core sites of the imperial center. Augustus's Mausoleum was one of the imperial structures included in this "landmark in classical archeology" (figure 7.1).[5] But these ruin-pictures are not mere archeological documents. Using a particular way of framing Rome's monumental structures, Piranesi who designed stage sets as a trained architect put Rome's ruins onstage.

In the previous chapters, I analyzed the importance of Greek and Roman stage architecture for ruin gazer scenarios. As Roman stages de-

7.1 Giovanni Battista Piranesi, *Reliquiae Mausolei Augusti* (ca. 1780).

7.2 Giovanni Battista Piranesi, *Veduta del Sepolcro creduto degli Scipioni* (1757).

veloped, perspectival painting did too, sometimes including "a distant cityscape."[6] Working from Vitruvius's chapters on theater architecture, the Italian eighteenth-century stage expert Bibiena developed ways of designing "scenes viewed at an angle" to create the maximum effect of depth on a flat surface.[7] Piranesi, who also designed stage sets, appropriated this *skenographia* for the *mise-en-scène* of Roman ruins. *The Tomb of the Scipios* is an example of Piranesi's use of this peculiar perspective (figure 7.2). Showing the ruin at a slight angle, Piranesi's engraving invites the implied viewer to step onto the Roman stage from the lower left-hand corner. The vanishing point's "effect of heightening" adds to this dynamic, staging the monumentality of overpowering architecture.[8] The overall effect is as dramatic as Bibiena's stage sets, echoing the ornate *scaenae frons* of imperial Roman theater.

While Polybios and Virgil staged the fall of empire as the ruination of the scene-house, Piranesi put the architecture of imperial Rome itself onstage. As I discussed in part 1, the Greek *skene* and the Roman *scaenae frons* represented the house of death, the house as palace, and potentially a ruin. Piranesi's Augustan Mausoleum and the ruined tomb of the Scipiones are monuments to Roman sovereignty.[9] They are also, and inevitably, houses of death. With these stagelike compositions, Piranesi re-creates the specific aesthetic of Roman ruin gazer scenarios, making their theatrical framing newly available to his contemporaries.

Imperial and anti-imperial intellectuals alike reinvented these staged scenes, inextricably tying modern Europe's imperial imaginaries to the sight of Roman ruins, the empire's end—and the figure of the new barbarian. As we will see, the natives of the South Pacific were, perhaps surprisingly, central to this imagination. In the context of eighteenth-century painting, Denis Diderot is known as the theorist of theatricality. In the context of postcolonial theory, he is known as the author of "Supplement to Bougainville's 'Voyage'" (1772), a polemical intervention in debates about the merits of European civilization, which includes a fierce critique of European explorers voiced by Orou, a Tahitian elder. Addressing Bougainville's translator, Orou asks: "If some day a Tahitian should land on your shores" and declare: "'This land belongs to the people of Tahiti,' what would you think?"[10]

In the literature on ruins, Diderot is known as having defined "the poetics of ruins."[11] Enchanted by one of Robert Hubert's scenographic ruin paintings, Diderot wrote: "Our glance lingers over the debris of a triumphal arch, a portico . . . and we retreat into ourselves; we contemplate the ravages of time, and in our imagination we scatter the rubble of the very buildings in which we live over the ground; in that moment . . . we are the sole survivors of an entire nation that is no more."[12] Inscribing the aesthetics of ruins into the discourse of the rise and fall of empires, Diderot discerns the "movement of anticipation" in Robert's ruinscapes.[13]

This experience of the ruin gazer, Diderot claims, is "the first tenet of the poetics of ruins."[14] Is the second tenet that the European ruin gazer ought not to change places with the non-European subject? That Diderot's Orou would not travel to Europe, that Europe's colonial subjects would not conquer the continent, that Orou would not contemplate the ruins of European empires? Gibbon's history of Rome's decline and fall connects Polybios's Carthaginian scenario to Cook's exploratory voyages in the South Pacific. This modern reinvention of the scenario is one of the core themes of part 3.

This chapter focuses on the French traveler and historian François de Volney (1757–1820) and the German theologian and historian Johann Gottfried Herder (1744–1803), both writing in the wake of eighteenth-century British and French voyages of discovery. Like Gibbon, these authors situate their ruin gazer scenarios in the context of reflections on neo-Roman mimesis. Continuing the convention of thinking about political history as grand theater, they created staged scenes of ruin gazing. While Herder rewrites Polybios's scenario at Carthage as part of a project of reinventing *world history*, Volney rewrites the Roman scenario as part of a treatise on political theory. Both historians reflect on the rise and fall of Rome, and more or less explicitly on the practice of neo-Roman mimesis. Drawing lessons from the past for Europe's neo-Roman empires, they voice an anti-imperial, anticolonial stance.

Their rewriting of Polybios's ruin scenario hints at something that is implicit in the latter's scenario: the replacement of the figure of the conqueror with the figure of the conquered, overlooking the ruins of the metropolis. As I argued in part 1, this revision was already part of the post-Polybian Roman scenarios, and in part 2 I analyzed a similar move in Garcilaso de la Vega's sonnet. In Herder's and Volney's modern ruin scenarios, ancient Roman enemies come back to life.

Both theorists argue against neo-Roman mimesis, and as modern thinkers, both reflect on the possibilities of breaking the cycle of empires rise and fall. At the same time, their political-philosophical texts and ruin scenarios continue to regenerate the imperial imagination, sketching imperial space and time, imperial sovereign subject and barbarians. In the imagination of the time, ruin travelers from the American colonies or the new Western empire will join travelers from the non-European world. Scipio wept at Carthage. Now ruin scenarios will be located on the shores of the Thames and the Seine.

Historical Mimesis: Herder's Theo-Historicist Histories of the World

Few images are as famous as Hegel's figuration of the philosopher's backward glance at the past: Minerva's owl taking flight when a "shape of life has grown old."[15] Spreading its wings at dusk, the owl sets out to understand what is no longer alive. In Piranesi's *Temple of Minerva Medica* (1751), there is no owl in sight. Instead, we find archeologists, another kind of specialist, in the backward gaze at Roman antiquity.[16] The eighteenth century saw a revival of universal history, the genre pioneered by Polybios. These eighteenth-century philosophies of history were written with a backward glance at Rome's fall, while at the same time paying attention to the non-European world recently made visible by exploratory travel and imperial ventures.[17]

For Herder, reinventing Polybian world history involved the concept of historical mimesis and his own version of the Scipionian scenario. In this section, my reading will focus on two texts: Herder's sketch for a world history, "This Too a Philosophy of History for the Formation of Humanity," published in 1774; and his *Ideen zur Philosophie der Geschichte der Menschheit* (*Reflections on the Philosophy of the History of Humankind*), published a decade later (from 1781 to 1791). Elaborating on the trope of history as spectacle, Herder narrates his world history as a drama to be observed by the historian closely tracking the path of providence. As we will see, the arrival of Rome on the world stage represents a climactic moment.

Having told his story about Rome, Herder intertwines two topics in his *Reflections on the Philosophy of History*: the representation of Rome as stage and a farewell to neo-Roman mimesis, pointing to the French revolutionaries' failed imitation. What do we learn from Roman history? Nothing but Latin words, Herder replied. When Roman history was "misunderstood," it "formed new Romans, none of whom ever equaled his model."[18] Not only was Rome's deadly spectacle of world domination unique. We should never wish for its "repetition" (I, 384).

What characterized Herder's world history? Herder combines this metaphorics of history as theater with the elevated viewpoint of the geohistorian, tracking the history of ever-expanding imperial space. Toward the end of "This Too a Philosophy of History," the theologian comes to occupy a celestial vantage point akin to what Kant termed "Weltbeschauer," or contemplator of the world.[19] Second, Herder's version of history is stadial and theological.[20] Here, Rome represents History's manhood, and "Northerners" the mature age.[21] His own historical moment—"our philosophical, cold European world"—is one of decline. Combining this stadial historicism and its implicit relativism with a theological version of the law of nature, he argued against eighteenth-century theories of history as "eternal revolution!" without "plan" and "progress."[22]

This theo-historicist story is a breathless account of incessant forward movement, culminating in contemporary Europe, but Herder's opinion of this old European world is far from positive. By the time of the Renaissance, Europe was already too enamored with an instrumental notion of progress. The Renaissance, era of science and exploratory voyages, revolutionized entire continents. Familiar with Las Casas's writings, Herder sees this revolution as a form of neo-barbarism, the conquest of the Americas a combination of looting and genocide.

Each of these stages of world history represented an increase in spatial expansion. This expansion took a significant leap first with the Phoenicians and then with the Roman Empire, eventually resulting in the global world of Herder's colonial present. Moreover, all nations and all historical transitions involve historical mimesis. That is, men continuously assimilate things similar to their nature. Rejecting what is alien, this active mimesis strengthens each people's soul. Romans were experts in this historical mimesis. Putting everything and everyone "in Roman dress," they acquired a firm core, enabling them to conquer the world.[23]

The entry of the Romans onto the world stage is the most dramatic moment in Herder's story of historical mimesis and spatial expansion. The Greeks' small actions on "a small stage" were replaced by the Romans' actions on the world's stage.[24] Quoting Virgil on the Romans' imperial mission, Herder announces this transition with considerable pathos. With a mixture of awe and horror, Herder contemplates this event, the rise of a world empire making everyone parts of "a great machine."[25] Oddly enough, Herder observed later, these barbarians never conceived of the idea of their own demise—with the exception of Scipio at the moment when the Romans' "courage" slid into "exuberant hubris" (I, 373).

One of the strands running through Herder's drama of the Romans' rise and fall is metaphorical: monumental buildings crashing to the ground. In the ruin gazer scenario from Herder's 1774 text, this theo-political architecture, the Romans' great "building" crashes, as did Polybios's *skene* and Virgil's *scaenae frons*.[26] With this critical scenario of late Rome, Herder's anti-imperial and anticolonial stance emerges once again. Turning to the present, Herder attacks the nations of Europe for their "barbarism," that is, their exploitation of the non-European world.[27] Imperialist hubris characterized both the emerging empires of his own age and the empire of the Romans; imperial expansion devastated Rome and the nations Rome conquered, and it would do the same to modern Europe and its non-European colonies.

The Ruins of Carthage and the Rubble of Rome: Against Neo-Roman Mimesis

Herder's 1774 sketch of world history is thus anticolonial in inspiration.[28] In *Ideen zur Philosophie der Geschichte der Menschheit* (*Reflections on the Philosophy of the History of Humankind*), Herder takes his critique of Roman and neo-Roman imperialism a step further with a ruin gazer scenario that introduces Hannibal's perspective. Here, Herder traverses world history's ever-expanding spaces, surveying the ruins of Rome and the wreckage left by bloody conquests in the Roman East and on Greek territory. Desolate, the landscape of Carthage still evokes "sadness" (I, 377). Had Polybios not become the friend and adviser of Scipio, had he foregone the project of writing a first universal history seen from Rome, he might have written the scenario of Scipio at Carthage the way Herder wrote it, displacing Scipio's gaze.

But let us first join Herder at Rome. In Herder's *Ideen*, the space of the former Roman Empire becomes a museum with blood-drenched grounds, filled with the "sunken treasures" of a bygone splendor (I, 366). The *Imperium Romanum* was a crude "machine" set on eradicating other nations, and the city itself, once built for eternity, is now a field of rubble. Returning to his architectural metaphor, Herder portrays the Roman state as a "war-building," whose violent death left nothing but a "pile of stones" (I, 371 and 370). This is a slight, but significant, shift in vocabulary. Rome's imperial ruins are not noble; they are "piles of stone"—worthless rubble.

Let us take a closer look at Herder's journey through Rome in his *Ideen zur Philosophie der Geschichte*. Hinting at an experience of the negative sublime, the historian-traveler stares at the city's monuments, feeling both enthralled and threatened. If at first, the onlooker's "eyes" and "soul" may succumb to grief, they also become conscious of being assaulted by Rome's power (I, 390). Unlike Scipio at Carthage, Herder will not weep at Rome. The philosopher of ethnic particularism cannot condone imperial Rome's drive to dominate and homogenize all cultures embodied in Rome's brutal monuments and equally brutal ruins.[29] These were the ruins of "barbarians" whom we have learned to "loathe" (I, 378 and 391).[30]

Tearing his gaze away from Rome to contemplate Carthage's ruins, Herder then sketches a postcolonial ruin scenario. He does not dignify the assault on the "betrayed republicans" of Carthage by reproducing Polybios's scenario. Instead, he discusses the Romans' brutality that rendered their history "daemonic" and predicts immortality for Rome's "courageous enemy" (I, 377). When Herder finally assumes the Scipionian gaze, the eye registering the violent traces left by the Roman conquerors might well be Hannibal's: "Wherever I direct my gaze from Carthage, I see destruction" (I, 377).[31] Resurrecting the Carthaginian by entangling his own authorial perspective with that of Hannibal, Herder then addresses him directly, asking why he did not save his country from ruin. With this gesture, Herder radically decenters the Polybian scenario. More radically yet, Herder turns his readers into ruin gazers looking not at the Romans' Carthaginian rubble, but Carthage's noble *ruins*.

Herder thus loathed imperial Rome with all the passion of a philosopher of cultural particularity, but Rome was part of God's plan. Connecting it to Daniel's chronosophy, he reaffirmed his theological version of stadial theory as subject to God's law, a theological variant of the Aristotelian law of nature: "Becoming, Being, Vanishing" (I, 395). Herder thus wrote his ruin scenarios in an anti-Roman and anticolonial spirit. The Roman Empire—and its neo-Roman imitators—are subject to the divine *law of nature*: a cycle of birth and death, and the *law of retaliation*. Directing the course of modern history away from the history of successive empires, Herder's modernity precludes imperial mimesis. Rome was Rome, its rise and fall obeying the laws of its particular soul.

Herder's concept of historical mimesis thus postulates that we are moderns, we are ourselves. Herder thus raised all of the topics that will concern us in part 3: the backward gaze at the Roman empire as worthy of imitation in the modern age—or not; the intertwining of the narrative about rise and fall with the stadial theories of the Scottish Enlightenment philosophers; the rethinking of the concept of barbarism and the barbarian in a neo-Roman age of discovery, colonialization, and the encounter with the noble/ignoble savage; the gaze of the historian-as-traveler, scanning the ever-expanding imperial spaces of history; and, finally, Herder's rubble and ruin scenarios, centered on the Roman and Carthaginian stage, the latter reversing the roles of conqueror and conquered.

Some Traveler Like Myself: Volney at Palmyra

Studying the wreckage and ruins left by the Roman Empire, Herder traveled to Carthage with Polybios and to Greece with Pausanias. In *Les Ruines, ou Meditations sur les Revolutions des Empires* (1791), the Comte de Volney—politician, philosopher, and professor of Oriental history—tells us about a different kind of journey: his travels to Palmyra, the Roman colony and desert city on the border between the Roman and Persian empires.[32] Studying the vestiges of imperial architecture, Volney too thought about the laws of nature, and the rise and fall of empires.

Volney's journey through territories that were part of the Ottoman Empire and had once been Roman took him across a landscape of "fields abandoned, villages deserted, and cities ruined" to Palmyra.[33] Or so he claimed, because Volney never made it to Palmyra and his descriptions of the city's fabled ruins are based on Robert Wood, *The Ruins of Palmyra, otherwise Tedmor, in the desart* (1753). Palmyra was the city of Zenobia, the Syrian "warrior queen," who led a revolt against Aurelian after her army invaded Roman Egypt around 270 CE.[34] With Saracens fighting at her side, Zenobia lost the city, and after a second rebellion in 274 CE, the Roman legions "razed it to the ground."[35] Watched over by a Roman garrison, the once-bustling trading city at the edge of the empire was reduced to a village, and eventually, to a small outpost of the Ottoman Empire.

Remaining an architectural hybrid, Roman Palmyra adopted the classicist architecture of the Roman Empire, with its thoroughfares and buildings based on the "concept of possessive location, of the clear and indisputable definition of space."[36] Palmyra's famous theater once fully restored but badly damaged by ISIS asserted a distinctly Roman presence. The theater's imposing scene-building or *scaenae frons* consists of five doors organized around a central *regia*, decorated with a niche that held statues of Roman emperors. While Volney never mentions the theater, he refers to the sight of Palmyra's ruins as "spectacle" and the ruin sites he encounters as "theatre" (RE, 4, 6; translation modified).

While Volney used *The Ruins of Palmyra* as his guidebook, Wood and his co-traveler, James Dawkins, followed British merchants who entered the city in 1691. Fascinated by the ruins, Wood regretted not knowing more about the city, Zenobia, and her minister, the rhetorician Longinus.[37] What the archeologists saw, they saw through British eyes: Palmyra was a "passage for the commodities of India."[38] In contrast, Volney's gaze was anti-imperial in nature. At the same time, both accounts are colored by a ruin aesthetic that celebrates Roman Palmyra's sublime splendor.

What did Volney see? Having traveled through the "Valley of Caves and Sepulchres," Volney was "suddenly struck with a scene of the most stupendous ruins" (RE, 4). Here were the remnants of the most splendid imperial architecture:

> a countless multitude of superb columns, stretching in avenues beyond the reach of sight. Among them were magnificent edifices, some entire, others in ruins; the earth everywhere strewn with fragments of cornices, capitals, shafts, entablatures, pilasters, all of white marble. (RE, 4)[39]

Fascinated by the spectacle before him, the ruinophile traveler decided to spend a few days at the site. Despite the exalted language of his text, Volney was no romantic; he sought "useful lessons" about tyranny, liberty, equality, and (political) history (RE, 1).

I want to draw your attention to a carefully staged scene, the moment when the French traveler sits down to contemplate Palmyra's Roman ruins.[40] Having decided to spend several days among the ruins, he climbs one of the hills, "from whence the eye commands the whole group of ruins and the immensity of the desert" (RE, 4). Not only does Volney tell us what he saw that night, he also paints a picture of himself seeing it. At the horizon, the traveler discerns the Syrian mountains, the rising moon lighting up the plains of the Euphrates, herdsmen and their camels. As darkness increases, "the pale phantasms of columns and walls" attract his attention (RE, 4). The traveler's field of vision then further narrows until we "see" nothing but him, the figure of a European traveler lost in thought:

> The aspect of a great city deserted, the memory of times past, compared with its present state, all elevated my mind to high contemplations. I sat on the shaft of a column, my elbow reposing on my knee, and head reclining on my hand, my eyes fixed, sometimes on the desert, sometimes on the ruins, and fell into a profound reverie. (RE, 4–5)

Pierre Tardieu's engraving shows our ruin gazer in Ottoman attire. Sitting under picturesquely entwined palm trees—Minerva's owl included—this European traveler overlooks a section of Palmyra's ruins, which Tardieu copied from Wood and Dawkins's panoramic view of the former merchant city in Roman Arabia (figure 7.3). The caption is a sentence taken from Volney's text: "Here, said I, here once flourished an opulent city, here was the seat of a powerful empire" (RE, 5).

Volney's *reverie* revolves around one question: What causes such "fatal revolutions" (RE, 7)? Do "empires" and "nations" all just "vanish" because of some "blind fatality" (RE, 6 and 8), or is this the work of men? Before Volney finds an answer to his question, he portrays himself again in the pose of the ruin gazer, but this time the pose is more despondent: "And sunk in profound melancholy, I remained motionless" (RE, 8). What pushes him into this paralyzing melancholia is not merely the idea of a "blind fatality" at work in the history of men, but the frightening image of the end of his own civilization:

> Who knows if on the banks of the Seine, the Thames, the Zuyder-Zee, where now, in the tumult of so many enjoyments, the heart and the eye suffice not for the multitude of sensations,—who knows if *some traveler like myself* shall not one day sit on their silent ruins, and weep in solitude over the ashes of their inhabitants, and the memory of their former greatness. (RE, 8; emphasis mine)

Volney's gaze, driven by a strong desire to see what is no longer there, here turns into a visionary gaze at the future: the ruins of empire as they might be seen by *another traveler*.

As we know, we can trace this scenario of imperial ruin gazing back to the moment when Rome destroyed the Phoenician Carthage.[41] Herder re-created the scenario, aligning his view of the ruin-strewn landscape left by the Roman Empire with Rome's enemy, Hannibal. Volney situates his future ruin gazer *at the heart of Europe*, overlooking the ruins of Paris or London. In Tardieu's engraving and in Volney's text, we are made to "see" with Volney, the European in Ottoman guise at the Roman ruins of Palmyra, while our gaze also rests on the figure of Volney. The same

7.3 François de Volney, Les *Ruines, ou Meditations sur les Revolutions des Empires* (1791), view of Palmyra.

perspective informs the mental image of the future ruin gazer at the shores of the Seine or the Thames that Volney conjures in our mind.

Volney's future ruin gazer is an ambiguous figure, leaving us to wonder whether this traveler will be a European "like" Volney—or not. The same ambiguity informs the perspectives that Herder's and Volney's texts are constructing. For we are encountering a ruin gazer scenario in which the European subject—the author and his readers—contemplates a scene of imperial ending together *with* the barbarian ruin gazer—in this case, the traveler who might or might not be like Volney. As I discussed in part 1, at stake in these scopic scenarios are the power relations between conquerors and conquered. This problematic also pertains to the constellation of the European authors of the neo-Roman age of empire and the colonized of these modern European empires. Neither Herder nor Volney cede scopic mastery to the colonized other.

Volney's Resurrectional Gaze

Keeping in mind Polybios, the historian and avid traveler, Scipio, the melancholy general, and Aeneas, the Roman empire's founder, let us now return to Palmyra and to what Volney called his "Reverie." Volney begins with the trope of imperial decline: "Here, said I, here once flourished an opulent city, here was the seat of a powerful empire" (RE, 5). With a sense for the drama of the clash between past and present, Volney continues to contrast presence and absence, what he sees and what he imagines. This drama—or "spectacle" (RE, 3)—leads to two things: an aesthetic act by which he resurrects the past in ruins, and his political reflections on the history of empires.

Before discussing Volney's political thought in more detail, I will briefly trace this act of resurrection. While Volney's politics were as anti-imperial as Herder's, his text nonetheless contributes, like Herder's, to the construction of a Roman zone, an imperial imaginary for the modern age. Volney's reverie makes the past visible, conjuring its imperial architecture and space with great precision, thus bringing Roman past and neo-Roman present into close proximity. Contemplating the ruins of the former Roman colony, Volney first beholds something *visible*—"what remains of this powerful city: a miserable skeleton!"—and something *invisible*: an "obscure remembrance!" (RE, 6). Then follows an accumulation of things seen, present and past. The series leads to the question obsessing Volney: Do all empires vanish? Finally, the ruin gazer steps into the foreground.

As his mind "revives" the stories of the past, Volney transforms memory into actual sight (RE, 6). Imagining "the Assyrian on the banks of the Tigris," he sees a Syria consisting of "a hundred flourishing cities and abounded with towns, villages, and hamlets" (RE, 6):

> whither vanished those brilliant creations of human industry? Where are those ramparts of Nineveh, those walls of Babylon . . . those temples of Balbec and of Jerusalem? Where are those fleets of Tyre . . . [and] work-shops of Sidon, and that multitude of sailors, of pilots, of merchants, and of soldiers? (RE, 6)

Now and *then*: Volney's gaze at the visible remnants of Zenobia's city turns more and more concrete, listing more and more detail—from landscape to town walls to workshops. Volney's gaze reconstructs the ruined landscape in its former totality; he reimagines what is no longer there by rebuilding the city and resurrecting those who once lived in it. And he does all this by tacitly drawing on the Book of Daniel, translating the *topos* of the succession of empires into the topography before his eyes.

The Ruins of Palmyra included engravings based on drawings done by Giovanni Battista Borra on site. As was archeological practice at the time, these drawings had a resurrectional aspect: sketching ruins in their "present state of decay," Borra measured the sites so that the authors would have an "idea of the building, when it was entire."[42] Palmyra seems to have been one of the first and most enduring sites for this resurrectional desire.[43] William Halifax, for instance, thought that Palmyra's ruins were so magnificent that "would if it be lawful to frame a *conjecture of the original* Beauty of that place *by what is still remaining*," no other city would rival its beauty (emphasis mine).[44] This *conjecturing by what is still remaining* or "guessing," whether accompanied by a soaring of the imagination or not, is part of the activity of all "ruin-seer[s]," be they professional archeologists or not.[45] It transforms the past into a visible (imperial) space and the historian into a traveler.

In *The Ruins of Palmyra*, Wood and Dawkins supplemented their panoramic vista of the ruins with more detailed plates of particular sites. The two panoramic views show the city's ruins and the explanations emphasize what can be seen ("F. a ruinous Turkish mosque, with its minaret") by pointing out what is no longer visible.[46] Some of the plates show ruined structures or parts of ruins restored by the artist. "[W]e could only guess" is the phrase that often accompanies these restorations.[47] These restored structures are as diligently drawn as the ruined remnants. Exact in the details, their mode of representation exemplifies what Said identified as

7.4 Robert Wood and James Dawkins, *The Ruins of Palmyra* (1753), view of Palmyra.

Orientalism's "descriptive realism."[48] Like Volney's textual descriptions of Palmyra, Borra's drawings and the engravings are informed by the traveler's archeological epistemology and resurrectional gaze. Volney described this empiricist epistemology in his *Voyage* and theorized it in his *apodemic*, *Questions de statistiques*. Wood and Dawkins resurrected Rome's eastern colony pictorially; Volney resurrected Roman Palmyra textually.

Palmyra's Anti-Imperial Lessons and the Advent of Liberty

Of course Volney's meditations on the revolutions of empires are not simply empiricist in nature; rather, they combine the sharp, empiricist gaze at what is left with a philosophical-political narrative about world history. In *The Ruins*, Volney rewrites this resurrectional gaze, obsessed with the (in)visibility of the past, as an imperial gaze by framing his ruin scenario with reflections on the fate of empires. Let us take a closer look at these reflections. There seems to be a law at work that propels all nations to become "empires of gigantic size," diminishing the "strength of states" and rendering the people's conditions "abject" (RE, 36). Volney's own Europe appeared to be heading toward decay caused by the pursuit of luxury and colonial exploitation. Pretending to engage in commerce, Europeans subjected "Africa to the most barbarous slavery," "desolated India," and "depopulated a new continent" (RE, 61). The *telos* of human history seems to lead toward the planet's utter ruination: "empires depopulated, monuments neglected and deserts multiplied" (RE, 40).

Yet gradually, Volney's colonial melancholia gives way to the enlightened lessons of Palmyra's ruins, "the sacred dogma of Equality" (RE, 1). Palmyra's Roman ruins also taught him that the cycle of imperial rise and decline could be broken. History to date has been a development from man's "primitive state" to imperfect, corrupt societies (RE, 22). As splendid as their ruins are, the great empires of the past were tyrannies. Once men create just societies founded on the "immutable" laws of nature, a new postimperial age begins (RE, 75). By declaring the equality of all men, the revolutionaries on the American continent and in Paris inaugurated this new age. An anti-imperial world republic was the ultimate political lesson that Volney derived from the silent ruins. Polybios's law of nature—the cycle of birth and decay—was thus replaced by natural law.

Volney's Ghost and *Scipio's Dream*

Volney's ruin gazer does not arrive at these lessons by himself; he is enlightened by an "apparition" (RE, 9). Who is this Palmyrene ghost? He argues against the ideas of "blind fatality," as did Polybios in his reflections on the proper writing of imperial history (RE, 9). Or is it the author of *Considérations sur les causes de la grandeur des Romains et de leur décadence* (1734)—the voice of Montesquieu, who adapted Polybios's natural law to Enlightenment historiography?[49] Or is it the voice of Rousseau, who faulted European civilization for corrupting human nature, finding noble savages in half-civilized territories and hoping for their return to Europe? Or the voice of the Scottish Enlightenment thinkers Adam Smith and Adam Ferguson, who refined "stadial theory," conceiving of history as progress from the savage to the barbarian to the civilized world of commerce?[50]

Volney's wordy specter with his anti-Roman, anticolonial lessons combines all of these voices—and many more. But there is one voice that we might overlook if we did not pay attention to the genre used by Volney in recounting the conversation between the young traveler and his philosopher-ghost. It is the voice of Scipio in "The Dream of Scipio," Cicero's *mise-en-scène* of the supreme imperial vantage point.[51] In this conclusion to Cicero's *Republic* (51 BCE), Scipio the Elder appears to Scipio the Younger, his grandson and destroyer of Carthage. Their conversation about glory and the supreme Roman virtue, patriotism, takes place in the vicinity of the "Milky Way."[52] Pointing to the city of Carthage below them, Scipio the Elder predicts his grandson's victory in the final Punic War and his triumph across the Roman stage. "Do you see that city," Scipio the Elder asks, "which, through my efforts, was forced to bend the knee to the Roman people?"[53] To this, Scipio the Younger adds: "he showed me Carthage from a high place."[54]

Noticing that his grandson keeps looking at the earth, the elder Scipio directs his attention to the whole "visible universe," to "that sphere called earth which you can see in the middle of this celestial space."[55] *Scipio's Dream* is "an act of spectatorship," to use Andrew Bell's felicitous phrase, combining political lessons with an exercise in visualizing space from a cosmic vantage point.[56] Unable to tear his gaze away from earth, Scipio the Younger is enthralled by what he sees. At the same time, he experiences an affect until then unknown to him: "[T]he earth itself seemed so small to me that I felt ashamed of our empire, whose extent was no more than [a pinprick] on its surface."[57] In response, the elder statesman explains that the earth belongs to that part of the universe where "everything is subject to death and decay."[58]

Cicero's *Somnium Scipionis* and its visualization of Roman/global/cosmic space had a long and contested afterlife. Scipio's intent yet relativizing gaze at the Roman Empire has been read as Cicero's critique of post-Republican Rome.[59] According to Harry Hine, Seneca first introduced the theme of imperial rise and fall into "The Dream of Scipio."[60] To Volney and his contemporaries, Seneca was known through Columbus as the Roman author who celebrated the empire's ever-expanding space.[61] This tension between the celebration of Rome and its ever-expanding space, on the one hand, and the warnings about the empire's end in ruins, on the other, was also present in Virgil, an author who also rewrote *Scipio's Dream*.

Cicero's cosmic imperial perspective and his critical distance structures Volney's text.[62] Asking again about the "secret causes" of imperial "rise and fall," Volney introduces the Ciceronian frame in chapter 4 (RE, 13). Pulled "to the regions above," Volney observes: "*from the aerial heights, looking down upon the earth*, I perceived a scene altogether new" (RE, 14; emphasis mine). Evoking Daniel's historical paradigm, the Palmyrene specter points out ancient empires and cities, describing their present state and the way they were before crumbling into "piles of ruins" (RE, 15). Volney's *Scipio redivivus* then sums up familiar lessons about ancient empires and laws of nature. As I wrote above, Volney's world history culminates in a new world order, ruled by a single humanity, not a single empire. It is this order that Volney is given to see, an assembly of "men of every race" and "region," people with different "features, and complexion," and in different outfits (RE, 73). The sight of this "multitude," Volney writes, affected him deeply (RE, 73).

Volney's Barbarians: "The Tattooed Races of the Isles of the Southern Ocean" and Palmyra's Dido

Writing in the wake of Cook's voyages to the South Pacific (1768–1771; 1772–1775), Volney, whose most avid reader was Mary Shelley's Frankenstein monster, paints a tableau of humanity moving from Europe to the South Pacific, from Europeans to "the tattooed races of the isles of the southern ocean" (RE, 75). That is, the Tahitians and the New Zealanders or Maori, whom Cook and his crew had so recently "discovered." From his Scipionian vantage point, Volney thus mapped the modern world as a postimperial space.[63]

Herder located his anti-imperial ruin gazer in Carthage. Volney conjured a ruin gazer from another continent, probably one of the citizens of the "tattooed races." Did he also have Zenobia in mind? According to Mary Beard, Roman historians turned Phoenician Zenobia into Dido. Injecting a good dose of Orientalism into his portrait of this Palmyrene Dido, Wood devoted most of his historical *précis* to Zenobia's war, reporting how Aurelian made her a spectacle in his triumph. Visualizing the "idea of Roman territorial expansion," this triumph displayed Zenobia and the Gallic chieftain Tetricus.[64] The Romans thus turned Zenobia into the rebel queen.[65] Volney resurrected Zenobia or al-Zabba, as she is known to

Arabic writers in the ruins of her city. She enters Volney's field of vision as *Justitia*, a rebel queen defending her city against Roman tyranny.

Edward Gibbon also depicted Palmyra's ruins through the eyes of Wood and Dawkins. To become a random assemblage of ruins inhabited by poor *fellaheen* was the fate of the city that once flourished in the "honorable rank of a colony."[66] Vividly depicting Aurelian's triumph, Gibbon also ends his story of Palmyra with Zenobia and Tetricus. Encountering Zenobia's descendants, Wood and Dawkins are struck by the women's appearance. Veiled, they "paint the ends of their fingers red, their lips blue, and their eye-brows and eye-lashes black," and decorate their ears and noses with rings.[67] The British travelers thought these natives of Ottoman Palmyra not only exotic in appearance, but because of that, also a potential threat. Gibbon discovered his own version of painted barbarians in the South Pacific.

EIGHT

Edward Gibbon and the Secret of Empire, or *Scipio Africanus* and the Savages of the South Pacific

Introduction

Starting his six-volume history of the Roman Empire in the age of Trajan and the Antonine emperors (98–180 CE) and concluding in 1453 with the Ottomans' conquest of Constantinople, the author of *The History of the Decline and Fall of the Roman Empire* (1776–1788) was one of the first to make the Ottoman Empire and Islam an integral part of his historical panorama.[1] Writing a history of Rome as a history of its decline and, more importantly, stretching its decline across a thousand years led others to question whether such a long period of decay would not signal the empire's strength, instead of its weakness.[2] Polybios thought of Rome's rise as the greatest showpiece. Gibbon considered the fall of Rome world history's "greatest, perhaps, and most awful scene" (DFIII, 1084).

Overlooking the ruins of ancient Palmyra, Volney found himself in the company of an owl perched on the branch of a tree. Gibbon's backward glance at Rome and Palmyra, long after their fall, does not paint gray in gray but resurrects the fallen empires in the most vivid colors, harnessing the power of ekphrastic *enargeia*.[3] This backward gaze at the empires of the past is itself imperial in nature, concerned with Rome and Europe's neo-Roman empires. Gibbon was a staunch believer in the benefits of the British Empire, and as its citizen he claimed epistemological privilege.[4] This vantage point, he thought, was the necessary condition to truly appreciate Roman remains. The proper "resurrection [of statues and other remains]" could not have occurred in an earlier age.[5]

Gibbon was writing about resurrection when neoclassical architecture began to spread across Britain and the British colonies. Captivated by Piranesi's idea of the "revitalizing uses of antiquity," James Adam designed the House of Parliament with "the Templum Mars Ultor" in mind.[6] Robert Adam designed "a classical pile" for Mysore's Governor, who presented himself as Augustus adopting a line from Virgil's *Aeneid* —"He extended the Empire over the Indians"—as motto.[7]

In his penultimate chapter, Gibbon takes his readers to the city of Rome and onto the ruined Roman stage. There, he mentally reassembled the broken bits and pieces for the modern age. Like Freud's archeologist, Gibbon stared at this ruined stage, trying to solve the enigma of Rome's decline. In a nutshell, Gibbon claimed that the fall was the result of Rome's imperial excesses. That is, Romans fatefully deviated from Augustus's decision not to further extend the borders of the empire, a politics of "moderation" maintained until the death of the last of the Antonine emperors. This study of Rome's golden age and its aftermath was meant as a warning to the British Empire, and it was received as such by his audience.

But Gibbon's concerns encompassed more than the fate of the British Empire. He wanted to know whether "the Europeans and their colonies" would meet the same fate as Rome—and he answered his own question with a resounding and confident no.[8] He believed in historical progress, in the possibility of breaking the cycle of rise and fall, and a future different from the past. Yet this confidence in breaking the cycle is not as assured as it first seems. The proliferation of classical and modern ruin gazer scenarios in Gibbon's *Decline and Fall* is one symptom of this unease. Zenobia and her Arab heirs, the indigenous peoples of the South Pacific, and other "savages" will play their part in the modern imagination of neo-Roman empires. In a chapter specifically devoted to the question of whether modern Europe with its colonies will suffer the same fate as ancient Rome, Gibbon explicitly and most anxiously muses about the state of barbarism in the modern world. His history, whose influence cannot be overestimated, was both a reaffirmation of the durability of empire and a warning: about "excessive" imperial ventures and *modern* barbarians.[9]

1776–1788: Edward Gibbon's Europe and Its Colonies

Let me begin by establishing some immediate context for the publication of Gibbon's *Decline and Fall*, whose volume 1 appeared in 1776 and volume 6 in 1788. These dates frame some major events related to the history and politics of the British Empire. The year 1776 was the year of the American Revolution, a revolution made by people fluent in Virgil and fascinated by Polybios's ideas about mixed government and the causes of decline.[10] They saw their colony as the Roman Republic on the rise and England as imperial Rome or Carthage in decline. During the crisis years preceding the American Revolution, the analogy of Imperial Rome and London "sprang to the lips of almost every commentator."[11] On both sides of the Atlantic, intellectuals and politicians argued that the corruption resulting from the influx of the "riches and luxuries of the East" had brought the British Empire to "the brink of ruin."[12] As Arendt wrote, the Americans "'ransack[ed] the archive of ancient prudence.'"[13] Joseph Warren donned the mask of Calgacus, the anti-Roman insurgent,[14] and John Adams cited Sallust, submitting that Great Britain found itself precisely at the point "where the Roman republic was when Jugurtha left it, pronouncing it a 'venal city, ripe for destruction.'"[15] Adams firmly believed in the "cycle of the rise and fall of empires," suggesting that Britain was waning.[16] Jefferson promised "modern Carthage" the same ruinous end: "And some *Scipio Americanus* will leave to posterity the problem of conjecturing where stood once the ancient and splendid city of London."[17]

Some colonists were thus "beginning to see [America] as the new modern equivalent to Rome."[18] In 1774, *Lloyd's Evening Post* published a ruin fantasy, set in 1974. Visitors from "the empire of America" tour London's ruins, "resembl[ing] Piranesi's drawings of the ancient city after the fall."[19] These American ruin gazers did not weep over the ruins of London, and neither did Gibbon, who followed the events in the colonies with great sympathy. Not fond of Montesquieu's decadence argument, Gibbon nevertheless remarked that the "décadence des Deux Empires, le Romain et le Britannique, s'avancent à pas égaux."[20]

The year 1776 did not only see the publication of volume 1 of *The Decline* and the American Revolution; it also saw the publication of *Wealth of Nations* by Adam Smith, Gibbon's friend. The *Wealth of Nations* was an unambiguously anticolonial book about the "plundering of natives," and a utilitarian critique of early modern empires and their imitation of imperial Rome.[21] Focusing on the Spanish and their shortsighted "thirst of gold," Smith argued that "the establishment of European colonies in

America and the West Indies arose from no necessity" and their "utility" was debatable.[22] The countries that Columbus discovered on his way to India were "uncultivated," their inhabitants "miserable savages."[23] Motivated by greed and the search for glory, this early modern empire's brutal economy in the Americas ultimately ruined Spain and the colonies.

Disdainfully discussing the Spanish crown's Roman masquerade, Smith describes the celebration of Columbus's return as "a sort of triumphal honours" drawing attention to "the principal productions of the countries which he had discovered" that "were carried in solemn procession before him."[24] While there were a few items of value, most of them "were objects of vulgar wonder and curiosity," the whole display "preceded by *six or seven of the wretched natives*, whose singular color and appearance added greatly to the novelty of the show."[25] Piranesi depicted the Romans' most ostentatious ritual in *The Triumphal Arch* (1750) as a luxurious exotic jumble of imperial relics. While Piranesi was in awe of the ancient empire's relics, Smith, the liberal economist inventing the concept of the world market, was not. Proper mimesis meant imitating the Romans' trading republic because the modern nation's purpose was the civilizing exchange of commodities, not the acquisition of worthless junk.

Smith started his economic critique of imperialism with an analysis of Greek and Roman colonies, based, he thought, on sound political and economic reasoning. His critique of imperialism arguably also implied a critique of the East India Company's practices of primitive accumulation. In 1788, when Gibbon published the last volume of the *Decline and Fall*, the impeachment trial against Warren Hastings (head of the East India Company and governor of Bengal) began. Attacking Hastings, Sheridan cited Gibbon on the nefarious effects of "oriental luxury."[26] Edmund Burke, an admirer of Virgil, played a crucial role in the trial.[27] Jacobins were "treating France like a country of conquest," he argued, and the East India Company exhibited the same "revolutionary" behavior.[28] And revolutionaries, Burke and Gibbon agreed, were barbarians and "cannibals."

Gibbon thus wrote *The Decline and Fall* at a time when "the pattern of imperial conquest" as well as its critique had been firmly established.[29] By the late eighteenth century, comparisons of the British to the Roman Empire had become common, with the ancient empire functioning as both "ideal" and "cautionary tale."[30] And sometimes as a model far surpassed. Thus, Horace Walpole declared in 1762 that it took the Romans three hundred years to conquer "three parts of [the world]" while "we subdued the globe in three campaigns."[31]

Yet, as we will see, like Smith's critique of the Roman-style territorial empire, Gibbon's critique of the East India Company did not amount to a radical break with imperialism. Instead, Gibbon followed the agenda of Smith, Hume, and Ferguson, advocating "empire by sea," leading to "the establishment of colonies for commerce."[32] Debating the pitfalls of expansion for Britain's second empire, British thinkers thus developed countermodels to territorial empire, including the idea that "Carthage bears the nearest resemblance to Britain."[33] Gibbon projected Smith's ideas onto the Roman past, privileging the "Golden Age" of the Roman Republic and its colonies.[34]

All of this—Smith's treatise, the American Revolution, the Hastings trial—belongs to the immediate context of the *Decline and Fall*. Let me add one more piece to complete the picture, Cook's exploratory voyages to the South Pacific. Both Cook's first voyage on the *Endeavour* (1768–1771) and the second voyage on the *Resolution* and *Adventure* (1772–1775) preceded the publication of *Decline and Fall*, while the onset of the third voyage of the *Resolution* and *Discovery* (1776–1780) coincided with the publication of Gibbon's first volume. Cook's journals were published in 1773 (by Hawkesworth), and by the British Admiralty in 1777 and then again in 1784. Georg Forster (1754–1794), the German Jacobin and world traveler who translated Volney's *Ruines* in 1792, accompanied Cook on his second voyage, publishing his own account in 1777.

Not only did the second voyage result in two competing accounts, it also attracted considerable attention for importing a visitor from Great Britain's "newest new world," a Ra'iatean man named Mai.[35] Joseph Banks, Cook's botanist, introduced the young Tahitian to British high society during his two-year stay, and the "savage" toured London's famous sites, St. Paul's Cathedral and the Houses of Parliament, before returning to the South Pacific in 1776.

Mai's arrival in London caused a predictable stir, and Sir Joshua Reynolds painted the visitor from the South Pacific (figure 8.1). Inventor of the "grand style," Reynolds created an Orientalist-neoclassical fantasy, a Tahitian visitor with tattooed hands in "spurious Tahitian garb" evoking "the Rajah and the Roman Senator."[36] Reynold's *Omai* is the portrait of a "savage" after his contact with Europe's civilizing mission, a fantasy about Great Britain's role in the progress of humanity that Gibbon celebrated in the conclusion of his "General Observations."

Reynold's portrayal of *Omai* competed with the more exotic portraits of New Zealand men. Maori men had a fierce reputation. Forster, for instance, referred to some of them as "having sunk to a state of barbarism."[37] Here are two of these portraits of New Zealand men, the first one in profile, the second a three-quarter view (figure 8.2). The engravings appeared in Hawkesworth's account of Cook's first voyage in 1773 and were based on

8.1 Sir Joshua Reynolds, *Omai* (1775).

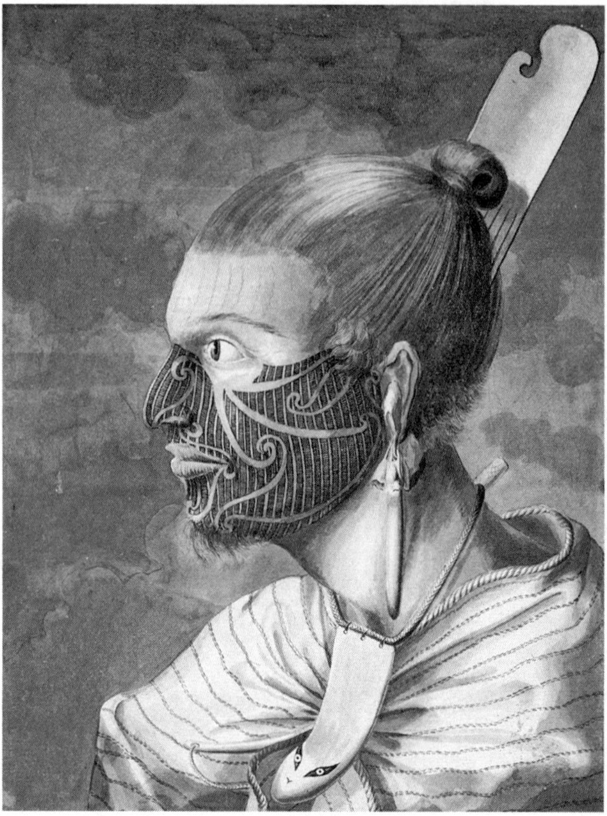

8.2 Sydney Parkinson, *Portrait of a New Zealand Man* (1773).

drawings of New Zealanders by Sydney Parkinson, Cook's scientific draftsman.[38] Among the most popular records of Cook's voyages, these painted Maori warriors, the "militant" natives of Oceania, represented the other, the barbarian face of Reynolds's noble Tahitian.[39]

James Cook's voyages played a crucial role in Great Britain's imperial rebirth. The three decades after the treaty of Paris in 1763 saw a "period of astonishing activity," where the loss of Great Britain's first empire in 1776 was followed by the pursuit of a second empire.[40] The composition and publication of Gibbon's *Decline and Fall* happened right in the middle of this decisive period. At the time when "nabobs" plundered India, and Gibbon analyzed "the decline and fall of an ancient empire," Britain was losing one "empire" while creating "another one."[41]

C. A. Bayly designated this era as *imperial meridian*, analyzing the period from 1780 to 1820 as a time when a "new style of imperialism" emerged out of a "world crisis" caused by the American loss, the threat of revolution from France, and conflicts in the Asian sphere of influence.[42] The transition to a more "vigorous world empire" involved new political practices and a shift in imperial culture, and this new "despotic" mode expressed the determination "to avoid the political fragmentation and economic uncertainty that was thought to have undone Britain's First Empire."[43] Overcoming earlier controversies about the desirability of empire, this new mode of rule was based on the assumption that Britain's empire was here to stay.

This shift brought with it a transition from the imagery of the noble savage (embodying a critique of metropolitan luxury and imperial excess at a time when the desirability of empire itself was debated) to the "'savage beyond all hopes of amelioration by culture'" (at a time when empire was no longer in question).[44] Written and published at the moment of the imperial meridian, Gibbon's *Decline and Fall* thematizes imperial mimesis, reflecting on the greatness of the Roman Empire—and obsessing about its fall. After the *Decline and Fall*, there would be no discussion of the British Empire that does not in one way or another refer to Gibbon's work.

Gibbon's Grand Tour: The Traveler-Historian

The desire to make the imperial world of the past as visible as possible sets Gibbon's volumes apart from the abstract Enlightenment histories of Rome. While Montesquieu harks back to Polybios's laws of nature, he abandons the detail that came with the Greek-Roman historian's gaze of the traveler. Gibbon reappropriates the thick texture of the latter. Contributing to the creation of the imperial imaginary of modernity's neo-Roman empires, Gibbon sketches his famous ruin scenarios. Reflecting on the four causes of the city's ruination in the very last chapter, Gibbon sketched one of these scenarios, starting the chapter with the story of two Romans ascending the Capitoline Hill in 1430. From the Capitoline Hill, they view the "prospect of desolation" and do what Gibbon never wanted to do: they "*moraliz[e]* on the vicissitudes of fortune" of empires (DF, 1062).[45] Gibbon, while sharing their emotions, was in principle opposed to this kind of "melancholy picture" (DF, 1064). He will search for the causes of decline—or what Bowersock calls the "secret of empire."[46]

Gibbon's multivolume history is a complicated edifice. We are indebted to Christopher Kelly for the analysis of one particular thread in this monumental text, the structure of the *Grand Tour*. The history of Rome's decline and fall is a "long journey" through fifteen centuries departing from and returning to "the metropolis of the world" (DF, 976). Assiduously footnoting classical and modern travel narratives, Gibbon referred to the "topographers of ancient Rome" and their "barbarous" successors, observing Rome's "visible remains" in the thirteenth century (DF, 1064).[47] He footnoted Cook's voyages, for instance, and referred to Roman and Greek reports about Palmyra as well as Wood and Dawkins's *The Ruins of Palmyra*. Gibbon also relied on Raynal's *Histoire des deux Indes* (1770), one of the first attempts "to write history as that of a world system," adding another layer to the global map that he asked his readers to imagine.[48]

If we combine the topographical range of Gibbon's history of Rome with the territories reached by the travelers whose work he footnotes, then the *Decline and Fall* emerges as a global history, a multilayered palimpsest that intertextually extends the geographical borders far beyond those outlined by Gibbon's actual story of Rome's decline and fall. Yet the empire's metropolitan stage remains the center of his journey. When Gibbon finally arrives back in Rome, he depicts the city in the "darkness of the middle ages" (DFIII, 979), sketching neo-Roman modernity's ultimate image of imperial ruination, an image that will remain imprinted on the minds of European intellectuals and artists: Rome's heart, the monumental stage of empire so carefully constructed under Augustus, is reduced to a pile of ruins, the surrounding Campagna is a wilderness, and the "provinces had been lost in the fall of the empire" (DFIII, 1083).

History as Spectacle, Imperial Space as Theater

As Bowersock points out, Gibbon's history has a "theatrical character."[49] His rendering of the battle of Constantinople is an excellent example of Gibbon's self-conscious deployment of this theatrical quality. He thematizes three things in this section: the trope of the historical event as spectacle that both historian and reader are witnessing as if they were present; the trope of the historian's sight; and, finally, the trope of the stage on which these events are taking place. Gibbon repeatedly acknowledged his debt to his classical predecessors and their techniques of conjuring up vivid images in their reader's mind of both the events narrated—the spectacle—and the space in which the spectacle unfolded before the reader's eyes.

Gibbon idealized the Antonine period (for reasons I will discuss later). If we direct our attention to Gibbon's *depiction of what was lost*, the empire in its "full meridian" (DFIII, 1066), we understand how Gibbon worked on and with his readers' spatial imagination. Outlining the geopolitical space of the period he idealized, Gibbon explained that the power and prosperity experienced under the reign of Nerva, Trajan, Hadrian, and the Antonines (96–180 CE) had much to do with their decision to stick to Augustus's legacy, "the advice of confining the empire" within "Nature['s]" limits: "on the west the Atlantic ocean; the Rhine and Danube on the north; the Euphrates on the east" and in the south, "the sandy deserts of Arabia and Africa" (DFI, 31).

To help his readers grasp the extent of the empire, Gibbon adds a description of Rome's provinces from Spain to Gaul, Britain, and Italy to Africa. Adding further details, Gibbon discusses the inhabitants, public works, and finally the great cities of the empire, praising the splendor of Rome, York, London, Paris, and finally the new Carthage, having risen "from its ashes" (DFI, 76). As he directs his gaze toward the East, he surveys the desolate landscapes of eighteenth-century "Turkish barbarism"—territory of former "Roman magnificence" that will one day become British colonies (DFI, 76). In these passages, historian and traveler merge into one figure, and the imperial gaze becomes a neo-Roman gaze: absence is made visible, and what becomes visible is the empire of the past, centered on its metropolitan stage.

Reassembling the Roman Stage

As I mentioned above, Gibbon starts his last chapter with a text by Poggio Bracciolini.[50] One of his declared goals is to isolate the four causes of the city's ruination, but in the process he did something that is of singular interest to us: he re-created the ruined stage of Rome. Gibbon quoted Bracciolini's account of what the two friends saw in 1453, tracing their reflections from their panoramic view of the remains to their minute description of them, a kind of stock-taking listing what is left, what is damaged, and how it happened. How did he begin? Rome's fall struck Bracciolini as "awful and deplorable" (DFIII, 1062). While Gibbon quoted Bracciolini, the latter in turn compared what he saw with lines from Virgil's book 8. Virgil described Rome, Bracciolini wrote, "such as she might appear in a remote age, when Evander entertained the stranger of Troy."[51] The Renaissance scholar then unfolds three layers of time: *at the time of Evander*, the "Tarpeian rock was . . . a savage . . . thicket"; *in the time of Virgil*, "it was crowned with the golden roofs of a temple"; and *today*, "the temple is overthrown" and weeds cover "the sacred ground" (DFIII, 1062). "[T]he wheel of fortune," Bracciolini wrote, "has accomplished her revolution" (DFIII, 1062). Once the Capitoline Hill was the empire's "head,"

Bracciolini observed, echoing with "the footsteps of so many triumphs," and filled with "the spoils" of many conquests (DFIII, 1062). In 1430, victory's route "is obliterated," Bracciolini writes, adding: "This spectacle of the world, how is it fallen!" (DFIII, 1063, 1062).

Having written this ruin scenario refracted through the sixteenth-century lens of Bracciolini, Gibbon continued quoting from the latter's text. Bracciolini did not remain on the level of metaphysical generalities, but instead wanted his readers to scrutinize the remnants closely, asking his readers to *cast their fifteenth-century eyes* on the Palantine Hill and to "seek among the shapeless and enormous fragments, the marble theatre, the obelisks, the colossal statues, the porticoes of Nero's palace." Bracciolini further asked them to "survey the other hills of the city," pointing out that "the vacant space is interrupted only by ruins and gardens" (DFIII, 1063). What else would they see? A Forum that "is now enclosed for the cultivation of pot-herbs" and "public and private edifices, that were founded for eternity," lying "prostrate, naked and broken"; "and *the ruin is the more visible*, from the stupendous relics that have survived the injuries of time and fortune" (DFIII, 1063). Bracciolini thus doubled his readers' lens, making them see simultaneously what was before their eyes and what had been visible, centuries ago. Standing on the Capitoline Hill, straining their eyes to see what was left of Rome's imperial architecture, they made the ruination of the Roman stage visible.

Gibbon objected to the melancholy metaphysics of Bracciolini's account, but not the latter's sharp-eyed gaze at the scene. After having quoted Bracciolini's text at length, Gibbon writes: "These relics are minutely described by Poggius," and then systematizes the fifteenth-century account by constructing a list of seven kinds of structures based on Bracciolini's observations, telling the reader what exactly "Poggio could discern" and what "the curious spectator" might have missed (DFIII, 1063): Vespasian's Temple of Peace, for instance; the theaters of Marcellus and Pompey; Hadrian's mausoleum turned into a "modern fortress"; and Augustus's mausoleum which, Gibbon writes, "could not totally be lost" if "only visible as a mound of earth" (DFIII, 1064). With this list, Gibbon reassembles the core of the theo-political metropolis renovated and built under Augustus and maintained by later emperors.

Complementing Bracciolini's report with that of an anonymous thirteenth-century "barbarous topographer," Gibbon's "diligent inquiry" into Rome's "visible remains" thus represents the same kind of labor that Piranesi performed at the dawn of the new age of imperialism: to make the Roman stage newly visible and thus available for the neo-Roman imagination.[52] The "path of victory was obliterated," Bracciolini wrote. Manetti, the papal commissioner of antiquity, had re-created the *Via triumphalis* for Charles V in 1536 (based on the labor of scholars like Bracciolini). With his systematizing listing, Gibbon clears the path symbolically for the conquerors of his own era.

That Rome functioned as stage in Gibbon's mind is obvious from Gibbon's genesis scenarios, explaining the origin of the *Decline and Fall*. In the very last paragraph of volume 6, Gibbon steps outside the story, alluding to his famous ruin gazing scenario: "It was among the ruins of the Capitol, that I first conceived the idea of a work which has amused and exercised near twenty years of my life" (DFIII, 1085). We have several versions of this scenario, among them the scene from Gibbon's memoirs. Arriving in Rome on October 2, 1764, Gibbon spent several months exploring the ruins. He portrayed his visit to the ruins of the Capitoline Hill and the shocking juxtaposition of the old and the new, of Catholic monks praying in a pagan site, as his moment of inspiration: "It was at Rome, on the fifteenth of October, 1764, as I sat musing amidst the ruins of the Capitol while the barefooted fryars were singing Vespers in the Temple of Jupiter, that the idea of writing the decline and fall of the City first started to my mind."[53]

At this time the Capitoline Hill, Rome's "most sacred place" and "ideological sign of Roman imperialism," was actually no longer a ruin site.[54] There were no ruins on the Capitoline Hill in 1764. The buildings of the hill and the ruins, Patricia Craddock writes, were "[v]isible only to the historian's imagination."[55] These imaginary ruins constituted the very heart of the Roman Empire, and Gibbon evoked "the power of the empire's ruins" to ask the question of the inevitable fall of all empires.[56] He "expected his readers to visualize the scene," to see "fragments of shadowy marble columns, the writer seated on a flight of broken steps amidst encroaching vines and underbrush."[57] His ruin scene does not merely repeat Bracciolini's "melancholy picture" (DFIII, 1064). Like Volney, he resumes the contemplative Aristotelian posture of Scipio. What his eyes rest on when his attention turns inward is the world-historical stage of Rome.

Bracciolini's way of thinking about ruination was foreign to his own.[58] And yet, Gibbon was not immune to the "edifying spectacle of ruin and desolation." On the contrary, he reported his youthful impression of Rome in 1764 as a form of intoxication in his memoirs. He would never forget, Gibbon wrote, "the strong emotions" when he first walked through "the ruins of the forum."[59] What transported him into this intoxicated state is the condensation of time into space, a theater of history and its heroes that can be apprehended in a single glance: "each memorable spot where Romulus stood, or Tully spoke, or Caesar fell, was at once *present to my eye*; and several days of *intoxication* were lost or enjoyed before I could descend to a *cool* and *minute* investigation."[60] For Gibbon, this experience of the past in its ruins was a prelude to "cool and minute investigation" and equally minute descriptions, intoxicated blindness giving way to the gaze of the modern historian synoptically making the past *present to his eye* and that of his reader. The result was the revival of the Roman stage on which all the great actions of the past had taken place.

In the neo-Roman imagination, like Augustus's *Res Gestae,* Roman ruins ask those who contemplate them with the idea of imitating Rome in mind to respond to the past, to devise strategies that will erase Rome's death by preventing that of the neo-Roman empire. Fond of the republic and its aristocratic elite, Gibbon adored Roman honor and virtue, its "masculine, vigorous liberty," celebrated in the triumphs of its generals, rituals artfully "display[ing] the theatre of Roman enterprises."[61] Coming to the end of his book, he laconically remarked that he had "described the triumph of barbarism and religion" (DFIII, 1068). Gibbon was famous for his anti-Christian animus or, more precisely, his aversion against an otherworldly religion that had drawn civic energies away from the republic, weakening Rome's civic spirit and institutions and thereby allowing the barbarian attacks to succeed. Yet this particular answer to the question of the *barbarians'* final victory over the Roman Empire was not the only one that Gibbon discovered. To the great distress of his commentators, Gibbon proposed different answers to the question. This restless search for the causes of barbarian triumph and Roman fall was ultimately a search for answers to the question of how to prolong the time of empire, the time before the end.

In "General Observations on the Fall of the Roman Empire in the West" (serving as a coda to chapter 38), Scipio reappears on the modern scene at the same time as Gibbon puts into place a philosophical line of argument based on his reading of eighteenth-century stadial theory as inexorable progress, excluding a return of the barbarian. In this text, Gibbon thus writes two different stories about the temporality of modern empires: the linear temporality of irreversible progress, and the cyclical repetition of rise and decline, one excluding the "awful revolution" (DFII, 511) of the Roman Empire and the victory of barbarism, the other not. As I argued in part 1, with his rubble gazer scenario Polybios introduced the threat of the barbarian, and thus contingency, into the logic of the natural cycle of (imperial) birth and death. He also introduced the idea of *slowing down* the movement of this natural law of ruin (through a combination of different forms of rule; see chapter 1), an idea that I traced from Polybios's political theory to Paul's concept of the *katechontic* sovereign. Gibbon reformulates these ideas for the modern age.

"A Repetition of Calamities": The *Katechontic* Function of Stadial Theory and the British Empire

In "General Observations," Gibbon interrupted the flow of his narrative to raise the question of whether the "awful revolution" of the empire may contain any lessons for the "present age" (DFII, 511).[62] Gibbon's "Observations" are indeed an essay about imperial Europe's present, not its past—and about Europe as the center of the civilized world. What is at stake is "the system of arts, and laws, and manners" that elevates "Europeans and their colonies" today "above the rest of mankind" (DFII, 511). Gibbon formulated the threat to Europe's empires in the idiom of eighteenth-century enlightenment: "The savage nations of the globe are the common enemies of civilized society." Increasing the urgency of his tone, he then proposed to examine "whether Europe is still threatened with a repetition of those calamities, which formerly oppressed the arms and institutions of Rome" (DFII, 511).

Polybios's *Histories* and his ideas about rise and fall are central to this chapter. While the latter glorified the sudden rise of Rome, Gibbon set out to explore the calamity of its slow decline. He started his "General Observations" with general reflections on historiography, discarding the Greek myth of Fortuna (leaving Athens for Rome) in favor of the ideas of a "wiser Greek," Polybios, who had opened the minds of his fellow colonial subjects to the "view of the deep foundations of the greatness of Rome" (DFII, 508). After briefly summarizing Polybios's explanation of the rise of Rome, Gibbon positioned himself as Polybios's successor.[63] The rise of an empire may merit "a philosophic mind," he wrote, "[b]ut the decline of Rome was the natural and inevitable effect of immoderate greatness" (DFII, 509). What follows is yet another synopsis of Gibbon's explanations for Rome's decline.[64] Returning to the effects of relentless imperial expansion, Gibbon stated that his "story of [Rome's] ruin is simple and obvious": *imperial excess* led to the destruction of not only the Roman republic, but the empire itself (DFII, 509). In volume 1, he credited Augustus with having introduced a "spirit of moderation," renouncing plans to conquer the world (DFI, 9). Once this politics was abandoned, the empire started to rot from within, becoming easy prey for barbarian invaders.

With "General Observations," Gibbon's Roman history thus moves squarely into the discourse of imperial mimesis and its pitfalls. What did all of this mean for Europe's neo-Roman empires and their "barbarians"? In part 1, I argued that the Roman idea of the barbarian is essentially a concept of the enemy. This also applies to Gibbon's meditations in this section where Gibbon addressed the issue of Europe's decline at the hand of barbarians from four angles: first, the Romans were not aware of the "extent of their danger," nor did they know the number of their enemies. This awareness now exists, Gibbon claimed, and, more importantly, the "reign of independent Barbarism is now contracted to a narrow span" in the eastern regions of Russia (DFII, 438). While he reassured his readers that these independent barbarians at the European periphery cannot possibly threaten "the great republic," he did not exclude the possibility that "new enemies, and unknown dangers, may possibly arise from some obscure people, *scarcely visible* in the map of the world" (DFII, 512). After all, Arabs and Saracens long languished in poverty before "Mahomet breathed into those savage bodies the soul of enthusiasm" (DFII, 512).

Second, even in this worst-case scenario of hitherto unknown barbarians spilling into Europe—from those blank spots, we may add, that older maps of the world designated as the regions where monsters may lurk—Europeans could escape to the "American world" (DFII, 514). Third, by the time these new barbarians had reached the military strength required to take the "fortifications" encircling Europe, they would no longer be "barbarous" (DFII, 514). For the advance in military technology would demand a much higher level of civilization than Rome's military equipment required of its "disciplined" and "educated" barbarians (DFII, 514).

Europe, Gibbon was trying to convince himself and his readers, was thus "secure from any further irruption of Barbarians (DFII, 514)." But not only did Gibbon discuss barbarians from the eastern reaches of the European continent, he also directed the reader's gaze toward Captain Cook's voyages and the new British subjects in the South Pacific. In this context, Gibbon introduces a new, fourth idea about what he calls "hope" (i.e., the barbarian victory will not be repeated) and what I analyzed in part 1 as *katechontic* strategies to delay the empire's end: stadial theory as the promise that European civilization is steadily advancing across the entire globe. In Gibbon's case, this *katechontic* strategy is of a double nature, involving both a philosophy of history, based on the idea of inexorable progress, and a historical actor, the benevolent British sovereign.

Let me begin with his version of stadial theory. We know, Gibbon wrote, from ancient and modern explorers and from the history of the "most enlightened nations," about the condition of early humanity, the "state of nature" (DFII, 515). As classicist, Gibbon offers two sources on this age of the "human savage": the testimony of Diodorus Siculus about the cannibals inhabiting "the shores of the Red Sea," and William Dampier's report about Australia's "natives" in 1699 (DFII, 515). "The discoveries of ancient and modern navigators," Gibbon writes, and enlightened Europeans' "domestic history" show "the *human savage*" (DFII, 515). But humans did not remain savages. Gradually evolving from "this abject condition," they now sailed the oceans and "measure the heavens" (DFII, 515). Although there were setbacks, we know one thing with certainty, Gibbon claimed: "[T]he experience of 4.000 years should enlarge our hopes and diminish our apprehensions." While we do not know how far humanity may advance "toward perfection," we can safely assume "that no people . . . will relapse into their original barbarism" (DFII, 515). The march of progress—at first "infinitely slow" and now of "redoubtable velocity"—will not be reversed (DFII, 515). Gibbon returns to this point: with every age, "the real wealth, the happiness, the knowledge and perhaps the virtue, of the human race" increases (DFII, 516). Following Adam Ferguson's and Adam Smith's story of progress, Gibbon insisted, that there will be no relapse into barbarism, not even among the new "savage" subjects of the British crown in the South Pacific.[65] The event of barbarians threatening Europe will not be repeated.

In the eighteenth century, the nexus of Roman ruins and neo-Roman empires thus generates scenarios of ruin gazing that are inextricably tied to the notion of progress, the hope that the cycle of rise and decline may be broken. Herder and Volney, committed anti-imperialists, opposed Roman mimesis, the latter putting his trust in new forms of government, and the overcoming of (religious) ignorance; Gibbon, admirer of Augustus, the Antonines, and the British crown, in the progressive narratives of stadial theory.

But that, it seems, was not enough for the Roman historian, worrying about the danger of barbarian invasions. Gibbon modified the standard stadial theories by underlining the active civilizing effects of world trade. Gibbon concedes that this progress has been irregular and slow, but it is unstoppable. Unlike the Spanish conquerors, who exported misery, Great Britain with its scientific voyages is exporting its civilization to the South Pacific: "Since the first discovery of the arts, war, commerce, and religious zeal have diffused, among the savages of the Old and New Worlds, these inestimable gifts: they have been successfully propagated; they can never be lost" (DFII, 515).

The concluding sentence of the "Observations," expressing Gibbon's faith in the progress of the "human race," is footnoted. With respect to the ever-looming threat of barbarism, this footnote is crucial. Referring to Cook's voyages to the South Pacific, the note simultaneously reintroduces the threat of barbarism and *denies it* one last time, by pointing to the improvements of civilization across the globe:

The *merit of discovery* has too often been stained with avarice, cruelty, and fanaticism; and the intercourse of nations has produced the communication of disease and prejudice. A singular exception is due to the virtue of our own time and country. The five great voyages successively undertaken by the command of his present Majesty, were inspired by the pure and generous love of science and of mankind. The same prince, adapting his benefactions to the different stages of society, has founded a school of painting in his capital; and has introduced into the islands of the South Sea, the vegetables and animals most useful to human life. (DFII, 516; emphasis mine)

This brief footnote is Gibbon's homage to the British Empire, to Cook's voyages to the South Pacific (1768–1771; 1772–1775), to his scientists and artists. Informed by Smith's attack on the Spanish-Portuguese mimesis of Rome, his reservations toward colonial conquest, and his advocacy of a system of world trade, it thematizes again the Roman historian's particular concern: the de-barbarization of the barbarian, achieved by scientific and commercial globalization.

Finally, this footnote claims the British monarch as the *katechontic* sovereign modeled on the Antonine emperors. Idealizing the latter period, Gibbon sketched the picture of a benevolent civilizing empire. In these "splendid days" (DFII, 516), Rome was a thriving cosmopolitan metropolis, "filled with subjects and strangers from every part of the world, who all introduced and enjoyed the favorite superstitions of their native country" (DFI, 60). "[E]xtensive empire" had its "evils," Gibbon wrote, but it also had some "beneficial consequences" (DFI, 78). Smith's vision of commercial society seems to inform Gibbon's ideal empire, where free trade might have created the vices of luxury, but also the "improvements of social life" (DFI, 78). With expanding trade came the diffusion of imperial art and culture across the entire empire. Britons began to read treatises on rhetoric; the barbarians of the Rhine and Danube are engrossed in Homer and Virgil.[66]

Polybios, Scipio, and Modernity's "Scarcely Visible Barbarians" (DFII, 512)

Far from being an antiquarian historian, Gibbon wrote his story of "the transactions of the past, for the instruction of future, ages."[67] The fall of the Roman Empire mattered to the British Empire at the dawn of what Hobsbawm called the age of empire. Gibbon's concern with the fall of Rome was a concern with the fate of the present—not merely with the present of his nation, but with the fate of Europe as the imperial center of the world system that had arisen with the Spanish and Portuguese conquests in the sixteenth century. Let us not forget the beginning of the "Observations": Rome's fall, "this awful revolution," he wrote, "may be usefully applied to the instruction of the present age" (DFII, 511). Gibbon was interested in the fate of empires of the *past* and the *present*—at the hands of "barbarians," or "savages," *ancient* or *modern*. Gibbon operated with the Greek notion of barbarian as the ones "on the other side of the frontier."[68] These "barbarians," "savages," and "near-savages" are now part of Europe's newly emerging colonial system—in Cook's South Pacific and Hastings's India.

Scipio's premonition of the empire's fall at Carthage was Gibbon's obsession. Recall that, according to Gibbon, Rome fell at Constantinople in 1453. And recall that Gibbon quoted Mehmet II quoting lines from a Persian poem, lines about the spider's web and the owl in the palace of the Caesars. What I did not mention is the following: Gibbon footnotes the sultan's quote, explaining that "Scipio repeated, in the sack of Carthage, the famous prophesy of Homer" (DFIII, 968). And he does this after having already alluded to Polybios's scenario of imperial endtime in the "General Observations," where he wrote that Polybios "excited the virtue of Scipio and beheld the ruin of Carthage" (DFII, 509).

Gibbon elaborates on this allusion to the Carthaginian scene, adding a footnote in which he paraphrases Appian's transmission of Polybios's text. The footnote, which raises the specter of repetition, reads: "While Carthage was in flames, Scipio repeated two lines of the Iliad, which express the destruction of Troy, acknowledging to his friend [Polybios] . . . that while he recollected the vicissitudes of human affairs, he inwardly applied them to the future calamities of Rome" (DFII, 509). With this synopsis of the Roman scenario, in which Scipio conjures the threat of the barbarian enemy as he contemplates the stage of an empire that had just fallen, Gibbon reinscribes the ancient ruin scenario into his text. At this point he also footnotes the Book of Daniel: "And the fourth kingdom shall be strong as iron; for as much as iron breaketh in pieces, and subdueth all things" (DFII, 509). As we know, the iron empire was Rome.

This is not the only section in which Gibbon alludes to the Roman ruin gazer scenario.[69] However, this textual layer reaching back to the ancient ruin gazer scenarios is most pronounced in the "General Observations." In the chapter's first paragraphs, the context for displaying the archive on rise and decline is Gibbon's celebration of the Roman Republic: its "temperate struggles," "firm and equal balance of the constitution," the mentality of "a people incapable of fear," dedicated to "conquest" and the "political virtues of prudence and courage" (DFII, 508). As I wrote above, telling the success story of Rome, Gibbon invoked Polybios as having witnessed Carthage's "ruin" (DFII, 509). It is this opening paragraph on Polybios's history of the "deep foundations of the greatness of Rome" that carries the weight of the footnotes on Scipio at Carthage (and Daniel's prophecy that the iron empire too will come to an end).

Linking rise and fall in this opening paragraph, Gibbon then narrates the rise of the Roman Empire, formulating the famous statements I quoted above: "[T]he decline of Rome was the natural and inevitable effect of immoderate greatness" (DFII, 509). It is this paragraph that establishes Gibbon as ruin gazer: "The story of [Rome's] ruin is simple and obvious," he wrote, and then summarized once more the causes bringing about the "deluge of Barbarians" (DFII, 510). Scipio had foreseen the end, and Gibbon labored in his "General Observations" against the repetition of this imperial fall, against the possibility of a barbarian "deluge." Yet Gibbon did more than argue against "the repetition of [Rome's] calamities" (DFII, 511). On this level of his text, engaging Polybios's scenario of imperial endtime, Gibbon linked the ruin gazer scenario to the figure of the modern barbarian—Dampier's Australian savages, Volney's "tattooed races of the isles of the southern ocean and of the continent of the antipodes" (RE, 75).

Linking Scipio's scenario to the modern barbarian, Gibbon produced a scenario of ruin gazing for the age of modern empires. No barbarians, Gibbon concluded, would ever again pose a threat to Europe's empire. But then why did he have to interrupt his story about Rome's decline with an essay about the "unknown dangers" that "may *possibly* arise from some obscure people, *scarcely visible* on the map of the world" (DFII, 512)? The obsessive repetition of Scipio's premonition in the ruins of Carthage belies the firmness of Gibbon's belief that Europe will not meet the same fate at the hands of modernity's barbarians. To use Volney's picture, Gibbon sought reassurance that there will not be "some traveler like myself" sitting "on [the] silent ruins" of Paris, London, or Amsterdam. For that was the scenario against which Gibbon mustered all his arguments: a subject of the British Empire, a barbarian, overlooking the ruins of London.

Conclusion

In the premodern and modern neo-Roman ruin gazer scenarios that I have explored so far, the history of European imperial mimesis takes place on a ruined stage. Built in the Augustan age, this theo-political stage has to be constructed anew for each imperial age, and the artists and authors I discussed in the past two chapters did so in their own media. Like Freud's archeologist, Herder, Volney, and Gibbon keep staring at the ruined stage, trying to decipher the enigma of Rome's fall and inventing strategies to either exit the cycle of rise and decline, or prevent the repetition of the fall. "Ever since Gibbon," Phiroze Vasunia writes, "the spectre of decline and fall haunted Britain."[70] We can safely add that this Gibbonian ghost kept scaring other Western imperialists.

Far into the modern age of imperialism, the Roman model meant the defense of civilization against barbarism. Or, in the words of a British archeologist: "[T]he Roman Empire was the civilized world; the safety of Rome was the safety of all civilization. Outside roared the wild chaos of barbarism."[71] Like Rome's barbarians, the conquered of the modern age will be restive. In 1806 a detachment of Sepoys attacked the British garrison at Vellore.[72] "Britons were terrified that the instrument they had created to dominate the subcontinent would now destroy them."[73] In the wake of the Sepoy insurrection, Charles Metcalfe reminded the British public of Polybios's truth that "Empires grow old, decay and perish."[74] Rephrasing Polybios's law of ruin, he also reminded his contemporaries of Polybios's cipher of contingency, the barbarian. Britain needed to maintain the "impression of invincibility," although it had now "reached 'premature old age' and its life could only be prolonged with care."[75] In the modern age, imperial time still is the time before the end, and the mission of the imperial sovereign is still *katechontic*: *to carefully prolong the empire's life*, to transform the imperial future into a carefully extended present.

Herder, Volney, and Gibbon resurrected the actors in the Carthaginian drama—sometimes Scipio and Hannibal, sometimes Scipio and Dido—reassigning them new roles and new masks. Participating in Cook's second voyage (1772–1775), Georg Forster experimented with the mask of Aeneas and, like William Hodges, discovered the mystery of the ruined stage in the South Pacific.

NINE

Aeneas Fragment and the Enigma of the End: Georg Forster's Voyage to the South Pacific and William Hodges's *Views of the Monuments of Easter Island*

Introduction: Rome, Rotting Corpse or Living Body?

At the turn of the eighteenth to the nineteenth century, a new wave of European imperial expansion started gathering momentum. The space of these modern European empires would soon exceed the size of the territory ruled by Augustus and his entourage of minor and major divinities. In the previous chapter, I mentioned Cook's exploratory voyages to the South Pacific in the context of Gibbon's *Decline and Fall*. The present chapter will deal with the voyages as a moment of conquest seen through the lens of Georg Forster. In chapters 11 and 12, I will focus on my second case of imperial expansion in the modern age, beginning with Napoleon's invasion of Egypt. In both instances, the Roman frame was applied from the outset. The Royal Society honored Cook in the Roman manner, and French sculptors and painters rushed to portray Napoleon, one of the "extraordinary men" sent to the "rescue of Empires ready to fall," in various

Roman guises: Caesar, Jupiter, even Scipio.[1] As I will argue in this chapter, Forster gingerly tried on the mantle of Aeneas at the very beginning of Britain's expansion into the South Pacific.

After Napoleon's demise, Hegel took a backward glance at Rome, theorizing modernity as the westward course of empire. Familiar with Gibbon's *Decline and Fall*, Hegel addressed the question of the "demise" of "peoples and states."[2] In these lectures on world history (held in 1822–1823), Rome's ruins signify a break with the past. "[T]he sight of the ruins of ancient glory," Hegel wrote, provokes profound sadness, adding: "everything seems to perish, nothing seems to remain"—or so it seems.[3] Yet there is no reason to adopt the pose of the melancholic since "the ruins of the past" are the foundations of each new stage of world history.[4]

This happy consciousness of breaking with the past is the core of the Enlightenment's progress narratives. This progressive consciousness drives the Enlightenment's imperial projects, their call for a break with the "uncivilized, barbarian" past of the countries they are conquering, or intend to conquer. If Todd Presner is correct, and Hegel's lectures are a form of travel narrative—a journey of the Spirit from East to West that is also a story of the westward course of empire—then Hegel's dialectical narrative is not a break with empire-building.[5] It is, however, a break with the Roman past and a break with Roman mimesis. Rome is dead, Hegel writes, redirecting his backward gaze on Roman ruins toward the future.

The imperial projects that I will analyze in the following chapters were characterized by the undeterred *gesture of repetition*, the belief that Rome is *not* dead. In Forster's case, this gesture was hesitant; in Napoleon's case, triumphant. Louis Bertrand defined France's colonial mission in Northern Africa as resurrection of the Roman Empire.[6] In each instance, the imperial thinkers allied with these projects of mimesis introduce ruin gazer scenarios: Forster by rewriting book 8 of the *Aeneid* with its archaic ruins; Fourier, the author of the historical introduction to the 1820 edition of the *Description de L'Égypte*, by reflecting on the *courte durée* of Rome's Egyptian ruins; and Bertrand by combining Catholicism and politics, Roman ruins and Paul's *katechontic* scenario.

Against Hegel's modern teleology, theorizing the break with ancient Rome, these political and discursive acts introduced neo-Roman repetition as one of the characteristics of European modernity. This modern mimesis is unhappy consciousness: as Herder, Volney, and Gibbon tell us, the sight of Rome's ruins continues to haunt those involved in neo-Roman imperial designs. Hegel hints at Rome's spectral presence. "What is past does not exist," he asserted, and then confronted his readers with the necro-trope of Rome's "spirit-less corpse," pullulating with maggots—the image of a past still uncannily alive.[7] The trope's literal excess—materiality that threatens to overpower the metaphorical register—signifies the uncanny dimension of imperial mimesis.

Hegel's trope reminds us of the labor of resurrection at the heart of all neo-Roman mimesis. The actors involved in modernity's neo-Roman projects continued to produce their own representations of the Roman past. Staring at the ruined stage—at Carthage, at Palmyra, at Rome—Herder, Volney, Gibbon brought back to life the empire of the past: the Roman actors and their enemies, Rome's conquests, and the empire's ever-expanding space. The men involved in Cook's voyages, Georg Forster and William Hodges, will do so too, in their respective media, the travelogue in Forster's case, the ruin painting in Hodges's.

Aeneas Fragment: Georg Forster on Easter Island's Barbarians, Their Ruins, and the Mystery of the End

Georg Forster (1754–1794) participated with his father, Johann Reinhold Forster, in Cook's second voyage on the *Resolution* and *Adventure* (1772–1775). A German Jacobin, he was involved in the founding of the Mainz Republic that emerged under French occupation in 1793. Before leaving for exile and Paris, Forster translated Volney's *The Ruins* in 1791. Forster saw the Roman Empire in a familiar light. Although the empire had preserved the "smashed remnants of Attic culture" as the legacy of European modernity, its imperial ventures enflamed "the most uninhibited moral corruption."[8] Yet, in his account of the journey, *A Voyage Round the World* (1777), Georg Forster compared himself to Aeneas and used classical references, often quoting directly from Virgil's *Aeneid*. Forster's use of Virgil's epic and other allusions to imperial Rome and its writers—Sallust, Horace, Pliny, Strabo, Juvenal—are scattered throughout the text without ever cohering into a strong conceptual framework for his story of exploration. On one level, these references represent conventional displays of classical learning and the use of a scientific archive. On another level, the use of Virgil's *Aeneid* is part of the (discursive and visual) imperial archive first established by the neo-Roman Spanish-Portuguese seafarers, and functions, I will argue, symptomatically. The question to ask, of course, is: What are these bits and pieces from the neo-Roman archive symptomatic of?

Forster's embrace of the *Aeneid* is nothing short of a contradiction. Forster, who praised William Hodges as being apt at imitating nature, also accused his co-traveler of neoclassical distortion, of painting men in Greco-Roman garb instead of Tahitian natives. This contradiction needs an explanation, and we might solve the puzzle if we think of Forster as someone trying on the costume of Aeneas, the Trojan-Roman traveler in the service of empire. This identification emerges at seemingly odd moments. Let me single out one instance where Forster quotes from Virgil: leaving New Zealand from Dusky Bay, Forster quotes Aeneas, addressing Dido, whose shade he encounters on his journey to the underworld: "Unwillingly, O queen, I parted from thy shores" (FE, 177).[9] On the one hand, these quotes are decorative flourishes about the perils and joys of seafaring. On the other, they track the Trojan-Romans' fateful journey to Rome, their departure from Carthage at the command of Jove, and arrival on the shores of Latium, Aeneas's final destination. They reach Italy after the Trojan-Romans' re-education in the underworld, where he learns about his imperial mission and the glorious future of the (Augustan) empire. In books 6 and 8 (i.e., the *katabasis* chapter and the crew's arrival in Latium), Virgil asks his readers to see Augustus behind the mask of Aeneas.

Aeneas's mask and his father's purple cloak, one of the famous "relics" that Aeneas saved "from burning Troy" (AFi, 204) and takes into exile, will play a crucial role in my reading of Forster's *Voyage*. Forster's *Aeneid* quotes frequently appear in the context of traveling in the footsteps of previous explorers. As the crew gathers on deck to catch a glimpse of Tahiti, Forster lists all the explorers who had previously stopped at the island: the island's "first discoverer" (Pedro Fernández de Quirós) in 1606, Captain Wallis in 1767, Bougainville in 1768, and Cook in 1769 (FE, 142). The British travelers arrive with "the highest expectations" about the island's beauty and the hospitality of its people (FE, 142), expectations raised by their precursors. Like Forster, they were avid readers of Virgil.

Joseph Banks, for instance, indirectly referred to Aeneas's arrival in the territory of Evander and his Arcadians, borrowing Virgil's "Arcadia" *topos*.[10] Banks followed Bougainville's lead, who contributed to the image of the noble savage and the enduring *topos* of the South Pacific as earthly paradise.[11] Referring to Tahiti as "Cythera," Venus's birthplace, Bougainville started his Tahiti chapter quoting Virgil's *Aeneid*.[12] Like Forster's quote at the beginning of his Tahiti chapter, this quote is taken from book 6 of the *Aeneid*, thus establishing Forster's opening as a gesture imitating Bougainville.

Bernard Smith traced the emergence of this Arcadia *topos* to eighteenth-century pictorial conventions, arguing that the neoclassical lens of painters like William Hodges trained in Italianate styles of portraiture, history, and landscape painting clashed with the tendency toward "close-focus realism" under the voyages' "pressure of empirical naturalism."[13] Bougainville, for instance, recognized "charming scenes" worthy of Boucher's anacreontic paintings.[14] I propose to trace the *topos* directly to Virgil's epic, thus claiming a strong form of *imperial intertextuality*. Intertextual relations involve the presence of one text in another, and this presence can be thematic or structural. If the latter is the case, we are dealing with a text akin to a palimpsest—the strongest form of literary mimesis.

Forster's *Aeneas Fragment* is such a palimpsest, in which the story of the modern explorers' travels in the South Pacific at times echoes the Trojans' erratic journey across the Mediterranean.[15] This mimetic desire, which we could read again as a response to the desire of the past (to Virgil's aspiration to have written *the* epic of the Augustan age and his heroic realism asking for both recognition and imitation), produces two instances in which the presence of the classical Roman text goes beyond mere thematic resonance. The first instance is the crew's arrival at Dusky Bay. Here, Forster engaged Virgil's book 1, the Trojans' arrival on Libyan shores. The second instance pertains to the Easter Island chapter and its relation to book 8; that is, the moment when Aeneas and his men, having finally arrived on the shores of Latium, enter Evander's terrain. Greek colonists hailing from Arcadia now live on the site where Saturn once civilized "savages."[16]

The status of these eighteenth-century exploratory voyages was ambiguous: on the one hand, they were scientific expeditions; on the other, they served imperial designs. Banks, for instance, writes of Arcadia as a country that the British will rule.[17] If Forster's occasional references to Virgil's imperial text seem somewhat hesitant, the Spanish and Portuguese explorers and conquistadors were far more explicit in their appropriation of Rome. As we know, they both identified as Rome's heirs and bragged about their superiority over the ancient conquerors. Sailing through the South Pacific almost two centuries after de Quirós, Forster and his companions constantly happen upon traces left by the sailors in the service of the Spanish crown. Depicting the inhabitants of Easter Island and their clothing, Forster noted a mixture of indigenous and European articles, among them "European hats," "cotton handkerchiefs," and worn-out coats that he calls "so many indubitable *testimonies* [*Denkmäler* oder *Überbleibsel*]," left behind in 1770 after the Spanish visited the islands (FE, 303; FG, 483).

The Spanish "presence" looms large in Forster's account, and it does so in Cook's journal, who also mentions these sartorial Spanish "Vistiges."[18] I propose to think about the Roman tropes and quotes in Forster's travelogue as "*Überbleibsel*"—literally as leftovers, remains left behind by the neo-Roman colonizers in the way Aeneas left his relics. They are Roman-Spanish fragments from the neo-Roman imperial archive, by now as worn as the shabby bits and pieces of clothing. For Forster, they function as mediators, opening access to a more sustained engagement with the original Virgilian text, its masks and cloaks, stories and tropes.

Forster was writing at a time when Spain's noble "armature of Greco-Roman antiquity" had already been under assault for a century and a half.[19] To Forster, as to Adam Smith, the Spanish represent imperial decadence, barbarians no better than New Zealand's "canibals" (FE, 281). The *Voyage*'s first two chapters deal with contemporary Portuguese possessions, and Forster's portrayal of the conditions in this "empire" (FE, 32) is critical. Preoccupied with the "pomp and glory of their greatness" (FE, 32), the Portuguese are too tired to civilize anyone.[20] Everything would improve, were the islands ruled by "an active, enterprising and commercial nation" (FE, 36)—it is safe to assume that he meant the British.

At the time of Forster's journey, British explorers started to think of themselves as the better Romans. Cook himself was made "Fellow of the Royal Society," an honor thought to be "equivalent to Rome's 'civic crown.'"[21] So let me reiterate my preliminary thesis: I propose to read Forster's sparse use of the Spanish-Portuguese remnants of the imperial epic as a cautious experiment with a Roman-British narrative of exploration and imperial mission, presenting himself and his fellow-explorers as the better Romans. However, Forster's travelogue is also an *Aeneas Fragment*. On the one hand, this fragment testifies to the ambiguous status of these voyages between imperial project and exploration. On the other, the fragmentary nature of this Roman-Spanish story hints at a gap between this neo-Roman framing and Forster's own often contradictory ideas about the voyages.

Forster's ambivalence emerges around the figure of O-Mai. Debating the benefits of these voyages, Forster uses the Society Island native brought to London on Cook's adventure in 1771 as a failed example. That is, Forster tells this story as the failure to improve the mind and morals of a man of "quick perception and lively fancy" (FE, 11). Having arrived in the "luxurious metropolis," and having witnessed the "civilized world's scenes of debauchery" among the British nobility, his heart remained "uncorrupted," but he learned no useful practical skills (FE, 11). Adam Smith criticized the Spanish for imitating the Romans and bringing colonial junk back from their colonies. Forster showed O-Mai imitating British luxury. Left in his "infant state," he returned home with useless objects (FE, 11).[22] In "Cook, the explorer," Forster then worked hard to contain his own doubts about the merits of European empire-building. In spite of the negative sides of exploration, Forster wrote, "enlightenment is advancing from experience to experience toward an unlimited future."[23]

Does the fragmentary, but insistent, presence of Virgil's epic in Forster's *Voyage* indicate his reservations about writing an imperial narrative modeled on the *Aeneid*? Is there more at stake than Forster's reservations? In order to answer these questions, I will focus on two sections of Forster's travelogue with their strong intertextual relations to Virgil's *Aeneid*: the part narrating the settlement at Dusky Bay and the chapter about Forster's stay at Easter Island and its ruins. While the first passage only obliquely refers to Virgil's *Aeneid*, the second passage does more: if Volney's text on the ruins of Palmyra represents a rewriting of *Scipio's Dream*, Forster's chapter on the ruins on Easter Island amounts to a rewriting of Virgil's book 8. However, before I trace Forster's *Aeneid* fragments in these two passages, I want to discuss Forster's reverie at Tanna, which presents the more general philosophical underpinnings of his travelogue.

World History: Meditations at Tanna

Exploratory travel transformed synchronic history into the diachronic picture of world history. In the wake of these voyages, Adam Ferguson and Adam Smith theorized stadial history, tracing the development of societies from the nomadic savage to the present, and inventing the non-synchronicity of civilized Europe and the uncivilized non-European world. Edmund Burke explained this new historical imaginary. "We need no longer go to History to trace it to all its stages," Burke wrote, because "the Great Map of Mankind is unrolled at once."[24] Europeans were now in a position to grasp with one glance every "Gradation of barbarism" and "mode of refinement": "The different Civility of Europe and China," for instance, or "The Savage State of North America and of New Zealand."[25] Forster's travelogue contributed to the creation of this new imperial space; it also contained sustained reflections on stadial theory.

On the second voyage (1772–1775), the British Admiralty provided Cook again with precise instructions or *apodemics*, hoping to make the South Pacific visible to Cook's metropolitan sponsors.[26] *Apodemics* required descriptions based on autopsy and empirical data. In Forster's account, this empiricist injunction coexisted with the philosophical explorer's musings on world history and its various stages.[27] His passion was people. What he wanted to know was which level of "savagery," or "civilization," each of the nations had attained.[28] Forster arrived at the conclusion that the inhabitants of Tahiti occupied one end of the spectrum (the level of near-civilization), the "barbarian" people of New Caledonia and the New Hebrides (especially the Terra del Fuegians) the other (see FE, 627–631). On the one hand, the "somewhat brutal Maori" or New Zealanders occupied an intermediate stage.[29] On the other, Forster discusses their "practice of eating human flesh" (FG, 279).[30]

The narrative of progress at the heart of stadial theory also informs his philosophical reverie on the island of Tanna. Here, Georg Forster portrayed himself overlooking a fertile valley where groups of natives were at work in the fields. Volney and Gibbon switched from reflections on the Roman past to the present. Forster switches from the empiricist description of the native culture before his eyes to philosophical reflections, assuming a familiar pose: "I fell from hence into a reverie" (FE, 549). That is, Forster's position at Tanna resembles Volney's at Palmyra. It also recalls Jupiter's cosmic vantage point in the *Aeneid* at the moment when he portrays Aeneas as civilizing hero, that is, one who will build a walled city (see AFi, 12).

Forster's reverie also deals with the future, the further evolution of a society under the benign influence of the neo-Roman European travelers. What induced such a "favorable" view of "mankind" (FE, 549), Forster suggests, is the idea that the inhabitants of Tanna—and the South Pacific in general—would benefit from their contact with the European travelers. This vision of civilizational progress, from which Forster distanced himself later, corresponds to the Smithian vision Gibbon outlined in his "Observations."[31] With his emphasis on the traveler's observations on the one hand, and systematic reflections on the different stages of human development on the other, Forster strove to "see"—and make us "see"—the synchronic tableau of the progress from barbarism to civilization.

Carthage on New Zealand

In this space, Forster encountered savages/barbarians and their ruins as Aeneas had done on his journey from Troy to Latium. Let us now take a closer look at Forster's use of Virgil's *Aeneid* in the chapter about the explorers' arrival at Dusky Bay, a reference that amounts to more than just a random selection of quotes from the West's imperial epic. In this section, Forster compared the crew's (temporary) settlement or "colony" on the southern shore of New Zealand to the *Aeneid*. More precisely, Forster condenses two things: the temporary *colonia* that the Trojans built upon their arrival on the shores of Libya; and the Tyrean *colonia* that Dido's people are in the process of building when Aeneas and his men arrive. Recall that when Aeneas leaves the ships, he wonders whether he will find "men or wild creatures" (AFi, 14). What he does find are hardworking

Carthaginians building a new city. Quoting Virgil, Forster paints a picture of men at work at Dusky Bay that he contrasts favorably with the state of "barbarism" (FE, 105). Aeneas's words—"How fortunate are these / Whose city walls are rising here and now!" (AFi, 19)—express Forster's message: civilization is being built at Dusky Bay as it was at Carthage.

This episode is framed by the *Aeneid*'s "master narrative."[32] After the Trojans' shipwreck on the shores of Carthage, Juno asks Jupiter: "What finish to these troubles will you give?" (AFi, 12; Latin quote in FE, 105). To this question, Jupiter replies with a prophecy about Aeneas's mission, the founding of the city that will be the metropolis of a future empire. Every time Forster makes use of the Virgilian archive, he touches on this imperial master narrative. But then, out of the blue, Forster places his Trojan-Roman-Oceanic idyll under the sign of rise and decay: "Sic transit gloria mundi!" (FG, 181). The sudden flowering of a "state of civilization" at Dusky Bay in the midst of "barbarism" will most likely remain a single brief moment of "Cultur," before the site will once again sink into its "original chaotic state" (FG, 180, 181). Weeds will cover every useful plant, Forster writes, and then he adds: "*From the point of view of the annihilating future*, moments or centuries of culture make no discernible difference" (FG, 181; emphasis mine).

How do we read this sudden eruption of pessimism into Forster's description of the settlement at Dusky Bay? Does this pessimistic tone derive from Forster's revision of his travelogue, inscribing his disillusionment with the explorers' civilizing mission and doubts about modern Europe's narrative of progress? Or do we read Forster's "*from the point of view of the annihilating future*" as another neo-Roman *Überbleibsel*, surfacing rather unexpectedly in Forster's text? This time, the *left-over* is not one of the Virgilian passages directly or indirectly related to the *Aeneid*'s imperial master narrative, but an echo of Virgil's many ruin gazer scenarios—the other integral part of the ancient text written by one of Rome's imperial thinkers. This would mean reading it as a symptom. Let us postpone the obvious question—symptom of what?—and continue with Forster from Dusky Bay to Easter Island.

Easter Island: Tattooed Savages and Archaic Monuments

Forster's chapter on the ruins on Easter Island amounts to a rewriting of Virgil's book 8—a literary form of mimesis as repetition-with-a-difference. I previously mentioned Claude Lorrain's neoclassical painting of Aeneas's arrival at Pallanteum. In this painting, we see the massive fortress of Evander's walled city towering above the landing point. As you may remember, Evander will show his new allies the prehistoric ruined fortress dating from the golden age of Saturn. Similarly, Forster and his companions will stumble upon archaic ruins among the "savages" of Easter Island, ruins that Forster will read as signs of an archaic, now-extinct culture.

But let us first look at Forster's description of the island's "savages" (FG, 482). It is among these Easter Islanders that he finds a group of people wearing the clothes left by the Spanish—"monuments" of their earlier presence.[33] Diderot praised Bougainville for his "quick eye" and his "real desire to see," qualities that are equally apparent in Forster's detailed visual description of the island's natives.[34] As soon as the European travelers arrived, Forster wrote, they saw a crowd of unarmed, "almost naked people" who "seem" to be of peaceful disposition (FG, 478). Forster is preoccupied with their painted bodies, creating the powerful images of the tattooed peoples of Oceania that remained imprinted on Volney's and Gibbon's memory.[35] Judging by their appearance, he writes, they were of the same tribe as the Tahitians, their entire bodies covered by "punctures" (FE, 301). Later, Forster singles out "a brazen fellow," drawing attention to his decorated ears, body tattoos, and the bone hanging from a string around his neck (FE, 302). Within a few hours, the man is dressed in a jacket, hat, and beads—British, not Spanish, leftovers.

What happens at the beginning of Virgil's book 7, that is, the moment when Aeneas's men land in Italy? Virgil begins the story of this momentous landing with another iteration of the *Aeneid*'s master narrative. Having landed at the Tiber's mouth, Aeneas sends some of his men to explore the "region and the people" and others as emissaries to the king, Latinus, who was told of "the arrival / Of tall men in strange costume" (AFi, 200 and 201). It is easy to see why so many modern explorers were attracted to Virgil's text. The emissaries ask for permission to build a settlement, offering in return some of Aeneas's Trojan relics, among them Priam's "embroidered purple" (AFi, 204).

Having conquered Latium, the Trojans meet with Evander, the Arcadian king who takes his new allies to his town and the ruined remnants of Saturn's golden age. These are Virgil's *imperial ruins*, the archaic foundations of the empire's metropolis. They are also ruins associated with savages, barbarians, and civilizing heroes: first Hercules, the "conqueror" who rescued men from the past's "barbaric" terrors (AFi, 236); then Saturn, the civilizing hero of Latium's golden age; and now Evander and his Arcadians, whom Virgil portrays as Greek forebears and yet less advanced than the conquering Trojans.

Ruins or the Mystery of the End

Narrating their sojourn on Easter Island, Forster returns several times to the island's "gigantic monument" (FE, 311), expending much guesswork on what they are, or what their function could have been. Forster traverses the island, often in Hodges's company, looking at these stones in several locations. Let us focus for a moment on Forster's description. How exactly did he describe the sites? First, there is the view from the ocean: "A great number of black pillars stood along the shore, many of which were elevated on platforms consisting of several ranges of stone" (FE, 301). They are able to "distinguish something resembling a human head and shoulders," but cannot figure out the "rude stone" at the base (FE, 301). Cook called these large stone columns or sculptures visible from afar "Monuments of Antiquity."[36] Forster referred to them as "pillars, columns, or statues" (FG, 486).

Forster uses the word "ruin" only once in this chapter. Hiking across the island, the voyagers come across two similar sites, and it is at the second site that Forster comes upon some stones that he perceives as ruins. Climbing the hills on the north side of the island, Forster writes, they find "some ruins of a crumbled wall on which might have stood a sculpture in ancient times" (FG, 498; translation mine). Did Forster hesitate to use the concept of ruin in this non-European setting? Did he think the concept of ruin was a European *left-over*? If so, why does he suddenly "see" ruins? Is it because this is a familiar sight: a crumbled wall? Or is it because Evander, showing Aeneas the "Monuments of the ancients," first points to "walls / Long fallen down" (AFi, 242 and 241)?

Like Aeneas in book 8, Forster discovers archaic ruins, and again like Aeneas, he does not know at first what he is seeing. While Evander makes Aeneas understand what he sees, Forster and his companions do not get much help from their native informants in deciphering these stones. Left to his own Virgilian devices, Forster concludes that the stones must be ruins left by a more advanced civilization, and again refers to these "surprising objects" as "*Überbleibsel*" (FG, 505) or "remains" (FE, 320). They once were "lasting monuments" built "to flatter the vanity of their princes by perpetuating their name" (FE, 320; FG, 505).

The Virgilian language of imperial ruins is thus present: ruined walls that hint at a structure from an archaic age; a monument built to last and built to glorify a ruler. The analogy between Evander's pre-Latin ruins on the site of what will become Rome's Capitol and the archaic ruins of Easter Island relates two sites testifying to a golden age. It also relates two presents. There is Virgil's glorious present, foreshadowed in Aeneas's dream about Augustus's marble metropolis before setting foot in Evander's Arcadian settlement. This is one of the moments when Virgil wants us to glimpse Augustus behind Aeneas's mask. And then there is Forster's present in which one imperial power, the Spanish-Portuguese Empire, is declining, and another European power, the British Empire, is rising.

Is Forster wearing the mask of Aeneas/Augustus? Before answering this question, we need to further explore Forster's Virgilian intertext. Book 8 is Virgil's book of Roman history, creating a sweeping arc from Latium's archaic prehistory to Rome's imperial present. Central to this story is Aeneas's shield, whose design recapitulates Roman history. Virgil's ekphrastic description of the shield re-creates Roman events and actors, ending with Augustus at his triple triumph. The point of view is now the emperor's, witnessing the procession. Aeneas, Virgil writes, did not understand any of these "images" from the future, but is ready to assume his destiny.

At the end of book 8, which began in Evander's Arcadian settlement and ended in Augustan Rome, Aeneas is thus ready to wear Augustus's mask. Is Forster ready to wear the Roman mask? He criticized depictions of toga-wearing South Sea islanders, and it is easy to imagine what Forster would have thought about the Roman toga worn by Mai in the portrait by Reynolds or in William Parry's *Omai, Banks, and Solander* (ca. 1776). However, in Forster's *Voyage*, Virgilian tropes are more than mere *Überbleibsel* of an earlier imperial formation that saw itself and its subjects through a Roman lens. When Forster finds himself at the ruin site on Easter Island, he is ready to wear the Roman mask in the service of the British Empire—if only for a brief moment.

Far from being a simple imitation of the Aeneid, *Voyage round the World* is its own modern genre, an *Aeneas Fragment*. Virgil's epic is present in the form of *left-overs*, but these fragmentary remnants are symptomatic of the presence of Virgil's imperial text, which consists of two core statements: that there is no empire without ruins and there is no empire without barbarians. Noble ruins that the empire celebrates as its founding ruins (at the very moment when its conquests produce city after city in rubble); and noble ruins that the empire will leave behind—once it has reached the end.

Let us reflect once more on Forster's sudden pessimistic framing of the flowering of civilization at Dusky Bay and his oddly violent expression: "*from the point of view of the annihilating future*" (FG, 181). I argue that the Dusky Bay chapter rewrites the beginning of Virgil's book 1, that is, the arrival of the Trojans at Carthage, the building of their temporary settlement on the shore and the rise of Dido's *colonia*.[37] With this rewriting and its flash of violence, Forster touches on Virgil's Carthaginian ruin gazer scenarios, thus emerging as an imperial thinker. In 1792, Forster then published his translation of Volney's anticolonial *The Ruins, or, Meditation on the Ruins of Empire*.[38]

William Hodges, or Piranesi in the South Pacific

Forster was not the only one who re-encountered Roman ruins in the South Pacific, surrounded by *savages*, and not the only one who imported—knowingly and unknowingly—the Roman imperial problematic to the South Pacific. Like Forster, William Hodges was fascinated with the monuments of Easter Island, and as in Forster's case there is a more direct neo-Roman *inter-visuality* at work than previous scholars detected. Virgil's *Aeneid* was Forster's intertext; in Hodges's ruin paintings, we find traces of Piranesi's images of Rome's imperial ruins.

Painters were part of Cook's crews on all three voyages because textual description alone was deemed to lack descriptive power. Some of William Hodges's sketches were included in Cook's account complementing Forster's textual descriptions, graphic records "drawn on the spot with the utmost exactness."[39] With Cook's voyages, European eighteenth-century conventions came in conflict with the desire to meticulously record the people, objects, and remnants of unknown cultures, setting in motion the

9.1 William Hodges, *A View of the Monuments of Easter Island* (1775).

9.2 William Woollett, *Monuments in Easter Island* (1777).

quest for new techniques of realist representation driven by the voyagers' epistemology of "empirical naturalism."[40] In *A View of the Monuments of Easter Island* [Rapanui] (1775), Hodges, Smith claimed, staged the tension between eighteenth-century ruin paintings and his own rendition of the ancient stones (figure 9.1). Here, Hodges gestured at the traditional *memento mori* motive by including a skull among the bones found at the monument and moving the skeletal remains closer to the center of our field of vision. The strong contrast of light and darkness also transfers the *vanitas* motive into the Pacific landscape.

Nevertheless, in Hodges's painting empiricist pressure indeed insists *against* eighteenth-century conventions. This becomes more apparent when we compare the painting with an engraving based on Hodges's drawings but executed by William Woollett, *Monuments in Easter Island* (included in Cook's report). Woollett's engraving pushed the Pacific site further in the direction of what his contemporary audience would expect: a site of tumbling stones gradually overtaken by nature (figure 9.2). Not quite ivy, the creeping plants in Woollett's engraving do recall more familiar scenes. And there is of course the figure of the shepherd, barely discernible as he walks under the broken columns. Bernard Smith compares the engraving to Richard Wilson's famous *Et in Arcadia Ego* (1755), pointing to this figure as the element common to both pictures.[41] Importing this kind of neoclassical imagery, Smith argues, helped create the idea of the Pacific as new Arcadia, the return of Europe's long-gone golden age.

What happens if we move from Smith's comparison of Woollett's picture to the eighteenth-century Italianate landscape with ruins to the contemporary eighteenth-century imagery of Roman ruins? In other words, what happens if we compare the South Pacific's Woollett's *Monuments in Easter Island* to Piranesi's monumentalist ruinscapes?[42] Let us begin with two *vedutae*, *Hadrian's Villa* (1751) and *The Temple of Juno* (1776–1778).[43] The composition of *The Temple of Juno* resonates with Woollett's *Monuments*: leaning on his staff, a shepherd is standing next to one of the enormous columns at Paestum, his eyes cast downward. In Piranesi's *Hadrian's Villa*, there are no contemplative shepherds and no bones. But again, there is a monumental ruin, dwarfing the inhabitants of the present, "natives," and inquisitive archeologists, like Forster and his companions, explorers of a remote past.

Woollett's Easter Island native in the guise of a neoclassical shepherd stands in the shadow of an over-towering structure. Similarly, Piranesi's archeologists work in the shadow of a large wall. But the proportions are reversed: in Woollett's engraving, the mountainous wall pressing in on the beholder's field of vision is a rock, located on the right side and extending out of the frame. Here, monumental nature dwarfs art; the opposite is true in Piranesi's engraving, where the remnant of Roman imperial architecture looms large. In Piranesi, not even nature is strong enough to vanquish Roman might. If there was a remote past on Easter Island, it was not of the Roman kind. Indeed, it is likely that Woollett intended to hint at a less glorious and more barbarian kind—witness the rather large skeleton, reducing the shepherd to a kind of Meissen miniature, dwarfed and utterly out of place in this primordial landscape.

Hodges's *The Monuments of Easter Island* restores the Piranesian dimensions, confronting the viewer with a high wall of four columns—Forster's "colossalische Monumente" (FG, 493). It also re-creates the basic composition of Piranesi's *Hadrian's Villa*: both pictures open away from the ruined wall onto a plain (enclosed by a range of low-level mountains)—Piranesi's to the right, arresting the viewer's gaze with a shepherd, Hodges's to the left, capturing the gaze with a group of "savages" near a cluster of similar but smaller rocks. As the Piranesi of the South Pacific, Hodges introduces the idea of the contrast between present decay and former greatness.

Putting Rome's ruins onstage, Piranesi often used Bibiena's angled views. In the case of *Hadrian's Villa*, this technique increases the walls' mass (reaching all the way to the top of the frame on the left) while opening up a large space in front of the wall. This angled view, I argue, echoes the theatrical aesthetic of Roman ruin gazer scenarios. What does this mean for our reading of Hodges's *Monuments*? The stone monuments are set on a low wall, the space in front of it filled with a pile of heavy stones,

9.3 Giovanni Battista Piranesi, *Remains of Funerary Structures along the Via Appia Antica* (1757).

a small skull, and two white bones, and this entire arrangement is located next to what appears to be a deep ravine. Was this a ritual site? There is no answer to this question. The space depicted by Hodges is utterly foreign to the eyes of eighteenth-century Europeans, rupturing their spatial imagination and refusing to be ordered.

Yet Hodges's stress on the foreignness of the scene does not exclude a connection to Piranesi's Roman ruins. Let me add a second example of Piranesi's allusion to the Roman ruin scenario's theatrical aesthetic, his view of the *Remains of Funerary Structures along the Via Appia Antica* (1756–1757) (figure 9.3). Here, the composition draws the beholder's eye to the three oddly shaped and rather precarious columns, remnants of a row of Roman mausoleums. They line a small open space on which we find two kinds of actors —archeologists, perhaps, debating the nature of these ruins, and a lonely observer sitting in the shade.

Closer to enigmatic structures in a dreamscape than Piranesi's other ruin sites, these monuments of death resonate strongly with Hodges's Easter Island columns. Hinting at a ruined Piranesian stage in the Pacific, Hodges reinvented the mystery of the end. Pushing us to muse about this secret, he simultaneously tells us that the answers to our questions will elude us. When Hodges worked in India, his ruin drawings of Bengal sites echoed Piranesi's staged ruins directly. Here, his "visual genealogy" and "hybrid aesthetics" were tied to Warren Hastings's ideas about colonial government.[44] As faint as it is in Hodges's *Monuments of Easter Island*, this visual genealogy nevertheless exists.

The ruins of Easter Island were one of the objects around which Forster and Hodges developed innovative techniques of description, inscribing the traveler's gaze while keeping Virgil and Piranesi in mind. Like Smith (who used the contrast between Hodges's and Woollett's ruin paintings to argue for Hodges's success in spite of the "remnants" of eighteenth-century Arcadian landscapes), and like David Bindman (who argued that Hodges succeeded because of these remnants), I have emphasized the paintings' visual genealogy.[45] But I have done so with a sideways glance at Piranesi's oeuvre, which I contend makes us notice the faded outlines of Roman ruins. I do not mean to suggest that the tension around the European aesthetic of ruins is absent. On the contrary, this tension between European eighteenth-century conventions of ruin painting and the aesthetic perception of the non-European object is very much part of the paintings. But Piranesi and his massive, towering ruins should not be left out of the discussion.

Let me summarize my argument before taking you to Egypt's Roman ruins. The fragmentary presence of Virgil's imperial text signals the gap between the voyage's mission and Forster's ambivalent stance toward this mission. These fragments are also signs of the mission's ambivalent positioning between exploration and conquest. Forster's text consists of two layers: first, the text of the ethnographer and travel writer who, working with the Virgilian *left-overs*, sees the world of Tahitians and Maori through the Roman lens and eventually realizes that not only the cloak of Aeneas, but the Roman pattern itself, does not fit. The second layer consists of the Roman imperial text reasserting itself, pushing Forster to wear Aeneas's mask.

As *Aeneas Fragment*, Forster's *Voyage* gives voice to his ambivalence toward the British mission and, ultimately, the idea of empire itself. At the same time, echoing Adam Smith, he holds on to his belief in the civilizing mission of "a trade-oriented people." My reading is not another intervention in the debate about Forster's ambivalence. Instead, I read Forster as an imperial thinker in the vein of Virgil: a thinker who understands the inevitable connection between empire and ruins, empire and barbarians. Similarly, I traced Hodges's reliance on the imperial archive.

In 1800 the philosopher Joseph Marie Degérando delineated a new global time map: "The philosophical traveler sailing to the ends of the earth," he wrote, is a time traveler, "exploring the past." Arriving in "those unknown islands," he reaches "the cradle of society."[46] Forster's travelogue and Hodges's ruins added another layer to this new mapping of time across the globe by making the South Pacific a neo-Roman space. These Europeans did not re-encounter history as repetition in the South

Pacific, they imported it—moving, like the Maori, "into the future with their eyes on the past."[47] That is, they brought with them the idea of linear time and teleological progress *and* the time of empire. As neo-Romans, they lived their present as the repetition of the Roman past and therefore as the repetition of imperial endtime: the present as duration, the space between violent beginning and violent end. As neo-Romans, they were people without history, for whom the present and the future are the repetition of the past.

TEN

Caught Up in "Eternal Repetitions": Napoleon in Egypt and Rome

Introduction

While Forster experimented with the mask of Aeneas, Jules Michelet declined to wear it. Guardian of the memory of the dead, Michelet, whose passion was the world of 1789, defined historiography as "Resurrection."[1] The historian was Orpheus, his backward glance potentially lethal because history's "beloved images" might pull him back into the realm of the shades.[2] Would it not be safer, Michelet wondered, if he took Aeneas as his model, who "entered [the underworld] sword in hand"?[3] Anti-Napoleonic to the core, Michelet dismisses the Roman model.

The imitation of Rome became again an all-consuming concern of European intellectuals once Napoleon presented himself as successor to the Roman Caesars. Herder and Volney hoped that Rome's imperial history would never be repeated; Gibbon thought about what it meant to repeat, and Forster became Aeneas—*malgré lui*. Michelet thought of empires as the creations of men, whose minds were caught in repetitive imitations. In his *Histoire Romaine* (1866), he attacked the very idea of imperial mimesis, sarcastically dismissing the great empire-builders: Alexander, Caesar—and "our moderns," Napoleon and his successors.[4] Their empire-building caught in "eternal repetitions," they never invented a thing because they were constrained by their "spirit of imitation."[5]

Michelet, Napoleon's republican critic, must have hated the Luxor obelisk, imported by the July Monarchy in 1836 and erected in Paris to commemorate Napoleon's Egyptian Campaign (1798–1801). The granite monument was the *Res Gestae* of Ramses II, inscribed with the achievements of his reign.[6] The obelisk's erection was organized as a grand spectacle, attended by Louis Philippe on the Place de la Concorde.[7] The remodeling of this square was undertaken in as conscious a manner as that of the Augustan Forum. Imagining a tour through Paris, a French man captured the obelisk's neo-Roman meaning. The visitor would perceive the monument "after having read on the Arc de Triomphe de L'Étoile the names of Aboukir, of Heliopolis, of the pyramids," he wrote.[8] Having admired the obelisk from afar, he would be impressed by "all the memories of science and glory" inscribed on its base.[9] "In recalling past triumphs, the obelisk becomes a new honor for our era because it makes seen that *we have executed in our turn what the Roman people alone had executed before us.*"[10]

The raising of the obelisk testified to the French state's successful neo-Roman mimesis: *we have executed what the Roman people alone had executed before us*. The event had been in the planning since 1801. Claiming to free the Egyptian people from their Mamelouk oppressors (who ruled Egypt in the name of the Ottomans), Napoleon had invaded Egypt in 1798 (eventually crossing into Syria). With this expedition, Napoleon embarked on the first stage of what was a French neo-Roman project of imperial mimesis stretching over three decades, from the Egyptian expedition to the conquest of Rome in 1808, to the first battles in Algeria in the 1830s. The 1836 installation of the Luxor obelisk in the middle of Paris would be the final act of this drawn-out performance.

What Napoleon Bonaparte and Michelet had in common was the desire to resurrect the past—the glorious past of the French Revolution in the ruins of the Bastille in the case of the historian, the monumental past of the Roman Empire in the ruins of Egypt in the case of the politician. Bringing the dead back to life, Michelet created a third space between past and present, "a city" in which the dead and the living mingled.[11] This imaginary third space is the same twilight zone in which much of this Napoleonic neo-Roman mimesis takes place. During the French occupation of Rome (1808–1814), French experts then designed and partially realized an ambitious remodeling program that re-created the classical Roman stage in their image.

The conquest of Rome was an interlude, but from the point of view of the neo-Roman imaginary a crucial one. The allies expelled French troops from Rome, but the memory of the beautifully ruined Roman stage had been successfully revived in this new neo-Roman imaginary. The Egyptian

10.1 Frontispiece, *Description de L'Égypte* (1809–1828).

Campaign too was an imperial venture that failed but, paradoxically, one which successive governments turned into the most memorable event of the postrevolutionary era. This drawn-out performance of imperial mimesis involved not only the Luxor/Paris obelisk but also state-commissioned paintings and a wave of texts, culminating in the publication of the *Description de L'Égypte* (consisting of ten folio volumes) between 1809 and 1828. This monumental work united texts and engravings by the scientists and artists who accompanied the French troops. The *Description*'s frontispiece echoes Piranesi's famous frontispieces (figure 10.1). Both of these engravings combine the jumble of ruins with an ordering gesture. In Piranesi's case, the *Antichità Romane* comes with a reconstructed map of the ancient city; in the case of the French engraving, our eyes are caught by a road leading through the pile of objects, referencing the introduction of the French future into the Egyptian present-as-past. The purpose of Piranesi's mapping was to make the ancient capital visible again as the empire's theo-political stage. The purpose of the Egyptian Campaign and the *Description* was to bring the spirit of Enlightenment to the East by finding, describing, and categorizing its architectural, artistic, and natural treasures.

But the *Description* is not a museum; rather, I will claim that it represents Napoleon's mausoleum, with the Egyptian obelisks that had framed Augustus's Roman-Egyptian mausoleum (celebrating victory at Actium, the conquest of Egypt, and the new imperial era) now placed on its frontispiece. As such, it responds to the imperial desire of the past and of the present. Like Augustus's mausoleum, this one is a monument to the past as much as a manifesto of the future, to France's imperial ventures in Egypt in 1798 *and* the conquest of Algeria starting in 1830.

I will conclude this chapter with a reading of Joseph Fourier's introduction to the *Description* as imitating the *Res Gestae* (first exhibited at Augustus's mausoleum; see part 1). Most intriguingly, this précis of world history, retelling the great deeds of Napoleon and the French Army, was written in the mode of the future subjunctive: what could have been. Published in 1828, Fourier's imperial manifesto created the campaign as a pivotal historical event to be remembered—and described what would have been had the campaign been successful. Fourier's text promised explicitly that there *will be* a French empire—not in Egypt, but in other parts of Northern Africa closer to Carthage. And it argued implicitly that a French Empire existed in Egypt. The writing and publication of the *Description* is thus another final step in the (post)Napoleonic mimesis of Rome.

Future Interrupted: Napoleon's Egyptian Campaign (1798–1801)

Before embarking for Egypt, Napoleon read Volney's *Travels through Syria and Egypt 1783–1785*.[12] The republican theorist drew imperial lessons from his visit to Syria and Egypt and like other revolutionary intellectuals supported the new emperor's Egyptian campaign.[13] Napoleon and his officers read Volney's travelogue together with the *Lettres sur L'Égypte* (1785) by Claude Etienne Savary. Both concluded that Egypt was in a state of decay from which it would not recover without outside help, attributing the decay to the rule of the Mamelouks, "barbarians" in Savary's mind.[14] Agreeing on the campaign, they differed when it came to its goals: Savary wanted to save Egyptians from Ottoman despotism, whereas Volney was interested in guarding Egypt's splendid past. The French, he opined, needed to salvage Egypt's ruins from Ottoman dereliction, sounding as if he were announcing the opening of a museum.[15]

Napoleon did not invade Egypt to provide the French with a museum of antiquity or to liberate the Egyptians; he and the Directorate had concrete geopolitical motives, involving the British presence in the Middle East.[16] Charles V left for Tunis with an entourage that included military men, scientists, and artists, and so did Napoleon. The so-called Army of the Orient was composed of military men and about 216 members of a scientific commission receiving instructions from Marie Caffarelli, the head of the commission, and quickly infected by the "Egyptian virus" (to count, to study, to report, to conclude).[17] Egypt was a stage littered with Roman ruins, and the project of making this stage as visible as possible was an integral part of the *mise-en-scène* of this modern act of Roman mimesis.[18]

"Egypt was a province of the Roman Empire," Talleyrand declared, and "she must become a province of the French Republic."[19] When the French Army left Toulon in May 1798, Napoleon addressed the soldiers as legionnaires of the Roman republic. Framing the Egyptian Campaign as a struggle with the British Empire, Napoleon took recourse to the analogy of Rome's wars against Carthage: "The Roman legions, *which you have sometimes resembled but not yet equaled*, fought the might of Carthage on this same sea and on the plains of Zama."[20] The Romans won because they "were disciplined."[21] Leaving for Egypt, the French soldiers were not yet Roman—and their general was not yet Caesar. Only the successful conquest of Egypt would convey reality on the imperial mimesis to which Napoleon aspired.

To overcome the gap between Napoleon's France and Caesar's Rome, the difference between past and present had to vanish in a twilight zone where the Roman past became the French present. Let me remind you of some of the core elements of imperial mimesis that are involved in this closing of the chronological gap: imperial mimesis is a performance, a story that revives the great men of the past by reenacting their great deeds. Imperial mimesis is thus the assumption of a subject position in an act that locates the subject in the past *and* in the present. This act of identification—wearing the mask of the dead—requires a stage.[22] For Napoleon this stage was Egypt, the country Augustus conquered (the victory being one of the first steps in establishing the Principate). And in this neo-Roman framework, the concept of barbarian reemerged. Systematically applied to the declared enemy, the Mamelouks, the concept sometimes shifted to the Ottomans, the conquerors' declared allies, and to the guerilla-like tribesmen who attacked the French Army once it moved toward Syria.

Napoleon's Egyptian campaign was an act of mimesis of the past carried out among the ruins of the imperial Roman past on an Egyptian terrain.[23] What exactly did imperial mimesis consist of? First and foremost, there were Napoleon's own speech acts or proclamations, comparing Roman past and neo-Roman present. Declaring that the invaders would respect Islam, Napoleon referred to the Roman precedent. Roman soldiers, Bonaparte explained, "protected all faiths," and his soldiers will "learn to accept" Egypt's "many different customs."[24] Articulating his imperial aspirations, he also stated that conquests required "one voice of authority," leaders who "should have even greater powers than those of Consuls in the armies of ancient Rome."[25] In one of his reports to the Directorate, he recounted his triumphal Cairo entry in 1799.[26] As we will see, Egypt's monuments and ruins played their role in the French conquerors' assumption of Roman masks.

The campaign's goal was the creation of an enlightened colony on the "ruins of the Ottoman Empire."[27] Napoleon's officers and scientists were expecting an Orientalist fantasy. What they saw was nothing but debris and ruins—a picture that they then used to justify their imperial project. The expedition's scientists were profoundly disappointed. "Shocked at this sight [of Alexandria]," the scientists "went to visit the remains of antiquity."[28] What they saw was a jumble of ruins, "columns of granite, some still standing, others promiscuously lying prostrate in the streets and squares, and even on the sea-shore, where they formed considerable piles; Egyptian monuments covered with hieroglyphics, serving for thresholds of doors, or benches used for seats."[29]

Moiret, a captain in the French Army, also recorded his disillusionment about Alexandria, a "hideous spectacle of misery, ugliness and squalor."[30] There was no beautiful Oriental city, and there were no splendid ruins. When Moiret finally comes across a site with some ancient stones, he strikes the pose of the Volneyan ruin gazer. Seated on one of Cleopatra's obelisks, he tells his readers: "Nothing remained of Alexandria's ancient monuments except *Pompey's column* in the middle and the two *obelisks* of Cleopatra."[31] At first glance, nothing too surprising is happening in this ruin gazer scenario, as Moiret predictably ponders the evanescence of all imperial power. What we ought to pay attention to is a small detail: the fragment of Roman, not Egyptian, power captured the ruin gazer's attention. This Roman column reminded Moiret of Paris, "look[ing] very much like the one in the Place Vendome in Paris."[32] Observing that the obelisk marked the site of Cleopatra's palace, Moiret's mind turned to Anthony's story. Egypt's ancient ruins are dead and will remain so, but Roman ruins are still alive—alive and available for the mimetic project of Napoleon in Egypt.

Napoleon's technicians of mimesis used Egypt's ruined Roman stage as the theater for their world-historical performance. On September 22, 1798, the army celebrated the founding of the Republic in Cairo, erecting a triumphal arch (dedicated to the battle of the pyramids) as well as an Egyptian-style obelisk (engraved with the names of the fallen French soldiers). Again Napoleon addressed his army, promising that they would be "crowned with laurels."[33] Thus, while the site for Napoleon's act of imperial mimesis is Egypt, its object was Roman—as were the props: arches and laurel wreaths.

The audience for whose eyes this spectacle of mimesis was performed was located in Europe, not here on the square in the decrepit city of Cairo. Egypt mattered only as backdrop. The French left the country in 1801, defeated but having revived imperial Rome and assumed its legacy—having completed the process of *their* imperial mimesis. Volney's prediction about Napoleon—"this will be the head of Caesar"—had come true.[34]

Act 2: The Aftermath of the Campaign

In his *préface historique* to the first volume of the *Description de L'Égypte*, Joseph Fourier reminded his readers in 1809 that Egypt had been the locus where not only Rome's fate but the fate of the entire world was decided.[35] Today, Fourier wrote, Egypt was the "theatre of Napoleon's glory."[36] After Egypt, Napoleon was Caesar—and Paris a new Rome. After having used the obelisk together with the triumphal arch as props in their mimetic performance in the center of Cairo, the Napoleonic architects of imperial power continued their work in France with the installation of the Luxor obelisk in 1836, at the end of act 2 of France's imperial mimesis.

When the Restoration edition of the *Description de L'Égypte* was published in 1826, a medal was struck in its honor bearing the words *Gallia Victrice Aegyptus Rediviva* (*Victorious Gaul Reviving Egypt*). The medal shows a Roman legionnaire standing in front of the pyramids and looking down at a reclining female figure while lifting her veil. Critics tend to draw attention to the message of Egypt's domestication.[37] I see the medal as a belated representation of imperial mimesis. Once a "pre-ancien régime national symbol,"[38] the Romanized Gaul is now a neo-Roman imperial warrior. The process of imperial mimesis has been completed—regardless of the fact that the act of possession was never realized.

And why should it matter that the French had to give up their civilizing mission in the Middle East? Napoleon famously hurried home in 1799, leaving Kleber in charge. Back in Paris, he staged his coup on the Eighteenth Brumaire, became the republic's First Consul, and in 1804 emperor of the French. Moiret observed that "this unhappy country," which was "once so rich and enlightened," seemed "condemned to barbarism, misery and the most appalling superstition."[39] Napoleon pioneered "a form of imperialism" that served as a model for France's later colonial projects.[40] The republican imperialist also set the stage for his coronation as neo-Roman emperor in 1804 by enacting a form of imperial mimesis in Egypt.[41]

In act 2 of this imperial mimesis, Paris became the stage. Two objects were at the center of this second act: the Luxor obelisk and Napoleon himself. Dominique-Vivant Denon, a veteran of the Egyptian Campaign, played a central role in organizing the second act.[42] In 1802 Denon published *Voyage dans la Basse et Haute Égypte*. His dedication thematized the logic governing the temporal imaginary of Napoleon's mimetic project: "To join the brilliance of your name to the splendor of the monuments of Egypt is to bring together the glorious splendor of our century to the fabulous times in history."[43] Denon's resurrectional metaphor was the reheating of Ramses's "ashes."[44]

In the aftermath of the Egyptian Campaign, Napoleon was not portrayed as Ramses, but as Roman. The empire's "nascent symbolism," Susan Siegfried writes, experimented with different incarnations of Napoleon.[45] When the Napoleonic Empire reached its greatest expansion in the summer of 1806, Denon, abandoning all other historical references, moved in the Roman direction. Politically, this meant stressing military success, iconographically, it meant a return to the mask that Napoleon had tentatively worn in Egypt: the mask of the Roman emperor.[46]

One of the projects signaling this shift was the Vendome column, modeled on Trajan's Column. Denon motivated this decision in a seemingly paradoxical way: "[W]e no longer have need of the illusion of centuries to search in the past for the heroes of France."[47] If we keep in mind that Napoleon had recently become Roman in Egypt, then Denon's statement is less paradoxical: in the wake of Egypt, Trajan's Roman past is more recent than Charlemagne's. Commissioned by Denon in 1806, the statue of Napoleon as Roman emperor "crowned the [Vendome] column from 1810 to 1814."[48]

Napoleon's Roman mimesis begins in Egypt, shades the portrayal of the First Consul and emperor upon his return to France, and then comes to the fore around 1806. Some of these portraits asserted imperial power by their colossal size and the use of the frontal "majesty posture," inspired, Siegfried writes, by Phidas's colossal statue of Zeus (the cult image at Olympia).[49] For instance, the gigantic bust of Napoleon, sponsored by Denon and installed on the outer façade of the Louvre in 1805, resonated with the frontal view of Ingres's portrait, *Napoleon I on his Imperial Throne* (1806). When Ingres's portrait was publicly exhibited in 1806, statues of Charlemagne, Alexander, Julius Caesar, and "Scipio the African" served as background.[50]

The *Battle of Jena* (1806) medal shows a youthful Napoleon with Jupiter's thunderbolt in hand, its celebration of "military conquest" again a belated reference to his Egyptian Campaign.[51] To these examples we should add the history paintings exhibited in the Salons between 1804 and 1810 depicting "Napoleon's triumphal entrance into vanquished cities," such as Charles Meynier's *Entrée de S. M. l'Empereur et Roi dans Berlin* or paintings of his Cairo and Alexandria entries.[52]

Act 3: Going Native in the Ruins of the Past: Napoleon in Rome

After the brief seizure of Rome in 1798, French troops occupied Rome from 1808 to 1814. Never having set foot in Rome, Napoleon named it "second city of the Empire."[53] During the occupation, Camille de Tournon was the conquered city's "civil head."[54] Leaving Egypt to Kleber, Napoleon led French troops across the Alps in 1800, "evoking images of Hannibal and Charlemagne."[55] He told an Italian sculptor that "[he was] of the race of the Caesars, and of the best of their kind, the founders."[56]

The Roman masquerade spanned from the first to the second conquest. In 1798 General Berthier declared Rome a republic, standing on the steps of the Capitol citing "Cato, Cicero, Brutus, and the sons of the Gauls."[57] The proclamation making Rome a "free imperial city" and part of France was read on June 10, 1809. Addressing the crowd in Napoleon's voice, the herald announced: "Romans, the greatest of heroes has reunited you with the greatest of states."[58] And then the absent emperor donned the mask of Augustus: he declared it "fitting" that the French people "should share the benefits of their laws . . . with those who, in another age, preceded them along the triumphal way."[59] In a neo-Roman reversal, he told Italians that they were joining "the Empire," invited "to share the triumph," granting Italians "a fate more worthy of your ancestors"—"after so many centuries of oblivion."[60]

Raised on "the classical stories of Rome," it was not hard for Napoleon to imagine himself "as the second Augustus."[61] The Egyptian Campaign put the framework for this Roman masquerade in place. Reestablishing the Roman stage, the architectural Romanization of eighteenth-century Rome provided the backdrop for its completion. In 1535, the papal commission restored Rome in preparation of the triumphal entry of Charles V. As soon as French troops entered Rome in 1808, commissions initiated the most extensive clearing, excavation, restoration, and restructuring of the city in the modern age. Under the aegis of these commissions, major ruins from the Augustan and post-Augustan age were cleared, repaired, and isolated. Used for the celebration of Napoleon's birthday, Augustus's Mausoleum, for instance, was to become a "'decorous amphitheatre' for public festivals."[62] In 1811, "an impossibly grandiose and destructive plan for an imperial palace" was proposed.[63] The complex encompassing the Palatine, Capitol, and Roman Forum would consist of ministries and theaters, its new avenues and triumphal arches opening completely new vistas.

Abandoning the idea, the *Commission des Embellisements* designed more realistic plans for a "picturesque" public garden on the Palatine, framing "the ruins of the imperial palaces."[64] The commission's purpose was to make the ancient monuments both accessible and newly visible. Much of this work involved demolitions. The commissions singled out ruins we are familiar with from the discussion of Augustan-era restorations: the Theater of Marcellus, for instance, and the Roman Forum. Other sites where work was planned or begun were the Colosseum and the Arch of Titus.

All of this demolition-*cum*-construction culminated in a grand spectacle resurrecting Rome's ruined imperial stage: "At night, the entire Capitol, the Forum, the Colosseum were illuminated."[65] By isolating the ruins, Tournon reported, the archeologists enhanced the "effect of these antique monuments." They attracted the viewers' gaze, "rendered more brilliant by the taste that had prepared them" for this illumination.[66] In a letter detailing his plans, Tournon prompted Napoleon to imagine his future Rome entry following an itinerary that would take him from "the Porta del Popolo" to his new "palace." Proceeding along "the Corso," now "extended through the Forum," Napoleon would pass through "the arches of Septimus and Titus."[67]

Piranesi or Gibbon reassembled the Roman stage in their respective media. Now Napoleon's colonial administrators and technicians worked on the same project. Having spectacularly resurrected Rome's theopolitical stage for one night, they continued working until allied troops drove them out of the city. The French conquest of Rome was as short lived as that of Egypt, but in Rome, the revolutionaries-turned-imperialists invented a remarkable neo-Roman paradigm: the constellation of First and Second City of the Empire, symbolically connecting Rome and Paris, the past and the present. This geo-spatial imaginary of an imperial past/present was supposed to have a future, but it didn't. This unrealized neo-Roman future—the future of what could have been—is the very topic of the *Description de L'Égypte*.

Description: Fourier's *Res Gestae*

Founded in 1826, the Egyptian gallery of the Louvre "did not so much reflect a secure empire as it cultivated imperial desire."[68] And this is what Joseph Fourier's introduction to the *Description* did: cultivate the imperial desire—of the present and the past. It is a document about the imperial desire of the past in two senses: first, because Fourier re-creates the Egyptian Campaign or "l'expédition memorable" and its "grandeur nouvelle" in all its aspects.[69] He also does this by re-narrating the military conquests in full immediacy. That is, he tells them in the realist mode. This mode of representation involves a second aspect: Fourier rewrites the *Res Gestae*, Augustus's account of his conquests, as the great deeds of Napoleon and his men in Egypt. Richard Wagner called the Romans' realist mode of representation the "most material" and "most absolute realism," letting them "revel in concrete and open bloodthirstiness, beholding human suffering set before them in absolute physical reality."[70] This Roman realism, I argued, also inscribed the desire to be imitated in the present and the future. Fourier's Napoleonic *Res Gestae* responded to this mimetic desire.

Fourier's historical introduction, written at the dawn of the Algerian conquest, cultivated the imperial desire of the present, because this text uses the Egyptian Campaign as a blueprint for France's imperial ambitions in the immediate present. The edition I am working with is the 1820 version, "authorized" by Louis XVIII. In the introductory paragraphs, Fourier (who served as minister of justice in occupied Egypt) touched on all the central topics: Egyptian history as a history of empires; the monuments testifying to the stability of Egypt's ancient governments; the "grand events" that have taken place in the region, and the great men that it attracted (FP, ii). In short, Fourier dealt with empire-builders, empire-building, and the time of empire, elaborating on the latter topic in striking ways.

The text is caught up in the contradiction between the reality of an imperial project that lasted all but three years and Fourier's effort to convey to this project "une grandeur nouvelle" (FP, viii). In his conclusion to this history of world empires focused on Egypt, Fourier attempts to overcome this contradiction by a montage of ruin gazer scenarios. In these pages, Fourier made a surprising move, contrasting Egypt and its monumental ruins with France and Rome—imperial powers that did not leave a "trace" on Egyptian soil. Yet this contrast did not signify that France and Rome were failed imperial powers; quite to the contrary, it established France's neo-Roman credentials.

But let's start at the beginning: Fourier introduced Egypt as a country that presented "great memories" and monuments so ancient they predated the Trojan War, and yet were "still standing" (FP, i). The French invasion is one of these great memories. The historian in the service of the French Empire will continue to make reference to these two aspects: Egypt as "the theatre of one of the grandest events of modern history" (FP, l) and Egypt as the country of massive ancient monuments.

Egypt has always inspired "imperial desire" (FP, iii), Fourier wrote, and recapitulated the history of Alexandria as having begun with Alexander and Augustus and ended with Napoleon—without naming the latter. Bonaparte is hidden behind the "illustrious princes" whom Egypt attracted and who "regulate the destinies of nations" (FP, i). Throughout this text in praise of the French nation and its kings, Napoleon remains unnamed and yet visibly present. For Fourier's explicit goal is to inscribe the Egyptian Campaign into the memory of the French, an effort he pursues quite relentlessly.[71] Once Fourier actually starts to relate the military campaign, the "order of events" of this "grand enterprise" (FP, lxix and lviii), he brings Napoleon back in: "[t]he presence of the victor [*vainqueur*] of Italy" (FP, lxvi) inspired confidence in the army and his corps of engineers, archeologists, and artists.

Augustus presented himself in the *Res Gestae* as military conqueror, politician, architect, and city-builder. As I wrote in chapter 6, he retold his military and political achievements in great detail, listing his campaigns and the work done by Roman engineers in the wake of these conquests as well as his involvement in the restoration of the Roman capital. Several times, Fourier interrupts his discursive reflections on the Egyptian project with a heroic narrative about the conquest. "The history of this campaign offers a series of fast marches, combats and successes" (FP, lxx). His *récit* of the French successes changes from the past tense into the present, heightening the drama at decisive moments of the battle. This epic retelling quickly took the reader to the next stage, the success of the expedition, which becomes apparent to all: "Egypt, delivered from its oppressors, finally commences to enjoy the benefits of laws . . . the sciences . . . and of the beaux-arts" (FP, lxxii and iii). The French "military accomplishments" attracted the attention of the entire world because, like the Romans, the

French "conquered and governed with care" (FP, lxix). "[R]especting their religious and civil customs," they provided their new subjects with "durable security" (FP, lxxv and lxxii).

Fourier portrays the Egyptian Campaign as an imitation of Roman colonialism.[72] Among the imperial powers ruling Egypt, the Roman Empire was most successful. The Romans, Fourier explained, administered the country with "wisdom" (FP, xxii), because they knew how to conquer and to rule. Through their form of colonial government (with its administrative measures, including infrastructural projects), the Romans brought "progress" to their province, "[making] their subjects forget their origins" (FP, xx and xxiii). With the reign of the Arabs, all progress came to a halt: conquering "barbarians," they did not know how "to found and perpetuate empires," leaving the country in an "abject" state (FP, xxvii and vi).[73] While "Egypt conserved all of the elements of its *ancient grandeur*," these "precious germs of a new prosperity" would only evolve under the "sage and powerful government" of Europeans (FP, liv).

Egypt's ruinous state of affairs is thus once again the justification for the invasion. At its imperial meridian, Britain turned from West to East, and in the wake of the American and Haitian revolutions, France followed suit, with Fourier outlining the program of French colonialism that inspired the campaign and was meant to inspire future imperial ventures in the region. This project in the Middle East, Fourier writes, had all the advantages that any "far away colony" lacked (FP, lvi).[74] Fourier's objective was a French settler colony "offer[ing] to its new inhabitants the image of their motherland" (FP, lxv).

"Never," Fourier summed up, "had this province been governed better" (FP, lxxxix). But that was exactly Fourier's problem: all of this didn't last. The Egyptians will always remember the success of the expedition and the progress of the sciences, he hastened again to assure his readers: "no event will ever efface the memory of this" (FP, lxxvii). And the "grand work" of the *Description de L'Égypte* will replace the *grand work* that was interrupted: all of the progressive changes implemented "during the duration of the expedition" (FP, lxxviii and cxi)—the very short duration of France's colonial venture in Egypt. The *Description* itself safeguarded the future of this past because reading this "monument," many generations will remember the campaign (FP, cxlix).

This replacement of the political project by the *Description* as commemorative monument is Fourier's first strategy for overcoming the contradiction between short-term occupation and Napoleon's long-term imperial designs, the establishment of a durable lasting order on the model of the Romans. Fourier retold the conquest and asserted its success. That is, he brings back the memory of the great battles and claims that Egyptians quickly understood the benefits of this occupation (changes involving the political and legal system as well as the country's dilapidated infrastructure, following the Roman model). This is Fourier's *Res Gestae* about the "memorable actions" of Napoleon, his generals and army (FP, c). It is a text that makes Napoleon a historical figure: a man whose deeds ought to be imitated in the French imperial present and in the future.

Fourier's second strategy for overcoming this contradiction involves writing a different kind of *Res Gestae* that outlines the invaders' modernizing program and then elaborates *in the future subjunctive* on the good society that this program would have produced, *if* it had it not been interrupted. Fourier spent as much time on the depiction of this interrupted imperial future *in the irrealis* as he did on his version of the actual events, the neo-Roman success story of French conquest and rule in Egypt. Fourier assured his readers that he had witnessed these successes, including the fact that the Egyptians started to think of themselves as no longer being "foreigners to the French nation" (FP, cxix). He then approached the topic of the imperial project's interruption, untimely in his view because "only time itself would have been able to test and affirm these new institutions" (FP, cxix). Because of the enemy, not a trace of this "memorable expedition" is left (FP, cxxvi): "war reversed them suddenly and didn't leave *a single trace*" (FP, cxix; emphasis mine).

What had been achieved? The Mamelukes' "bizarre government" was "at least interrupted for three years" (FP, cxxvii). Now Egypt was again "the prey of [the Arabs'] barbarism" (FP, cxxvi). Fourier then returns to the topic of the interrupted imperial future, listing in the future subjunctive all the improvements that would have taken root if the French had stayed in Egypt and governed based on the vast knowledge of the country they had gathered and would have continued to gather. Toward the end of his introduction, Fourier returned once more to this theme, claiming that had the French stayed in Egypt, "the most desirable advantages" would have resulted (FP, cxlvi). Painting the image of a perfect colony, including the exile of the more recalcitrant Arab tribes to "the far reaches of the deserts" (FP, cxlvi), he once more concluded: "Such would today be the state of Egypt"—if the French had not been rudely interrupted (FP, cxlvii).

Interruption and "prolonged influence" or presence thus are the categories organizing Fourier's *Res Gestae*. Augustus did not doubt that he had installed a durable empire. And yet we know that Rome's imperial thinkers thought of this duration in terms of the duration before the end. In a paradoxical move, Fourier reenacted this knowledge in the last pages of his modern *Res Gestae* by portraying the Roman Empire as short lived. This strategic move contradicted what he had done earlier when he established Rome as the model for the neo-Roman Napoleonic conquerors. The trope of Egyptian stability and duration plays a central role in this move.

Let me for a brief instant take you back to Fourier's discussion of Egypt's weighty monuments and the Romans' Egyptian mimesis. Fourier claimed that the Romans learned from Egyptian monumental architecture, modeling their public buildings on the Egyptians' "durable witnesses of power" and raising Egyptian obelisks in Rome (FP, xxi and ii). He returned to this topic of Egypt's durable monuments at the end of the introduction. These "durable works" (FP, cl) were the result of the Egyptian character. Egyptians built useful and "durable" things (FP, cli), thinking their "grand public monuments" would contribute to "their empire's stability" (FP, cliii). In this the Romans imitated them.

Fourier thus opened up an enormous gap between the *vanished traces* of the French presence in Egypt and Egypt's eternal monuments, "constructed several centuries before Greek cities were founded" (FP, cl–cli). In a ruin gazer scenario with its gaze trained on the European future, Fourier then opened an equally abysmal gap between Egyptian monuments and Europe's future ruins. The Egyptian monuments witnessed "the grandeur of Tyre, Carthage, and Athens rise and vanish." People already called them "antiquities in the time of Plato," he explained, and later generations "will still admire them when, in all other places of the globe, there will be nothing left but vestiges of the buildings standing today" (FP, cli). Politically, this leads Fourier to praise the French king's efforts to maintain order in postrevolutionary France. Egypt taught us, Fourier writes, the value of laws and a "stable government" (FP, cliv). To this politics corresponds an aesthetics of "solid and durable objects," of "stability and grandeur" (FP, clv).

The trope of stability and duration is an arresting conclusion to Fourier's obsession with the sudden interruption of Napoleon's imperial project. We have seen that Fourier presented the expedition as a neo-Roman project, inspired by Rome's wise colonial venture in Egypt. Nothing in this section hinted at the idea of Rome not having had a stable government at the time. In this concluding section, Rome appears as yet another empire that did not leave a trace. Discussing Egypt's eternal ruins and the ruins of the future, Fourier claimed that discovering "on the shores of the Nile the ruins of Roman edifices is *barely possible*" (FP, cli). Napoleon's army did not leave a trace, and Rome left but a few.

Fourier thus leaves us with three temporalities: the *longue durée* of Egypt, the short *durée* of the Roman Empire, and the even shorter *durée* of the Egyptian Campaign. Napoleon's conquest of Egypt was interrupted, but the imperial mimesis begun in the sands of Egypt was resumed in Rome and then in the public squares and exhibition halls of Paris. Imperial time is the time before the empire ends—few imperial endeavors confirmed this ancient Roman knowledge in a more radical manner than this Egyptian Campaign. Act 2 of the French imitation of Rome, the era of Louis Philippe, struggled to deny this newly recovered insight. Let us return one last time to the Luxor/Paris obelisk and the obelisks that Augustus erected in front of his mausoleum, marking the beginning of a new imperial era. These obelisks, "lacking hieroglyphic inscriptions," flanked the bronze tablets with Augustus's *Res Gestae*.[75] Signs of the longevity of the Pharaohs' rule, the granite monuments testified to the Roman Empire's duration—the *longue durée* of the imperial present before its inevitable end in ruins. It was this meaning—"tremendous longevity"—that French commentators attributed to the Luxor/Paris obelisk.[76]

In 1836, six years after France had started the conquest of Algeria, the July Monarchy installed the obelisk bearing the inscription "Recentis Gloriae ad nilum Armis Partae."[77] With this reference to the Egyptian Campaign, the installation of the obelisk turned an interrupted imperial venture into act 1 of the French state's neo-Roman mimesis, connecting the recent experience of a sudden imperial ending to the *longue durée* of the Roman imperial present and the deep time of ancient Egypt. Virgil had founded Augustan Rome on the pre-Arcadian ruins at Rome's very center. The French state placed an obelisk at the center of its imperial metropolis. A neo-Roman gesture, this massive object fetishistically disavowed the end of a conquest, leaving no trace among the Roman ruins on the Egyptian stage.

ELEVEN

Repetition of a Repetition: The Conquest of Algeria, and Louis Bertrand's North African *Latinité*

Introduction: On the Carthaginian Stage

In the wake of the French Army's occupation of Rome, J. M. W. Turner painted *Snow Storm: Hannibal and His Army Crossing the Alps* (1812). Toward the end of the Napoleonic Wars, Turner completed his Carthaginian allegories *Dido Building Carthage, or the Rise of the Carthaginian Empire* (1815), and *The Decline of the Carthaginian Empire* (1817), inspired by Claude Lorrain's Aeneas and Dido narratives.[1] Having witnessed "the spectacle" of rise and fall, Turner captured in *The Decline* the moment before the city's destruction, the painting's architectural composition framing Carthage's harbor as a stage set.[2] Set at a dramatic angle, a pictorial convention going back to Vitruvius's reflections on the stage-building, the canvas invites the viewer to step onto the Carthaginian stage, entering the painting from the lower left, and to join the group of spectators mesmerized by the setting sun (figure 11.1).[3] At the same time, the beholder is kept in place in front of the painting, her eyes caught by the radiant golden sun setting over the luxurious cityscape. Carthage's majestic white marble architecture that the rising sun lit up in muted tones in *Dido Building Carthage* now begins to fall under the encroaching shadows of the empire's death. With this dra-

11.1 J. M. W. Turner, *The Decline of the Carthaginian Empire* (1817).

matic staging and its "'ensanguined'" sunset, Turner transmitted both the violence of the Polybian scenario and its theatrical aesthetics.[4]

Anti-Napoleonic in spirit, the Carthage pictures' "classical architecture" also alludes to the British Empire.[5] Critics "have long suspected that he intended the audience to draw a parallel between the fate of Carthage and the prospects of a newly victorious Britain."[6] With *Regulus* (1828), Turner revisited the Carthaginian scene, positioning the spectator right at the edge of his world-historical stage (chapter 3). At the end of this chapter, we will journey back to the ruined Carthaginian stage with another architectural fantasy about Dido's city.

Scholars of imperialism emphasize the nexus of territorial conquest and scientific exploration. Military conquest is the phase when ideas and images become ever more precise. I analyze this initial phase as the moment that activates the imitation of Europe's "archetypal" empire and its claim to "have conquered the world."[7] This process of fixing Roman images begins with the tracking of Roman ruins and their symbolic conquest. The mimetic act that took place in Egypt was repeated by the French military on Algerian territory, their mimetic experts working again with Rome's "world-symbols."[8] None of this Algerian activity is original; it is a repetition of a repetition.

What is original in the Algerian case is the theo-politics of Louis Bertrand (1866–1941). Having taught in Algeria from 1891 to 1900, Bertrand came to be known as one of the theorists of African *Latinité*. The "organic intellectual" of Algerian settlers, Bertrand never wavered in his support of French imperialism.[9] The second part of this chapter concentrates on Bertrand's novels, essays, and lectures, texts in which he keeps returning to his political epiphany in the Roman ruins of Tipasa: the discovery that the ancient (Christian) Roman past was alive on African soil.

Among the last versions of this theo-political experience in the Roman ruins of Tipasa is Bertrand's 1930 speech in Carthage at the occasion of the centenary of the conquest of Algeria.[10] Bertrand, who arrived in Algeria with an *agrégation* in Classics, created North Africa's Roman ruins in his texts as theo-political sites where the Roman past was resurrected, and the postconquest work of French archeologists played a central role in the development of his political and aesthetic project.

Bertrand's project of African *Latinité* was as deeply anchored in this definition of North African Muslims as the French Empire's enemy as it was in his radical conservative critique of late nineteenth-century capitalist-urban modernity.[11] Decadent France needed to be re-barbarized, and Algeria was the terrain where this would happen because here, French soldiers and *colons* were engaged in fighting their barbarian enemy. Bertrand's African *Latinité* was predicated on the idea that the imperial present was repeating, had to repeat, the Roman past. The reign of "the Arab" led to "misery, anarchy, and barbarism," Bertrand wrote in 1905, but it was nothing more than the "momentary eclipse of Rome"—a brief episode between Roman and neo-Roman Empire.[12]

Conquering Roman Algeria, 1830

In Bertrand's view, the mission of the French Empire in North Africa was to recuperate this ancient Roman space, save it from being "Orientalized" in the same way Rome wrested the area from the East when it attacked Carthage. His own mission was the reawakening of the spirit of the Roman Empire *and* early Christianity. As I wrote above, North Africa's Roman ruins were the sites of this theo-political resurrection. Among these sites, none were more important to Bertrand than "Roman Carthage."[13] Tipasa was his Gibbonian site, the site of the genesis of his life's work in a moment of revelation surrounded by Rome's ruins, but the ruined Roman stage of Carthage, Bertrand hoped, would become the French Empire's North African Rome.

Many of the military men who arrived in Algeria in 1830 shared Bertrand's view of this neo-Roman mission. Thirty years after Napoleon's soldiers had left Egypt and sixteen years after the occupation of Rome, the French Army landed in Algeria, capturing Algiers in 1830 and Kabylia in 1857. In 1848 the French government declared Algeria a region of France, keeping it under military administration until 1871, the year of the Kabyle rebellion and end of the Second Empire.[14] In 1894, Paul Monceau declared: "Roman Africa has . . . become French territory."[15]

As Patricia Lorcin and others have argued, Algeria's Roman past played a crucial role in the history of French rule in Algeria, both as model and as justification. As they conquered the country, the army advanced along Roman roads, forts, cisterns, and aqueducts, repeating the Romans' conquest by using their infrastructure.[16] Once Algiers was captured, the French king ordered troops "to complete the conquest of Algeria in order to return to the civilized world the bank of the Mediterranean, which had been in the grip of anarchy and barbaric methods since the fall of the Roman Empire."[17]

From the vantage point of Algeria, the Egyptian Campaign was "the initial step" in creating an association between imperial France and imperial Rome in Africa.[18] The scientists of Napoleon's Campaign had uncovered the monumental architectural remains of the Roman Empire in Egypt. In 1840 and 1842, French architects conducted the first "inventories" of historical monuments in Algeria.[19] These officers and scientists dug deep into Algeria's Roman past in order to erase the Arab and Berber presence. Like Napoleon's experts, they used these Roman traces to justify their conquest as much as they used the *topos* of Islamic devastation and stagnation.[20] With its triumphal arch, Djemila was one of the main sites of Algeria's Roman-ness explored since 1839. And excavations of the Roman cities of Tébessa, Lambaesis, and Timgad, "home to the Roman Empire's third legion," were undertaken early on.[21]

The conquerors of Algeria emulated the *Description*, setting up commissions to study the Roman presence.[22] The official equivalent to the *Description*'s volume on Egyptian antiquities was *Monuments Antiques de L'Algérie* (1901) by Stéphane Gsell, an archeologist.[23] Like his Napoleonic predecessors, Gsell, tracing pre-Roman, pre-Christian Roman, and Christian Roman ruins, tirelessly pointed out that many of the cities, fortresses, and churches were destroyed by Arab-Muslim invaders or "barbarians."[24]

Arriving in Algeria in 1890 from Rome, Gsell published *L'Algérie dans l'Antiquité (1903)*. This history about Rome's presence concluded with the Arab invasions and the end of the Roman Empire in the seventh century. Claiming ancient Algeria for the West, Gsell painted a "rosy picture" of the Roman conquest, while portraying the Arab invasion as a "'great shipwreck.'"[25] Roman civilization vanished except for the "immense ruins and

11.2 Stéphane Gsell, *Monuments Antiques de L'Algérie*, photo, Arch of Caracalla at Tebessa.

the memory of the power of the 'roumis' [Romans]."[26] What the French encountered in 1830 was a "barbaric country," a "'corpse'" in need of resuscitation.[27] In Gsell's view, studying Rome's remnants in Algeria taught salutary lessons, chief among them the Romans' failure to build a military infrastructure in Algeria strong enough to block "the roads for invaders."[28]

The two volumes of Gsell's *Monuments Antiques de L'Algérie* delineated the imperial fortifications and triumphal arches built across the African province (figure 11.2). Gsell's early predecessors were the president of the

Algerian Historical Society, who worked on archeological digs "toward the uncovering of Algeria's past," and Amable Ravoisie, who traveled along the northern coast of Africa exploring ancient sites, including Caracalla's triumphal arch in Djemila. While Ravoisie's exceedingly precise "graphic restoration[s]" resembled those of the *Description de L'Égypte*, they were of a purer classicist spirit, their form thus accentuating "the parallel between the glory of the [Algerian] conquest and that of Rome."[29]

As early as 1837 the scholars at the Algerian *Académie* prepared instructions for archeological, historical, and geographical research. Like Napoleon's scientists, they mapped French space onto Algeria using its Roman past, frequently relying on classical texts. Classicists like Gaston Boissier addressed the issue of native policy going back to Sallust (and his Jurgurthine Wars); Edouard Lapène thought that Tacitus's text on *Germania*'s barbarian tribes might explain Algeria's Berbers.[30] By 1850, "the meshing together of Rome and France, as different stages of the same oeuvre, was well-established."[31] In 1900, copies of the classical antiquities collected by Gsell and his precursors were displayed in the Palace of Algeria of the Universal Exhibition in Paris.[32]

Rediscovering the Barbarian: Tocqueville's Roman Model

Appropriating Algeria for Western civilization, Rome's legacy also revived the idea of the barbarian. Alexis de Tocqueville became an important voice in the debate about how to conquer and rule Algeria, with his essays and letters addressing the question of direct or indirect rule. Advocating a mixture of the two, he claimed in 1837 that this policy (together with separate legal systems for settlers and natives of Algeria) would one day succeed in "amalgamating the two races."[33] The Roman example proved the efficiency of this mixed rule. When the Western empire fell, Tocqueville wrote, two kinds of laws were in place, "barbarian laws" for "the barbarian" and "Roman laws" for Romans.[34] This Roman system should be imitated "because it is the only way we can hope safely to negotiate the transitional period that elapses before two people of different civilizations can manage to refound themselves as a single whole."[35] Tocqueville operated with the distinction of Romanizable and non-Romanizable "barbarian[s]."[36] He excluded the Kabyle, who ferociously resisted conquest as barely having "reached the first stage of civilization."[37]

At the height of the debate about how to begin the transition from conquest to domination, Tocqueville intervened again, emphasizing the urgency of the situation: "time is pressing."[38] Starting with the specter of decline, Tocqueville argued against leaving Algeria. He repeated the logic at the core of empire: imperial powers must keep expanding. If they do not pursue this course, they "visibly enter[ed] the period of [their] decline."[39] He again points to the Roman example, specifically the way they mixed "domination and colonization" by simultaneously seizing the central government and establishing settlements.[40]

Taking recourse to the Roman model, Tocqueville thus outlined a program for an Algerian settler colony at a moment when French forces were engaged in brutal warfare with Abdel Kader, their Muslim enemy and leader of the army of recently united Arab tribes. Haunted by the possibility of Algiers "fall[ing] back into the hands of the Muslims," Tocqueville called for brutal warfare against "Muslim barbarians."[41] Arriving in Algeria decades after this brutal conquest, Bertrand remained committed to Tocqueville's militant views about Algeria's two cultures and the country's "barbarian" inhabitants. He described his discovery of the country as a twofold journey. One took him through the streets of Algiers, where he shed his Orientalism, discovering Algerians as Muslim and Latin settlers as neo-Roman barbarians. The other journey took him through the country's ruin sites, making him aware of the country's deep Roman past. Let us start with the latter.

Bertrand's Discovery of Neo-Roman Algeria

In the spring of 1895, Bertrand and Gsell visited the ruins of Tipasa, the former Roman *colonia* and ancient Phoenician town. Gsell was at the time in charge of excavations at Tipasa and Timgad, the "Pompei Africaine."[42] Bertrand later told his French Carthaginian audience that he had followed "this track of ruins" since his arrival in Algeria in 1891.[43] Spreading across ancient Africa "from Leptis Magna to Tangiers," these Roman sites had been or were being excavated at the time when Bertrand began to write.[44] Bertrand continued this work of making the ruined Roman foundations of French imperialism visible in his own medium and with his own resurrectional techniques.

Bertrand also befriended Charles Lavigerie, archbishop of Carthage and Algiers who, fond of the ruins of the early North African church, dreamt of re-creating Augustine's Roman Church.[45] To Lavigerie and Bertrand, the ruins of the Roman Empire and the early church, visual reminders of Algeria's Roman past, became signs of France's Catholic mission to recivilize Roman Africa.[46] They also shared their disdain of the French state's official policy of tolerance toward Islam.[47] Bertrand thus believed in the power of

French imperialism to resurrect ancient Rome and early Christianity. He also firmly believed that this resurrection had the power to delay the empire's end. "Let us remain Latins to preserve the empire" [*Restons des Latins pour garder L'Empire*] was Bertrand's admonition to his countrymen.[48] Finally, as I mentioned above, he was also convinced that the conquest of this "grand classical landscape" would in turn help resurrect the French metropole.

Algerian *fin-de-siècle*: The Enemy and the Re-Barbarization of the French

Gustave Flaubert, author of *Salammbo* (1862) and avid reader of Michelet's *Histoire Romaine*, with its lurid chapters on the Punic Wars, was one of Bertrand's models.[49] Flaubert's ambition to resurrect the Carthaginian past was born out of his anti-modern affect. It was his aversion against modern life that motivated him to resuscitate Carthage. This anti-modern affect strongly resonated with Bertrand's own. His friend Maurice Barrès referred to the petit-bourgeois of the *fin-de-siècle* French republic as lifeless "barbarians."[50] Bertrand discovered the "man of instinct and passion," whom Barrès was longing for, in Algeria's Latin *colons*.[51] More precisely, he found in the French, Italian, and Spanish settlers of Algeria new Romans, virile and re-barbarized. Their Algeria was a different modernity, one that had not broken with the rural past and its traditions. Coexisting with the country's indigenous *barbarians*, these settlers lived a life on high alert. This colonial encounter would *re-barbarize* Latin settlers, creating an entirely "new race" of people, conquerors stirred into action.[52]

Moreover, the contact with the Muslim enemy would eventually re-barbarize the Parisian petit-bourgeois as well.[53] Bertrand saw his neo-Roman utopia realized in Italy when Mussolini came to power.[54] In Bertrand's texts, scenes of bloody combat are missing, but images of the *enemy*—the Muslim *barbarian*—are omnipresent. Arthur de Gobineau, the author of *The Inequality of Human Races* (1853–1855), who reawakened the specter of *the barbarian*, was as strong an influence on Bertrand as Barrès and Flaubert. Patricia Lorcin shows Bertrand adopting Gobineau's terminology of *barbarism*, his definition of race and belief in racial inequality and, finally, his core thesis that intermingling with the colonized would lead to degeneration.[55]

While reinvigorated by Algeria's Muslim population, Latin Africans had to keep separate from them. This was the lesson that Bertrand drew from reading Gobineau's inquiry into the causes of Rome's fall. "[W]e have seen the fall of many empires," Gobineau stated, and we never tire of being fascinated by the reasons for their demise.[56] He rewrote the Roman ruin gazer scenario with a biological twist, his book a search for this "principle of death."[57] Gobineau's criterion of a race's "vitality" is its "aptitude for conquest and domination."[58] Rome was such a race, driven by a strong "original impulse."[59] So what is Gobineau's answer to the secret of imperial decline?

Decline set in when unequal races started to mix—and this was the cardinal mistake committed by the Romans.[60] This process is gradual. For a while the institutions, customs, and laws of the "dead master" will continue to exist, "sapless and rotten."[61] For a while, this civilization will still seem alive: "as long as even their shadows remain, the building stands, the body seems to have a soul, the pale ghost walks."[62] But eventually a point is reached when "[n]othing remains: the civilization is dead,"[63] and a vast landscape of ruins is born. Gobineau's story was uncompromising: European civilization with its "Germanic" core will repeat Rome's death.[64] It will do so because, like the Roman Empire, this imperial civilization included more than it absorbed. The "sad end" of this civilization (superior with respect to knowledge and, therefore, conquest, but inferior with respect to the arts) will be "inevitable."[65] And then Gobineau revived Volney's traveler: "When our day has drawn to its close, and the ruins of our towns and monuments cover the face of the land," Gobineau wrote, "the traveller will discover nothing, in the forests and marshes that will skirt the Thames, the Seine, and the Rhine, to rival the gorgeous ruins of Philae, Nineveh, Athens."[66]

Seeking to resurrect decaying Parisian culture from its periphery, Bertrand resisted this scenario and Gobineau's iron law of ruin. Arguing that "[c]ivilization is incommunicable," Gobineau used the example of Algeria.[67] But there is another part of Gobineau's argument that Bertrand accepted. "[T]he savage races of today have always been savage," Gobineau maintained, and "will continue to be so, until the day when they vanish."[68] The Greco-Roman concept of the barbarian was still accurate in the modern age: "*Barbarians*, this name that remained as testimony to a justified distrust."[69] The eternal existence of the barbarian enemy is exactly what Bertrand thought he understood in Algeria. The territory of Latin Africa—"the old Mediterranean civilization of the Greco-Latin era"—represented a place where all Mediterranean races mingled with "barbarian" natives; this terrain would always be subject to an imperial master.[70] Centuries ago the Romans were here; now it was the French.

Having left France, Bertrand suddenly found himself "in an imperial country" where he witnessed the renaissance of "l'Afrique latine."[71] The people of Western Europe, including France, were decadent, while the French in Algeria found themselves in close contact with "rude men" [*hommes rudes*] and were in the process of "reinvigoration."[72] Empires need their barbarians—that was part of Gobineau's and Bertrand's neo-Roman story.[73]

Bertrand's view of Algeria and its barbarians changed between his arrival in the country and the writing of his memoirs. At first, there was the fascination of Orientalism. On nightly walks through Algiers searching for "barbarie" and "sauvagerie," he lived his first encounters in the register of Flaubert's feverish visions.[74] Later, Bertrand criticized the "vieux mirage oriental" of Eugène Fromentin, Orientalist author and painter, as outmoded.[75] And yet, modern France had gone through a process of disenchantment that made Bertrand long for Algeria. Bertrand's ambivalent "murder of Romantic orientalism" leaves him with the Orientalist excess of his figure of the barbarian.[76] In his 1936 memoirs, Bertrand claimed: "Nothing is more complicated than the barbarian."[77] He was as fascinated with Algeria's "savages" as he was repulsed by them, praising them for their "vigor" and brutality.[78]

Immersed into these "black Semitic depths," the contact with Algeria's natives had re-barbarized the settlers of Algeria.[79] The opposite of their French compatriots, they were men of violent instincts and passion. This much is familiar to us. Here is what is new: in these simple workers, artisans, soldiers, and merchants, Bertrand rediscovered "the man of the classical epochs"—they reminded him of the men he had read about in Virgil's *Aeneid*.[80] Maurice Barrès's elitist, Nietzschean ideal thus found its paradoxical incarnation in Algeria's *colons*. Here, in neo-Roman *fin-de-siècle* Algeria, Bertrand discovered Barrès's Parisian barbarian, who embodied decline after a century of democracy, metamorphosed into his contrary: a rejuvenated barbarian Frenchman.

What accounted for this transformation was not only the close contact with Algeria's indigenous barbarians and their coarse lives, but also the *colons'* renewed sense of "the enemy."[81] Framing his Algerian experience as the reaction of the Alsatian who always had a better sense of the enemy than his fellow-countrymen, he asserted in his memoirs: "As soon as I had arrived [in Algiers] *I sensed the Enemy* [in the Algerian native]."[82]

Rediscovering the Roman concept of the barbarian as enemy, Bertrand traces his awakening to Algeria's dangers in some detail. Convinced that the "African Muslims" belonged to a dying civilization, Bertrand saw them at first as mere decorative figures against an exotic backdrop.[83] With time, he understood that the Muslim population's patience was not a sign of decline but veiled a dangerous enemy—one "who doesn't forget, who doesn't forgive, and who does not lay down his weapons."[84] In the long term, they would do what all barbarians had done: take revenge. Bertrand concluded these reflections on the enemy with a statement of outright antipathy. Having become aware of their "latent hostility" and the "backward state of barbarism" in which they languished, he turned toward the "people of his own race."[85]

Tipasa: Bertrand's Epiphany

All this Bertrand realized while studying the "Roman ruins so plentiful in Algeria," proof that this "new Africa has deep roots in the past."[86] And indeed, what better place to escape modernity's banality than the sites of antiquity's ruins? But Bertrand insisted that he had left all Romanticism, all Orientalism behind. While metropolitan Paris reveled in the Orientalist dioramas and "transported indigènes" in the Palace of Algerian Attractions at the Universal Exhibition, Bertrand had unmasked the colony's exotic appearance, uncovering its hostile essence.[87]

As I mentioned above, Bertrand told the story of his visit to Tipasa several times, and he did so with varying emphases. In *Jardin de la mort* (1903), he insisted that his love for Africa's Roman ruins did not mean that he had fallen back into Chateaubriand's "cult of Death and Ruins."[88] Retelling his conversion from Romantic Orientalist to neo-Roman colonizer, he claimed sobriety and a clear gaze. On the one hand, this vision resulted from a better understanding of Africa's deep Roman roots; on the other hand, it was the effect of Roman ruins being better preserved here than anywhere else. North African ruins were more "saisissantes"—a word we might want to translate conventionally as "more striking." But it also hints at the idea that these ruin sites have a superior power to seize or capture the spectator's eye and imagination.[89]

Shell-shocked by the French Revolution, the "cannibals" dancing in the streets of Paris, Chateaubriand, son of a Breton slave trader, decided to travel.[90] Serving as Napoleon's ambassador in Rome, he arrived at Carthage in 1807.[91] As he surveyed the peninsula from the Byrsa, the city's acropolis, Chateaubriand's thoughts went to Dido as he "contemplate[s] the vast plains where the legions of Hannibal, of Scipio, of Caesar are buried."[92] Then, his gaze turning inward, Chateaubriand writes: "[T]he terrible vandals, the light-footed Moors passed one after the other through [the theater of] my memory, which offered to me, as the last *tableau*, Saint Louis, expiring in the ruins of Carthage."[93] Everything perishes, and the only thing that counts is the memory of the Catholic crusader.

Europe's old politico-theological order, Chateaubriand believed, could only be mourned, not resurrected. Bertrand disagreed. In Chateaubriand's text, the Carthaginian ruin site is the setting for his theater of memory, the Roman past nothing but scraps of fleeting memories. In Bertrand's texts, the Roman ruin sites are solid, real, and intensely alive, testifying to the "mysterious influence of the old Latin imperialism."[94] The conquest of Algeria and Tunisia was a "re-taking of possession" in the spirit of this ancient Latin imperialism, alive in the monumental ruinscapes it left behind.[95] In contrast, the Arab conquest proved "ephemeral," leaving nothing behind but a "fragile décor."[96]

All this Bertrand began to understand at Tipasa when he arrived with Gsell in the spring of 1895.[97] As I mentioned above, Bertrand told the story of his visit with varying emphases. In *Jardin de la mort* (1903), he insisted that his love for Africa's Roman ruins did not mean that he had fallen back into the Romantics' cult of death and ruins. His epiphany was of a different kind. In his 1930 address at the Eucharistic Congress in French-occupied Tunisia, he formulated the experience in religious terms as a "vision," a "revelation," even.[98]

What was this revelation? Wandering through the ruined graveyards of Tipasa, Bertrand communicated "with a very ancient world," realizing that the ancient Christian Roman past was alive on African soil.[99] Looking at the ruins that Gsell had recently unearthed, Bertrand saw an "unforgettable spectacle," the image of a ruined city fully restored in his mind's eye as "an African municipality in the first centuries of Christianity."[100] In this Volneyan vision, the ancient Christians who once prayed in the cathedrals lining the African coastline came alive in his imagination. The vision of the eleventh-century Pope Leo IX, Bertrand told his audience assembled in modern Carthage to celebrate French colonialism, finally had become reality: Carthage had been resurrected.[101]

Bertrand's right-wing theo-politics with its story of ruins and resurrection represents one of the ways in which French colonialism entwined its fate with Rome in the wake of Napoleon's "grand project" in Egypt, and the occupation of the Roman stage. "The resurrection," Bertrand declared in 1930 in Carthage, "is accomplished."[102] After defeating their Carthaginian enemy, Bertrand reminded his audience, the Roman Empire became a world power. Their world empire, the Romans thought, was without "precedent."[103] Bertrand envisioned the unprecedented rise of a neo-Roman French Empire in the same ancient Punic territory.

Performing on the Ruined Stage, or Fighting to the End

As I mentioned above, Bertrand thought of the colonizing of Algeria and Tunisia as a French reconquest. In 1905 Bertrand declared that "this retaking of possession is definitive."[104] Yet he also wrote: "Whatever happens, we have to persuade ourselves more and more [that this is the case]."[105] Decades after the conquest of Algeria and the army's bloody battles with Algerians, the danger of losing the empire to the heirs of Abdel Kader remained alive. What was Bertrand's answer to the question of how to "maintain" a French Empire "in Africa"?[106] Recall Bertrand's admonition to his countrymen: "Let us remain Latins in order to preserve the empire!"[107] To Bertrand, this meant first and foremost fighting the Enemy. Conquest is a never-ending struggle between *re-barbarized* Latins and the indigenous "Barbarian."[108] Second, this fight against barbarians repeated the Romans' struggles: "Faced with our domination the Maroccan's attitude," Bertrand wrote in 1921, one year into the so-called Rif War, "is that of the Numidian king confronted by Romans."[109]

This unending conquest took place on the solid terrain of North Africa's deep and enduring Roman foundations. Archeological excavations helped us "to become conscious of our heritage" and "the Empire's expanse and depth."[110] Bertrand's metaphors reinforce this idea of the neo-Roman project's enduring foundations. The "chain" of ruined Roman towns in Northern Africa was the Roman "armature of the old African soil."[111] While Africa might not be "Latin in its vertebrae and bone marrow," this skeletal armature proved how deeply this territory had been penetrated by "la latinité."[112]

From the point of view of this *Algerianiste*, the country appeared as an "empty space, an abandoned Latin property," covered with Roman ruins.[113] Since the Roman Empire, nothing has "moved" in these Roman ruinscapes.[114] The Berbers crossing this ancient terrain, he thought, unconsciously "perpetuate the gestures and the thoughts of the ancient men who created them."[115] In these nomads dressed in white, the Roman Empire's "*gens togata*" survived.[116]

When Bertrand looked at these ruin sites, they turned into stage sets, sites of a theater where the same actors kept performing the same actions and plots. Moroccans were Numidians, and Algeria's settlers were Latins, heirs of Rome still fighting the same rebels: "The dramas of the past repeat themselves in those of the present."[117] Walking through these Roman ruins taught him yet another lesson: "the prime causes [causes primitives] still operate behind contemporary events."[118] The "causes" that drove the action now and then were the laws about race, about imperial masters and their subjects, that Bertrand had gleaned from his reading of Gobineau. Bertrand never tired of asserting that the ancient Roman-Christian territory of North Africa had to be defended: "Here we are the masters: here we have to remain masters."[119]

The trope of the barbarian avenger thus reappears once again in the ruins of the Roman Empire—this time in the guise of North Africa's Muslims. Bertrand's politics and resurrectional aesthetics rested on the idea that the legions of Scipio and Hannibal's hordes never vanished, that the same causes drove the same plots, that the stage was still the same stage. Bertrand wanted his readers to see the Roman "background" behind the "scene" of the present.[120] The Arab or Ottoman presence in North Africa amounted to nothing but flimsy stage sets, the "Islamic décor."[121] The true stage of the empire was North Africa's ruined Roman stage.[122]

The Roman Empire thus had been resurrected, but like all empires, this new French Empire on African territory had to be maintained with care—as long as it lasts, for the time that remains: *Restons des Latins pour guarder l'Empire*. As I wrote above, to Bertrand, being Latin translated first and foremost into being prepared to fight the barbarian enemy. This antagonism was the essence of the colonial situation. "Those who live on the territory of Islam," Bertrand wrote in his *Sens de L'Ennemi*, "have to be constantly on guard."[123] For, he continued, "one never knows when the [next] massacre will begin."[124] The trope of the barbarian avenger thus reappears once again in the ruins of the Roman Empire—the ancient figure of Hannibal in the guise of Algerian and Tunisian Muslims.

Bertrand "used religion" as legitimation.[125] What merits pointing out once more is that Bertrand's neo-Roman theo-politics was of the most militant, most belligerent kind. Like Lavigerie, he referred often to Augustine, Berber, and Bishop of Hippo (a city in Roman Numidia and modern Algeria). Yet the theologian whom he emphasized in his 1930 Carthage speech was Tertullian, the militant "author of the *Apologeticum*."[126] To Tertullian, the Roman Empire and its emperor mattered because it had the function of the *katechon*: fighting the armies of the antichrist, it delayed the Second Coming of Christ and, thus, the end (chapter 5). In Bertrand's militant theo-politics, the Roman Empire was still the *katechon*, and in Islam he had discovered the new face of the antichrist.

Reconstruct Carthage!

Ancient Rome and neo-Roman France was the empire of Western civilization, Bertrand believed, and Islam was the "barbarity" of the Asiatic East.[127] There was only one "lesson" to be drawn from the ruined triumphal arches of the ancient cities of Timgad and Djemila, Bertrand wrote in his autobiography (1936): "We need to maintain the *Arc de triomphe*!"[128] While Michelet did not think that Rome was a model for the modern age, he was nevertheless carried away by Rome's defeat of Carthage, motivated by a kind of anti-Semitic anti-capitalism that led him to identify Carthage with London.[129] Dido's perverse Semitic world of trade and rapacious colonialism, Michelet thought, deserved to die, and he looked with deep satisfaction—and a measure of horror—at the unprecedented devastation of decadent Carthage.[130] To Bertrand too, Carthage mattered more than any other North African site because here Rome saved the West from becoming "orientalized."[131] On this ancient terrain, history endlessly repeats itself. The "same struggles await us at Carthage," the same "actors" and the same "dramas."[132]

Urban designers remade Rome into the Napoleonic Empire's Second City. Describing the view from the Byrsa, Carthage's acropolis, Bertrand proposed in 1921 to "resuscitate Carthage."[133] He meant this in the most literal sense. The excellent work of the military, the archeologists, the historians—all of their books, their descriptions, and images rendering the picture of North Africa's Roman ruins "more precise"—will never convey the true "spectacle" of these cities.[134] To achieve this effect, the existing ruin sites—desolate "voids" or dead archeological sites whose ruins were "scraped to the bone" and "reduced to a skeletal condition"—had to be restored.[135] Above all, the French Empire needed Roman Carthage restored. Only a fully restored Carthage would represent Latin Africa to the future visitors as vibrantly alive.

Bertrand's programmatic essays in *La Revue des Deux Mondes* 1920 and 1921 demonstrate that this desire to rebuild Carthage involved more than the political-aesthetic project of remaking Carthage for "our occidental imaginations."[136] Neo-Roman Africa needed its own ruined Roman stage, its own theo-political center. The Arab invaders' white city was made of materials that did not endure; turned inward, it was the architectural materialization of Islamic "particularism"—a "dead" city.[137] Roman Africa's golden city was made of stone; "open like the Empire," it was "dominating, conquering, legislative"—the city of Roman and neo-Roman sovereignty.[138] "Re-taking possession" of Carthage's ancient Roman stage would create the most beautiful of Northern Africa's "golden cities"—a neo-Roman city eclipsing "Islam's white cities."[139]

How did Bertrand envision this new African Rome? Did he have Turner's golden city in mind, the way the painter depicted it in *Dido Building Carthage or The Rise of the Carthaginian Empire*? Neglected after years of archeological excavations, Bertrand wrote, the ruins of "Dido's hill" presented a desolate sight.[140] Encircled by "neo-mauresques" villas, the ancient core of Carthage was surrounded by a modern city whose suburbs turned the entire Punic peninsula into a shabby "banlieue nicoise."[141] Bertrand wanted the French state to transform the ancient city into a museum encircled by new "Roman-style villas" and "real archeological reconstitutions."[142] Why not reconstruct an amphitheater? After all, did not Septimus Severus replicate Carthaginian building in his Roman palace?

These were not architectural "fantasies" but suggestions for refashioning modern Carthage as "analogous" to Rome with its "islands of ancient ruins."[143] To achieve this effect, the ancient city ruins would have to be fully restored. In Bertrand's mind, this could easily be done. Carthage's theater and its scene-building, for instance, could easily be reassembled. If we execute these proposals, Bertrand wrote, we will succeed in "our mission to resuscitate" Roman Carthage.[144] Imagine the colossal statues of Victory reinstalled on the Byrsa, Bertrand prodded his readers, their "vast wings spread out," dominating the ancient hill sung by Virgil.

Conclusion

Toward the end of his long life as a literary author closely connected to the French Catholic right, Bertrand attended a Nazi Party rally in Nuremberg and a conference on colonialism in fascist Italy in 1938. Spanning the period from 1830 to 1930, this chapter extended into the era when the imperial thinkers of Italian fascism reinvented *romanità*. With the next chapter, we will revisit the Napoleonic Wars from the perspective of Germania's barbarians.

TWELVE

Maori in Europe: Ruin Gazing and Scopic Mastery

Introduction

In 1938, the author of a German article asked his readers to imagine the following situation: an inhabitant of one of the islands in the South Pacific happens to come upon reports about Europeans polemicizing about the Spanish Civil War. Skimming the material, this islander first accepts that humanitarian virtue seems to be on the republican side, while Franco's allies are barbarians. Yet, as he continues reading, the Pacific Islander becomes more and more confused about this issue of who is and who is not a barbarian, and gradually feels his longing for Europe evaporate. Pacific Islanders, he concludes, are the better humans.

The author of this piece on the Spanish Civil War is Joseph Goebbels, the Nazi with a doctorate from the University of Heidelberg.[1] Having been trained by the art historian Friedrich Gundolf, it is conceivable that Goebbels heard about Denis Diderot's Orou, the fictional Tahitian translator who criticized imperialist Europe. We do know that Goebbels was acquainted with the work of Emil Nolde, the painter and Nazi sympathizer. In 1913–1914, Nolde participated in an expedition to the German colony of New Guinea, financed by the *Reichskolonialamt*.[2] Upon his return, he produced his South Sea paintings, among them *Neu-Guinea-Wilde* (*New Guinea Savages*) (1915) (figure 12.1). Diderot's Orou was a philosopher of peace. Nolde's New Guineans are warriors. On a boat with Maori, Nolde believed himself in the company

12.1 Emil Nolde, *Neu-Guinea-Wilde* (New Guinea Savages), Painting, 1915. © Nolde Stiftung Seebüll. 73 × 100.5 cm (Wvz. Urban 669).

of "cannibals," experiencing their stares as potentially lethal.[3] The thick black outlines that Nolde added to his vibrant color scheme distinguish *New Guinea Savages*, introducing a threatening dimension further accentuated by the central figure locking the beholder in his fierce gaze.[4] The Maori had rebelled against British authority in the 1840s, and Nolde's frontal composition, in which the threatening warrior faces the onlooker, might well be one of the afterimages of these rebellions.[5]

In the wake of Volney's, Forster's, and Gibbon's texts on Cook's voyages, the Maori or New Zealander emerged, somewhat counterintuitively, as one of the iconic ruin gazers of the nineteenth and twentieth centuries. These depictions of the South Pacific Islander, the modern age's cipher of the neo-Roman "barbarian," vacillate between noble savage and savage warrior. Using the most iconic example, Gustave Doré's New Zealander, gazing at the ruins of London, I want to conclude part 3 with a few remarks on the scopic configurations of power in the neo-Roman scenarios. It was T. B. Macaulay, the British historian and colonial administrator, who invented this enduring image of the New Zealander in 1840.[6] Commenting on the strength of Catholicism, Macaulay observed that "it may still exist in undiminished vigor when some traveler from New Zealand shall, in the midst of a vast solitude, take his stand on a broken arch of London Bridge

12.2 Gustave Doré, *The New Zealander* (1872).

to sketch the ruins of St. Paul."[7] In the journal that he kept on his trip to Italy in 1838, Macaulay again "looks at Rome but thinks of London": "Yet—to indulge in a sort of reflection which I often fall into here, the day may come when London, then dwindled to the dimensions of St. Martin's and supported in its decay by the expenditure of wealthy Patagonians and New Zealanders may have no more important questions to decide [than the wording on the tomb of a baker's wife]."[8]

Attuned to Volney's suggestion to imagine a future *visitor like myself* sitting on the shores of the Thames, Macaulay reversed Volney's scene at Palmyra: in Macaulay's scenario, it is the non-European from the (still) colonized world who is overlooking London's ruins. Rendered by Gustave Doré in 1872, Macaulay's Maori brings to mind a young English gentleman on his Grand Tour, sketching pad and pencil in hand, as he surveys the antique sight, with the ruins of the European metropolis spread out before him like a stage set.

Successors to Piranesi, the artists who accompanied Napoleon to Egypt painted similar figures, often inscribing their own gaze at the ruined monuments. *Vue générale du tombeau d'Osymandyas* is such an example. The engraving is centered on the ruin itself; in the lower left corner, one of the French explorers points at the tomb, while the other works on a sketchbook that he is holding in his hands. Doré structures the trajectory of the beholder's gaze differently, by moving the dark figure of the New Zealander toward the center of the image, and centering the ruins of the city on Saint Paul's Cathedral, lit up by the clouded sun.[9] In chapter 12, I analyzed J. M. W. Turner's *The Decline of the Carthaginian Empire* (1817), drawing attention to the way in which the architectural composition turns the city's harbor into a stage set. Doré echoes this stagelike quality, but while Turner invites the viewer to step onto the proscenium and into the moment before the end, Doré puts the stage at a contemplative distance. Turner had the end of the Napoleonic Empire in mind; in *The New Zealander*, we are witnessing a moment long after the end of the British Empire.

But how exactly should we read Doré's neo-Roman Maori?[10] A liberal imperialist, Macaulay had written extensively on Roman Britain, whose barbarian inhabitants he thought were "little superior to the natives of the Sandwich Islands."[11] In 1844, Macaulay was put in charge of frescoes for the new Houses of Parliament whose subject was British history, spanning Roman Britain, sunk in barbarism, and modern Britain, "instructing the savage."[12] Cook in Tahiti was the subject of the fifth fresco. Macaulay had also written an essay about British imperial pedagogy, a key text about the project of colonial mimicry, the vexed identity formation analyzed by Homi Bhabha. "We must," Macaulay wrote, "do our best," to shape a group of people, "Indians in blood and color, but English in taste, in opinions, in morals, and in intellect."[13]

Depending on how we read Macaulay's views of the British Indian subject, we might argue that Doré's Maori, who is the object of our gaze, embodies a colonial subject ironically or patronizingly offered to the

European gaze; or, even more harshly, that this English gentleman in blackface expresses all the ridicule nineteenth-century colonizers felt toward their subjects—including O-Mai. Or—and this is the point I would make—we might focus on the threat embodied by this figure and his ruined surroundings, despite the ironizing strategies at work in Macaulay's style and Doré's composition. Macaulay is famous for his statement that the Indian was "an enigma of mysterious origin and constitution"—potentially British in taste but possibly as violently "barbarian" as the Maori.[14] Reading Doré's scene with all of the earlier European ruin gazers in mind, it is worth remembering that the Maori were seen as violent cannibals. At the end of the nineteenth century, the "barbarians" of the British Empire had long been restive, and this iconic image condenses the images of modern *barbarians* we encountered in the previous chapters.

In 1806 a detachment of Sepoys had attacked a British garrison in India. Their insurrection created panic, and led Charles Metcalfe to muse about the time of empire: "Empires grow old, decay and perish."[15] Britain needed to maintain the "impression of invincibility," although it had now "reached 'premature old age' and *its life could only be prolonged with care*."[16]

Contributing to the debate about the East India Company in 1833, Macaulay too raised the issue of the empire's duration, reverting once more to the comparison between the British and Roman empires. As Britain's case proved, ancient Rome's civilizing mission was a success. Having encountered "a great people sunk in the lowest depths of slavery and superstition," the Romans governed Britannia in a way that fostered Britons' desire and capacity for self-government.[17] This was proof that "there are triumphs which are followed by no reverse."[18] Macaulay defined these "triumphs" as "the pacific triumphs of reason over barbarism" and "empire" as "the imperishable empire of our arts and our morals, our literature and our laws."[19] Speaking about Britain's civilizing mission, Macaulay then proclaimed: "There is an empire exempt from all natural causes of decay."[20]

Macaulay's scenario raised the same worrisome issues—perishable empires and modern barbarians—in a different way. The scenario of the imperial ruin gazer creates an imaginary space that organizes the power relations between the imperial subject and his "barbarian" other. Polybios first inscribed the Roman conqueror's craving for visual mastery over the images of the new, post-Carthaginian world into his rubble scenario; inspired by Virgil's version of the Carthaginian scenario, Silius Italicus created a scene that narrated Hannibal's fierce gaze at the Roman stage in ruins, and so did Herder. In contrast to Scipio's hungry gaze or Hannibal's annihilating desire, Doré's New Zealander quietly contemplates a ruinscape, dominated by the crumbling cathedral named after Paul. Doré's scenographic scenario brings back a problematic that arose with Silius's and Herder's scenes: the question of who will be occupying *the position of scopic mastery*.

Doré structured the scene in ways that subordinate the gaze of the colonized to the gaze of the European beholder. That is, while Doré shows the Maori in quarter-profile, contemplating the ruins of London, he preserves the scopic mastery of the metropolitan subject, who is the one looking at the Maori looking at the ruins. In this, Doré follows the visual logic of Macaulay's text: the reader's mental image forms as she "follows," so to speak, the visual trajectory of the narrator, looking at the New Zealander contemplating the ruins. While both the colonizer and the colonized look at the ruins of empire, the true object of desire in this scenario is the gaze itself, the scopic mastery exerted over the colonized.[21] In the end, the imperial subject is still the one who is looking. To preserve this position of mastery is one of the things that neo-Roman ruin gazing will try to repeat, far into the twentieth century. Again and again, acts of imperial mimesis will be generating scenarios of scopic mastery that either hold the colonial other in the field of vision of the subject's gaze—or ban him from the picture altogether.

Let me briefly return to the stagelike framing of London's ruinscape in Doré's engraving. Turner revived the Roman framing of ruin gazer scenarios as scenes from the theater of history for the Napoleonic age. Yet his Carthage is in decline, not ruined. Inspired by Turner, the British-American painter Thomas Cole took a step further into the future, depicting the ivy-covered remnants of an imperial city long after its fall in a painting entitled *Desolation* (1833–1836), which belongs to a cycle entitled *The Course of Empire*. The most arresting characteristic of these four allegorical paintings is their "overt theatricality" (figure 12.3).[22] In this panoramic view of a ruined city located on a harbor, closely echoing Turner's Carthaginian topography, a gleaming white column rises in front of a wide row of smaller columns that might well be the remnants of a Roman-style theater.

Doré's dense, wall-like accumulation of ruined buildings also calls to mind the monumentality of the imperial *scaenae frons*.[23] Intriguingly, this British *scaenae frons* is not dominated by the *porta regalis* of the Roman stage but the crumbling cathedral, named after Paul, the theorist of the *katechon*, that is, the imperial sovereign who stalls the empire's inevitable end (see chapter 5). *To prolong the life of empire with care* was Louis Bertrand's neo-Roman obsession. Bertrand's texts on the resurrection of the Roman Empire in the French colonies with their long history of insurgencies are replete with ruin gazer scenarios, organized around the French imperial

12.3 *The Course of Empire: Desolation* (fifth in series) by Thomas Cole, 1836; oil on canvas, 39 ¼ × 63 ¼ inches. Gift of the New York Gallery of the Fine Arts. Digital image created by Oppenheimer Editions; object #1858.5.

subject in the position of scopic mastery. We saw Fourier reoccupying the position of the neo-Roman ruin gazer after the disaster of the neo-Roman Egyptian campaign. I also discussed Forster's ambivalent search for Virgil's archaic ruins in the Pacific, and his equally ambivalent portrayal of the Maori. Like Volney, Forster was able to think of the possibility of a barbarian in the position of the ruin gazer; and yet, like Volney, he held on to the position of scopic mastery.

Between the late eighteenth and early twentieth centuries, the Maori thus emerged as the cipher for the modern barbarian. As I wrote above, even Doré's iconic contemplative image emanates this threat, however faint. In the North African campaign of World War II, Maori will return as a very real threat to the Italian allies of their former colonizers, and Goebbels's propaganda apparatus soon began to portray them as savage "scalp hunters."[24] In the modern age, the Roman trope of the barbarian avenger, the ancient figure of Hannibal, was thus reimagined as South Pacific Islander in the wake of Cook's voyages to the South Pacific.

But Maori were of course not the only incarnation of the "barbarian" enemy in the (pre)modern age. Starting with the military campaigns of Charles V at Tunis and Vienna in 1535 against the Ottomans, North African Muslims were made into the other iconic figure of the barbarian enemy. In the context of his bellicose theories about African Latinity, Louis Bertrand worked especially hard to make Muslims Western Europe's most threatening enemy. In *Le Sens de L'Ennemi* (1917), Bertrand wrote: "I use the word Barbarian in the widest sense, ranging from foreigner to savage and enemy of civilization."[25] With this statement, he captured the essence of the modern concept of the barbarian.

In this text, Bertrand also passionately argued that Europeans needed to understand that all Muslims agree that Europe far "exceeds its rights" whenever it "imposes its sovereignty on a people of Islam."[26] Muslims will never accept being dominated, and neither will they assimilate. Their sole goal is "to endure" against us.[27] That Muslims were barbarians was the premise of many texts written in the wake of the conquest of Algeria. The Arab conquest of North Africa was, historians and archeologists agreed, the return of barbarism. Gibbon famously concluded his *Decline and Fall* with the Ottoman conquest of Constantinople in 1453, the moment of "Grief and terror of Europe" (DFIII, 974). Including the Ottoman Empire was a remarkable decision for an eighteenth-century historian of Rome. Gibbon's story about the arrival of Mehmed/Mahomet II in the Roman emperor's palace is equally noteworthy. Entering the city through the "gate of Saint Romanus," the Ottoman sultan "gazed with satisfaction and wonder at the domes and palaces" (DFIII, 967). Passing in triumph through the city, the sultan arrived at the ruined residence of the Byzantine emperors. As he entered Constantine's mansion, a "melancholy reflection on the vicissitudes of human greatness, forced itself on his mind," Gibbon reported, adding that Mehmed II recited verses from a Persian poem: "The spider has wove his web in the Imperial palace; and the owl hath sung her watch-song on the towers of Afrasiab" (DFIII, 968).[28]

Much is condensed in this scene: the Muslim enemy visually taking possession of the ruins of the Eastern Roman Empire, the Muslim conqueror seemingly voicing Scipio's imperial *tristesse*—and the imperial historian of the West maintaining scopic mastery. But, most importantly, Gibbon wants us to know that there are ruin gazer scenarios other than those of the Western tradition, opening a tiny crack in the armature of the ruinous neo-Roman imaginary.[29]

PART FOUR

From Germany's Anti-Roman Barbarians to the Ruin Gazer Scenarios of the Conservative Revolution

Preface

Jürgen Osterhammel periodizes the long nineteenth century lasting from Koselleck's *Sattelzeit* (1770–1830) to the end of the long *fin-de-siècle* (1880–1930). He agrees with C. A. Baily's characterization of the era between 1760/1770 and 1830 as a "first epoch of global imperialism," leading to the "great conflict of the imperia between the years of 1793 and 1815."[1] He also understands the nineteenth century in terms of two "master narrative[s]," the stories of emerging nation-states and the enduring power of empires.[2] The German *Reich* exemplified this entanglement of two stories: Germany's foundation in 1871 as a "nation state" (whose constitution authorized a German *Kaiser*, or emperor) was soon followed by the formation of an "overseas '*Reich*,'" whose first colonies were acquired under Bismarck in 1884.[3]

I reconstruct the European history of neo-Roman mimesis as a series of historical snapshots, a story that meanders across national and chronological boundaries. In this part, I shift the focus entirely to the German case. Here, the dominant discourse about the Roman Empire changed radically in the course of the nineteenth century. At the beginning of the century, the resistance to Napoleonic France engendered an anti-Roman discourse in politics, philosophy, and the arts. With the *Kaiserreich*'s acquisition of colonies between 1884 and 1900 and its rise to world power, neo-Roman mimesis became part of the Second Empire.

Part 4 thus starts with a discussion about the philosophers and artists of the anti-Napoleonic movement, among them Johann Gottlieb Fichte, Heinrich von Kleist, and Caspar David Friedrich, and concludes with a chapter about two of the imperial thinkers of the *Kaiserreich*: Friedrich Ratzel, the historical geographer, and Oswald Spengler, father of the so-called conservative revolution. That is, in terms of the topography of *The Conquest of Ruins*, I will ask you to leave France's North African colonies, and in terms of chronology, I will temporarily reverse course, starting with Fichte's *Addresses to the German Nation* in the wake of Prussia's defeat in 1806 and ending in 1933 with Oswald Spengler's *Jahre der Entscheidung* (*The Hour of Decision*).

Fichte, the philosopher, and Kleist, the playwright, recuperated Tacitus's anthropological portrait of Germania's barbarian tribes for their politics of national insurgency against the Napoleonic Empire, which claimed Rome as its Second City. In chapter 14, I single out Fichte's lectures held in Berlin during the Napoleonic occupation, and Kleist's drama of insurrection, *Die Hermannsschlacht* (*The Battle of Herrmann*), written immediately after the Prussian defeat. Fichte agitated for a German culture, nation, and future *Reich* defined in contrast to its Romanized occupiers. Kleist's play mobilized the history of the Germanic tribes' rebellion against the Romans in 9 CE, promising a French Empire in ruins and portraying the site of the battle as Germania's heart of darkness. I will trace this latter trope in one of Caspar David Friedrich's anti-Napoleonic ruin paintings.

In chapter 15, I focus on the German *Kaiserreich*, inquiring into the forms that neo-Roman mimesis takes at this moment. Here I single out festivities like the 1886 anniversary of the Prussian Academy of the Arts, which included a Pergamon panorama; Theodor Mommsen's involvement in the excavations of Roman sites on the territory of the new *Reich*; or the novel *Der Kampf um Rom* (*The Struggle for Rome*) (1876), written by author-historian Felix Dahn. The resurrectional realism of Dahn's historical novel corresponds to the visual techniques of the new immersive media. Both media opened up access to the Roman world of the past as the *Kaiserreich* acquired its first colonies in the South Pacific.

These artists and historians thus laid the groundwork for the Second Empire's neo-Roman mimesis as the transformation of the anti-Roman barbarian into the neo-Roman imperialist. Fichte lectured about the imitation of Rome, touching on the concept of mimesis. Chapter 16 deals with the way this concept was theorized by Friedrich Nietzsche and narrated by Wilhelm Jensen in his novella *Gradiva: ein pompejanisches Phantasiestück* (*Gradiva: A Pompeiian Fancy*) (1903). Nietzsche was the *Kaiserreich*'s theorist of neo-Roman mimesis in the modernist mode and Jensen's novella was a Nietzschean text about imitation.

Chapter 17 focuses on two of the *Kaiserreich*'s most influential imperial thinkers, the geographer Friedrich Ratzel and Oswald Spengler, author of *Der Untergang des Abendlandes* (*The Decline of the West*). This chapter reconnects to Louis Bertrand, whose reflections on empire, barbarian enemies, and imperial ruins resemble those of Germany's conservative critics of modernity such as Ratzel and Spengler. Latecomers to the exploitation of the non-European world, these German thinkers reflected on the problematic of empire-building—of duration and ruination—taking advantage of their belated knowledge.

Spengler reconceived world history radicalizing the cyclical paradigm of rise and decline. Analyzing *Civilization*, or Western imperialist modernity, as the decay of *Kultur*, Spengler prophesied the inevitable end of the Occident in ruins and introduced the concept of the *Caesarist* sovereign as decelerator. Theorizing imperial expansion in terms of spatial instinct, Ratzel thematized the nexus of empire and ruins. He spent less time thinking about barbarians than Spengler, whose political manifesto, *The Hour of Decision* (1933), was a long rant about the barbarians at Europe's gates.

With the help of his double lens of nation-state and *imperium*, Osterhammel analyzes nineteenth-century nationalism as a formation that establishes a demarcation against "neighbors and distant 'barbarians.'"[4] Nineteenth-century German culture and politics began with the idea of some barbarians very close at hand, and the *Kaiserreich*'s neo-Roman mimesis involved the conversion of anti-Roman barbarians into Romans fighting their own "remote barbarians." In 1897, Rome's ancient enemy, Hannibal, was still vividly alive for Sigmund Freud, whose *cathexis* of the Carthaginian hero was an act of *Besetzung* articulating the tensions around his Jewishness in the *fin-de-siècle* capital of the disintegrating Habsburg Empire. Part 4 traces the ways in which German intellectuals and artists rearticulated the concepts of empire and imperial mimesis. Reinventing scenarios of ruin gazing for their particular cultural and political contexts, they also revived the ancient image of the barbarian. Some did this by enacting a *cathexis* of the barbarian similar to Freud's, while others took possession of the model of the Roman conqueror ready to fight the barbarians in the remote colonies of the Second *Reich*.

THIRTEEN

Anti-Roman Barbarians: Johann Gottlieb Fichte, Heinrich von Kleist, C. D. Friedrich, and the Fight against Napoleon in the Ruins of *Germania*

Introduction

Napoleon's self-stylization as Roman hero was heralded by some intellectuals in the occupied German states, despised by others. Eyewitness to the emperor's triumphal entry into the city of Düsseldorf in 1811, Heinrich Heine gleefully celebrated Napoleon's defeat of Prussia. The German Jacobin sees a man who is both body and statue, his hand of "gleaming marble," his face "of the same color as the ancient Greek and Roman [marble] busts."[1] This is a neo-Roman sovereign whose Roman mask is part of his being, and whose gaze is that of the conqueror, swiftly embracing with one glance "all earthly things, while other mortals could only see them one by one."[2] In a poem about Bonaparte in Egypt from 1799, Karoline von Günderrode also idealized Napoleon as the revolutionary hero who revived "Roman vigor."[3] Her later poems then depicted him as a tyrant.

German intellectuals and artists of the anti-Napoleonic movement rediscovered two Roman texts as their weapons,

Tacitus's anthropological treatise on the barbarian German tribes and Virgil's *Aeneid*.[4] I will discuss two exemplary cases: Johann Gottlieb Fichte, the Romantic philosopher, who made constant use of Tacitus's *De Germanorum*; and Heinrich von Kleist, who used Virgil's *Aeneid* as a kind of intertextual skeleton for his *Battle of Herrmann* [*Hermannsschlacht*] (1807), a piece of guerilla theater ending with a vision of Rome/Paris in ruins.[5] I will then propose to read one of Caspar David Friedrich's ruin paintings as a kind of Tacitean *Description de l'Allemagne*. The chapter concludes with a transitional text, Theodor Mommsen's *Roman History* (1856).

The Struggle against Rome: Barbarians and Their Anti-Napoleonic Ruins

The Holy Roman Empire (a vast formation of sovereign units in the middle of Europe ruled by the Habsburgs) died with the Prussian defeat at Jena and Auerstedt in 1806. The defeat put an end to the German Romantics' Jacobin enthusiasms, replacing it with a wave of "hatred" focused on Napoleon.[6] Fichte's lectures in Berlin, *Addresses to the German Nation* (1807–1808), were among the most popular events of the first decade of the nineteenth century. Staging his lectures as a "collective event," Fichte expressed his fear that the political occupation of the German territories might lead to Germany's spiritual decline.[7] Advocating a program of national pedagogy predicated on Germany's national specificity, Fichte frequently referred to Tacitus's view of the rebellious German tribes of the first century.[8] These lectures were based on the idea of a radical break with the past and an equally radical renewal, inaugurating an era in which nations would begin to act freely.

It was Fichte's opinion that Germany alone had preserved a sense of freedom, since Germans had opposed the idea of *imperium* and chosen the nation as their political form. This spirit had to be reawakened. Fichte understood this reawakening in a political and cultural sense, making the imitation of Rome a central problematic. Ever since the fall of the Roman Empire, the German tribes had understood themselves as a loose confederation of fraternal *Völker* who never submitted to an *imperator*. Some of these tribes, Fichte argued, adapted Rome's language; others did not. In Fichte's mind, the choice of language was a matter of life and death: German is a language connected to "life," whereas Romanized languages were essentially dead languages, the product of nations that lacked their own "images" and "culture," since all they had done was to imitate Rome.[9]

Imitation kills: what the assimilated tribes were left with in their eagerness to remain close to Rome was "the flat and dead history of an alien culture."[10] Out of the Roman Empire thus emerged the difference between "foreign countries" and "motherland."[11] In Fichte's lectures, foreign country means above all the French enemy. Politically, the French are engaged in unproductive mimesis, philosophically they are producing fluff, and artistically they merely decorate—all because they imitate Rome.

But there is also a life-giving form of imitation: tracing German culture back to Greece, Fichte argued that Germany had preserved a "sense for profundity" and a connection to nature and life.[12] If the French triumphed over the Germans' motherland, robbing it of its independence, then both would perish. For France would cut "the last remaining thread," Fichte wrote, by which it was still connected to "nature" and "life."[13] By vanquishing Greek Germany, Roman France would die a "spiritual death"—a death that has been shown to be France's very essence. As a result of this Napoleonic victory, *all of Europe*—Rome's imitators included—would fall back into "barbarism."[14]

Fichte's lectures were thus anti-Napoleonic to the core.[15] Let us remember that these lectures took place after the French Army's victory in 1806, the ensuing occupation of Prussia, and the dissolution of the Holy Roman Empire.[16] Like other German intellectuals, Fichte glorified Arminius's anti-imperial resistance against the Romans. Quoting Tacitus, Fichte reminded his listeners that Arminius's Germans chose freedom and death over slavery. Refusing to become "half Romans," the Germanic tribes avoided the loss of their "particularity by fighting against the Romans' intention to conquer the world."[17] In Fichte's lectures, the repetition of Arminius's anti-imperial struggle was not a hollow form of mimesis, but a spiritual form of resurrection.[18] His first lecture concluded with a poetic image, hinting at Lucan's *Pharsalia* and Erichtho's resurrection of a dead soldier. A later lecture framed the reanimation of the nation's dead body in Christian terms.

Quoting Fichte, Carl Schmitt reminded his readers in 1934 that the philosopher defined *volk* as "a group of people" unified by their "common history" toward the "constitution of a Reich," arguing that a *volk*'s "autonomy" resided in this capacity "to evolve into a *Reich*."[19] If this "striving toward an empire" encountered that of another *volk/Reich*, Schmitt clarified, its members had the duty to join this "'life-and-death' struggle."[20] In 1813 Prussia officially declared war, and anti-Napoleonic militias were founded. Describing the mood among Berlin academics, Bettina von Arnim ironically depicted Fichte with "shield and dagger."[21] While Fichte connected *volk* to *Reich* in 1813, he most certainly did not think the Germans' *Reich* would masquerade as Roman.[22]

Jacobins like Heine and Georg Forster mocked Fichte's *völkisch* patriotism; Heinrich von Kleist, the German playwright, took him seriously. One of the "greatest haters," Kleist urged "Germania's children" to "color all public squares . . . white with their bones" and "to build a dam in the Rhine with their corpses."[23] Like Fichte, Kleist was attracted to Tacitus's *Germania* or *De origine et situ Germanorum* (written ca. 98 CE), the Roman historian's travel narrative about Germania as the Romans' dark continent. Tacitus celebrated the simplicity and purity of the German tribes. Living in villages hidden away in their impenetrable forests, they were more virtuous than the Romans living in their decadent cities—in fact, these barbarians were more Roman than the Romans. In their fight against the new Romans, the German freedom fighters responded enthusiastically to this glorification of their barbarous ancestors.[24]

Tacitus's scenes of the German tribes' brutal revenge were well known. In 1794, Herder reminded his readers of Tacitus's story about the arrival of Germanicus's legions in the Teutoburger Wald. Six years after the defeat of Varus's army, the dead still lay unburied. As the Romans arrived at the "sad site," Herder quoted Tacitus, "they see Varus' camp" and "the field [still] covered with white bones."[25] There were "broken lances" lying next to dismembered horses—all this scattered around "a half-ruined breastwork," Tacitus wrote, "where the last remnants [of Varus's army] had gathered."[26] And then they saw the skulls, "heads nailed to tree trunks," and "nearby in the forest" archaic "barbarian altars, on which tribunes and centurions had bled to death."[27] In Tacitus's *Annals*, this Germanic forest was the Roman Empire's heart of darkness.[28]

In *The Battle of Herrmann* (1807), Kleist retold the story of Hermann/Arminius luring the Roman legions into the barbaric forests. With his usual excess, Kleist celebrated Germania's barbarians, ending with Arminius's appeal to his tribal followers to march on Rome. Set at the time of Augustus, the play moves toward a climactic battle between the leader of a Germanic tribe, *Arminius the Cheruscan*, and the Roman troops of Varus.[29] It was apparent to Kleist's audiences that Augustus (and his stand-in, Varus) was Napoleon. The analogy is more than transparent when Kleist ridicules Varus's assurances that his emperor respected the Germanic gods—mimicking Napoleon's statements to Cairo's Muslim inhabitants.[30] The opening lines belong to one of Herrmann's chieftains, lamenting Rome's imperial reach and power.[31] With cunning appeals to their patriotism, Arminius unites the tribes, starting a movement that he promises will liberate all of Germania—and the world—from the foreign invaders.

In his patriotic texts, Heinrich von Kleist outlined the mission of the anti-Napoleonic struggle: the constitution of "Germania's sacred soil," a geographic space that Fichte drew onto the ruined map of the Holy Roman Empire.[32] This geopolitical constitution, Kleist wrote, was the "foundation stone" of the new Germany's "community."[33] And here South Sea islanders made another appearance on the German scene. This community of German philosophers, scientists, artists, kings, wrote Kleist, would be so splendid that "if the savages of the South Sea knew [this community] they would rush to protect it."[34]

Kleist read Forster's *Voyage 'Round the World* and, like Forster, he knew his Virgil, whose *Aeneid* provided Kleist with the structural skeleton for his play. The decisive battle with Varus ends with Teutoburg "in rubble."[35] When one of his comrades in arms tells Arminius that "all of Teutoburg now lies in ash and rubble!" he merely answers: "But we'll build ourselves a better one."[36] Replacing Virgil's Troy with Teutoburg, Kleist takes hold of one of the *Aeneid*'s ruin gazer scenarios, Aeneas's tale about Troy's destruction and his melancholic contemplation of the fresco in Juno's temple depicting the last day of Troy. But Kleist has no patience for Virgil's Augustan moment of compassion. In *The Battle of Herrmann*, there is no regret, only the desire to destroy. Like Augustus, the French Romans might claim to be compassionate; their barbarian enemies do not know such compassion—and in this they are closer to the guerillas Napoleon encountered in Egypt than to their fellow Europeans.

Herrmann's ultimate goal is the annihilation of Rome/Paris. The play ends with Arminius's plan to march on Rome, the project of the constitution of Germania turning at the end of the play into one of conquest.[37] The scene culminates with Herrmann's vision of Rome reduced to rubble: "Because the world will have no peace / From this murderous brood / Until we have annihilated the outlaw's lair, / And nothing remains but a black flag / Fluttering over its desolate pile of rubble!"[38] Virgil had readers imagine Rome as Carthage, the capital of the empire being destroyed as thoroughly as the capital of its Punic enemy. In *The Battle*, the Germanic rebel promises that Rome/Paris will be Carthage. The battle at Teutoburg did not spell the end of the Roman Empire—Kleist's audience knew that. Napoleon was still in power. However, Kleist has Varus, the defeated general, understand his defeat as a sign of the end: "And so Rome's world dominion falls / By the cunning of a savage."[39] Rome fell—and Paris will fall too.

Narrating the Romans' "first contact with the inhabitants of Germania," Mommsen praised Caesar for having recognized in Germania's tribes the "antagonists of the Romano-Greek world."[40] Carl Schmitt thought *The Battle of Herrmann*, which gave this enmity a modern shape, was "the greatest partisan poem of all times."[41] Like Schmitt, Kleist's guerilla warriors were certain who their enemies were. Kleist's staging of the decisive battle in the Teutoburg Forest again refers to Virgil's *Aeneid*. More precisely, it refers to Aeneas's descent into the underworld: as the Romans err through the dark forest, having lost their way, they encounter a German witch, whom Varus, addressing her as "Roman sybil," interrogates about the way out of these dark barbarian woods.[42]

More strikingly, the anti-Napoleonic writer famously played with the limit separating barbarian and non-barbarian. Two of the play's central episodes involve acts that turn one woman into a "barbarian" and use another in a display of barbarian violence.[43] In Kleist's play, Dido returns as the avenging Germanic barbarian. These acts are part of Arminius's new strategy of guerilla warfare, and in his anti-Napoleonic fever Kleist happily risks the descent into "barbarism." Kleist's anti-Napoleonic guerilla theater thus appropriated Napoleon's imperial mimesis of the Romans, glorifying anti-Roman "barbarism" and reveling in the idea of Germany as the wilderness that the Romans would never penetrate.[44]

Caspar David Friedrich's *Description de L'Allemagne*, or the Cold, Dark Ruins of Germania

Since Strabo, political geography has been intimately linked to ideas about the scopic regimes of empire. These reflections concern the elevated, far-ranging gaze of the ruler and the searching gaze of the conqueror. In 1903 Friedrich Ratzel wrote about the geographer's experience of the sublime, the mixture of elation and terror so often invoked in discussions of Caspar David Friedrich's landscape paintings. When he surveys the country from a mountaintop, Ratzel wrote at the zenith of Germany's colonial empire, the geographer's panoramic gaze penetrates to the very "limit of the visible"—and in his eyes is mirrored his "mastery of the world."[45] In an earlier piece, Ratzel introduced the point of view of the Roman conquerors, reminding his readers of the Romans' incursion into impenetrable German territory. Romans, he wrote in 1896, depicted Germany as a "country of barbarians," most of it covered with dense forests.[46] No wonder, Ratzel wrote, that "the Roman [soldier] found it difficult to find his bearings in this dark-humid world."[47]

Caspar David Friedrich painted two ruin landscapes, *Abbey in the Oak Forest* (1809–1810) and *Cloister Cemetery in the Snow* (1817–1819), in which he depicted Northern German landscapes during the era when Napoleon's armies invaded Germany. When these French legionnaires entered Egypt, they saw vast sandy deserts shimmering in the unbearable heat, ancient

Egyptian ruins and less ancient Roman ruins. What did they see, Friedrich seems to wonder, when they entered German territory?

The commonplace about Caspar David Friedrich's paintings is that they are melancholy, but some of them are also fiercely anti-Napoleonic. Let us first consider two paintings whose iconography positions them in proximity to Kleist's anti-Roman project. For instance, Friedrich's contemporaries discussed ruin paintings such as *Hünengräber* (1812) as patriotic. The religious component of Friedrich's landscape paintings is strong, often infusing them with an apocalyptic sensibility. But paintings like *Ulrich von Hutten's Grave* (1823–1824), with its anti-French iconography, have a strong resurrectional quality (figure 13.1). The stark contrast between dark interior and the golden light streaming in through the Gothic windows (and illuminating the tree growing on top of the roofless structure) forces the idea of a new life, if not resurrection, upon the beholder. This particular painting, with its German-Lutheran theme, does not self-reflexively stage the tension between the empirical and metaphysical, the real and the idea, the visible and the invisible (as Joseph Koerner argues with respect to other paintings).[48] On the contrary, the viewer's upward glance further reinforces the resurrectional dimension—*Hutten's Grave* is the worst kind of anti-Napoleonic ruin kitsch.

But what about Friedrich's *Abbey in the Oak Forest* (1809–1810), or his later painting, *Cloister Cemetery in the Snow* (1817–1819)? In these ruin landscapes, contemporary with Kleist's play, Lutheranism meets the remnants of a German Gothic, that is, pagan "Nordic-German" past.[49] The ruined structures depicted here are a response to an empire in a state of disintegration. But they are not the same: *Cloister Cemetery in the Snow* again introduces the theme of resurrection by erecting the lighter Gothic structure above the dark and withered ruins of the abbey (figure 13.2). More significantly, the beholder's eyes are drawn away from the scene that figures death—the abbey and its graveyard—toward the elegant Gothic arch, and then guided upward by the fact that the trees that are framing the abbey and cathedral diverge, opening up beyond the painting's upper limit.

Something entirely different is going on in Friedrich's earlier *Abbey in the Oak Forest* (1809–1810), another of his ruins "in the wilderness" (figure 13.3).[50] The division into darker ground and lighter upper half is more pronounced, and no ethereal structure transcends the two. We might be justified in reading the contrast between light and darkness, between a sky that attracts our gaze and the darkish ground where objects are so hard to discern and which so conventionally thematize death, as the promise of resurrection. But these ruins are not only dead; they are cold skeletons, as

13.1 Caspar David Friedrich, *Ulrich von Hutten's Grave* (1823–1824).

are the oaks surrounding them. More than that, both the ruins and the distorted, barren trees are threatening, as threatening and uncanny as the derelict graveyard with its fallen crosses.

What is this threat? Is it the threat of death that the dark ruins, graveyard, and neglected tombs evoke? Or is the threat more specific, involving a perspective that invites us to shift our gaze from the sky, from the source of light in the upper right corner, to the darkness on the ground?

13.2 C. D. Friedrich, *Cloister Cemetery in the Snow* (1817–1819).

13.3 C. D. Friedrich, *Abbey in the Oak Forest* (1809–1810).

A perspective that asks us to imagine what it would feel to traverse this landscape on the ground surrounded by "deathly darkness," barely able to see?[51] Listening to the distant "savage shouting and triumphant songs" of Arminius's "partisans"?[52] I am proposing that we read Friedrich's abbey in the wilderness as a painting that looks at Germany from the invaders' perspective, depicting the country as the heart of darkness—a dark, empty, cold land where semi-barbarians lived dressed in dark robes silently filing through graveyards at night.

A country dangerous in many ways—and not so dissimilar to Egypt, where Napoleon's grand army had experiences that its soldiers, artists, and scientists would spend many years trying to understand. Just listen again to Tacitus's report about the "Teutoburgian Wood" with its bones and its ruins.[53] "Caecina was sent ahead," Tacitus reported, "to reconnoiter the dark woods."[54] What they saw lived up to the soldiers' "horrible" expectations: the white bones, the fragments of spears, the human heads, the ruined earthworks, the "outlandish" altar.[55] Having been sent to repress the barbarian uprising, Germanicus was taunted by Arminius, sneering at the "wages of slavery."[56] Tacitus reported that the Roman general was haunted by a terrible dream: "Varus, covered with blood, seemed to rise out of the morass, and call him."[57] Tacitus did not report whether the dream about Germania and its barbarians kept haunting Germanicus when he toured Egypt after Tiberius named him governor of Rome's eastern provinces.

Dreams of a Roman Stage: Schinkel's Triumphal Arch and Mommsen's Roman History of Germany

In the wake of Napoleon's defeat, the Prussian architect Karl Friedrich Schinkel began translating classical scenographic architecture for post-Napoleonic Berlin. In 1813 Schinkel designed a monumental Gothic cathedral for Leipzig Square, intended as a resting place for the heroes of the wars of liberation. The project was never realized, but in 1818 Schinkel completed the *Neue Wache*. Located on Prussian Berlin's main boulevard (which Schinkel hoped to turn into a *Via triumphalis*), the building was modeled on a Roman military camp or *castrum*.[58] Decorating the front with a panel depicting a battle scene above a row of six columns, Schinkel added six small Victory statues.

Schinkel's painting, *Triumphbogen (Ruhmeshalle)* (1817), an architectural fantasy, combined the Gothic cathedral with an immense Triumphal Arch built around an equally immense equestrian statue of Fredrick Wil-

13.4 Karl Friedrich Schinkel, *Hall of Fame (*1817). Bpk Bildagentur/Art Resource, NY.

helm III, entering Berlin after the victory over Napoleon (figure 13.4). Like Piranesi and Hubert Robert, Schinkel used the arch as "entry gate leading onto the stage."[59] Darkened by age, the painting is of excruciating precision, depicting the triumphal procession with hundreds if not thousands of civilian onlookers and military men marching toward the cathedral as well as every single decorative detail of the Roman-style arch with its crowded battle reliefs. This is Schinkel's dream of Germany's might, an imperial fantasy of anti-Napoleonic barbarians having become Romans parading on their own neo-Roman stage.

While Schinkel created the architectural armory of empire for Berlin, Theodor Mommsen's *The History of Rome* (1856) nourished the *Kaiserreich*'s fascination with its image in the Roman mirror. Gibbon patiently reassembled the ruined Roman stage. Similarly, Mommsen took his readers on a tour of "*Roma quadrata,*" the earliest settlement on the Palatine hill, depicting a Rome that no longer existed.[60] This imaginative restoration is grounded in the rhetoric of Roman history as grand spectacle. Caesar's coming to power, Mommsen wrote, represented "the last act of this great world historical drama."[61]

Mommsen opened *The History of Rome* with a panoramic view of the Mediterranean, inviting the reader to follow the historian's gaze across this geo-historical space. Reformulating the trope of the succession of empires with a Herderian concept, the idea of the irreducible particularity of ethno-cultural regions, Mommsen then outlined a civilizational space whose historical apexes are tied to the names of four cities: Thebes, Carthage, Athens, and Rome.[62]

For Mommsen, the Romans provided the model for German nation-building and Caesar prefigured Bismarck. Beginning with the first Latin settlements, Mommsen tells the history of Rome's war with "Semitic" Carthage and its "capitalist" regime, the city's "rotten basis," led by a "decayed" class of merchants, and finishes with a portrait of Caesar as the head of Rome's first "military monarchy."[63] More importantly, Mommsen argues that this process of nation-state formation was *imperial* in nature. He thus had no qualms about colonial expansion *per se*. On the contrary, Rome's occupation of Gaul, for instance, followed a "natural law."[64] For world history was a struggle between nations "as hard and flexible as steel" and those doomed to perish.[65] Characterizing the conquered as "barbarians" or "natives," Mommsen justified the annexation of Gallia and Caesar's brief excursions into Germany and Britannia in terms of the Romans' superior Hellenist culture and more vigorous race.

The 1851 World's Fair in London marked the British Empire's emergence as the hegemon of the world-system. Writing the history of Rome in this context, Mommsen compared the Romans' subjugation of the West to the British Empire's colonization of India. In Mommsen's text, Caesar imitated, so to speak, the military conquests of the British Empire in taking his legions across the Alps. Analyzing Roman and neo-Roman spatial imaginaries, Mommsen also compared the effects of Caesar's conquests and Roman expansion to the exploration and conquest of "barbarian landscapes" of the Americas.[66] The Romans' westward expansion constituted a world-historical event of the same magnitude as the exploration of the Americas. Like these early modern explorers, Caesar changed the way the Romans imagined the world. This analogy to modern colonialism and its civilizing mission informed Mommsen's conclusions about the subjugation of Western barbarians: Caesar's Romanizing of the West was both inevitable and beneficial.

Two logics thus operate at once in Mommsen's *History of Rome*: on the one hand, a critique of Napoleon's imperial ventures; on the other, a justification of imperial expansion and concomitant approval of the neo-Roman imperial projects of the Spanish-Portuguese and British conquerors. Mommsen thus was not in principle opposed to the imitation of Rome. Like all historians of Rome, Mommsen wrote a ruin gazer scenario. He asserted Western European durability and displaced the threat of ruination toward the Ottoman Empire. Of Alexander's Hellenist Empire in the East, nothing is left but rubble. Caesar's solid "edifice," however, is eternal.[67] It still "stands erect," having endured "for thousands of years" as history relocated the "center of civilization."[68] This edifice might have been incomplete, but it was—and is—not a ruin.

Some empires perish but others endure—this is Mommsen's conclusion in 1856. That is, at the moment when a united German state was still a mirage and three decades before the Second German Empire acquired its first colony. Like Gibbon, Mommsen attributes Rome's durability to Caesar's moderation. Alexander aimed for an empire without limits; Caesar did not. With this history of state formation as inextricably linked to imperial expansion, Mommsen did preparatory work for the Second Empire's neo-Roman mimesis, whether intentionally or not. Caesar, who "built on and from ruins," he implied, should be Bismarck's model.[69] And Rome, the city that developed from primitive settlement to metropolis, was the model for Berlin.

FOURTEEN

The Second German *Reich*: *The Struggle for Rome*, or Barbarians Becoming Romans

Introduction: Being Roman

Pergamon was among the excavations financed by the new *Reich*, and by 1880, the first fragments of the Pergamon Altar (ca. 180 BCE) were on display in the Royal Museum in Berlin.[1] For the 1886 anniversary of the Prussian Academy of the Arts, the organizers commissioned a Pergamon Panorama, consisting of a giant 180-degree painting. A curious architectural hybrid, the structure built for the Panorama mixed elements from the Pergamon Altar and the Zeus Temple of Olympia (ca. 460 BCE). In front of this "archeological collage" stood an obelisk, and the wide stairway was flanked on either side by the plaster copies of six panels from the Pergamon Altar.[2] Located on the site of the anniversary exhibit at Berlin's Lehrter train station, the temple provided the background for the exhibit's opening event, a "Pergamene Celebration."[3] Here, 1,500 Berlin artists reenacted a triumph held in 184 BCE by Attalus II celebrating victory over Celtic barbarians.

Entering the temple, visitors found themselves in the dark interior of the Panorama's rotunda. A masterwork of resurrectional realism, the panorama-picture obeys Aristotelian rules about the unity of time, place, and action, striving to transport the beholder to the locale that it represents.[4] Advised by an archeologist, the artists Max Koch and Alexander Kips depicted the ancient city and its acropolis "at the time of its flourishing under the Roman emperors."[5] Among the most striking aspects of this particular history-machine is the spectators' position: they joined a group of guests on the terrace of the villa of a rich Roman, located on a hill across from Pergamon's acropolis.[6] It was thus as Roman colonizers that German visitors surveyed the world of Roman Pergamon, their experience given a new "sensory intensity" by the novel medium.[7]

The pleasure of this kind of "image-machine" consists in the ability to grasp the image of an ancient city at a single glance.[8] As the authors of the guidebook wrote: "Like the relatives and friends of the villa's owners on the platform," the panorama's visitors "were able to look past the tall cypresses and pines and across terraces and gardens at the . . . [city's] hilltop, covered with magnificent buildings."[9] But these kinds of paintings are also designed to immerse the spectators in the classical past, allowing them to tour the city vicariously. In the case of the Berlin Panorama, the artists used two main strategies of panoramic scenography to achieve this effect. "[C]leverly chosen hints" directed the viewers' gaze, Wulf-Rheidt explains—hints like the tall cypresses that direct the eye toward the large theater located on the slope of the acropolis.

The artists also "pulled the viewers into the city" by making them witnesses to a yearly celebration, which took place, the guidebook explained, during the era when Roman emperors ruled the city.[10] Attracting the spectators' eyes to the Pergamene crowd, advancing toward Pergamon's acropolis, the artists made them walk with the ancient Pergamenes, first winding their way through the city and then entering the Roman-style theater. Located on a steep slope, the performance space descends toward a barely visible *scaenae frons*. The artists painted the theater as it was slowly filling with the city's inhabitants, and added a lavishly decorated "loge of the Roman governor."[11] With this staging of Roman Pergamon, Greco-Roman ocularcentrism and the theatricality of the ancient empire became part of the *Kaiserreich*'s society of spectacle.

A New German Empire

At the moment when the Pergamon Panorama's visitors imagined themselves among the Roman governor's guests in 1887, they were citizens of a *Reich* that had recently joined the ranks of Europe's colonial powers. In 1900, Germany acquired the last of its overseas colonies in Samoa and the newly founded *Reich* reached the peak of its imperial power. Like Britain and France, Germany now had colonies in Africa, the Pacific, and China; it had its pro- and anticolonial debates, its colonial scandals and colonial novels, its colonial exhibits and conferences.

In 1879, Friedrich Fabri published a *plaidoyer* for overseas colonialism entitled *Bedarf Deutschland der Kolonien?* His manifesto was soon followed by the founding of the Colonial Union in 1882 and the Society for German Colonialization in 1884.[12] This colonial movement agitated in a Social-Darwinistic vein, convinced that if Germany did not capture its part of the world, the German *Reich*, despite its present economic and political vigor, would soon join the ranks of the dying nations. Fabri too argued along these lines. Once Germany's greatness rested on its "powerful expansion" into the East.[13] Today Germans faced the alternative of becoming a world power or a nation in decline.

A mere eight years after the *Reich*'s founding in 1871, the Imperial Chancellor Bismarck ceded to the pressure to expand overseas. In 1885, Heinrich Goering, the father of Hermann Goering, arrived in German Southwest Africa as "Imperial Commissary."[14] In 1884–1885, Berlin was the site of the Congo Conference, presided over by Bismarck, and in 1900–1901, the German *Reich* participated in the international expedition forces sent to suppress the Boxer Rebellion. In 1896, Germany's first major Colonial Exhibition staged its newly acquired colonial subjects. The catalogue announced reenactments by "Hottentots and Herreros," performing for the emperor and empress.[15] In 1904, the German state reacted to the Ovahero Rebellion with massacres and the invention of concentration camps.[16]

Clearly the *Kaiserreich* had now joined the ranks of Europe's colonizing powers, and the *Kaiser* soon joined the British monarchy in its performance of imperial spectacles.[17] The most famous of these royal tours was Queen Victoria's proclamation as empress of India in 1876 in Delhi. Lord Lytton, the newly appointed viceroy and governor general of India, had organized the procession into Delhi, inaugurating a "culture of ornamentation" that culminated in Queen Victoria's Diamond Jubilee in 1897, a splendid Roman-style pageant through London.[18] The journey to the Middle East that took Wilhelm II from Vienna to Venice, to Istanbul, Haifa, and Jerusalem, in October 1889, and then back through Beirut, Damascus, and the ruins of Baalbek, expressed this new imperial self-confidence.[19] The *Kaiser*'s journey had specific symbolic dimensions: first, the *mise-en-scène* of the continuity of the Second *Reich*, Holy Roman Empire, and Roman Empire (with the German *Kaiser* retracing the journey of Friedrich II to the Holy Land); second, the presentation of the German *Reich* as one of Europe's major colonial powers. The trip also demonstrated the close relationship to the Ottoman Empire. In good imperial fashion, Istanbul underwent radical changes to its urban fabric, turning the visit into a triumph.[20]

The European struggle over empire was a struggle over the ruins and remnants of antiquity, and Germany jumped into the fray. The *Kaiser*'s trip to the Middle East was embedded in the increasing archeological activity explicitly rivaling the archeological exploits of the British Empire.[21] Meeting the emperor at Miletus, Theodor Wiegand explained the importance of the ancient trading city, and in 1908 the city's monumental Roman market gate arrived in Berlin. The last station of the *Kaiser*'s trip was the Roman ruins of Baalbek. Wilhelm II, who revered Antoninus Pius, took a guided tour through the ruins at dusk and then spent the night in a tent erected inside the Roman Temple, said to have been built by Antoninus.[22]

By the late nineteenth century, Germany started financing large-scale archeological projects to acquire what was left of the world's great treasures.[23] Besides the excavations at Pergamon, Germany also financed digs at Olympia in 1875. Writing about the Pergamon Altar in 1879, the Prussian education minister Falk noted with satisfaction that the German museum now owned "a Greek work of art of dimensions that are equal (or nearly) to the great rows of Attic and Asia Minor sculptures in the British Museum."[24] Like in London or Paris, Greece represented in Berlin the poetic realm of exalted *Bildung*, Rome the prosaic domain of politics.[25] Pieces from the Roman Miletus gate were first exhibited in the Pergamon Museum; from 1925 to 1929, the gate was reconstructed in its entirety.

Mommsen's connection of ancient Rome and contemporary German politics did not end with the publication of his *Roman History*. Involved in the revised edition of the *Res Gestae* (1883), he actively pursued in the 1890s the creation of a commission tracing the Roman Empire's outer border, the *limes*, and its fortresses, erected by the Romans after Varus's defeat in 9 CE.[26] The commission's actual archeological research into the *Kaiserreich*'s Roman prehistory came in the wake of a conference on Roman-German archeology in 1890. This research, Mommsen proclaimed, would address the problem of the "all too blank pages of Roman-German history."[27] In 1900, Wilhelm II used the foundation ceremony for the reconstructed Roman *limes* fortress in Bad Homburg to reenact a triumph with locals dressed as Roman soldiers and barbarian Germans.[28]

The *Kaiser*'s restaged triumph expressed the tension between the nation's identification with barbarian ancestors and the empire's imitation of Rome, a tension present in all Romanized empires.[29] *Thusnelda in the*

14.1 K. T. von Piloty, *Thusnelda in the Triumphal Procession of Germanicus* (1873).

Triumphal Procession of Germanicus by Karl von Piloty thematized the same tension. Exhibited in 1873 at the Vienna World Exhibition, Piloty's painting depicted a single day in Rome, May 26, 17 CE, when the Romans celebrated Germanicus's victory over Germania's barbarian tribes (figure 14.1). Piloty's crowded painting represents Germanicus's triumph after his retaliatory campaign. Among the captives paraded through the streets of Rome were Arminius's wife and son. As Mary Beard notes in her reading of the painting, it is not Germanicus himself, or his emperor, Tiberius, but Thusnelda, the painter's heavy-handed allegory of the German nation, who attracts the eyes of the participants and the contemporary beholder.

Piloty combined two attitudes toward these imperial spectacles: on the one hand, Strabo's enthusiasm for Germanicus's "brilliant" *mise-en-scène* of imperial power in 17 CE;[30] on the other, Tacitus's cynical discussion of the ceremony as another sign of Roman decadence—the ostentatious display of a victory not yet achieved.[31] Piloty's procession was thus both a celebration of Germany's victory over the French enemy and a reflection on the decline and decadence of empires—at the time of Tiberius, and in 1873, in Rome and in Paris. Piloty's painting testified to the enduring memory of Napoleon's neo-Roman mimesis and the equally enduring presence of the multivalent figure of the (post)Roman barbarian.

Felix Dahn's Gothic *Aeneid*

Like Piloty, Felix Dahn celebrated Germanic barbarians in his popular novel *A Struggle for Rome* [*Ein Kampf um Rom*] (1876), but he did so by transforming them into the better Romans. Like Gibbon, Dahn relied on the Byzantine historian and eyewitness Procopius for his history of the Gothic wars. A professor of ancient history, he presented his historical novel as "pictures from the sixth century in the shape of a novel," based on the conceit of history as drama or "Schauspiel," literally translated as a play-to-be-viewed.[32] Dahn tells the story of the Ostrogoths. Having heeded Theodoric's call to follow him to Rome, they stand "on the soil that [their] fathers had wrested" from the Romans "as victors."[33] These barbarians are heroic, self-sacrificing, manly. We are already familiar with this celebration of German barbarity from Kleist's *Battle of Herrmann* (1809) and Tacitus's contrast of decadent Romans and unspoiled Germans. However, these unspoiled barbarians, while rooted in their own *volk*, are steeped in Greco-Roman culture—they are the better Romans, or put differently, they are closer to the original, authentic Roman warriors before the empire entered its decadent stage.

Dahn focuses on Theodoric's successors, Totila and Teias. Theodoric learned how to run an empire from Augustus, and his successors are now planning to restore the Augustan Empire, fighting against Justinian and his generals. Cethegus, a patrician Roman, supports Justinian's "oriental despotism" while conspiring to rebuild Augustan Rome on the "rubble" of the Byzantine Empire.[34] Procopius regrets not having been Scipio's historian and rather melancholically explains to Cethegus that Rome's world rule is finished. Yet Cethegus persists, thus allowing Dahn to tell the story of his failed attempt to repeat Aeneas's act of re-foundation.

Dahn's novel thus combines two projects of imperial re-foundation. For a brief period, the neo-Roman Ostrogoths seem to have restored the Roman Empire under Totila, proudly wearing Augustus's death mask. Yet the melancholic Teias keeps foretelling their impending doom. And he seems to be right. After Totila's death, Teias leads the Goths into their last battle at Mount Vesuvius, but here their fate suddenly changes. Viking ships arrive, annihilate the Byzantine fleet, and the Ostrogoths are saved. The story of defeat turns into one of re-foundation when the dying Teias commands his young protégé to lead the remaining Ostrogoths to the North.

Like Kleist's *Hermannsschlacht*, this historical novel about the Second *Reich*'s imperial prehistory is a Virgilian text. Gibbon ends the account of the Gothic wars with Teias's head "exalted on a spear," announcing the barbarians' defeat (DFII, 757). Dahn's novel ends with a grand finale, a performance of neo-Roman sovereignty: the Ostrogoths' procession toward the coast, which Dahn describes as the triumph-*cum*-apotheosis of their dead, legendary king, Theodoric, seated on his throne, his purple mantle glowing in the dusk. With the spectacle of a falcon's soaring flight embodying the emperor's immortal soul, Dahn transforms the vanquished into future victors.

Dahn interweaves this story about the Ostrogoths' *völkisch* northward turn with reflections on imperial rise and fall. While Teias is convinced that all empires are destined to crumble, Totila, whom Gibbon called a "wise barbarian" (DFII, 749), dreams of a new *Roman-Gothic Reich*, defending Theodoric's post-Augustan legacy. In a kind of colonial manifesto, Totila appeals to the Italians for help against Justinian, promising them a "new Empire [*Reich*]," combining Italian "civilization" with Gothic "strength."[35] The novel proves that this project is ultimately doomed to fail. Dahn gives us two reasons for this. The first is the relentless hatred of the colonized. More importantly, Dahn questions the very idea of an empire on foreign soil. Italy is not their soil, the Italians are not of their *volk*.

The scene that deals most explicitly with imperial rise and fall is staged before a frieze that Totila and his Roman friend Julius discover depicting a Roman emperor's victory over Germanic barbarians. All former empires "blossomed, ripened, and faded away," Julius observes; paraphrasing the Book of Daniel, he declares that "Romans [have their] allotted time."[36] Why, he then asks, should the Goths have a different fate? Totila's answer is simple: "We are made of better stuff."[37] Totila, this most Roman barbarian who sees himself as successor to Augustus, also dismisses the idea that ethnicity divides Goths from Romans. Dahn's text will side with Julius's analysis of the relationship between Goths and colonized Italians: the age-old hatred of the conquered will ultimately gain the upper hand. Like Aeneas's men, the Ostrogoths will have to re-found Rome, their ruined city, elsewhere.

While Dahn's *völkisch* epic argues against colonialism, it still dreams about another *Reich*, one where Dahn's barbarian neo-Romans won't feel that they "have been swept into an alien world."[38] Directing German colonial desires north and east, Dahn fueled imperial desires that anticipated the Nazis' eastward expansion. In the fall of 1941, Hitler told his dinner guests that the Ukraine would soon carry the name "Gothenland."[39] Castigating critics who dismissed his imperial plans for the "desolate Eastern territories," he reminded them that "in the eyes of the ancient Romans, all Northern Europe offered a spectacle of desolation."[40]

Dahn's novel matters in our context not only because of its plain ideological text but because of what it asks its readers to do: to imagine a (post) Roman world that no longer exists, to imagine *being* in a world that they know only as ruined. Or, as the narrator repeatedly reminds his readers, in the days of his story, Rome looked very different. This well-written middlebrow novel works visually, constructing history as a spectacle to be brought before the readers' eyes, busy setting the stage on which the historical characters are acting. The novel's length has much to do with the accumulation of passages that initiate this transition from the narrator's (and thus reader's) perception of a ruined to an unruined state. Like Mommsen, Dahn sends his readers on walks through Rome, ruined now, unruined at the time of his story. Explaining where Hadrian's monument was located at the time of his story, he concludes this topographic excursus with Cethegus, walking along the monument's walls, "his eyes capturing 'his' Rome."[41] And as this Roman's gaze seizes the picture of Rome as it was in the past, so does the reader's, finding herself immersed in a past that no longer existed.

I have already mentioned the panorama, this other nineteenth-century medium of resurrectional realism, positioning spectators in a way that allows them to dominate an ancient city at a glance. *Panorama* derives from the Greek words for "everything, whole," and "to see."[42] The exhibition park of the 1888 anniversary celebrations of the Prussian Academy also contained several so-called *Kaiserdioramas*, representing high points of German colonial expansion, such as the deployment of the German Navy on the African coast.[43] In 1888, ancient Rome itself was the site of another panorama by Josef Bultmann and Alexander Wagner, entitled *Antique Rome with the Triumph of Emperor Constantine*.[44]

In this 360-degree panorama, characterized by the visual excess of excessive realism, the Roman stage is fully restored. The painting locates the viewer on a hill. Looking across the top of Constantine's triumphal arch, the viewer sees Roman crowds assembled to watch Constantine's entry. The city is filled with ancient Romans in togas and uniforms, people watching and others performing their parts in the imperial cortège winding through the streets; there are statues everywhere, and buildings whose architectural details are rendered in painstaking detail. Precursors of film, these historical panoramas were exercises in the imperial imagination, recreating antiquity as living present, while its ruined remnants were exhibited in the newly built Prussian museums in the center of the city.

FIFTEEN

Friedrich Nietzsche's Modernist Mimesis and *Gradiva*'s Splendid Act of Imitation

Introduction

With his praise for the Roman warrior and the modern neo-Roman barbarian, in *Genealogy of Morality* (1887), Friedrich Nietzsche played a crucial role in the *fin-de-siècle* reinscription of the image of the modern barbarian that I discussed, for instance, in chapter 12 in the context of Louis Bertrand's African *Latinité*. Nietzsche also participated in the *Kaiserreich*'s project of imitating Rome with his reflections on historical mimesis and the paralyzing excess of history. More precisely, problematizing imperial mimesis at the dawn of German imperialism, Nietzsche theorized a modernist version of neo-Roman mimesis.

The 1886 Pergamon Panorama and Mommsen's and Dahn's intensely visual texts, I argued in the previous chapter, took their readers back into the Roman past. Or, put differently, with their techniques of immersion they taught readers and viewers *to be* in this past—albeit only for a brief, fleeting moment. Moving in the imaginary space of neo-Roman mimesis, viewers and readers learn how to live in a world where the shadowy world of the unruined Roman past emerges into the neo-Roman present. In chapter 6, I discussed this imaginary space with Freud's example of the city of Rome as an impossible site where every building ever constructed still exists. In this twilight zone, Rome's remnants remain as "lively" or vivid as the ruins of childhood memories that Freud excavated in Pompeii.[1] Reading Wilhelm Jensen's novella *Gradiva: A Pompeiian Fancy* (*Gradiva: Ein Pompejanisches Phantasiestück*) (1903), I will further explore this aspect of neo-Roman mimesis—the exercise of *being* in the Roman past. However, the more intriguing aspect of the novella is this: *Gradiva*, I will claim, is a post-Nietzschean text, exploring the problematic of the relation between original and copy, *and* staging the perfect act of imitation.

Nietzsche's Roman Warriors and the Act of Mimesis

In the previous chapter, I wrote about the artists who laid the groundwork for the Second Empire's practices of neo-Roman mimesis as the transformation of the anti-Roman barbarian of the Napoleonic era into the neo-Roman imperialist. In 370 CE, the philosopher Themistius wrote: "There is in each of us a barbarian tribe, extremely overbearing and intractable—I mean temper and those insatiable desires, which stand opposed to rationality as . . . Germans do to the Romans."[2] Nietzsche asked his contemporaries to rediscover this German barbarian *and* to learn to wear the Roman mask.

In *On the Uses and Disadvantages of History for Life (Vom Nutzen und Nachtheil der Historie für das Leben)*, Nietzsche reflected on the practice of historical mimesis. Written between 1873 and 1874, this essay dealing with the (public) uses of monumental, critical, and antiquarian history is often discussed as a critique of German historicism. Reading it as a meditation on modernity and modernism in the wake of the French Revolution, Elco Runia writes that the essay startled its contemporaries with its unprecedented "attempt to start history anew."[3] This reflection on modernity addressed again the very conditions of heroic, decisive acts—in the Roman mold. I propose to read the essay as an interrogation of neo-Roman mimesis in the vein of Marx's 1852 text on the Eighteenth Brumaire. I base this shift in perspective on two ideas: first, Nietzsche understood the political condition of his age as imperial in nature, and second, monumental history is predicated on the idea that the greatness of the past is "possible for a second time."[4]

Nietzsche liked to wear the mask of Columbus, because philosophy, he thought, was a voyage of discovery, the philosopher-explorer sailing into uncertain terrain.[5] Let me begin with the more familiar aspect of Nietzsche's essay on history, his polemic against the "fever of history" consuming his contemporaries (OU, 60). This excessive preoccupation with the past was in his eyes destructive, the sign of a decadent age, of men weary of life *and* death. Action requires a break with the past, a stepping outside the past—a moment of forgetting, not remembering. Those who always remain within the horizon of their past—an individual, a people, or a culture—will "feebly waste away"; those who seize this "ahistorical" moment will be "healthy, strong, and fruitful" (UL, 90). Philosophical, aesthetic, political creativity was one of Nietzsche's main concerns.

Sometimes this politics of the passions and heroic acts might be informed by models from the past—the actions of Rome's heroic men, for instance. Indeed, these models are necessary. Here, Nietzsche entered the terrain of *historia magistra vitae*, this Roman concept of history based on the desire to imitate the past and to be imitated in the future. "History belongs above all to the man of deeds and power," he writes, reminding his readers that Polybios wrote his "political history" holding up his "[men] of deeds" as teachers providing lessons about how to govern (OU, 67). The "soul of historiography," *monumental* history provides "the great stimuli" for the "man of power" (OU, 70). Conceiving of the past "as worthy of imitation, as imitable and possible for a second time," this mode of using the past introduces the possibility of repeating heroic actions and events (OU, 70).

The risks of historical mimesis are multiple: "There is," Nietzsche wrote, "a degree of historical sensibility that injures and ultimately destroys all living things" (UL, 89). The man who remains entangled in the past will "not find his way back to crude wanting and desiring" (UL, 91). "[T]he capacity to live ahistorically," Nietzsche concluded, is ultimately "more significant and more originary" (UL, 91). We encountered similar ideas about the risks inherent in historical mimesis in Marx's 1852 text. Let me quote Nietzsche's famous conclusions about the dangers of historical mimesis at length: "The ahistorical is like an enveloping atmosphere in which alone life is engendered," Nietzsche wrote and asserted: "only when the human being, by thinking, reflecting, comparing, analyzing, and synthesizing, limits that historical element, only when a bright, flashing, iridescent light is generated within that enveloping cloud of mist—that is, only by means of the power to *utilize the past for life* and to *reshape past events into history* once more—does the human being become a human being" (UL, 91; emphasis mine). What is at stake is the capacity to begin: "in an excess of history the human being ceases once again, and without that mantle of the ahistorical *he would never have begun and would never have dared to begin*" (UL, 91; emphasis mine).

Mere repetition and modernity—as the beginning of something new—

are at odds. Individuals, peoples, cultures search for "inspiration to imitate or do better" yet successful neo-Roman mimesis—as the creation of life, not death—would have to *reshape past events* into great *historical deeds in the present* (UO, 68). Referring to B. G. Niebuhr, the author of *Römische Geschichte* (*Roman History*) (1811–1832), Nietzsche introduces the concept of "a *suprahistorical* vantage point" (OU, 65). Like Mommsen, Niebuhr discovered a model for German post-Napoleonic politics in Roman history and argued that only "impassioned commitment"—the acts of great men—counts (OU, 65). This, Nietzsche thinks, is the vantage point proper to monumental history.

Far from being a mere repetition, this creative imitation does two things: first, the act of imitating the great men and deeds of the past risks death, disdaining the desire: "to live, at any cost" (OU, 68). Second, it obeys the demand that the moments of "greatness" last forever (OU, 68). Monumental history is the command that "the great moments in the struggle of the human individual constitute a chain, that this chain unites mankind across the millennia like a range of mountain peaks, that the summit of such a long-ago moment shall be for me still living" (OU, 68). Like monumental architecture, the practices of monumental history aim for continuity and duration.

Finally, theorizing this process of genuine imitation, Nietzsche takes recourse to Herder's ethno-mimesis and his concept of mimesis. There is a universal law, Nietzsche writes, pertaining to all living things. If a living being "is incapable of drawing a horizon around itself, and at the same time too self-centered to enclose its own view within that of another, it will decline" (OU, 63; translation modified). From this Herderian perspective, imitation is a process of transformation and incorporation (*umbilden* and *einverleiben* are Nietzsche's words).[6] Reflecting on the imitation of the past by the present and more specifically, "the boundary at which the past has to be forgotten if it is not to become the gravedigger of the present," Nietzsche introduces the Herderian question about "the *plastic* power of a man, a people, a culture," and a Herderian answer to this question, defining plastic power as the ability to "transform and incorporate into oneself what is past and foreign" (OU, 62).

The act of imitation involves a moment of recognition: "Behold, greatness already exists!" (OU, 72). In Nietzsche's essay, monumental history's backward glance captures a very specific image. The figure embodying the successful act of imitation is Victoria, the goddess whom Romans worshipped in her temple on the Palatine: "He who cannot sink on the threshold of the moment, who cannot stand balanced like a goddess of victory without growing dizzy or afraid, will never know what happiness is" (OU, 62). This Roman figure embodies Nietzsche's ideal and that of post-Nietzschean decisionism: the man "who acts," the one who "recognizes the rights only of that which is now to come into being" (OU, 64). More importantly, with this Roman goddess of victory, ethno-mimesis becomes neo-Roman mimesis.

Victoria is one connection to the Roman past, the language of masks that accompanies Nietzsche's reflections on the modern condition another. Nietzsche searches for a "German unity in the highest sense," meaning "the unity of German spirit and life after the abolition of the antithesis of form and content" (OU, 82). If this German unity will be found, it may cause the downfall of contemporary culture. Does he also mean to say that it will help Germany achieve victory over all other cultures? The modern era, he writes, is a time of "convention and masquerade" (OU, 85). People wear "masks" hiding the fact that they lost their will to live and act (OU, 84). Even before he has told us that he read Gibbon's *Decline and Fall*, Nietzsche compares this situation to the late Roman Empire:

> [M]odern man suffers from a weakened personality. As the Roman of the imperial era became un-Roman in relation to the world which stood at his service, as he lost himself in the flood of foreigners which came streaming in and degenerated in the midst of the carnival of gods, arts, and customs, so the same must happen to the modern man who allows his artists in history to go on preparing a world exhibition for him: he has become a strolling spectator. (OU, 83)

Without the stimulus of monumental history, life degenerates and people remain spectators instead of becoming *actors*. When monumental history is used to celebrate the great men of the past at the expense of the present, the man who imitates is not a historical actor but merely a man wearing a "masquerade costume" (OU, 72).

The Roman death mask has to be brought to life by the "dark, driving power" of life (OU, 76). Germans are not yet ready to do so because Germans are still marked by a "barbaric" exterior (OU, 79). Indeed, were "an ancient Greek transported into our time," he would take Germans for "barbarians" (OU, 79). How does Nietzsche explain this cultural barbarism, and what exactly does it mean? In the past, Germans imitated French culture. Today, they celebrate German "inwardness," distrusting convention as "vestment" or "disguise" (OU, 81, 80). As a result of this anti-French move, Nietzsche writes, content and form are falling apart. Their "barbaric" exterior now half-heartedly imitates French culture while their interior is too weak to produce "an outward effect and endow itself with a form" (OU, 79, 81). Having failed to create their own "style," the culture of the Germans resembles a "handbook of inward culture for outward barbarians" (UO, 79, 80).

English men are genuine human beings; Germans are not. What does this entail? Among other things, the fact that Germans are not able to act like Romans. As Shakespeare's dramas show, these "flesh-and-blood Englishmen" wear "the Roman toga" exceedingly well (OU, 85). Only genuine human beings are able to bear the weight of Roman death masks. To imagine Germans in Roman togas simply does not work, since Germans are nothing but "abstractions made concrete," hiding behind their "slovenly" imitated French masks (OU, 86).

Let me summarize the core of Nietzsche's thinking about the uses of history with respect to neo-Roman mimesis. Using the language of masks and death masks, Nietzsche re-theorizes Herder's ethno-mimesis, that is, the very ability of a people to fashion an authentic self from material foreign to it—as foreign as the great men of imperial Rome and their goddess of victory. Monumental history is a "hard relay-race" and represents a way of relating to the past through which "greatness goes on living" (OU, 68). Acts of neo-Roman mimesis—acts so successfully performed by his British contemporaries—actualize this greatness in the present, thus serving life and the future.

At the end of the essay, Nietzsche veers away from ancient Rome toward ancient Greece and the culture that he argues was made by men who had found their style. "There were," he writes, addressing German youth, times when Greeks were confronted with the "danger of being overwhelmed by what was past and foreign, of perishing through 'history'" (OU, 122). Never isolated, their culture was "a chaos of foreign, Semitic, Babylonian" and "Egyptian forms" (UO, 122). In this they resembled late imperial Rome or the *Kaiserreich*. But Greeks took once more "possession of themselves" by taking possession of the other (UO, 122). Their culture did not know dissimulation and the antithesis of inner and outer. It was this "unanimity of life, appearance and will" that helped Greeks achieve "victory over all other cultures" (UO, 123).

With this ending, Nietzsche makes a concession to those of his contemporaries who claim the particularity of Germans to consist in being "descendants of antiquity" (UL, 141). He accepts the premise on the condition that Germans think about their identity as "successors" in the "proudest sense" (OU, 103). Germans thus need to decide whether they are content with being "pupils of declining antiquity" (OU, 103). Nietzsche is not. He wants Germans to take a step *beyond* neo-Roman mimesis. At some point in the future, Germans should "claim credit for having developed the spirit of Alexandrian-Roman culture so nobly," Nietzsche wrote, "that we might now as a reward be permitted to set ourselves the even mightier task of striving to get behind and beyond this Alexandrian world and boldly to seek our models in the original ancient Greek world of greatness, naturalness and humanity" (OU, 103). These Greco-Germans would achieve "victory over all other cultures" not as successors to antiquity's decline, but as practitioners of a mimesis reviving the "astonishing powers of antiquity" (OU, 123, 103).

What is Nietzsche's cultural and political program in "The uses and abuses of history for life"? Here, neo-Roman mimesis—the repetition of the acts of great men—requires a Greco-German foundation, requires the memory of an "unhistorical" culture that dared to begin (UO, 103). Eventually, however, this neo-Roman mimesis will give way to a Greco-German politics of unprecedented acts—of the creation of something radically new, something radically different from Europe's neo-Roman imperial culture.[7] But let us remain in Nietzsche's present and examine briefly what else he had to say about Rome and the Roman warrior who occupied such a crucial place in Nietzsche's later thought. In *On the Genealogy of Morality* (1887), written when the *Kaiserreich*'s imperialism was approaching its zenith, Nietzsche praised the Roman warrior. In doing so, he proposed his own theory of re-barbarization, celebrating history's noble races, which proudly "left the concept of barbarian in their traces."[8] Although Nietzsche was not an advocate of colonial expansion, he did have a vision of imperial politics—a politics different from the "decadent 'particularism'" of his time; this vision concerned a new united Europe, not Bismarck's overseas empire; it was tied to Nietzsche's image of Rome and its leaders.

Rome, he wrote in *The Anti-Christ* (1894), was an example of "grand architecture" whose "construction was designed to prove itself through thousands of years."[9] What animated this empire was "the will to tradition," he wrote in 1889, "to authority, to responsibility for centuries to come, to the solidarity of chains of generations, forward and backward *ad infinitum*."[10] In *Genealogy of Morality*, Nietzsche wrote about Roman leaders, whom he deeply admired: they were "[men] of war," not slaves, who still continued to live in Homer's violent world.[11] Concerned above all with the preconditions of ecstatic-heroic action, Nietzsche contrasted the warrior, who delights in destruction, with the Christian: in ancient Rome, the word "bonus" referred to warrior, Nietzsche wrote, not to the man committed to Christian slave morality.[12]

Writing in the wake of the Berlin Congo conference, Nietzsche alluded in *Genealogy* to the brutal conquest stories of non-European territories.[13] The Philistines turned into "uncaged beasts of prey," he wrote, enjoying their "freedom from every social constraint" once they entered the "world outside where the strange, the foreign begins."[14] Having committed their atrocities, they walk away with their "spiritual equilibrium" intact.[15] Noble races, however, are "conscious of this and indeed proud of it"; more than that, they deeply enjoy the "debauches of victory and cruelty." And then Nietzsche added what would become his most infamous sentence: "At the centre of all those noble races we cannot fail to see the beast of prey, the magnificent *blond beast* avidly prowling round for spoil and victory; his hidden center needs release from time to time, the beast must out again, must return to the wild," and in this respect, "Roman, Arabian, Germanic" or "Homeric heroes" are all the same.[16] The concept of the "barbarian" is, Nietzsche proposed, the creation of these noble warriors. For it is their own traits and desires that we find condensed in this figure: what is barbarian is their "'daring,'" their "unpredictability," their scorn for safety, body, life, and their "delight in all destruction." All of this, Nietzsche believed, was condensed "in the image of the 'barbarian,' the 'evil enemy.'"[17] This concept of the barbarian is still alive in the characterization of the colonized, Nietzsche implied. More importantly, it is a concept that Nietzsche himself celebrated, a figure that he contrasted with the weak, decadent men of the *fin-de-siècle*.

When Nietzsche discusses "great politics" between 1881 and 1885, Roman warriors thus play a central role.[18] In conclusion, let us return to one of Nietzsche's passages about monumental history. Here, Nietzsche explains that this use of the past necessarily rests on mere analogies: "[T]hat which was once possible *could present itself as a possibility for a second time* only," he writes, "if the Pythagoreans were right that when the constellation of the heavenly bodies is repeated the same things, down to the smallest event, must be repeated on earth" (OU, 70). Only if this were the case could we conclude "that whenever the stars stand in a certain relation to one another . . . Columbus will again discover America" (OU, 70). Yet while the world is a stage, history is not cyclical: "the earth's drama" does not start over again once the fifth act ends (OU, 70). Genuine mimesis as the *conscious* wearing of Roman masks sustains the "hard relay-race of monumental history" from Polybios to Nietzsche, Augustus to the imperial rulers of European modernity (OU, 68). And this is Nietzsche's novel contribution to the theory of neo-Roman mimesis: the gap between original and copy, Roman and neo-Roman masks, is the mark of imitation in the modern age, the characteristic of a modernist practice of mimesis. And this gap—though he does not say this—opens up the possibility that the new neo-Roman empire will not suffer the same fate.

Gradiva's Ruined Stage, or the Perfect Act of Imitation

Like Dahn's *Struggle for Rome* or the Pergamon Panorama, Wilhelm Jensen's *Gradiva: A Pompeiian Fantasy* (1903) is an exercise in resurrectional realism. That is, through the eyes of its protagonist, the classicist and archeologist Norbert Hanold, it performs the imaginary reconstitution of the ancient Roman world out of its ruins, and by doing so transports character and reader into the past. At first glance, the two novels seem very different: Jensen's love story is located in the modern world, not the sixth century; it focuses on a young classicist, Norbert Hanold, and his beloved, Zoe Bertgang, not Ostrogothic warriors and their enemies; its project is to cure the protagonist of his obsession with the past, not the re-foundation of an empire. Moreover, this story about Hanold's journey to Pompeii, where he encounters Zoe, his childhood friend, and rediscovers his love for her, has no apparent connection to the topic of (post)Roman Empire. On the contrary, the text seems to argue insistently for a life in the present, free from any attachments to a dead past.

This is the logic that Freud discerned: Hanold has to overcome his attachment to Gradiva, the Roman woman represented on a frieze adorning his study, in favor of the living Zoe. At the end of the text, they return to the vibrant modern city, with Hanold having opted to live in the present. And yet, the Pompeiian journey was a necessary detour. Equating Roman ruins and childhood memories, European history and psyche, Freud argues that Hanold needs to return to the past in order to live in the present. Looking at Jensen's Pompeiian stage, he sees Hanold discover Zoe, the original object of his desires, and jettison Gradiva as mere mask.

With this reading, revolving around Hanold's neurotic *cathexis* of a Roman image, Freud misses the novella's political text. It is precisely the question of original and copy, Gradiva and Zoe, which connects the novella to the problematic of neo-Roman mimesis. Let us begin with the relief or, rather, plaster cast, which Hanold acquired on his previous journey to Rome. Hanold thinks of aesthetic mimesis as the successful imitation of life. The point where art captures life is the "act of walking," more specifically the moment when the young woman is about to step forward, lowering her right foot.[19] Fascinated with this gait, Hanold decides to name the young woman Gradiva in analogy to *Mars Gradivus*, the Roman god of war setting out for battle. Yet Hanold's "Roman virgin" is no exalted mythical figure but someone from the sphere of daily life (GRA, 7).[20]

Driven by the experience of a lack that he vaguely associates with the *Gradiva*, Hanold travels to Rome and then to Pompeii, where he encounters Zoe, sitting in the Casa di Meleagro. Mistaking her for Gradiva, it will take Hanold the entire length of the story to understand that this apparition is not a long-dead Pompeiian beauty inexplicably still alive, but the charming Zoe, who lives in the same German city, indeed in his own neighborhood. Once he has regained his "reason" and the *Gradiva* has become first "Zoe-Gradiva" and then "Zoe," his "dear life and lovely present," Hanold asks her to imitate the *Gradiva* by walking over the stepping-stones of a Pompeiian street (GRA, 138).

As I mentioned above, Freud reads this moment as the story's *telos* and final affirmation that Hanold has been cured of his historical fever. I propose to complicate the reading of this final scene, approaching *Gradiva* as a story about ruined stages and Roman masks. When Hanold encounters Zoe for the first time in the Casa di Meleagro, she is sitting before a wall, adorned with a Greco-Roman stage set.[21] Like all true neo-Roman stages, this is a ruined one: the room's mosaic floor is "fallen to decay and weather worn" (GRA, 63). Composing the ensuing scene centered on a moment of (mis)recognition, Jensen might have been inspired by one of the many Pompeii photographs circulating at the turn of the century.[22] We are staring once more at an enigmatic scene on a ruined stage, waiting for the story to unfold. Only this time, the drama does not concern the causes of Rome's fall. In this novella, the ruined Roman stage with its Pompeiian *scaenae frons* mural is the setting of an act of recognition: the recognition of Gradiva—as the necessary condition for Zoe's act of neo-Roman mimesis. Besotted with the Roman woman, Hanold *recognizes* Gradiva in the woman sitting on the stage. "He had found what he was looking for" (GRA, 65).

When he returns the next day and finds her again in the same ruined hall, he tells Zoe, still recognizing her *as Gradiva*, that he recognized her again "at first glance" (GRA, 80). Slowly realizing Hanold's obsession with this long-dead woman, Zoe begins to act *as if she were Gradiva*. In a manner of speaking, Zoe follows the suggestion of Roman muralists, who in a gesture of "representational self-reference," painted theatrical masks into their *scaenae frons*, adorning Pompeiian houses.[23] At the end of their conversation, Hanold asks Zoe, still believing her to be Gradiva, to imitate the latter's walk. He would be happy, he tells her, to observe her "walking as you do in the bas-relief" (GRA, 84). Zoe complies, and when Hanold notices a slight discrepancy, Zoe explains it away.

Nietzsche condensed the practice of historical mimesis in the image of the man who "stand[s] balanced like a goddess of victory"—balanced like the goddess perched on the victory column in Berlin. Let us not overlook the fact that Hanold invents Gradiva as a Roman steeped in Greek culture. As I mentioned above, before ever meeting the woman, Hanold names her after the Roman god of war. Once he decides that she lives in Pompeii, Hanold concludes that she is the patrician daughter of a Roman town magistrate, with the Greek education appropriate to her background.[24] In other words, the woman Zoe learns to imitate is the perfect Hellenized Roman of Jensen's time and the time of Augustus.

When Hanold finally recognizes his childhood friend, Zoe's Roman masquerade ends. Let me remind you of Freud's reading of the novella's penultimate moment when Hanold asks Zoe to copy Gradiva's way of walking: observing this act with the loving gaze and hard-won intellectual distance of the archeologist, he recognizes Zoe as Gradiva's original, and is finally ready to leave the ruins of the past behind. Freud uncharacteristically simplifies this moment. For when Zoe walks across the street, Hanold sees her *acting* as if she were Gradiva, sees her wearing Gradiva's mask. With this act of imitation—an act demanded by Hanold—the Roman woman of Greek genealogy, who was first Gradiva, then Zoe-Gradiva, has now become "Gradiva *rediviva* Zoe Bertgang" (GRA, 139).

Zoe's act is the perfect act of neo-Roman mimesis. This act of wearing the Roman mask produces a new identity—the Roman goddess of war, revived for the present. And only now does Hanold recognize that Zoe resembles Gradiva, noting their "extraordinary resemblance": "What luck, though, that you are not Gradiva, but are like the congenial young woman!" (GRA, 132). Proper imitation of the past works by analogy, conscious of the gap between past and present—this was Nietzsche's insight. Freud famously ignored this moment of "extraordinary resemblance," or the reappearance of Gradiva, yet it is crucial to Jensen's argument about the relationship between past and present. It is only in the Roman past that the German present finds its image.

Jensen's text portrays Hanold's act of recognition of Gradiva on the ruined Roman stage as an act that responds to the desire of the Roman past. When Hanold buys Gradiva's image, he feels himself respond to the "life" that he detects in the frieze (GRA, 8). Standing in the ruins of Pompeii, Hanold detects something still alive in this "site of debris" and Pompeii suddenly shows him an "entirely changed *face*" (GRA, 49, 50; translation modified). Instead of being "alive," the Roman city's "face" appears to him "completely petrified in dead immobility" (GRA, 157). Despite this change, the Roman past is not dead. For Hanold now experiences "a feeling that death was beginning to talk" (GRA, 50).

Under the attentive gaze of this classicist, the dead are waking up, beginning to speak a language only he understands. In Jensen's story, the Roman past addresses Hanold, calls on the German classicist by turning its "other face" toward him (GRA, 52; translation modified). Far from being deluded, Hanold is a specialist in detecting the desire of the past. It is he who encounters this desire, recognizes it as the desire to be imitated, and thus prepares the moment of perfect imitation by asking Zoe to imitate Gradiva.

Jensen's novella thus begins with reflections on aesthetic mimesis—on the lifelike nature of the image—and ends with mimesis as the imitation of an act of the past in the imperial present. I want to end this discussion of *Gradiva* with some brief observations on the novella's resurrectional realism. A passionate archeologist, Hanold is endowed with an unusually vivid "imagination," allowing him to imagine the past as if it were the present (GRA, 11). Under the spell of the frieze, Hanold begins to think about Gradiva in his Berlin study, deciding that she must have lived in Pompeii. Then Jensen writes: "*Thus he saw her*" (GRA, 11). As Hanold's eyes follow her crossing the street, Pompeii's urban center "rose before his imagination as if it were actual, material reality" (GRA, 11; translation modified).[25]

Answering Gradiva's desire, Hanold acquires the power of her sight and enters the past. No longer ruined, the ancient Roman city now "stood vividly before Hanold's eyes," as Jensen's realism conjures up its streets, houses, people, statues, ending again with the image of Gradiva stepping across the stones (GRA, 12). Just as Zoe learns to become *Gradiva rediviva Zoe Bertgang*, Hanold—and through his eyes, the reader—learns to "see" the past, arising from its ruins, learns to enter this in-between space of the imperial imaginary in which the past exists in the present, somewhere between "dreampicture" and "reality" (GRA, 58).

In part 1, we accompanied Aeneas and Evander through the ruins of the archaic settlement that will be Rome, the latter acting as Aeneas's guide. In *Gradiva*, Zoe-Gradiva leads Hanold into the ruins of the past, enabling him to imagine Pompeii as if it were alive. Like Dahn's *Struggle for Rome* and the panoramas of ancient Rome and Pergamon, *Gradiva* is thus a veritable training exercise in the ruin gazing imagination. Jensen's tale, celebrating the German present (its vibrant modern capital and its charming inhabitant, Zoe, who is not a long-dead Pompeiian beauty, but very much alive), is thus not a story that leaves the past behind. It is a story about discovering the past and its desire to be imitated, and about an exemplary act of responding to the desire of the past by imitating it in the service of the imperial German present.[26] Zoe's final act of imitation on the ruined stage of empire is a veritable triumph of neo-Roman mimesis in the modernist mode, informed by the classicist's Nietzschean knowledge that such willful acts are always only approximations, marked by the inevitable gap between original and copy.

Conclusion

The politicians who ruled the Second Empire were not Nietzscheans, interested in modernity as the creation of something radically new. On the contrary, they were set on imitating their rivals and joining them in the imitation of Rome. With the *Kaiserreich*'s rise to world power, neo-Roman mimesis became part of the imperial culture of the Second Empire. Polybios, Josephus, and Paul; Gibbon and Adam Smith; Volney, Michelet, and Fourier—all of these authors reflected on the (neo)Roman imperial projects of their times. Friedrich Ratzel and Oswald Spengler did the same during the *Kaiserreich*. Jensen took his readers into the impossible space of the neo-Roman imperial imaginary where ruins are un-ruined and the distance between past and present begins to shrink. In this twilight zone, Rome's remnants persist as vividly as the ruins of childhood memories that Freud excavated in Pompeii.[27] Committed to the Roman model, Spengler provoked his readers to imagine living in the ruins of the future.

SIXTEEN

Empires, Ruins, and the Conservative Critique of Modernity: Friedrich Ratzel and Oswald Spengler

Introduction: Stranded Objects

At the moment when Louis Bertrand left Paris for Latin Africa, mobilizing the power of Roman ruins against Parisian decadence, Max Nordau wrote *Degeneration* (1895). Like Bertrand, Nordau thought of metropolitan France as decadent. Unlike Bertrand's ruins, the ruins in Nordau's text are metaphorical, signs of a cultural disturbance caused by the collapsing of the walls between past and present, the space of Europe and the non-European world. He believed his mission was to "demolish historical ruins and remove their rubbish," making room for a healthy modern culture.[1] Residing in metropolitan Paris, the Hungarian author dismissed the city's late nineteenth-century imperial culture as an incongruous assemblage of *Überbleibsel*, stranded objects similar to the ones that Forster had encountered in the South Pacific. Women wear their hair like Roman matrons, Nordau complained in his "diatribe of cultural criticism,"[2] and their bedrooms were "harem[s]."[3] This mixing of ages and cultures was a sign of metropolitan Paris's *un-organic* culture. Georg Forster felt ambivalent toward this kind of colonial *leftovers*. Nordau read their presence in metropolitan Paris as the sign of a dying people.[4]

Paving the way for the discourse about authentic *Kultur* and inauthentic *Zivilisation*, Nietzsche argued that modern culture was the product of "pitiful imitation[s]," lacking the "instinct" to make a people's "soul" and its cultural forms coincide (UO, 78, 79). In particular, "'German' culture'" was "a struggling chaos of all the West and of all past ages" (UO, 122). In the realm of culture, the remedy was style, in the political domain the Nietzschean mode of neo-Roman mimesis. Based on analogy, not the naïve donning of Roman masks, this modernist answer to the Roman past, a past "evoking great effects" (UO, 103), not minor fashions, had the power to propel Germany into the grander realm of imperial politics.

The opposition of organic *Kultur* versus inorganic *Zivilisation* permeated the writings of Friedrich Ratzel (1844–1904) and Oswald Spengler (1880–1936). One a geographer, the other a mathematician and philosopher by training, they thought about the imperial present by comparing it to the Roman Empire translating the contrast between *Kultur* and *Zivilisation* into the opposition between two forms or stages of expansion, state-led conquest and economic imperialism. Like Nordau anxious about borders, they privileged *Kultur* and its controlled forms of expansion over *Zivilisation* as boundary-dissolving imperialism.

Retheorizing imperial space and time in the context of the newly emerging German Empire and its neo-Roman mimesis, these conservative critics of modernity also wrote their ruin gazer scenarios with the contrast between *Kultur* and decadent *Zivilisation* in mind. Ratzel's geo-historical gaze scanning Roman ruins and Spengler's baroque scenarios are part of their reflections about the scopic regimes of (post)Roman empires and the spatial imagination proper to these regimes. Moreover, both Ratzel and Spengler addressed the topic of imperial endtime. When Ratzel looked at Roman ruins, he saw witnesses to the ancient empire's enduring power. When Spengler looked at Rome's ruined stage, he saw the West's predetermined end, the course of a history subject to an iron "logic" (DI, 3).

Finally, to their reflections on *Kultur* and *Zivilisation*, conquest and imperialism, ruins, and scopic regimes, Ratzel and Spengler added the dichotomous image of the modern barbarian. On the one hand, the barbarian will remain the imperial other; on the other hand, the barbarian becomes the re-barbarized imperial subject and sovereign. With his praise for the Roman warrior and the modern neo-Roman barbarian in *Genealogy of Morality* (1887), Nietzsche partook in the re-articulation of this image (see previous chapter). Caesarism was Spengler's answer to Nietzsche's ideas about this new kind of leadership based on the will to power. Glorifying this Caesarist leader, Spengler invested him with the delaying or *katechontic* power that Polybios, Paul, Tertullian, and their successors attributed to the imperial sovereign.

Ratzel merely held up the Roman Empire as the model of a particularly solid imperial formation; he was not interested in Nietzschean questions of national style or the aesthetics of imitation. Spengler, however, influenced by Nietzsche's ideas about the unity of content and form, reflected on the authenticity of neo-Roman mimesis. Dismissing all forms of neoclassicism, Spengler found a genuine form of imitation in the paradoxical affirmation of Western civilization's techno-rationalist modernity, the Caesarist politics of world hegemony, and the hard style of Weimar *Sachlichkeit* or sobriety. Mourning the decline of Faustian *Kultur*, Spengler thus simultaneously advocated Roman late civilization and its imperialism as a political model for the twentieth century.

Friedrich Ratzel's Mastery of Space: Mapping Global Space and Rome's Sturdy Ruins

The first volume of Ratzel's *Anthropo-Geographie* (1882) appeared just three years after Fabri published his manifesto for German colonialism. Providing the theoretical underpinnings for the *Kaiserreich*'s overseas expansion, the historical geographer proposed the concept of *Raumbewältigung*, or mastery of space.[5] Like Mommsen, Ratzel saw nothing wrong with imperial mimesis. On the contrary, Ratzel welcomed the *Kaiserreich*'s renewed colonial vigor, writing that Germans were now recognizing "the lack of a space well suited to the expansion whose necessity has been recognized for a long time."[6]

As an imperial thinker, Ratzel was concerned with stability and duration. German colonialism developed late, reaching its zenith after Bismarck's death. Ratzel seized the advantage of the latecomer, surveying and categorizing all forms of expansion, in his *Politische Geographie* (1897). Settler colonialism, he argued, was more durable than others. Underlying this ideal model of colonization is a conservative critique of capitalist modernity. Genuine expansion, Ratzel believed, was a state-led project, whose "mastery of space" was of a "spiritual" nature.[7] Ratzel's conservative anti-capitalist ideas about settler colonialism rested on the dichotomy of state versus society that is so central to much conservative thought.

Ancient Rome functions as the central reference point for Ratzel's analysis of space and expansion. Today's world is Europeanized, he argued, because of Europe's peculiar generative power. Today, Europe is what Rome once was "when it founded its world empire."[8] Like Polybios or Mommsen, Ratzel based his imperial theory on a natural law. Every people, Ratzel asserted, is animated by "the drive to expand" (AGI, 117). The desire to conquer and master space, he argued, is "characteristic" of being a *volk*, and the more nations become conscious of global spatial relations, the more they engage in a "struggle over space."[9]

Imperial *power*, Ratzel argued, followed the logic of concentration and expansion, and his model for this pattern was Rome. This picture of the Roman Empire as a "mastering, creative force" (AGI, 121–122) revolved around the problematic of imperial duration. The early *fortification of the nation* created the precondition for the sudden imperial leap characteristic of all expansive world powers; it also determined the *duration* of this expansion. Rome matters, because Rome, Ratzel argued, taught the world how to build and maintain empires over vast stretches of land. Since Rome, empires rose and continued to exist for centuries. This Roman lesson, Ratzel wrote, argued against the popular idea of the "transience of world empires" (AGI, 160). Every *volk*'s power to expand will eventually weaken, but there is, Ratzel insisted at the height of Europe's imperial age, no "deeply determined law of the decay of great empires" (AGI, 161). To Ratzel, the trope of the cycle of rise and decline was no more than a pesky remnant of Europe's century-long conversations about empire that he dutifully addressed. Rome endured, and so do all empires with a strong *volk* at their core. The idea that large spatial organizations necessarily fall apart because of the increasing ethnic differences that such empires embrace, Ratzel wrote, is simply wrong.

In the context of Rome's world-historical significance, Ratzel expanded on his concept of the *imperial imaginary*. A certain *visual regime* is both the precondition and product of expansion. That is, expansion demands and creates a "wide-angle view," strengthening the "visual power" of the (mind's) eye (AGI, 163). One of the goals of Ratzel's new global geography is to train people to acquire a new "political-geographic gaze."[10] In this geo-historical imaginary, ruins as visible remnants play their part.

Antiquity's ruined cities are the sites where a specifically historical way of looking is born. Like the archeologist, the historian works by conjecture, completing the picture in his mind. In the process, he gains a "depth-gaze," complementing the geographer's wide-angle view (AGI, 121). Following in Herder's footsteps, Ratzel assumes this superior gaze, mapping and categorizing ruins across the globe.[11] The core dichotomy that organizes his categorization is the contrast between "Kultur" and "Barbarei," between peoples at the higher end of cultural achievement and peoples lacking culture (AGII, 513). There are thus barbarian rubble and non-barbarian ruins. Another way of mapping the world's ruins is Ratzel's concept of "*ruin countries*" (AGII, 516). Ratzel's *ruin countries* fall into two categories: the countries of former "Kulturvölker," and those whose rubble is not worth discovering, "territories of nomads," where frequent wars and the perpetual "transition into the ruin-like" constitute a form of life (AGII, 513). These countries are full of "rubble" without any "grandeur" or "duration" (AGII, 512). Much of this is reminiscent of postcolonial studies' analysis of the colonizers' representation of rubble and ruins. While the ruins of *Kulturvölker* reveal to us the complexity of the cultures in question, Ratzel writes, the remnants of *Naturvölker* signify little more than "Here, too, there were once human beings" (AGII, 519).

As important as Rome itself are Rome's imperial ruins. They stand out, because they were left by a powerful people with a "sense of the monumental" (AGII, 515). If one were to map the world's distribution of ruins, the outcome would be predictable: we would find "countries rich in ruins" in exactly those places in Europe where the Romans once ruled (AGII, 515). Great empires thus come with great ruins. The debris that the conquistadors found in the New World was a sign of the complete rupture between present and past; the existence of Rome's "monumental traces" is a symbol of the presence of this past (AGII, 515).

The key concept of duration thus informed Ratzel's discussion of different forms of imperialism and his categorization of ruins. Representing "legacy," imperial ruins tend to accumulate on the *borders* between world empires (AGII, 512).[12] Macaulay traced the Roman ruin belt in North Africa, and Louis Bertrand wrote about Roman ruins in North Africa. Here, the stamp of the empire remained visible everywhere, its ruins "perpetuating the obscure memory of this (secular) tradition."[13] Ratzel thus held up the Roman Empire as the model of a particularly solid imperial formation, a solidity manifest in its enduring ruins. The Roman Empire, with its territories defined by powerful imperial ruins, served as a paradigmatic model in Ratzel's theory of planetary spaces.[14]

Spengler had a weakness for heroes and heroic deeds, defining the Faustian culture of the *Abendland* or Occident as "a culture of the will."[15] Not surprisingly, he counted Napoleon among such men, animated by the "Faustian world-feeling of the deed," his ethos grounded in the willing confrontation with "death" (DI, 355; DII, 274).[16] Deeply influenced by Nietzsche, Spengler thus participated in the Weimar cult of the voluntarist Caesarist leader who dares to act.[17]

Imagining a "Future That Is Already the Past":[18] Spengler's Theory of Neo-Roman Imperialism

Oswald Spengler (1880–1936) published volume 1 of *Der Untergang des Abendlandes* or *The Decline of the West* in 1918, volume 2 in 1922. With this book, Spengler set out to prove that Rome's end was the destiny of all empires. He announced his project as follows: the book's immediate concern was the "analysis of the Decline of that West-European Culture which is now spread over the entire globe" (DI, 50).[19] Its broader theme was the "meaning of all historic 'declines'" (DI, 106; translation modified). Because the picture of the "'Decline of Antiquity'" stands before our eyes "with the most well-defined outlines," it lets us predict the "'Decline of the Occident'" (DI, 106; translation modified). The decline of Antiquity and the decline of the Occident, Spengler thus maintained, were analogous events as distinct as they were similar.

The Decline is infamous for its critique of European modernity as decaying, that is, as the moment when organic *Kultur/culture* is gradually sliding into inorganic *Zivilisation/civilization*. As a result of this transition, a Great Culture's "soul" (DI, 183), born in a particular geographical space and firmly rooted in its soil, degenerates into the calculating reason of rootless, soulless, urban civilization. From this conservative perspective, culture is dominated by politics, whereas civilization is characterized by the reign of money. This portrait of urban civilization partakes in the anti-Semitic discourse about modernity and its urban culture common among conservative critics of modernity. Men acting in the service of an idea belong to the *Abendland*'s stage of *Kultur*—as do peasants, poets, and thinkers. Their counterparts are the men of decaying *Zivilisation*, the rootless urban masses whom Spengler calls *fellaheen*;[20] and the rootless urban intellectuals, embodied in the Jewish intellectual.

Less known than Spengler's conservative *cultural critique of modernity* is the fact that he was also a theorist of empire and the imperial imaginary. Equally unnoticed remains the fact that the Roman Empire constitutes the centerpiece of Spengler's theory of late European modernity. Analyzing the transition from early to late Roman *civilization*, Spengler arrived at the conclusion that imperialism is *civilization* in its most "unadulterated" form (DI, 136), and that world empires were the inevitable end product of all civilizations.

Spengler claimed to have discovered an inexorable "logic" at work in world history, the unstoppable course of "life" toward death (DI, 3).[21] The Nietzschean concept of analogy at the heart of this grand metaphysical project provided the epistemological ground for Spengler's comparison of ancient Roman to modern *civilization*/imperialism and his prediction that the *Abendland* was destined to repeat Rome's demise.[22] Rome's ruins, Spengler argued, were Europe's fate—and at some point in the far future, someone from another Great Culture as yet unknown to us would be looking at the ruins of the West just as the "red-haired barbarians" of Northern Europe have been scrutinizing Roman ruins for centuries (DII, 42).

Spengler repeatedly pointed to the so-called Second Morocco Crisis in 1911 as the moment when the idea for *The Decline* arose in his mind. In the immediate prewar period, the analogy of Roman and neo-Roman empires was common. "The memory of the imperium Romanum," Ludwig Dehio wrote for instance, "inevitably emerged from the mists of what had been supposed to be distant history."[23] Equally common among German politicians and generals was the comparison of the British Empire with Carthage, the German *Kaiserreich* with Rome. Spengler thought of Agadir, the brief standoff between Britain, France, and Germany in 1911, as Hannibal's defeat at Zama and as the moment that announced the final battle between twentieth-century Carthage (or London) and Rome (or Prussian Germany).[24] The result of this coming world war, he hoped in 1911, would be the "long-term foundation of German global hegemony."[25]

Spengler's prophetic stance is deliberately paradoxical: announcing, indeed celebrating, the birth of this new imperialist *civilization,* he also set out to convince his readers that the *Abendland* was coming to its predetermined end.[26] In the course of this long endtime, neo-Roman Prussia would reach its political zenith, but only if a twentieth-century form of *Caesarism* emerged. Spengler understood his imperialist politics and advocacy of Caesarism as hardheaded realism. In this theory of imperialism, the Caesarist leader takes on the familiar *katechontic* function but with a new twist, combining strategic deceleration and symptomatic acceleration. However, while the logic of decline can be decelerated, it can never be reversed. According to Spengler, all that remains is the heroic stance of the modern stoic. Mourning the decline of Faustian *culture,* Spengler thus simultaneously advocated Roman late *civilization* and its imperialism as a political model for the twentieth century.

In the following sections, I will trace Spengler's arguments in detail, focusing on the ways in which his definition of *civilization* informs his "historical parallel" between ancient Roman and modern Western *civilization.*[27] A theorist of (neo-Roman) empire, Spengler also proposed his version of the imperial imaginary. Theorizing the nexus of imperial space and visual imagination, Spengler analyzed the West's scopic regime. Spengler's epistemology and aesthetics of ruins (a topic I touched on in the introduction) is proper to the Occident's Faustian regime of scopic desire and visibility.

Like Polybios's *Histories* or Gibbon's *Decline and Fall*, Spengler's *The Decline* operates with the metaphor of world history as grand spectacle. To the imperial theorist, history consists of world-historical encounters and heroic deeds occurring in front of the "scene building of the world-stage" (DI, 5; translation modified). As I mentioned above, in Spengler's morphological world history the ruined stage of Rome is not a singular phenomenon. Founding his entire political analysis, Spengler's historical parallel between the first and twentieth centuries also informs his ruin gazer scenarios. Spengler asserted that the global cities of the twentieth century were now emerging in their full civilizational splendor, just as Roman cities did in the time of Augustus. Sites of reason and money, not soul and politics, these mega-cities signal the beginning of the Occident's ruinous end. Like Rome, London, Paris, and Berlin will become petrified global cities. Once Europe will have passed through its imperialist stage, they will disintegrate into urban deserts inhabited by "fellaheen" masses lacking any sense of history or destiny, working diligently, suffering in silence (DII, 434).

Nothing could be further removed from Ratzel's evolutionary optimism than Spengler's heroic-fatalistic view of his own times and his morphology's iron logic of decline. Spengler's *Decline* is a fascinating exercise in repetitive ruin gazing. Obsessively directing his and his readers' gaze at the ruined metropolitan stage of the past and the ruined stages of the future, Spengler reassembled the ruined Roman stage as he kept staring at the scenes from world history's theater. The peculiar nature of his staged ruin gazer scenarios, the Faustian historian's fortified gaze, will be the object of my analysis in the concluding part of this chapter.

Spengler's retheorizing of European empires in analogy to the Roman Empire generates two figures: the (modern) barbarian and the Jewish intellectual. At the end of the nineteenth century, racial thinking combined with a "virulent political anti-Semitism."[28] Spengler shared Nietzsche's anti-Semitism and was deeply influenced by the latter's idea that a new imperial age would see a new breed of neo-Romans, Prussian barbarians.[29] Yet all empires have their barbarian others, and Spengler's 1933 publication, *Jahre der Entscheidung (The Hour of Decision)*, painted this danger of barbarians at the *Abendland*'s gates in ways more reminiscent of Gobineau than Nietzsche.[30]

Jeffrey Herf thinks of Spengler as reactionary modernist,[31] Gilbert Merlio sees him as extreme nationalist, and Massimo Ferrari Zumbini locates his politics close to the organizations of the new radical right that emerged in the 1890s.[32] In light of Spengler's deliberately paradoxical stance, combining his unambiguous privileging of *Kultur* (which he claims lasted in Western Europe from 1000 to 1800) with his equally unambiguous celebration of *Civilization* and *imperialism*, I prefer the term "conservative revolutionary," and see *The Decline* as the founding text, *The Hour of Decision* as one of the manifestos of this movement.[33] Welcoming Mussolini's revolution, Spengler had only disdain for traditional conservatives. People mesmerized by the bygone age of *Kultur* were incapable of making history. In the twentieth century, history had to be made under the conditions of and with the means of neo-Roman imperialist *civilization*.

Rewriting World History: Spengler's "Comparative Morphology" (DII, 44)

Let me begin my inquiry into Spengler's theory of (neo)Roman imperialism and imperial imaginary with a brief discussion of his methodological premises. Spengler redefined world history as the coming and going of Great Cultures appearing as suddenly as they vanish. According to Spengler, the Faustian *Culture* of the Occident provided the morphological historian with a privileged vantage point over this process. Only he was in a position to grasp the whole of world history. This assertion of the epistemological privilege of the Western historian contemplating the theater of world history is the core premise of Spengler's historiography.

At the same time, like Ratzel, Spengler attacked Eurocentric linear narratives of world history. He claimed to bring about a Copernican revolution in historiography by taking into account "our" new way of thinking in terms of continents. Producing a *spatialized view*, the global colonial world thus intruded into Spengler's morphology just as it did into Ratzel's *Anthropo-Geographie*. Western Europe likes to think of history as a sequence of "great Cultures" centered around a European core, an invention which, according to Spengler, is nothing but the result of European vanity (DI, 18). Spengler proposes instead to spatialize our historiography. According to his morphological view of separate, unique "singular worlds," Chinese, Aztec-Mayan, or Persian-Jewish-Arab cultures exist next to classical antiquity and the West without the latter occupying any privileged position (DI, 18; translation modified).[34]

Spengler thus replaced the linear paradigm of "Antiquity—Middle Ages—Modernity" (whose origin he traces to the Book of Daniel) with a spatialized study of eight separate autonomous world cultures and their gradual unfolding from birth to death (DI, 18; translation modified).

While Spengler devotes space to all eight, he concentrates on three: first, the *Faustian Culture* of the Occident, whose *Vorzeit* or prehistory starts with the barbarian invasions into Roman territory, the age of *culture* around 1100, and its *civilization* at around 1800. Second, the *Apollonian Culture* of classical antiquity, whose birth he situates around the time of Homer. Antiquity's Hellenist culture comes to an end with Alexander's imperial ventures; its *civilization* flourishes at the time of the Scipios, enters its late stage with Caesar, and Augustus's *Pax Romana*, and its final stage with the so-called soldier-emperors in the third century. And, third, the Orient's *Magian Culture* or the Persian-Jewish-early-Christian-Arab world.[35]

Fate or "destiny" was the word Spengler used to name the logic at work in world history (DI, 120). This iron logic of "life," derived from Goethe's morphology, allowed Spengler to make nonsynchronous comparisons between the respective life stages of the world's advanced *Cultures*.[36] Thus, late Rome and late Europe, for instance, run parallel—one of the aspects of Spengler's "strange journey through time."[37] Each of these eight advanced cultures evolved from their birth in their prehistory to the awakening of their unique soul at the onset of "*culture*," and then to *civilization*, the stage of their decline, before falling back into their "primitive," barbarian prehistory, and thus death (DII, 431). As these world cultures pass from prehistory back to prehistory, each of these stages in turn followed a pattern, evolving from childhood to youth, flowering, decline, and death.[38]

Moreover, each of these stages obeyed their own temporality, ranging from the slow movement of prehistory to the increasingly accelerating time of *culture* and *civilization* to the deceleration setting in during the decline of this fourth stage, ending in the ossification of all structures and modes of thought, and then, finally, the stagnation characterizing a culture once it returned to prehistory. In this time before the end, the time of biology or sheer "duration" reasserts itself (U, 615). As they are dying, all advanced *Cultures* return "from their world of perfect forms back to their primitive [state]" (U, 1101). In "these *very late* stages" when the metaphorical and material ruins of civilization slowly turn to dust, time itself has decayed into the "cosmic-ahistorical" (U, 615, 1101; emphasis mine).

Spengler thus proposes a morphological logic at work within eight autonomous, nonsynchronous *Great Cultures* inexorably moving through predetermined stages and inexorably moving toward their ruinous death. According to Spengler, the relation between these advanced *Cultures* is defined by a feeling of profound alterity. At the height of a Great Culture's development, politics means war. Yet as soon as they encounter *members of a different Culture*, the nations of a Great Culture unify around the "feeling of their souls' relatedness" (DII, 170; translation modified). At the same time, this encounter generates "the notion of the *barbarian*"—someone with a different soul, Spengler wrote, someone who at best belongs to one's culture in appearance, not in essence (DII, 170).

How exactly does Spengler understand the essential differences and different stages of the world's Great Cultures? Let me begin with a first sketch of how Spengler characterized the dichotomy between the stage of *culture* and that of *civilization*, the flowering of a Great Culture and the period of decay that all Great Cultures traverse before turning once more into a "demonic stone desert" (DII, 99).[39] In Spengler's conservative critique of modernity, "inorganic" *Civilization* is abstract reason, *culture* the "expression of [a Great Culture's] soul" (DI, 44, 180). Like other conservative critics of modernity, Spengler added a whole string of antitheses to this opposition of cosmopolitan civilizations versus rooted cultures: country versus city, *volk* versus urban masses, genuine culture or *Bildung* versus shallow mass entertainment, state versus "society," politics driven by national versus economic interests, the ethics of war versus the will to (economic and political) power—and, ultimately, state-led conquest in the service of a theo-political idea versus capitalist imperialism (DI, 33).

Urban civilization, the site of the "homeless financial capital," severs people from their soil and traditions.[40] This separation from organic *culture* in turn diminishes their sense of fate and embeddedness in "the cosmic beat of [his] being" (DII, 102). The changing experience of time is a crucial aspect of Spengler's *culture-civilization* dichotomy. Every new culture and its unique soul arise from a defining moment of terror, a "sudden glimpse of death" (DI, 167). This intense experience of "world-fear" gives birth to a *Culture*'s unique "world view" and its very soul (DI, 166). Moreover, from this encounter with the ultimate limit of existence emerges the perception of time. Being human means apprehending "the uncanny nature of time" (U, 161).[41]

Reflections on the course of time are at the core of Spengler's metaphysical project. Transferring the study of morphology from the realm of nature to that of world history, Spengler argued that Great Cultures have to be studied as living organisms. Two aspects of this vitalist paradigm are important for us: Spengler's emphatic insistence on life as time and his Nietzschean conception of life as relentless drive or will. Historicists collected dead facts; Spengler wanted to discern history's "organic structure," to trace life's process-of-becoming (DI, 5). This meant two things. First, that life *is* time: with birth comes death, and "with fulfillment the end" (DI, 123). Second, like all living things, *Cultures* are subject to life's "direction," its "movement-quality," "drive," and "will" (DI, 122). Spengler thus ultimately rearticulated Aristotle's natural law—which he paraphrases as

"*Every thing-become is mortal* [*Alles Gewordene ist vergänglich*]" (DI, 167; U, 216)—with a Nietzschean philosophy of life.

What does this have to do with Spengler's theory of imperialism? With respect to the political realm, Spengler defines *civilization*'s logic as economic, *culture*'s logic as political. *Civilization* is *culture* decayed, and imperialism has to do with the decay of *culture*'s political forms. *Culture*, this was Spengler's basic tenet, gave *form* to life's relentless drive, while *civilization* was the age of increasing *formlessness*. Put differently, as life begins to die, so do its forms. Losing the ability to shape its world, a culture slowly begins to perish, surrounded by ever-more-ossifying forms, eventually leaving behind ruins or dead forms.

With respect to a *Culture*'s way of experiencing the world, Spengler saw the effects of life's weakening as increasing abstraction, leading from a life of ideas based in lived experience to rigidly systematizing forms of thought and, finally, instrumental rationality. In the realm of the arts, genuine style gives way to various forms of neoclassicisms and their random assortments of dead forms. In the political domain, this means the unleashing of the drive toward ever-increasing expansion, imperialism unbounded by space or time. Empires, Spengler writes, are rigid "petrifacts," the inevitable end product of all *civilizations* (DI, 36).

I will return to Spengler's theory of imperialism and the "daemonic" logic at its core later (DI, 37). Here, I want to draw your attention to Spengler's grand conclusion. Criticizing Eurocentric world histories, Spengler also dismissed the idea of progress underlying the linear Faustian paradigm. Casting his eyes over the world's cultures, Spengler states apodictically that there is no single "'mankind,'" and "'mankind' does not have a telos" (DI, 21; translation modified). Instead, there is a diversity of Great Cultures, each of which has its own *telos*: its own predetermined end.[42] Polybios argued that certain forms of rule might resist the course of empire ultimately predetermined by Aristotle's law of nature: all things perish. Edward Gibbon tried to demonstrate that the cycle of rise and fall might be broken—all the while keeping Polybios's scenario alive. Spengler dresses the Aristotelian law in the metaphysical garb of Faustian morphology. His "biological determinism" is a reassertion of an inexorable law of ruin at work in all Great Cultures, a relentless movement toward death.[43]

There is thus a kind of repetition at work in world history whose basic pattern, Spengler argued, escaped those historians whose eyes remained fixed on the ever-changing stage sets of world history. "The future of the West," Spengler intones, "is not a limitless tending upwards and onwards" taking place in "time-spaces of fantastic dimensions," but "a unique historical event encompassing a few centuries" (DI, 39). It is "strictly limited" with respect to "form and duration" and inescapably determined (DI, 39). While the *Abendland*'s era of *civilization* was entering its zenith in the wake of WWI, its final stage, Spengler did not hesitate to predict, would end around the year 2000.

In the following section, I will explore Spengler's ideas about the irreducible uniqueness of each Great Culture and its being in the world. In these reflections, the Occident emerges as the culture with a privileged relation to the nexus of will and space, and Spengler as the Faustian theorist of the imperial imaginary and its scopic regimes.[44]

Retheorizing Space: Faustian *Culture*, Imperial Imaginary, and Scopic Regime

Friedrich Ratzel isolated the "natural law" of *space-mastery* as the driving force of world history. At the heart of Spengler's definition of *Kulturkreis*, we find a *concept of space* that is post-Ratzelian—that is, post-empirical—and post-Kantian—that is, historicized. While each *Kulturkreis*, or *Culture*, moves through the same stages, each *Kulturkreis* revolves around its own unique *ur*-phenomenon. It is each *Kulturkreis*'s conception of *space* that constitutes this *ur*-phenomenon and that characterizes its unique *soul*. As we saw above, this soul, or, as Fernand Braudel put it, this "mystical being,"[45] is formed in the confrontation with death. It also manifests itself in a culture's specific aesthetic, religious, and political forms, and these forms are inextricably linked to the way in which *a culture imagines and lives space*. Once a *Great Culture* enters the stage of *civilization*, these forms dissolve into *civilization*'s formlessness.

Spatial imagination—and the way a world culture creates its world and lives it in accordance with this imagination—thus constitutes one of the core premises of Spengler's retheorizing of world history. Historicizing Kant's theorem of space as an *a priori* category of thought, Spengler proposes a specifically Faustian definition of space:[46] the idea of boundless, "infinite extension" (DI, 308). At the moment of the Occident's awakening, Gothic "will-culture" expressed its soul by building cathedrals, fighting crusades, and conquering and settling the East (DI, 308). The study of architectural style is thus one way of gaining access to a *Culture*'s experience of space and consequently its worldview. Spengler thematizes this sense of space when he discusses the Apollinian, Faustian, and Magian or Oriental soul.[47] In this context, he also theorizes sight and the different ways of looking characteristic of "Classical Culture," "Western Culture," and Magian or "Arabian Culture" (DI, 183).

As I mentioned above, Spengler ties the birth of culture to the experience of the uncanny nature of time. In his reflections about architecture, Spengler argues that at the moment of its awakening, the Faustian soul invented "immortality" as "endless space" (DI, 188). Gothic architects translated this nexus of infinite space and time into soaring cathedrals. The Faustian man longs for distant shores, and remote futures, experiencing the world historically by looking back at "the distant past" (DI, 14). In contrast, the ancient Greeks remained within the limits of their optically restricted sensuality. Of limited mobility, their culture expressed the "corporally-present individual thing" (DI, 198). The experience of the world proper to Greek culture finds its political expression in the idea of the state as a body made of citizens; its architectural expression is the temple as body, mysteriously circling around its center.

None of the ways in which classical antiquity lives space allow for the idea of a space extending into geographical or historical distance. According to Spengler, the Greek *skene* is the best expression of their limited horizon and ahistorical being. Comparing "the skene of Attic theater" to the polis, the smallest stage of Being, Spengler argued that Greek "being" lacked depth perspective and the Faustian sense for open horizons by pointing to the "flat back-wall" of the scene-building as a feature that restricted the space of the Attic stage (DI, 147; translation modified).

Each *Culture* also has its particular views of sight and the act of seeing itself. Greek philosophers theorized the act of seeing as a penetration of the body by material particles emanating from the object, and sculptors focused this gaze on the materiality of the body. In contrast, Faustian artists draw the beholder's attention to the statues' "eyes look[ing] into the distance" (DI, 216). Egyptian friezes force the beholder's gaze in one direction only, whereas Western painting liberates the viewer's gaze into infinite space. Like everything else, the Faustian soul and its gaze, scanning the far horizons, decline in the transition from *culture* to *civilization*.

Spengler connects the Faustian experience of space and acts of seeing to the mastery over that which is foreign. Summing up his revision of Kantian philosophy, Spengler writes that "[s]pace as *a priori* form of perception" involves "an assertion of supremacy of soul over the alien [das Fremde]" (DI, 310). There is no difference between "will" and "space-as-depth" (DI, 310). Faustian *Culture*, Spengler concludes, is unique because it is centered on the notion of a "pure space" as the effect of the Faustian desire to expand "into the distance." While penetrating all forms of Occidental *Culture*, this way of conceptualizing and experiencing space as expressing the will to dominate is fundamentally foreign to other cultures.

The identity of "*space*" and "*will*" informs the projects of all Faustian men striving to master "world space" (DI, 310; translation modified). Spengler locates a tension at the core of this imperial way of seeing, experiencing, and dominating space, an unsettling confrontation with infinite space. The solitude that characterizes Faustian heroes is the feeling of a tension in this "void without limits" that is ultimately uncanny: the desire "to penetrate the Infinite" stems from both a *longing for* and fear of the void (DI, 186, 187).[48]

It is precisely at this point that Spengler emerges as one of the major theorists of modern neo-Roman empire and imperial imaginary. For what Spengler does in these sections is to theorize the West—its politics and culture—as colonial and imperial in essence. He does this by historicizing and culturally contextualizing ideas about space, spatial imagination, and expansion. In Ratzel's political geography, all nations follow the natural law of expansion. Similarly, in Spengler's paradigm, all cultures expand, but their forms of expansion differ, because their conceptions of space are unique. As we just saw, according to Spengler, Faustian culture is defined by the nexus of will and space. Essentially passive, Antiquity, Spengler contends, lacked this connection. Comparing Napoleon, the West's first politician to think in terms of world empire, to Caesar, Spengler claims that the former's will is not the same as the energy directed at the outside world that characterized Caesar.[49]

Second, Spengler's analysis of a culture's way of imagining space leads him to theorize that culture's *scopic regime*, that is, its field of vision and its limits, and the subject of this field of vision and its scopic desires. Only the Faustian soul is driven by a desire to go beyond the empirical, beyond that which is visually apprehended. Spengler understands this longing to conquer "empty space" as the iron "will to overcome and break all resistances of the visible" (DI, 185–186). In this discussion, sensory perception refers primarily to the visual; this is a culture that strives to "transcend every optical limitation" (DI, 198). In Spengler's view, the Faustian subject is driven by his scopic desire for mastery and "suffers under this limitation of our sense-perception" (DI, 332). This is *in nuce* a theory of the imperial imaginary, one that Carl Schmitt will return to in 1940, analyzing the Third Reich.

The concept of the West's expansive force and will to expand is central to Spengler's theory of the imperial imaginary. Let me elaborate in more depth on his ideas about the difference between the spatial imaginations of classical antiquity versus the West. One of the key contrasts that emerge from these discussions ranging across Occidental *culture* and *civilization*, as well as Hellenist *culture* and Roman *civilization*, is the opposition between

Heimat and *Weltraum*, limited versus limitless expansion. In his chapter on the forms of the soul, Spengler traces this radical difference. While Greeks and Romans heard about Egyptians' and Carthaginians' journeys along the coast of Africa, the news left them entirely unmoved. Accentuating the opposition between Faustian longing for adventure and Greek caution, Spengler contrasts the fifteenth-century Spanish and Portuguese conquests and the Hellenic colonization of the eighth-century-BCE Greeks, averse to leaving the polis, who experienced *Heimat* as "the ground on which [their] city was built" (DI, 335). Their *narrow field of vision* did not encompass the infinity of the oceans; rather, beyond their home territory began "the alien, the enemy [die Fremde, der Feind]" (DI, 334).[50] *The scopic regime of Antiquity's Hellenist culture* thus remained well circumscribed, its subject situated in place, and in a clearly demarcated distance from its barbarian "others." Even the Romans, Spengler argued, never attempted to penetrate Africa's interior. *Patria* always meant *Urbs Roma*. Devoid of any symbolic urge to expand, Romans fought wars in order to secure their possessions. No *Reich* spanning the entire globe comparable to that of the Spanish Habsburgs existed. There was imperialism, but it was not of the European kind. While the space of classical antiquity and its scopic regime thus remained territorially delimited, Faustian *Heimat* is compatible with "restless wanderings" (DI, 335). Eventually, Faustian *Culture* acquired a "planetary character" transforming the entire "globe into a single colonial and economic system" (DI, 334, 335).

The Faustian Ruins of the Past

If the Faustian scopic regime is characterized by a particular desire to overcome the realm of the empirical, that is, the visible, then it comes as no surprise that ruins—these material remains of the past that invite the beholder's gaze beyond the realm of the empirical—play a crucial role in Spengler's ideas about Faustian *Culture*. Faustian *Culture* is obsessed with the ruins of the past, its gaze responding to their provocation to re-create what is no longer visible. Spengler describes this Faustian fascination with the fragments of the past as a kind of scopophilia: they invite the eye to fill the empty space. He theorizes a kind of resurrectional drive, basing it on a Faustian longing for boundless space and the will to overcome and "break all resistances of the visible" (DI, 185–186). It is in this context of Faustian fascination with infinite space that Spengler theorizes ruins, their particular epistemology and aesthetics. The Faustian experiences a kind of "secret piety" for "the rubble-like [das Trümmerhafte]" (DI, 254). Like so many ruin theorists, he claims this fascination did not exist in antiquity (see introduction). In contrast to these Faustian ruins, representing the "triumph of time," Greek ruins merely signify the triumph of barbarism over style (DI, 254, note 3).

Spengler offers both an epistemology and an aesthetics of ruins. Faustian *Culture* is obsessed with ruins and the act of imagining them as whole. Using Winckelmann's fascination with the mutilated remains of Greek art, Spengler gives an imperial twist to the eighteenth-century account of the Faustian gaze at the fragmented statues, linking the wide spaces of empire to the scopophilia that drives the *Abendland*'s obsession with the fragments of the past. In contrast to statues, the wounded torso of Heracles, for instance, is surrounded by something "pointing into the distance," he claims, inciting our eyes to fill "the empty space of missing limbs with the pulse and swing of invisible lines" (DI, 255). If we were to repair this ruined remnant of a body, we would destroy its effect, Spengler writes, because "the secret charm of endless possibilities" would come to an end (DI, 255).

In Spengler, the desire for empire and the desire for ruins belong together. Both are expressions of the Faustian (scopic) desires for mastery of space and time. Ruins function like Winckelmann's famous mutilated statues, setting in motion this exploration of unlimited possibilities, infinite ways of visually complementing what is not there to see. Patina on bronze statues, blackened marble, or the broken limbs of a statue—all these vestiges left by age provoke visual trajectories in both the literal and metaphorical sense, since they "abolish for our inner eye the limitations of time and space" (DI, 255). The Western European gaze, Spengler concludes, is the master's gaze (see DI, 38). Set on transgressing the borders of the visible, Faustian *Culture* is above all a culture of explorers and a culture obsessed with the past and its ruins—territories beyond the borders of the visible.

Thus, while Ratzel argued that a *volk*'s drive toward expansion gradually gives birth to its way of conceiving space, Spengler reversed Ratzel's causality, arguing that a Great *Culture*'s spatial imagination determines whether—and in which form—it will expand its territory. More significantly, Spengler's history of rise and decline is also a history of particular scopic regimes, their fields of vision, and their subjects' scopic desires and gaze—a field and a gaze which, in the case of Faustian *Culture*, eventually becomes completely unbounded and ultimately decays. This process, the waning of the Faustian gaze, is the effect of Spengler's law of ruin affecting all cultures as they transition into civilization. What is important for our analysis of Spengler's ruin gazing scenarios is this: with the transition into *civilization*, the Faustian gaze loses the power to take hold of its objects.

The literal and metaphorical Faustian drive toward infinite space thus characterizes all thought and practices of the *Abendland*, among them the desire to "see" faraway places. The scopic regime proper to Faustian *Culture* also shapes the historian's view of the past. World history, Spengler writes, demands a Faustian eye, whose perspective Spengler defines as both synoptic *and* contemplative. Spengler's new landscape of diverse cultures thus requires a specific optics as the morphological historian's gaze at the past tries to grasp the wide expanse of the Faustian world at a glance—and from an elevated point of view. We are familiar with this wide-angle view—from Roman theorists of empire to Gibbon, from Scipio to Fourier. But let us not forget Spengler's premise: our own gaze is transient, because it belongs exclusively to a particular *Culture*. Reconstructed under conditions of *civilization*, the Faustian historian's imperial perspective is inherently unstable and inherently in need of stabilization.[51]

As I wrote above, this conception of the Faustian historian's gaze has consequences for Spengler's ruin gazer scenarios. Posing as the *Abendland*'s last ruin gazer, Spengler writes his endtime scenarios as the staging of the Faustian historian's fortified gaze. Yet, before analyzing Spengler's scenarios and their gaze in more depth, we do need to explore Spengler's "grand parallel" between Roman first-century and neo-Roman twentieth-century imperialism. I will begin this discussion with another look at Spengler's *culture* versus *civilization* dichotomy. *Culture*, Spengler agued, is the stage of conquering states and their settler colonies, *civilization* the stage of amorphous, ever-expanding empires. At the core of this dichotomy, we find the opposition between form-conscious and formless expansion, politics and economics. There is conquest at the moment of Faustian *Culture*'s awakening—the Teutonic Knights' settling of the East, for instance; and there are *civilization*'s imperial ventures—Charles V, Napoleon, and Cecil Rhodes. With late *civilization*, sovereign states decay, leaving only political parties, defending private interests, not those of the nation.[52] Spengler shares this view, privileging politically motivated conquest over economically driven imperialism, with other radical conservative critics of capitalism and parliamentary democracy, along with their longing for a strong state and a strong leader.

In a second step, I will discuss in more detail Spengler's views of the Roman Empire as a model of this process. Spengler's grand analogy between Roman and Western *civilization* actually involves two analogies: first, the analogy between the heroic era of Rome's early *civilization* (the age of the Scipios and the Punic Wars) and the early twentieth century; and second, the analogy between Rome's later *civilization* (the age of Caesar, Augustus, and the post-Augustan emperors) and the twentieth century's later decades. I will focus on Spengler's conception of the ancient empire in terms of this difference, and Spengler's version of Caesarism as an integral part of Antiquity's transition to Roman imperial *civilization*. It is the function of Caesarist leaders to overcome the fragmentation of the state and society through his alliance with the urban masses—however distasteful they are to Spengler's aristocratic sensibility.[53]

Spengler's Grand Parallel: First- and Twentieth-Century Imperialism/Caesarism

Spengler associates *culture* with nation, and imperialism with the decline of the nation and loss of its soul. In this context of politics and sovereignty, the soul in turn is linked to a (nonbiological) notion of race, designating the attitude of elites acting in the service of a national idea. Representing a *Culture*'s "race-ideal," this nobility experiences "belonging to a nation" as its "historical mission" (U, 780 and 774). This intense spiritual experience lived by only a few men is a form of "being awake" (U, 780).[54]

What Spengler argues here are two things: 1) history means the fate of a nation and the nobility's heroic struggle in the service of this idea; and 2) the very concept of history is limited to Faustian culture. Only Faustian people, Spengler writes, "are conscious of the telos of their history." And *culture* is the only stage when nations make history, deciding to be history's subject. Spengler frequently cites the example of the Hohenstaufen dynasty and the northern crusades they started in the twelfth century. To Spengler, this eastward expansion and settlement is the moment when Faustian culture starts to awaken to its full potential.

Spengler's Nietzschean noble elites embodying the nation's being thus have a sense of fate. Committed to an ethics of action, their actions are based on their will to power. Moreover, they have the idea of race as "deeply felt genealogy" (U, 775).[55] At the same time, all Great Cultures contain a second minority for which Spengler has nothing but contempt: "book-people," "eternally scared," who are the "waste" produced by all Great *Cultures* in their transition from *culture* to *civilization* (U, 781). Weary cosmopolitans, they are animated by their hatred of the idea of "history as destiny"; their *culture* is "behind them and no idea of future before them" (U, 781, 454, 455). At home in the emerging mega-cities and cynical about the heroic act, these intellectuals are the "spiritual leaders of fellah-dom [Fellachentum]" (U, 781).

In Spengler's conservative critique of modernity, *culture* thus obeys a political logic. Its very essence is politics, connected to notions of destiny,

Heimat, and the will to power. The quest for power in the age of *culture* is profoundly political, indeed guided by a theo-political idea, as Spengler's example of the Hohenstaufen shows. Moreover, this will to power finds its form in the absolute state. It was, however, not only the theo-political idea of the state and its sovereign that defined the age of *culture*. The nations of a Great Culture define their very being by waging war against other nations. With *civilization* ends the idea of service to the state, leaving nothing but the naked will to power. This power devoid of any traditional legitimation characterizes the Caesarist leader.

The rise of Caesarism in the transition from *culture* to *civilization* is a Roman story. Hellenist Athens was *culture*, and imperial Rome *civilization*. Representatives of Antiquity's endtime, Romans did not have a soul, but only intellect. "[B]arbarians" blessed with a practical imagination, they built an empire spreading from Rome to a global network of "world-cities" (DI, 32). Economics, not politics, explains the Roman Empire—and by implication, Spengler's own era. However, Rome's increasing obsession with economic issues transformed it from a strong state into a weak empire. The heroic age of Rome's *civilization*, Spengler implies, was the era of the Punic Wars when Rome conquered Carthage. At this moment, Rome, Spengler writes, represented early, and Carthage late, *civilization*. That is, Rome was still in *civilization*'s beginning phase, the "time when states are waging wars" (U, 1088) about world hegemony, and Carthage lost because the Carthaginians subordinated politics to their economic interests. With the victory of Scipio the Younger, Rome itself entered its mature imperialist era, when "money triumphs in the form of democracy," eventually leading to the disintegration of traditional political structures and Caesarism with its endless wars for the private possession of the world (U, 1102).

Dismissing debates about the difference between the late Republic and the Principate, Caesar and Augustus as meaningless, Spengler locates the emergence of the prototype of the Caesarist leader embodying nothing but "personal authority" as early as the third century BCE (U, 1101).[56] From this perspective, Augustus's restoration of traditional Roman culture becomes a mere "costume" or mask, hiding the fact that the Caesarist leader is no longer legitimated by political office but "personal talent"; that his will to power is no longer based on Roman tradition but military force (U, 1104). *Divus* is an empty formula and the Augustan Principate a form of formless, absolute rule. In this late *civilization*, Spengler writes, nothing matters but "purely zoological questions of powers" (U, 614).

Like all epiphenomena of *civilization*, Caesarism is itself subject to decay. In other words, there is a Caesarism worth imitating and one which is the symptom of a *civilization* in its death throes. After Caesar and Augustus, the best form of Caesarist leadership emerged in the era from Nerva to Marc Aurelius (ca. 96–180 CE). The endphase of Rome's *civilization* then saw "ever more negro-like struggles for the title of Caesar" fought by soldier-emperors ruling over subjects without "history" and "soul" (U, 616, 617). With Septimus Severus (the emperor born in Roman Africa who ruled from 193 to 211 CE), late *civilization* entered the phase when *Cultures* revert back into barbarism.

Discussing Antiquity, Spengler thus again argued that the logic of *late civilizations* is relentless expansion for territorial and economic gain. One aspect of Spengler's theory of *civilization* and its imperialist core deserves further attention. I mentioned how Spengler connected the weakening of *culture*'s forms in *civilization* to the unleashing of imperialism's drive. According to Spengler, civilizations are subject to an iron imperialist logic beyond human volition, "something daemonic" and ultimately uncanny (U, 51). Discussing the coming and going of Great Cultures, Spengler formulates his vitalism in a language that comes surprisingly close to Freud's. When a Great *Culture* is born and its soul separates itself from "formlessness," the *Culture*'s "living Being" consists in the "struggle of the idea [that defines it]" against the chaos of the outside world—and against "the unconscious within" (U, 143).

Writing about the decisionist form that politics takes in Faustian *culture*, Spengler again puts a psychoanalytic twist on his Nietzschean power politics of imperial expansion: "What is often termed these days vital energy [vitality], that 'id' that is within us, that will go forward and upward at any cost, our blind, cosmic, longing drive [Drang] for recognition and power" (U, 1109). On the basis of this concept of a "cosmic 'id,'" Spengler then articulated his version of imperialism's totalizing law: "For one can only *grow or die out*. There is no third possibility" (U, 1109; emphasis in original). As the soul loses its power to create coherent forms, the relentless drive of this unconscious is unleashed in the age of civilization. All *late civilizations* are subject to this demonic tendency operating independently of the will of any individual or *volk*. They are "seized" by this uncanny force, pressed into its service (U, 51).[57] Germany's acquisition of colonies is one of Spengler's examples; the other is the Roman-style Prussian imperialism of the future.

The Return of Scipio and the Future Prusso-Germanic Empire

How exactly did Spengler then imagine the demise of Rome? Rome's "typical final state," Spengler contended, was not the result of barbarian attacks, but occurred as "extinction from within" (U, 144). The violent end of Antiquity at the hand of barbarians distinguishes it from other *Great Cultures*. Invaded by Germanic tribes, Antiquity came to an end before living out its "endstage" (U, 687). Like all *Cultures*, Antiquity reached the stage of *civilization* by following its history's "organisch-logische Folge" (U, 43). This was Antiquity's "fate," and when Germanic tribes sacked imperial Rome, the empire's late *civilization* was already in the process of dying (U, 43). The end of Antiquity was thus caused not by a precipitous fall but by decline and death. In other words, empires do not fall; they perish.

Not surprisingly, Spengler finds his ideas about the inevitable end of Rome confirmed by Polybios. Defining the Punic Wars as the "era of warring states" at the onset of Antiquity's entry into *civilization*, Spengler reminds his readers of Scipio the Elder's "fear about the fate that a polis faced when burdened by the tasks of ruling the world" (U, 1089). Scipio's efforts to "avoid all future conquests" were in vain because "imperialism is a necessary event in every *civilization*" (U, 1089). Ultimately, all nations will be forced into their predetermined "role of master" (U, 1089). The uncontrollable drive to expand characterizes *civilization* as much as the ever-more-decaying forms of Caesarist leadership. Scipio the Elder lived at the early, Scipio the Younger at a later stage of *civilization*, when the *orbis Romanum* had devolved into a "formless world" (U, 1089). Here, Spengler alludes to Polybios's ruin gazer scenario. Scipio the Younger chose "imperialism," although "this clear-eyed leader foresaw the fate of his city" (U, 1099–1100).

Within Spengler's iron logic of decline, the Caesarist leader's function exceeds that of preventing the empire's precipitous fall by fighting against barbarian assaults. Caught in *civilization*'s rush toward the end, the Caesarist sovereigns temporarily delay the inevitable decline and death, delay the moment of *civilization*'s final "return to Nature" (U, 977). In this version, the Caesarist leaders of early and late *civilization* are thus both accelerator and delayer. Once *civilization* reenters the terrain of prehistory, the utterly decayed forms of Caesarism lose the power to resist the course of time.

In Spengler's reflections on the Prusso-Germanic Empire of the future, the Caesarist leader occupies a central role. As I wrote above, making the relentless pursuit of ever greater expansion for territorial and economic gain central to *civilization*, Spengler also asserted that Faustian culture's drive to expand exceeded that of all other Great Cultures. Nothing captured this logic better than Cecil Rhodes's slogan that "expansion is everything" (DI, 37). With this slogan, Spengler wrote, Rhodes outlined the very essence of the "remote, Western, Germanic, and especially German future" (DI, 37, translation modified). Rhodes is Spengler's model for the

Caesarist leader who might be able to postpone the end of this relentlessly expanding imperialism of the future. Under the strong leadership of the Prussian monarchy, Germany had fought its classical wars: 1813, 1870, and 1914. This time is over, and Europe will now see an epoch in which politics becomes Roman.

What will the *Abendland*'s remote future look like? Expanding its hegemony across the entire globe, the Occident will be ruled by a new Caesarist leader, a Prussian dictator, straining to give form to economic interests becoming ever more autonomous from the state. Having reached its zenith in the course of the twentieth century under these new forms of rule, the West will repeat Roman *late time* and its slow decay. The inevitable endform of all *civilizations*, Roman-style empires become ossified formations, lingering for centuries before they finally perish, leaving behind ruins going to dust. They die because they are subject to the inexorable law of ruin, which manifests itself as imperialism and Caesarism, *civilization*'s decayed forms of conquest and political leadership.

Destined to repeat Rome's transition from *culture* to *civilization*, from heroic conquest to unfettered economic imperialism, the *Abendland* will thus repeat Rome's ruinous fate. Before exploring Spengler's ideas about the Occident's last empire in more detail, I will briefly return to Spengler's Nietzschean concept of analogy, grounding his comparatist morphology or the comparison of the nonsynchronous. For analogy is the concept at the heart of Spengler's thinking about the possibility of neo-Roman mimesis.

Neo-Roman Mimesis: Repetition and Analogy

Let me begin with a statement that seems at first glance inimical to the very idea of neo-Roman mimesis. In Spengler's morphological picture, classical antiquity and the Occident were two radically different *Cultures*. By arguing the West's superiority, Farrenkopf writes, Spengler betrays signs of "hostility toward antiquity."[58] By emphasizing the continuity between modernity and classical antiquity, his contemporaries, Spengler polemicized, repeated the Romans' practice of inventing their prehistory. Germans felt too close an affinity to the ancients. By analyzing the distinct souls of Antiquity and Occident, he set out to demonstrate "how immeasurably alien and distant these things are from our inner selves" (DI, 27). There was, for instance, a radical difference between the Occident's historical consciousness and Antiquity's "determination to banish distance, in every aspect, from its world-consciousness" (DI, 9). In Greco-Roman

Antiquity, the idea of cosmos does not name a world that *is becoming* but one that *is*.[59] And yet, Spengler maintains, in contemplating Antiquity's evolution we may find "the constant alter ego of our own actuality" (DI, 27). Revealing the similarity and difference of Antiquity and Occident, his analogical method allowed us to see beyond the mere resemblance of world history's "stage sets" (DI, 5; translation modified).

There has always been, Spengler wrote, a sense that events from the Roman past were repeated in the present. Napoleon's contemporaries compared him to Caesar, the Jacobins thought of themselves as Romans, and Rhodes collected biographies of Caesar. This sense of repetition, Spengler maintained, was grounded in superficial knowledge, whereas his own analogical understanding of the phenomenon rested on the sober "technique of analogy" (DI, 5). With these reflections on analogy, Spengler explicitly referred to Goethe, implicitly to Nietzsche. Recall his idea that the core of monumental history was analogy because history *was not cyclical*, because the drama did not start over again once the fifth act ended. With his determinist logic, Spengler reintroduced the cyclical model of birth and death into world history. Second, recall that Nietzsche proposed a specifically modernist form of neo-Roman mimesis, a self-conscious act of analogical practice that would result in a unified German-Roman style of the political. Asserting world history's morphological structure and the synchronicity of asynchronous historical moments, Spengler claimed that "eras, epochs, situations, persons [do repeat] themselves true to type" (DI, 4).

The basic structure of Roman *civilization* is in the process of repeating itself in the West—this was Spengler's theoretical intervention. Making his contemporaries aware of the deep similarities between past and present in order to lay the groundwork for a genuine imitation of imperial Rome was his political project. Spengler's morpho-logic thus encompassed a model of imperial mimesis as the deep affinity between Rome's *civilization* and the Faustian present. A lengthy passage revolving around the Colosseum and Spengler's reflections on genuine Roman ruins lets us understand Spengler's ideas about the relationship between nonsynchronous comparison (the laying bare of the structural similarities between distinct historical moments) and imperial mimesis (as the self-reflective practice based on this comparison).

Like so many authors writing about ancient Rome, Spengler penned his moment in ruins in his diary. This scene about having been moved to tears in front of an "*insignificant* ruin" betrays the melancholia at the heart of Spengler's flamboyant stoicism.[60] The West's "love of Antiquity" strikes him as a puzzle that needs solving.[61] Here is a puzzle for us to solve: What is the opposite of an "insignificant" ruin? In *The Decline*, Spengler told his readers that only structures like the Colosseum with the "brown massiveness of their brick construction" express "the *real* Rome," the "practical sense" of Rome's engineers (DI, 44). There are thus authentic Roman ruins, powerful structural skeletons. The colosseum would leave him cold, Spengler added, if the emperors' statues and all the other "pretentious" decorations were still visible (DI, 44). These ruins embodied genuine Roman-ness because they were stripped of Roman neoclassicism.

Spengler made these comments with plaster models of ancient Rome in mind displayed at the 1911 Italian World's Fair. Comparing the *Kaiserreich*'s mass culture to the late Roman classicism on display, Spengler wrote that the reconstructed "imperial fora" with their baroque ornamentations were as "empty" as a "modern International Exhibition" (DI, 44). Late *civilizations* replace style with neoclassicist "simulacra" (U, 255). Like imperial Rome, his own neo-Roman era is marked by the contrast between the stylistic looting characterizing the *Kaiserreich*'s "architecture" and the magnificent, highly intellectual forms characterizing steel mills (DI, 44).

Genuine neo-Roman mimesis foregoes neoclassicism. Only the austere modernism of industrial design captured the essence of Roman-ness embodied in the Colosseum. Spengler's model for twentieth-century mimesis thus involved a particular aspect of late Roman civilization: "Rome, with its rigorous realism—uninspired, barbaric, disciplined, practical, Protestant, *Prussian*—will always give us, working as we must by analogies, the key to understanding our own future" (DI, 26).

Before the End: Faustian Imperialism and Caesarism

Spengler's infamous *Kulturkritik* or analysis of Western modernity as decadent is thus both a conservative critique and a stoic celebration of the Occident's coming imperialist *civilization*, expression of "pure intellect and purely extensive" (U, 685). Let me remind you again of the paradigm informing Spengler's comparison of Antiquity's past and the Occident's present and future: "[Studying] another biography we come to know ourselves" and who "we will be" (U, 612). These comparisons between his present and the successive stages of Antiquity's *civilization*, Spengler argued, constituted the firm ground for his prophecies. The Occident's incipient neo-Roman *civilization*, whose "arena" will be the "entire earth," will cover whatever remains of older *cultures* with "an ever denser layer of west European forms of life" (U, 610). And then the Occident will repeat Antiquity's decline.

Spengler determined his own moment as the stage when *civilizations* unfold their essence and perpetual war over "world hegemony" begins (U, 1097). What is his picture of the *Occident*'s imperial future? Spreading *civilization* across the entire globe was the "mission of the Germans as the Occident's last Nation." Modeled on the late Roman Empire, this future empire will surpass it by the unrivaled "force" of its expansion (U, 598). Roman-style Caesarism, the era of the "last Führer," is now on the agenda (U, 1101). Spengler's Caesarist leaders, I argued above, act as both accelerators and delayers. They are at the mercy of *civilization*'s uncanny drive toward ever greater territorial and temporal expansion. Yet, as heirs to Prussia's exceptionally strong political tradition, Spengler's future Caesarists will have the strength to delay: *"We, who still have History and make History"* (U, 612; emphasis mine).

Once Faustian *civilization* enters its final stage, Caesarist leaders of a new kind will rule, reincarnations of Rome's third-century soldier-emperors. Spengler thus rethinks the *katechontic* leader: on the one hand, the Caesarist leader is a symptom of *civilization*'s accelerating trajectory toward its demise; on the other hand, by overcoming *civilization*'s inexorable corrosion of Faustian *Kultur*'s political forms, the Caesarist sovereign will temporarily delay the Occident's repetition of Rome's end. Put differently, Roman *civilization*'s early form of Caesarism is a strategy for slowing down imperialism's inexorable movement toward this late and final period of decline, a second barbarism. Like the *Imperium Romanum*, the West's future Prussian empire might ward off this ruinous end—but only for a while.

Spengler's Roman Ruins of Modernity

According to Spengler, the work of the Occidental historian consisted in translating the scenes from world history's theater into a "memory picture" (DI, 103) of all those cultures that have been—and all those that will have been. Contemplating the theater of his memory, Spengler sees ancient Roman ruins in the landscapes of the future. Beginning with the scopic dimensions of ruin gazer scenarios and returning to the problematic of the Caesarist leader, I will explore the specificity of Spengler's scenarios. Ratzel and Spengler both theorized empire, space, and ruins with an eye toward the Roman Empire. Ratzel surveyed the world's ruins and ruin countries, expressing both awe and desolation. Spengler's *Decline* is a text of ruin gazer scenarios, centered on the scopic mastery of the imperial subject.

Spengler positioned himself as the Occident's last ruin gazer. He analyzed world history as a relentlessly accelerating movement, leaving the occidental visionary standing "on the summit, the point where the fifth act begins. The last decisions are taken. The tragedy ends."[62] Like all aspects characterizing Faustian *Culture*, its scopic regime—its desires and its clear-eyed, unblinking gaze—declines in the transition from the stage of *culture* to *civilization*. Yet Spengler deliberately does *not* stage the shattered gaze of *civilization* afflicting his contemporaries. His ruin scenarios are characterized by the same hard realism suffusing his imperialist politics. These are fortified scenarios, staging again and again the imperial theorist's synoptic view *and* the fortified gaze of the heroic realist in the age of *civilization/imperialism*. Spengler took pride in this cool, detached gaze attuned to the sobriety of the *Spätzeit* that he inhabited. His "hunter's eye," Adorno observed, "mercilessly scrutinizes the cities of mankind as though they were the wilderness they really are."[63] This is the fortified gaze of Scipio the Younger, whom Spengler called clear-eyed, alluding to Polybios's scenario.

And yet the heroic, detached stance of the anorganic intellectual crumbles when faced with the spectacle of Rome's ruins. Spengler repeatedly asked his readers to remember the ancient historians' depiction of Rome and their accounts of the "appalling depopulation" draining the empire's core. There are many of these haunting descriptions in Polybios's, Strabo's, and later Pausanias's texts, Spengler wrote, directing his readers' gaze at his own ruin picture: abandoned rows of houses slowly crumbling, "while in the Forum . . . herds of cattle are grazing and the amphitheater is a sown field, dotted with emergent statues and hermae" (U, 683).[64] These Rome pictures decidedly do not resonate with cold, heroic pathos, but are filled with a profound sense of grief, mourning Rome's transition from culture city to megalopolis. Discussing the death of Rome and the Roman Empire, Spengler's detached gaze disintegrates, resonating with the emotions of centuries of ruin gazing: grief, awe—and terror.

The Caesarist leader's mission is to prolong the era of *civilization's* maturity, the stage *before* late *civilization* descends into utter ruination. Here, I want us to linger with Spengler's picture of "these very late conditions," the era when *civilization* reaches its definitive form but has not yet given way to barbarian prehistory (U, 615). In these petrified imperialist endtimes, temporality is reduced to "solemn duration" and Caesarism itself is decaying (U, 615).[65] As the empire of Scipio and Augustus went to ruin, nomadic warlords and their roaming barbarian hordes fought endless wars. Once Prussia's future world empire will begin to crumble, "ghosts" of ancient Gothic warlords will reawaken (U, 1106).

Staring far into the future, Spengler experiences this "spectacle" of the West's final end as "sublime" (U, 1107). Of the West's last *imperium*, nothing will remain but barren landscapes where former world cities are "empty shells of an extinct soul in which an a-historical humanity tries to find shelter" (U, 1107). This—an empty stage, a ruined *skene*—is Spengler's picture of the future to come. His political project—a Prussian dictatorship modeled on the late Roman Empire, its military technology, and its Caesarism—is ultimately a project of imperial *slowdown* conceived to ward off the advent of *a particular moment*: the Occident's inexorable descent into a second barbarism.

Unlike Ratzel's desolate ruinscapes, Spengler's future ruins are not located in Africa, Middle America, or some unspecified territory of nomads—they will appear in the Occident's metropolitan core long after *culture* has been replaced by *civilization*. To European eyes, this future ruinscape is a familiar sight because it recalls Rome's death. We now understand "the Imperium Romanum," Spengler concluded, "as the normal product of a strict and energetic, megalopolitan, predominantly practical intellect and *as typical end state* which has occurred often enough though it has only been identified as such in this instance" (DI, 38; translation modified; emphasis mine).

Spengler's 1933 Intervention, or the Post-Nietzschean Call for a New Barbarism

Spengler thus arrived at the conclusion that Rome's end was the destiny of all empires.[66] Like time, empires are uncanny. As I mentioned above, the morpho-logic of *The Decline* leaves open the possibility of the scenario of the *barbarian* ruin gazer from another *Culture*, who arrives on the scene after the Occident's death. In *The Decline*, Spengler considered two endings: the inevitable passing of all world cultures and the premature fall at the hand of barbarians (U, 687). In *The Hour of Decision* (1933), Spengler envisioned the latter scenario.[67]

Those who in Roman times were called "'savages' or 'barbarians,'" Spengler warned, were waiting at the gates.[68] The ultimate *telos* of the West's struggle will be a neo-Roman "*Imperium Mundi*" with Prussia at its center (H, 204). Deep inside, these new Prussians remain Nietzschean barbarians, ready to conquer.[69] Spengler thus reinvented the notion of "the barbarian" for the twentieth century—noble Prussian barbarians and ignoble non-Prussian barbarians. Insisting on the accuracy of his analogy, Spengler writes that the late classical age offers us "an exact picture of events" similar to "those toward which we are irrevocably moving" (H, 205). From the time of "Hannibal and Scipio" to the battle of Actium, Romans fought for control over "the coming *Imperium*" (H, 31). European powers fought the same fight before 1914. Now the time had come for the decisive battle: "Caesar's legions are returning to consciousness" (H, 229). The barbarian threat to this new global empire is much stronger than it was at the time of late Rome because now the barbarians are "lurking *within* the field of white power" (H, 208). Like Bertrand, Spengler warned of a "deep agitation" among Muslims, and the sudden appearance of a Caliph on the North African scene.[70] This barbarian threat needed to be met by the barbarism of the West.

In 1933, Spengler thus positioned himself as *Europe's last ruin gazer*. Now the scenario of the *barbarian* ruin gazer had become more than a mere possibility derived from a relativist historiography—this scenario was now a hysterically voiced threat.[71] There is an interesting logic at play in this new Spenglerian project. Having reached the stage of *civilization*, Europe was now in the process of turning into a ruinscape. And we know that ruins legitimized colonization. Recall Louis Bernard, who argued that French colonizers had to push aside Ottoman debris as they followed in the tracks of the Romans. In a similar vein, Spengler's Caesarist leaders would follow in the tracks of the Romans, trying to recivilize a ruined continent by wresting the last shreds of culture—of a Prussian spirit—from the ruins of its *civilization*. Spengler's *Hour of Decision* was thus a paradoxical colonial tract of imperial mimesis, turning Europe's imperial logic back onto itself by proposing to recolonize a ruined continent with the model of the Romans in mind. "Restons des Latins," Bertrand had written, "pour garder l'empire."[72] Bertrand's project was to resurrect an African *Latinité* among the Algerian *colons*; Spengler hoped to reawaken Germany's Prussian spirit in the ruins of *civilization* in order to re-imperialize the West and its bored *fellaheen* masses who imported "Negro dancing to perform the Death March for a great Culture" (H, 227–228).

Conclusion

Ratzel believed that state-led forms of settler colonialism would guarantee imperial duration and read Rome's monumental ruins as signs of Rome's monumental power. Like Ratzel, Spengler was invested in the idea of duration but believed this to be a problem of delaying the Occident's inevitable end. Spengler seems caught in a paradox: celebrating the Faustian "mastery of planetary space," he privileges the form that expansion takes in *culture* (wars and conquest in the service of a theo-political idea) over the form it assumes in *civilization* (economic imperialism) (U, 31). At the same time, he thinks of the late Roman Empire and its political form of rule, Caesarism, as the only solution to the cultural and political problems of twentieth-century imperialist modernity.

From the perspective of the deep history of imperial thought, Spengler does no more than take the *katechontic* politics of empire to its extreme by arguing that Caesarism was the only means to decelerate the inexorable movement toward the end. In Spengler's *Decline*, the historical process is ultimately neo-Roman repetition-in-ruins. Reflecting on this process—the inexorable degeneration of *civilization*/imperialism—he reinvented the concept of the barbarian enemy. Bertrand warned against North Africa's Muslims, Spengler the "colored races." These reflections are also linked to *fin-de-siècle* anti-Semitism, and the reemergence of the trope of the rootless, wandering Jew.

His text entangled in anxieties about Europe's internal other, Nordau theorized the *fin-de-siècle* subject as one perennially crossing borders. His picture of degenerate moderns foregrounds the intrusion of other times and other cultures into the metropolis. Here, ruins represent time out of joint and "the degenerate" is someone who dwells on the "borderland."[73] Compulsively "seeking [to be always] *somewhere else*," a student of Charcot's thought, was a form of pathology proper to Jews, "Israelites [who] never hesitate to leave their homes for an important business affair."[74] In Spengler, this anti-Semitic figure is Paul, the intellectual of Roman *civilization*. Drawn to the abstractions of the law and the rootless urban masses, Paul pulled the early Christian community into the "urban demagogical public sphere of the Imperium Romanum" (U, 461).

PART FIVE

With the End in Mind: The Nazi Empire's Neo-Roman Mimesis and the Ruined Stage of Rome

Preface

Explaining the difference between "Kaffirs" and people with history, Heidegger used Hitler's visit to Venice in 1934 as example of "historicality": "When the airplane takes the Führer from Munich to Venice, of course, history happens."[1] Having informed Mussolini about the history that was about to happen in Austria, Hitler flew back to Germany, paying a visit to the construction site for the Nazi Party's Rallying Grounds. Here, work had just begun on the *Zeppelinfeld*'s main viewing stand, a perfect example of Speer's monumental version of Rome's scenographic architecture and the site where his famous ruin value theory was born. Hitler, Speer explained later, had returned convinced that Mussolini's politics of imperial rebirth would not have been possible, were it not for the Roman *imperium*'s architectural remnants. With the Third Reich's future ruins in mind, Hitler ordered Speer to build "in granite."[2]

In part 5, I will start in Rome with Hitler's 1938 visit (chapter 17), resuming the story of this visit (taking place during the Italians' bimillenary celebrations of Augustus's birth) in chapter 22. Hitler's Rome visit represented a signal moment in the Nazis' imitation of Rome. My overarching thesis in part 5 is that the Nazis took neo-Roman mimesis to its extreme: their empire would be the greatest *Reich* ever, and Germans would be left with the most imposing ruins ever seen. In other words, Hitler proposed to conquer a vast continental empire and to build a new metropolis—and in doing the latter, he and Speer imagined building their own Roman ruins, their own ruined stage.

In the eyes of much of the world, Nazis were not Romans, they were barbarians. This portrayal of Nazi Germany was the result of many voices. Nehru wrote about the Nazis' "barbarism."[3] Thomas Mann saw the Nazis' "imperialism" as a "relapse into barbarism."[4] Here, South Sea islanders made another appearance, as Mann compared their ecstatic dancing to fascist mass rallies.[5] Spengler had this to say: "[The Nazis] created a kind of barbarity that is not that of the ancient Germans, but of cannibals."[6] And Mussolini reminded Hitler that when Romans ruled the world, Germans were still barbarians.[7] Writing in the wake of Hitler's state visit to Rome, Simone Weil agreed with Mann's portrayal of the Nazis. Unlike Mann, the philosopher and member of the French resistance believed that the Nazis were barbarians precisely because they were the best imitators of Rome. "Hitler alone," she wrote, "has understood correctly how to copy the Romans."[8] Weil's views are those of a Hellenist who equates Greece with freedom and creativity, the Roman Empire with numbing repetition and the will to power. This will to power suffused everything, from the Romans' ruthless conquests to their scenographic architecture. Today, Weil thought, this Roman will to dominate animated the Nazis' belief in their destiny, the "sovereign mastery" over other nations.[9]

The Nazis' "Germanic frills," Weil thought, merely distracted from the fact that they were Rome's most "remarkable imitator."[10] Hitler's ancestor was not Arminius, the rebel, but Caesar, the ruthless conqueror, who invented the art of "imposing submission by terror."[11] Weil explained the Third Reich through the Roman lens (and with the help of Nietzsche). I will explore how Nazi leaders and intellectuals thought of and presented the Nazi empire as Roman. Looting the neo-Roman archive of classical antiquity, they created their own form of neo-Roman mimesis, mixing the Roman with the Germanic, and at various moments rewriting the story of Rome's battle with Carthage.

Analyzing this specific form of imitation, I will trace the serial production of ruin gazer scenarios characteristic of the Third Reich's fortified ruinous imaginary. Spengler reinscribed the occidental subject's position of mastery in his ruin scenarios and invented the Caesarist leader as the imperialist sovereign who assumes power with the West's end in sight (chapter 16). Awed by ancient Rome's power and obsessed with its fall,

Hitler, Himmler, and the Nazi empire's leading intellectuals all stared at Rome's ruined stage, looking for the "deepest and ultimate cause" of the empire's fall and searching for strategies to postpone this fall (MK, 310). Convinced that the course of history followed the law of rise and fall, and certain that they would postpone this fall for at least a thousand years, the Nazi leadership acted with the picture of a vast imperial ruinscape in mind, stretching from Berlin/*Germania* to the far reaches of the East.

Two things thus characterized the Third Reich. On the one hand, there was the promise of *durable imperial foundations* and equally *durable ruins*. On the other hand, there was a proliferation of racialized scenarios of decline and fall, scenarios that involved the endless production of barbarian enemies, from Rosenberg's Judeo-Bolshevists to Hitler's Polish Maori to Goebbels's Carthaginians. In a gesture of defiance and rivalry, National Socialists deliberately deployed ruin scenarios, making the Third Reich into a truly neo-Roman project. Rome rose and fell, and so will the Third Reich, these authors wrote, while at the same time asserting mastery over this process—political and symbolic mastery.

Obsessed with this problematic of duration and ruination, the Nazis went to work on making their empire endure, thinking about ways of fortifying the empire they set out to conquer. Both literal and symbolic, these labors of fortification involved monumental architecture and scopic mastery—mastery of the spaces of the empire and the empire's new metropolis, of the Roman past, and of the new barbarians. One of the goals of part 5 will be to explore the spatio-temporal imaginary and its fortified scopic regime underlying the neo-Roman theories and performances of these murderous twentieth-century imitators of ancient Rome.

The 1938 state visit to Italy constitutes a pivotal moment because here, Hitler and his large entourage witnessed the Italian fascists' elaborate *mise-en-scène* of their imitation of ancient Rome and the powerful effects of their techniques of resurrectional modernism. This visit, taking place in the context of the two-thousand-year anniversary of Augustus and in the wake of the new *imperium*'s victory over Ethiopia's "barbarians" and the successful completion of the North African campaign's "civilizing mission" in 1937, was the moment when the Nazis' previous appropriations of classical antiquity began to consolidate around imperial Rome. In all likelihood, Martin Heidegger had this Rome visit in mind when he later wrote his diatribes against the Nazis' "verrömerte[n] Antike," or "Romified" antiquity, disdainfully dissecting their "historicist" conquests of antiquity taking possession of the past in the spirit of Western instrumental modernity by defining it (chapter 25).[12]

With their resurrectional efforts, the Third Reich's leading classicists and artists played a central role in this neo-Roman mimesis and the production of the Nazi empire's imaginary. I will begin this fifth part with Hitler's 1938 visit and the Italian project of *romanità*, or fascism as the rebirth of the *Imperium Romanum* (chapter 17). Chapter 18 begins with a discussion of how this visit shaped Hitler's thinking about empire, and then examines texts by Hitler, Heinrich Himmler, and Arthur Rosenberg about the empire they thought they were in the process of building. Here, I will focus on the role that Rome's fall played in their thinking. In chapters 19 and 20, I will then move from the problematic of the ruined stage, captured by Hitler's, Himmler's, and Rosenberg's racialized ruin gazer scenarios and their ideas about imperial temporality, to the issue of the Third Reich's neo-Roman imaginary. Together with Nazi leaders, classicists and artists worked on the transformation of distance from Rome's "far-away past" into imaginary closeness. In chapter 19, I will explore texts by leading Nazi classicists (often close to the circles of the conservative revolution) focusing on their labor of constructing the imaginary zone opening the Third Reich's present onto the classical past, the resurrectional performances in texts devoted to Augustus, and the obsession with the (neo)-Roman leader's gaze.

In chapter 20, I turn to two Nazi modernists, Leni Riefenstahl and Gottfried Benn, and their exercises in resurrectional modernism, first analyzing the prologue to Leni Riefenstahl's film on the 1936 Olympic Games, and then tracing Gottfried Benn's post-Nietzschean poetics. They too established the proximity of the classical past to the Nazi present. Heidegger's "Romanified" antiquity perfectly captures Riefenstahl's Greece in the prologue to *Olympia* (1936), and Benn's Sparta in his essays on aesthetics and politics. Taking their spectators/readers into the space of the Nazi empire's neo-Roman imaginary, both artists also staged a fortified gaze. In ways similar to the Nazi classicists, these modernists elicit their readers-viewers' scopic desires in the service of the Nazis' imperial project.

Chapter 21 then explores the enactment of Roman mimesis in architecture and Berlin/*Germania* as the Nazis' version of the Roman architectural stage. Revisiting Hitler's and Speer's ruin theory and the link between empire-building and ruination, I will draw attention to their project of making Germans into Romans. Their building program emphasized scenographic monumentality in the Roman vein, envisioning a solid metropolis at the core of an equally solid, fortified empire. The incessant foregrounding of this monumentality was the most literal response to the story of rise and decline.

Having opened part 5 with Hitler's visit to the Roman stage, and his tour of the *Mostra Augustea della Romanita*, the exhibit devoted to the Augustan age, I will return in chapter 22 to a specific moment of Hitler's Rome visit, his nighttime journey through the ancient ruins of Rome. Analyzing the ways in which the German press staged this performance of ruin gazing, I will revisit the issues of scopic mastery inscribed in that scenario. Part 5 concludes with Hitler's very last ruin gazer scenario in his *Political Testament* (chapter 23). The framing context here is the Nazis' revival of the Punic Wars in the final months of the war.

SEVENTEEN

Hitler in Rome 1: Visiting the *Mostra Augustea della Romanità, 1938*

Introduction

When Hitler visited the exhibition at the center of the bimillenary celebrations of Augustus's birth, on May 6, 1938, he encountered the statues and stories of the great founders of the Roman Empire, from the mythical Aeneas to Augustus.[1] As Italian newspapers noted, Hitler lingered in the exhibition halls dedicated to the Roman emperor, one of which housed a plaster cast of the front of the Augustus Temple at Ankara, inscribed with the emperor's *Res Gestae*. It was this Augustan text about imperial conquest and rule that attracted Hitler's particular attention.[2]

Hitler's guide was Giulio Giglioli, the archeologist in charge of the Augustan bimillenary and director of the exhibit.[3] After they entered the building through the façade's modernist version of a triumphal arch, Giglioli took Hitler and his entourage to the "Hall of Empire," which offered "a grandiose representation of *romanità*: scenes of triumph, sacrifice, combat, barbarian prisoners and victorious soldiers."[4] We may safely assume that Giglioli did not miss the chance to draw his visitors' attention to the colossal statue of a barbarian woman depicting Thusnelda, the wife of the German hero who led the uprising against Augustus's legions.

From the "Hall of Empire" and Augustus's Ancyra Temple, the visitors then strolled through a series of rooms telling the history of the city of Rome, beginning with its legendary founder, Aeneas. The first hall was devoted to the golden age of Augustus's reign, opening with a mosaic of Virgil. The visitors then passed a translation of the entire *Res Gestae* as well as plaster models of the *Ara Pacis* and the *Mausoleo di Augusto*.[5] The remaining Augustan rooms (Sala IX to XVI) presented the emperor himself, detailing the spread of his cult across all of the empire's provinces. Here, Giglioli might have used the illuminated map to demonstrate the gradual growth of the *imperium*. In the rooms reserved for the Roman military, the German visitors might have scrutinized the list of the provinces where the Roman legions were stationed, ranging from Roman Tunis to London, from Palmyra to Spain. This list included German Saalburg and, of course, the Teutoburg Forest.

When the German visitors arrived at the main floor's last hall, *Sala XXVI*, they were instructed in the "Immortality of the Idea of Rome, and the Rebirth of the Empire of the New Fascist Italy."[6] Here, the curators quoted Mussolini's statements about *romanità*, or the rebirth of ancient Rome. "We dream of a Roman Italy," Mussolini said in 1922, "disciplined and imperial"; this new Italy will exist because "the immortal spirit of Rome has risen again in Fascism."[7] Italians were again Romans.

Giglioli's own text for *Sala XVI* echoed Mussolini's trope of Rome's rebirth, updating its meaning for the late 1930s: "with the will of the Duce, every ideal, every institution, every Roman deed will return to shine in the new Italy, and after the epic conflict of combatants on African soil, the Roman Empire rises up out of the ruins of a barbarian empire."[8] This barbarian empire was the empire of Haile Selassie, whose defeat Mussolini announced on May 5, 1936. Italy's "Roman gladiators" and Roman "civility" had "triumphed," Mussolini bragged, "over barbarism," and Italians were now celebrating the *imperium*'s "reappearance . . . on the fated Hills of Rome."[9]

Let us speculate: Giglioli, leading the German delegation through *Sala XVI* dedicated to Italy's new status as *imperium*, mentioned *Scipione l'Africano* (1937), a "spectacular historical film" reenacting Rome's victory over African Carthage during the African campaigns.[10] And let us pause for a moment and wonder about the Germans' reaction to one of the rather remarkable aspects of this room, depicting the fascists' North African conquests. Did Hitler or any of his friends notice that using the trope of rebirth, both Mussolini and Giglioli omitted any reference to Rome's ancient ruins, and that in their story of resurrection, ruins belonged to the conquered Ethiopians? Furthermore, did they take note of the even more intriguing fact that Giglioli's text erased the story of Rome's decline and fall, barely mentioning the fact—"L'idea imperiale romana non si estinse con la caduta dell'Impero d'Occidente"—before leaping across centuries into the fascist era?[11]

Of course we do not know whether Hitler noticed any of this. What this room with its story of empire, rebirth, and ruins tells us is that the Italians' neo-Roman mimesis had its origin in a voluntarist act of resurrection that depended on a remarkable act of oblivion if not obliteration. More than other neo-Roman projects, the Italian fascists' mimesis embraced Rome's ancient ruins as signs of power while simultaneously combatting the specter of Rome's end, hovering over the city's ruinscape. It thus makes sense that Mussolini, putting the fascists' "resurrection of the Roman Empire" under the sign of *romanità*, constantly felt compelled to emphasize that the "cult of Romanness" was not "a nostalgic contemplation of the past, but hard preparation for the future."[12]

I will return to this willed forgetting of Rome's fall in the *Mostra Augustea* in the context of the fascists' decade-long reconstruction of the city's ruined imperial stage, which complemented the obsessive reconstruction of Rome inside the walls of the Augustan exhibit. Let us first rejoin Hitler, who was so fascinated by the Augustan exhibit that he returned the next day for a tour of the second floor. This time he was accompanied by Goebbels, Himmler, Hess, Ribbentropp, and other uniformed members of the Nazi *nomenclatura*, and Giglioli was replaced by Giuseppe Bottai, onetime governor of Addis Ababa, minister of education, friend of Heidegger's, and one of the most influential theorists of *romanità*.

Exhibiting "Europe's shared Roman heritage," this second floor documented the Romans' presence across the entire empire, using photographs, models, maps, and artifacts to demonstrate that "there really was a time when almost all of Europe shared a single civilization."[13] Celebrating Roman feats of engineering and construction, there were rooms devoted to Roman roads, bridges, and aqueducts, to theaters and funerary monuments, to the acropolis of Baalbek (Syria) and the Roman cities in the empire—among them Cologne and Vindobona (Vienna). Let us speculate again. Did Bottai explain to Hitler that the city was one of the principal Roman fortresses on the Danube, pointing to the city plan displayed on the wall, marking the *castrum* as the heart of contemporary Vienna?[14] Perhaps he did, because we do know from Italian journalists that the Führer slowed down, captivated by the Roman artifacts found in Germany.

Fascist Techniques of Resurrection

Every new act of imperial mimesis, I have been arguing in this book, created the image-object of that which it wanted to imitate. The Italian fascists engaged in this repetitive labor of imitation-through-creation from the moment they took power. Having witnessed the Italians' efforts to become new Romans, and taking aim at the entire European tradition of neo-Roman imperialism, Weil and Nehru belittled the imitators as mindless copiers. Romans were slavish imitators of Greek culture, Weil thought, and these neo-Romans were nothing but "bad imitations of undistinguished conquerors."[15] Nehru too thought that Roman culture was but a "pale shadow of Hellenic civilization," and that Romans and Britain's neo-Romans "were both singularly devoid of imagination."[16] In the light of Weil's and Nehru's statements, it is rather ironic that the curators of the *Mostra Augustea* displayed objects that in most cases were plaster casts or other kinds of copies. For instance, they used hundreds of plaster models to draw the viewers' eyes to reconstructed temples, triumphal arches, and theaters. Among these models was the Roman theater at Sabratha. By the time of the exhibit, this theater was a familiar sight to Italian audiences because of Mussolini's tour of Libya in 1937. Seated with a view of the theater's magnificent *scaenae frons*, he attended a production of Sophocles's *Oedipus Rex*.[17]

The *Mostra*'s most famous *pièce-de-resistance*, however, was a huge model of imperial Rome, displayed in a room entitled "Reconstruction of Imperial Rome," and showing the restored city at the time of its greatest expansion.[18] The official museum narrative encouraged visitors to begin their exploration of the ancient city, pointing first to Augustus's mausoleum, Apollo's Temple, the "gnomon," and the *Ara Pacis*, thus foregrounding the Augustan-era building program. On one of the walls of this exhibition hall (*Sala LX*), the curators added city plans of the Spanish *Augusta Merita*, Algerian Timgad, and Syrian Palmyra, thus once more underlining the reach of the Roman Empire and civilization.

Giglioli wanted people to "*see* the spirit and the works accomplished by the greatest Empire there ever was."[19] The unstated goal of the techniques of restoration used by the designers of the *Mostra Augustea* was to abolish the intervening centuries between the Roman past and the neo-Roman present. As I mentioned above, inside the exhibit, the dominant mode of the representation of the city and empire was that of resurrection through restoration: while the *Mostra Augustea* displayed photographs of the Roman sites in their ruined state, the visitors' attention was focused

17.1 Via dei Trionfi, Rome (1938).

on the plaster models and full-scale reconstructions. These techniques invited visitors to participate in the resurrection of the ancient empire, made present in an almost excessive manner of restorative display.

Outside of the *Mostra Augustea*, the Italian fascists' scenographic architecture reframed Rome's classical ruins, turning the ancient ruined stage into a performance space for the mimetic practices of the new Romans. On May 4, 1938, Mussolini's experts in political spectacle provided the backdrops for the military parade on the *Via dei Trionfi*, a new thoroughfare leading straight toward the Arch of Constantine (figure 17.1). Mussolini wanted Rome's ruins to be visible. Announcing the restructuring of Rome's ancient core as early as 1925, he demanded that "[the] millennial monuments of our history must loom gigantic in their necessary solitude."[20]

Reframing imperial Rome's ruins as the "ruins of romanitas" in the 1930s,[21] the Italian fascists thus took possession of Rome's ruined stage, making it their own. Driven by "space-lust,"[22] they demolished the vernacular architecture that had grown up around the ruins of ancient Rome, re-creating the center as a "city-wide stage."[23] Italian classicists, historians, archeologists, and other experts in things Roman thus worked hard on the connection between Roman Empire and Italian fascism. As we will see later, many of the leading German archeologists and classicists were involved in this work of re-creating the image of imperial Rome, which involved "conservation, excavation, and interpretation."[24] And the German press reported frequently on their contribution to this "salvation of European civilization."[25]

Wilhelm Weber, a Nazi classicist famous for his 1936 exegesis of the *Res Gestae*, lectured about Rome's rebirth in 1940. Weber, one of the many conservative revolutionaries among the classicists, portrayed the Duce as "founder of a new Reich," who transformed the picture of Rome in a spirit both "revolutionary and conservative."[26] He also praised the Italian leader for having reinvented the "stage of the world's amphitheater."[27] Welcoming Mussolini's project of a new *imperium* on African soil, Weber envisioned a time when Italy would reclaim "Carthaginian Tunis."[28] Weber situated the remaking of Rome in a wider context: the rebirth of imperial Rome was an event testifying to the present's "planetary vision" and concerned the entire *Abendland* or "white race."[29]

Mussolini's Ruined Architectural Stage

In 1937, Mussolini had visited Berlin. For this occasion, the Nazis transformed Berlin's streets into "ceremonial avenues," decorated with cardboard pylons topped by "gilded eagles," a *mise-en-scène* that Speer later found "hideous."[30] In 1938, Mussolini's experts in political spectacle designed an itinerary for Hitler's state visit that offered a very different spectacle, based on "Mussolini's cultivation of Roman ruins as imperial stage sets."[31] What the German delegation saw in Rome was not made of cardboard, but the solid result of more than a decade of fascist planning. Radically reimagining and re-creating Rome's ruined center, this project also contributed to Mussolini's image as Rome's third founder, the heir to Aeneas and Augustus.

Many of these interventions into the urban fabric focused on Augustan-era monuments and ruins. This extensive work of de- and reconstructing Augustan Rome—including not only the demolition of vernacular architecture and the "liberating" of existing ruins like Constantine's Arch, but also multiple excavations, and relocations of major monuments like the *Ara Pacis*—all of these interventions had one goal: to showcase the ancient remnants. Mussolini insisted specifically that no structure ought to "block . . . a view of the Arch of Constantine."[32] Once more, the power of ancient Rome was being made visible to the world.

This "symbolic conquest" of the ancient city included the construction of major avenues, the *Via dei Trionfi* and the *Via dell'Impero*.[33] Starting at the Piazza Venezia where Mussolini's office was located and paralleling the *Via Sacra* (the ancient road through the Roman Forum), the *Via dell'Impero* led straight to the Colosseum.[34] The purpose of these new thoroughfares was twofold: to serve as triumphal avenues and to open new vistas on Rome's ancient monuments.[35] As I wrote above, many of these interventions focused on Augustan-era ruins. Excavations at the Theater of Marcellus and the Forum of Augustus, for instance, took place between 1924 and 1930. Once its façade was exposed, the theater presented a "clean, symmetrical face."[36]

The *Ara Pacis* underwent more elaborate restoration. The altar was first reassembled, and then relocated to a new site where this "'radiant expression of Roman imperium'" was encased in a "Bauhaus-inspired" shell.[37] Inscribed on the base of the altar, the *Res Gestae Divi Augusti* was once more displayed in the city center. A plaque marking the event of the altar's erection echoed the section of the *Res Gestae* in which Augustus presented himself as the city-builder by reminding visitors that the Duce had ordered the remaking of the *Ara Pacis* and "'the extraction of the mausoleum from the shadows of the centuries.'"[38]

As we know, the Augustan mausoleum "carried special meaning," not only because of its association with Augustus, but also because of its subsequent history: in 1811, Napoleon's birthday was celebrated in the mausoleum during the six-year occupation of the city, which then bore the title second city of the empire (see chapter 10). The mausoleum also played an important role in the making of Mussolini's image. In 1921, the Italian fascists held their Congress in the *Augusteo*, and in 1926, the poet Valerio Ratti praised the new Augustus, addressing his audience, assembled "among the live stones of the tomb of Augustus"; they were here "to celebrate . . . the resurrection of imperial Rome in the world."[39] Like Napoleon before him, Mussolini had his urban planners reconfigure the *Augusteo*, transforming the crumbling edifice into an "authentic Roman ruin."[40] By the time of Hitler's visit, the *Augusteo* "was freestanding again," its "grandeur and abandon" reminding one observer of Piranesi's etchings.[41] The new square, *Piazzale Augusto Imperatore*, designed to showcase the dynastic tomb and the *Ara Pacis*, was still under construction.[42] A "sanctuary" to fascist *romanità*, Aristotle Kallis writes, the square functioned as a "visible threshold into a different dimension of time,"[43] a sacred space of "time-lessness" connected to myth. The "time-lessness" of this space, I would argue, is that proper to the neo-Roman imaginary with its dissolution of the boundaries between present and past.

Undertaking a radical restructuring of the historical center, the fascist planners thus integrated these ancient monuments into their "urban scenography."[44] This disciplining of space eliminated the "chaotic, colorful Rome of the Grand Tour" with its "moss-covered ruins."[45] Doing so, it reconnected with the very Piranesian desire to resurrect the power of ancient Rome. Recall that Piranesi expressed this power by depicting its ruins as massive, regular structures. It was this effect of massiveness that the urban restructuring recaptured. Like the *Mostra Augustea's Sala X*, this "liberation" of ruins from the accretions of centuries closely connected ancient and modern Rome, erasing the memory of the empire's fall and all the centuries between the golden era of Augustus and the new Italian Empire.

When Mussolini promised in 1925 to change the city, he explained that he had a center in mind that would function not only as Italy's "political and moral capital" but as the world's symbol of a "truly 'universal civilization.'"[46] By 1938, Italy was an empire. One of the restored structures, the Basilica of Maxentius and Constantine, bore witness to this fact. Five large marble wall maps were mounted on the basilica's "retaining wall," tracing the gradual geographic expansion from the city to the Roman Empire, with the last map outlining the borders of the fascist empire with its new colonies in East Africa, for which the neo-Roman cartographers used Latin names, that is, Tripolitania and Cyrenaica.[47]

Ruins and Death Masks

As we saw above, Mussolini insisted that the celebration of *romanità* was oriented toward the future, not the past. In the service of this future, the symbolic conquest of Rome's imperial ruins transformed the ruins from dead into living objects. When Mussolini announced this de- and reconstruction in 1925, he framed it as a fight against decadent liberalism. Belonging to this decadent past, the ivy-covered ruins revered by the travelers of the Grand Tour were replaced by the clean iconic monuments of a new vital empire. In this act of demolition and the constant reference to Italy's imperial future, the dynamism of Italian futurists still resonates.[48]

But what about the tension between life and death inherent in the imitation of the ancient empire that ruin gazer scenarios visualize? The narrative of the *Mostra Augustea* glossed over the fall of Rome and its end in ruins, while the reordering of ancient ruins addressed the inevitable entanglement of mimetic resurrection and death, in the streets of Rome. Mussolini claimed that his act of founding a Third Rome had overcome this problematic. Rome's new, clean ruins were living objects, not dead witnesses to the fall. If this was the case, then why did Mussolini's main architect, Marcello Piacentini, design an entirely new city on the periphery of the old, a city copying the basic features of ancient Rome arranged around an axial design? Here is how Scobie describes Piacentini's design for the E42 (also called EUR): the "new town was to have a *cardo*, the *Via Imperiale*, which at its northern end was to pass beneath a vast triumphal arch, the Porta Imperiale," while the town's *decumanus* would run straight through the city from west to east.[49] Axial plan and buildings "were to convey the 'senso di Roma,'" with some of the latter modeled on specific Roman structures.[50] Thus the "triumphal entry arch," for instance, replicated the arch of Trajan at the western end of Timgad's *decumanus*.[51] This new imperial center would also include a *Piazza Imperiale, a Teatro Imperiale*, an administrative Palace, a Palace of Culture, *Palazzo dei Congressi, Palazzo della Difensa della Razza*, and an "altar" modeled on the *Ara Pacis*.[52] Conceived in the fascist style of "'*romanità* of modernity,'" the design exuded "calm classical austerity."[53]

Mussolini planned to open this neo-Roman metropole with the *Universal Exposition of Rome* in 1942. He wanted a "global theater with a monumental stage" extolling the eternal values of Roman empires past and present.[54] Oddly enough, this international fair would house yet another Roman exhibit, the *Mostra della Civiltà Italiana*, taking visitors across "seven floors of maps, portraits, and statues," proving that Roman civilization was universal, constituting the very core of the West.[55] The new *Ara Pacis*, Piacentini explained, "will praise for all times and in a [monumental] Roman style the triumph of the new world order."[56] Italian newsreels started showing the construction site of E42 in 1939, alternately presenting their spectators with aerial views of the plaster model of E42 or zooming in on the individual buildings.

There is more at stake in this construction of a Third Rome than the pragmatic reason of urban expansion or the desire for government buildings that by their "grandiosity and monumentality" would suit the future *imperium*.[57] By duplicating on the city's periphery what lay in ruins in the center of Rome, and including an improved version of the *Mostra Augustea* (renamed *Mostra de la Romanità*), the urbanists and architects of project E42 countered the threat lingering over Rome's ruined zone—kept lingering despite the fascists' symbolic conquest of this uncanny terrain.

Mussolini proudly wore the mask of Augustus, defiantly embracing the ruined stage of the ancient empire. That is, he planned to stay in the Duce's residence, the Palazzo Venezia, in the midst of all these fragile, albeit recently reinforced, witnesses to the death of the Roman Empire. But how could he not be uneasy about wearing the emperor's death mask?

The future *imperium*, he decided, would be governed from a new and solid Roman stage, one that sported a triumphal arch made of steel, taller and wider than its Timgad antecedent. E42 was built, but the arch was never completed. A tall Egyptian obelisk still stands at the center of the building complex, but Piacentini's city never became the metropolis of an Italian Empire. Instead, in 1942, New Zealand's 28th Maori Battalion arrived in Italian Libya, driving through the Marble Arch (unveiled on March 16, 1937, in the presence of Mussolini), and in June 1944, American and British troops arrived in Rome.[58]

Curzio Malaparte, embedded journalist, described the columns of Sherman tanks entering the city through the *Via Appia Antica*, the "noblest road in the world," taken by the emperors when they "returned from the Orient, Greece, Egypt, Africa."[59] Commenting on the arrival of the American troops, Mussolini himself cast a melancholy look at what remained of his "Empire" that once stretched from "Tripoli to Mogadishu, from Bastia to Rhodes and Tirana." Not long ago, Italians ruled in Addis Ababa, he wrote, but "today, Africans bivouac in Rome."[60]

EIGHTEEN

Roman Lessons: Theorizing Empire, Conquering the East

Introduction

Reporting on Hitler's coming Rome visit, an American journalist described the fascist renovations as a theatrical façade superimposed onto the "grandeur" of ancient Rome. Nonetheless, he still believed in the power of Augustan ruins to "remind" Hitler that the dictator's life is "ephemeral."[1] Hitler didn't need reminding; he already was obsessed with Rome's downfall. As I will argue in this chapter, Hitler shows himself as an imperial theorist in the neo-Roman vein, fascinated by the question of why Rome fell. He visited the empire's ruined stage in his writing and speeches long before he toured Rome in 1938, and long before he began to work with Speer on Berlin/*Germania*. Like Hitler, Heinrich Himmler thought of world history in terms of the rise and fall of empires, so much so that the problematic of Rome's ruined stage functioned as an organizing subtext of his thinking about the future Germanic World Empire.

This chapter begins the analysis of the Third Reich's Roman mimesis with a reading of the role that the fall of the ancient Roman Empire played in the Nazis' theories of their empire to come. Hitler fully embraced this neo-Roman identity after his state visit to Rome in May 1938. That is, Hitler's discourse about empire gradually foregrounded Roman history at the expense of his story about "Aryan" world history, portraying Nazis as heirs to anti-Roman barbarians and Roman conquerors. The tension between barbarian past and imperial present is characteristic of all neo-Roman empire-building. In the Nazi case, the tension between anti-Roman barbarians and neo-Romans reappeared in a specific guise. Kleist's *Battle of Hermann*, pitting German barbarians against Romans, saw a revival on German stages.[2] The preoccupation with the Germanic tribes was one strand of fascist ideology; Hitler's, Goebbels's, and Speer's privileging of classical antiquity, another.[3] More importantly, the Nazi discourse about the Third Reich's Germanic legacy was essentially Romanized. Himmler was drawn into the imaginary of Western imperialism and Arthur Rosenberg, another leading Nazi known for his Germanic worldview, glorified Rome's destruction of Carthage, one of the "Semitic-Jewish command centers," holding up the ancient conquest empire as a model for the fight against "Judeo-bolshevism."[4]

I will begin this chapter with a brief discussion of the repercussions of the 1938 Rome visit on Hitler's thinking about empire. The Nazis' imperial project involved the genocidal creation of a territorial empire to the east of Germany. In other words, the Third Reich was exceptional.[5] However, like other European imperialists, the Nazis and their collaborators connected this new kind of imperial formation to the Roman Empire in their speeches, writings, architecture, and performances of imperial mimesis. Setting out to build this vast continental empire, they redefined the barbarian, generating a bewildering mass of imperial enemies—Slavic *Untermenschen*, half-Germanized Slavs, worthless Slavicized Germans, "Ghetto Jews," wandering Jews, and Jewish imperialists, among others.

Roman Aftereffects: Germans as the Better Romans

Victor Klemperer noted in 1938 that the Italians should let their new emperor represent them in a more imperial fashion "if they are going to play at empires."[6] After Hitler's state visit, the Germans would begin this playing at empires in earnest, and the Rome visit itself turned out to have been a pivotal moment in the way in which Hitler, Goebbels, and Himmler thought about their empire, wars of conquest, and *Pax Germanica*. As I mentioned in the previous chapter, strolling through the *Mostra Augustea*, Hitler lingered in the rooms dedicated to the Roman emperor. What I did not mention was that Giglioli had also guided him through the rooms narrating Rome's "Triumph over Carthage," filled with maps tracing Hannibal's invasion of Italy, busts of the Scipios, and quotes from Polybios's history about the unprecedented rise of the Roman Empire.

On the eve of World War II, which turned the Third Reich into a conquest empire, Hitler thus encountered Aeneas, Rome's mythical founder, Scipio, the conqueror of Carthage, and Augustus, the emperor and city-builder. He also witnessed the modern practices of imitating Rome and encountered, in the person of the Duce, a modern imitator, a man whom the *Mostra Augustea* presented as the heir to Augustus. In an article entitled "Italia docet," Moeller van den Bruck wrote that the Italians excavated their imperial destiny "from the Italian ruins."[7] Hitler eagerly followed Moeller van den Bruck's advice, learning his Roman lessons.

Simone Weil saw the imitation of Roman emperors as tedious, mindless repetition. Hitler saw it as a challenge, hastily occupying Mussolini's territory of neo-Roman mimesis in an act of imperial rivalry. Having just ordered the attack on the Soviet Union, Hitler explained to Heinrich Himmler and other dinner guests that ancient Rome was the *Reich*'s "only rival in the world."[8] Witnessing the practices of *romanità* changed Hitler's thinking about imperial conquest and empire-building. Consolidating his earlier ideas about Roman history, politics, and architecture, the Rome visit further pushed Hitler and other Nazi leaders in the direction of a German form of neo-Roman mimesis in which Rome's ruined architectural stage would play an unprecedented role.[9]

Before his visit, Hitler had dismissed Mussolini's neo-Roman mimesis. Looking over plans for the E42, Hitler judged it "a meaningless copy without any impact."[10] Despite their profound familiarity with Mussolini's plans for the new metropole and their extensive involvement in E42, Hitler and Speer rarely mentioned the Italian fascists' new Roman city.[11] Instead, Hitler kept reminiscing about his Grand Tour in 1938, leaving no doubt that he was deeply impressed by Mussolini's ancient Roman capital. The Nazis' copy of ancient Rome would not be trivial; it would not lack strength.

Thanks to Alex Scobie, Alexander Demandt, Johann Chapoutot, and others, Hitler's statements about the Roman Empire are well known.[12] We find the traces of his Rome visit not only in the 1942 edition of *Mein Kampf* but also in Hitler's table talks. In the former, Hitler famously reflected on Roman history as the best teacher. In his so-called *Table Talk*, Hitler continued to reminisce about his trip, his remarks culminating in the widely quoted statement from 1941 that "The Roman Empire never had its like. To have succeeded in completely ruling the world! And no empire has spread its civilization as Rome did."[13] Outlining a new *orbis Germanorum*, a continental *Reich* modeled on Rome's spread of its civilization across the known world, Hitler then told his captive audience: "If Russia goes under in this war, Europe will stretch eastwards to the limits of Germanic colonization."[14] Looking back across the centuries, Hitler thus found a way to think of his grandiose plans of conquest and rule.

Thinking beyond the era of conquest to the era of imperial rule, Hitler focused on the new empire's architecture, working with Speer to build the *Reich*'s own architectural Roman stage. They named this stage *Germania*—a Latin name testifying to the fact that they saw their imperial metropolis through Roman eyes. Returning from Rome, Hitler not only saw the future *Reich*'s capital through Roman eyes, he also began to see Germanic tribes from the perspective of their Roman conquerors. In 1942, he discovered among the Germanic tribes of the past and the German farmers of the present men with Roman and Greek profiles. Moreover, Hitler, who never forgot Mussolini's quip about German barbarians, argued that Rome would not have maintained its power if Roman society had not been "constantly regenerated" by "Germanic blood."[15]

Hitler thus had little interest in reviving the ancient anti-Roman barbarians as model Germans. Instead, he invented a genealogy that merged Germanic tribes and Roman conquerors. This neo-Roman perspective led to some rather striking propositions. In one instance, the idea that the Nazis were Rome's true heirs produced a convoluted line of argument about German neo-Roman conquerors and ancient German barbarians that somewhat unexpectedly involved the iconic figure of the Maori warrior. Trying to make sense of his plans for the territories east of Germany in 1942, Hitler came across the "Maoris" as an example of barbarians in need of civilizing.[16] Distancing himself from Himmler's idealization of the Germanic tribes and hero-worship of Arminius, Hitler first compared present-day Poland to ancient *Germania* in 1941: "For any Roman [soldier], the fact of being posted to *Germania*" was similar to contemporary Germans being "sent to Posen."[17]

Hitler then elaborated on the analogy, comparing the Germanic tribes' resistance against the Romans to the Maori's struggle against the British Empire. These Germanic tribes, he explained further, were at the time as uncultured as the Maori were in the present, and thus were, by implication, the Poles. The Germanic tribes' "level of civilization cannot much have surpassed that of the Maoris."[18] Reflecting on Romans, Germans, and the people he was in the process of enslaving, Hitler thus leaves us with an identification of Nazis and Romans, and a curious chain of equivalences: Germanic tribes—Maori—Poles. Hitler intended to be on the side of the colonizers, not the colonized, and thus firmly sided with the Romans. Germans might once have been barbarians, but now they would become the better Romans.

The Nazi empire was a conquest empire, lasting a mere six years. The imperial project of the Nazi leadership thus never attained a coherent form, but instead consisted of a lethal array of different projects and strategies—a kind of hideous experiment in empire-building that finally precipitated toward its defining form, the mass killings of Jews and other enemies in the death camps.[19] After 1938, the will to imitate and ultimately surpass ancient Rome was a crucial part of this imperial experiment. However, while the Roman model only came to the fore after 1938, it was present from the start.

Again, Italian fascists provided the material that Nazi leaders and intellectuals registered attentively. In 1934, for instance, a monthly entitled *Volk und Reich* published a series of photographs of the four marble maps outlining the Roman Empire's gradual expansion, recently embedded in the back wall of the Basilica Maxentius, as well as a map of the Italian "sphere of power."[20] The daily scrutiny of these marble maps was a training exercise, the authors implied, a daily education in the spatio-temporal imaginary of fascist empire-building. While Mussolini directed the Italians' gaze toward Africa, Hitler, as I will discuss in more detail later, advocated "Eastern orientation."[21] In 1941, Hitler berated fellow-party-members for using the cliché of "desolate Eastern territories," reminding his entourage that "in the eyes of the ancient Romans all Northern Europe offered a spectacle of desolation."[22] In August 1942 he told his guests: "We have never before driven into empty spaces."[23] Like Italy's new imperial space, these empty spaces needed to be made visible. Goebbels, for instance, commissioned a photo-essay in 1942, entitled *Deutscher Osten: Land der Zukunft* (*German East: Land of the Future*). Like Mussolini's marble cartography, this photo-text is a training exercise in the imperial gaze. Addressing their readers as future settlers and directing their "burning" gaze eastward, the authors explained that Germans now undertook the "enormous task of reconstruction" in the former Prussian territories and the new *General Government* in Poland.[24]

A German *Reich* from the Atlantic to the Urals

With the Third Reich, a new form of empire arose in Europe. Such was the claim on the part of the National Socialist theorists. Werner Best, one of the SS's *völkisch* theorists of empire, for instance, wrote in 1942 that contemporary Germans are not "the grandchildren of an old order, but the ancestors of a new one."[25] And such was the reality: the Third Reich was "exceptional," as historian Ulrich Herbert writes, representing the "violent attempt to impose a new imperial 'völkisch' order onto [Western and Eastern] Europe by means of genocide."[26] With his paradigm of nonsynchronicity, Spengler rewrote the history of empire as the repetition by the British and German states of Roman hegemony, or *Pax Augusta*, as *Pax Britannica* in the nineteenth century and *Pax Germanica* in the twentieth.[27] With this deadly *Pax Germanica* as his goal, Hitler told his entourage in 1941 that their most urgent and immediate task was "to conquer."[28]

The Nazis' imperial ambitions involved Africa and the European continent, the idea of regaining Germany's former African colonies and a continental *Reich* that would reach deep into Russian territory.[29] Hitler thought of his mission as a radical spatial revolution that would redirect the nation's gaze toward the territories east of Germany. When the Nazis directed their gaze at eastern territories, they thus saw desolate landscapes asking to be conquered, their "natives" born to be slaves.[30] Hitler called Poland "Urwelt," and on his journey through the country, Himmler's secretary experienced it as a vast terrain waiting to be recivilized.[31] After the victory parade in Warsaw in 1939, Hans Frank, the future *Generalgouverneur* of Poland, claimed that "colonizing and resettlement" of the East had begun.[32] In 1940, the *SS Office for the Strengthening of Germandom* began to develop the General Plan East, a blueprint for the Germanizing of the eastern territories. In the wake of the attack on the Soviet Union in 1941, these "SS settlement plans" pushed the boundaries of the future German *Reich* deep into Russian territory.[33]

Emboldened by the initial success of the invasion, Hitler told his guests in 1941 that the "Russian space" would be the *Reich*'s India, its "natives" exploited for labor and supplied with "glass beads and everything that colonial people like."[34] In the same year, Hitler made Alfred Rosenberg minister for the Occupied Eastern Territories.[35] Heinrich Himmler and Reichsmarshall Göring were the other men in charge of the empire's necro-politics of settlement, resettlement, and genocide in the conquered countries. Among those who theorized the Third *Reich*'s expansion eastward, we find at one extreme the exterminationist concepts of *Lebensraum* discussed by Hitler, Goebbels, or Goering and the SS theorists like Werner Best, Reinhard Höhn, and Wilhelm Stuckart, who argued in terms of *völkisch*-racial superiority.[36] At the other extreme were *Reich* theorists like Hans Freyer or Carl Schmitt, uneasy about the invasion of the Soviet Union but equally adamant about expanding the Third Reich's eastern borders.

Rome's ruined stage, I wrote earlier, was central to the Third Reich's imperial imaginary. In the next part of this chapter, I will analyze texts by Hitler, Rosenberg, and Himmler, proving the centrality of the story of Rome's rise and fall to the Nazi leadership's thoughts about empire. These texts range from one of Hitler's earliest speeches, "Why We Are Anti-Semites"

(1920), in which he revisits the Roman stage, to Himmler's infamous Posen Speech, delivered in the fall of 1943, when many Nazis saw the writing on the wall. These men philosophize about world history with a genocidal empire reaching to the Ural Mountains in mind.

Drawing racist and anti-Semitic lessons from Rome's fall, Hitler sketched racialized ruin gazer scenarios and—implicitly or explicitly—proposed strategies for prolonging the existence of this new empire, and Himmler followed suit, outlining the *Reich*'s imperial future in the East while inventing his own ruin gazer scenarios. Promising both solid foundations grounded in the laws of nature and a glorious end in ruins, the Nazi leadership took the tension between triumphant imperial present and anticipation of the end to an extreme. Or, put differently, the Nazis imitated Rome by imitating the end.

Thinking Empire, or Hitler's Roman Lessons

We know Hitler's *Mein Kampf* as an anti-Semitic tract about Aryans as the master race. It is also the text of a would-be theorist of empire who, straining to equal Spengler, writes about world history as the rise and fall of empires. "Thus cultures and empires [Reiche] collapse," Hitler writes, concluding one of his world-historical panoramas (MKe, 296). All of world history is a struggle to conquer and subdue the world. Second, this world history is also one of two opposing empires, Aryan and Jewish. German history, Hitler promises his readers, will culminate in a struggle with "international Jewry," whose ultimate goal is the "economic conquest" and "political subjugation of the world" (MKe, 321). The danger he foresaw was "Jewish world Bolshevization" (MKe, 662), a concept borrowed from Rosenberg.

Like Spengler, Hitler proposed a *reconquest* of Europe under German leadership. More precisely, Germans would reconquer not only Europe but the entire Eastern space. The Nazis developed their imperial ambitions in contrast to England and France; their *Reich* would be continental, their civilizing mission directed at the vast regions east of Germany.[37] Speaking to generals in February 1933, Hitler presented this orientation toward the East in world-historical terms, stating that the era of sea-based colonial powers had come to an end, and the era of the colonization of the great land masses of Europe was beginning. In the chapter on the empire's orientation toward the East, Hitler outlined the Nazis' historical "mission," promising to lead the German people "to new land and soil" (MKe, 646). The main obstacle to this new empire, Hitler announced, would be Jews, the *Reich*'s "mortal enemy" (MKe, 662).

This was the Augustan text of *Mein Kampf*, the story of great leaders, and their future conquests, taking place on the stage of world history.[38] Hitler's concept of empire was a racialized version of Ratzel's *völkisch* law of *Raumbewältigung* or space-mastery: each people needed the amount of space proportionate to its racial quality.[39] His theory of empire is based on a cyclical theory of history reminiscent of Spengler's. Hitler's gaze at the past presents him with a "picture of becoming, of being active, and declining" and a *single cause* of "the conquerors'" decline: the infringement against the "iron logic of nature" to preserve racial purity (MKe, 293; translation modified; 292). His historical panoramas let us discern the template of familiar stories about Rome's rise and fall. Creating cultures in their own image, these conquerors eventually—"[a]fter a thousand years and more"—merge with the conquered (MKe, 292). What follows is a Spenglerian picture of ruination and, finally, relapse into "barbarism" (MKe, 292). Hitler's conclusion doesn't come as a surprise: forgetting history's iron law is the "deepest and ultimate" cause of imperial decline (MKe, 283). The cycle of imperial history thus keeps revolving, from a thousand-year period of rise to a thousand-year period of decline.

In "Warum sind wir Antisemiten?" (Why Are We Anti-Semites?), Hitler presented his ideas about the fate of empires as early as 1920. More importantly, in this speech he took his audience onto the ruined stage of Rome, explicitly connecting his thoughts about a Nordic race and Jews to ideas about the Romans' fatal mistakes, and the lessons to be drawn from these mistakes. In this early speech Hitler already told a version of world history, which begins with Nordic immigrants to Egypt, claims Greco-Roman antiquity, and ties modern imperialism to the trope of Jewish finance capital and world domination. Jews did not create states but caused their collapse, he stated, and then addressed the fall of Rome. No state was more systematically destroyed by Jews than "the state of rising Rome."[40] To the explanation of Rome's decline at the hands of Jewish merchants, Hitler added Spengler's anti-Semitic version of Gibbon's thesis about the link between Christianity and the fall of Rome. The culprit was Paul, ruining Rome by postulating the equality of all men.

In 1920, Hitler thus believed that he had witnessed the *Ur-Scene* that had been performed on Rome's ruined stage a long time ago—the setting, the actors, and the plot that explained why Rome fell and when. The conclusions Hitler drew from his analysis of the causes of Rome's fall are unfortunately predictable: if Jews had destabilized Rome from the moment of its *rising*, then the Nazis needed to eliminate Jews from the very moment they set out to build a new *Reich*. Eliminating the other race *from the beginning* was one strategy that would assure that the Third Reich would not repeat Rome's decline.

Hitler's conjectural history thus defined the coming Nazi empire *ex negativo*: as the neo-Roman empire that is the *pure* Rome—the *non-Jewish* Rome. Jews destroyed ancient Rome; they would not destroy this modern empire. Second, this empire would differ from modern imperialism. The Nazi empire would be rooted in the occupation of the land, not in the "colonial and commercial policies" of Western imperialism (MKe, 654). In other words, Hitler's concept of empire combined exterminationist anti-Semitism and Spengler's conservative critique of modernity with its distaste for capitalism.

From these early reflections about the cycle of empire and the causes of Rome's fall, Hitler's thought moved toward neo-Roman mimesis. In 1920, Hitler depicted world history as the migration of Aryan races. By 1941, the story had changed and Hitler was convinced that he was leading not only the strongest but also the most Roman *volk*. Mussolini, we saw, positioned fascist Italy as the guardian of European civilization, resting on Roman foundations. At the moment of conquest, Hitler claimed this role, which he defined in 1941 as guarding the border between West and East in his address to the *Reichstag* about Operation Barbarossa. "The fall of Rome," Alexander Demandt writes, "was no academic problem for Hitler, but an urgent problem for the present."[41]

Pausanias, or the Weimar Republic in Ruins

The men whom Hitler put in charge of conquered Poland was Heinrich Himmler, who surrounded himself with a staff of SS theorists, many of whom had moved from the circles of the conservative revolution into the orbit of National Socialism, working out their versions of the new imperial order, or what Werner Best called "Großraumordnung." The other man in charge of the East, I mentioned above, was Alfred Rosenberg, a Baltic German.[42] Like Hitler, Rosenberg visited Rome's ruined stage, translating his reflections about the empire's fall in *Der Mythus des 20. Jahrhunderts* (*The Myth of the 20th Century*; 1930) into a Pausanian ruin scenario. Familiar with Spengler's *Decline* and committed to a new *Reich*, Rosenberg too argued the necessity of reconquering Europe. This was the task of Nordic Germans, inheritors of ancient Rome's "*völkisch* state" and racial vigor.[43] The mission now was to launch the final battle between the Nordic and the Jewish soul.

For his ruin scenario, Rosenberg drew on Pausanias's *Guide to Greece*, equating ancient Greece and the Weimar Republic. In this montage, consisting mainly of quotes from Pausanias's travelogue about Greece under Roman rule, Rosenberg visualized the Greek states' decline for his readers: of Arcadia's "Megalopolis," he wrote, nothing remained but a "'great solitude.'"[44] The explanation for this ruination of Greece and Weimar was again racial mixing. Since Rome repeated Greece's mistake, Germans had to return to Arminius and his German barbarians.

Rosenberg's wacky metaphysics of history as a struggle between the Apollonian Germanic-Greek lineage and the Dionysian (the "Asiatic-African underworld" and the Jewish-Oriental world) seems to argue against understanding the Third Reich in terms of neo-Roman mimesis.[45] However, as I mentioned above, Rosenberg thought that Rome, the destroyer of Semitic Carthage, was worth imitating because it saved Europe from the "foul pestilential emanations of this Phoenician city."[46] With the invasion of the Soviet Union, the Third Reich had turned into a conquest empire whose defeat Hitler and Goebbels later began to narrate as the moment of the Second Punic War.

The Greatest Empire Ever: Himmler's *Posen Speech* (1943)

As a student, he fantasized about a life in Turkey, dressed up as an Arab, but mostly dreamt about life as a settler in the East. Like Hitler, Heinrich Himmler envisioned an empire that would last, outlining the strategies that would guarantee this duration. Hitler had discussed the end of Rome. Himmler combines visions of a future *Reich* that will last for centuries with ruin scenarios set in an equally remote future. Himmler delivered this so-called *Posen Speech* on October 4, 1943.[47] That is, at the very moment when even some Nazis were starting to wonder whether the war in the East was lost.[48] However, this tension between asserting the empire's long duration and conjuring scenarios of its fall, set in an even more remote future, is not primarily due to this state of exception; rather, as the reading of Hitler's texts showed, this tension characterized the Third Reich's spatio-temporal imaginary.

Heinrich Himmler is known for the role he played as one of the principal engineers of the Holocaust. This was not "the ultimate goal of his policies but rather the precondition for much more extensive plans for a bloody 'new ordering' of the European continent."[49] In 1942, Himmler and his SS intellectuals went to work on their "grand scheme of Germanizing the East."[50] Around 1942, Himmler's thinking about the new world empire underwent a significant shift. Before 1942, Himmler believed that it would take several generations to achieve the goal of creating a Greater Germanic Reich. Having abandoned the phrase *Greater Germanic Reich*, Himmler began using it again in 1942, convinced that "he had successfully laid the foundations of [this *Reich*]."[51] In September 1942, Himmler outlined his long-term vision of a Germanized East in his Ukrainian model colony, Hegewald: millions of German settlers would inhabit the East "in 400–500 years."[52] Genocide, resettlement, and Holocaust were preparatory work, the "first step" toward a qualitatively "new form of supranational" racial regime under totalitarian rule.[53]

Himmler's moment of imperialist delirium did not last long. First the Allies' landing in North Africa in November 1942, then Stalingrad in the winter of 1942–1943, and finally Mussolini's fall in the summer of 1943 radically changed the situation. By October 1943, Himmler had decided to postpone colonial settlement plans for the postwar era and joined in the war of annihilation, removing or killing "primitive Slavs," making room for German settlers, and rendering cities "uninhabitable."[54]

What do we learn about the centrality of Rome's ruins from Himmler's 1943 speech at Poznań? Unlike Hitler, Himmler never mentions the Roman Empire in his so-called *Posen Speech*. However, Himmler's ideas about the Germanic world empire of the future are deeply enmeshed in tropes of imperial rise and fall. Given his background, this Roman grammar is not surprising. Himmler's father taught German literature and Classics, and considered touring Greece's ancient ruins a mandatory part of his education. In 1910, Himmler enrolled at a Grammar School specializing in the transmission of classics.[55] He devoured Felix Dahn's *A Struggle for Rome* (1875), enthralled by the story about "perfidious Latins" and "fine and truly Germanic people."[56]

Thinking in terms of empires and their rise and fall thus came naturally to the future head of the SS, who translated this inherited knowledge into his own pseudo-philosophical worldview. At the opening ceremony for a Germanic sanctuary, Himmler spoke in 1935 about an ancient German law: "ascendancy is followed by downfall and downfall then followed by new life, as long as the will and strength of blood live on in an earthly being."[57] Himmler "probably used the term 'greater Germanic empire' for the first time" in 1938, declaring that the SS would create "the greatest empire that has ever been achieved by human beings and that the earth has ever seen."[58]

More importantly, the Third Reich was a work in progress, involving a wide range of scholars, researchers, and theorists—hard-core Nazis as well as radical conservative collaborators. One of those was Werner Best, part of a group of "*völkisch*-radical intellectuals," theorists of the SS and its Security Service (SD).[59] Best published a key essay during the preparations for the attack on the Soviet Union, entitled "Principles of a German *Great Space* Order" (1941). If his historical analysis of empires and imperial forms of rule set a specific research agenda, Best put the study of the Roman Empire at the top of this research agenda. Future research, he wrote, would prove that Rome's "great space-administration" was "exceptionally steady."[60]

Spengler fantasized about colonialism, Himmler dreamt about being a settler in Russia, and Werner Best always wanted to become the "governor" of a German "colony."[61] Best started his essay from the premise that the "[earth-]space in which the German volk exercises indirect or direct power" was rapidly increasing. This situation demanded the revision of "all concepts, principles, and forms, in which the exercise of ordering power hitherto has been thought and executed."[62] At stake were "the creation," the "preservation and further development" of "a new order in this space" and the strategies that would "guarantee its duration" (GV, 33).[63]

Best's analytical category of *great space order* encompassed different *völkisch* forms (like German *Reich* or Roman *imperium*). Deeply influenced by Fichte's *Addresses to the German Nation*, Best connected this geopolitical notion to "*völkisch*-organic" ideology.[64] The "subject of history" was *volk*, not race, and each *great space* consisted of "leading peoples" and weak *völker* in need of being ruled (GV, 42). This Fichtean geopolitics combined metaphysical high-mindedness with genocide. *Völkisch* laws of life, Best wrote, have to be respected, since the ultimate purpose of any *great space administration* is to preserve the *völker* of this spatial order. Some forms of rule neglect this law. In this context, Best addressed the growing use of the term "Helots-people" (GV, 43), or the idea of making Poland into "a master-less worker-volk."[65] Imitating Sparta left only the choice between apartheid, which was bound to fail, and assimilation, which inevitably led to "blood mixing" and "the danger of slave rebellions" (GV, 43). Best argued that *great space*-building in the East would include the annihilation of "undesirable volk."[66] This anti-Spartan program of *völkisch* order meant deportation, resettlement, and death. Jews, Best thought, were also *völkisch* enemies.[67]

The Third Reich was thus an empire *sui generis*. Discussing the "Roman imperium," Best wrote that "Reich" was a concept referring exclusively to "the German [here used in the sense of 'theudisk,' meaning German] life-orders of all *Germanen*"; it should never "be used for [other] foreign *völkisch* orders."[68] And yet the imperial problematic is the same: how to guarantee that the *Reich* will last. The fact that the Roman Empire existed for 500 years, a "duration" never again achieved by any other great space order, made Rome a "model" (GV, 50). In 1942, Best published an anonymous essay raising the question of whether the Nazi empire was about to repeat Rome's fall. I will discuss this essay in the context of Carl Schmitt's articles also addressing the topic of imperial rise and fall in the early 1940s. It is thus far from surprising to find that the template of Rome's rise and fall deeply structured Himmler's thinking.

In 1943, Himmler concluded his speech at Poznań with a vision of a postwar German East, extending to the Ural Mountains—a territory settled by German peasants, ruled by a German elite or SS *Führungsschicht*, and protected by fortified SS garrisons along its easternmost border. Addressing an audience of SS officers, police commanders, and other high-ranking Nazis, Himmler defined the Nazis' goal as "Germanic World Empire" and World War II as a means "to keep the path to the East open."[69] The *Posen Speech* is known above all for a section euphemistically entitled "Evacuation of Jews" (PR, 25).[70] As Longerich writes, with this passage Himmler told the audience that the first part of the SS's mission was accomplished: the work of Judeocide was done. After setting the "Final Solution" in motion in 1942, "the Jews receded more and more as the principal enemy" in Himmler's mind, and were replaced by the image of the Asian enemy.[71] Addressing the "conflict with Asia," Himmler told army officers in the spring of 1944 that there would be no "hate-filled avengers" in the future.[72] A little later, he wrote that having solved "[t]he Jewish question," no Jewish "avengers" would survive.[73]

The *Posen Speech* is about the work of the present and the tasks of the future. Empire-building, Himmler told his audience in 1943, is postponed, and the war against the barbarians of the East, the "Slavic Mongolian human masses" (PR, 5), has to take center stage. Himmler reminds his audience again that the stakes have been raised: Germans are no longer fighting for a Germanic Reich, but a Germanic "world empire" (PR, 20). "We will be settling!" Himmler announced, and concluded the speech by outlining once more his plans for a Germanized East, governed by a ruling elite, the SS, the vast new space marked by a ring of fortified towns (PR, 40).

Ruin gazer scenarios are a prominent part of Himmler's speech. More precisely, Himmler depicted two scenarios of imperial ruination, similar with respect to the way they conceptualize imperial temporality, but different with respect to the representation of the barbarian enemy. Let me begin with the first scenario. Speaking about "the long history that we have before us" (PR, 41), Himmler places this imperial project into a vast temporal horizon of future struggles. In this vision of the imperial future, time is measured in terms of "eons," not "the life-span of human beings"

(PR, 27). The tone is prophetic ("We are seeing far into the future"), and the vision outlined depicts the dangers of a defeat not in the present, but in "the remote future" (PR, 41). The SS will settle the East, fortifying its borders. Once this process is accomplished, the SS will begin to create a strong German settler population, using the methods of selection as their tool. Only then will the preconditions exist for Europe to overcome "Asia" in the final battle (PR, 41). If Europe loses this final battle, all "beauty" and "creativity" will come to an end (PR, 41). This was Himmler's version of Spengler's scenario, *a scenario set in the far future*: the *Abendland* in ruins, overrun by Asia's "cannibals."[74]

Earlier in the speech, Himmler asked his audience to *think in temporal categories of the long, if not the very long, term*. Here, Himmler names the laws of the SS: the law of nature and the "law of selection" (PR, 26). The core of the passage with Himmler's second ruin scenario reads as follows: "The moment we begin to forget the *law of selection* and hardness against ourselves," he explains, "*we will be perishing like every human organization*, like every flower in this world will eventually come to an end." And then he explains the SS's mission: to extend the era of the "flowering" of the German *volk* "for as long as possible and—do not be shocked—to possibly extend it for thousands of years" (PR, 27; emphasis mine).

We can dismiss these ideas as genocidal Darwinism, and the emphasis on the *longue durée* of the Germanic Empire as propaganda in a state of exception. And we would be right to do so. As Michael Geyer argues, by summer 1942 the Armed Forces High Command and Hitler knew that the war was lost. Deciding to wage "a war to the death," they accelerated and intensified "the machinery of destruction and annihilation."[75] General Jodl explained the rationale behind this decision in 1945: "can you give up an empire and a people, before you have lost the war?"[76] In other words, Hitler and many generals were living the end of empire.

But there is something else at stake in Himmler's scenarios of imperial ruination. Himmler sketches scenarios of imperial ending while at the same time gesturing at the solid foundations of racial history. On the one hand, he introduces a law of nature that he does not name as such: the Polybian/Aristotelian law (which he had already reformulated in 1935) that everything will perish—eventually. On the other hand, he defines the SS's mission as making this empire last, extending its duration for millennia to come by the SS's mastery of the laws of nature. Himmler's ruin gazer scenarios thus revise Polybios's law of nature and of imperial endtime—the most extreme version yet. Moreover, in a speech full of images of imperial enemies—of barbarian Slavs and Jewish nonhumans—Himmler completely eliminates the barbarian enemy from this racialized scenario of imperial endings and endtimes. In Himmler's 1943 fantasy about a world without barbarian avengers, fate is in the hands of the SS, who are in charge of the process of selection. In this state of emergency, Himmler articulates the new empire's imperial imaginary in its most extreme form.

Let me briefly summarize my argument. Hitler and Himmler connected scenarios of imperial endings to race, deploying their images of the barbarian enemy, ranging from Paul's heirs, the modern world's Jewish imperialists, to Himmler's Asiatic cannibals. Second, Himmler and Hitler restaged the tension inherent in the time of empire as duration and endtime. Promising a *Reich* that would last for centuries, they claimed to master the threat of imperial decline by restoring the iron laws of nature, whose rule modernity had suspended. While pursuing a reckless politics of conquest and extermination, risking the new *Reich*'s fall with every decision, the *Reich*'s leader and the leader of the *SS* thus introduced their version of imperial temporality into this German future: the very *longue durée* of racialized history, a history made to last by the twin practices of annihilation and selective breeding that accompanied the conquest in the East. This was a new use of Polybios's natural law (in the last instance, all things perish), articulating the surface temporality of accelerated empire-building with the deep slow-moving temporality of nature's movement.

In the fascist imaginary, empire's time—the time that remains—thus combines both the accelerated temporality of conquest and annihilation, and the decelerated time of nature. Foregrounding racial enmity and the project of restoring the laws of nature, these hard-core theorists of empire drew their lessons from two centuries of theorizing about the racial causes of Rome's fall. The strategies of postponing the end that they came up with were simple: eliminating their enemies, and fortifying their empire, literally and symbolically. In the next chapter, I will explore the construction of the Nazi empire's Roman zone, the ways in which the nation's gaze was directed toward the faraway past of the Roman Empire, its heroes and its Greco-Roman culture.

NINETEEN

Creating the Twilight Zone of the Third Reich's Neo-Roman Imaginary: German Classicists, Resurrectional Performances, and the Trope of the Neo-Roman Conqueror's Fortified Gaze

Introduction

Spengler prided himself on his cold detached gaze at the *Abendland*'s ruinous future. Hitler portrayed himself as the neo-Roman founder of a German *Reich*, heroically facing the ruins of the future. Himmler too struck the heroic pose of the imperial leader, conquering time by mastering the laws of nature. Karl Haushofer, a former general and the Nazis' leading political geographer, transformed the existing ruin gazer scenarios into his own post-Spenglerian fantasy about the risks of empire-building. The "mastery of space," Haushofer argued, constituted the "decisive question of every founding of a Reich."[1] Unlike many of his contemporaries, Haushofer saw a hidden optimism in Spengler's European "ruinlandscape."[2] Having studied Ratzel's ideas about space and instinct, young and old nations, Haushofer translated them into the Nazi project of a rejuvenated Europe, led by a *völkisch* state. In his 1934 geopolitical handbook, Haushofer explained that the Third Reich needed *Volksgenossen* who at all times kept their eyes fixed on long-term goals—or on the end, a heroic end in smoke, flames, and ruins. Haushofer's grandiose conclusion to his *Weltpolitik* included a ruin gazer scenario, translating Spengler's heroic pessimism into equally heroic geopolitical decisionism. Germans had no choice but to face up to the deadly abyss of world politics. Quoting Horace ("Si fractus illabatur orbis / impavidum ferient ruinae"), Haushofer promised that "world-political self-education" would enable Germans to perish "knowingly."[3] Not every German, only men of action, commanded such a superior point of view.

Most Nazi intellectuals were familiar with Spengler's analysis of the Faustian gaze. Wilhelm Weber (Roman historian and, like Haushofer, best described as a conservative revolutionary converted to Nazism) idealized Roman emperors as Spenglerian heroes, who stared "with wide-open burning eyes" into the "infinity" of space, intent on mastering it.[4] This fortified imperial gaze would be thematized and staged in the early years of the Third Reich as classicists and artists reflected on, and performed the relationship of, the classical past to the neo-Roman present. In particular, the trope of the neo-Roman leader's gaze was part of the resurrection of Augustus's image in the context of the Augustan bimillenary. Thematizing the relationship of the present to the classical past, some of the Third Reich's leading classicists captured the image of Augustus in a series of resurrectional performances. Bringing the Roman emperor back onto the stage of world history, they presented him as the ideal *Führer and* they recreated his image in their scenes of contemplations, drawing attention to the act of looking—theirs and Augustus's. Two studies preceded this labor of revivification: Wilhelm Weber's influential *Princeps* (1936), and Joseph Vogt's equally influential study of the Romans' *Raumlust*, or lust for space. Drawing on Spengler's ideas about scopic regimes and Haushofer's geopolitics, Vogt analyzed as inextricable the connection between spatial instinct and consciousness, the desire to "see" and to conquer.

German Classicists: Embracing the Neo-Roman Present

There are three areas in which the work of classicists is relevant to my argument about the Nazi empire's neo-Roman imaginary and its scopic regime. These areas also correspond to three different stages in the fascists' consolidation of power and conquest of the East: first, in the mid- to late

1930s there was the focus on Augustus prompted by the bimillenary and Hitler's Rome visit. Second, toward the end of the war, essays about the Second Punic War were commissioned. Third, as the German Army attacked the Soviet Union in 1941, classicists discussed the Roman Empire as a model of imagining, conquering, and securing a vast imperial space. Disdainful of parliamentary democracy, these classicists favored a strong (Caesarist) leader.[5] Their politics was close to that of the Nazi leadership and, increasingly, marked by racialist thinking.

Joseph Vogt, a friend of Schmitt's, made the case for neo-Roman mimesis most explicitly, arguing in his lectures in 1940 and 1941 that the "Imperium Romanum" was the Third Reich's ancestor.[6] People admired the Roman Empire for centuries, because a single state managed to create "a firm power formation" across an immense space (RR, 5). Due to its racial superiority, the "Reich *volk*" now assumed the "position of mastery" occupied by the "Roman citizenry" under Augustus, a "genuine" Führer.[7]

Vogt's collection, *Vom Reichsgedanken der Römer* (1942), appeared in the same year as Helmut Berve's *Das neue Bild der Antike* (1942), a two-volume collection of essays produced as part of the so-called *Aktion Ritterbusch* and drawn from a Berlin conference held right after the assault on the Soviet Union.[8] Between 1940 and 1942, a series of articles appeared, exploring ancient Rome as the model empire. Ernst Kornemann, for instance, known for his work on Augustus and the *Monumentum Ancyranum*, lectured on the rise and fall of the Roman Empire in the winter of 1940–1941.[9] In 1942, Berve published a lecture under the title *Imperium Romanum*.[10] And in 1940, Weber contributed an entry, entitled "Roman History to the World Empire's Decline," to the *Propyläen World History* (1940).[11]

Appearing at the moment of conquest, these texts were published after Hitler's pronouncements about the model character of the Roman Empire and in the wake of Carl Schmitt's *Großraum* lectures (held in 1939) as well as the competing publications on the concept of *Großraum* and the reordering of Europe and the Soviet Union by SS theorists like Werner Best. I will discuss some of these texts in more detail in later chapters. Their key aspects are the articulation of the study of antiquity with Haushofer's geopolitics or the competing *Großraum* theories, and with race science, the latter then shaping the ideas about the causes of Rome's fall. Two prestige objects of the Third Reich, the re-edition of *Knaurs World History* (1935) and *Propyläen World History* (1940), exemplify these trends. Haushofer, in charge of editing the former, advocated a rethinking of world history along geopolitical lines.[12] Beginning with Ratzel, geopolitics was intimately connected to *völkisch* thinking, often veering into racism. While Haushofer refrained from outright biological racism, the editor of the later *Propyläen*

World History (1940), Willy Andreas, advocated the reconceptualization of world history in terms of race science.[13]

That these post-Spenglerian conservatives attributed Rome's fall to the waning of the Romans' *völkisch* and/or racial substance comes as no surprise. Claiming Spengler's "synchronous gaze," Berve, for instance, wrote about late Romans' loss of "race instinct" and the empire's "racial decomposition."[14] Vogt too thought that assimilation was one of the reasons why Romans eventually lost the desire to act for their *Reich*. Weber's version of the drama that he pieced together from his contemplation of Rome's ruined stage was no different. Rome died because the ruling elite disappeared into the mass of assimilated citizens, losing the will to dominate the "foreigners" whom they had educated in their "way of life."[15]

"A Foreign Historical Zone": Inventing the Third Reich's Historical Imaginary

As I wrote above, German classicists did not merely advocate Rome as the model empire. They also contributed to the creation of the spatiotemporal structures of the Third Reich's imperial imaginary. In this section, I will focus on a particular aspect of this contribution, that is, the ways in which classicists thematized the project of bringing Roman past and German present into close proximity. Acts of neo-Roman mimesis come with their own imperial imaginaries, visualizing the existence of the Roman past in the neo-Roman present. They do so in different ways. While Spengler's discussion of the Roman Empire still maintained a tension between distance and closeness, difference and imitation, Nazi theorists and artists drew the imperial past ever closer to the present. In 1930, a conservative Catholic diagnosed a "painful 'synchronicity'" with the Augustan era.[16] Fantasizing the birth of a Spartan Germany out of the depths of the *Abendland*'s decline, Gottfried Benn wrote: "Antiquity is very close, is completely inside of us."[17] Hitler stated in his first cultural address that "Greeks and Romans suddenly stand close to *Germanen*."[18]

Like the Italian theorists of *romanità* and specialists in mimetic strategies before them, German classicists eagerly pursued the project of erasing the distance between classical antiquity and twentieth-century Germany. They did so in two ways: first, they reflected on the trope of the present's close proximity to the classical. Second, they staged this trope in their texts, writing scenes of revivification, veritable performances of resurrection centered on Augustus. Historical distance was thus transformed into closeness, difference into sameness. No one made the case for this "naturally close relationship" more passionately than Helmut Berve.[19] In *Das neue Bild der Antike* (1942), Berve claimed that because of their "racial awakening," Germans now experienced Greeks and Romans "as being of our blood."[20] That is, the Germans' organic relationship experienced the Romans' "political instinct" as informing "our own corporeal and spiritual existence."[21]

As I wrote above, classicists combined reflections on the trope of proximity between antiquity and the contemporary moment, with the (textual) staging of resurrectional performances. Here, their language is drenched in the visual register of the imaginary and its structures of mirroring and the desires for (re)cognition. Berve outlined this resurrectional paradigm at the Nazi empire's zenith in 1942, writing that the effect of the Nazi revolution was a new "exhilarating proximity": antiquity's "great spirits [Geister]" were "now [stepping] into the harsh light of historical reality."[22] Forsaking previous scholars' "fleeting glimpse" at antiquity, Nazi classicists would bestow "unity" and "form" on Europe's future order by creating a new image of Greco-Roman antiquity.[23] Vogt also discussed this question of proximity and distance between Greco-Roman antiquity and modern-day Germany in *Vom Reichsgedanken der Römer* (*The Romans' Idea of Empire*; 1942). Even if some people may find it questionable to apply contemporary concepts to "a remote past, a remote historical zone," the concept of *Reich* belonged to the things that antiquity and *Abendland* had in common.[24]

Devoting themselves to the effort of transforming Rome's *faraway past* into imaginary closeness, Nazi classicists also fabricated images about ancient Rome and Romans, new death masks for contemplation and use. They did not do this naïvely. As classicists, they were as aware of the projections involved in turning antiquity's "foreign historical zone" into familiar territory as were their nineteenth-century predecessors. Ernst Rhode, for instance, wrote that historical objectivity remained an illusion, since antiquity was, after all, a "ruined . . . wonderland."[25] Ulrich von Wilamowitz took the thought a step further. If "tradition is dead," he wrote, then "our task is to resuscitate the life of the past," while remaining aware of the role of "imagination," because "the tradition offers up only ruins."[26] Antiquity's dead, "the spirits we summon demand the blood of our hearts," Wilamowitz wrote, yet philologists were not sufficiently aware of their projections or that "something of us has entered into them, something strange."[27] Alluding to these debates, Berve wrote that if too closely tied to the "desires" of the present, the "new view of antiquity" risked being the product of "an easily excited fantasy."[28] But like all collaborators in the Nazis' new imaginary, Berve did not struggle too hard to rein in what Wilamowitz called this "strange" thing.

What had been nothing more than a way of speaking for nineteenth-century classicists, the textual-visual resurrection of a faraway past that blurred temporal boundaries became a form of symbolic politics not only in fascist Italy but also in Nazi Germany. In this neo-Roman twilight zone, the Roman dead were made to live again. Moving from the early 1940s backward in time to the Augustan bimillenary, the next section of this chapter deals with the ways in which classicists and artists staged this spatio-temporal imaginary in scenes of resurrection, revolving around Augustus. Thematizing and staging the fortification of the neo-Roman gaze, these scenes reawakened Augustus's mimetic gesture, the desire to be imitated inscribed into the realist text of the emperor's *Res Gestae*.

A Burning Desire for Augustus: Refashioning the Emperor's Death Mask

With the *Mostra Augustea*, Giglioli and his specialists in resurrection brought Augustus back onto the imperial stage, making him "the central protagonist of *romanità*," and Mussolini Augustus's heir.[29] In a literal act of identification, the entrance to the exhibition displayed two colossal statues of Augustus and the Duce.[30] Whether the Duce truly identified with Augustus ultimately doesn't matter. What matters is that Italian intellectuals like Bottai constantly urged this identification. German classicists eagerly joined in this celebration of model and copy. Ernst Kornemann, for instance, fond of Spengler's ideas about Caesarist leaders, lectured in Rome about Augustus's unique creation of "leadership [Führertum]," implying continuity with Mussolini if not Hitler.[31] Wilhelm Weber compared the Duce to Caesar and Augustus.[32] In the context of the Augustan anniversary, German classicists then called the Roman emperor onto the German stage. Weber published *Princeps* (1936), and the journal *Die Antike* devoted a special issue in 1937 to the Italian celebrations, opening with a sentence from Augustus, expressing the wish to be remembered as "the founder of the best [political] order."[33]

Discussing Augustus as the model *Führer*, the authors contributing to this issue (Gerhart Rodenwaldt, professor of archeology and art history; Johannes Stroux, one of the editors of *Die Antike)*, as well as Carl Weickert (an archeologist who directed the *Antiken-Sammlung* of the Berlin museums), thematized and performed this act of making the ancient emperor part of the neo-Roman present. Moreover, these authors all wove Augustus's *Res Gestae* into their analysis. While Gerhart Rodenwaldt explored the realist aesthetic of Augustan art, Carl Weickert recalled the mimetic power of the *Res Gestae*: "in many respects I [Augustus] left to my successors examples worthy of imitation."[34] It is this desire of the past—Augustus's "IMITATE ME"—that their articles reawaken and their responses to Augustus's images rekindle.

Let us begin with Gerhart Rodenwaldt, the longtime director of the German Archeological Institute, whose work on the aesthetics of the Augustan era decisively contributed to the creation of the Nazi empire's imaginary Roman zone. Like Vogt, Rodenwaldt portrayed the Third Reich as the rebirth of Rome. He too thought that Romans and Germans were "related tribes," and in his *Kunst um Augustus* (*Art around Augustus*; 1939), Rodenwaldt contributed a series of images of resurrected Romans, proving Rome's "proximity to the present."[35] In these scenes, Rodenwaldt used the Winckelmannian tropes of emotional closeness to the artwork, and the Rome traveler's scenarios of bringing the torso to life.

Rodenwaldt (who participated in the Augustan anniversary as head of the *Deutsche Archäologische Institut [DAI]*) was deeply invested in making Rome matter to a German intellectual tradition committed to its Hellenistic heritage. To make his point, Rodenwaldt compared the Parthenon of the era of Pericles to the Augustan *Ara Pacis*, "the highest form of political propaganda."[36] Rodenwaldt argued that the Greek friezes celebrated not reality, but a utopia: the Greek city-states' democratic community. In contrast, the Roman altar represented the "historical reality" of Augustus's achievements (the empire's pacification) as an integral part of a Roman history told in Virgilian terms, which included Aeneas.[37]

Rodenwaldt's text interpreting Augustan art and the *Ara Pacis* in particular relied on reproductions of the restorations done for the Augustan bimillenary exhibitions. The subject of the altar's Greek friezes was myth, Rodenwaldt argued; that of the Roman panels (the so-called processions decorating the altar's sides) was the political history narrated in Augustus's *Res Gestae*. While Rodenwaldt's description of the figure of Aeneas in the *Ara Pacis* panel remained in the discursive register, his descriptions of the many statues of Augustus reproduced the emotional closeness that we know from Winckelmann's journeys into the Greek past. Having quoted at length from the *Res Gestae*, Rodenwaldt selected the Augustus statue found at Prima Porta, positioning himself and the reader in front of the work.

Rodenwaldt wrote this encounter with the Roman statue as an intense experience. Negating the difference between present and past as "we" behold it, the power embodied in the statue of Augustus provoked a "burning desire" to imitate.[38] All European nations had reasons to remember this man who "influenced" the course of world history.[39] Continuing Rodenwaldt's paean to Augustus, Johannes Stroux also mixed his portrayal of the "founder of our occidental world" with discussions of the *Prima Porta* statue.[40] Both Rodenwaldt and Stroux quoted extensively from the *Res Gestae*, the realist text in which Augustus offered his death mask to later conquerors presenting himself as a model sovereign. To Stroux, the document spoke "in the [emperor's] living voice."[41] Carl Weickert also cited the *Res Gestae*, combining his reading of Augustus's principate with interpretations of the many busts and statues of Augustus. The political subtext of Weickert's portrait, and the analogy between Augustus and Hitler informing it, is easy to read: many expected Augustus, the "revolutionary," to become a "tyrant"; instead, he became the "ideal picture of the ruler," glorified by Virgil.[42] But let us return to Weickert's enthusiastic acts of contemplating Augustus's likenesses. Portraits of the passionate young man conveyed the "impression of the uncanny."[43] Contemplating the *Prima Porta* statue, dating from the time of Augustus's victory at Actium, Weickert experienced the full impact of perceiving "hard," "sober," "powerful" Roman-ness.[44]

Rodenwaldt's art history, Stroux's analysis of the *Principate* as *Führertum*, and Weickert's exploration of Augustus's portraits appeared one year after the publication of Wilhelm Weber's *Princeps* (1936), the influential study of Augustus's principate, and his *Res Gestae*. Weber, *the* "representative of Roman history" in the Nazi era, was deeply marked by the Second Reich's defeat in 1918.[45] In 1933, Weber believed salvation had come to a defeated Germany in the guise of "a soldier."[46] His *Princeps* (1936) contributed decisively to the resurrection of Augustus as model leader.[47] Weber read the *Res Gestae* as a performative text, in which Augustus created his own myth.[48] Carefully crafting the figure of the divine sovereign, Augustus created the Roman Empire's political theology.[49] Weber thus added a theopolitical version to Spengler's notion of the Caesarist leader.

In *Knaurs Weltgeschichte* (1935), Weber's celebration of Augustus anticipated the core theses of his *Princeps*. The story he told about Augustus's rise to power resonated with Weickert's story—and Hitler's own myth: a "revolutionary," Augustus put an end to the "state of exception," establishing his "reign of peace."[50] In Weber's exalted language, the Roman leader is a man whose eyes radiated "divine power."[51] In his contribution to *Die Neue Propyläen Weltgeschichte* (1940), the divine Augustus again played a central role. A kind of monument to the Roman emperor, the entry included the full text of the *Res Gestae* accompanied by a photograph of the original text at the Ancyra Temple. Weber's introduction to the emperor's manifesto hinted at his interpretation of the *Res Gestae* as reflecting "the personality of the 'sublime [one]' in its uniqueness."[52]

Like Rodenwaldt, Weickert, and Stroux, Weber thus revived Augustus, celebrating the leader's visionary gaze. In the 1943 edition of *Kunst um Augustus*, Rodenwaldt, gesturing at the precarious situation of the German *Reich*, wrote that world-historical epochs always turn toward "the greatest men and the greatest deeds."[53] Since the bimillenary celebrations, he wrote, "world events have made the figure of the Roman Empire's founder come to the fore ever more powerfully."[54] In other words, between 1937 and 1943, the image of Augustus emerged from the remote past into the imaginary twilight zone of the Nazi empire.

Joseph Vogt's Study of the Roman Empire's Scopic Regime

With the beginning of the war, Weber started to speak the language of geopolitics, commenting for instance about Mussolini's efforts to add "Carthaginian Tunis" to Libya as the imperial ventures of a man acting according to the "law of blood and space."[55] By 1940, Weber had thus fully absorbed Haushofer's ideas about geopolitics as actions taking place on the stage of world history and Joseph Vogt's theses on the Romans' spatial consciousness and scopic regime. Mussolini, Weber pointed out, had recognized in the ruins of Rome the "stage of the world's amphitheater."[56] The radical alteration of Rome's urban fabric testified to the "planetary vision and events of the present."[57]

Rodenwaldt, Stroux, Weickert, and Weber revived the image of Augustus and the Romans' imperial gaze. What did Vogt contribute to this project with his *Vom Reichsgedanken der Römer* (*The Romans' Idea of Empire*; 1942)? In this post-Spenglerian study, Vogt embedded the topic of the leader's imperial gaze in a larger analysis of the Romans' scopic order. As I mentioned above, Vogt approached the topic of the relation between classical past and fascist present from the angle of geopolitics. States conquered territory, and conquest established law—this was the core premise of Vogt's thought. Taking the theory of *Reich* and the scopic regime of empires onto classical Latin terrain, Vogt analyzed the Romans' native policies and then their spatial imagination. To Vogt, Romans mattered because they conquered and secured a vast imperial space and because they imagined this vast space.

The first chapter of *Reichsgedanken der Römer* was based on a lecture held in April 1942. Here, Vogt explained that Rome gave birth to the very concept of *Reich* (which he defined as a power that rules and serves many *völker* in a large space) and explicated his thesis that the Romans, driven by intense *Raumlust*, had excelled in thinking and imagining imperial space.[58] Applying Spengler's Faustian scopic regime to the Roman Empire, Vogt wrote that to the Romans, the future itself was a "space to be captured by their gaze" (RR, 44). Vogt's second chapter is devoted to the ways in which conceptions of space shaped Roman politics. This meant studying the process of how the Romans elevated "the stirrings of space-instinct into consciousness" (RR, 36). Endowed with this particularly alert "spatial instinct," Romans practiced visualizing "their position in the great space" (RR, 38).[59] Generating a scopic regime containing spatial instinct through spatial consciousness, this articulation of *Raumlust* with efforts to "perceive and dominate" large spaces shaped the empire (RR, 43). Reflecting on the transformations of *Raumbewußtsein* as a symptom of the later empire's political fragility, Vogt also connected spatial consciousness to decline. The moment of "Scipio's Dream" (RR, 76) was the moment when Romans began to worry that their expansion had reached its limits.

Conclusion

Vividly mimicking nineteenth-century rhetoric about the reawakening of the classical past, Berve argued in "Antike und der nationalsozialistische Staat" (Antiquity and National Socialist State; 1934) that the Romans would be of central importance to the new *Reich*. His methodological essays, Rodenwaldt's art history, Stroux's analysis of the *Principate* as *Führertum*, Weickert's exploration of Augustus's image, and the work of Weber and Vogt participated in the reinvention of a neo-Roman imperial imaginary and its visual regime. The Third Reich's classicists thus took their audience into the Roman zone. Like all historical imaginaries, the Nazi empire's imaginary was as much about "facts" and discursive readings of the past as it was about the production of images. Nazi classicists contributed to this imaginary's thick layer of (textual and visual) images. Circulating Augustan images for acts of identification and dis-identification, they invented vivid scenes of contemplation, drawing attention to their own acts of looking while depicting again and again the imperial leader's commanding gaze. Riefenstahl and Benn joined this project of resurrection as committed modernists.

TWENTY

Resurrections in a Modernist Mode: Greeks, Spartans, and Wild Savages, or the Restoration of Civilization's Shattered Gaze

Introduction

After his Rome visit, Hitler's eyes were fixed on the Roman model. And so the nation's gaze had to be directed toward the distant territories of the East, and the distant past of Greco-Roman antiquity. No one resurrected this faraway past more effectively than Leni Riefenstahl in her *Prologue in Images* to *Olympia* (1936), the film about the Olympic Games in Berlin. Hitler commissioned the *mise-en-scène* of the Olympic Games, and Speer, Riefenstahl, and her staff choreographed the Games with an eye toward the film.[1] The Games were supposed to demonstrate the *Reich*'s peaceful nature, to reassure Germany's own population and allay the world's fears about Nazi aggression.

Reports in the German press about excavations in Olympia underscored this legitimatory move. In addition, the architects of the *Reichssportfeld* laid claim to classical Greek culture, nowhere more so than with the *Dietrich-Eckart Freilichtbühn*, the open-air theater on the Olympic grounds.

Modeled on Pausanias's favorite theater at Epidaurus, this theater featured in the Nazi press as a site where Greek antiquity was reawakened.[2] An article in the *Völkische Beobachter* underscored the faithful reproduction of the Greek original, listing every single architectural element of the site, from the orchestra to the *Bühnenwand* or *skene*, the theater's focal point.[3] This Greek-style theater, part of the Roman-style architectural setting of the Olympic grounds, signaled what the Nazis' neo-Roman architecture was about: the reinvention of the ocularcentrism of Augustan culture, oriented toward stage- and scene-building as the stage of world history and the site of imperial sovereignty.[4]

Journey into the Present: Leni Riefenstahl's *Prologue in Images*

Riefenstahl clothed the Third *Reich* in her own modernist neoclassicism—or rather, unclothed it: Riefenstahl's opening sequence builds up to a striking scene, a carefully choreographed filmic superimposition, in which a famous statue, the *Disc Thrower* by the Greek artist Myron, slowly comes to life as a present-day German athlete wearing very little. This scene staged the resurrection of ancient Greek warrior-athletes. To this striking moment of resurrection, Riefenstahl added a series of images of athletes in movement (the graceful movements not of sports, but modern dance). Turning her resurrectional beginning into a story about historical continuity, Riefenstahl takes the spectator on a journey from Greece to the Aryan north, from the ruins of the Acropolis to the newly renovated stadium in Berlin. We follow several Olympic torchbearers, running toward Berlin. The first of these runners emerges again from a resurrectional scene (in which a group of women slowly "burns away" while the young athlete comes into sight). The travel sequence consists of shots of the actual runners as they exchange the torch, images of maps, and aerial scenes as well as photographs of easily recognizable architectural sites, such as the Charles Bridge in Prague. These images take us from the most medieval to the most modern architectural sites. By the time the runner enters the Berlin Stadium to light the flame, he has become an easily recognizable Aryan figure, thus repeating the moment of resurrection a third time.

On the one hand, Riefenstahl invented a conventional ruin story in which fragments are integrated into a new whole and continuity emerges out of a seemingly unbridgeable break between past and present. I am, however, more interested in the resurrection of this past, the forms that this resurrection took, and the aesthetic strategies that Riefenstahl developed in the film. While Winckelmann re-created mutilated torsos as a whole, Riefenstahl started with a statue that was intact. Yet her mode of representation is as invested in bringing this statue alive as was that of Winckelmann, who visualized the torso's missing limbs as he imagined the body in motion.

In her filmic work of resurrection, Riefenstahl displayed her Winckelmannian fascination with Greek statuary and Greek ruins, reveling in the aesthetic power of her modernist medium. Her *Prologue in Images* is driven by the desire to close the gap between past and present and to bring the past back to life. To do so, Riefenstahl developed realist strategies of resurrection in a modernist medium. In this prologue, Riefenstahl "[renounces] language," visualizing the film's story as a modern journey from the ruins of the Greco-Roman past to the ritual sites of the Nazi present.[5] We first follow her camera as it circles around the ancient ruins of the Acropolis. Accompanied by classical music, the camera approaches the remnants of the Greek stadium from ground level. At first we see nothing but unconnected stones and weedy grass—rubble. Only slowly do we then get to see more substantial vestiges, which we start to recognize as ancient ruins.[6]

Riefenstahl thus systematically engaged the viewers' scopophilia in the process, sharpening their gaze at the objects put before their eyes. As soon as the camera moves from rubble to ruin, Riefenstahl starts to introduce moments of superimposition so that the image of one ruin slides into the other. In addition, she begins to intersperse shots of sculptures and busts. By the end of the sequence, Riefenstahl consistently keeps the viewer in a spectator position that is overawed by the view of monumental ruins—sometimes from up close, other times from farther away, but always from below (figure 20.1).[7] Riefenstahl intensifies this sublime view with a curiously dizzying acceleration of camera movements, lending a modernist sensibility to her appropriation of antiquity.[8]

She repeats this move in the prologue's core sequence: the camera again first circles around a series of sculptures and busts before it focuses on a single statue, the *Disk Thrower*.[9] Myron's statue then comes to life in the slow, graceful movement of the contemporary German *Diskuswerfer*. As I mentioned above, the moment of resurrection is carefully constructed, and a detailed analysis reveals a significant detail: during Riefenstahl's superimposition, the camera slows down substantially, letting us see every step in the process of resurrection—as if to sharpen the spectator's vision. This is certainly not the "fleeting gaze" at antiquity dismissed by Berve; instead, Riefenstahl creates an intent, scrutinizing gaze, grasping the ancient image "in the light of the new day"—to again use Berve's metaphors.[10] This

20.1 Acropolis. Leni Riefenstahl, *Olympia* (1938).

sequence thus repeats what characterized the rubble-ruins sequence, that is, a deliberate provocation of the viewers' epistemophilia, fastening their gaze on a series of objects.[11]

How does this work? Riefenstahl has the German athlete assume the exact same pose as Myron's statue. There is but a brief moment of exact superimposition before the athlete starts to move with slow, sweeping movements (figure 20.2). However, there is never a "pure" moment of superimposition, as their naked bodies never seamlessly meld into each other. For the large, muscular body of the German athlete appears as a dark silhouette around the statue, which then gradually disappears from the viewer's sight. That is, in Riefenstahl's prologue, the Greek statue slowly comes to life as the contemporary athlete, as the viewer's gaze becomes "pre-occupied" with the Aryan male body—the present takes over from the past. The Greek past fades from view—leaving us with the German reincarnations—solid, muscular bodies, statues in their own right.[12]

In Riefenstahl's film, ancient Greece is left behind—a beautiful memory image that lingers but shortly, overpowered by Aryans, on whom Riefenstahl fixes our gaze. There is not a trace of Winckelmannian melancholia about the loss of the past in these scenes of resurrection.[13] Riefenstahl's prologue evokes antiquity as legacy, as a genealogy that she brings into the imaginary space of the present for a brief moment—and then abandons it. These steeled bodies in the present, constantly in motion, are what Riefenstahl's imaginary is built around—not the immobile statues of the past. And yet these modern bodies would not signify what they do without their antique shadows. They are born in what Vogt called the foreign historical zone of the past.

20.2 Disc Thrower. Leni Riefenstahl, *Olympia* (1938).

In the same year that Riefenstahl resurrected her Greek statue as Aryan athlete and Aryan runner, making them part of the modern present's *corporeal existence* (to use Berve's phrase), Jacques Lacan undertook his own journey, supposedly visiting Berlin to attend the Olympic Games. Lacan was on his way back from Marienbad, where he had just delivered the first version of his mirror stage essay at the 14th International Psychoanalytic Congress. When Lacan later justified his trip that took place three years after students burned Freud's books and the psychoanalytic journal *Imago* in Berlin, he spoke of tracking "the air of the times."[14] We don't know whether Lacan actually attended the Games (or whether he ever saw Leni Riefenstahl's film about them). But since Riefenstahl's prologue to the film is an act of mimesis that negotiates difference and identity, proximity and distance, structured around ideal bodies and statues, we can assume that the French analyst would have had a lot to say about the film's use of desire and scenes of (mis)recognition in the context of the Third Reich's neo-Roman mimesis.[15]

"The Eye's Possession": Gottfried Benn's Spartan Gaze

The Greeks invented the term "barbarian," and acts of neo-Roman mimesis involve the reinvention of imperial enemies as barbarians. Gottfried Benn, who had read a lot of Nietzsche and too much Spengler, welcomed the Nazis as the twentieth century's new barbarians. Fascinated by primitivism, Benn glorified the archaic forces beneath the thin veneer of modern urban civilization in the 1920s. In March 1933, polemicizing against the left's discourse about Nazism as barbarism, Benn wrote that the Nazis might well be "a horde of savages," but that this was testimony to the historical moment: "All new historical movements," he claimed, "have barbarian beginnings."[16] Human consciousness incessantly created new worlds by positing "the great objective idea," thereby giving the world political and artistic form.[17] History has no *telos*; it is great men and their ideas that give it direction, creating a "chain of races and *völker*" and demanding sacrifices.[18]

"Dorische Welt: Eine Untersuchung über die Beziehung von Kunst und Macht" (Dorian World: A Study of the Relationship between Art and Power; 1934) is Benn's contribution to Nazi ideology and to the outline of a post-Nietzschean aesthetics suited to the *Reich*'s symbolic order. Like Heidegger's 1933 *Rektoratsrede*, Benn's reflections on power and art marked the moment when he positioned himself squarely on the side of the fascist movement. Heidegger believed that Germany's intellectuals will either "will" the "greatness of the beginning [Aufbruch]," or else the "spiritual power of the West breaks down" and its moribund civilization will collapse.[19] Benn was a bit more optimistic. History, Benn thought in 1933, had just begun.[20] A conservative revolutionary by sensibility, he compared National Socialism to a regenerative force, pouring "the stream of its vitality heavy with tradition [ahnenschwer] across dead European plains."[21]

Benn's text is invested in the power of looking. Reveling in the rupture with Weimar's formless civilization, Benn wrote: "Man has [only] a blurred backward gaze, no forward gaze at all."[22] With "Dorische Welt," Benn created this "backward gaze" by sharpening the gaze at the past. Like Riefenstahl's *Prologue with Images*, Benn's resurrection of the Dorian world is an act of mimesis that negotiates difference and identity, proximity and distance. And like Riefenstahl, Benn resurrects past worlds, first Greece and then Sparta, the gray, "anti-feminist" Dorian world of "camps" with its warrior heroes standing behind the silhouette of pan-Hellenic Greece – the golden age of the "white race."[23]

Benn's enthusiasm for Sparta and its "beautiful bodies" was not the idiosyncratic obsession of a medical doctor turned author. Rather, it was part of the revival of Sparta studies that Best alluded to and whose authors were in some cases critical of the *Reich*'s Roman mimesis. Helmut Berve, for instance, published his Spenglerian critique of modernity, arguing the contemporary world's "proximity" to Sparta's "mastervolk" and manly warriors.[24] A "bulwark" against "barbarians," the Spartan "Führer-State" led a "campaign of extermination" against their Persian enemies.[25] This existential struggle between the "Orient's non-human formlessness" and Sparta's master race constitutes the core of Berve's history.[26] While Berve ultimately preferred Rome to Sparta, Walter Eberhardt, the most racist among these classicists, remained deeply attached to the Spartan model. The "rebirth of the German volk" would lead to a "rebirth of antiquity," a coming alive of the past grounded in "blood, instinct, and ur-relatedness."[27] In Eberhardt's eyes, Greek statues, "present in their blood," did not elicit cool distance.[28] They turned into mirrors. Like Riefenstahl, Eberhardt wanted living, moving bodies, not the "plaster figures" populating the dusty "museum" of bourgeois classical studies that Eberhardt ridiculed in 1935.[29]

Eberhardt's model empire was not Rome, but Sparta. The Nazi classicist mixed Nietzsche's critique of historicism and its love for a dead past, and Jakob Burckhardt's revisionist view of "barbarian" Greece, with Rosenberg's *Mythus* and Hans Günther's race theories, situating himself in the camp of intellectuals close to Himmler. As I mentioned above, Rosenberg invented "Germanic-nordic" antiquity, glorifying Arminius. Reevaluating the past in terms of Germany's "racial self-consciousness," Eberhardt shifted the accent from Rome to Greece.[30] By the end of Eberhardt's essay, Germans are no longer Spartans but "barbarians."[31] To Germans, the memory of Rome is a memory of enslavement. Having started with an act of identification with Spartan warriors, Eberhardt now speaks in the voice of the barbarian, using the word with some irony, but also a considerable amount of hostility.

Benn was not Berve, or Eberhardt, and the historical sources from which he assembled his palimpsestic text were more respectable—among them Pausanias's *Periegesis*.[32] Unlike Berve, who served the Third Reich to the very end, Benn was attacked by the SS in 1936 and reverted quickly to a worldview more nihilistic, more elitist than Spengler's, if such a thing were possible.[33] Benn's elitism and his avant-garde aesthetics with its Nietzschean insistence on art as autonomous, a "lonely elevated world," was prone to alienate him from his new allies (DW, 150). It is also safe to claim that Benn evinced little interest in Arminius, the anti-Roman insurgent. Yet, like Eberhardt, he participated in the (not-entirely) ironic description of Nazi Germans as barbarians. And like Berve, Benn held up Sparta's political idea, the growth of ordinary politics into the "spatial [Raumhafte] and imperial," and drew his readers' eyes to the statue of the Spartan warrior, made of stone and based on bodies perfected in the gymnasium and on the battlefield (DW, 151).

In "Dorische Welt," Benn's Spenglerian essay, he exhibited Spartan statues four times, putting them directly before his readers' eyes: "The figures are naked. Dorian, that is skin, but skin that is being moved, the skin that covers muscles, manly flesh, the body" (DW, 137). These are "pure" bodies, "tanned by the sun, the oil, the dust, the brush, and the cold baths, used to air" (ibid.). Here, every "muscle" and "joint" are sculpted and "worked into each other, the whole warrior-like" (ibid.). The second time, Benn assumes the pose of Winckelmann, encircling the antique statue. This statue, he writes, belongs to a later stage of Sparta's artistic development:

> The general stance and the whole movement, nature in other words, that is the meaning of the figures, these are statues of pure limbs, they barely contain the spiritual element, these are the limbs of the gymnast, the warrior, the wrestler. (DW, 142)

"Such a statue is firm," he continued, "its limbs and its torso have weight, one can walk around it, and the beholder becomes conscious of its mass" (ibid.).

And then he returns a third time, in a less descriptive and more discursive mode, tracing Sparta's artistic development to the moment when nature becomes *Geist*: "At the beginning purely materialist . . . then more and more taking the laws from the material, the eternal material of stone" (DW, 144). At this point, Benn introduces the point of view of the Spartan artists who scrutinized the "anatomy" of perfectly bred naked bodies (ibid.). This sight "has long become *the most precise possession of the eye* [der genaueste Besitz des Auges], now the inner eye separates reality from all particularities and the contours of victors and gods emerge freely" [emphasis mine] (ibid.).

The final image that Benn invokes is again the image of a warrior: the "stela of the dying runner," representing Spartan law: "A law against life, a law only for heroes" (DW, 153). Retrieved from the bottom of the ocean, this stele speaks to the present: "Our eyes follow the Dorian world, the people with style" (ibid.). They vanished, "their time is over," yet they "still call out a law to those who come later, from the depth, the shards," or the "bronze statues," all recovered from ships sunk to the ocean floor (DW, 152–153).

With these four different descriptions of the Spartan warrior, Benn thus moves from Riefenstahl's mimetic resurrection of the Greek warrior to an aesthetically and discursively mediated resurrection of a statue, repeating the transition from "naturalist" reproduction to *art pure* (or what Benn calls *style*) and from Winckelmann's neoclassicist reconstitution of a wounded torso to Rilke's modernist reflections on the power of classical art (which did not reconstruct the fragment as a whole).

With both modes of resurrection, Benn sought to establish a link between the present and a Spartan past that to his contemporaries might have seemed so very distant. Benn begins and ends the essay with passages evoking this classical past, present only in its ruins—ruins that magically attract the viewer's gaze. To the image of a world sunk to the bottom of the ocean corresponds the image of Greek antiquity in the opening paragraph: "This world, which is part of our movements and on whose remnants our tense, shaken [erschütterten], tragic-questioning eyes are resting" (DW, 124). And to these passages about the classical past's past-ness, and the desire to retrieve it, corresponds the image with which Benn captured the moment of 1933: "All the old contents are sinking [into the ground], but can't yet sink/vanish completely," Benn wrote, and then asked: once these remnants of a decaying civilization have been removed, "what are we then supposed to do with the emptied space?" (KM, 200). In "Dorische Welt," Benn "filled" this void by retrieving the fragments of a more glorious past, and resurrecting them for the present.

The series of images of Sparta's warriors and statues punctuates a text that raises questions of politics and aesthetics, celebrating both Sparta's great idea (the transformation of politics into the spatial and the imperial) and the style that arose with this idea. Moreover, Benn connected politics and aesthetics with a sustained Spenglerian reflection on acts of looking at the past and the present, while performing a new gaze. The idea expressed in a phrase we encountered above—*Besitz des Auges*—will prove to be central to Benn's retrieval of the Spartan past, which in essence represents a Romanized Greece with its foregrounding of military might and the dominance of the political.

Retrieved from the ocean, the statue of the "runner" embodies Sparta's law, "the law of the [clean] outline" (DW, 153). It was in Sparta where art was born from power, it was in Sparta that artists *seized* bodies with their gaze, turning them into statues, it was in Sparta where the dream arose that defines the Occident's *Great Culture*, the culture of the "white race" (DW, 134). Benn reawakened this culture for Nazi Germany: the dream of "selection and eternal youth, equality with the gods, strong will, the strongest aristocratic belief in race" (DW, 135). He believed that "we are seeing a new world," a "world of forms" built on the only two principles: art and power, "the warrior and the statue" (KM, 201). These principles are strong, and they sustain a strong idea: "selective breeding" (ibid.).

Benn did not start the essay with Sparta, with warriors and statues. Instead, he first lured his readers into a historical zone more familiar to them, Athenian Greece. For this purpose, Benn, the inveterate modernist, reinvented resurrectional realism, having his readers accompany a "refined Athenian," walking through Athens (DW, 130, 128). Benn disliked nothing more than realist novels, and yet in 1934, he described in the minutest detail the moment before this resurrected Athenian leaves his house. As he walks in the direction of the harbor, crosses the marketplace, stops at the main street, and finally reaches the theater located outside the city, Benn's Athenian becomes fully visible. This is the effect of the kind of descriptive writing, obsessed with everyday details and obsessively listing them, that we know from realist literature, from travelogues and historians, aiming for the most vivid evocation of a past that no longer exists.[34]

In these passages, Benn creates an imaginary space, the "Greek space" that his protagonist traverses and that we "see" through the protagonist's eyes (DW, 131). The backdrop to Benn's story is reconstructed ruins; Benn's Athenian strolls through an intact city.[35] Yet at the same time as he resurrects the past in the realist mode, Benn signals repeatedly that he is describing what others have described before him: "A world in a light that frequently has been described" (ibid.). The purely imaginary dimension of this mimetic resurrection of the past comes to the fore in these hyperrealist passages, which let us trace the desire to be in the past, *and* to "see" the past through the eyes of the past—an aesthetics of immersion that restores the moderns' shattered gaze, the "eyes of today's civilization" (ibid.). Yet this exercise in resurrectional realism with a modernist touch is embedded in discursive prose, making "Dorische Welt" a text that conveys difference and identity, proximity and distance (ibid.). Benn thus maintains an ironic distance toward this desire of bringing imperial past and imperial present into close proximity and its textual manifestation, that is, the creation of an effect of immediate presence in/of the past.

Having introduced the Athenian citizen—so familiar to Germany's *Bildungsbürgertum* as a figure of identification—Benn then redirects his searching gaze toward another object: the Spartan warrior. Benn glorifies Sparta as the military, disciplined, masculine model for the new Nazi state and its art.[36] Sparta is a "city of warriors," whose inevitably brutal "soldier mentality" constitutes the very foundation of the entire Greek world. Benn celebrates Sparta's power to spread its warrior culture, driven by "space panic [Raumpanik]"—the echoes with Spengler and the analogy to Nazi Germany are again hard to miss (KM, 150). That this empire will involve colonial domination seems self-evident to Benn.[37] And of course, Benn praises the education of the young Spartans, who learn above all how to slaughter and subject their enemies. If necessary, they practiced "city-racism," depriving some of their citizens of their rights for the good of the community (DW, 133). This hard, firm mentality makes Sparta a community of men not motivated by profit, but by honor.[38]

Sparta was Spenglerian *culture*, not *civilization*, and like all genuine cultures it still had a hard, barbarian core. Hard is Sparta's style, expressing race and power like the city itself. Spartan art is public, weighty, solid—statues made of stone, testifying to the "birth of art from power" (DW, 145).[39] The gaze that Spartan artists cast at bodies, turning them into art, is also hard. Benn begins the entire discussion of the relation between ancient past and modern Germany with a Spenglerian reflection on "civilization's" scopic regime, and civilization's longing for this past in ruins. "Our eyes/gazes that [today] are so destroyed [*unsere heute so zerstörten Blicke*]," he writes, are drawn to the "remnants" of this Dorian world, searching for "art, for perfection" (DW, 124; emphasis mine). The denigration of Sparta is symptomatic of this wrecked, ruined, shattered gaze. For the Spartan world represents the part of the Greek past that liberals did not want to see, Benn claimed. Or rather, they were not able to "see" Sparta the way it was—to see its significance and its power—because the era of liberalism shied away from violence: "[the liberal era] was unable to seize *Völker* and men with their eyes [ins Auge fassen]—'to seize' that already sounded too violent to them" (DW, 141).

Averting its eyes from Sparta, the liberal era fastened its gaze on the exotic spectacle of wild savages, financing "expeditions to savage peoples" as a form of entertainment (ibid.). This phrase: "ins Auge fassen"—to grasp an object with one's eyes, to take hold of it—plays a key role in Benn's political aesthetics, as does the exotic spectacle of "primitive[s]" (DW, 146).[40] Politics and aesthetics are inextricably entangled: liberals not only abhorred violence, they also gave up on slavery—they not only failed to "seize" these primitives with a firm gaze, they stopped seizing them *tout court (ibid.)*. Greece, on the other hand, was built on slavery.[41]

At its core, Benn's essay is a revision of Nietzsche's aesthetics, prompted by the spectacles of a colonial world. Records of colonial encounters with "primitive *Völker*" force us to reevaluate Nietzsche's Dionysians differently (KM, 146). In contrast to Nietzsche's privileging of the Dionysian over the Apollonian, Benn argues, ancient Greece needs to be derived from Sparta; it is the tension between the "Doric-Apollonian" that characterizes the Greek (ibid.). Greeks, even Spartans, were a "primitive" people, he grants Nietzsche; "primitive" meaning "a people close to intoxication [rausch-nahes Volk]" seized by "great, intoxicating waves of excitation" (ibid.). But these Spartan "primitives" were different from the "primitives" that we see in contemporary travelogues and films: "By now we have become acquainted with primitive *völker* [seen] in travelogues and films, especially races of Negros [Negerrassen], whose entire existence seems to be a series of intoxicated states without [these states] creating any art" (ibid.).

What these colonial images prove is that ecstasy alone does not produce art, Benn argued. For art to arise from ecstasy, a third element needs to intervene: the "Spartan-Apollonian" or Apollo as the "great disciplining [züchtende] force" (DW, 144). In other words, a military state with manly Prussian virtues. If this form-giving law does not intervene, we are left with Benn's savages and their formless ecstasy, or what Berve in his history of Sparta called "the orient's inhuman lack of form."[42]

For Benn, the year 1933 is thus a foundational moment in which things are given form. That which gives form is (Spartan) style, a "species-specific [arthafte] aesthetic law," proper to the Occident's "Kulturkreis" (DW, 151, 150). State and style have similar functions in Benn's Spartan world: while state power guards against the state of nature, style transforms nature into style: style "no longer originates in nature in unmediated form" (DW, 150). Returning to the trope of Weimar's savages, Benn argued that ecstasy remains close to nature, expresses nature, while style transforms "material" into "form"—in the art of the white race, there is no nature left (DW, 150, 151). Genuine art, "Spartan-Apollonian," is born from power—that is the essay's main thesis. It is also born out of *acts of seeing that seize bodies and objects*: "By now the anatomy of nakedness, studied in gymnasia and wrestling stadiums, has been the possession of the eye for a long time; now the inner eye separates reality from all particularities and the contour of the victor and the gods emerges freely" (DW, 144). The Spartan artist's gaze took visual possession of the warrior's body, and so does Benn.

As I mentioned before, the final image on which the reader's gaze comes to rest is again the image of a warrior: the "stela of the dying runner." It is this image with its clear-cut outlines, not the dissolving outlines that characterize European civilization, which Benn's fortified, heroic gaze retrieved from the depth of history. In "Dorische Welt," Benn brought this dead warrior figure back to life, and in the process he restructured civilization's crumbling scopic regime. European civilization has lost its Faustian drive to see beyond the visible, to (visually and literally) seize the worlds of the past (remember the Faustian gaze's fascination with ruins) or the "primitives" located beyond Europe's borders.

Benn invites his audience to wander into the invisible world of the past and to take hold of it with their eyes. As I mentioned above, Benn begins the essay with civilization's shattered gaze, and he ends with a fetishistic invocation of the newly strengthened gaze, its grasping, seizing quality. Only a fortified gaze will grasp Sparta's vanished past in its true significance, and only a fortified gaze will bring this vanished past back to life from its ruined remnants, redrawing their former outlines instead of leaving them as blurry, indistinct shapes.

The truly imaginary dimension of Benn's essay is located in the fortification of the scopic regime that brings this Spartan gaze back to life. For that is what Benn does: he brings back to life the gaze of the Spartan artist seizing the naked body with his eyes, making it its "possession," and turning the warrior into art. It is here that the identification takes place; it is here where the *object a*—that object which completes the subject's existential lack and around which the work of fantasy develops its complicated visual scenarios—is located: in the eyes of the past. Benn's resurrection of the Spartan world is also an attempt to resurrect what he thought was its scopic regime.

Benn takes his readers into the foreign zone of the imaginary: proximity to the past replaces distance from it. At the heart of the new Germany, we find Sparta: "One cannot claim [that antiquity, all of] this is far away," he writes, and adds: "Antiquity is very close, is totally inside of us" (DW, 147). Correcting Spengler, who claimed that the occidental *Kulturkreis* was about to end, Benn wrote: "the Kulturkreis has not yet been closed" (ibid.). With the onset of the *Third Reich*, Germany is about to enter the height of a new culture, not the depth of civilization.[43] "Die Antike ist sehr nah, ist völlig in uns"—this statement articulates a political-ideological project: Benn affirms Nazi Germany's classical genealogy—or, in terms of the imaginary, he thinks of the *Third Reich* as a Spartan empire and Sparta as the *Third Reich*.[44]

Riefenstahl and Benn celebrate Greek bodies. Yet, like the Winckelmannian scenes centered on Augustus, written by Rodenwaldt, Stroux, Weickert, and Weber, their work is part of the Third Reich's neo-Roman mimesis. For the picture of antiquity that Benn and Riefenstahl produced has ultimately more to do with Rome than Greece. Benn's Spartans certainly fit into this Romanizing of Greek culture. Around 1939, Heidegger began to theorize National Socialism as the last stage of Western metaphysics, of the self-assertion of the Western subject. Heidegger now saw Nietzsche as someone who "'sees the Greek world exclusively in a Roman way, i.e., in a way at once modern and un-Greek.'"[45] I discussed Nietzsche's admiration for the Roman Empire and Roman warriors in chapter 15. It is this *verrömerter or "Romified"* Nietzsche whom we find in Benn.

Antiquity's Other Barbarians, or the Enemy's Body

We know that Benn's fascination with Sparta was as intense as it was brief. By 1937, Benn faulted Greece for having invented the "totalitarian claims of the state."[46] And in 1948, threatened by the Red Army and surrounded by rubble, Benn wrote: "Antiquity has come to an end; when we started out, the archeological finds once more unveiled its splendor, today . . . it can no longer be reawakened."[47] Yet, as we saw in the previous chapter, other intellectuals continued working on the resurrection of the classical past and the neo-Roman gaze. Like Riefenstahl and Benn, Rodenwaldt, Stroux, and the like took readers into the twilight zone of their historical imaginary on the terrain of art, aesthetic theory, and art history, in the medium of film, text, and the reproduction of works of art.

Their images, retrieved from a distant ruined past, helped give form to the new *Reich*'s symbolic order, with its thick imaginary layers. The proliferation of these images of classical bodies sustained a historical imaginary that made the Greco-Spartan and Roman past newly visible. More than idealized Aryan bodies, the body of the Greek athlete, the Spartan warrior, and, finally, the body of Augustus, the Roman emperor—all of these bodies were part of the Third Reich's imperial mimesis, visually embodying the presence of the past and giving voice to a strong mimetic desire.[48] There were of course also the images of the new empire's enemies. Eberhardt wrote in 1935: "We recognize ourselves in the enemy's otherness."[49]

Benn made this "being other" corporeally visible with an anecdote from Spartan life: Agesilaos has his men undress the Persian captives, and then the Greeks start laughing, "full of contempt for their enemies" (DW, 138). Returning to Sparta, Benn finds Greek barbarians ("beautiful bodies, large bodies, bodies for selective breeding") and Persian barbarians, bodies that attract the gaze and bodies that provoke distain—Spartan form and Oriental formlessness (DW, 138).

Hinting at genocide, Veit Harlan's *Der ewige Jude* (*The Eternal Jew*; 1940) also renarrates art history from classical antiquity to European modernism. This art historical sequence begins with cross-fades, slowly arranging the façade of a Greek temple and Greek and Gothic sculptures into a harmonious whole. As the sequence switches to an expressionist portrait by Emil Nolde, the soundtrack suddenly shifts from classical music "to African rhythms," and accelerating cuts produce "visual chaos."[50] The radical conservative author Moeller van den Bruck saw the specter of "Africa" creeping into the heart of Europe.[51] Spengler thought that the bored masses' fascination with "Negro dancing" was a symptom of the dying of "a great culture."[52] Reflecting on the concept of *volk*, Martin Heidegger told his students that "Kaffirs" belonged to those "who have no history," and in 1939, he still lamented the juxtaposition of photographs of the Acropolis and a "negro kral."[53] Against this backdrop, Riefenstahl and Benn resurrected what Benn called the "German-occidental genetic mass" (KM, 198). Taking their readers and spectators into an imaginary zone, where ruins are made whole and the classical past becomes the fascist present, the filmmaker and the poet fashioned Greek and Spartan counterimages—Nazis going native in Athens and Sparta.

Conclusion: Entering the Roman Zone—Architecture

The overall effect of the Nazis' Greek masquerade in 1936 is rather ambiguous. Riefenstahl's prologue and the Olympic Games seem to privilege Greek culture. However, recall that Riefenstahl took her spectators on a journey to the neo-Roman present, the newly built Berlin Stadium modeled on the Roman Colosseum. Based on the Roman axial structure, the Olympic grounds' architecture, the film's extradiegetic setting, also brings to mind Heidegger's "Romified" antiquity.[54] The idea of a Romanized Greek style applies even to the most Grecianizing element, the theater with its weighty bulky stage-building. Pausanias preferred the elegant "composition" of the Epidaurus theater to the "magnitude" of the Roman theater at Megalopolis.[55] The architecture of the Dietrich-Eckart-Stage breathed the spirit of Rome, more bunker than *skene*.

Roman style means power, and the entire *Reichssportfeld* exuded the threat of this new German power. Friedrich Tamms, a member of Speer's staff, defined heroic monumentality in terms of sheer "mass"—"real, i.e., massive"—embodying the *Reich*'s "will" and the Führer's "hardness."[56] Tamms here touched on the myth of the leader's steely gaze. In the past two chapters, I argued that the *act of visually imagining the ancient Greco-Roman past* was articulated to *a fortified gaze,* an imperial gaze that seized its objects. Moving to Hitler's and Speer's scenographic architecture, I will argue that the neo-Roman *spaces of the new empire* were similarly joined to the *Führer*'s fortified gaze.

TWENTY-ONE

Berlin/*Germania*: Seeing with Roman Eyes, Building a Roman Stage

Introduction

In 1940, the "aryanized" *Propyläen* publishing house revised its world history, urging contributors to think in racial terms. Wilhelm Weber followed the directive, characterizing Carthage as the empire of "merchants of a foreign race."[1] What distinguishes this piece on the Roman Empire's rise and fall is the thick textual-visual representation of ancient Rome and its ruins. The *Mostra Augustea* brought imperial Rome back to life. Weber's illustrated essay aimed for the same effect. Of course, this essay was not a German *Mostra Augustea*, yet like all richly illustrated texts it did have an exhibitionary quality to it. Readers were invited to glance at photographs of statues of famous Romans; at *sarcophagi* in the family tomb of the Scipios; and at Hadrian's Wall. Their eyes lingered on photos of the *Ara Pacis*'s relief panels and Pompeiian murals; they scrutinized ruin photos of the Acropolis at Sardis (Turkey) and Trier's *Porta Nigra*. Weber also guided his readers through Rome's archeological sites: the Tarpeian Rock, the Roman Forum, and many others. And he visualized for them the empire's expanse, using, for instance, a foldout map of Rome's world. Finally, Weber added the *Res Gestae* (chapter 6) accompanied by a photograph of the original text from the Ancyran Temple of Roma and Augustus.

The *Mostra Augustea*'s symbolic conquest of the Roman

stage had its material equivalent in the simultaneous restructuring of the city. Conversely, Weber's symbolic *Bildnahme* of the Roman stage for the Germans' neo-Roman project had its material equivalent in the architectural planning and practice of Hitler and Speer. Goebbels noted during their Rome visit that Germany lacked the "great history" of "ancient Rome" and mused that this lack might be remedied "in the realm of monumental architecture."[2] In the spirit of imperial rivalry, Goebbels added: "There is much that we cannot do, much that we will do better."[3] I will explore this form of mimetic practice, focusing on the Berlin/*Germania* project, the metropolis that Hitler and Speer imagined as the center of the future German world empire.[4] As mimetic practice and as discourse about it, the Third Reich's classicist architecture was a crucial aspect of the Nazis' project of creating a spatio-temporal imaginary.

The Nazis promised a strong and enduring empire, fortifying spaces in both the literal and the imaginary mode. Scenographic and monumental, Speer's architectural plans (often based on Hitler's drawings) were supposed to provide the weighty stage sets for the empire of the future and its metropole. As we know, imperial imaginaries of the neo-Roman kind are ruinous imaginaries, centered on the ruined stage of ancient Rome. In the case of the Third Reich, this preoccupation with the ruined architectural stage took on a new form. Simultaneously thinking about their building program and ruin theories, Hitler and Speer set out to construct two neo-Roman stages, one monumental, the other monumentally ruined. Promising that the empire would endure for thousands of years, they also promised a ruined neo-Roman stage that would endure into the far future. With their building program, Hitler and Speer thus enacted a particular form of neo-Roman mimesis: the mimesis of Rome's end.

Most scholars emphasize two aspects of Nazi architecture: first, excessive monumentality as the expression of the Third Reich's power, and second, the affinity of this architecture to stage sets.[5] To this scholarship about scenographic monumentality, I add the neo-Roman lens, arguing that the Nazis' reconstruction of Berlin as *Germania* has to be understood within the framework of Western European discourses and practices, of neo-Roman mimesis. Berlin/*Germania* is another iteration of the (re)construction of the Roman stage as imperial center within another iteration of imperial culture as ocularcentric.[6]

As I discussed in previous chapters, Nazi leaders, geopolitical theorists, and classicists were acutely aware of the nexus of imperial expansion and spatial imagination. Having read Spengler, Hitler spoke of conquest as spatial revolution. According to Karl Haushofer, a superior spatial consciousness, the faculty to produce a "geopolitical world-picture" that grasps the "expansive potential" of *völkisch* space, is the necessary precondition of conquest.[7] Romans, Haushofer wrote, echoing Vogt, excelled at this spatial imagination. Conquering Europe and the East was one way of expanding the spatial consciousness of the Third Reich's citizens. The other was the invention of a new spatio-temporal imaginary with the help of a Roman-style architecture centered on the future empire's stage.

Remade in stone, *Germania*'s new urban landscape would inscribe the imperial gaze as a neo-Roman one centered on the empire's stage. By having their subjects step onto this new Roman stage, Hitler and Speer's urban planners did not only want them to be awed by power or participate in the spectacles of power. They also wanted them to enter the Roman zone of the Third Reich's imperial imaginary. On his trip to Rome, Hitler understood that Italians rediscovered their *romanità* by reviving their ancient past and reinscribing it into their urban center. Now, Germans too would become Romans, seeing their world as Romans.

This is precisely what Gerhart Rodenwaldt argued. Wanting his contemporaries to realize the strong parallels between the Third Reich and imperial Rome, he based his argument on Nazi architecture. In 1937, discussing Augustus's *Res Gestae* of the Divine Augustus together with Vitruvius's dedicatory preface to his architecture books, Rodenwaldt declared architecture the "most Roman of all arts."[8] Vitruvius related Augustus's expansion of the *orbis Romanum* to public architecture, arguing that Roman edifices needed to express the empire's majesty. In 1939, Rodenwaldt took his readers on a virtual tour on the *Via dell'Impero*, again discussing the Vitruvian "essence of imperial architecture" and the ways in which it "teaches seeing," while reasserting the German visitor's experience of "being related to the ancient Romans."[9]

In 1943, Rodenwaldt then claimed that the "Reichssportfeld" in Nuremberg resembled Trajan's Forum; that the Berlin stadium had the shape of a Roman amphitheater, etc. More significant for our context are Rodenwaldt's ideas about the visual effects of these Romanized urban spaces: "When we experience that [the re-created] architectonic ensembles . . . produce a new effect through the liberation of their axes and the completion of their spatial composition, we organize and *see in a Roman way and with Roman eyes*."[10]

Traversing the Roman Zone

Berlin/*Germania* would not exist until 1950, but Germans could begin to imagine and experience their new capital and its monumental spaces with

Roman eyes. In his 1942 essay on Roman state architecture, Rodenwaldt analyzed the features that made Rome an imperial capital, recalling Constantine's visit to the city in 357 CE. Ammianus Marcellinus, Rodenwaldt explained, reported the strong impressions that the imperial capital's *fora*, monumental buildings, and axial structure made on the emperor, helping us imagine what it felt like to traverse this city. Unfortunately, we moderns, Rodenwaldt continued, can only repeat this "experience" in "our fantasy."[11] With the help of the classical travelogue and an appendix mixing contemporary photographs of Roman architecture, ground plans, and sketches of reconstructed buildings, Rodenwaldt then made his readers see what was no longer there: the architectural stage that Augustus built and that the Germans were now in the process of imitating.

Like Rodenwaldt, Hitler and his architects wanted Germans to take imaginary walks, experiencing what did not yet exist: a new architecture, representing the power of the Nazi empire and the "political will" of its sovereign.[12] Starting in 1936, numerous books appeared, showing the conversion of the "built environment into a gigantic stage."[13] Photographers like Walter Hege further exaggerated the proportions of these enormous monuments and broad avenues. *Die neue Reichskanzlei (The New Reich Chancellery)*, a booklet about the Third Reich's new site of sovereignty, guided readers-viewers through each single room. Photographs emphasized the stage-set-like nature of the Court of Honor, the *Mosaiksaal*, or Hitler's study with his *Medusa*-desk and the Virgilian wall tapestry.[14]

One of the most widely distributed films about the building program, Kurt Rupli's *Das Wort aus Stein* (*The Word Made of Stone*) (1938), took its title from one of Hitler's speeches.[15] Like Walter Hege's *Die Bauten Hitlers* (*Hitler's Buildings*) (1939), *Wort aus Stein* worked primarily with scale models. Both films did so in a way that made their viewers *see* the *Reich*'s future, filming the scale models of various cities as if they were already built. There is an entire archive of photographs showing Hitler and his entourage scrutinizing architectural city models of the future *Reich*. By 1939, Speer's team had built a large wooden "model of the master plan for Berlin."[16] Speer's team placed the model on movable tables, allowing viewers to enter the central axis or "Große Straße" at any point.[17]

Numerous photographs showed Speer and Hitler bent over the plans and models of *Germania*, or what Speer later called "cosmopolis."[18] Some of the photographs drew attention to the model itself or one of its featured buildings. Thus, one of these images showed Hitler contemplating the *Monument of the Movement* in Munich, foregrounding Trajan's column. Other photographs showed Hitler alone, sunk in the contemplation of an unbuilt future. One of the more widely known photographs focuses on

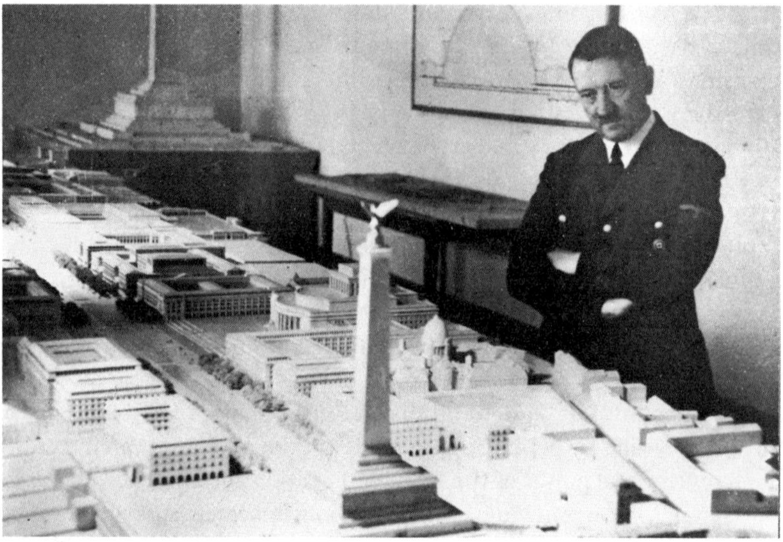

21.1 Hitler contemplating city model for Linz, Austria. Bpk Bildagentur/Art Resource, NY.

Hitler's contemplative pose and ultimately his gaze (figure 21.1). As Speer reported in his memoirs, Hitler liked to assume "the position of the traveler" when he studied Speer's model of Berlin's grand avenue, imagining how this traveler would admire the Great Hall standing at the heart of the avenue (SM, 133). This was a leader who knew about the connection of power and architecture;[19] he visually took hold of things and excelled in imagining the space of the future *Reich* and its new capital.

Theodoric the Great asked Rome's architects to restore the damage inflicted by time and "barbarian" attacks. The purpose was "[t]o leave to future generations, to humanity, monuments that will fill them with admiration."[20] Germany did not have a classical Rome to rebuild, but like this long-dead Roman emperor, Hitler and Speer wanted the glory of their capital to be remembered. Thirty years after the publication of Spengler's *Decline*, in an act of fateful hubris, Albert Speer set out to re-create the very preconditions for the ecstatic ruin gazing that Spengler had described in his *Decline of the West.*

Ruin Theories: Roman Ruins, Jewish Ruins, and a "Future That Is Already the Past"[21]

Munich and the Nuremberg Party Rally Grounds were the first major architectural projects. At Nuremberg, Speer fully assumed the role of "the architect as stage manager."[22] Excessively monumental, Speer's scenographic design of the tribune put Hitler at the center of the audience's field of vision (figure 21.2).[23] Supervising demolitions in Nuremberg, Speer realized that modern buildings would make "dreary" ruins (SM, 56). He did not want to be responsible for "rusting heaps of rubble" but wanted to create "structures which even in a state of decay, after hundreds or (such were our reckonings) thousands of years would more or less resemble Roman ruins" (SM, 56).

To make his point, Speer prepared a "Romantic drawing" in the genre of the anticipated ruin.[24] Among the most famous practitioners of this genre were Joseph Gandy, the British architect, who depicted the newly constructed Bank of England in picturesque wreckage, Caspar David Friedrich, who ruined the *Jakobikirche* at Greifswald in 1815, and Robert Hubert, who decayed his newly constructed Louvre in *Imaginary View of the Grande Gallery of the Louvre in Ruins* drawing the viewer into "the depths of the ruin" (figure 21.3).[25] Speer's own drawing depicted the *Zeppelinfeld*'s viewing stand after "generations of neglect": "overgrown with ivy, its columns

21.2 Grand Stand at the Nazi Party Rally Grounds, Nuremberg (ca. 1938). Bpk Bildagentur/Art Resource, NY.

21.3 Robert Hubert, *Imaginary View of the Grande Galerie in Ruins* (1798–1799).

fallen, the walls crumbling here and there, but the outlines still clearly recognizable" (SM, 56). While Hitler's entourage was outraged by Speer's ideas, the Führer himself was fascinated by his architect's invention, the "'law of ruins'" (SM, 56). Hitler could, like Speer himself, easily "conceive of a period of decline for the newly founded *Reich* destined to last a thousand years" (SM, 56).[26] At the foundation ceremony for the Nuremberg Congress Hall, Hitler framed the copy of the *Colosseum* in terms of "this new way of ruin-construction,"[27] explaining that this "giant" will speak its language of power long after "the movement has fallen silent."[28]

Writing about Italy, Medina Lansky observed: "The built past provided great raw material for Fascist rhetoric."[29] Hitler and Speer decided to provide future Germans with this raw material of the past. That is, Hitler and Speer planned to build their own ruined stage: Berlin would be reborn as *Germania* with its future as a city of imperial ruins in mind—a beautiful *Germania ruina*, a monumental ruinscape that would reveal itself after the fall of their thousand-year empire. This paradoxical act of architectural mimesis was inspired by Mussolini's Rome, and the latter's symbolic occupation of Rome's ruined stage. It was Augustus who first perfected this stage; it was Napoleon's experts who restructured it into the French Empire's Second City. Hitler and Speer did something much more radical: they began their building program with Rome in mind, setting out to construct their Rome—and anticipating Berlin/*Germania* as their ruined Rome.

If the monumental ruin of the Roman emperors had not survived, Speer remembered Hitler asking after his Rome visit, "[w]hat would still bear witness to them today?" (SM, 55). In a paradoxical take on Polybios's natural law, Speer thus invented a form of neo-Roman monumental architecture that promised monumental ruins that would last as long as the ruins of Rome. How would this be achieved? The granite monumentality of Berlin/*Germania* and the reorganization of the city through wide, axial boulevards would ensure that the ruins of the future would one day resemble "the 'framed' relics of the Roman palimpsest" that Mussolini's urbanists created in the 1930s.[30] As Friedrich Tamms explained, building ruins meant building according to the "law of the monumental," imitating Roman architecture's signifier of "durability," its raw materiality.[31] To achieve the ultimate Roman ruin effect, Speer would use hard materials that would go to ruin as "clearly recognizable ruins," not rubble (SM, 56).

Hitler's derivative thoughts on the history of art and architecture are the foundation of Speer's ruin theory. At the core of these thoughts, we find the contrast between modern and ancient cities, between private, capitalist architecture and public, state architecture. In a Spenglerian vein, Hitler outlined his own apocalyptic vision of the Weimar Republic's ruins of the future: "If the fate of Rome should strike Berlin," he wrote, then "the future generations would some day admire the department stores of a few Jews, as the mightiest works of our era," the expression of "our culture" (MKe, 265).[32] Empires need their "ideological-religious" center, expressing their rulers' "concept of power."[33] Modern cities will leave nothing but modernist ruins behind—ugly remnants of particularist Jewish-capitalist interests.[34]

Rome's monumental ruins were thus the model for the future ruins of Berlin/*Germania*. Obviously there is a lot of Spengler in these texts about modernity's decadence, and a lot of Mussolini. Yet we should not forget the resonances with Friedrich Ratzel's distinction between *Kulturvölker* likely to produce durable ruins and *Naturvölker* that left nothing behind. Hitler saw Jews through the same lens. Lacking creativity, Jews never left anything behind, no art, no buildings—and no ruins. Sublime imperial ruins would be the legacy of the Nazi empire, and "even when deeds will no longer speak, the stones will."[35]

Referring to Augustus's report on his building activities in the *Res Gestae*, Rodenwaldt wrote about the duty of imperial leaders to erect public buildings.[36] The architect August Stürzenacker celebrated Vitruvius as Augustus's collaborator, translating the latter's "heroic world view" into

Roman classicism.[37] Hitler and Speer thus did not only collaborate on the designs of a monumental capital, they also fantasized about rebuilding Rome as *Germania*, the city that would eventually—that is, in thousands and thousands of years—crumble into beautiful, awe-inspiring ruins. Promising sturdy ruins, they aestheticized ruination, inscribing the Third Reich into their imperial temporality of the *longue durée*. Leader and architect thus shared a common ruin imaginary, whose temporality is best described as anticipation of the past: an imaginary in the future perfect—this will have been. The future of the *Reich* was a future of beautiful imperial ruins.

Berlin/Germania

In 1940, Hitler sent out a memorandum to his architects that "Berlin must as soon as possible receive its new architectural form as capital of a strong, new Reich." Hitler saw this construction as "the most important contribution to the final securing of our victory" and announced its completion for 1950.[38] In 1941, imitating Mussolini imitating Augustus, Hitler proclaimed that everything "ugly" would be removed in Berlin. The scale of the new buildings would stun future visitors. Rome, the *Führer* said, will be "our only rival."[39]

Germany's rebuilt cities would be even more monumental in size than ancient Rome. The excessive monumentality, Speer explained after 1945, had to be seen against the backdrop of a future empire, not the existing nation-state. They were, after all, "on the point of creating an empire" (SM, 142).[40] The urban designs and models included the usual markers of imperial monumentality: Munich's new center would be dominated by a *Monument to the Movement* modeled after Trajan's column; and *Germania*, the Romanized capital, would include a Triumphal Arch of gigantic size, a *Führer Palace* resembling a fortress, and a Great Hall that would have reduced the Brandenburg Gate to a miniature. Like Trajan's Column, the Arch was based on Hitler's sketches.

This was Hitler's architecture of conquest made of "granite."[41] Coming back from Italy, Hitler envisioned this new capital as a center whose Latin name would give every German, "however far away from the capital he may be," the sense of belonging to the "Reich."[42] Reminiscing about his Rome visit, he made his guests imagine how they would see and experience *Germania*. In this vision of the future, Hitler imagined the *Reich* Chancellery as the site of imperial sovereignty as the destination: "One will arrive there [at the *Reich* Chancellery] along wide avenues containing the Triumphal Arch, the Pantheon of the Army, the Square of the People—

21.4 Great Hall seen through the Triumphal Arch. Bpk Bildagentur/Art Resource, NY.

things to take your breath away!"[43] Once the metropolis with its new axial grid existed, they would have "a magnificent perspective, stretching from the southern train station to the Triumphal Arch, with the cupola of the People's Palace [Great Hall] in the distance."[44]

In Speer's 1978 book, the photograph of the Arch frames the view onto the Great Hall, the composition reminiscent of Schinkel's painting of a triumphal arch (figure 21.4; see chapter 13). Would this restructuring of Berlin turn Germans into Romans? Rodenwaldt, commenting on Speer's plans in 1942, thought that the Nazis had succeeded. That is, he argued that plans for the restructuring of Berlin successfully emulated Roman architecture's appropriation of monumentality's "ethos," embodied by the Greek temple.[45]

Rodenwaldt drew a comparison between the successful creation of Rome as the capital of the Roman *imperium*, and Speer's *Germania*. Speer's architectural designs, the basis for the creation of "the Reich's capital . . . pro maiestate imperii," Rodenwaldt wrote, "equal the creations of Roman state architecture," because here too "we find the axis, the intensity of the spatial directions, the coordination of streets, squares, and great interior spaces."[46] Augustus's neoclassicism, which put Greek forms in the service of "Roman spirit," had its equivalent in Hitler's and Speer's new architectural language.[47]

Reorganizing ways of seeing through monumental architecture modeled on Rome (and its appropriation of the Greek temple) would be Hitler's and Speer's project. In this respect, Speer's monumental scenographic aesthetic corresponded to the efforts of fortifying the neo-Roman gaze that I discussed in the previous chapter. Recall, for instance, that Benn too was thinking of transforming modern ways of seeing, or what he called in his essay on Greco-Spartan art "our gazes that are so shattered today" (DW, 124). The multiplication of scenographic elements made this fortified gaze an integral part of Speer's designs. Providing the stage sets for the performance of sovereign imperial power wherever he could, Speer firmly aligned the spectators' gaze with that of their leader. Inside the Great Hall, Speer made the enormous speaker's podium, from which Hitler would address the subjects of "his future empire," the hall's vanishing point.[48] Speer's imperial sovereign was as distanced from the crowd as the deified emperors performing on the Roman stage.[49] The single, central entrance to the *Führer Palace*, a tall "gate with a balcony," again put the sovereign at the center.[50] Yet no stage was more intricately centered than the Nuremberg Grandstand, Speer's most archetypical "architectural stage-set."[51] Speer's persistently scenographic architecture thus strove to reproduce the Roman stage as the "stage of the world's amphitheater," to use Weber's phrase.[52] *Germania*'s stage would structure the "present's planetary vision and events," and it would do so in the most monumental form.[53]

An Empire Built in Granite

Neoclassical monumentality is nothing new.[54] What is new is simply the grandiose scale of the Nazi projects: an *Arc de Triomphe* in Berlin/*Germania* bigger than the one in Paris; a Congress Hall in Nuremberg bigger than the Colosseum; a North-South axis for *Germania* wider and broader than the axis that Mussolini rammed through Rome. Hitler's Mausoleum in Munich would be "slightly smaller" than Hadrian's Pantheon.[55] Nazi monumental architecture thus created an imperial, neo-Roman space and inscribed a new scopic regime, a Roman gaze. These monumental dimensions represented the Nazis' most literal response to the trope of imperial rise and decline. What Hitler, Speer, and the entire army of National Socialist architects built was a weighty imperial structure with fortresses along its borders, and a heavy solid core in its metropolitan center. The Nazi empire promised unlimited expansion, but within a framework of extraordinary stability—a country made of stone.

The obsession with this fortified empire appeared as an obsession with

21.5 Erich Mercker, *Marble for the Reich Chancellery* (1937).

a particular material, granite. Hitler had promised granite foundations. At a time when many Germans started to wonder whether the empire was reaching the point of overextension, Hitler reasserted imperial state power by again promising a rock-solid frame for Germany's future *metropolis*. German granite, the most enduring material, would be used for *Germania*. The *Reich*'s future, Hitler promised in 1941, would be solid: "In ten thousand years these buildings will be standing just as they are."[56] Nazi painters depicted not just the labor but also the materials required for this massive effort to build an imperial structure made of granite (figure 21.5). Mercker's painting shows workers and stone masons in a quarry painted as massively monumental in its proportions as Speer's actual *Reich* Chancellery would be. Joseph Thorak and Arno Breker then provided the suitable sculptures, classical monsters, made from marble, bronze, and sometimes granite.[57]

The Nazis' mimesis of Roman imperial architecture also included plans for the demarcation of imperial frontiers. Within Germany, the Nuremberg Party Rally Grounds combined Roman elements with fortification; outside the *Reich*, the Nazis' extensive Eastern plans included fortified settler cities. Speer was involved in Hitler's plans for the "settlement and development of the conquered eastern territories," modeled on antiquity's "colonial cities" in Sicily (SD, 156), or, as Scobie points out, Rome's African "veteran colonies."[58]

Moreover, to visibly mark the *Reich*'s frontiers, Hitler thought of a series of fortress-monuments to honor the fallen of his future wars and Wilhelm Kreis began to design *Totenburgen* or fortresses to the dead like the massive cube in Northern Africa or the "archaic round pyramid" in Russia.[59] Tamms compared Kreis's necro-monuments to Greek temples as "witnesses to empire," while Gerdy Troost thought they expressed the *Abendland*'s "will to order" in the midst of the "barbarian east."[60] Kreis's sketches strongly resembled Piranesi's studies of the Augustan mausoleum. Since Augustus's golden age, monumentality signified duration, fortress architecture a rigid topography of inclusion versus exclusion. For the occupied East, this meant a rigidly enforced separation between the new imperialists and those over whom they ruled.[61] Again, the model for this creation of imperial space was imperial Rome and the chain of ruins marking its former periphery. Romans, I argued, invented the concept of imperial ruins. Hitler, and his architects and artists, invented an imaginary featuring the solid, granite-based *Reich* of the present and the equally solid, but ruined, *Reich* of the future.

Conclusion: Imitating Ruins

Mussolini planned to open E42 with a world exposition in 1942. The completion of Berlin/*Germania* was scheduled for 1950. With anticipatory haste, Hitler envisioned a foundation ceremony when he would declare the "world Empire," and open a "world exposition" "on [*Germania*'s] eternal stage."[62] In 1950, the Third Reich would have its own *orbis Germanorum* and its very own Roman stage. Deeply convinced that the course of history followed the law of rise and fall, and equally certain that they would postpone this fall for at least a thousand years, the Nazi leadership thus acted with the picture of a vast imperial ruinscape, stretching from *Germania* to the far reaches of the East, in mind. Building their neo-Roman stage, they imagined it as ruined from the moment it was conceived, anticipating a stage-in-ruins more monumental than that of ancient Rome.

Reveling in the tension between triumphant architecture and glorious fall, Hitler and Speer thus created the conditions of future ruin gazing by writing Polybios's law of nature into the very foundation of Berlin/*Germania*. Closely working with Hitler, Speer contributed to this imperial imaginary centered on their neo-Roman stage. This was imperial mimesis of the end, enacted in their architectural constructions and designs, based on the re-creation of Berlin as Roman stage and their theories of ruin construction.

During his visit to Rome, Hitler performed the mimesis of the empire's end on Mussolini's neo-Augustan stage. Revisiting this moment in chapter 22, I will begin with Hitler's carriage ride through Rome's historic center at night, and an in-depth exploration of this performance of imperial mimesis and the staging of the imperial ruin gazer in the capital of the imperial past. With this analysis of Hitler's nighttime ride, we will return to the scopic dimensions of the ruin gazer scenario and the core issues of scopic mastery.

TWENTY-TWO

Hitler in Rome 2: The *Führer* as Ruin Gazer, 1938

Introduction

On the evening of May 3, 1938, Hitler arrived at Rome's Ostia train station. Reminiscing about "[having] seen Rome," Hitler later explained to his dinner guests that Mussolini conjured the idea of a "modern imperium" out of the ruins of ancient Rome.[1] The technicians in charge of the *mise-en-scène* of *romanità* made sure that in the course of this first evening, Hitler experienced the rebirth of empire in fascist Italy with all the intensity they could generate. Mussolini's experts in things Roman had worked hard on the connection between Roman Empire and Italian fascism, providing the urban spaces and monumental backdrop for the project of reviving the Roman Empire in the twentieth century and the spectacles of *romanità* in the ancient capital. The orchestration of Hitler's journey through the city's ruined core represented in their eyes and the eyes of the world the highpoint of this spectral politics.

The journey's planners worked under the direction of a Roman stage designer, whose sketches of each section of this journey along Rome's new avenues dramatized the depth of central perspectives. Enhanced by the effects of stage-lighting techniques, this *mise-en-scène* "made Hitler into the protagonist of [their] performance."[2] On this evening, the visitors moved in the twilight zone of their hosts' neo-Roman imaginary, who invited them to participate in a triumphant act of ruin gazing, an act that asserted mastery over the ancient empire's end in ruins by celebrating the beginning of a new *imperium* on African soil.

From the Ostia train station built for this special occasion, Hitler and his train of Nazi leaders and journalists drove onto the Roman stage through a newly created entry route that took them across the reframed ancient ruinscape to the Piazza de Venezia. The carriage with Hitler and the Italian emperor passed under the balcony from which Hitler and Mussolini would address the crowds on the following day before stopping at the Palace. This route started at the city gate, named after Paul, the author of the first text about the *katechontic* sovereign. This new entry route through the *Porta di San Paolo* (once the *Porta Ostiensis)* was expressly modeled on the triumphal entries of ancient and less ancient emperors. More precisely, Mussolini's urban planners built a new route into the city that repeated the itineraries of ancient Roman triumphal processions, and "the 1536 arrival of Charles V."[3] During a 1923 ceremony commemorating the march on Rome, one of the speakers reminded the audience that Charles V had marched through the Roman Forum (see chapter 6).[4] Because of this new entry route, what was a metaphorical act of repetition in 1923 was now reality for Hitler.

Coming through the San Paolo Gate, one of the stage managers wrote, Hitler would be seeing "a long succession of scenes."[5] The moment the Italian emperor and his guest drove across the "square in front of the Porta Ostiense" lit by "torches mounted on top of the city gate and the adjacent walls," they entered the twilight zone of the Roman past.[6] Staging a journey through the very heart of classical Rome, Mussolini's technicians used the ruins to resurrect imperial Rome. The horse-drawn carriage turned from the new *Viale Hitler* at the Ostia station onto the *Viale Africa,* then the Imperial Avenues, the *Via dei Trionfi,* and finally the *Via dell'Impero,* ending at the Piazza Venezia. The planners of this nighttime carriage ride ensured that Hitler caught sight of the Obelisk of Axum, moved from Ethiopia in 1937; the Temple of Venus and Roma; the Colosseum, where red light and smoke emanated through the window openings, leaving the outer wall dark. The *Via dell'Impero* took the visitor through the classical *fora*—the Forum of Augustus, Caesar, Nervi, and Trajan—and past the Basilica Maxentius with its marble maps of the Roman and Italian imperia.[7]

The itinerary, timing, and well-orchestrated light sources of this tour across the ruined stage apparently created an unforgettable event. Setting off the ruins against the dark night sky, the stage designers and specialists in resurrectional realism intended to give Hitler an "unexpected" and "immediate vision" of a revelatory nature.[8] "Colossal candelabras," with multiple gas flames creating a fiery red glow, were installed along the *Via dei Trionfi*.[9] One observer noted that the lights from the Colosseum "threw into ghostly relief the Palatine and Oppian hill, and the temple of Venus and Rome."[10] And from the *Via Africa*, the "ruins of the ancient imperial palaces upon the Palatine hill" were visible.[11] Gothic seems the appropriate word for the particular mode in which the ancient ruins were resurrected for this journey into the past.

On the night of May 3, 1938, imperial Rome became real, its "heroism in ruin" a renewed presence.[12] Masters of the resurrectional mode, Mussolini's technicians opened a space, an imperial imaginary, in which the boundaries of past, present, and future had collapsed. Against the backdrop of Rome's "imperishable symbols of power," this *mise-en-scène* of imperial power invented its participants as neo-Roman travelers made to experience the mastery that comes with the power of giving life to the past.[13] This fascist spectacle also interpellated the participants as imperial ruin gazers, putting them in a position of scopic mastery. Crossing Augustus's ruined stage, they had access to an unencumbered view of Rome's urban center and a god's-eye view that allowed them to look both backward and forward—to their imperial past and to the future of their empire. Most importantly, however, the specter of barbarian ruin gazers had been chased from the urban ruinscape: it was Mussolini who had orchestrated the scenario and Hitler who looked at Rome's ruined stage, reoccupying Spengler's privileged position (see chapter 16).

As I mentioned above, the resurrectional spectacle made Hitler both spectator and performer. The role that was assigned to him was that of the victorious Roman general. The carriage passed the Arch of Titus. When it arrived at the *Via dei Trionfi*, a spectacular vista opened onto the Arch of Constantine, ablaze in light—and Hitler was then driven through Constantine's Arch. During the military parade, the Arch of Constantine was again used as a backdrop as troops marched through the wide-open space around it, followed by tanks. Still in the thrall of this experience, Hitler regaled his dinner companions in the fall of 1941 with the idea of future triumphal processions through *Germania*. Every year, they would guide a "troop of Kirghizes through the capital of the *Reich*, in order to strike their imaginations with the size of our monuments."[14] One of the monuments the future *Reich's barbarians* would encounter as they would be driven through the streets of Berlin would be the gigantic *Arch of Triumph* that Hitler had been planning since 1936.[15]

The *Führer* as Ruin Gazer

"Whoever has emerged victorious participates to this day in the triumphal procession in which the present rulers step over those who are lying prostrate."[16] When Benjamin wrote this sentence, he was not merely thinking in metaphors. The Nazis appreciated Mussolini's fantasy and used the visit for their own purposes. Ribbentropp's foreign ministry published *Der Schlüssel zum Frieden* (*The Key to Peace*) on May 17, 1938, documenting Hitler's state visit from the moment the *Führer* left Berlin's *Anhalterbahnhof*, to his return triumphantly staged at the Brandenburg Gate. The book is a collage that resembles one of the Nazis' weekly newsreels. The text tells two stories: the story of the "*Triumphzug*" of Hitler, the statesman, and of the Grand Tour of Hitler, the artist and architect.[17]

The book's title thematized the politics of the Axis, its subtitle (*Führertage in Italien, or The Führer's Days in Italy*) the narrative of Hitler as artist on his Grand Tour.[18] The lavishly illustrated travelogue stages the *Führer* as contemporary ruin gazer, triumphantly testifying to the possibility of imperial rebirth—in Italy, where, Hitler tells his audience, Mussolini "founded a new Imperium," and in Germany, where a "new Germanic Reich" has arisen.[19] Showing Hitler touring ancient Rome, the editors of *Führertage* also seized the opportunity to portray him once more as post-Augustan builder, by including reports from the Italian press calling Hitler the "the greatest architect of all times" and publishing a series of photographs of the Third Reich's new monumental architecture.[20]

The Germans wanted to communicate that Mussolini was not the only imperial leader, which explains the overall frame of the political narrative, the *Führer*'s own "*triumphal procession*."[21] *Schlüssel zum Frieden* documented this event on the Berlin stage, orchestrated once more by Speer. Before showing Hitler at the Berlin train station leaving for Italy, the booklet documents a mass meeting held in Berlin's very own Colosseum, the Olympic stadium. The outer wall is illuminated by floodlights bringing out the resemblance to the Roman model. *Schlüssel zum Frieden* also documents Hitler's re-entry through the Brandenburg Gate, greeted by the assembled masses at night. Watching newsreels about the events, Victor Klemperer noted that Hitler's return was celebrated as "a triumphal welcome."[22]

While this *Triumphzug* story positions Hitler in the shadow of Rome's emperors, the narrative of the *Grand Tour* takes up the Roman theme from a different angle. Rome visited is always Rome revisited. Thomas Macaulay, the inventor of the Maori on Grand Tour, admired the "majesty" of the Colosseum on his own journey in 1838.[23] *Führertage* thus presents the

22.1 *Der Schlüssel zum Frieden* (1938). Giovanni Battista Piranesi, *Coliseum*.

Führer as *Italy traveler* in the vein of Goethe.[24] Among other things, this section consists of an excerpt from Goethe's *Italienische Reise* (*Italian Journey*) and concludes with Piranesi's *Coliseum* (1760) (figure 22.1).[25] As I mentioned in an earlier chapter, with his *Antichità Romane*, its reconstructed map of Italy, and the monumental, often reconstructed ruins of the Augustan city, Piranesi had rendered the metropole of the Roman Empire newly visible for a new imperial age. On a smaller scale, *Führertage* attempted to do the same thing for the twentieth century.

The excerpt from Goethe's journey consists of two paragraphs: first, Goethe's general reflections on the "new" and "old" Rome and the difficulty of separating the two, and then his more subjective reaction to the city, a feeling of being overwhelmed. The purpose of including these lines is obvious: beyond the legitimatory claim (Goethe as Hitler's precursor), there is the self-reflective gesture of uncovering the meaning of Rome's past for the present.[26]

What the editors of *Führertage* left out is an intriguing story of masks. On his journey, Goethe identifies with Georg Forster, the explorer, and behaves with his friend, the painter Tischbein, like New Zealanders "when they caught sight of a war vessel."[27] Overwhelmed by the "non-form [Unform] of ruins," and experiencing Rome's reality as "monstrous," Goethe read Herder, discovering Rome as the center of world history.[28] Returning to the ruins, he then imagined himself as citizen of ancient Rome, a spectator, gaping at the emperor's triumph and basking in the glory of the ancient empire.[29] In Goethe's *Italian Journey*, these masks—of the ex-

22.2 *Der Schlüssel zum Frieden* (1938). Hitler contemplating the *Ara Pacis* relief.

plorer, of the Maori, of the Roman—are part of the aesthetic and very real pleasures of his journey.[30] When Hitler wore the mask of the Roman, he was, as always, dead serious, a tedious bore. A separate section of *Führertage* documents Hitler's day in Rome, studying Augustus's Mausoleum, touring the *Mostra Augustea*, the Pantheon, and the Colosseum, and listening to Ranuccio Bandinelli, archeologist and art historian, explaining the *Ara Pacis* panels still kept in the *Museo Nazionale* in Diocletian's baths (figure 22.2).[31] *Schlüssel zum Frieden* also included photos of the models of the ancient imperial metropolis exhibited in the *Mostra Augustea*, and concludes Hitler's tour of Rome with a visit to the Colosseum, the photograph showing Hitler listening to his guide, Bandinelli, against the backdrop of the Colosseum's massive walls.

Hitler's Journey through the Ruins: Performing Scopic Mastery

Recapitulating Hitler's journey through the imperial capital of the ancient Roman Empire, *Schlüssel zum Frieden* represented the tour of the ancient city at night as the highpoint of this performance of imperial mimesis. The core of this section consists of a photograph of the *Führer* himself (in a carriage with the Italian king), and three of the dramatically illuminated ruin sites displayed for Hitler's gaze (figure 22.3). A brief text entitled "Römische Impressionen" then narrates the carriage ride for the German readers in the present tense, observing that the "Rome of the *imperatores* seems to have awakened to . . . life," quoting the welcoming words of the Roman governor, who expressed the Roman people's elation about receiving the *Führer* "in the midst of the monuments of its ancient power and the signs of its renewed imperium."[32] The political story of *Schlüssel zum Frieden* thus is one of the triumphant rebirth of empires, south and north of the Alps. The story of Hitler on his Italian tour is inextricably linked to this imperial politics.

For all imperial projects, I have been arguing throughout this book, Rome is *the* traumatic site. Hitler toured Rome at a strategic moment, when he was preparing for his expansionist war of conquest. The Nazis' repetition of Mussolini's dramatic *mise-en-scène* of ruin gazing—the display of photograph after photograph of the *Führer* in the ruins of Rome—turned this performance of imperial mimesis into a paradigmatic act of ruin gazing. To have Hitler perform this act of imperial mimesis by staging him as ruin gazer is a defiant gesture, a gesture of mastery promising a *Reich* that will last a thousand years. This promise of durability involves the strategies

22.3 *Der Schlüssel zum Frieden* (1938). Hitler's carriage ride through Rome at night.

of fortification at work in this display of the imperial ruin gazer scenario. With the photographs of Hitler's nightly carriage ride through Rome's ancient imperial ruins, Ribbentrop's propagandists reinstalled the Occidental ruin gazer in his position of scopic mastery. Spengler's *barbarian* and Doré's *Maori* were pushed out of sight, their memory erased.

The elaborate staging of the Roman scenario thus aimed at restabilizing the scenario of ruin gazing, firmly installing the European subject in the position of scopic mastery. In Speer's and Hitler's imaginary, there would be a future ruin gazer, but he would be an Aryan German. They did not imagine the ruin gazer to be the empire's victorious subject—the one who would be gazing at *Germania* would not be a Pole, or Russian, or Jew. Hitler thought that *Germania*'s ruins would function as a bridge reminding future generations in times of weakness of their mighty imperial past—Germans, not their subjects-turned-victors (chapter 23). And as I mentioned above, Hitler fantasized about an annual *Triumphzug* with German "masters" leading the natives from the East across *Germania*'s imperial stage (SM, 417). Yet this archaic scenario of triumph and victory too remained uncanny. For who was to guarantee that it would be an Aryan descendant whose gaze would rest on the remains of the Third Reich? Who was to guarantee that it would not be one of the *barbarians*? Behind the awed and cowed "natives" lurks forever the uncanny shadow of Spengler's *barbarian* ruin traveler from another *Kulturkreis*, scrutinizing the remnants of a dead civilization, the iconic colonized subject, whom Hitler at one point imagined as *Slavic Maori*.

At the time of Hitler's visit to Rome, Walter Benjamin created his famous Angel of History. Was it Mussolini's grandiose historicist parade through Roman ruins that Benjamin had in mind when he wrote his *Theses on the Philosophy of History* in Paris? Did this spectacle prompt him to argue that the resurrection of the past had to be in the service of the defeated, not the victors? Was it Mussolini's ideological junk heap of dehistoricized rubble that piled up in front of Benjamin's angel, terrifying him to death? Or, even more intriguingly, did the exiled philosopher of history reconceptualize Spengler's *barbarian* or Hitler's *Slavic Maori*—petrified, their eyes wide open?

With their neoclassical architecture and ruin gazer scenarios, the Nazis wanted to create an imperial gaze, not this panicked stare. In part 5, I have been arguing that they celebrated their new Roman Empire *and* invented their own story of imperial decline with their architectural projects, ruin theories, and the staging of Hitler's tour through Rome. As Hitler contemplated the remains of Rome, so another Aryan leader will drive through Berlin/*Germania*, the public's eyes centered on the imperator and his steadfast gaze fixed on the remains of the Third Reich, its noble ruins. Imperial decline was unavoidable—but Hitler and Himmler projected this decline into the remote future.

As Hitler's visit to Rome was meant to demonstrate, the inevitable end could be mastered. That is, it could be given form, a form-giving that included the creation of imaginary spaces in which past and present converged, and the fortification of ruin scenarios. This fortification involved three aspects: the object of representation (sturdy, well-defined ruins that allowed the beholder to imagine them intact, asserting the neo-Roman conqueror's power of imagination); the fixing of the power constellation (the exclusion of the empire's subject from the position of mastery); and finally, the imperial conqueror's gaze.

Spengler maintained that each morphological stage invents its own scopic regime with its specific acts of looking at the visible world and what lies beyond that visible world—at the present, but also the past and the future. Vogt made similar arguments about the Roman Empire. Hitler defined his imperial mission as the radical transformation of the existing scopic regime. Riefenstahl made a remote past visible by strengthening the modern spectator's gaze, and Benn made this gaze the object of desire. Hitler's performance of imperial mimesis on the Roman stage was another part of this story. Re-fortifying once more the scopic constellations of the ruin scenario, it placed the imperial subject, the conqueror, in a position of mastery.

This fortification also involved the master-subject's gaze. *Schlüssel zum Frieden* is a document that not only fastens the readers' eyes on the image of Hitler but includes several photographs of Hitler in the act of looking. In the first of these photographs, Hitler posed in profile, putting on the Augustan death mask, the mask of the conqueror and founder of empire with the commanding Roman gaze—a gaze that masters the power of ruins and the power of the enemy.[33]

Conclusion

So let me summarize what I think is involved in this moment of mastery on the ancient Roman stage: the assertion of equality with and superiority over imperial Rome, the elimination of the barbarian threat, and the fortification of the ruin scenario's scopic dimensions. Yet there is another aspect involved in the Nazis' staging of imperial sovereignty in the ruins of Rome. I have been arguing that in the long history of European imitations of Rome, the ubiquity of ruin gazer scenarios is symptomatic of the encounter with the ancient empire's death. That acts of wearing Roman masks are encounters with death is, however, not only the confrontation with an empirical fact. There is something else at stake, something particular to empire as a political formation that resonates with the formation of the subject in language.

From a Lacanian perspective, every sentence is a project, escaping the subject's mastery, a process where meaning emerges only in hindsight, once the sentence has been completed. In Lacan, the speaking subject is a subject in the future perfect: *I will have been*. Likewise, empire is a project escaping the sovereign's intention and mastery (sovereign here referring both to individual and state). Let me explain why I think this is the case. All definitions of empire emphasize size, but more significantly, the ceaseless, never-ending expansion of sovereignty and space. Empires are large and expand relentlessly. Sheldon Pollock, listing the set of convictions shared across imperial formations, names as the very first one that "power had to be extended as far as power could be extended."[34] Discussing this expansive drive, Pollock quotes Herodotus's admiring comment about Xerxes's project to "extend the Persian territory as far as the Gods' heavens reach."[35] And we know Virgil's statements on the matter of empire without limits.

Like the unpredictable adventure of the sentence, empires driven by ever-increasing, relentless expansion can only be grasped from their limits, the limits of space and time—the limits of the empire's death. Thus, empires too obey the logic of the future perfect: *the empire will have been*. The imperial sovereign is never more sovereign than during these performances on the ruined Roman stage. In each case, these scenarios enact the neo-Roman empires' very own version of Rome's story and the connection of this story to their own. In the case of Hitler's performance in Rome, this act of mastery is taken a step further: what Hitler, Himmler, and the like believed was that mastery lies in telling the story of their own end, a story about *what the Third Reich will have been*—a monumentally ruined *Germania* at the center of a vast imperial ruinscape reaching into Northern Africa.

Eric Michaud reads Hitler's statements on antiquity's ruins as "death threat directed against his people" and Nazi politics and aesthetics ruled by the accelerating "structure of anticipating the end" as symptom of an eschatological (death) drive that has its origin in the Nazis' resistance to modernity's acceleration.[36] I argued in chapter 18 that in the fascist imaginary, empire's time—the time that remains—combined both the accelerated temporality of conquest and annihilation, and the decelerated time of nature. The Nazis' ruinophilia did not originate in their resistance to modernity's acceleration, but in the neo-Roman scripting of their necropolitics of conquest and empire-building.[37]

Hitler's 1938 performance inaugurated the era of imperial conquest, and by 1941 the German Army was fighting on the territory of Rome's African colonies. With the British victory at El-Alamein (Egypt) and the landing of British and American troops in the fall of 1942, the fight for Tunisia suddenly acquired unexpected significance. In the fall of 1943, the tanks of the Africa Corps began moving west, occupying Tunisia for a year. When the German-Italian forces surrendered in Tunis on May 3, 1943, Italy lost most of its "African empire," and German plans to take over the oil fields of the Middle East turned to dust.[38] In these North African campaigns, Macaulay's iconic ruin gazer from New Zealand suddenly reappeared in the very real guise of Maori soldiers, priding themselves on their warrior culture, and the myth of savage "scalp hunters" spread quickly.[39]

Jérome Carcopino, a member of the Vichy government inspired by Louis Bertrand's *Latinité*, compared the battles in French North Africa to Scipio's victory over Hannibal at Zama.[40] The North African defeat followed the surrender at Stalingrad. On February 18, 1943, Goebbels had called for total war, spewing out images of the barbarian enemy pouring into German space. The *Abendland* will die, Goebbels yelled, unless Europe unites against the onslaught of the barbarian hordes. To his Spenglerian vision of Asia's invasion of Europe, Goebbels added the belligerent appeal to fight modern-day Carthage—New York, the city of Jews.[41] A few months later, Goebbels wrote that the fall of Tunis subjected the North African territories to a Jewish "reign of terror."[42]

By the spring of 1945, the battles in North Africa had long been lost, the fascist *imperium* had fallen, and Mussolini had witnessed the arrival of "Africans" in the ruins of Rome. Now the Germans' "monstrous Reich" was collapsing, its core overrun by the armies of Hitler's enemy, "the Jew," from the West, and "barbarian hordes" from the East.[43] In the guise of "cannibals" from the easternmost regions of the Soviet Union, the ghost of Macaulay's New Zealander and Virgil's Hannibal was now taking residence in Germany's ruins.[44]

TWENTY-THREE

Return to Carthage, or Hitler's *Aeneas/Dido Fragment*

Introduction

In the previous chapter, I analyzed Hitler's performance of imperial mimesis in Rome tracing the theme of imperial ruin gazer and barbarian enemy in the chapter's conclusion to the moment of the Nazi empire's collapse in the spring of 1945. Here, I will discuss a particular episode in the history of this fall, Hitler's last neo-Roman performance, taking place on the eve of his suicide on April 30, 1945, in the *Reich* Chancellery's bombing shelter. At this moment, Hitler, writing his *Political Testament*, reached for Roman *and* Carthaginian death masks, taking us back to the ancient city of Dido and Hannibal.

As Friedländer argues, this *Political Testament* contains "the essentials" of anti-Semitism as Nazism's core ideology, again summoning Jews as the "phantasmal" enemy.[1] I will read Hitler's will, organized around his last ruin gazer scenario, as a text about fracturing neo-Roman subject positions. Reassembling core elements of the Nazis' imperial imaginary, the text leaves this imaginary as ruined as the *Reich* Chancellery where Hitler revised his will, hidden away in his bomb shelter. Where Hitler's nighttime carriage ride through Rome in 1938 constituted the triumphalist assumption of the position of the imperial ruin gazer at the moment when the German *Reich* readied itself to enter an era of conquests, the *Political Testament* enacted the breakdown of the Nazis' ruin gazer scenarios, the shattering of the effort to write the power constellation of imperial subject and barbarian other in stone.

To access the full meaning of Hitler's last act of neo-Roman mimesis as the unraveling of the Nazi empire's neo-Roman imaginary requires that we pay attention to the Nazi leadership's increasing preoccupation with the Punic Wars, their deployment of stories equating Rome with Berlin and Carthage with London/New York and Moscow, the Nazi empire's "capitalist-bolshevist-Jewish" enemy. This Carthage-centered act of imperial mimesis begins in 1943, when the Nazis' wars of conquest reached their final "turning point" on the North African terrain of the ancient Punic Empire, shortly after the defeat at Stalingrad.[2] In the context of this double loss, Hitler and Goebbels mobilized the *topos* of Carthage for a populist critique of (Anglo-American) capitalist decadence with strong anti-Semitic overtones.[3] In this campaign, Hannibal, his deep-seated hatred of the Romans, and his victory at Cannae in the Second Punic War loomed large.

Fighting Carthage

In this context, classicists were mobilized to define the nature of the war, portraying the Nazi empire as successor to the Scipios' conquering empire, and the *Reich*'s enemies as Carthaginians. In 1943, Joseph Vogt edited a volume entitled *Rom und Karthago*, arguing that the ancient conflict was racially motivated, leading to a "war of annihilation."[4] Helmut Berve lectured on "Rom und Karthago" between May 1942 and September 1944, addressing academics and Wehrmacht officers. Berve too argued that the Punic Wars remained a testimony to "fanatical enmity among races," annihilating "Semite-dom" in the Mediterranean.[5] By heroically mastering the catastrophe of Cannae, Rome became the *Abendland*'s leading power, laying the foundations of European culture.

Intensifying his propaganda campaigns in the spring of 1945, Goebbels revived the memory of Hannibal and his Roman enemies after reading Theodor Mommsen's *Roman History*. Did he imagine himself as Scipio overlooking Carthage's ruins as his total war neared its catastrophic end? Or was he plagued by visions of another ruin gazer, a Carthaginian barbarian triumphantly surveying the smoking remains of Speer's Berlin? Reading his diaries, I think he did both, veering between despair and hope for a last-minute reversal. In January 1945, Goebbels proposed to Hitler to use the Punic Wars as a precedent in his propaganda campaigns, and in March

1945, Hitler ordered him to publish articles on the wars in the German press.

The analogy between the Punic Wars and World War II armed Goebbels with models of Roman fortitude, "the courage of the Roman people and its leadership."[6] In addition, the Punic Wars, the greatest example of a "world-historical decision," were used as an explanatory model for military losses.[7] Accentuating the importance of the Second Punic War, Berve and others had already argued in 1943 that Rome's path to world domination was long and arduous.[8] Goebbels echoed the classicists' story about Rome's long rise to power, writing that the conflict was not "decided" in a single war.[9] In 1944, he lectured factory workers about the Romans' "decade-long" struggle and their refusal to "capitulate" when Hannibal appeared at the city's gates.[10] In 1945, Goebbels then ordered journalists to focus on the Second Punic War as a prelude to Rome's final victory.[11]

Published in the spring of 1945, the articles left no doubt that the Nazis were Romans, their enemies Carthaginians, the age-old *topos* of the Semitic merchant city fitting perfectly with Hitler's idea of a final battle against his Jewish-capitalist-Bolshevist enemy. In April 1945, the *Völkischer Beobachter* ran an article by Hugo Landgraf, entitled "Roms Triumph über Hannibal: Die Widerstandskraft einer Soldatennation entschied den zweiten Punischen Krieg" (Rome's Triumph over Hannibal: A Soldier Nation's Power to Resist Decided the Second Punic War). On April 8 and 15, Goebbels's weekly *Das Reich* published Walter Frank's "Hannibal vor den Toren. Senat und Volk von Rom in den Punier Kriegen" (Hannibal at the Gates: Rome's Senate and Volk in the Punic Wars). In this state of emergency, the articles turned a whole phalanx of Roman generals of the First and Second Punic Wars into easily recognizable stand-ins for Hitler or his generals, focusing on Scipio the Elder and the Younger and relentlessly returning to the trope of Hannibal as Rome's most terrible enemy.

In 1944, the *SS Guidance Booklet* had already published an essay on the Second Punic War, entitled "Cannae." The account of the Roman soldiers' encirclement and Hannibal's "blood bath" begins to hint at the allegorical nature of this story; the glorification of Lucius Aemilius Paullus, one of the Roman generals, completes the allegorical reading of Cannae as Stalingrad.[12] More significant is another aspect of the argument: Rome's hegemony was established by Scipio's later victory over Hannibal at Zama. The articles published in the last months of World War II shared the idea that the decisive military conflict was still to come.

Hugo Landgraf's essay "Roms Triumph über Hannibal" appeared in April 1945, arranged around a short text, a call to arms, pushing Germans to resist the Red Army and inciting burning hatred and the lust for revenge.

Landgraf's article relies on the same emotions. Here, Hannibal, Dido's hate-filled avenger, is Rome's "fiercest enemy."[13] Landgraf (1895–1946), a journalist and *SS-Untersturmführer* who fought in Russia, might well be the author of "Cannae." His essay tells the same basic story about Cannae as the first step toward victory, yet makes the analogy between antiquity and the present, Scipio and Hitler, more explicit. Walter Frank, the director of the *Reichsinstitut Geschichte des neuen Deutschlands* (*Reich* Institute for the History of the New Germany) and author of a biography of Carl Peters, belonged to the *Reich's* intellectual elite. His long article, "Hannibal vor den Toren. Senat und Volk von Rom in den Punier Kriegen," revisited the entire history of the Punic Wars. He too portrayed the Carthaginian general as Rome's "most terrible" and "most dangerous" enemy, harboring a "burning hatred" of Rome.[14] Relying on Polybios, Plutarch, and Livy as well as Ranke and Mommsen, Frank included the famous scene of Hannibal's father, demanding that the son swear eternal hatred of Rome.

Frank, another Spenglerian who discovered salvation in Hitler's *Reich*, was anti-Semitic to the core, and interpreted the wars as a "race war in the modern sense."[15] He finished his historical panorama with Scipio the Younger "avenging the dead of Cannae" at Zama, and the destruction of Carthage in 146 BCE. By the end of the article, Frank has driven home the point that Hitler was Scipio and that Germany's situation in the spring of 1945 was that of the Romans in the Second Punic War. Toward the end, Frank's essay takes a literary turn. This section is a bombastic exercise in resurrectional realism and neo-Roman mimesis at the moment of the Nazi empire's collapse, transforming the vanquished into future victors.[16] Narrating Scipio's triumphal procession through Rome, Frank makes his readers watch Scipio, the "avenger of Cannae's dead," followed by legions of dead soldiers from the Third Punic War. And then there are more shades, women killed by "black Numidian riders."[17] Painting visions of barbarian hordes, Frank finished his triumph with delirious visions of a future *Pax Germanorum*.

Rome's heroic conquerors and rulers, and Hannibal, Dido's raging avenger, thus reentered the stage, asked to play their part in the Nazis' last act of neo-Roman mimesis. Clinging to the idea of some last-minute reversal of fortune, Goebbels used his propaganda machinery in 1945 to mobilize the fear of "Jewish liquidation squads."[18] Rage and revenge were no longer reserved for Hannibal. The time for "revenge," the time of "suffocating hatred," Goebbels noted in his diary in April, had come.[19] Hitler killed himself on April 30, Goebbels on May 1, and eight days later, Frank committed suicide, indignant about having to deal with the American Army's "Black" soldiers.[20] The *Political Testament* with its Punic War resonances is Hitler's last attempt to give meaning to the deadly world he had created, presenting himself as the founder of the future German *Reich*.

Hitler Leaves the Stage, or Dido/Hannibal in the Bunker

In April 1945, Mussolini's Rome was occupied by Allied forces and the battles in North Africa had long been lost. Hitler, immobilized in his bombing shelter, saw his empire invaded by the barbarian hordes from the East and the armies of his mortal enemy, "the Jew," from the West.[21] Berlin's monumental stage was turning into a bomb-scarred wilderness and the Nazi leadership was now literally living in the ruins of their empire. Massive American bombing raids had destroyed parts of the *Reich* Chancellery in February, driving Hitler and his retinue into the building's underground shelters. Here, Hitler composed a personal letter nine days before his suicide, sketching his view of the state of affairs: united, Germany's enemies, "Bolshevism and the troops of Jewry," were "push[ing] our continent into chaos."[22] The letter was addressed to Mussolini at Salò. "The struggle that we are leading for our sheer existence," Hitler wrote, "has reached its culmination."[23]

When the news of Mussolini's execution and the public defilement of his dead body reached Hitler in his bunker on April 28, he started preparing for his suicide. On April 29, Soviet soldiers reached the *Reich* Chancellery and Hitler revised his *Political Testament*. Writing with an eye on posterity, he presents his suicide as a deliberate political act, a heroic sacrifice and refusal to play any role in the "spectacle" that he believed his Jewish enemies were already planning.[24]

Speer claimed later that Hitler remembered Felix Dahn's story about the Ostrogoths' final battle at Mount Vesuvius as the ring of Red Army soldiers closed around the *Reich* Chancellery.[25] As I will argue in this section, the memory of Dahn's story is but one of the fragments of a disintegrating neo-Roman imaginary. In his *Political Testament*, Hitler reaffirmed his commitment to *Germania*, the "Reich's capital."[26] Reasserting once more his self-image as neo-Roman conqueror-city-builder, he cast his eyes once more on the metropolis that he designed with Speer. Or, to be more precise, he let his eyes rest on the capital's neo-Roman ruins. Listen to his story: having made up his mind not to leave Berlin, Hitler wrote, he had to end his life now that the site of the *Reich*'s sovereignty, "the Führer's seat [of power]," could no longer be secured.[27] The last act of the world-historical drama in which Hitler saw himself as the lead actor had begun, and he was determined to stage his own exit.

Hitler's *Political Testament*, written in his Berlin shelter and dramatizing his last entry on the stage of world history, takes him into Carthage's ruins as he dons the death masks of neo-Roman conqueror *and* Dido/Hannibal. This is, I argue, the way in which we need to read Hitler's text, whose introductory section rushes toward Hitler's last imperial ruin gazer scenario. Having stated that he put his entire life at the service of the "Reich," Hitler writes: "Centuries will pass but from the ruins of our cities and our monuments *hatred will arise again* against the people that bears the responsibility in the end, the one whom we have to thank for all of this: international Jewry and its acolytes!"[28] Here, as in other parts of the testament, Hitler directly blames his enemies for not only the war but the Holocaust.[29] In the wake of Friedländer's reading, this particular speech act needs no further comment. The question I want to ask is: Who is speaking?

Ten days earlier, Goebbels had broadcast *his* last speech. Barely coherent, the speech claimed Nazi hegemony over Europe while simultaneously acknowledging the empire's fall. Goebbels did not see *Germania*'s Roman ruins of the future but Spengler's *Abendland* "falling into rubble,"[30] and Spengler's prophecy had come true: Germans were "living the last act of a great tragedy."[31] Yet Hitler still had a role to play because for Goebbels, he personified "resistance against the falling apart of the world [Weltverfall]."[32] The crumbling of the world that surfaces in Goebbels's speech as logical incoherence surfaces in Hitler's *Political Testament* as the breaking apart of the scripts that were supposed to master reality and organize psyches. Or, put differently, the text consists of fragments of identities, ruins left after the disintegration of imperial fantasies.

There is, on the one hand, a reassertion of his role as neo-Roman conqueror. In a postscript to the will, Hitler reasserts the imperial aims of the war: "to win territory in the East for the German people."[33] The theme of the imperial future also appears in the concluding passage of the *Testament* itself. Expressing the hope that his "spirit" will continue to animate his chosen successors, Dönitz, Goebbels, and so on, Hitler asks them to keep in mind that "our task, the further extension of a National Socialist state, will be the work of centuries"; he then impresses on them again the importance of the law that keeps all neo-Roman empires from declining: the "compliance with race-laws."[34]

With this in mind, let us return to his *Political Testament*. As I mentioned above, Hitler refers several times to his decision to remain in Berlin. This emphasis on "the city which is the capital of this empire" brings back his self-conception as imperial ruler and architect. But is it this neo-Roman ruler-builder who speaks when Hitler writes about the "hatred" that will arise "out of the ruins of our cities and monuments"—after centuries have passed? In this sentence, Hitler does indeed continue to speak as the (anti-Semitic) neo-Roman conqueror and city-builder, the one who claims the legacy of Aeneas, Scipio, and Augustus. Yet, and this is the point I want to make, there are other subject positions at play. In this ultimate version of his ruin gazer scenario, Hitler also exists as Dido/Hannibal. For Hitler's text here echoes Dido's grand scene on the funeral pyre, in which she prophesies the destruction of Rome at the hand of her avenger, Hannibal, who will, she exclaims, rise from her ashes. Virgil, I argued in chapter 3, wrote the scene in Dido's palace as a piece of theater, and it is this stage that Hitler enters, sliding into the role of Dido as he imagines his avenger arising from "the ruins of our cities." Or, put differently, Hitler, the neo-Roman conqueror, trying to define his neo-Roman world and the role he plays in it one last time, takes the place of the Carthaginian queen, who burned herself alive in her palace, calling out to Hannibal as her avenger.[35]

As I argued, Virgil prompted his readers to imagine the crashing of the imperial scene-building—in Carthage and in Rome. In Virgil's *Aeneid*, the reader knows that the Carthaginian *skene* will crumble; in Hitler's last play, the Chancellery already has. Yet Hitler's ruin gazer scenario is still located in the far future—a time when the burning wreckage of war will have changed into beautiful ruins. As we saw above, Hitler, the imperial ruler, commands his heirs to continue the war, a war that history, he writes, "will remember as a people's fullest and most courageous will to live [Lebenswille] despite all of the set-backs." Hitler speaking as Dido fixes his gaze on the ruinscape of the future.[36]

Dido in the *Reich* Chancellery

Given the prominence of the stories about the Punic Wars, the idea of Hitler grasping for the Roman and Carthaginian masks that the neo-Roman arsenal has to offer, at the moment of crisis, is not surprising. Hitler himself used the Punic analogy as early as November 1941. When the German Army's expansion into the East encountered its first resistance, the "autodidact" who liked to hide his lack of formal education behind monologues about classical antiquity[37] compared the attack of "Asia mobilized by Bolshevism" to "the Carthaginians' expedition against Rome."[38] Yet this war discourse was only one source for Hitler's sliding identifications with Scipio/Augustus, Dido, and Hannibal. When Hitler visited Rome in 1938, his guides explained Augustus's *Res Gestae* in the *Mostra Augustea* and at the Mausoleum. They also took him to see the *Ara Pacis* panels with their Aeneas and Augustus figures (see chapters 17 and 22). How could

23.1 *Venus Tells Aeneas and His Friend Achates to Go to Carthage*, 1679. Giovanni Francesco Romanelli (Italian, 1610–1662), Michael Wauters (Flemish, 1679). Tapestry weave: silk and wool; overall: 411.3 × 294.5 cm (161 ⅞ × 115 15⁄16 in.). Cleveland Museum of Art, Gift of Mrs. Francis F. Prentiss, in memory of Dr. Dudley P. Allen, 1915.79.1.

writing a letter to Mussolini a few hours before the *Political Testament* not activate the memory of the Roman/Carthaginian matrix?

There is a third source for this chain of identifications at work in Hitler's *Political Testament*, a set of Aeneas and Dido tapestries that Speer, the man who provided Hitler with the bits and pieces of classical antiquity, had installed in the *Reich* Chancellery. Recall that Charles V commissioned Flemish tapestries celebrating his victory at Tunis depicting battle scenes in front of Roman Carthaginian ruins (see chapter 6). Speer, following a time-honored neo-Roman tradition, personally selected the seventeenth-century Flemish wall tapestries from the inventory of Vienna's *Kunsthistorisches Museum*.[39]

The *Reich* Chancellery was one of the central components of Speer's architectural stage set, the new neo-Roman Berlin. Hitler's study, in turn, was designed as the building's central room. The first of the eight tapestries in the *Reich* Chancellery, *Venus Telling Aeneas and His Friend Achates to Go to Carthage* (1679), hung on the wall behind the desk in Hitler's study (figure 23.1). Aeneas, the founder of the city that will give its name to the future world empire, is thus the main protagonist depicted in this first scene.

With the fourth tapestry, the cycle moves from Aeneas to Dido, from the Roman to the Carthaginian ruler who "founded a noble city" (AFa, 150). Under the title *Dido Shows Aeneas the Plans for the Fortifications of Carthage* (1679), the artists portray Dido as city-builder, visiting the Carthaginian construction site (figure 23.2). Pointing to the city plans in the hands of the architect kneeling at her feet, Dido addresses her explanations to Aeneas, wearing full military garb. The group is surrounded by men working on the construction site. In the picture's lower left, a stone mason is busy with hammer and chisel; behind him, men are lifting a stone pulling on ropes. In the upper right-hand corner, we see what might be Dido's palace. These tapestries thus contribute to a field of subject positions that allow for the sliding from neo-Roman to Carthaginian that I described above.

23.2 *Dido Shows Aeneas the Plans for the Fortifications of Carthage*, 1679. Giovanni Francesco Romanelli (Italian, 1610–1662), Michael Wauters (Flemish, 1679). Tapestry weave: silk and wool; overall: 416.4 × 563.6 cm (163 ⅞ × 221 ⅞ in.). Cleveland Museum of Art, Gift of Mrs. Francis F. Prentiss, in memory of Dr. Dudley P. Allen, 1915.79.4.

23.3 *The Death of Dido*, 1679. Giovanni Francesco Romanelli (Italian, 1610–1662), Michael Wauters (Flemish, 1679). Tapestry weave: silk and wool; overall: 414 × 466.5 cm (162 15/16 × 183 5/8 in.). Cleveland Museum of Art, Gift of Mrs. Francis F. Prentiss, in memory of Dr. Dudley P. Allen, 1915.79.8.

The Death of Dido is the theme of the last of the tapestries, showing Dido on her bed, holding on to Aeneas's armor, and Juno hovering above the dying queen ready to take her to "the dark world below" (AFa, 152) (figure 23.3). In the *Aeneid*, Dido dies a violent, bloody death, destroying Aeneas's "effigy," herself, and her "new city" (AFa, 145 and 151). Here, Dido dies a decorous romantic death. Passionate love and sorrow, not passionate rage and revenge, are the emotions that the artists conveyed, and Hannibal is nowhere to be seen. But let me remind you of Dido's curse. Calling on Hannibal to avenge her, her first sentence is about "hatred":

> And you, my Tyrians, harry with hatred / all his [Aeneas's] line, his race to come: / . . . come rising up from my bones, you avenger still unknown! / to stalk those Trojan settlers, hunt with fire and iron, / now or in time to come, whenever the power is yours. (AFa, 149)

From the *Reich*'s ruins, Hitler promises in the core scene of his *Political Testament,* "the hatred" against the enemy will rise—again and again. As Goebbels and his propagandists kept repeating, Hannibal was known above all for his immense hatred of Rome. Buried in his underground shelter, grasping for stories and scripts as he writes the final version of his *Political Testament,* Hitler disappears behind the masks that the Nazis' neo-Roman archive put at his disposal: the mask of Aeneas, the Roman conqueror, city-founder, and ancestor of Augustus; the mask of the dying Carthaginian architect-queen; and, finally, the mask of Hannibal.[40]

Hitler's drama of fragmenting subjectivity and unmoored identifications thus takes him to the Carthaginian side, to the furious rage of Dido and the relentless hatred of her avenger, Hannibal. Let me be clear: I am not interested in Goebbels's or Hitler's psyche, but in the subject positions that are at Hitler's disposal in the moment when he attempts to write the role of the dying leader. Responding to the desire of the past in the moment of crisis, the neo-Roman leader's identification fractures into the identities of the imperial Roman and the Roman's Carthaginian enemies. These dispersing identities we should think of as the ruins of neo-Roman identity, indeed, as the signs of the ruination of the neo-Roman imperial imaginary. Structured around a scene of ruin gazing, Hitler's final *mise-en-scène* confounds not only Roman and barbarian, speaking in the voice of both Aeneas/Augustus and Dido. Hitler's post-neo-Roman drama also confounds the Roman and the Carthaginian stage. Speaking as Aeneas/Scipio/Augustus, Hitler speaks from Rome, his gaze resting on Rome's future ruins. Speaking as Dido, Hitler speaks from Carthage, his eyes resting on the Roman ruins left by Hannibal.

In 1945 General Jodl had this to say about Hitler: "He had himself buried on top of the ruins of his Empire."[41] In Jodl's apologetic text, Hitler "acted like all heroes have acted in history."[42] Hitler never identified publicly or privately with Augustus or any other Roman emperor. And yet in these very last moments, he attempted to inhabit or, rather, was compelled to inhabit the subject position of the neo-Roman sovereign—the conqueror, ruler, and city-builder. Georg Forster deliberately tried the mantle of the Roman conqueror, leaving us his *Aeneas fragment.* Hitler's *Dido and Aeneas fragment* is the effect of the breakdown of a symbolic order and its imaginary, a European order with a long history and an immense structuring power over those engaged in empire-building.

Conclusion

In his postwar memoirs, Rudolf Rahn, one of Hitler's special envoys to the Middle East, described the Germans' defeat at Carthage. In May 1943, Rahn found himself in Tunis, watching British and American tanks roll into the city.[43] For years, he had traveled through the region, arming insurgents in their fight against the British Empire and advising a "pro-Axis coup" in Iraq.[44] Rahn fought in battles at Palmyra, and in his spare time he toured the ruins of Baalbek and Nineveh. During the German occupation of Tunis (November 1942–May 1943), he worked at the German Consulate, residing in Hamam-Lif, an ancient Punic costal town. A few weeks before the last German officials fled Tunis by plane, Rahn found himself in the Djebel Zaghouan mountain region, overseeing the completion of anti-tank barriers. The men working on these barriers were Jewish inmates from the labor camps, among them the Tunisian author Albert Memmi.[45] This area close to ancient Carthage with its Roman ruins is familiar to us. One of these ruins is Hadrian's aqueduct, the backdrop in the tapestries designed to celebrate the Tunis Campaign of Charles V in 1535. The event organized by Rahn to celebrate the completion of the work also took place in "a half-ruined arena" dating from the time of Roman Carthage.[46]

Fittingly, Rahn, a conservative revolutionary and one of the Third Reich's most imperially minded officials, ends the Orientalist description of this last Tunisian-German evening on Carthaginian territory with the matter-of-fact observation that "the end was now approaching rapidly."[47] Having left the stance of the heroic Spartan behind, Gottfried Benn affected Spengler's pose of philosophical detachment: "Everything is as it will be and the end is good."[48] Calmly reflecting on Germany's future, Ernst Jünger saw Rome: "Perhaps," he thought, "only sheep will be grazing on the rubble as in [the images] one can see on the old paintings of the Forum Romanum."[49] Looking at the Third Reich's ruins, the protagonist of Jünger's *Heliopolis. Rückblick auf eine Stadt* (1949) quotes from the Book of Daniel.[50] With Hitler, Rahn, Benn, and Jünger, we have thus come full circle: back to Rome and Carthage, to Scipio and Hannibal, to Daniel, Polybios, and Paul.

PART SIX

Romans or Greeks? Carl Schmitt and Martin Heidegger

Preface

In April 1947, Robert Kempner, the US prosecutor, interrogated Carl Schmitt about his role as one of the Third Reich's theorists of *Großraum*, or Great Space. Literally writing for his life, Schmitt explained in one of his memoranda for Kempner that Hitler engaged in an "inferior, ultimately totally desperate politics of power and expansion," hoping to convince Kempner that his "scientifically grounded theoretical constructions" differed substantially from the "politics of conquest" of a "primitive" leadership.[1] Schmitt's theorizing resulted in *The Nomos of the Earth in the International Law of the Jus Publicum Europaeum* (1950), completed in the spring of 1945.

In part 5, I explored the Nazis' neo-Roman mimesis as *mimesis of imperial endtimes and a future in ruins* and their peculiar efforts to connect *Landnahme* and *Bildnahme*, neo-Roman empire-building, and the creation of a neo-Roman imaginary. I explored this empire-building on different levels, beginning with the ways in which Hitler and others reinscribed the tension between imperial ending and the empire's *longue durée*, and concluding with the juxtaposition of Hitler's triumphant ruin gazing in Rome and the crumbling of his ruin scenario in his *Political Testament*. The Third

Reich, I argued, was characterized by the tension between the promise of solid foundations and equally solid ruins.

In chapter 24 I will explore how Schmitt evolved into *the* neo-Roman theorist of empire, imperial mimesis, and imperial imaginary by observing the rise, and then the fall, of the Third Reich. With his *katechontic* theory of empire, Schmitt sums up the entire neo-Roman imperial tradition. Polybios developed his ideas about imperial endtimes at the moment when Rome conquered Carthage. Schmitt's idea of the *restrainer* who postpones the empire's end emerged in the early 1940s, when Werner Best, the leading SS-*Großraum*-theorist, argued that the Nazi empire might be in the process of repeating Rome's fall while the *Reich*'s leadership was still celebrating its victories.

I will conclude *The Conquest of Ruins* with a conservative revolutionary thinker as controversial as Carl Schmitt, briefly exploring in chapter 25 Heidegger's thinking about empire and imperialism. Coming to Heidegger's defense, Arendt stated that the philosopher lacked the capability to think politically. Arendt should have said that when Heidegger thought politically, he thought in Spenglerian terms. Hitler, Himmler, and Speer proposed a thousand-year *Reich* and thousands of years of glorious ruins. Schmitt devoted himself to the neo-Roman problem of how to prolong the time before the fall by returning to the first century. Privileging ancient Greek readiness to face the end, Heidegger analyzed and criticized this Roman desire to endure. In contrast to Schmitt, when Heidegger thought about *Reich*, he did not return to Rome but turned to archaic Greece.

We will hear echoes of Schmitt's (and Best's) reflections on empire in Heidegger's thoughts about (Jewish) Western imperialism. But the strongest voice in Heidegger's diaries, the so-called *Black Notebooks*, is that of Oswald Spengler. Like Schmitt, Heidegger belonged to the long tradition of conservative revolutionary thinkers of empire that I traced beginning with Louis Bertrand and Oswald Spengler.[2] With Heidegger's immersion in Spengler's theory of Caesarist imperialism and his implicit dismissal of Schmitt's version of the Pauline *katechon*, *The Conquest of Ruins* ends.

TWENTY-FOUR

Katechon: Carl Schmitt's Theology of Empire

[I]rgendwann ist Schluss. JAKOB TAUBES[1]

Introduction: "Kaffirs" and Other Barbarians

Observing that Schmitt initially supported the Nazis' seizure of power, Robert Kempner asked Schmitt whether his work had legitimated their "expansion of Grossraum by force."[2] Schmitt smugly explained his collaboration as a satisfying new experience akin to that of the "ethnologist" coming in contact with "a new tribe of Kaffirs."[3] To think of Nazis as "Kaffirs" having taken over Europe was something that came quite naturally to Schmitt and his friends. Visiting Ernst Jünger in Paris in 1941, Schmitt compared himself to Benito Cereno, the Spanish captain of a slave ship in Herman Melville's novella of the same name who was held captive by a "Caffre guard of honor."[4] The situation of the "white captain dominated by black slaves," Schmitt explained to Jünger, resembled that of conservative intellectuals in Nazi Germany.[5]

Whether Schmitt went native or kept his distance from his German "Kaffirs" is of course the question hovering over all discussions of Schmitt.[6] However, Schmitt the collaborator is not my topic. Schmitt the neo-Roman theorist of empire, imperial mimesis, and imaginary is. Yet we simply cannot make sense of Schmitt's writings on *Reich*, *Grossraum*, and *nomos* if we do not place him in the context of the Nazis' neo-Roman mimesis to which he contributed long after having been marginalized by the SS and SD intellectuals around Werner Best and Reinhard Höhn.[7] Schmitt's comparison of Nazis to "caffres" tells us not only about Schmitt's need to differentiate himself from other Nazis, but also about the ultimate horizon of his politics and political theory: Europe and its neo-Roman empires.

Schmitt's ideal was the Spanish-Portuguese Empire and its imperial theology, which he glorified in *The Nomos of the Earth (1950)*. The "reconquest" of Spain, Schmitt noted in 1948, was the precondition for the "conquest of a new world" since only the experience of defeat "provides the momentum to go out and conquer the world."[8] Imperial beginnings need imperial endings, and the subsequent renewal of the empire's political theologies—in the confrontation with the empire's enemies, with Muslims, Jews, and the pagans of the new world. Defeat thus intensifies friend-enemy constellations, and the resolve to act. It also awakens the acute awareness that all empires will eventually end.

In the present chapter, I will explore how Schmitt evolved into *the* neo-Roman theorist by observing the rise, and then the fall, of the Third Reich from the elevated vantage point of *Scipio's Dream*. With his *katechontic* theory of empire, Schmitt sums up the entire neo-Roman imperial tradition, returning to the first and second centuries—to Rome, Paul, and Tertullian—in order to find the definitive answer to the question of how to postpone the end. I will begin my exploration of Schmitt's *katechontic* theory of empire with his reinvention of the political as friend-enemy constellation, and of the decisionist state/sovereign in the years before Schmitt set out to theorize empire first as the nexus of *Reich* and *Grossraum* and then as *nomos*.

The Sovereign Decision and the Politics of Enmity

In 1919, Hans Freyer, author of *Revolution von rechts* (1931), theorist of *Reich* and *Volk*, and a close friend of Schmitt, reviewed Spengler's *Decline of the West*. Freyer agreed with Spengler's organic conception of cultures and his *German* socialism but vehemently disagreed with his pessimistic prognosis. Striking the "voluntaristic note" so typical of postwar radical conservatives, Freyer passionately defended "the risk of the [political] act."[9] Schmitt too longed for heroic politics, admiring Sorel because he remained true to the "impulse of an intensive life," to "warlike and heroic conceptions."[10] And it was Schmitt, the "Anti-Leninist" of the radical right, who theorized this wager of the act in *Political Theology* (1922; 1934) and *The Concept of the Political* (1927; 1932).[11]

These essays revolve around ideas that will be crucial components of Schmitt's *katechontic* imperial sovereignty and its ruin scenario: the decisionist sovereign and the enemy. While Schmitt's analogy of miracle and state of exception constitutes the most intense articulation of this rediscovery of the political, I will focus on the concept of decisionism and the political as the readiness to "see" the enemy—and to kill him. Moreover, I will argue that Schmitt's concept of the enemy is shadowed by the notion of the barbarian by drawing on earlier texts. Discussing the post-1933 edition of *The Concept of the Political*, I will then argue that his concern with rendering the enemy visible locates his reflections within the (Nazi) empire's imperial imaginary. Finally, where these thoughts on the decisionist sovereign engage the work of Donoso Cortés, they already touch on the eschatological problematic of Paul's letters (chapter 5).[12]

Reacting to the French Revolution and 1848, Schmitt argued, Donoso believed that European history was reaching its eschatological endzone. According to Donoso, the yearning for a great decision emerged as capitalism gradually subordinated politics to economics, and dictatorship was his solution. Schmitt loved Donoso's attack on liberalism (for hoping in vain that parliamentary debates could avoid "the decisive bloody battle") but criticized the formalist theory of the state underlying his decisionism.[13] Secular modernity had severed the state from its theological grounding, and instead of developing a *new* form of legitimacy, Schmitt wrote, Donoso collapsed eschatology and political history, believing that the moment of the last battle had arrived. Schmitt's critique of Donoso's decisionism thus revolved implicitly around the problem addressed by Paul: the eschatological temporalities of waiting for the end of the world in the near versus remote future. While Schmitt shared Donoso's eschatological sense of politics as taking place in a state of exception, he was looking for ways of relegitimizing political sovereignty that would not fall back into the latter's metaphysical nihilism, or Spengler's equally nihilist reduction of politics to Caesarist voluntarism and personal dictatorship. Schmitt's answer will be the *katechontic* sovereign. Donoso failed, Schmitt argued later, because he lacked the concept of a *katechontic* sovereign who *creates a space* for political action in this world.[14]

How did the making visible of the barbarian enemy figure in these reflections on decisionism? Schmitt's definition of the sovereign is one of his most famous lines: "Sovereign is he who decides on the exception."[15] In *The Concept of the Political*, Schmitt introduced the concept inextricably tied to this decisionism (establishing a new order in the midst of chaos): the political defined as the degree of intensity of the relation between friend and enemy. Schmitt, it turns out, was as invested in fortifying the sovereign gaze as the gaze seizing its object as were Gottfried Benn or Leni Riefenstahl. For the state of exception as the moment when the political reaches its greatest intensity is also the moment when the enemy is most clearly *visible*. Or, more precisely, when the enemy is *made* visible and his image firmly captured.

This concept of the enemy remained tied to that of the barbarian. In *Roman Catholicism* (1923), Schmitt operated within the paradigm of culture versus barbarism.[16] Starting from his core idea that the political is "something more than the economic," Schmitt argued for the Catholic Church's political power as the power to give form.[17] I am interested in the conclusion to this essay and its Spenglerian equation of form/*culture* and formlessness/barbarism. From "the standpoint of traditional West European culture," Schmitt wrote, Europe's urban proletariat and Russia's masses were "barbarians," and the west's "economic-technical thinking" was helpless against the "formlessness" of these masses led by their leaders' "barbarian instinct[s]."[18]

This paradigm of (post)Roman *culture* versus barbarism left its traces in *The Concept of the Political*. Here, Schmitt notoriously defined the enemy as "der andere, der Fremde," or "the other, the stranger."[19] The enemy's essence, Schmitt wrote, is defined by being "existentially something other and foreign."[20] This definition concerned war: the being-other of the enemy potentially constituted the "negation of one's own existence" and thus legitimized killing.[21] Although these passages seem to define the external enemy, other statements make it abundantly clear that Schmitt also had internal enemies in mind (I will return to this point).

At the end of *The Concept of the Political*, Schmitt returned to the question of what characterized political thinking, namely, the will and ability to distinguish friend and enemy.[22] Three things are significant about these concluding pages: first, the Spenglerian statement that the "inability and unwillingness" to make this distinction is symptomatic "of the political end," the symptom of a declining civilization.[23] Second, Schmitt's examples of enemies are European and non-European; and third, he emphasizes the *visibility* of the enemy.

Discussing moments of decline, Schmitt moves from Russia to imperial Europe. Just as "the *declining* classes" in prerevolutionary Russia "romanticized the Russian peasant," so the confused bourgeoisie of Europe "searched all sorts of exotic cultures for the purpose of making them an object of aesthetic consumption."[24] Had this bourgeoisie not been a *declining class*, it would have "seen" its enemy: the Russian peasant, Europe's colonial subjects, the kinds of enemies whom Schmitt called "barbarians" a decade earlier, and whom, Gottfried Benn thought, Europeans had tired of wanting to seize—with their gaze and with their weapons (chapter 20).

In contrast to the leaders of this declining class, sovereign leaders like Kleist's anti-Napoleonic hero or Cromwell distinguished friend from enemy. Drawing attention to the latter's deictic gesture, his appeal *to look at the enemy*, Schmitt wrote: "Let us thus consider [betrachten] our enemies."[25] Cromwell's speech, Schmitt explained, represents one of the "moments in which the enemy is, in concrete clarity, recognized [erblickt] as the enemy."[26] Times of "great politics" are always eruptions of "enmity."[27] At such moments, the decisionist sovereign holds the image of the enemy captive. Executing the decision is thus as much a process of *looking* as of *making* visible and *seizing* the image.[28]

This is again the problematic of the sharpened, fortified gaze—the gaze of the sovereign who, to use Schwab's apt metaphor, "suddenly awakens" at the very moment "when a normal situation threatens to become an exception."[29] Raphael Gross analyzed Schmitt's definition of the political with an eye toward seizing the image of the *internal* other, that is, assimilated German Jews.[30] Schmitt's anti-Semitic resentment comes with a language of masks, of veiling and unveiling the other. With every new stage of history, Schmitt declared in 1936, Jews execute a "monstrous, uncanny change of masks."[31] After the war, Schmitt put it bluntly: "the true enemy" was "the assimilated Jew."[32] Like other conservative revolutionaries, Schmitt would have hesitated to use Goebbels's vocabulary.[33] The exterminationist language is not the point of overlap between official Nazi anti-Semitism and Schmitt's anti-Semitic anti-modernism, but the discourse of the enemy's visible mask and invisible essence and the construct of "Jewish-capitalist" imperialism is.[34]

In 1934, Schmitt was thus ready to think about empire and the heroic politics of imperial conquest and domination. He did so in *völkisch* terms, distinguishing between *völker*, attached to space and thus able to imagine space, and those who lack this faculty. Moreover, by the early 1930s, Schmitt already thought in terms of rise and decline. He had argued for a strong state, and he would now argue that the German *Reich* needed this strong state at its core. He had developed his ideas about politics and enmity, and he already had the state's enemies in his line of sight: internal enemies and external enemies, European and non-European. It was but a small step to think of imperial enemies. All of this will coalesce into Schmitt's *katechontic* concept of empire and his version of the neo-Roman imperial imaginary—an imaginary that visualizes time, space, barbarians, and other enemies.

Katechon: Theology and Politics

Schmitt defined the *katechon* as the "power that prevents the long-overdue apocalyptic end of times from already happening now."[35] A theo-political power, it "opens the space of secular politics."[36] Schmitt rediscovered the concept of the *katechontic* sovereign—referring to political figures, or institutions such as *Reich*—at the precise moment when the Third Reich had reached its zenith and Werner Best, Himmler's *Großraum*-theorist, "rediscovered" the fall of Rome. Focused on questions of imperial beginnings and endings, on the fall of the British and the rise of the German empire, Schmitt begins to theorize the concept in the early 1940s in a series of articles on the war, and in his *Land und Meer: Eine weltgeschichtliche Betrachtung* (*Land and Sea: World-Historical Reflections; 1942*). These texts reveal that Schmitt is an imperial thinker who retheorized empire as the inextricable articulation of beginning and end: the time of empire is the time that remains.[37] He did so with the end *in sight*, observing the fall of the Third Reich, which he and his friends started to anticipate by 1942.[38]

In the wake of his 1939 lectures on the concept of *Reich* and *Großraum* (which I will discuss in some detail later), the *katechon* touches on central issues in Schmitt's work: his attempts to retheorize *empire* (first as *Reich* and *Großraum*, and then as *nomos),* the process of *imperial mimesis*, and the spatio-temporal structure of the *imperial imaginary*. Although I trace the ways in which Schmitt redefined *Reich* in 1939, I am not concerned with Schmitt's concept of empire *per se*. Instead, I will concentrate on his post-Spenglerian reinvention of the imperial imaginary, and the central role that the *katechon* plays in this reinvention. The *katechon*, I will argue, represents Schmitt's version of the scenario of the imperial ruin gazer. Like all ruin gazer scenarios deployed during the *Third Reich*, Schmitt's *katechon* invited his contemporaries to imagine the end of empire, to imagine ruins and ruination as that which will be—sometime in the future, not now, not yet.

A closer reading of Schmitt's essays on the war and his world-historical reflections, *Land und Meer*, uncovers a crucial fact: not only does the concept of the *katechon* as *restraining force* change radically, acquiring a positive meaning; more significantly, it emerges in the context of traditional ways of thinking about empires, about their rise and fall.[39] While I basically agree with Gross and colleagues that this changing valence points to a (temporary) dampening of Schmitt's *raum*-revolutionary fervor, I think it is more important that Schmitt takes his readers back to the articulation of this early Christian concept with the Roman Empire. In other words, he situated himself within the long history of neo-Roman imperial thought.

Paul cautioned his followers in the Second Letter to the Thessalonians that the end of time had not yet come, explaining that the battle between the antichrist and the one still restraining him will precede Christ's Second Coming. Schmitt adopted the interpretation proposed by the Carthaginian theologian Tertullian. Tertullian identified the *katechon* with the Roman Empire, and, Schmitt argued in *Politische Theologie II: Die Legende von der Erledigung jeder Politischen Theologie* (1970), represented a "specific-theological decisionism."[40] Schmitt thus worked with an exegetic variant of the concept closely tied to Roman and neo-Roman imperial discourse.

Two things are important: first, going back to these first-century theorists of the Roman Empire's political theology, Schmitt theorized the ruin gazer scenario as a *constitutive* component of empire. Second, Schmitt did so at a moment when the Nazi leadership and the Nazis' conservative collaborators deployed these ruin gazer scenarios—in a defiant gesture of mastery or as a warning, but always with the Third Reich's stability and duration in mind. Schmitt too was invested in the question of how empires endure—how imperial endtime might be prolonged.

Toward an Imperial Genealogy of the *Katechon*

The concept of the *katechontic* sovereign inevitably takes center stage in debates about the theological grounding of Schmitt's politics and political concepts.[41] This debate also touches on two related questions: first, whether Schmitt abandoned decisionism in favor of *Ordnungsdenken* (as he himself announced in his preface to the 1934 edition of *Politische Theologie*);[42] and second, if this was not the case, what was the nature of Schmitt's decisionism after the Nazis seized power in 1933 and established what Schmitt called their new state's "concrete order"?[43] Much recent Schmitt scholarship has thus focused on the theological dimension of his concept of *katechon*, sketching different genealogies or political and philosophical contexts. Andreas Koenen portrays Schmitt as a radical Catholic conservative whose growing preoccupation with the Christian concept of *katechon* in the early 1940s signifies a return to his *Reich-theological* foundations.[44] Characterizing Schmitt as a Weimar theologian of *Reich*, committed to the lineage of Roman Empire, Holy Roman Empire, and Third Reich, Koenen leaves out the neo-Roman genealogy of European imperialism. Building on Koenen's work, Raphael Gross also neglects this imperial dimension of Schmitt's thinking. Presenting Schmitt as a radical Catholic anti-Semite, Gross makes the *katechon* the crux of his argument about anti-Semitism as the founding logic of Schmitt's political thought.[45] He situates Schmitt in the context of Germany's radical conservative movement, whose proponents emphasized modernity's "dark side" and understood capitalist rationality as inherently Jewish.[46]

In contrast to Koenen, Gross emphasizes the conservative revolutionary thrust of Schmitt's thought and thus his affinity to Spengler.[47] So does Günter Meuter, who explores Schmitt's concept of decisionism (its transcendent foundations, or lack thereof) in a discussion of Schmitt as conservative revolutionary. Tracing the "remainder of the transcendental substance" that sustains Schmitt's pre-1933 decisionism as much as his post-1933 "Order-Thinking," Meuter comes to the conclusion that Schmitt's political theory is best characterized as "katechontic theology," with the *katechon* as *the* point of crystallization of the metaphysical excess that sustains Schmitt's theorizing.[48]

Arguing that Schmitt never abandoned decisionism, Ruth Groh also identifies the *katechon* as the basis of Schmitt's pre- and post-1933 metaphysical legitimation of the political order established by the sovereign's decision. Discussing Schmitt as an anti-Judaic Catholic critic of post-religious modernity, Groh argues that Schmitt's political theology focuses on the decisive final battle against the antichrist. Schmitt's "katechontic theology of history" thus finds the *meaning* of history "in enmity and in the struggle against enemies who are defined politically/theologically."[49]

While I agree that Schmitt belongs in the context of the (anti-Semitic) conservative revolution and that his reactionary stance is shaped by his theological commitments, I think the existing literature has failed to fully grasp the imperial dimension of Schmitt's thought.[50] After 1939, Schmitt was first and foremost a theorist of empire. This involves what Meuter defines as the reactionary modernist's *katechontic* theology of history. In 1947, Schmitt wrote: "To me the katechon represents the only possibility of understanding history as a Christian and finding it meaningful."[51] In *Nomos*, he elaborated on this statement, proposing the concept of *katechon* as a "bridge" between eschatology and historical thought: "The belief that a *restrainer* holds back the end of the world provides the only bridge between the eschatological paralysis of all human events and the tremendous historical power of the Christian empire of the Germanic kings."[52] In *Politische Theologie II*, Schmitt then spelled out the implications of this *katechontic* view for his understanding of historical time. Instead of being "a long march," the Christian era "is a single long waiting," a space located "between the appearance of the Lord in the time of the Roman emperor Augustus and the Lord's return at the end of time."[53]

"Within this long interim" between the reign of Augustus and the end of time, "there emerge continually new worldly interims," different time horizons which Schmitt names "In-Between-Times."[54] In *Nomos*, Schmitt conceptualized these *in-between-times* as the *longue durée* of *nomoi*, translating his *theology of history* into the time of empires. Or, put differently, Schmitt writes an eschatological horizon into his world history as the articulation of the always limited time of specific empires with the time of world history. Taubes presents Schmitt as the apocalyptic thinker of the right who knew that "time is limited."[55] Apocalyptic urgency characterizes the time of the *katechontic sovereign*.

At the danger of repetition, let me state my main thesis once again: the *katechon* is first and foremost a function of imperial logic. More precisely, it is the effect of Schmitt's engagement with the trope of imperial rise and decline, and with the scopic scenario that is part of all imperial mimesis: the sight of an empire in ruins. I will thus trace a genealogy that takes us onto a different discursive terrain, that is, the terrain of European imperial thought.[56] *Nomos* contains Schmitt's definitive version of the *katechon* as a *scopic scenario* that articulates imperial space and time. The Christian *Reich* of late antiquity, Schmitt wrote, was essentially characterized by the fact "that it was not eternal":

> It always had its own end and the end of the present aeon in sight. Nevertheless it was capable of being *a* historical power.[57]

Schmitt thus defined the *katechon* as a kind of *ruin gazer scenario*: the imperial sovereign—empire or emperor—who, with its or his eyes fixed on the end of time, prepares for political battle to delay that very end. This battle is both military and ideological, fought in the case of Rome in the name of the divine Caesars, and in the case of the Spanish-Portuguese Empire, in the name of the church.[58] Far from being a passive figure, the *katechontic* sovereign thus acts by preparing "the final decisive battle against the eschatological enemy."[59]

"When Empires Collapse":[60] Carl Schmitt's Theory of *Volk-Reich-Großraum*

In 1939, Carl Schmitt held his famous lecture on *Großraumordnung* or *great space order* and the principles of international law at Kiel University. He published a revised version, entitled "Völkerrechtliche Großraumordnung mit Interventionsverbot für raumfremde Mächte: Ein Beitrag zum

Reichsbegriff im Völkerrecht," in 1941. Here, Schmitt outlined his thinking about a new spatial world order and the spatial imagination of the world, or "conceptions of planetary space" that would accompany such an order (GO, 270). He proposed to move away from what he saw as "despatialized political ideas" and "designified spaces" by replacing the empty, neo-Kantian concept of *Raum* (*GO*, 282).

In the wake of the German-Soviet nonaggression pact (which he celebrated as the sign of a new non-universalist order), Schmitt transferred the "Great-Space-Thinking" of the Monroe Doctrine to Middle and Eastern European space (*GO*, 283). The lecture was as concerned with the concept of *Großraum* as it was with the reinvention of *Reich* (and its link to *volk*) as the strong core of any *Großraum*. Schmitt's ultimate goal was the "introduction of our concept of Reich" (GO, 300). The intention here is revolutionary. With the birth of a new "powerful German Reich" as the "strong and unassailable center of Europe," its intellectuals needed to create new words and new concepts (GO, 306). *Großraum* was one of these concepts. Schmitt redefined the originally *economic* concept of *Großraum* as a *political* entity.[61] In a first step, Schmitt defined *Großraum* as a planned "realm of human planning, organization and activity" (GO, 272). A single "great political idea" would govern this space, represented by the German *Reich* as the political body in which sovereignty is located (GO, 306).

Schmitt connected this second concept, *Reich*, to the political idea of *volk*. Celebrating Hitler's imperial success in the lecture's climactic paragraph, he wrote that *Völker* are "an empirical reality determined by species and origin, blood and soil" (GO, 306).[62] A *Großraum*, Schmitt argued, cannot exist without *Reich* as the political body combining "conscious discipline" and "heightened organization" (GO, 303). While not all *Völker* had the capacity to create states, let alone *Reiche*, Germany commanded the discipline required for this "new spatial ordering" on the European continent (GO, 304).

Having redefined the conventional economic notion of *Großraum* in political terms, Schmitt spent considerable time redefining the concept of *Reich*. *Reich* was more than an enlarged state, and certainly not identical with *Großraum* (GO, 309). Outlining his justification for the Third Reich as a continental empire, Schmitt told his audience that he refused to submit to the concepts used by Western democracies. Instead, he proposed translating the concept of empire into the German context. The *Third Reich*, Schmitt wanted his audience to understand, did not engage in facile mimesis; something completely new was about to emerge that was more than just an "afterimage."[63]

Schmitt approached the issue of genuine imperial mimesis, of creative innovation as opposed to mere repetition, by discussing the available terminology—*Reich*, empire, *imperium*, and "*Weltreich*" or world empire (*GO*, 286). Schmitt reminded his audience that all efforts to translate *Deutsches Reich* inevitably fail because every genuine political entity has its own historical specificity. "[O]ur German Reich," he argued, "is essentially defined by ethnic homogeneity and is essentially a non-universalist legal order based on respect for all other ethnicities" (GO, 297). In contrast, "imperium" tended to signify a "trans-völkisch formation," which was seen by many as "universalist," encompassing "the world and all of humanity" (GO, 296). The word *Reich*, Schmitt declared strategically, remained "untainted" by the negative connotations that imperialism had acquired since the end of the nineteenth century: "economic-capitalist methods of colonization and expansion" (GO, 297).

Unlike the British Empire, the German *Reich* with its *Großraum* extending into Eastern Europe would thus be governed by a political logic. The *Reich*'s ultimate function was the protection of "the sacrality of a non-universalist, völkisch order of life" (GO, 297). The German *Reich's Großraum* would be guided by the idea that the *Reich* accepted the "cultural and *völkisch* autonomy" of its members in the "Eastern space [Ostraum]" (GO, 294). In Schmitt's mind, this entailed a rearrangement of this space, affecting what he called, in the jargon of the times, the "Jewish problem" (GO, 292).

Reich differed therefore not only from Western capitalist imperialism, Schmitt argued, but also from the late Roman Empire, because "a völkisch concept of Reich that would respect all völkisch life" contrasted sharply with the conception of ethnicity characterizing the "declining Roman Imperium" (GO, 297). The political logic of the German *Reich* imitated the early Roman Empire, the Rome of the Scipios; or Rome at the time of the Augustan restoration, with its reinvention of *romanitas*.[64] In this privileging of the early empire, Schmitt followed Spengler and post-Spenglerians like Heidegger. Like the latter, Schmitt thus theorized the new *Reich* in opposition to the universalist, assimilationist *Imperium Romanum*.[65]

Despite his insistence on the difference of *Reich*/*Großraum* from British Empire and Roman *imperium*, Schmitt's project of rethinking the spatio-political ordering of the world as a constellation of great spaces thus unfolds within the discursive formation of neo-Roman mimesis. Schmitt's reference to the Roman Empire is just one sign of the presence of this discourse. The theological echoes in Schmitt's language—the "sacrality" of the *völkisch* order—hint at a neo-Roman imperial theology, not at Catholic *Reich* ideology. Schmitt started from the premise that the history of international law is "in reality a history of empires" (GO, 309). While

Schmitt approached his new "Großraumordnung" from the perspective of the Monroe Doctrine, the historical lineage he set in place in this discussion of the concept of *Reich* is a familiar one: Babylon, Persia, Macedonia, Rome, and finally the "Reiche der Germanen" (GO, 298).[66] Each of these ancient imperial powers was situated in a specific constellation with "rival empires" and was at all times "ready for war" (GO, 298).

Discussing the situation in 1939, Schmitt took recourse to the discourse of imperial rise and fall. Proposing to think of the present moment as transitional, he observed that the contours of the international order connected to the West's "old empires" become most visible "[w]hen Reiche collapse and battles are fought over new forms of order" (GO, 308). What was Schmitt's answer to the question of why empires fall? On the one hand, he pointed to the internal contradictions of the old international order; on the other, quoting Ratzel about "the mastery of space" as "the defining feature of all life," he claimed that the struggle among *Völker* and their empires was the very motor of history (GO, 318). Each *Reich* needed a "volk" ready for this "task" (GO, 305).

According to Schmitt, the entire global space was in transition in 1939. What did this contemporary transitional epoch reveal about the previous order? First, the era that was coming to an end, Schmitt wrote, was characterized by the British Empire's hegemony and its global network of territorially scattered and unconnected colonies (GO, 308). Second, two things attract attention at such moments of crystallization: "the imagination of planetary space specific to each system of international law" and "of a spatial distribution of the earth" (GO, 308). However, the main topic of Schmitt's lecture is the rise of a new European empire, and the tone is belligerent. The advent of a strong continental *Reich*, Schmitt promised in 1939, would radically change the global order *and* the ways in which people visualize this order (GO, 308).

Schmitt announced a radical "Raumrevolution" or spatial revolution—to use the term that Schmitt coined in his decisionist imperial fervor.[67] With the German-Soviet Pact, a new stage in the history of *Reiche* and their great spaces had been reached. This new order would protect itself and Europe's "eastern space" against two "spatially foreign" great spaces and their guiding political ideas. "The German Reich," Schmitt wrote, was situated between two universalist empires: the "liberal democratic, ethnically assimilating West" and the "bolshevist-revolutionary East" (GO, 297).

The 1939 lecture was Schmitt's contribution to the Nazis' collective endeavor to redefine *Reich* for the German context. As a *Reich*, he argued, Germany had become Europe's "unassailable center," whose mission was to defend the continent against "powers alien to the space and its ethnicity" (GO, 306). Schmitt described the future presence of the Third Reich in the East euphemistically as "radiating into the central and east European space" (GO, 306). While Schmitt clearly hoped that the lecture would position him as the Third Reich's leading theorist of empire, his attempt to bring analytical order to the ongoing discussions on empire and empire-building earned him a second round of attacks from racially oriented SS-theorists of *Lebensraum*.[68] Insisting on the racial dimension of *Großraum*, the *Reichsamtsleiter* Werner Daitz, for instance, proclaimed that the Third Reich's task was to strengthen "the European continent as the core space of the white race."[69] Opposed to the notion of *Lebensraum* and the idea of "natural" borders, Schmitt redefined *Lebensraum*, strategically referring to the various geopoliticians who were *en vogue* at the time: Friedrich Ratzel, Karl and Albrecht Haushofer, and his adversaries Reinhard Höhn and Werner Best.

The Nazi empire was an experimental work in progress, and one that involved a lot of researchers and theorists. For a while Schmitt was, as Jan-Werner Müller writes, useful to the Nazis.[70] Although definitely a "Catholic anti-Semite" of the radical right, Schmitt was not a National Socialist theorist of *Lebensraum* and genocide.[71] A theorist of empire, imperial mimesis, and imperial imaginaries, he was one of the many conservative revolutionaries who became inextricably entangled in the Nazis' imperial project.

Imagining Imperial Space: "[As] I Kept Turning My Eyes Repeatedly Back to Earth"[72]

Schmitt defined (German) *Reich* as "combination of a *Großraum*, a Volk, and a political idea" (GO, 297). The National Socialist act of the taking-of-land or coming *Raumrevolution* would fundamentally change established ways of thinking and "seeing" space. For in Schmitt, the act of Landnahme or *land-appropriation* is also an act of *Bildnahme*, or taking-of-a-picture. Schmitt rewrites world history as both time-space and "*Seh-Raum*," or scopic space.[73] That is, as a space surveyed by the imperial theorist's gaze and as a contingent sequence of empires or *nomoi* and their corresponding scopic regimes. Schmitt's utopia was a well-ordered global space visible as the assemblage of "precisely drawn" great spaces (GO, 315). In a later essay, Schmitt outlined his vantage point: "*I am contemplating the earth*," he wrote, "the planet on which we live, as a whole, as a globe and I am scrutinizing it for its global division and order."[74]

Like Volney, Schmitt thus inscribed the supreme imperial vantage point of Cicero's *Scipio's Dream* into his text. This cosmic imperial perspective—with its equally cosmic distance toward empire—structures much of Schmitt's writings about *Reich*, *nomos*, and the moments of their radical transformation. It also sustains Schmitt's *katechontic* ruin gazer scenarios. Schmitt's Scipionian vantage point gradually acquired the critical distance coloring Cicero's view.[75] But let us return to Schmitt's reflections on spatial imagination in the concluding section of his 1941 article on *Reich* and great space. Following in the tracks of Spengler, Schmitt contended that Kant's concept of space as an *a priori* category was ahistorical and consequently had to be retheorized. This revision of Kantian concepts constitutes the core of Schmitt's theory of the imperial imaginary as a spatial imaginary. In 1941, the anti-Semitic Spenglerian dimension of his critique of the "Jewish" neo-Kantians' theories of space is explicit.[76] Jewish intellectuals, he argued, lacked the very capacity to *imagine* space other than as empty or measurable. In contrast to these Jewish intellectuals and their calculating, nomadic imagination, *völker* capable of building empires are set on the "mastery of empty space" (GO, 318).

So what was the non-Jewish theory of space that Schmitt had in mind? Schmitt started his exploration of contemporary "changes in the spatial picture and conceptions" by arguing that neo-Kantian legal theorists inherited the "spatial imagination" shaped in the early modern period when exploratory voyages and conquests changed the "planetary image of the earth and the world" and the reigning concepts of space (GO, 318). This "raum-revolutionary transformation," Schmitt maintained, transformed lived political space into empty, measurable space (GO, 318). Abstract scientific space is thus the effect of a *particular* form of spatial expansion. Connecting this way of conceiving space specifically to the British Empire's rise in the sixteenth century, Schmitt argued that the "universalism of the Anglo-Saxon sea-based hegemony that transcends space, is foreign to the land and therefore limitless" (GO, 320). In contrast, Schmitt wrote, German theorists attempted to overcome universalist ways of thinking about space, referring to Ratzel's concept of "mastering space" (*GO*, 318).

Schmitt's analysis of empty, abstract versus *völkisch*, concrete space elaborates on Spengler's opposition of culture versus civilization, and his connection of civilization's tendency toward formlessness to imperialism's expansionist drive. Schmitt elaborated on the conceptualization and imagination of space in *Land und Meer* (1942; *Land and Sea*, 2015), and then in "Raumrevolution: Vom Geist des Abendlandes," also published in 1942 in *Deutsche Kolonialzeitung*, the latter essay openly acknowledging his debt to Spengler. "Raumrevolution" outlines the history of *empires* as a history of three major *Raumrevolutionen*, or spatial revolutions, closely following Spengler's analysis of the world's eight Great Cultures and their unique spatial consciousness. Schmitt opened this Spenglerian text with a question: "What is a spatial revolution [*Raumrevolution*]?" (RI, 219). All major historical transformations affect the ways in which people picture their "spaces of historical existence" (RI, 219). The transformation of spatial concepts and peoples' "picture of space" is more complete the more radical the territorial expansion.[77] Spatial revolutions thus occur when the concepts' actual structure changes (RI, 219).

Schmitt thus retold world history as a sequence of *Raumrevolutionen*. He isolated three particular instances: the Roman Empire in the first century CE, the Renaissance, and his own era. In the first genuine *Raumrevolution*, "the field of vision," Schmitt wrote, "expanded" because of Rome's exploratory expeditions and "wars of conquest," especially Caesar's westward expansions (RI, 219). The empire's political theology spiritually unified this Roman space, ranging from Spain to Persia, the people from the most "distant regions" now experiencing "a common fate" (RI, 219). With Spengler's help, Schmitt analyzed the ability to think and visualize the empire as part of the globe—in short, the Romans' imperial imaginary. Quoting Seneca's famous prophecy about the Roman Empire going beyond the earth's known limits, Schmitt defined the imperial imaginary. This "beginning of a new era," Schmitt wrote, "was connected to the consciousness not only of time's fullness but also of the fullness of the planet and of the planetary horizon" (RI, 219). This is an imaginary in which concepts of space and time are concrete, "filled" with imperial meaning: the time of empire extends into a future without limits, and the imperial space will transgress all boundaries. It is the Augustan imaginary of Virgil's *Aeneid*, the promise of *imperium sine fine*.[78]

Spengler celebrated the Faustian *Abendland* as driven by the Faustian desire to transgress the limits of space and time, and thus by a longing for faraway places both spatially and temporally. If readers did not catch Schmitt's Spenglerian subtext, the title of the article's next section, dealing with Europe's second *Raumrevolution* as the "most consequential transformation of the planetary world-picture," spelled it out: "The Faustian Experience of Space" (RI, 220). Schmitt attributed this radical transformation to the Faustian soul, to its desire to "[expand] into the cosmos" and its "imagination of infinite empty space" (RI, 220). The "cause" of this powerful "idea of infinite, empty space," Schmitt wrote, was not merely geographical expansion. Rather, it was the effect of the transformation of all spatial concepts pertaining to all realms of life.

Like Spengler, Schmitt unapologetically celebrated the age of European empire-building. This neo-Roman *Raumrevolution* brought about "the rational superiority of the European." Resulting in the subjection of "non-European peoples," it left them with the "dilemma to either adapt to European civilization, or to sink to the level of a mere colonized people" (RI, 221). From the Renaissance's neo-Roman *Raumrevolution* and *Landnahme*, Schmitt took his readers to the contemporary world—a world in which the Third Reich dominated Western and Eastern Europe and was in the midst of a third *Raumrevolution*. In 1942, the nations east of Germany, Schmitt seemed to think, faced essentially the same dilemma as the "new world" did in 1492.

In his article on *Reich* and *Großraum* and the first part of "Raumrevolution," Schmitt thus mapped out the imaginary imperial space, in which the *katechontic* sovereign is situated. The second part of "Raumrevolution" and his subsequent essays circled around the trope of imperial endings, adding another element to his scopic scenario. In these texts thematizing the *katechon*, we can trace a movement from the revolutionary assertion that the British Empire will come to an end and the German *Reich* will begin, to the seemingly detached—and, as I will argue, ambivalent—analysis of the end of the Third Reich and the beginning of a new Anglo-American *nomos*. Schmitt thinks of these imperial endings in the present in analogy to the Roman Empire and the Spanish-Portuguese Empire.

Imperial Endings: *Katechon* as a Negative Concept

At the end of the 1942 essay on the Occident's "Raumrevolution," Schmitt turned from his Spenglerian account of the nature and genesis of Roman and neo-Roman imperial imaginaries to the significance of past and present wars over acts of *Landnahme* among European powers.[79] The present moment, Schmitt claimed, revolved around the *translatio imperii Britannici*. The end of the British Empire *was* in sight. Schmitt argued his story about the end of one empire and the rise of another by drawing a parallel between the sixteenth and twentieth centuries, between the Spanish-Portuguese *conquista* and the Nazis' expansion in the East. The Occident's "Christian-European civilization and order," Schmitt wrote, persisted even in the "bloody wars" of the sixteenth century (RI, 221). Compared to the "fact that all of Europe participated in the seizure of land in the new world," these wars were insignificant (RI, 221). Schmitt invited his readers to translate these political conditions into their twentieth-century context. Nazi Germany's war of aggression in the East, this was Schmitt's analogy, was a European war fought in the service of the Occident's civilizing mission—an idea voiced more hysterically by Goebbels in 1943.[80]

Establishing this analogy between *conquista* and Third Reich, Schmitt asked his readers to imagine the fall of the British Empire. Concerned with imperial beginnings, Schmitt's line of argument led to the topic of imperial decline. In "Die Raumrevolution: durch den totalen Krieg zu einem totalen Frieden" (1940) and "Beschleuniger wider Willen" (1942), Schmitt then further shifted the emphasis from imperial beginnings to imperial decline, conjuring images from Europe's archive of ruin scenarios. In the latter essay, he discussed the *katechon* for the first time, albeit in negative terms.

The essay "Die Raumrevolution: durch den totalen Krieg zu einem totalen Frieden" (1940) again clarified what Schmitt thought was at stake in terms of the *translatio imperii* from Great Britain to the Third Reich, and the successful form of imperial mimesis that such a process would require. This essay on World War II as a "space-ordering war" evoked the imperial ruin scenario by using Virgil's *Aeneid* (RII, 391). His readers were witnessing, Schmitt wrote, "the spectacle of a British exodus from Europe" (RII, 391). Schmitt compared this "modern exodus" to Virgil's story about Aeneas's Trojans, leaving their ravaged city, hoping to found a new empire on Italian soil: "When Aeneas left burning Troy, he took with him," Schmitt reminded his readers, "the sacred images" (RII, 391).

This exodus, Schmitt wrote, makes us think about the "succession of a 'translatio Imperii Britannici'" (RII, 391). Nothing, Schmitt told the readers of *Das Reich* in 1940, would prevent the birth of a new "European spatial order" and "imagination" (RII, 391). More than that, reordering the European continent for a genuine peace would rearrange the entire "space of the earth" and the established ways of thinking about it (RII, 390). Drawing on "Virgil's great epic," Schmitt counted on his readers' knowledge of Virgil's analogies, with the imperial ruins of the Roman past—Troy and Carthage—representing a warning about the future ruin of the Roman Empire. With this allusion, Schmitt provoked his readers to imagine the sight of London in ruins (RII, 391).

While Schmitt writes at length and with considerable *raum*-revolutionary enthusiasm about imperial rise and decline, he does not yet use the concept of the *katechon* in this 1940 essay. It is in "Beschleuniger wider Willen" (April 1942) that Schmitt discussed the *katechon*'s genesis in Paul's Second Letter to the Thessalonians. In tune with his celebration of the Nazis' imperial project as "accelerator" of world history, Schmitt portrayed the United States as a *katechontic* power, which he defined here as "decelerator of world history"—only to then turn it into the paradox of the "accelerator despite itself."[81]

The concept of *katechon* thus emerged when Schmitt was focused on the topic of the British Empire's end and the question of its successor. The concept is squarely located in a discourse on rising and falling, young and old empires. Delaying world history, Schmitt maintained, was the law of all "aging empires" (BWW, 436). Under the sway of this law, Schmitt wrote, England resisted "change," and the same applied to the United States (BWW, 436). As successor to the British Empire, the United States had become entangled in contradictions that undermined the political function shared by all old empires: to become "restrainers and decelerators" (BWW, 436). The only remaining function was "accelerator against its own will" (BWW, 436). While Great Britain was the "restrainer" and the United States "accelerator *malgré lui*," the Third Reich played the part of "great mover" in Schmitt's world-historical drama (BWW, 436).

Here, Schmitt introduced the Paulinian *katechon* and Tertullian's interpretation of the concept as the Roman Empire. In antiquity, Schmitt wrote, people believed that a "mysterious delaying power" existed, called "'kat-echon' (from the Greek for 'to hold down')" (BWW, 436). This mysterious power "prevented the long-overdue apocalyptic end of times from already happening now." Tertullian understood "the old Imperium Romanum as the delayer which, through its mere existence, 'held' ['*hielt*'] the eon, causing a delay of the end" (BWW, 436). Great Britain's political existence had been ruled by this *katechontic* law governing aging empires since the late nineteenth century, and the United States was now subject to the same logic. Firmly situated on the side of the *Beweger* or young empires, Schmitt thus turned Tertullian's praise for the "old" Roman Empire into a curse—only to reverse this evaluation as the end of the Third Reich came into focus.

Werner Best's Decline and Fall

Before I continue tracing the emergence of the *katechon* in Schmitt's texts, I want to thicken the context for this crucial moment when Schmitt moves from a negative to a positive understanding of this idea. As I mentioned above, Schmitt and Freyer, uneasy about the attack on the Soviet Union, started to anticipate the fall of the Third Reich by 1942, a pessimism based on Schmitt's view that "the Reich [was] no longer a sovereign ordering power."[82] In this situation, Werner Best published an article anonymously, entitled "Herrenschicht oder Führervolk?" (1942). One of the Nazi empire's governors and theorists of *Großraum*, Best raised the specter of Rome's decline, asserting that "*the laws of rise and decline* continue to be operative."[83] He did so at the moment when the Third Reich had reached its greatest expansion and men like Himmler, Goering, and Rosenberg were implementing their genocidal settlement policies in the occupied territories.[84]

Drawing an analogy between the rising Roman Empire and the Third Reich in 1942, Best warned that the new German empire might repeat Rome's fall. The article opened with a sentence touching the very heart of all neo-Roman mimesis: "History does not repeat itself" (HS, 122). Having asserted difference, Best then justified exploring sameness. There were universal "laws of life" governing a "*völkisch Reich*," whose infringement led to "race-death"—"in the long run" (HS, 123, 128, and 130). Establishing his *völkisch* Fichtean approach, Best raised the neo-Roman problematic by addressing "the cliché" that mixed marriages, legalized by Caracalla, "the son of the African L. Septimus Severus and the Syrian Julia Domna," had caused the empire's death (HS, 128, 127). Best watched a different drama: the true cause was "the 'race-death' of the Roman-Italian volkdom" occurring long before Caracalla's edict (HS, 131).

Best's article was a pointed intervention in debates about how to rule the conquered East, aimed at the so-called Spartan model—the idea of imposing a strict apartheid "system of 'racial separation'"—popular among some Nazis (HS, 128). Going Spartan, Best warned, would lead to the *Reich*'s fall. More precisely, the danger that Best saw looming on the horizon in 1942 was that of Germans becoming a "master *volk*" instead of a "leading *volk*" (HS, 133). Romans erred "in the decisive era of the imperium's creation" following the Punic Wars when they opted for an *imperium* where the entire Roman *volk* participated in the exploitation of the "conquered territories," and Germans were about to repeat this momentous error (HS, 126).[85]

The use of conquered peoples as worker-slaves was the true cause of the "barbarization" of the "old peasant state."[86] As soon as a *volk* abandons "its living totality" by "making itself the ruling elite over other *völker*" or "the masses of Helots," Best wrote, then "*the laws of rise and decline* continue to be operative" (HS, 130; emphasis mine). Having neglected these laws, the Romans were defenseless against the worker-slaves from lower races infiltrating Roman society.[87] Best already warned in 1941 that imitating Spartan apartheid would provoke endless slave insurrections (GV, 43). In this 1942 essay, he also argued against abandoning the Germanizing of the East (chapter 18). To endure, the *Reich* needed German settlers in the East because only members of a *völkisch Reich* remained vigilant against their "adversary" (HS, 138).

Far from being bothered by the expulsion, resettlement, and mass killings, Best considered annihilation part of empire-building. What he advocated was a way of creating a "*völkisch* Reich of the future" not set on the inexorable path toward *barbarization* (HS, 138).[88] While Best's argument resonates with Spengler's picture of early Rome versus Roman imperialism, he did not believe in Spengler's thesis of the inevitability of decline or his concept of Caesarism as the radically secularized *katechon*.[89] On the contrary, in the hands of a strong *volk* and its *völkisch* leader, a durable imperial order was possible.

Schmitt, who between 1940 and 1942 thought of the Third Reich as a space-revolutionary conquest empire, might have disagreed with some of the annihilationist premises of Best's 1942 essay, but he too was invested in the question of how empires endure—how imperial endtime might be prolonged. Building and maintaining a neo-Roman empire was a question of solid foundations, decisive actions, and firm ideas about who the empire's enemy was. The positive concept of the *katechon* with its scenario of postponed but inevitable ending was central to this project.

Writing with the End in Sight: *Katechon* as Positive Concept

Discussing the British Empire in "Beschleuniger wider Willen" (April 1942), Schmitt wrote that the *katechon*'s historical meaning resided in resisting the "reasonable" movement of world history. Schmitt then introduced the *katechon* as a positive notion at the onset of *Land and Sea: A World-Historical Meditation* (1942; 2015). Here, Schmitt invited his readers "to cast a glance at certain developments of the great history of the world from the point of view of this battle between land and sea," ranging from Greek antiquity to "the declining Roman Empire" and the beginning of the Arabs' maritime reign over the Mediterranean after reconquering Carthage in the seventh century.[90] Crediting the Byzantine Empire with having "held out" against Islam for "many centuries," he introduced the idea of empire as "Katechon." As the "genuine 'restrainer' ['Aufhalter']," Schmitt wrote, the Eastern Roman Empire prevented Muslims from settling in Italy (L, 17; translation modified).

Mehring argues that Freyer alerted Schmitt to the concept of *katechon*.[91] Schmitt's beginning indeed mirrored Freyer's conclusion to his *Weltgeschichte Europas* (*World-History of Europe*; 1948).[92] Here, Freyer implied an analogy between the end of the Byzantine Empire and the end of the Third Reich, between Islam and the Soviet Union. Besieged for years, Freyer wrote, the Byzantine Empire brought Islam's "great expansion" to a standstill.[93] "The ring that the Roman arts of state craft had forged at its greatest moment is now torn apart by Islam's cold fire," Freyer wrote, "900 years after Publius Cornelius Scipio vanquished Carthage."[94]

Let us return to Schmitt's *Land and Sea*, the text in which Schmitt traced the rise of England as Europe's dominant sea-based world power. Schmitt concluded his text with a scenario of ruin gazing, predicting the end of Europe's older sea-based *nomos*—and thus the end of the British Empire. What we are witnessing today, Schmitt wrote in 1942, is the "inexorable" growth of "the new nomos of our planet" (L, 93). Many of his contemporaries might not see it this way, Schmitt conceded:

> Many shall see in [the end of the old *nomos*] only death and destruction. Some believe themselves to be experiencing the end of the world. In reality we are only experiencing the end of the relation between land and sea, which had held up to this point. Still, human angst [Angst] in the face of the new is often as great as the angst in the face of the void, even when the new is the overcoming of the void. Thus the many see only senseless disorder where in reality a new sense struggles for its order. (L, 93)

This scenario, with its story of transition, is rather opaque, allowing multiple readings. We could read it as promising a new beginning, involving the Third Reich's victory and the establishment of an air-based *nomos*.[95] How does the text support such a reading? Schmitt opened *Land and Sea* with a strong decisionist appeal, vehemently arguing against historical determinism by asking what it would take to overcome "distress and danger" (L, 10). Being aware of "the possibility of rebirth," Schmitt wrote, "man has the strength to historically conquer his existence [*Dasein*] and consciousness" (L, 10; translation modified). Moments of danger in particular required the heroic decision to begin "a new collective form of his historical existence" (L, 11). With his grandiose ruin gazer scenario, Haushofer turned Spengler's heroic nihilism into fascist decisionism. Here, Schmitt did not sound all that different. Relying on the Spenglerian trope of the fear of the void and the Faustian desire to overcome infinite space, he promised that a new world would arise out of the ruins of the old, hinting that this new *nomos* would be ruled by the Nazi empire, with the air force as its "space force" (L, 90).

By extending the *raum*-revolutionary analogy between the Spanish-Portuguese and German conquests, Schmitt's authorship in the 1942 edition of *Land and Sea* seems to confirm this reading about new beginnings after the war. Framing the text as a story about the "Jewish secret doctrine" of Leviathan and Behemoth told to his daughter, Schmitt added: "This is how Jews interpret world history."[96] Readers did not find it too hard to decipher Schmitt's parable in 1942: Leviathan was sea-based Great Britain, while Behemoth stood for Germany, the land-based power. According to Schmitt, "the Jews" thought of themselves as the detached observers of this mythical battle.[97] Schmitt singled out Isaac Abravanel, treasurer to the Portuguese and then the Castilian king, who lived "in the age of great discoveries" and thus "knew what he said," as the most likely author of the tale (L, 16). Schmitt implied that he too occupied a position close to power at a time of imperial land-appropriations. By setting up his world history as an alternative story to the Jewish-Kabbalistic tale of Abravanel, the voice that Schmitt invented in this text is the voice of the non-Jewish imperial world historian.[98] "This is how *non*-Jews interpret world history"—such could be the epigraph of *Land and Sea*.[99]

But does Schmitt's concluding passage really tell this revolutionary decisionist story? Is he observing the Third Reich on the verge of making a great decision? Or is this a story about *katechontic* power? The latter reading is, I think, entirely plausible. To make my point, let me single out two sentences from Schmitt's concluding passage quoted above: Many see in the end of the old *nomos* only death and destruction, Schmitt wrote, and: Some people think they are experiencing the end of the world. With these sentences, Schmitt paraphrased Paul's story of the Thessalonians' mistaken expectation of the end. This Pauline paraphrase in turn invites us to recall Schmitt's portrayal of the Byzantine Empire as *katechontic*, based on Freyer's Tertullian reading of Paul. If we do so, we are dealing with a text analyzing the Third Reich as an empire, acting under the *katechontic* law to postpone its own end—and an empire about to end.

We are also dealing with an imperial theorist who writes with his eyes on the empire in ruins. This is the gaze of the *katechontic* imperial theorist who knows that all empires will eventually come to an end. Let us not forget that Melville's novella confronted Schmitt in 1941 with scenes of imperial ruin. In this story about the encounter of two empires, one falling and the other rising, Melville portrayed the Castilian ship as ruin, a "relic of faded grandeur" that still carried signs of a once-powerful empire.[100] The text's evocative visualization of this imperial end in ruins must have struck Schmitt with some force. The decaying Spanish-Portuguese ship—once a "very fine vessel," which "still, under the decline of masters, preserved signs of former state"—is seen through the eyes of Delano, the "blunt-thinking" American captain, turning him into the archetypical ruin gazer.[101] As the ship appears on the horizon, Delano takes note of its decayed state: the ship's tops are "in sad disrepair," hanging "overhead like three ruinous aviaries . . . battered and moldy"; to Delano, "the castellated forecastle" looks like "some ancient turret, long ago taken by assault and then left to decay."[102] The quarter galleries' balustrades are overgrown with "sea-moss."[103] The Castilian coat-of-arms has been supplemented by a "rudely painted" inscription reading: "'Seguid vuestro jefe' [follow your leader]."[104]

So how should we read Schmitt's concluding passage? While Schmitt's anti-Abravanelian authorship supports the heroic reading, equating two imperial *beginnings*—the Spanish-Portuguese and German *Landnahmen*—the connection to the Spanish-Portuguese Empire simultaneously directs our attention to a *katechontic* scenario announcing the Nazi empire's end in ruins. These two different readings are not alternatives, but signal a basic tension in the text. Schmitt was either unaware of this tension, or more likely, he maintained it deliberately. As so often, Schmitt was hedging his bets.

The *Katechontic* Scenario

What *Land and Sea* left much less vague is the authorial position that Schmitt constructed in this text. The vantage point from which Schmitt writes his concluding passage is literally "air-based," akin to the imperial perspective of *Scipio's Dream*. Schmitt's authorship thus soars to Ciceronian heights. Joseph Vogt linked this Scipionian vantage point in 1942 to the era of Roman decline, but he was far from the only classicist recalling Cicero's lesson. In 1943, Wilhelm Weber published "Aufstieg und Untergang Roms," an article ending with an excerpt from Cicero's *Dream of Scipio*. While the younger Scipio beheld the "tiny earth," Weber explained, Scipio the Elder—"defeator of Hannibal"—urged him to keep fighting.[105]

In Schmitt's texts, this Ciceronian vantage point at the edge of imperial endtime signaled the detached world historian's downward gaze at the empire he once helped theorize—a deliberate strategic gesture on Schmitt's part, and one that would provide the foundation for his work after 1945. In other words, Schmitt was getting ready to position himself as the *katechontic* theorist not of *Reich*, or of *Großraum*, but of *nomos*—a theorist still animated by the same conservative revolutionary spirit he so admired in the Spanish-Portuguese conquistadors and their successors, Salazar and Franco.[106]

Against the background of recent scholarship that reads the *katechon* as symptom of the theological foundations of Schmitt's critique of secular modernity, I began this chapter arguing that Schmitt's concept of the *katechon* needs a deeper genealogy. Most of these critics locate Schmitt in the context of the conservative revolution, with its political-cultural critique of modernity and hopes for a new *Reich*. Schmitt's concepts of *Reich, Großraum, and nomos*, I argue, represent attempts to theorize empire beyond the narrow domestic notion of *Reich*. The discursive formation that we call the conservative revolution had a strong imperial dimension that we miss if we keep working with the narrow concept of *Reich* that informs existing scholarship. The *katechon* is symptomatic of Schmitt's engagement with this wider context of European neo-Roman imperial thought *and* its imperial imaginary as *Seh-* and *Zeitraum*, scopic space and time-space. More than that, Schmitt's *katechontic* scenario represents a radical reconceptualization of the imperial imaginary, forcing into the foreground the knowledge driving all ruin gazer scenarios: that time is running out.

Contemplating the end of the British and then German Empire, Schmitt began to theorize the time of the imperial imaginary as the *time of the exception*. Situated in the *nomotic Zwischen-Zeit*—the time-space between imperial beginnings and imperial endings—the *katechon* acts when the end of times *is near*. All previous ruin gazer scenarios visualized the time of empires as limited, but Schmitt intensified this temporal imagination by reviving the apocalyptic urgency of the *katechon*.[107] Far from having abandoned decisionism in favor of *Ordnungsdenken*, Schmitt reconceptualized the decisionist act as central to his *katechontic* theory of empire.[108] The *katechon* is the restrainer—alert and always ready to act, ready to seize the moment.

This decisionist *katechon* is Schmitt's post-Spenglerian response to the ruin scenarios of the conservative revolution's first imperial thinker.[109] As the imperial sovereign who acts with an eye toward the end (or, more precisely, who *strategically* prepares for the final battle that will bring about the end, thus postponing it by stabilizing worldly affairs for the time being), the *katechon* is Schmitt's response to the urgent question that has haunted all neo-Roman empires: when (and how) to act in order to prevent imperial decline. Hans Freyer summarized this post-Spenglerian politics of empire once more in the spring of 1945: "Decline [Verfall] always happens when it is not countered by political action."[110]

The empire's enemy is part of Schmitt's decisionist *katechontic* scenario. Acting by preparing "the final decisive battle," the *katechontic* sovereign confronts this enemy.[111] Much of the literature on Schmitt's *katechon* has been devoted to the question of this eschatological enemy, this antichrist. While Gross analyzed Schmitt's definition of politics as friend-enemy constellations with an eye toward the *internal* other (i.e., assimilated German

Jews), I argue that the neo-Roman barbarian shadows Schmitt's concept of the external enemy.[112] Nazi leaders and intellectuals discussed Jews in the context of their own empire-building, and in the next chapter, I will discuss Heidegger's thoughts on the matter. These theories of "Jewish" imperialism erased the distinction of Jews as internal and external enemies. Schmitt's *katechontic* scenario thus narrates the confrontation with Europe's others—with the colonized subjects overseas and in the East. Moreover, Schmitt's scenario maintains the constellation of power characterizing ruin gazer scenarios. That is, it keeps the imperial subject in a position of scopic mastery.

In Schmitt's case, we are thus dealing with an *imperial theology* characterized by a strong decisionist thrust. Let me briefly return to the discussion of decisionism and the question of its theological foundations. Mehring reads Schmitt's wartime essays and *Land und Meer* as pivotal texts in which Schmitt's *political theology* turned into a *theology of history*.[113] According to Mehring, the reason for this shift is twofold: first, confronted with the coming defeat of the Third Reich, Schmitt abandoned the concept of *Reich*, turning to world-historical reflections and raising the question of the *katechon*. Under these conditions, Schmitt was no longer able to identify the *katechontic* function of restrainer with any really existing political order. Second, Mehring defines the *theology* of history as grounded in the idea that the *katechon* conceives of the end as "*historically meaningful*."[114]

In contrast, I propose that we understand Schmitt's *katechon* as a reconceptualization of imperial decline, a reconceptualization that does *not* require the idea of a *meaningful* ending—merely the understanding that empires do eventually come to an end.[115] What it does require is a decisionist concept of sovereignty. Imperial legitimacy is founded on the *katechontic* power to delay the empire's end. In sum, we are not dealing with a *theological politics of empire* that has eschatology as its very substance, but a form of *imperial theology*, that is, a *politics of empire* that feeds on the remnants of eschatological history and their abandoned meanings.

Katechon and Imperial Mimesis: Rome as Theo-Political Stage

Schmitt's *katechontic ruin gazer scenario* thus designates a specific form of imperial sovereignty. In this scenario, the *katechon* is the *Reich*'s sovereign, ready to fight the final battle—his eyes fixed on the ruins of the future. This scopic scenario thus imagines the confrontation with the empire's enemy and translates eschatological time into the time of empire. There is an aspect of the Schmittian *katechon* that I have neglected so far, namely, that the *katechon* is also the concept through which Schmitt theorized imperial mimesis, in its proper and improper forms. Establishing a distinction between German *Reich* and Western *imperialism,* Schmitt addressed imperial mimesis in his 1939 lecture on Großraum. In *The Nomos of the Earth* (1950; 2003), Schmitt retheorized the issue in the context of his final version of the *katechon.*

Here, the *katechon* is more than the restrainer or imperial sovereign postponing the end. In *Nomos,* Schmitt makes the *katechon* the central figure/instance in his theory of imperial mimesis as the articulation of imperial ideology or political theology with a particular territorialized imperial space and time. Rethinking the notion of imperial *succession,* Schmitt writes in these key passages that "[t]he decisive concept of this continuity was that of the restrainer [Aufhalter], of the katechon."[116] Replacing the political theology of pagan Rome with its own Christian version, Schmitt argued, meant that this new *Reich* represented "the historical power to restrain the appearance of the antichrist and the end of the present eon."[117] The Christian *Reich,* Schmitt continued, "was a power that withholds [*qui tenet*], as the Apostle Paul said in his Second Letter to the Thessalonians."[118] This translation of pagan into Christian imperial theology rests on two basic tenets that I discussed above: Schmitt's appropriation of Tertullian's reading of the *katechon* as the Roman Empire, and his idea that any *nomos*—produced by the law-founding act of the seizing of land—combines *Ordnung* with *Ortung,* order and its territorialization around a sacred (pagan or Christian) center.

In *Nomos,* successful neo-Roman mimesis thus has to do with "the concrete orientation to Rome."[119] In *Political Theology II,* Schmitt elaborated on this idea by exploring in depth the parallel between Augustan Rome's pagan theology and later Christian forms. Virgil was the author who contributed to Augustus's restoration "in the spirit of pagan Italian piety."[120] Centered on imperial Rome, this Virgilian "religion of loyalty in the Empire" is the core of the Romans' political theology.[121] Explaining this "*theologia politica,*" Schmitt relied on Varro's distinctions between mythical, philosophical, and "political theology, whose place is the polis and the urbs."[122] Based on this latter definition, Schmitt argued that *nomos* and political theology are inseparable because theology's function was to create "a public sphere through the cult of the gods, the sacrificial cults, and ceremonies."[123] Political theology thus "takes and gives space," Schmitt wrote, creating power as *visible* and *public.*[124] Empires that endured needed sacred centers, sites like the Roman capital rebuilt by Augustus as the world's stage, according to the empire's pagan theology.

In its mature version, Schmitt's *katechon* is thus the instance bringing about a successful process of imperial mimesis by maintaining the "identity of space" while changing the content of this very space.[125] The *conquistadors* replaced the Romans' pagan political theology with their Marian theology, but the city of Rome remained the center of the empire/*nomos*. Before the caesura of 1942, Schmitt's idea of a successful imperial mimesis involved the *Reich*'s political theology of *volk*, centered on Berlin as the empire's stage.[126] The *katechon* is thus central to any *genuine* process of imperial neo-Roman mimesis. That is, to any creative innovation that avoids mere repetition.

Die große Parallele:[127] Schmitt's return to Tertullian

In 1971, Schmitt reaffirmed his reading of the Paulinian concept of the *katechon*. The *katechon*, he stated in an interview, was his *idée fixe*, and he then explained the notion:[128]

> In Thessalonians 2:6, I think, it says: "der katechon," ho katechon, and then immediately after: "to katechon." Thus once masculine and once neuter. That means nothing but: "Ho katechon" is the ruling emperor [der jeweils regiernde Imperator], "to katechon" is the imperium. And as long as the imperium exists, the world will not go under.[129]

With this categorical statement, Schmitt ended a discussion about his political theology. The core questions of this theology were: Why is the end not coming, and who is the "Aufhalter" or delayer?[130] Augustine reported Tertullian's reading of the *katechon* as Roman Empire, Schmitt stated, but he did not adopt it. He, the legal scholar in the tradition of Tertullian, did.

Schmitt thus returned to the first-century problematic—Paul's *katechon*—via Tertullian's *Apologeticum*, a critique of Roman modernity that appealed to Schmitt's revolutionary-conservative leanings. Criticizing Roman decadence, Tertullian assured the Roman emperor that Christians were his most loyal subjects, praying for the empire's duration. Hans Blumenberg criticized Schmitt's Tertullian concept of *katechon* as a "bridge" between "eschatological faith and historical consciousness," arguing that this "mysterious imagination of delaying the events of the end" never was a genuine eschatological idea.[131] Rather, Tertullian's *katechontic* version of history put eschatology in the service of politics.[132] Eschatology and politics, Blumenberg insisted, simply do not mix, because the expectation that the end is near or "immediate expectation" is a state of emergency negating "every type of durability."[133]

Blumenberg was not a theorist of empire. Schmitt, however, was a neo-Roman imperial thinker, who understood that imperial sovereignty operated in the endzone—was a state of both exception *and* duration. Building and maintaining a neo-Roman empire was a question of solid foundations, decisive actions, and firm ideas about who the enemy is.[134] Schmitt's concept of the *katechon* remained central to this project, and his postwar texts testify to the central role that the Roman Empire continued to play in his political theory. Schmitt is the twentieth century's post-Paulinian theorist of empire, who continued scanning the ruined stage, searching for ways of delaying the end—right into the era of decolonization.

TWENTY-FIVE

Empire and Time: Martin Heidegger's Anti-Roman Intervention

Introduction

In essence, Carl Schmitt argued that the Nazi empire failed because it lacked the *katechontic* theo-politics and imaginary of the pagan empire of ancient Rome or the Christian empire of the Spanish crown. Instead, he told his American interrogator, the Nazi leadership pursued a debased politics of imperialist expansion doomed to repeat Rome's fall. Spengler, who located the origins of thinking in the "meditation upon death" (DI, 166), related (techno-capitalist) *civilization* to imperialism, arguing that the former unleashed a relentless drive toward expansion. Decelerating *civilization*'s rush toward its inevitable relapse into barbarian prehistory was the mission of the Caesarist leader (chapter 16). Immersed in Spengler's analysis of Caesarist imperialism, Martin Heidegger took leave of his dream of a *völkisch* German Empire in the early 1940s.[1] Posing as the late-twentieth-century Spenglerian prophet, Heidegger declared that the world was witnessing the dawn of a global empire, in thrall to the logic of technological progress.

Heidegger was far from being the only conservative revolutionary turned Nazi who fell back on Spengler's ideas in the 1940s. Two years after Best's 1942 article about the potential reoccurrence of Rome's fall, Karl Haushofer proposed a Spenglerian analysis of the imperial unconscious, hinting at the failure of the Nazis' neo-Roman mimesis. Haushofer's erratic reflections circled around the tension between limited and unlimited expansion, state-led empire-building and (Jewish-capitalist) imperialism. Referring to the fall of Tunis in 1943, Haushofer argued that in contrast to Italian colonialism, the imperialism of the "merchant-people" driving the Italians out of their African colonies lacked any ethical grounding.[2]

Haushofer formulated his core problematic as follows: What directed the "national *unconscious* onto the path of expansion," and was there an "ethically justified transition from nationalism to imperialism?"[3] If states expanded *not* because they needed "*Lebensraum*" for their *volk*, and if this *volk* had *not* reached "the highest stage of culture," then "the [genocidal] law of the jungle will rule."[4] According to Haushofer, there was always a tension at work in colonialism between "spatio-political instinct" and the nation's "spatio-political consciousness."[5] Connecting this critique of imperialism's genocidal logic to a familiar Roman model, Haushofer wrote that "Augustus insisted on limits."[6] Reviving Spengler's Nietzschean theses about imperialism's unconscious expansionist drive, Haushofer implied that the Nazis failed to heed Augustus's ethics of restraint.

Thinking Imperial Politics with and against Spengler and Nietzsche

After years of passionate investment in the idea of a German *Reich*, Heidegger also began to criticize the Nazis' neo-Roman project in the early 1940s, but not because he thought they imitated Rome incorrectly. On the contrary, like Simone Weil, he thought they were Romans, driven by the will to power into fantasies of ever greater expansion of their Germanic empire. We would expect a minor theorist like Haushofer to recycle Spengler's ideas. That Heidegger did so still causes unease among some Heideggerians.[7] And yet, Emmanuel Faye's analysis of the centrality of Spengler's reflections on late Western modernity for Heidegger's thinking is as compelling as his analysis of Heidegger's investment in the idea of a new German *Reich*.[8]

In the seminar on "*Hegel, On the State*" (winter 1934–1935), Heidegger told his students that it was their task to define this *Reich*. He explained that "the state will continue to exist beyond fifty or one hundred years," adding that it will then require "something *from which* it exists."[9] This something is "spirit."[10] Posing the question about the "long-term durability of the Nazi state" more explicitly, Heidegger raised the question of succession.[11] Since "the Führer" will no longer lead the state "[i]n sixty years," he stated, "what becomes *then* will depend on *us*."[12] In the lectures entitled *Basic Concepts* (winter 1941), Heidegger then made the case against Hitler's and Himmler's neo-Roman desire for "the greatest possible duration" of their future empire.[13] This transition from a concern with the essence of the *völkisch* state to a critique of neo-Roman imperialism was mediated by Heidegger's reflections on Nietzsche and Spengler.

Heidegger saw himself in the role of the Nazis' master thinker, training the "'political nobility'" for Hitler's "Führerstaat."[14] Convinced that he was witnessing a *völkisch* revolution, Heidegger thus reserved the definition of this revolution for himself and the new elite he would educate.[15] Together they would think about the nature of this state as the embodiment of the German people's "metaphysics," finding the answers to the fundamental questions raised by this conservative revolution: "What is *this* people we ourselves are?"[16] What is its "historical destiny" and "[spiritual-*volklich]* mission"?[17]

In the seminar on *Hegel, On the State*, Heidegger explicated his decisionist politics on the basis of Spengler's book on the state, lecturing about "the conception of the political as self-affirmation" and "assertion of Führung."[18] In the *Black Notebooks*, or diaries covering the years 1931–1941, Heidegger returned to Spengler. While he criticized Spengler's idealization of "Roman-dom [Römertum] and Caesarism," he praised him for having understood the "Caesarist brutality of power."[19] In *The State* (1924), Spengler argued that the age of the transition from parliamentarism to Caesarism was beginning. Condemning what Spengler lauded, Heidegger adopted his analysis of Caesarist imperialism as the political formation of Occidental civilization's last neo-Roman stage.[20] As a conservative revolutionary committed to *völkisch* particularity, Heidegger could imagine a German *Reich* in the vein of Herder, Fichte, and Best. The era of Caesarist imperialism, however, meant the end of the *völkisch* movement that he supported.

In the *Black Notebooks*, Heidegger's analysis of imperialism as the political form of late modernity—or what he now saw as the end stage of the West's "metaphysics as machination"—begins with his ruminations on the life worlds of the Nazis' enemies, characterized, he thought, by "the unconditional unfolding of subjectivity into pure *rationality*" (ÜXII, 257, 235). This Western metaphysics driven by the Roman will to power would ultimately lead to the "unfolding into absolute planetary domination" (ÜXII, 190). With his "idea of the eternal recurrence of the same," Heidegger thought, Nietzsche articulated the "essence" of this "will to power" (ÜXII, 93). This was the voice of the Roman Nietzsche who "[repudiated] Greek-dom [Griechentum] in favor of Roman-dom [Römertum]," and thus "the will to power" as the will to "'Technik'" (ÜXII, 198).[21]

The opposition between Rome and Greece, the Greek city-states' colonial empires and Roman imperialism, will remain the central pivot of Heidegger's emerging critique of Nazi imperialism as subject to the same logic of "the gigantic" as the rest of the Western world.[22] Thinking with and against Spengler and Nietzsche, Heidegger thus discovered that modern imperialism, or what he would call "*planetarism*" (ÜXII, 260), was Roman in nature.[23] In the notebooks, he pursued this line of thought at first with respect to the Western allies (and, to some extent, the Soviets). England began "to construct the modern world," and in its essence, this modernity, Heidegger wrote, was "aiming for the unleashing of the machination of the entire planet" (ÜXII, 243). Moreover, England's "'mastervolk'" was the servant of Americanism, the highest form of Western imperialism that erased all *völkisch* particularity because it represented the global "victory of unconditional 'Abstraction'" (ÜXII, 258, 268). The Occident's future was thus American world dominion, Heidegger asserted in the early 1940s, eventually leading to "modernity's perishing [Verendung] into desolation" (ÜXII, 257). That is, a Hobbesian state of nature or, from the perspective of Spengler's theory of late Western modernity, the relapse of calculating, abstract *civilization* into barbarian prehistory.

These reflections culminate in the notorious passage about the role of "world Jewry" in this historical process, written after Hitler declared war against the Soviet Union: "The idea of an agreement with England in the sense of a just distribution of the possessions of [all] imperialisms does not touch on the essence of the historical process that England is now bringing to a close," Heidegger noted, "within Americanism and Bolshevism and that means simultaneously, also within World Jewry [Weltjudentum]" (ÜXII, 243). To think of "the role of World Jewry [des Judentums]" in "racial" terms is wrong, Heidegger wrote.[24] Instead, this is a "metaphysical question" concerning "the nature of a type of humanity [Menschentümlichkeit]."[25] And this Jewish way of being human, he believed, was "the absolutely unbound [schlechthin ungebunden] capable of assuming the world-historical 'task' of uprooting all beings from being."[26] These "imperialisms," Heidegger mused, were using World War II for a "new ordering of the 'earth'" (ÜXII, 193). The process—the striving for world domination—was merely a stage in the development of the West, the very "last step of [machination's] power," Heidegger wrote, "on the path to devastation [Verwüstung]" (ÜXII, 260).

This "rootless," capitalist-Jewish imperialism is the opposite of the Nazi empire or, rather, the *völkisch* German *Reich* of the Heideggerian kind.[27] Discussing Schmitt's modernization of the concept of the barbarian enemy, I accentuated his insistence on making the enemy visible. A few years later, Heidegger—infamously—wrote about enmity in terms of a people's existence and the fierce "struggle" needed "to catch sight of the enemy as such, to bring the enemy into the open [and] to prepare the attack looking far ahead with the goal of total annihilation."[28] In his *Black Notebooks*, "World Jewry" figures as "unfassbar" or "ungraspable" (ÜXII, 262).[29] There is a lot of Herder and Fichte, and certainly more than a trace of Spengler, Best, and other radical conservatives' ideas about imperialism in these reflections—and needless to say, this resonates strongly with Hitler's, Himmler's, and Goebbels's ideas about capitalism, imperialism, and Jews.[30]

At the moment when the Nazis assaulted the Soviet Union, Heidegger's nationalism and allegiance to the idea of a Third Reich was still intact. By 1942, however, Heidegger was speaking in the voice of the Spenglerian prophet: "At the earliest historicity may again be [possible] around 2300" (ÜXII, 225). The reason for this possible return of (genuine) history? By then, Heidegger wrote, "Americanism [would] have exhausted itself because of the surfeit of its emptiness" (ibid.). Like Spengler, Heidegger sees this future "Prussian absolute Über-Americanism" as the "condition of civilized barbarity" (ÜXII, 270, 225).

By 1942, Heidegger was convinced that modernity's drawn-out or "protracted perishing [Verendung]" was beginning (ÜXII, 225). That is, rethinking Spengler's picture of late modernity, he also started retheorizing Spengler's notion of *Untergang*. Addressing the Nazi leadership's discourse about "*The Occident and Europe*," Heidegger asserted: "'Europe' is the realization of the *Decline of the West*" (ÜXII, 274). Redefining decline, Heidegger also redefined his role, assigning to philosophy (and poetry) the task of thinking outside Western metaphysics, and the act of preserving the memory of a different way of being. What this act of remembrance entailed, Heidegger first explained when he lectured about Friedrich Hölderlin's poetry in 1936 at the German Institute in Rome.[31] The poet's task, Heidegger told his audience, was the rediscovery of an archaic Greek way of being in the world that he theorized as the other of Western modernity.[32]

In 1941, Adorno credited Spengler with having foreseen the "real possibility of a regression to barbarism."[33] By 1942, it was no longer clear whether Heidegger still distinguished between the Third Reich and its imperialist enemies or whether he then thought of the Nazi empire as one of these "imperialisms." The historical moment when the "final self-devastation of the entire modern humanity" would become reality, he now thought, was approaching (ÜXII, 256). In this situation, Heidegger defined his task as salvaging "a beginning or commencement of German Being beyond the now unfettered and definitive self-devastation of modern humanity" (ibid.). Looking at this American future, Heidegger asked: "When will the being of the fatherland be spoken?" (ÜXII, 275). With this question, Heidegger then finds his future role: "Der weit vorauswesende Augenblick der Entscheidung zum Wesen der Geschichte—ist den Deutschen zugesprochen" (ÜXII, 235). Essence of *Occidental* history would be the more precise formulation, because Heidegger remained committed to the conservative revolution's key concept, the *Abendland*.

Empire and Death, or Romans versus Greeks

By the early 1940s, Heidegger had abandoned the project of educating the elite and thus the task of "contributing to the longevity of the Nazi state."[34] In *Basic Concepts*, Heidegger criticized the Nazis for their Roman, and in his mind Nietzschean, desire to master time, to endure. In these lectures held in the winter of 1941, Heidegger reflected on time and empire in the context of theorizing the "inception," that is, the radical break with Western modernity (BC, 6). As I mentioned above, this break required the remembrance of another, a Greek, beginning or commencement—and, he argued in *Basic Concepts*, a return to the Greek experience of empire and imperial temporality.

"[W]hat distances modern man from the inception of his history," Heidegger stated, is "the changed mode of world-interpretation and the basic position in the midst of beings." This "modern position is the 'technological'" (BC, 14). Technology determined modern being, Heidegger argued, and it was "an already decided mode of world-interpretation" (ibid.). Or, put differently, "the practical mastery of technology already presupposes a metaphysical subjugation to technology" (ibid.). It is here that Heidegger introduced the question of temporality echoing Spengler's ideas about *civilization*'s will to master time almost verbatim: "Accompanying this subjugation within us is an attitude that grasps everything according to plan and calculation, and does so with a view to vast time-spans in order willfully and knowingly to secure what can last for the longest possible duration" (ibid.).[35]

The critique of technological modernity and the will to power, striving for world domination, erasing *völkisch* particularity and transforming time into meaningless succession, the "endlessness of continuing in the form of giganticism" (ÜXII, 270)—this critique now includes the Nazi empire as empire modeled on Rome.[36] Built to last a thousand years, the Third *Reich* is the same as all other imperialisms, following the logic of modernity as "machination" (ibid.). "It is one thing," Heidegger wrote, "when empires endure for millennia because of their continuing stability" (BC, 14). As we know, to merely *let* empire endure was not exactly Hitler's or Himmler's project of imperial fortification. "It is something else," Heidegger continued as the German Army was invading the Soviet Union, "when world dominions are knowingly planned to last millennia and the assurance of their existence is undertaken by that will whose essential goal is the greatest possible duration of the greatest possible order of the largest possible masses" (ibid.). Heidegger called this will "the concealed metaphysical essence of modernity" (ibid.). As the "will to man's unconditional mastery over the world, and the execution of this will," it shaped all of "modern world-history" (BC, 14, 15).

Heidegger thus connected the Nazi leadership's Roman desire to make empire endure to Spengler's analysis of Western *civilization* as imperialism.[37] This reflection about imperialism as the highest stage of Western metaphysics coincided with Heidegger's reconceptualization of Spengler's notion of *Untergang*. Problematizing the "refusal of decline," Heidegger addressed this topic in his Hölderlin lectures (winter 1941–1942).[38] Here, Heidegger's redefinition of decline is based on his founding thesis about being that he formulated in his Aristotle lectures as ruinance and tersely reformulated in the Hölderlin lectures: "To man's being belongs his non-being."[39] In the latter text, Heidegger distinguished between "*Untergang,*" or decline, "*Verschwinden,*" or disappearance, and "*Verenden,*" or perishing.[40]

As I mentioned above, Heidegger thought about the future of the American world empire as a form of perishing, not decline. His reading of one of Hölderlin's poems explains why he chose this particular word and how he understands the difference between decline and perishing or dying. Here, "evening's dusk" and "morning's dawn," "decline" and "rise," are linked, with "night" as a positive term, a space of "transition," that "receives" decline and "prepares" the rise.[41] Like night, decline functions as a positive term: "Decline is not mere vanishing or dying."[42] In Heidegger's mind, the concept of *Verenden* is linked to a meaningless life, *Untergehen* to a world of meaningful, ultimately tragic existence: "Only the great has the capacity to decline, the small [or insignificant] never does; it either continues to endure or it merely ends."[43] Declining means "[knowing] how to abandon [oneself] to that which has been."[44] The philosopher-poet is the custodian of decline, of that which "declines in a truly historical sense," thus preparing the future rising.[45]

Let us return to *Basic Concepts*. Here, Heidegger explained that this refusal of decline was a very un-Greek desire. "The will to preservation, and that always means the will to enhance life and its lastingness, works essentially against decline and sees deficiency and powerlessness in what lasts only a short while" (BC, 15). Taking his discussion of empire and time back to ancient Greece, Heidegger reasserted the difference between *Untergang* (decline) and *Verenden* (perishing or dying): "for the inception of our history, for the Greeks, decline was unique, momentary, laudable, and great" (ibid.).

This distinction between endings then becomes the foundation of a different conception of world history, an alternative to the idea of the cycle of rise and decline, and the repetitive succession of empires. Heidegger begins his reflection on this other history by further clarifying his distinction between the two different ways of coming to an end, "between decline while entering into something unique and perishing while clinging fast to the ordinary" (ibid.). Perishing, or what Heidegger called in his early work "ruinance,"[46] is linked to the desire for the continuation of the same, decline to the inception as the creation of something radically new. "What is imperishable in the inception does not consist in the longest possible extension and breadth of its effects," Heidegger writes, "but in the rarity and singularity of each varied return of what is originary in it" (ibid.).

Romans and neo-Romans desire modernity's sameness, and they imagine world history as the eternal repetition of the same imperial rise and fall. Thinking in terms of the inception, however, means thinking of endings as modernity's originary difference that returns throughout history but always in a different form. If empire, Heidegger seemed to suggest, then empire as a radically new beginning and a new end, instead of the mindless repetition of the same beginning and the same end—empire modeled on the antagonistic Greek city-states and their colonies closely tied to the polis, not the universalist Roman Empire. From this perspective, neo-Roman empire is repetition, a monotonous, meaningless, universal formation doomed to a monotonous, meaningless death. And what would an empire in the spirit of the ancient Greeks be? A *völkisch*, Fichtean *Reich*, mindful of the particularity of its leading *volk* and the subject people it ruled? A particularity in dialogue with the "foreign" that is "one's own"?[47] Heidegger of course does not spell this out. But we may extrapolate from the above that this other *Reich*, a meaningful political entity, would die a meaningful, tragic death.

Heidegger thus proposed to exit from the Nazis' *verrömerte* or "Romified" antiquity. Invested in duration, their ideas about empire and ruins, Heidegger's reflections implied, "slipped out of the danger zone of *Dasein*," refusing the experience of the "being seized by terror" that Heidegger's other beginning required and which, he argued, characterized Greek colonial politics.[48] An attack on the Nazis' imitation of Rome, this was also an implicit critique of Schmitt's version of the Pauline *katechon* who, while residing in the danger zone, acted in order to postpone the end as long as possible.[49]

Recognition, not Imitation: Heidegger's Anti-Historicist Assault on Neo-Roman Mimesis

In these lectures of the early 1940s, Heidegger thus devoted himself to the remembrance of, and recognition in, modernity's other Greek inception. Along the way, Heidegger criticized the Nazis' conquest of the classical past. Western metaphysics counts, calculates, and appropriates, and Heidegger sees Nazi historicism as a way of approaching the irreducible particularity of the past from this vantage point.[50] Historicists look at the past as a "possession"; they "find" it and use it as "models to be imitated" whenever they are needed for the present (ÜVII, 212). The aesthetics of Western metaphysics—the "re-presentation" of the world in the service of technological rationality—provides the "means of representation" for this instrumental use of the past (ibid.).

By establishing "the classical" as the "exemplary" or model, *per se*, classicists disavowed their instrumental, calculating approach to the past by idealizing it (ÜVII, 158).[51] Was Heidegger here thinking of Hitler's inane dictum about Roman history as teacher? Of Rodenwaldt's resurrection of Augustus? Of Weber's *Princeps*? Of Speer's designs for Berlin/*Germania*? Heidegger certainly was aware of the many lectures, held in the context of Augustus's bimillenary, lectures like the one by Friedrich Matz, in which the latter expressed the hope that "German being" would arrive at the "true awareness of itself in the contemplation of antiquity."[52] And it is entirely plausible that he had the new, luxuriously illustrated Nazi world histories in mind when he made the following statement: "All historical instruction" and "selective, illustrated reporting about 'Worldhistory'" lacked a meaningful "relationship to history" (ÜXII, 51).

Heidegger thus applied his early critique of historicism to the Nazis' appropriation of antiquity, dissecting their acts of defining and taking possession of the past as Nietzschean conquests.[53] When he lectured in 1936 in Rome, the terrain of the fascist ideology and practice of *romanità* as the resurrection of ancient Rome, about *Hölderlin* and the search for German being, Heidegger had already made neo-Roman mimesis the object of his anti-historicist critique. "One cannot amass," Heidegger told his audience, "one's own" as if comparing imperial conquest and the Nazis' historicist relation to the past.[54] What we are looking for, Heidegger insisted, cannot "be replaced by some kind of rebirth of antiquity, indeed it *cannot be found* in a historicist manner."[55] This was a critique of neo-Roman mimesis of the Italian and the German kind, whose theorists and practitioners were busy conquering the Roman past, caught in their own present, their own will to power, and their own metaphysics. For Heidegger, to think historically involved a different journey, a journey of discovery, searching for the otherness of the past. This originary otherness of the West could only be rediscovered in the encounter with ancient Greece in the *future*, through the work of remembrance reserved for philosophers and poets. With this swerve away from politics, Heidegger ended his mission to reinvent the theory and politics of empire as thinking and acting in the danger zone.

In 1947, Speer insisted that "we were not just a gang of world conquerors babbling nonsense about master races" (SD, 57). His generation was attracted to the Nazis because of a shared "European pathos" and belief in new beginnings (ibid., translation modified). By the end of the war, Speer said later, Spengler's prediction seemed to come true that the "primitive people will prove superior" (SM, 185). Hitler couched the attack on the Soviet Union in Spenglerian terms, and in 1943 Goebbels echoed the idea that the clash between East and West concerned the entire Christian *Abendland*. Fighting this last battle was Germany's "historical mission."[56] Joseph Vogt, Karl Haushofer, Martin Heidegger, Werner Best, Carl Schmitt, and many other minor theorists I have discussed in this book shared this *Abendland* pathos—and they all ended up supporting National Socialism, invested in the question of whether or not to prolong the time of empire—and if so, how.

Epilogue: Anselm Kiefer's *Zersetzungen/ Disarticulations*

Jede konkrete Verortung ist . . . eine Art von Sichtbarkeit. CARL SCHMITT[1]

In 1969, Anselm Kiefer traveled through France and Italy and then published a series of photographs entitled "Besetzungen," or Occupations. These photographs depict the artist "occupying" different European sites, his right arm raised in the Hitler salute.[2] The series starts with Kiefer, shot from below as he stands on top of a government building, performing the *Sieg Heil* gesture, and ends with the artist facing the Baltic shore, his right arm again raised in the fascist "gesture of conquest."[3] We see Kiefer's back, and both setting and pose recall paintings by Caspar David Friedrich—not one of the mountain landscapes that Nazi artists copied with their granite quarries, but Friedrich's *Wanderer above the Misty Sea* (ca. 1818).

This last shot of the series is preceded by two photographs of Kiefer—facing us as he stands first in front of the Colosseum, then inside (figure E.1). The photographs of Kiefer at the Colosseum follow upon a shot of him, standing amid the ruins of *Paestum*—those "Doric" temples that Speer admired so much on his Grand Tour to Italy in 1935. Kiefer introduces the theme of the Nazis' neo-Roman mimesis early in the series with two shots: the occupier in Arles's Roman graveyard and the artist in Montpellier, standing in front of

E.1 Anselm Kiefer, *Occupations* (1969). From: Interfunktionen No. 12. Various Artists. Harvard Art Museum/Busch-Reisinger Museum, Antonia Paepke DuBrul Fund, 2001.206. Imaging Department © President and Fellows of Harvard College.

a Roman warrior. Barely visible in front of the giant statue, Kiefer's body imitates the Roman's gestures.

With *Besetzungen,* Kiefer revived the Third Reich's neo-Roman imaginary and the mimetic desires of all those conquerors and architects involved in monumentalizing empire. Dwarfed by the monumentalism of the Colosseum, Kiefer launched an attack on the Third Reich's imperial project and the gaze sustaining it, transforming imperial *Besetzung* into postimperial *Zer-Setzung*. In 2006, Kiefer's exhibit in the Grand Palais, *Sternenfall/Chute d'étoiles*, continued this demolition work. In this first *Monumenta* exhibition dedicated to a single artist, Kiefer shattered the entire scopic structure of the ruin gazer scenarios that I analyzed in this book.

The Paris show oscillated between unforgettable images and rather heavy-handed ruin kitsch. At the center of the exhibit stood two concrete towers, one in the process of falling, the other already collapsed, spewing its rubble across the floor of the Grand Palais. The layers of imperial decline that the central tower evoked were multiple: the fallen tower's gray material evoked the bunkers that the Nazis built along the Atlantic Ocean; a miniature submarine stranded among the rubble of the first tower reinforced the Hitlerian association. And who would not think of the watch towers guarding the most western border of the Soviet empire? But in 2006, the two collapsing towers were of course not objects devoid

E.2 Anselm Kiefer. *Tower* (2006). Photograph George Steinmetz.

of more contemporary associations. Kiefer made sure that we would not miss his allusions, commenting in the introduction to the exhibit that "everything collapses; we know everything collapses, we know that one day there will be grass growing where New York is now, we already know that."[4] What distinguished Kiefer, the neo-Romantic artist, from us was his ability to see the future in ruins: "But I can already see it," Kiefer stated. "I can already see the grass growing over New York." The exhibit's French commentator then made the point that "what we have here is the aspect of his [Kiefer's] recent work . . . closest to what is called the poetry of ruin."[5]

Tracing this ruin aesthetic from the eighteenth century to Kiefer, the commentator omitted the reference that sprang to my mind as soon as I heard Kiefer articulate his prophetic vision of the postmodern world's metropolis, Spengler's *Untergang*. Kiefer's *Chute d'étoiles/Sternenfall* could be read as a staging of Spengler's ruin gazer scenario with a crucial difference: on the one hand, Kiefer, the artist, emphatically positions himself as future ruin gazer: "I can already see it"—New York in ruins; on the other, the work of art itself does not allow for a singular gaze or scopic mastery. On the contrary, if you look again at the photograph of the tower, you will notice that the object is displayed in such a way that it disperses this gaze into a multitude of acts of looking. Or, put differently, there is not one position from which the crumbled tower can be fully apprehended. This *constellation of scopic dispersal* is very different from the tensions that characterize Spengler's scenarios of ruin gazing. And the constellation differs radically from the many scenarios of ruin gazing deployed by the Third Reich. For, as we know, those scenarios were designed with a sole purpose in mind: to keep the European ruin gazer in a position of mastery. With his broken tower, Kiefer took apart the entire imaginary hardware of neo-Roman mimesis.

Notes

INTRODUCTION

1. François-René de Chateaubriand, quoted in François Hartog, *Regimes of Historicity: Presentism and the Experience of Time*: 75.
2. Mary Beard, *SPQR: A History of Ancient Rome*: 15.
3. Saint-Just, quoted in François Hartog, *Anciens, modernes, sauvages*: 84.
4. The full quote reads: "The world has been empty since the Romans, and only their memory fills it and still prophesies liberty." Saint-Just, quoted in Friedrich Engels and Karl Marx, *The Holy Family or Critique of Critical Critique*: 164.
5. Hannah Arendt, *On Revolution*: 212.
6. Ibid.
7. George Washington praised the enlightened foundations of the American "imperium." Quoted in Helmut Anton Prantner, "Imperium USA: Die aktuelle englischsprachige Argumentation": 135.
8. See, for instance, George Steinmetz on US imperialism as "nonterritorial form of empire." Steinmetz, "Return to Empire: The New U.S. Imperialism in Comparative Perspective": 340. See also Julia Adams and George Steinmetz, "Sovereignty and Sociology: From State Theory to Theories of Empire." The United States changed from "benevolent hegemon" to empire, making Europe one of the subcenters. Herfried Münckler, *Empires*: 161.
9. Charles Maier, *Among Empires*: 41. In Michael Hardt and Antonio Negri's *Empire* (2000), imperial Rome was the model for the new world order. Ibid.: 20. On these debates, see Neville Morley, *The Roman Empire: Roots of Imperialism*: 6–8.
10. One of the chief examples is Jane Burbank and Fred Cooper's *Empires in World History* (2010).

11. Catharine Edwards, ed., *Roman Presences: Receptions of Rome in European Culture, 1789–1945*: 15.
12. Greg Woolf, "Inventing Empire in Ancient Rome": 312. Rome, Simon Goldhill put it, is "the Mother of Empires." Goldhill, "Introduction," in *Being Greek under Rome: Cultural Identity, the Second Sophistic and the Development of Empire*: 25.
13. The story of empires is a deep history of "repeated imitations of empire." Sheldon Pollock, "Empire and Imitation": 188. Arguing for a particular Western strand in this history of imitations, Pollock begins with an analytical caveat: the core elements of empire (rule over a vast and expanding territory, forms of communication across this imperial expanse, and the use of imperial culture and religion, signifying symbolic authority and unifying the "geobody") were assembled before Rome (182). Taking Rome as their model, the early modern and modern empires of the West continued to invent solutions to the "general imperial problem of how to rule large and differentiated dominions," inflecting the model in different ways (185). Burbank and Cooper observe that the "Roman model" lasted "for millennia, in political imagination." Jane Burbank and Fred Cooper, *Empires in World History: Power and the Politics of Difference*: 13 and 38.
14. Neville Morley, *The Roman Empire*: 2.
15. Many classicists and modernists have explored the afterlife of the Roman Empire during specific historical periods in specific national contexts. *The Conquest* would not have been possible without this body of research.
16. This book continues my work in "Imperial Ruin Gazers, or Why Did Scipio Weep?," published in *Ruins of Modernity*, ed. Julia Hell and Andreas Schönle: 169–192.
17. For the rest of the book, I will not use quotation marks around the concept of the barbarian.
18. David J. Mattingly, *Imperialism, Power, and Identity: Experiencing the Roman Empire*: 23.
19. It is because of this powerful effect on the history of the imperial West that Rome needs to be studied as much as its continued effects. On this point, see Morley, *The Roman Empire*: 13. What Greg Woolf defines as our *conventional* understanding of empire is the result of this endless imitation. See Woolf, *Rome: An Empire's Story*: 24.
20. Michael Hardt and Antonio Negri, *Empire*: 20. Immanuel Wallerstein best theorized this being-in-crisis with a world systems model that articulates contingent historical development and structural rise and decline. See, for instance, his *The Decline of American Power: The U.S. in a Chaotic World* (2003).
21. By locating the Third Reich in the context of this political and cultural legacy, I add historical depth to the existing scholarship on the imperial dimensions of the Third Reich. See, for instance, Mark Mazower, *Hitler's Empire: How the Nazis Ruled Europe*; Dirk Moses, "Empire and History: Reconceptualizing the Colonial Transfer Debate in National Socialism and the Holocaust"

and "Redemptive Anti-Semitism and the Imperialist Imaginary"; Birthe Kundrus's excellent piece "Colonialism, Imperialism, National Socialism: How Imperial Was the Third Reich?"; and Geoff Eley, "Empire by Land or Sea? Germany's Imperial Imaginary, 1840–1945."

22. Hannah Arendt, "Understanding and Politics (The Difficulty of Understanding)": 309.
23. Barbara Fuchs introduced the term in "Imperium Studies: Theorizing Early Modern Expansion": 71. Fuchs explores "links between metropolitan sovereignty and expansion abroad, and the cultural productions that sustain them both" (71). See also Fuchs's important contribution to the *theories and methodologies* section of *PMLA* 130.2, entitled "Another Turn for Transnationalism: Empire, Nation, and Imperium in Early Modern Studies," and the introduction to the section by Sahar Amer and Laura Doyle, "*Reframing Postcolonial and Global Studies in the Longer Durée.*" On ruin studies, see the introduction to *Ruins of Modernity*, ed. Julia Hell and Andreas Schönle: 1–14.
24. In theoretical terms, this approach pushes postcolonial theory into the longer *durée*, a point I will return to in the sections on "Interventions."
25. I explain the reasons for a break in this chronological organization at the end of the introduction.
26. An analytical narrative intertwining several threads, *The Conquest of Ruins* also allows readers to follow a particular strand. Imperial theorizing and the question of Rome's end, for instance, leads from Polybios to Volney, Herder, Gibbon, Bertrand, Spengler, Himmler, Schmitt, and Heidegger.
27. See Frederic Spotts, *Hitler and the Power of Aesthetics*: 358. Speer used Hitler's sketches for the Great Hall and the Arch.
28. Ibid.: 364. Germania's core would include museums like Wilhelm Kreis's "race museum" (361).
29. Albert Speer, *Spandauer Tagebücher (hereafter ST)*: 160. See also Speer, *Spandau: The Secret Diaries (hereafter SD)*: 107; translation modified.
30. Ferdinando Galli Bibiena, *L'Architettura civile*: 60. Piranesi also draws on the "stage-like compositions" in Claude Lorrain's *Küstenszene mit Landung des Aeneas* (1650), one of three allegories about the rise and fall of Rome, based on Virgil's *Aeneid*. Martin Sonnabend and Jon Whiteley, *Claude Lorrain: Die verzauberte Landschaft*: 47.
31. Speer calls it "Trauertuch," or a cloth of mourning (ST, 160).
32. Speer, *Inside the Third Reich: Memoirs (hereafter SM)*: 56. The law was based on Hitler's "theory of ruin value" (SM, 56).
33. It is an imperial past, contemplated in the postimperial present. On the anticipatory structure, see Hermann Sturm, "Gegenwartsformen der Vergangenheit—Zu einer Ästhetik des Diversen": 106.
34. Speer's imitation of Piranesi, the artist who defended Roman culture against eighteenth-century Hellenism, is more complex. Part of his later self-stylization as the neo-Romantic artist in love with Greek ruins (in contrast to Hitler's fascination with Rome's monumental ruins), Speers's drawing

combined Roman monumentalism (*Führerbau*) with Romantic Hellenism (Paestum-style columns).

35. Arendt, "Understanding": 320.
36. Ibid.: 312. The author who saw the Nazis as the Romans' best imitators, driven like the latter by the will to power, was Simone Weil (see preface to part 5). It is safe to assume that Arendt was familiar with Weil's 1940 essay.
37. Arendt, "Understanding": 319.
38. Ibid.: 321. Arendt privileges new beginnings over endings: "For whatever the historian calls an end, the end of a period or a tradition or a whole civilization, is a new beginning for those who are alive." Ibid.: 320.
39. Ibid.: 321.
40. Ibid.
41. Ibid.
42. Arendt argues against the first comparison, because it uncovers misleading "motives"—lust for conquest instead of economic imperialism (which is her argument in *The Origins of Totalitarianism*). The second comparison is not concerned with motives, but an existential situation. Nevertheless, the fact remains that she sees the Nazi empire as similar to Rome. The effect of the Nazis' Roman mimesis was powerful, creating a discursive reality that did not vanish after 1945. The Nazi regime eventually caused Arendt to reevaluate Roman authors like Cicero as "practical" philosophers and inventors of tradition. See Joy Connolly, "The Promise of the Classical Canon: Hannah Arendt and the Romans": 12.
43. A political formation, whose aim was to eradicate the very capacity for new beginnings, that is, subjectivity itself, reducing human beings in the camps to bare life.
44. Hannah Arendt, "Franz Kafka: A Revaluation" (1944): 74.
45. Ibid.
46. Ibid.
47. Ibid.; emphasis mine. In *Origins*, Arendt argued against the "temptation" to "yield to the mere process of disintegration," which "has assumed the spurious grandeur of 'historical necessity.'" Arendt, *The Origins of Totalitarianism*: vii–viii. The book was written to resist this temptation to give in to "growing decay" and the "belief in an unavoidable doom" (vii).
48. The house analogy is based on Aristotle, *METAPHYSICA (Metaphysics)*: 727.
49. Arendt, "Kafka": 74.
50. Ibid.; emphasis mine. This discussion of bourgeois notions of history as progress and of man's return to nature foreshadowed Arendt's thoughts on totalitarianism as ruination, as a return to the state of nature. Hobbes, the imperial philosopher of the bourgeoisie, is at the origin of a development that will displace the logic of expansion from the realm of the economy to that of politics. This imperial logic will destroy the nation-state, and ultimately its subjects.
51. Arendt is in dialogue with Walter Benjamin and Martin Heidegger: she di-

rectly draws on the former's critique of Marxist determinism and concept of messianism; and she indirectly engages Heidegger's 1921–1922 lectures on Aristotle, where he introduced "Ruinanz" as "Grundsinn der Bewegtheit faktischen Lebens." Martin Heidegger, *Phänomenologische Interpretationen zu Aristoteles*: 131. On "ruinance," see also Ryan Coyne, *Heidegger's Confessions: The Remains of Saint Augustine in Being and Time & Beyond*: 80.

52. Arendt, *Origins*: 469.
53. *Pleasure of Ruins* is a "perverse book" because "we are now living in a ruinous world (in which there are, above and under the earth, far more ruined than unruined buildings)." Macaulay, *Pleasure of Ruins*: vii.
54. And the experience of a fragile world: listing the crumbling castles of English kings and Ottoman sultans, Macaulay condenses her law of ruin into an image of accelerated decay, observing that "there is no security, which is what we always knew." Macaulay, *Pleasure*: 452.
55. Ibid.: xv.
56. Ibid.: 454.
57. Ibid.: 453 and 454.
58. Ibid.: xvii.
59. Ibid.: 454.
60. Ibid.: 455.
61. Ibid.
62. She does so through her exceedingly precise descriptions, the montage of texts by other ruin gazers, and illustrations. In the German context, we find a similar effort: Hans Vogel, *Die Ruine in der Darstellung der abendländischen Kunst* (1948).
63. Arendt, "Understanding": 308.
64. Macaulay, *Pleasure*: xvii. Macaulay was as committed to the British Empire as T. S. Eliot, who in 1944 declared Virgil's *Aeneid* Europe's foundational text. Virgil was the poet of "a moment of order and stability, of equilibrium and harmony"—in other words, the modernist's aesthetics is not that far removed from Macaulay's neoclassicism. T. S. Eliot, *What Is a Classic?*: 119.
65. As Alexander Demandt points out, people have found 210 causes for this decline. Demandt, *Der Fall Roms: Die Auflösung des römischen Reiches im Urteil der Nachwelt*: 695. This book emphatically does not add the 211th cause. I too study the centuries-long conversation about the fall of Rome, but unlike Demandt, with a focus on the connection between empire and ruins.
66. Like Heidegger (and Arendt via Heidegger), Polybios turned to Aristotle for his concept of the natural law of ruin. "[N]othing," Aristotle wrote, "will be eternal or unmovable; for all perceptible things perish and are in movement." *METAPHYSICA (Metaphysics)*: 724. No history of Rome omits Polybios's scene. See, for instance, Beard, *SPQR*: 172.
67. There is already a double logic at play in Polybios's text: the inexorable logic of rise and fall and the logic of contingency or the unpredictability of historical events.

68. Polybios thus turned the Romans' victory over Carthage in 146 BCE into an "irrevocably new event." Arendt, "Understanding": 320.
69. This study of the conceptualization of empire's time contributes to the research into Western "regimes of historicity" and the multiple layers of "historical temporalities" (or different ways of "conceptualizing time") that Alexandra Lianeri proposes in her introduction to *The Western Time of Ancient History: Historiographical Encounters with the Greek and Roman Past*: 15 and 10.
70. Ando, *Roman Social Imaginaries*: 21.
71. Ando, *Roman Social Imaginaries*: 4. Background understanding means "the common understanding that makes possible common practices and a widely shared sense of legitimacy" (ibid.).
72. Ibid.: 5.
73. And sometimes, negotiations and the trading of colonies among empires.
74. Arendt, *On Revolution*: 206. To avoid potential misunderstandings, the unexpected event (which I discussed earlier) is different from Arendt's concept of beginning.
75. Ibid.: 212.
76. Ibid.: 213.
77. Arendt thinks of the idea of a *new beginning* as proper to (European) modernity. However, conceptualizing the aim of a new beginning takes Arendt back to the Greek polis (as space of political action) via the "buried concept" of freedom, the ultimate goal of new beginnings. This is "a conceptual return" to antiquity. Miriam Leonard, "Arendt's Revolutionary Antiquity": 54, 61.
78. Ibid.: 206. Among the Romans' long-lived innovations was the "idea of '*humanitas*'": civilization as "the distinguishing possession of insiders with the right to rule barbarians," which became the foundation of the West's notion of the civilizing mission. Burbank and Cooper, *Empires*: 41.
79. On the Russian case, see Katerina Clark, *Moscow, The Fourth Rome: Stalinism, Cosmopolitanism, and the Evolution of Soviet Culture, 1931–1941*.
80. This chronology is based on Wallerstein's analysis of the "long sixteenth century" as the moment of the emergence of the capitalist world system and Charles V's failed "alternative." Immanuel Wallerstein, "Charles V and the Nascent Capitalist World-Economy": 365.
81. The theory and practice of post-Roman mimesis is at certain times more pronounced than others, coming to the foreground most strongly during periods of conquest. I thus differ from Duncan Bell, who argues that Rome's fall was not an issue as long as British writers thought this eventual fall belonged to the "distant future." Duncan Bell, *The Idea of Greater Britain: Empire and the Future World Order, 1860–1900*: 223.
82. The boundaries are rendered both obsolete and meaningful, since every single nation at some point claims to be Rome's true inheritor.
83. As the case of the *Kaiserreich* and the Nazi empire will show, the post-Roman theme is much more prevalent in the German case than we previously assumed.

84. Barbara Fuchs explores "state-sponsored mimesis" in the imperial context in *Mimesis and Empire: The New World, Islam, and European Identity*: 5. Natasha Eaton studies *Mimesis across Empires: Artworks and Networks in India 1765–1860*. On the transnational context, see Kader Konuk, *East West Mimesis: Auerbach in Turkey*.
85. J. Laplanche and J.-B. Pontalis, *The Language of Psychoanalysis*: 318.
86. My use of Freudian categories takes into account Simon Goldhill's discussion of Stoic debates about "the faculty of vision" in the wake of Plato and Aristotle and the idea of "'the soul's desire to see.'" Goldhill, "Refracting Classical Vision: Changing Cultures of Viewing": 23.
87. It is this position of scopic mastery that Speer rescued with his post-1945 ruin images.
88. Julia Hell, "Ruins Travel: Orphic Journeys through 1940s Germany": 127. Here I explore the nexus of scopic scenarios and ruins in the context of the empiricist epistemology of postwar realism.
89. Or articulations of "philosophical, aesthetic, and technological assumptions and practices." Martin Jay, "Scopic Regimes of Modernity Revisited": 55.
90. Ancient Greek historians and poets thought of history as a spectacle performed under the gaze of the gods.
91. Richard Jenkyns, *God, Space & City in the Roman Imagination*: 8. Initially, Latin *scaena* meant "'backdrop,' then more broadly 'stage' or 'setting'" (8).
92. This empiricist epistemology (foregrounding visible appearances against non-visible laws or structures) informs Lacan's concept of the imaginary, a register in which we experience the world as visible, and we experience it as understandable *because* it is visible—discernible to our gaze, the empiricist gaze of the spectator, scanning the stage and the world's surface in search of its meaning.
93. Ando, *Roman Social Imaginaries*: 5. Inviting "historical reflection on the imbrication of linguistic-cognitive shift and contextual change," Ando aims for "an inquiry into the distinctive flavour of Roman ordering of the world" and the study of "distinctive ways of being and reflecting" (ibid.).
94. I borrow the term from Martin Jay, who introduced it into the study of the visual cultures of modernity; see his "Scopic Regimes of Modernity Revisited": 51–63.
95. Beginning with military conquest, "land-appropriation" inaugurates the "process of order and orientation that is based on firm land and establishes law." Schmitt, *The Nomos of the Earth*: 80.
96. Ibid.: 194. Being master of the territory is the condition for the sovereignty-exception nexus Schmitt theorized in *Political Theology*.
97. Schmitt, *The Nomos*: 70 and 68. That is, it was derived from the "original distribution of land," not one based on some universalist rule of law (68).
98. "Raum und Rom" or space and Rome, he wrote later, "is the same word." Carl Schmitt, "*Raum* und *Rom*—Zur Phonetik des Wortes Raum" (1951): 491.
99. Schmitt, *The Nomos*: 70.

100. *Nomos* derives from the "taking," "distributing," and "use," representing three different acts in the "Ur-Drama of human history in three acts." Carl Schmitt, "Der neue Nomos der Erde" (1955): 518. The most explicit program to educate "the power of visualization" of the empire's citizens as the condition for grasping the drama taking place on "the world-wide stage" is H. J. Mackinder's "The Teaching of Geography from an Imperial Point of View, and the Use Which Could and Should Be Made of Visual Instruction" (1911): 80, 81.
101. See David Atkinson, "Hitler's Grand Tour: The Triumphal Entrance to Rome 1938": 10.
102. Spiro Kostof, "The Emperor and the Duce: The Planning of Piazzale Augusto Imperator in Rome": 287. In the process they transformed the crumbling edifice into an "authentic Roman ruin" (289).
103. This interminable process of reassembling the ruined Roman stage with the aid of various media also involved Carthage's Roman stage.
104. My use of "resurrectional" is based in Virgil's use of the verb *resurgere* (see chapter 6).
105. Walter Benjamin, "The Work of Art in the Age of Mechanical Reproduction": 223. Critically analyzing mass culture in a reified world, Benjamin simultaneously argued that mass media enabled the resurgence of a phylogenetically and ontogenetically older "creative form of mimesis." Susan Buck-Morss, *The Dialectics of Seeing: Walter Benjamin and the Arcades Project*: 263. This mimetic faculty involves recognizing and producing similarities. See Benjamin, "On the Mimetic Faculty" (1933).
106. On this nexus of ruins and description, see my "Ruins Travel": 126–128. The classical texts on the descriptive aesthetics of colonialism are Edward Said's *Orientalism* and Svetlana Alpers's *The Dutch Art of Describing: Dutch Art in the Seventeenth Century*. Analyzing the appropriative aesthetic of Orientalism, Said coined the term "descriptive realism" as an aspect of "radical realism." Said, *Orientalism*: 87, 72. Alpers explored this descriptive mode in the context of Dutch colonialism. See also Alex Potts on the "particularities of a form of description" in Winckelmann's writings "that sits on the boundary between scientific knowing and aesthetic experience," the former drawing on the "empiricism" of the enlightenment's "regimes of description," a practice developed among other things in travelogues. Potts, "Disparities between Part and Whole in the Description of Works of Art": 135 and 136.
107. Julia Hell and Andreas Schönle, "Introduction": 7.
108. Peter Geimer, *Die Vergangenheit der Kunst: Strategien der Nachträglichkeit im 18. Jhd.*: 123.
109. Ibid.: 122.
110. Ibid.: 122.
111. Hell and Schönle, "Introduction": 7.
112. Geimer, *Die Vergangenheit der Kunst*: 123.
113. Humboldt (1804), quoted in Geimer, *Die Vergangenheit der Kunst*: 123. In the

context of post-Roman mimesis, the inability to avert the gaze from Rome's remains is caused by the obsession with Rome's fall.

114. Digital media have taken these reconstruction and immersion techniques to a new level. See, for instance, the chapter entitled "Rome: Jumping over the Line" in Todd Presner, David Shepard, and Yoh Kawano, eds., *HyperCities: Thick Mapping in the Digital Humanities*: 128–133. See also the website for Andrea Caradini, *The Atlas of Ancient Rome: Biography and Portraits of the City*, 2 vols., http://atlasofancientrome.com; or the digital printing of Palmyra's destroyed arch.
115. Arendt, *The Life of the Mind*: 76.
116. "There is no simple Roman model to follow," Beard writes in *SPQR*: 535. I would add that there were many Roman models created by post-Romans.
117. I concentrate on public performances of identification. This is thus not an argument about an individual ruler's psyche and psychic investments, though there is enough literature to support the claim that Mussolini, for instance, deeply identified first with Caesar, then Augustus.
118. Like Roman, post-Roman imperial imaginaries are thus discursive formations that are not identical with, but tilt toward, the register of the imaginary. That is, they operate according to the identitarian logic and draw on the capacity proper to the imaginary to call forth an image of what is absent.
119. Volney's description of Palmyra is an act of resurrectional realism. Scrutinizing ruins, he asked readers to imagine the city before its ruination, thus switching from the register of the imperial to the post-Roman gaze.
120. Alpers, *The Dutch Art of Describing*: xxi.
121. I also gestured at Lacan's imaginary, the register of being in the world that obeys the empiricist logic of visibility and identity/sameness. The imaginary is also the register of scopic desire, of a subject in search of images confirming that elusive identity. However, the moment of specular identity already involves the symbolic as the register of the desire for scopic *mastery*: in the imaginary, we are positioned at the center of the field of vision, but haunted by the knowledge that we are ourselves an object in the field of vision of the other—and desiring this other gaze.
122. On Freud's later anti-empiricism as the step from discovering the laws of nature to a theory of the unconscious and its mechanisms, see Anthony Elliott, "Psychoanalysis and the Theory of the Subject."
123. Freud, *The Complete Letters of Sigmund Freud to Wilhelm Fliess 1887–1904*: 285. In Polybios's scene, Hamilcar Barca asks his son to swear that he will "take vengeance on the Romans." Polybios, *Histories*: 189. The link between "Semitic defiance" and Jewish anxiety includes Dido. Ellen Oliensis, *Freud's Rome: Psychoanalysis and Latin Poetry*: 129. Freud's ambivalent relationship to Rome is legendary. Identifying with Hannibal, Freud also implied that his ancestors followed the Romans to Cologne, *colonia* in Barbarian territory. See David Damrosh, "The Politics of Ethics: Freud and Rome": 121. Freud, *An Autobiographical Study*: 8.

124. Christopher Bollas, *Hysteria*: 118. Freud traced his obsession with Hannibal to his fascination with archeology. Freud, *The Interpretation of Dreams*: 196–198.
125. Freud, "Fragment of an Analysis": 12; "Bruchstück einer Hysterie-Analyse": 92.
126. Freud, "The Aetiology of Hysteria": 193.
127. Ibid.: 192; and Freud, "Zur Ätiologie der Hysterie": 54.
128. Freud, "The Aetiology of Hysteria": 192. On the importance of Heinrich Schliemann, see Richard Armstrong, *A Compulsion for Antiquity: Freud and the Ancient World*: 114ff.
129. Freud, "The Aetiology of Hysteria": 192.
130. Ibid.
131. Ibid.
132. Ibid.
133. The English version of the text contains translates "*Trümmerfeld*" ("Zur Ätiologie der Hysterie": 54) as "expanse of ruins" ("The Aetiology of Hysteria": 192). Yet so far, Freud has not yet used the word; instead, he writes about "Trümmer[feld]," remains (as in *Mauerreste*), fragments (as in *Bruchstücke*), and then "Schutt," or rubbish/debris ("Zur Ätiologie der Hysterie": 54).
134. Freud, "Zur Ätiologie der Hysterie": 54.
135. Freud, "The Aetiology of Hysteria": 192; translation modified and "Zur Ätiologie der Hysterie": 54.
136. Ibid.
137. Freud, "Zur Ätiologie der Hysterie": 54.
138. Freud, "The Aetiology of Hysteria": 193; "Zur Ätiologie der Hysterie": 55. The example of the "traumatic scene" that Freud then adduces traces the symptom back to an "experience" that is once again visual: "the sight of a decomposing dead body." Freud, "The Aetiology of Hysteria": 194.
139. Freud, "The Aetiology of Hysteria": 193.
140. Freud, "The Aetiology of Hysteria": 192–193.
141. And second, what is the role of the explorer's interpretation of the stones—for clearly, they do not speak. See Andrew Collier, "Critical Realism," for a discussion of psychoanalysis and its surface/depth model in terms of (critical) realism.
142. Freud, "From the History of an Infantile Neurosis": 41; translation modified.
143. Ibid.: 38, 45, 35.
144. Freud, *Aus der Geschichte einer infantile Neurose*: 154.
145. All political thinkers from Plato and Aristotle to Cicero defined the "real business of politics" as "evading the threat of natural decline." Reinhart Koselleck, *Futures Past: On the Semantics of Historical Time*: 98. Proposing mixed constitutions to stave off this decline, they "shared the idea of a space of political experience limited by nature" (ibid.).
146. Virgil, *The Aeneid* (hereafter AFa), transl. Robert Fagles: 115.
147. Aaron Seider, *Memory in Virgil's Aeneid*: 89.

148. Maier, *Among Empires*: 286.
149. Heiner Müller, *Mommsens Block* (1993): 258.
150. More specifically, Rome's fall is traced to racial mixing and the Romans' practices of assimilating the barbarians they had conquered, and in Hitler's case, to the corroding influence of Jews.
151. He did so on the terrain of native policy. Addressing London's Classical Association. Cromer began his lecture entitled *"Ancient and Modern Imperialism"* (1909) with a gesture of legitimation: "Imperialism is as old as the world." Lord Cromer, *Ancient and Modern Imperialism*: 4. The body of Cromer's lecture was devoted to asserting the superiority of British imperialism over its Roman predecessor, a superiority that was based on a fundamental similarity between the Roman and British character and methods of rule—the difference resulting from Britons being the better Romans.
152. As Duncan Bell writes, they "became a fixture in the entrance exam for the Indian civil service." Duncan Bell, *The Idea of Greater Britain*: 216.
153. Lord Cromer, *Ancient and Modern Imperialism*: 37 and 36.
154. Ibid.: 3.
155. On this topic, see for instance Mark Bradley's "Introduction" to *Classics and Imperialism in the British Empire*: 1–25.
156. Simon Goldhill, "Introduction," in *Being Greek under Rome*: 25. In turn, scholars of antiquity using postcolonial theory have been accused of anachronism.
157. Michael Taussig, *Mimesis and Alterity: A Particular History of the Senses*: 236.
158. In *The Devil's Handwriting: Precoloniality and the German Colonial State in Qindao, Samoa, and Southwest Africa*, George Steinmetz explores the processes of identification of colonizers with colonized.
159. This triangulation is part of David Quint's *Epic and Empire*; Fuchs's *Mimesis and Empire*; Sabine MacCormack's *On the Wings of Time: Rome, the Incas, Spain, and Peru,* and the work of other authors analyzing early modern Western empires.
160. At stake is the history and theory "of how Europe had consolidated itself as sovereign subject by defining its colonies as 'Others,' even as it constituted them, for purposes of administration and the expansion of markets, into programmed near-images of that sovereign self." Gayatri Spivak, "The Rani of Samur: An Essay in Reading the Archives" (1985): 247.
161. Sometimes in the context of heightened rivalry among imperial powers. Woolf, *Rome: An Empire's Story*: 22.
162. The concept of sovereignty, Fuchs argues, never lost its link to the Roman concept of *imperium* because the "political and cultural authority" of European "imperialism and nation formation" are grounded in the idea of "*translatio imperii.*" Fuchs, "Imperium Studies": 72, 73.
163. Morley, *The Roman Empire*: 17.
164. Ibid.: 17. Augustus was the first to use the phrase "imperium populi Romanum" to mean empire in the territorial sense. He did so in his *Res Gestae*

Divi Augusti. Karl Galinsky, *Augustus: Introduction to the Life of an Emperor*: 159. He also distinguished between the magistrate's *potestas* (power) and his *auctoritas* as power "rooted in personal leadership qualities and initiative." Ibid.: 70. The change from "a command" to "territorial empire" occurred in the decade before Augustus's reign. Woolf, "Inventing Empire in Ancient Rome": 313.

165. Galinsky, *Augustus*: 71.
166. By adding to this personal dimension that Augustus's power ultimately "rested on his control of the army," Galinsky points in the direction of later concepts of Caesarism. Galinsky, *Augustus*: 71.
167. This is centralized, absolute power in theory, not practice. Empires are "polyethnic, multicultural," and, most importantly, "politically centrifugal." Osterhammel, *Die Verwandlung der Welt: Eine Geschichte des 19. Jahrhunderts*: 610.
168. Arendt, *On Revolution*: 203.
169. In *Political Theology*, Carl Schmitt famously argued that modern political concepts carry the shadow of theological concepts, elaborating on the connection to Roman pagan theology later (see chapter 24). The concept of the post-Roman imperial sovereign, I propose, never sheds the Roman shadow of the ruler legitimated by theology, pagan or otherwise. This imperial angle locates the imagination of the sovereign in the *longer durée* thematized by Ernst Kantorowicz in the wake of Schmitt. "[T]he substance of the idea of the King's Two Bodies had been anticipated in pagan Antiquity," especially in the "duplication" at work in practices concerning the "divinity" of Roman emperors. Kantorowicz, *The King's Two Bodies: A Study in Medieval Political Theology*: 505, 501, 500.
170. See Johannes Fabian, *Time and the Other: How Anthropology Makes Its Object* (1983), on the denial of "coevalness" (31ff).
171. Jay originally proposed four scopic regimes or characteristic "epochal configurations." Martin Jay, "Scopic Regimes of Modernity Revisited": 57. Analyzing the role of visuality and visual regimes in the context of empire, the editors and contributors of *Visions of Empire* extend the reach of the concept of scopic regimes into non-European domains and alternative modernities.
172. On the most abstract level, I am thus moving closer to the Lacanian concept of (Western) modernity and its visual regime.
173. In Aristotelian rhetoric, *topos* is the point of departure of an argument; here, the topos is a never-ending argument about the end of empire.
174. Although sometimes they become "new barbarians." On the Benjaminian notion of "positive barbarism," see Hardt and Negri, *Empire*: 215.
175. Morley, *The Roman Empire*: 13.
176. For the opposing view foregrounding racialization, see Alejandro Colas, *Empire*: 117ff.
177. Mattingly, *Imperialism*: 23.
178. Osterhammel, *Die Verwandlung der Welt*: 610.

179. Mattingly, *Imperialism*: 23.
180. Anthony Pagden, *The Fall of Natural Man: The American Indian and the Origins of Comparative Ethnology* (1982): 16.
181. Ibid.: 16. Greek was the language of reason, the faculty indispensable for the creation of community.
182. Ibid.: 16 and 18.
183. François Hartog, *Memories of Odysseus: Frontier Tales from Ancient Greece*: 101.
184. Beard, *SPQR*: 67; and Caesar, *Seven Commentaries on The Gallic War*: 80. To Aristotle and Cicero, barbarians "lacked the necessary qualities for membership of the civitas." Anthony Pagden, *Lords of All the World: Ideologies of Empire in Spain, Britain and France c. 1500–c. 1800*: 21. In contrast to Aristotle, for whom "'barbarians' hovered on the very edge of humanity," Cicero thought that the empire's subjects "were entitled to just rule despite being 'savage and barbarous nations'" (24, 22).
185. Cicero already thematized the tensions around exclusion versus inclusion that were "to persist in all later European conceptions of empire." Pagden, *Lords*: 23.
186. In this instance, the Germanic tribes east of the Elbe.
187. Bertrand, quoted in Patricia Lorcin, *Imperial Identities: Stereotyping, Prejudice & Race in Colonial Algeria*: 205.
188. Mattingly, *Imperialism*: 34.
189. Edward W. Said, *Orientalism*: 172, 170. A "degenerate surface," the Orient was only valued for the "contacts it had with a distant European past" (171, 85).
190. See chapter 11 for the Algerian case, for instance.
191. *An Absence of Ruins* is the title of a novel by Orlando Patterson, a reference to Derek Walcott's poem "The Royal Palms . . . an absence of ruins" (1962), which Patterson uses as one of his epigraphs. See Patterson, *An Absence of Ruins* (2012): no page nrs.
192. The correspondence of ruin (as material object) and allegory (as ruin in thought) rests on the analysis of modern historical consciousness as experiencing eschatological history in ruins. See Benjamin, *The Origin of German Tragic Drama*: 159–182. The Benjaminian paradigm informs *Irresistible Decay: Ruins Reclaimed*, ed. Michael Roth, Claire Lyons, and Michael Merewether.
193. Oswald Spengler, *Der Untergang des Abendlandes (hereafter U)*: 329.
194. Oswald Spengler, *The Decline of the West*, vol. 1: *Form and Actuality*, transl. Charles Francis Atkinson (hereafter DI): 254. I will also use *The Decline of the West*, vol. 2: *Perspectives of World History* (1996; hereafter DII), transl. Charles Francis Atkinson. Where Atkinson's translation is not accurate or in need of updating, I will use Spengler, *Der Untergang des Abendlandes (U)*.
195. On the contrary, in classical antiquity, people "cleared out of sight everything that did not speak of the present" (DI, 254). "We," on the other hand, not content with painting ruins, even create them artificially in our gardens. On Spengler's reinvention of the imperial imaginary and the epistemology of ruins, see chapter 16.

196. Michel Makarius, for instance, asserts that before the fifteenth century, there was only rubble: vestiges, wreckage, broken things—useless *"Trümmer."* Makarius, *Ruinen: Die gegenwärtige Vergangenheit*: 9. Ruins are "[r]emnants to whom one ascribes a symbolic and aesthetic dignity" (9). Living the experience of a new world by resurrecting the past, the intellectuals of the Renaissance appropriated antiquity by establishing it as "absolutely different" (22). Depicting ruins was one way of doing this. Signs of a new era, their ruins also expressed a deep nostalgia for an archaic, irretrievably lost, totality of meaning. See also *Ruinenbilder*, ed. Aleida Assmann, Monika Gomille, and Gabriele Rippl (2002). Here, Margaret M. McGowan begins with Petrarca's Rome visit in her "Unwillkürliches Gedächtnis": 19. See also Andreas Schönle, *The Architecture of Oblivion: Ruins and Historical Consciousness in Russia*; and Helmut Puff, *Miniature Monuments: Modeling German History*.
197. Her examples of pre-Renaissance ruin pleasure and fear include the Book of Daniel, Greco-Roman ruin landscapes on Pompeiian wall paintings, and a letter from Cicero about Corinth. "[T]he sudden sight of the ruins," Cicero wrote in this letter, "had more effect on me than on the actual inhabitants, for long contemplation had had the hardening effect of length of time upon their souls." Macaulay, *The Pleasure*: 5.
198. Ibid.: 6. As Ahuvia Kahane states, the ruin "is as much an ancient idea as it is a product of modernity." Kahane, "Antiquity and the Ruin: Introduction": 631. On the need for further study of the ruin in classical antiquity, see ibid.: 637. This special issue on the *Ruins of Antiquity* (2011) ranges from Greco-Roman antiquity to the twentieth century.
199. Macaulay, *The Pleasure*: 7.
200. For the multilayered meaning of this concept of imperial ruins, see the preface to part 1 and the end of chapter 4. In *Writing Rome*, Catharine Edwards explores the representation of the city as a "multi-layered" place, including the ancient ruins of the city's Latin past. See the introduction to her *Writing Rome: Textual Approaches to the City*, and 31. In a recent piece, Edwards reads the ruin as "traces of violent ruptures in the history of [the] city." Edwards, "Imagining Ruins in Ancient Rome": 645. In contrast, Richard Alston argues for a "dialectic between the ruin and the imperial state." His ultimate goal is to argue against Hegelian narratives that "force us to overdraw distinctions between, for instance, the ideologies of empire, ancient and modern, between the structures of domination in different times." Alston, "Seeing Caesar in Ruins: Towards a Radical Aesthetics of Ruins": 697, 711. While I sympathize with Alston's project of studying the nexus of empire and ruins across the antiquity/modernity divide, I disagree with Alston's—more indirect than direct—thesis of a continuous Western totalitarianism.
201. See, for instance, Simon Goldhill, "Refracting Classical Vision: Changing Cultures of Viewing" (1996).
202. James Porter, "Reception Studies: Future Prospects": 476.

203. With Ulysses as the "the bourgeois subject's Ur-image," Horkheimer and Adorno introduced the longer *durée* into the study of subjectivity. Max Horkheimer and Theodor W. Adorno, *Dialectic of Enlightenment*: 43; translation modified. Recovering this deep historical dimension of critical theory, I argue that in the course of the long history of post-Roman mimesis, the Roman conqueror/emperor emerged as the *Ur-image* of the West's imperial sovereign.
204. Since Arendt's *The Origins of Totalitarianism*, the connection between imperialism/colonialism and Nazi genocide and war of annihilation has been researched extensively. See, for instance, Jürgen Zimmerer, "The Birth of the Ostland Out of the Spirit of Colonialism: A Postcolonial Perspective on the Nazi Policy of Conquest and Extermination."
205. Arendt, "Understanding": 319.
206. In her own words: "only as the end and the culmination of everything that happened before." Ibid.: 319.
207. Ibid.
208. Arendt writes about tracing the "crystallizing elements" that produced totalitarianisms. Ibid.: 310.
209. Arendt, "Understanding": 319.
210. This is still the case despite Hitler's well-known pronouncements on the Roman model and, more importantly, the excellent scholarship on the Third Reich and antiquity. That Nazi leaders and intellectuals raided classical antiquity is now well documented. See, for instance, Johann Chapoutot's monumental *Greeks, Romans, Germans: How the Nazis Usurped Europe's Classical Past*; and the work of the architectural historian Alex Scobie in his *Hitler's State Architecture: The Impact of Classical Antiquity*. See also Näf's study of the discipline of classics, Beat Näf, ed., *Antike und Altertumswissenschaft in der Zeit von Faschismus und Nationalsozialismus*.
211. In view of the Western tendency to downplay the brutality of the ancient empire, Mattingly demands a "demolition job." Mattingly, *Imperialism*: 13, 22. The Nazis' post-Roman mimesis, I would argue, took care of this demolition by revealing the face of death behind the Roman mask. However, let us not forget Beard's plea not to "demonise" the Roman Empire. Beard, *SPQR*: 536. For instance, unlike citizenship in Greece, Roman citizenship was not based on ethnicity. On this topic see Beard, *SPQR*: 48, 49. Beard also reminds us that "modern critiques of imperialism" have their precedents among Roman authors (536).
212. For a definition of the term, see François Hartog, *Regimes of Historicity*: xv.
213. Reinhard Koselleck, "'Progress' and 'Decline': An Appendix to the History of Two Concepts": 235. More precisely, Koselleck argued that progress shed its "natural background meaning," while decline didn't, emerging "again and again as the aporia of progress" (221 and 231).
214. On nineteenth-century British "cyclical vision[s]" of empire, "following pre-

determined trajectories," for instance, see Duncan Bell, *Reordering the World: Essays on Liberalism and Empire* (2016): 119–131.

215. Beard, *SPQR*: 536.
216. There is an excellent body of scholarship on the role of classics in the training of colonial officials (Spanish-Portuguese; British; French); and intellectual histories about the discourse about Rome.
217. Peter Longerich, *Heinrich Himmler*: 13. As Karl Galinsky and his colleagues demonstrate in *Memoria Romana: Memory in Rome and Rome in Memory*, the Roman political and intellectual elite set up their canon of political and philosophical texts as well as works of art and architecture with later generations in mind. European imperialism's post-Roman mimesis is one of the ways in which Rome was remembered—and had itself remembered.
218. The British Empire, Lord Roseberry insisted in 1883, "has made its own history; it is creating its own precedent," pursuing "its [own] path into the future." Quoted in Duncan Bell, *The Idea of Greater Britain*: 223.
219. Suleiman I, Ottoman ruler and opponent of Charles V, eschatologically legitimized his reign as "Emperor of the Last Age" by drawing on the Book of Daniel. Anthony Pagden, *Worlds at War: The 2,500-Year Struggle between East and West*: 278. On Mehmed II and eschatology, see Kaya Sahin, "Constantinople and the End of Times: The Ottoman Conquest as a Portent of the Last Hour."
220. Contemporary report, quoted in Can Bilsel, *Antiquity on Display: Regimes of the Authentic in Berlin's Pergamon Museum*: 39.
221. Arguably, this formation also includes Virgil, committed to the Augustan restoration of the traditional theo-political values of the Italian soldier-farmer.
222. Morley, *The Roman Empire*: 2. Morley's study comes with a plea for self-reflexivity: "the way that Rome has been claimed as one of the foundations of our entire civilization, is precisely why we need to keep studying it: the Roman Empire is still ruling us" (13). *The Conquest of Ruins* is another contribution to "break[ing] its power over the modern imagination" (135).

CHAPTER ONE

1. And will become a "tributary empire." Woolf, *Rome*: 98.
2. Morley, *The Roman Empire*: 16. Founded by Phoenician settlers, Carthage created overseas colonies as "trading centers." Adrian Goldsworth, *The Fall of Carthage*: 27.
3. Morley, *The Roman Empire*: 16.
4. Woolf, *Rome*: 64.
5. Morley, *The Roman Empire*: 17.
6. That Romans made the city inhabitable by sowing salt is a legend, and some ruins were left for touring visitors. R. T. Ridley, "To Be Taken with a Pinch of Salt": 142.

7. Pliny the Elder, *The Natural History*, ed. John Bostock, at Perseus Digital Library, vol. 35, 7.4.
8. Appian, *The Punic Wars*, ed. and transl. Horace White, at Perseus Digital Library, chapter 20, section 134. On Appian, see David Potter, "The Greek Historians of Imperial Rome": 328–329.
9. Ibid.
10. Originally intending to narrate Rome's rise from 220 to 168 BCE, Polybios expanded *The Histories* to cover the period from 264 to 146 BCE.
11. Ellen O'Gorman, "Cato the Elder and the Destruction of Carthage": 101, 102.
12. Ibid.: 102, 103.
13. Polybios, *The Rise of the Roman Empire, transl. by Ian Scott-Kilvert, selected with an introduction by F. W. Walbank* (hereafter R): 528. For an outline of the *Histories*, see Brian McGing, *Polybius' Histories*: 223–239.
14. The transmission of the forty books of the *Histories* is incomplete. While parts of the final books are missing, they were reported by Appian. For this crucial passage about the destruction of Carthage, I am using the Loeb edition of Polybios's *Histories*, where the missing pages are replaced by Appian's text. This form of transmission allows us to read it as Polybios's text. On the transmission, see Walbank, "Introduction": 35–37; see also Pocock, *Barbarism and Religion*, vol. 3: 35.
15. Embracing the "entire oikoumene," the Roman conquest represented a "real break and the beginning of a new era of history." Hartog, *Memories*: 152.
16. This set the agenda for the "historians of the late Republic and early Principate." David Potter, "The Greek Historians of Imperial Rome": 316.
17. Hartog, *L'histoire d'Homère à Augustin*: 142.
18. *Sunopsis* means two things: "seeing everything simultaneously" and, in Stoic philosophy, "the ambition to seize (understand) the totality." Hartog, "Polybius and the First Universal History": 35, 36. Polybios is the first in a long line of historians of empire who "by their ocular observations render the conquest easy [to grasp]," thus acting as "custodians of the imperial imagination." Pagden, *Lords of All the World*: 32.
19. Koselleck, "Transformations of Experience": 62; and Hartog, *L'histoire*: 141.
20. Hartog, "Polybius and the First Universal History": 38. Polybios turned the distinction between poetry and history against Aristotle "by slipping from the general (*to katholou*) to the catholic (*historia katholike*)" (38).
21. Hartog, *L'histoire*: 141. Polybios's synoptic view rests on the historian taking up the "point of view of Fortune" (141). I will return to this point later. See also Koselleck, "Transformations of Experience," on Polybios's "unity of geographically differentiated histories" (61).
22. It is futile to expect to garner an "impression of the shape, arrangement and order of the whole world" by traveling to the empire's various cities, writing their separate stories. Reading these various "reports and events" separately would amount to "behaving like a man who, when he has examined the

dissected parts of a body which was once alive and beautiful, imagines that he has beheld the living animal in all its grace and movement" (R, 45).

23. Tonio Hölscher, *The Language of Images in Roman Art*: 32.
24. Hartog, *Memories*: 152.
25. Augustine, *Concerning the City of God*: 72.
26. See chapter 7.
27. R. G. Collingwood, *The Idea of History*: 34.
28. Ibid.: 34.
29. Frank W. Walbank, "The Idea of Decline in Polybius": 43.
30. According to Walbank, "the future fall of Rome" does not concern Polybios. "The Idea of Decline in Polybius": 42. I will argue the contrary.
31. Walbank, "The Idea of Decline": 53. Polybios was the first to combine mixed constitution and *anacyclosis* into a "naturalistic sequence of constitutional forms" from birth to death (49–51). He called this the "cycle of constitutions [politeion anakuklosis]." McGing, *Polybius' Histories*: 177. The cycle is "driven" by "nature," and constitutions eventually "return to their original form" (177). See McGing on the debate about Polybios's "internal inconsistency," his welding together of "the concept of cycle and the linear progression of the biological pattern" (from birth to death) (176).
32. Aristotle, *METAPHYSICA (Metaphysics)*: 724.
33. Ibid.: 727.
34. Walbank, "The Idea of Decline": 42.
35. Ibid.: 41. To Polybios, the Macedonian Empire's end was a "shattering event" (ibid.). His positive teleology (on the one hand, Rome as the strongest of the four empires; on the other, the empire's limited duration) is an instance of a "relative model of progress," relative because there is no "path" toward "further progress," no "opening up into the future" as is the case in modern conceptions of time. Koselleck, "'Progress' and 'Decline'": 222.
36. Frank W. Walbank, *Polybius, Rome, and the Hellenistic World: Essays and Reflections*: 233.
37. Robert B. Strassler, ed., *The Landmark Herodotus: The Histories*: 3.
38. Martin Jay, *Downcast Eyes*: 25.
39. Appian, *The Punic Wars*, chapter 19, section 129.
40. Ibid. Archeological digs give credence to Appian's "lurid description." Goldsworthy, *The Fall of Carthage*: 352.
41. Appian, *The Punic Wars*, chapter 19, section 130.
42. Ibid. Appian writes from the Roman viewpoint, including at times the perspective of the conquered. See Pocock, *Barbarism and Religion*, vol. 1: *The First Decline*: 39. On the latter convention, see Harald Fuchs, *Der geistige Widerstand gegen Rom* ([1933] 1965): 17.
43. Goldsworthy, *The Fall of Carthage*: 352.
44. Pocock, *Barbarism and Religion*, vol. 1: 40, 39.
45. Polybios, *The Histories*, transl. W. R. Paton, vol. 6: 437.
46. A footnote in the Paton translation references *Iliad* 6: 448–449.

47. Polybios, *The Histories*, vol. 6: 439; emphasis mine.
48. Ibid., vol. 6: 439.
49. Stephen Halliwell, *The Aesthetics of Mimesis: Ancient Texts and Modern Problems:* 168. *Energeia* in turn involves *phantasia* as the capacity "in virtue of which an image occurs for us." Aristotle, *De Anima (On the Soul)*: 587.
50. On this transformation of prose into "stage set," see Albrecht Koschorke, *Wahrheit und Erfindung: Grundzüge einer Allgemeinen Erzähltheorie*: 71.
51. Hannah Arendt, *The Human Condition*: 15.
52. Contemplation is without a practical goal. Aristotle, *Nichomachean Ethics*: 1104.
53. Aristotle, *De Anima (On the Soul)*: 595. "Knowledge" is "the state of having seen." Bruno Snell, quoted in Jay, *Downcast Eyes:* 24. Remembrance is also connected to this faculty of "'presentation.'" Aristotle, *De Memoria et Reminiscentia (Memory and Reminiscence):* 609.
54. Arnaldo Momigliano, *On Pagans, Jews, and Christians*: 40.
55. Homer, *The Iliad*, transl. Robert Fagles: 210.
56. Simon Goldhill, "Refracting Classical Vision: Changing Cultures of Viewing": 17.
57. Graham Ley, *The Theatricality of Greek Tragedy*: 103, 104. The chorus created strong images, its strophe setting up a "concrete well-visualized image," the antistrophe giving meaning to the image. David Wiles, *Tragedy in Athens: Performance Space and Theatrical Meaning*: 97.
58. Greek historians used the paradigm of "imperial succession" beginning with Herodotus. Hartog, *Regimes*: 12. See also Momigliano, *On Pagans, Christians, and Jews*: 42. Momigliano refutes the idea that Appian introduced the paradigm (41). On the transmission of the schema, see also David Potter, *Prophets and Emperors: Human and Divine Authority from Augustus to Theodosius*: 183–192.
59. Hartog, *Regimes*: 11.
60. Ibid.: 12, 33.
61. Daniel 2, verse 44. New International Version of the Bible.
62. Momigliano, *On Pagans*: 43. A "forged letter from Hannibal" existed, promising the Athenians victory over the "ancestors of the Romans" (ibid.).
63. Polybios attributed Hannibal's reputation for cruelty to the fact that his journey exposed him to the "savage nature of the barbaric inhabitants of the countries" he traversed (R, 401).
64. Sigmund Freud, *The Interpretation of Dreams*: 197.
65. Hannibal regrets that the "noble empires" of the Carthaginians and Romans ignored the "limits" set by "Nature" craving "possessions outside Italy" and "Africa" (R, 470, 469).
66. The "barbarian rented hordes of Carthage" become a *topos*. See Barthold G. Niebuhr, *Römische Geschichte*, vol. 3: 498.
67. Appian, *The Punic Wars*, chapter 18, section 118. Emphasis mine.
68. Hartog, *Memories of Odysseus*: 166.

69. Maier, *Among Empires*: 286.
70. "Aristotle's Ethics," *Stanford Encyclopedia of Philosophy*: 30.
71. He did so long before Virgil grasped that it is impossible to "insure institutional immortality" of empire "although he sought to pretend otherwise." Maier, *Among Empires*: 286.
72. Ibid.: 286.
73. Johann Gottfried Herder, *Ideen zur Philosophie der Menschheit* (1794–81): 380; emphasis mine.
74. Aristotle, *Nichomachean Ethics*: 1105.
75. Andrea Wilson Nightingale, *Spectacles of Truth in Classical Greek Philosophy: Theoria in Its Classical Contexts*: 69. Contemplation is a journey: "[viewing] beautiful things, one after another in a correct way, he will suddenly see, at the end, a wonderous . . . vision." Plato, quoted in Nightingale, *Spectacles*: 84.
76. Ibid.: 68. On the *theoros* as the historian's precursor, see Hartog, *Memories*: 109.
77. Nightingale, *Spectacles*: 45.
78. Ibid.: 55.
79. Graham Ley, *The Theatricality of Greek Tragedy: Playing Space and Chorus*: 8.
80. Nightingale, *Spectacles*: 56. These festivals opened "Athens to the gaze of foreigners" (58).
81. Ley, *The Theatricality of Greek Tragedy*: 8.
82. Graham Ley, *A Short Introduction to Ancient Greek Theater*: 23. According to Vitruvius, Agatharchos was the first to use perspectival scene painting for Aeschylus's plays. Richard C. Beacham, *The Roman Theatre and Its Audience*: 64.
83. Ley, *The Theatricality of Greek Tragedy*: 9 and 27.
84. Ibid.: 62. See Simon Goldhill on the question of whether the building's collapse actually happened onstage or was imagined. Goldhill, *Reading Greek Tragedy*: 279.
85. See Aeschylus, *Agamemnon*, transl. Sara Ruden: 67.
86. Pausanias, *Guide to Greece*, vol. 2: 452.
87. Beacham, *The Roman Theatre*: 18.
88. Ibid.: 20.
89. Eleanor Winsor Leach, *The Social Life of Painting in Ancient Rome and on the Bay of Naples*: 104.
90. Beacham, *The Roman Theatre*: 164.
91. Ibid.: 57.
92. Ibid.: 60. *Scaena* is also painted scenery.
93. He describes the "large *skene*" of a triumph's temporary stage and compares declamatory writing to "scene-paintings." Polybios, quoted in Beacham, *The Roman Theatre*: 64.
94. Aristotle, *DE POETICA (Poetics)*: 1461; and *ETHICA NICOMACHEA (Nichomachean Ethics)*: 1098; emphasis mine.
95. Sigmund Freud, "Triebe und Triebschicksale" (1915): 129; and "Instincts and Their Vicissitudes": 130.
96. That is, a drive exercising more pressure to attain its final aim.

97. Goldhill, "Refracting Classical Vision: Changing Cultures of Viewing": 26. In this key essay, Goldhill traces this new connection between "viewing and desiring" to a "major shift in the discussion of the epistemological status of viewing" (23) after Plato and Aristotle. Plato "worked to separate the faculty of vision from true knowledge" (23). Stoic philosophers begin to see "*phantasiai*" or "'presentations'" as connecting "the physics of vision and the process of conceptualization" (23, 24). This led to reflections about whether "eyes merely see or are already part of an erotic economy" and questions about "the relation between desire and the viewing subject" (24).
98. Freud, "Instincts": 132.
99. Karl Galinsky, "Introduction," in *Memoria Romana*: 1.
100. The "leadership" of the "senatorial aristocracy and the *nobiles*" was based on mnemic strategies. They controlled "the collective discourse of what history is or should be," "the contents as well as the media, textual and visual," "the language and semantics of monuments as well as the syntax of rituals and ceremonies and their meanings and messages." Karl-J. Hölkeskamp, "In Defense of Concepts, Categories, and Other Abstractions: Remarks on a Theory of Memory (in the Making)": 69.
101. Mary Beard, *The Roman Triumph*: 211, 44; and Paul Zanker, *Roman Art*: 98.
102. On *imagines maiorum*, see Harriet I. Flower, *Ancestor Masks and Aristocratic Power in Roman Society*: 59.
103. Zanker, *The Power of Images in the Age of Augustus*: 210.
104. Kuttner, quoted in Karl-J. Hölkeskamp, "In Defense": 68.
105. Ibid.
106. Cicero, "The Dream of Scipio," in his *The Republic*: 86–94.
107. Tacitus, *The Annals of Imperial Rome*: 110.
108. Pocock, *Barbarism and Religion* vol. 3: *The First Decline*: 37. Livy also wrote about the "dangers of overextension," which "would haunt" later empires. Anthony Pagden, *Peoples and Empires*: 35.
109. Sallust, *Catiline's War, The Jughurtine War, Histories*: 83. Sallust is the "theorist of the so called *metus hostilis*, and its significance for the internal order." Marco Walter, "Between Fascination and Deterrence: Roman Decadence and Empire": 5.
110. Sallust, *The Jughurtine War*: 83.
111. Beard, *The Roman Triumph*: 117.
112. Appian, quoted in ibid.
113. Ibid.

CHAPTER TWO

1. I combine the idea of the imperial capital as "symbolic center" (Lawrence J. Vale, *Architecture, Power, and National Identity*: 11) with the scholarship on Rome's politics of spectacle. "The word [*scaena*/scene] is recurrent in descriptions of public life: great men knew that their lives were acted out upon a

stage." Richard Jenkyns, *God, Space, & City in the Roman Imagination*: 8. By Cicero's time, the metaphor of public performance as "piece of theatre" was a "cliché" (8).

2. Chapters 19, 20, and 21 of the *RGDA* consist of lists of structures built and restored. See Alison E. Cooley, ed., *Res Gestae Divi Augusti: Text, Translation, and Commentary*.
3. Karl Galinsky, *Augustus: Introduction to the Life of an Emperor*: 61.
4. Ibid.: 67.
5. Woolf, *Rome*: 166.
6. Galinsky, *Augustus*: 63.
7. By first "demobilizing armies, touring and securing the provinces," and creating a working relationship with the Senate. Woolf, *Rome*: 166–167.
8. Solving "the domestic problem of What did an emperor do?," this period of "world conquest" ended with the "disastrous defeat in Germany in AD 9." Woolf, *Rome*: 167.
9. Josephus, quoted in Neil Elliott, "The Anti-Imperial Message of the Cross": 168. In 4 BCE, Varus crucified two thousand Judean rebels before making off for the forests of Germania.
10. Elliott, "The Anti-Imperial Message of the Cross": 171.
11. Woolf, *Rome*: 167.
12. Cooley, ed., *Res Gestae Divi Augusti*: 58.
13. Winsor Leach, *The Social Life*: 114. The line was used by Greek actors as they exited the stage.
14. Ibid.
15. Capturing this self-consciousness of the Roman official, Cicero wrote about "seeing himself acting as if within a theater of the entire world." Winsor Leach, *The Social Life*: 109.
16. Roman "performance culture" was one of the appropriations of Greek culture, where the theater organized a "sense of collective participatory spectatorship." Goldhill, "Refracting Classical Vision": 19.
17. Quoted in David Karmon, *The Ruin of the Eternal City: Antiquity & Preservation in Renaissance Rome*: 29.
18. Nicolet, *Space, Geography, and Politics in the Early Roman Empire*: 16.
19. Ibid.: 15.
20. Ibid.: 24.
21. Nicolet puts the accent on the *Res Gestae*'s topographical descriptions and their "visual" nature (ibid.: 23).
22. Karmon, *The Ruin*: 33.
23. Vitruvius, *Ten Books on Architecture*, ed. Ingrid W. Rowland and Thomas Noble Howe: 26.
24. Vitruvius, *De Architectura, Liber Primus*: lines 13 and 14.
25. See Eric Santner, "Freud's *Moses* and the Ethics of Nomotropic Desire": 3–41.
26. Ellen O'Gorman, "Cato the Elder and the Destruction of Carthage": 116. This opposition of decadent sea-based and traditional land-based empire and the

(anti-Semitic) trope of merchant Carthage continued to play a role in the conservative critique of imperialism.

27. Cicero, quoted in O'Gorman, "Cato the Elder": 116.
28. Ibid.: 115.
29. William L. MacDonald, *The Architecture of the Roman Empire*, vol. 2: 141. Visibility was achieved by clearing space around the structures, for instance. In addition, vertical lines dominated, as did secure construction and "solid fabric" (142).
30. Ibid.: 132.
31. Diane Favro, "Making Rome a World City": 260. On the Schmittian concepts of order and territorialization, see the introduction.
32. Jenkyns, *God*: 331.
33. Ibid.: 1.
34. Zanker, *The Power of Images in the Age of Augustus*: 66.
35. Augustus created "a permanent bureaucracy" in charge of the city's infrastructure. Karmon, *The Ruin*: 32.
36. Ovid, quoted in Galinsky, *Augustan Culture*: 99.
37. Jenkyns, *God*: 78.
38. Zanker, *The Power of Images*: 77.
39. Edwards, *Writing Rome*: 34. The staff of religious officials repaired the hut whenever "any part of it is injured." Dionysius of Halicarnassus, quoted in Edwards, *Writing Rome*: 33. On the hut as Augustan "fiction," see also Karmon, *The Ruin*: 26.
40. Edwards, *Writing Rome*: 34.
41. Vitruvius, *Ten Books on Architecture*: 34 and 33.
42. MacDonald, *The Architecture of the Roman Empire*, vol. 2: 159.
43. Zanker, *The Power of Images*: 76 and 84.
44. Nicolet, *Space*: 16.
45. Zanker, *The Power of Images*: 73.
46. Nicolet, *Space*: 16.
47. Orietta Osini, *ARA PACIS Guide*: 6.
48. Zanker, *Roman Art*: 88.
49. Ibid.: 91. On the different readings of the goddess figure in the "panel of Tellus," see Orietta Osini, *Ara Pacis guide*: 36.
50. Nicolet, *Space*: 17.
51. Diane Favro, "Making Rome a World City": 250.
52. Favro, "Moving Events: Curating the Memory of the Roman Triumph": 89.
53. On Cicero's "theoretical segregation of the stage and the political life of the state," see Andrew Feldherr, *Spectacle and Society in Livy's History*: 169–172.
54. Hölkeskamp, "In Defense": 69.
55. Beacham, *The Roman Theatre and Its Audience*: 164.
56. Vitruvius, quoted in Winsor Leach, *The Social Life*: 94–95.
57. In 58 BCE, one of the *aedile* "built the theatrical extravaganza of all times," a three-story-high *scaenae frons*. Winsor Leach, *The Social Life*: 103.

58. Gilles Sauron, "Mythe et Pouvoir: La Mystification Augustienne": 33.
59. Winsor Leach, *The Social Life*: 94. The residential complex that includes Livia's house was Augustus's residence.
60. Winsor Leach, *The Social Life*: 110.
61. Ibid.: 113.
62. In *Writing Rome*, Catharine Edwards traces this long textualization.
63. Strabo, *The Geography of Strabo*, vol. 2: 409. Strabo's universal geography is equivalent to Polybios's universal history; see Jas Elsner, "From the Pyramids to Pausanias and Piglet": 235–238.
64. Strabo, *The Geography of Strabo*, vol. 2: 407.
65. Jenkyns, *God*: 331.
66. Ibid.: 2.
67. Beard, *The Roman Triumph*: 160, 161. Triumphs "[brought] before the eyes of the Roman people a vivid impression of their achievements." Polybios, quoted in Beard, *The Roman Triumph*: 162.
68. Diane Favro, "Moving Events: Curating the Memory of the Roman Triumph": 160 and 123. Beard, *The Roman Triumph*: 145.
69. These "participatory rituals" encouraged "participatory looking." Kuttner, quoted in Hölkeskamp, "In Defense": 68.
70. Elliott, "The Anti-Imperial Message of the Cross": 170.
71. Ovid, quoted in Jenkyns, *God*: 31.
72. Nicolet, *Space*: 99, 101.
73. It also depicted the army building infrastructure across "untamed nature." Jon Coulston, "Transport and Travel on Trajan's Column": 130.
74. Tacitus, *The Annals*: 310.
75. MacDonald, *Architecture of the Roman Empire*: 269. Combining Roman and Hellenistic elements into a "stylistically coherent whole," this classicist architecture allied Greece and Rome (180).
76. See Karen E. Ros, "The Roman Theater at Carthage": 483.
77. Nicolet, *Space*: 112.
78. Don Fowler, "The Ruin of Time": 195.
79. The eternal city "is a concept of infinite duration in the future." Jenkyns, "The Memory of Rome in Rome": 19.
80. During the Augustan age, Romans seem "to have held a linear view of historical progression." David Potter, *Literary Texts and the Roman Historian*: 50. Friedrich Vittinghoff analyzes the Augustan era's "static view of history" and the "religious metaphysics" informing the belief that the "imperium was the time-less end stage of history." Vittinghoff, "Zum geschichtlichen Selbstverständnis der Spätantike": 549 and 547.
81. Quoted in Anthony M. Tung, *Preserving the World's Great Cities*: 36.
82. Ibid.: 36–37.
83. Louis Marin, "Fragments of a Walk through Poussin's Ruins": 143.
84. Macaulay, *Pleasure*: 137.

85. Ibid.: 137, 138, and 136.
86. Ibid.: 138. Macaulay implies that Britain was better at Roman mimesis than the Nazis.
87. Ibid.: 139.
88. See Zanker, *The Power of Images*: 315.
89. Catharine Edwards, *Writing Rome*: 31.

CHAPTER THREE

1. T. P. Wiseman, "Popular Memory," in *Memoria Romana*: 56.
2. David Quint, *Epic and Empire*: 183. In the Roman victors' ideology, Dido represents the "anarchic forces inherent in the [barbarian] East," a "monstrous irrationality" (28, 109).
3. Ibid.: 112.
4. Turner resisted "academic principle" by decentering the protagonist. Barry Venning, *Turner*: 197.
5. Horace, *Poem 16*, line 8 in *Epodon Liber*, http://data.perseus.org/citations/urn:cts:latinLit:phi0893.phi003.perseus-lat1:16; and Augustine, *Concerning the City of God*: 72.
6. J. D. Reed, *Virgil's Gaze: Nation and Poetry in the Aeneid*: 96.
7. Translation in ibid.: 129.
8. Virgil, *The Aeneid (hereafter AFi)*, transl. Robert Fitzgerald: 3.
9. Philip Hardie, *Virgil's Aeneid*: x.
10. Virgil implored the gods not to thwart Augustus's plan to restore the civil wars' "world in ruins." Virgil, *The Georgics*, transl. L. P. Wilkinson: 72. The *Aeneid* portrays a "new kind of hero appropriate for Augustan Rome." Dufallo, *Ghosts*: 101.
11. On Virgil's ideology of empire, see Reed: *Virgil's Gaze*: 138; and Quint, *Epic and Empire*: 23ff. W. R. Johnson foregrounds ideological ambivalence in *Darkness Visible*.
12. Duncan F. Kennedy, "Virgilian Epic": 146.
13. Ibid.: 146.
14. See Reed, *Virgil's Gaze*: 9.
15. See Jas Elsner on the ekphrasis of the frescoes in his *Roman Eyes: Visuality and Subjectivity in Art and Text*: 79ff.
16. Quint, *Epic and Empire*: 61ff. Troy's fall forces the Trojans into traumatic repetitions, trying to recover their loss as they visit a "parade of replica Troys" (ibid.: 61).
17. For the temporal structure, see also Karl Galinsky, "Virgil's *Aeneid* and Ovid's *Metamorphoses*": 344.
18. See also Miles on Carthage's re-foundations (including the third, in 29 BCE by Augustus) and the city's role in the Roman imagination, in "Rivaling Rome": 131ff.

19. Zetzel, "Rome and Its Traditions": 188.
20. "Through his visions of Rome as she is not he invites his readers to look with the mind's eye on Rome as she is." Jenkyns, *God*: 115–116.
21. On the lament, see Reed, *Virgil's Gaze*: 135.
22. The description of Aeneas's shield in book 6 renders Virgil's interpretation of Rome's entire "history and destiny." Zetzel, "Rome and Its Traditions": 189.
23. Reed, *Virgil's Gaze*: 141.
24. See also Virgil's statement in the *Georgics* about the inevitable end of all cities. Reed, *Virgil's Gaze*: 147.
25. Quint, *Epic and Empire*: 111.
26. Virgil's "'subjective' style" allows "readers to enter the world of the poem from the perspective of the participants." Ioannis Ziogas, "Singing for Octavia: Vergil's Life and Marcellus' Death": 6.
27. On this topic, see Philip Hardie, "Virgil and Tragedy": 312–315.
28. Ibid.: 322.
29. Elizabeth Young, "Homer in a Nutshell: Virgilian Miniaturization and the Sublime": 61.
30. Ibid.
31. Karen E. Ros, "The Roman Theater at Carthage": 483.
32. "[O]verlooking the Carthaginian ramparts," Aeneas has a godlike vantage point. Young, "Homer in a Nutshell": 61. This gaze creates the spectator-position grounding Virgil's proleptic ruin gazer scenario: as Aeneas stares down at the Carthaginian stage, the reader stares down at the ruined *scaenae frons*.
33. Reed, *Virgil's Gaze*: 24 and 42. With the "domineering" Roman gaze, "desire becomes a figure for imperial subjection" (42).
34. Aristotle, *De Poetica (Poetics)*: 1471; see also Halliwell, *The Aesthetics of Mimesis*: 20.
35. Dido's consciousness draws the Roman reader into her own world. See Reed, *Virgil's Gaze*: 79ff.
36. Dido "foretells" the story "of the conquered who refuse to stay conquered," questioning the epic's ideological closure. Quint, *Epic and Empire*: 111. On the power of Dido's curse (in the context of the Spanish-Portuguese conquests), see Quint, "Voices of Resistance": 252ff.
37. Aeneas's first sight of Carthage was "a proleptic vision of Rome, the city he is destined to found." Young, "Homer in a Nutshell": 58. Dido's simile is the proleptic vision of Rome's end in ruins.
38. On *katabasis* in Virgil, see Alan Itkin, *Underworlds of Memory: W. G. Sebald's Epic Journeys through the Past*: 23–47.
39. Hardie, *Virgil's Aeneid*: 69. Using cosmic religion for an imperialist cause, Virgil here connects cosmology and political eschatology (70).
40. Dufallo, *Ghosts*: 104.
41. Hardie, *Virgil's Aeneid*: 76. On this intertextual connection, see Hardie, *Virgil's Aeneid*: 79.

42. Virgil's *Aeneid* ends with a scene in which "Aeneas is monumentally captured," killing Turnus. Don Fowler, "The Ruin of Time": 217. Monumentalizing founding violence, Virgil freezes time.
43. Robert Ginsberg, "The Terminology of Ruin": 286.
44. Fowler, "Even Better Than the Real Thing": 94.
45. Silius, quoted in ibid.: 102.
46. Ibid.: 105. "Hannibal dreams of a Punic epic and a Punic Hadrian's column." Ibid.: 104.
47. Silius, *Punica*, quoted in ibid.: 105.
48. They never existed, but Silius makes us infer that they must have been installed at Liternum before the outbreak of the Second Punic War.
49. Silius, *Punica*, quoted in Fowler, "Even Better Than the Real Thing": 104.
50. K. W. Grandsden identifies this as the *Ara Maxima* and Porta Carmentalis. "Commentary," in Virgil, *Aeneid: Book VIII*: 123.
51. Virgil, *Aeneid, book 8*, line 356, http://data.perseus.org/citations/urn:cts:latinLit:phi0690.phi003.perseus-lat1:8.337-8.369.
52. Discussing razed cities, Strabo writes that "although only *traces* of cities were left, *those traces have become famous* because of the sojourn which Aeneas made there." Strabo, *The Geography*, book 5, chapter 3, transl. H. L. Jones. Debris is no longer meaningless because the *ruinae* of Rome's ancient cities have become *famous traces* by their association with Rome's foundational myth. Strabo uses the Greek word *ichnos,* meaning trace, track, or footstep. Thanks go to Alan Itkin.
53. Grandsden, "Commentary": 124. Using the word *conditor* or founder, Virgil makes Evander the forerunner of Aeneas and Augustus.
54. See James E. Zetzel on Virgil's use of hard and soft primitivism, state of nature versus Arcadian golden age. "Rome and Its Traditions": 190–191.
55. Catharine Edwards, *Writing Rome*: 31.
56. The reading is plausible, since Evander's historical account narrates a series of degenerations, which Augustus's restoration of the golden age overcomes. Grandsden, "Commentary": 126. This era might be succeeded by a new cycle of degenerations.
57. See also Catharine Edwards, "Imagining Ruins in Ancient Rome": 649.
58. See Karl Galinsky for Virgil's redefinition of the golden age from *Eclogues* to *Georgics* to the *Aeneid*. *Augustan Culture*: 92–99.
59. Book 8 is evidence that "the palimpsestic idea of Rome" originated with Virgil. Jenkyns, "The Memory of Rome in Rome": 24. This accumulation of historical layers involves ruin consciousness.
60. Philip Hardie, *Virgil's Aeneid*: 97.
61. The description of the shield slows down as soon as it reaches the age of Augustus. Actium, the conflict between western Augustus and eastern Egypt, is told with dramatic flair.
62. This is the other Virgil, who observed the principate's beginning with "anxiety and foreboding." W. R. Johnson, *Darkness Visible*: 137.

63. Zetzel writes: "[T]he possibility that peace will endure is by no means a certainty." "Rome and Its Traditions": 200. Referring to Zetzel's reading, Catharine Edwards points out that Evander might be gesturing at a time "in the future when the Capitol will once again be overgrown," eventually "resembling the overgrown monuments built by Janus and Saturn." Edwards, *Writing Rome*: 31.
64. On Propertius's tour of Rome, tracing the contrast between Augustan and Evander's Rome, see Fowler, "The Ruin of Time": 206–207.
65. Jane Wilson Joyce, "General Introduction": xii.
66. Ibid.: xviii.
67. Quint writes that as first "anti-imperial poet," Lucan founded the tradition of "epics of the defeated" by his "allusions" to and "imitations" of Virgil's "epic of the imperial victors." Quint, *Epic and Empire*: 8. Lucan, I would argue, is anti-*imperialist* since he laments the end of the republican empire.
68. Wilson Joyce, "General Introduction": xxiii.
69. Lucan, *Pharsalia* (*The Civil War*) (hereafter CW): 9.
70. Virgil, *Georgics*: 72.
71. On regimes of historicity as specific articulations of past, present, and future, see Hartog, *Regimes*: 19 and 27ff.
72. On the Book of Daniel and the relation between Jewish and Christian apocalyptic thought, see Arnaldo Momigliano, *Essays on Ancient and Modern Judaism*: 88–100. On Jewish readings of the Book of Daniel and the eschatological expectations expressed in these texts, see Lester Grabbe, "A Dan(iel) for All Seasons": 242.
73. Hans Blumenberg, *The Legitimacy of the Modern Age*: 41. On Stoic philosophy as a moral justification of empire, see Andrew Erskine, *The Hellenistic Stoa: Political Thought and Action*: 181–210.
74. Civil war "remained the political nightmare of Roman society." David Potter, *Literary Texts and the Roman Historian*: 52.
75. Wilson Joyce, "General Introduction": xxii.
76. Virgil is a "gloomy optimist," Lucan the "angry pessimist." Ibid.

CHAPTER FOUR

1. On the "remaking" of "Greek sites in Italy" in "poetry, gardens, and interiors," see Bettina Bergmann, "Meanwhile, back in Italy . . . : Creating Landscapes of Allusion": 156, 159.
2. Diderot, quoted in Ginsberg, *The Aesthetics*: 287.
3. Makarius, *Ruinen*: 14.
4. Macaulay, *Pleasure of Ruins*: 14, 42.
5. Peter Geimer, *Die Vergangenheit der Kunst*: 122.
6. Augustus, quoted in Morley, *The Roman Empire*: 41.
7. On Josephus's "liminal position," see Maud Gleason, "Mutilated Messengers: Body Language in Josephus": 54.

8. Flavius Josephus, *Bellum Judaicum* or *Jewish War (hereafter J)*: 381 and 832.
9. Goldhill, *Jerusalem*: 171.
10. Feldherr, *Spectacle*: 15–16.
11. See Josephus, *Jewish Antiquities*: 437–438.
12. Richard Horsley, "Paul's Counter-Imperial Gospel: Introduction": 146.
13. Morley, *The Roman Empire*: 38.
14. Hartog reads his travelogue (on Arcadia as "the most authentic, Greece") as anticolonial *tractatus*. Hartog: *Memories*: 133. James Porter discusses Pausanias as theorist of memory, analyzing the "mood" of Greek patriotism. Porter, "Ideals and Ruins": 70.
15. Hadrian prided himself on having toured the outer reaches of the empire. See Raymond Chevallier, *Voyages et déplacements dans l'empire Romain*: 190–194.
16. Hartog, *Memories*: 144.
17. Porter, "Ideals and Ruins": 73.
18. Hartog, *Memories*: 144.
19. Elsner, "From the Pyramids": 252.
20. Ibid.: 250.
21. Hartog, *Memories*: 144.
22. The narrative of Greek freedom declining echoes Herodotus. See Elsner, "From the Pyramids": 252.
23. Pausanias, *Guide to Greece* (hereafter G2), vol. 2: 437.
24. Hartog, *Memories*: 134 and 139.
25. See Pliny the Elder on the painter of these landscapes, in John R. Clarke, "Augustan Domestic Interiors: Propaganda or Fashion": 273–274.
26. On the paradoxical nature of these landscape scenes, see Zanker, *The Power of Images*: 285–287; the revival of the simple life and the Italian farmer-soldier was the ideological ground for Augustan rule.
27. Virgil, *Georgics*: 92. See 91–93 on the *topos* of the decadent city: the theater's decadent pleasures; the "frantic Forum"; the luxurious palaces; the people wearing clothing from across the empire. All of this is modern and un-Italian.
28. Sir Joshua Reynolds, quoted in Clare Pace, "Claude the Enchanted: Interpretations of Claude in England in the Earlier Nineteenth Century": 734.
29. Jas Elsner, *Roman Eyes*: 57.
30. He uses the phenomenological aspect of travel—the "I have seen and experienced"—in the service of the past. Writing as if the rituals at the sanctuary at Olympia were in progress, Pausanias describes what is left to see for the second-century visitor. See John Elsner, "Structuring Greece": 12.
31. Porter, "Ideals and Ruins": 70. Porter reads Pausanian ruins through the Lacanian lens as "sublime objects of the past," designating absolute, idealized loss (70).
32. Tim Whitmarsh, "Quickening the Classics": 374.
33. David Wiles, *Tragedy in Athens*: 37.
34. Porter, "Ideals and Ruins": 73.

35. Pausanias introduces "time into 'things Greek'" as the trajectory from "greatness to ruins." Hartog, *Memories*: 143.
36. Morley, *The Roman Empire*: 38.
37. Pausanias, *Guide to Greece*, vol. 1: 47.
38. Porter, "Ideals and Ruins": 74.
39. Augustine, *City of God: 42.*

CHAPTER FIVE

1. At stake is thus the conception of the imperial present with respect to the expectation of the nearness or remoteness of the end, in pagan imperial time, Jewish messianic time, and early Christian eschatology.
2. Blumenberg, *The Legitimacy of the Modern Age*: 45.
3. Koselleck, "'Progress' and 'Decline'": 222. Thucydides has a model of relative progress: 1) the present "civilized" state of affairs is better than the state in which barbarians live; and 2) the Greeks themselves once lived under such "barbarian" conditions (222).
4. Ibid. Romans lacked the "surplus of expectation" characterizing modern articulations of past, present, and future (ibid.).
5. On the context of later Jewish and Christian readings of the Book of Daniel and the eschatological expectations expressed in these texts, see Grabbe, "A Dan(iel) for All Seasons": 236ff.
6. Blumenberg, *The Legitimacy*: 45, 43.
7. Dieter Georgi, "God Turned Upside Down": 151.
8. Richard A. Horsley, "Paul's Counter-Imperial Gospel": 144.
9. Paul, *First Letter to the Thessalonians*: 183.
10. Creston Davis and Patrick Aaron Riches, "Metanoia: The Theological Praxis of Revolution": 29.
11. Georgi, "God Turned Upside Down": 151.
12. And their state of "eschatological indifference." Giorgio Agamben, *The Time That Remains (hereafter T)*: 20.
13. Koselleck, "'Progress'": 223.
14. Hartog, *Regimes of Historicity*: 60, 61.
15. Ibid.: 61.
16. Blumenberg, *The Legitimacy*: 45, 44.
17. Tertullian, *Apology*, transl. T. R. Glover: 159.
18. Ibid.: 105; translation modified.
19. Ibid.: 155; translation modified.
20. Tertullian, quoted in Agamben, *The Time*: 109; emphasis mine.
21. Blumenberg, *The Legitimacy*: 44.
22. Ibid.: 44. Tertullian defined "Romanness" as "a more desirable, more comfortable, more stable, as well as more just, way of life than any which the 'barbarians' who came under Roman rule could have enjoyed beyond the limits of the Roman world." Anthony Pagden, *The Burdens of Empire, 1539 to the Present*: 3.

23. On other theologians characterizing the empire as restrainer, see Potter, *The Roman Empire at Bay AD 180–395*: 4.
24. Vittinghoff, "Zum geschichtlichen Selbstverständnis": 538.
25. Agamben argues that Paul "decomposes the messianic event into two times: resurrection and *parousia*, the second coming of Jesus at the end of time" (T, 69). This decomposition results in a "paradoxical tension between *an already* and a *not yet* that defines the Pauline conception of salvation" (T, 69).
26. According to Agamben, *parousia* "literally signifies next to; in this sense, being is beside itself in the present," and not a second messianic event (T, 70). *Parousia* was used for "the arrival of a king or an emperor." Koester, "Imperial Ideology and Paul's Eschatology in 1 Thessalonians": 158.
27. Agamben, "The Time That Is Left": p. 1 of printed text.
28. Paul, quoted in Horsley, "Paul's Counter-Imperial Gospel": 146.
29. Also "law that is simultaneously suspended and fulfilled" (T, 104).
30. Davis and Riches, "The Theological Praxis of Revolution": 30.
31. Carl Schmitt is of course one of those theorists.
32. The *katechon* opens "the mundane space of the political as such." William Rasch, *Sovereignty and Its Discontents: On the Primacy of Conflict and the Structure of the Political*: 100.
33. Agamben's reading is part of the literature debating Paul's "counter-imperial theology." Davis and Riches read Paul's gospel as "the casting of empire as parody." Davis and Riches, "The Theological Praxis of Revolution": 30, 29.
34. Ibid.: 30.
35. David Potter, *Ancient Rome: A New History*: 304.
36. Woolf, *Rome*: 251.
37. Ibid.: 252.
38. Ibid.: 240.
39. Ibid.: 253.
40. Augustine, *Concerning the City of God against the Pagans* (hereafter C): 7; and G. R. Evans, "Introduction": xiv.
41. He relies on Varro's concept of "civil theology" (C, 234).
42. Horsley, "Paul's Counter-Imperial Gospel": 147. By overcoming the civil wars, the intellectuals of Augustus's generation also overcame the "moods of decay and doom" informing "Jewish and Christian apocalyptic thought." Vittinghoff, "Zum geschichtlichen Selbstverständnis": 548.
43. Vittinghoff, "Zum geschichtlichen Selbstverständnis": 564.
44. Ibid.: 548.

CHAPTER SIX

1. Sigmund Freud, "The Economic Problem of Masochism": 168.
2. Identifications retain their "object-cathexis." Freud, "Group Psychology and the Analysis of the Ego": 114.
3. Reflecting on the workings of mimesis in the context of the early modern

Iberian empire, Barbara Fuchs discards Auerbach's understanding of mimesis. See Fuchs, *Mimesis and Empire*: 5. I propose to return to the ancient concept of mimesis that informed Auerbach's.

4. It is worth recalling that Bhabha's scenarios analyze the production of a form of colonial subjectivity desired by the colonizer. It is not a model of colonial subjectivity *per se*.
5. Lupher, *Romans in a New World*: 32. The Iberian elites' classical education provided them with models to understand their conquests. On this topic, see also Sabine MacCormack, *On the Wings of Time*: 170–202.
6. Quint, *Epic and Empire*: 381, note 1. Like other Spanish texts of the period, Villagra's *Historia* revived Dido's epic curse, giving voice to indigenous resistance against the conquerors.
7. The Aztec capital was compared to Jerusalem and Carthage.
8. Tzvetan Todorov, *The Conquest of America*: 231.
9. Fuchs, *Mimesis and Empire*: 7. Fuchs introduces Islam as a "third pole in such mimetic exchanges" (7).
10. Pagden, *Lords of All the World*: 44.
11. On the concept of *translatio imperii* and Charles V see Pagden, *Lords of All the World*, 40ff.
12. Burke, "Presenting and Re-Presenting Charles V": 422. We know the maxim in Virgil's ideological formulation as *imperium sine fine*.
13. Wallerstein, "Charles V and the Nascent Capitalist World-Economy": 365.
14. Ibid.: 370, 371.
15. The form of world-empire or universal monarchy resists the "primacy" of capital accumulation. Ibid.: 391.
16. Burke, "Presenting and Re-Presenting Charles V": 400.
17. Fuchs, *Mimesis and Empire*: 50.
18. J. H. Elliott, *Empires of the Atlantic World: Britain and Spain in America*: 23.
19. Friedrich Heer, *The Holy Roman Empire*: 166.
20. See Pagden, *The Burdens of Empire: 1539 to the Present*: 10.
21. Pagden, *Lords of All the World*: 42, 43.
22. Ibid.: 42.
23. Burke, "Presenting and Re-Presenting Charles V": 418.
24. The Ottoman army reached Buda in 1530. After the capture of Tunis, Sepulveda published its history as *De bello Africo*.
25. Charles's "enterprise of 'self-representation'," Burke writes, was a "collective project." Burke, "Presenting and Re-Presenting Charles V": 439.
26. Hendrik J. Horn, *Jan Cornelisz Vermeyen: Painter of Charles V and the Conquest of Tunis*, vol. 1: 15.
27. Richard Helgerson, *A Sonnet from Carthage: Garcilaso de la Vega and the New Poetry of Sixteenth-Century Europe*: 25–26.
28. Spanish authors transposed the "triumphalist genre" of the epic to the New World and the post-*Reconquista* setting. Fuchs, *Mimesis and Empire*: 38.

29. From then on, the tapestry served as a regular backdrop at Habsburg dynastic events. Helgerson, *A Sonnet*: 26.
30. Hendrik J. Horn, *Jan Cornelisz Vermeyen*: 189 and 235 (original Latin text). The tapestries had three different texts: a Latin poem at the bottom; small tablets in Spanish at the right (about locale); and an analysis of the action in Spanish at the top (175).
31. Ibid.: 189.
32. Ibid.
33. If we take up the position that the text describes, we have a line of vision from the ruins to Galeta, with Tunis to our right. Horn, *Jan Cornelisz Vermeyen*: 201.
34. Helgerson, *A Sonnet*: 29.
35. Ibid.
36. Ibid.: 82.
37. See Burke, "Presenting and Re-Presenting Charles V": 422.
38. Ibid.: 415.
39. Ibid.: 433. In Naples, a triumphal arch allegorically depicted "conquered Africa," and in Florence, Charles was celebrated with a series of paintings about Tunis (434).
40. Karmon, *The Ruin*: 102–103.
41. Makarius, *Ruinen*: 44.
42. See Burke, "Presenting and Re-Presenting Charles V": 433.
43. See Karmon, *The Ruin*: 106.
44. Ibid.: 105.
45. Burke, "Presenting and Re-Presenting Charles V": 433.
46. Karmon, *The Ruin*: 103.
47. Lugard, *The Dual Mandate in British Tropical Africa*. Thanks to Andrew Zimmerman for this reference.
48. Joseph Conrad, *Heart of Darkness*: 10–11.
49. Greg Woolf, "Inventing Empire in Ancient Rome": 313.
50. Plato, *The Republic, transl. Tom Griffith*: 84.
51. Ibid.: 84.
52. Ibid.:4. The goal of the imitation of exemplary men is "to become like them," implying a "faculty for transformation." Gebauer and Wulf, *Mimesis*: 53, 56.
53. Plato, *The Republic*: 87.
54. Ibid.: 318.
55. Ibid.
56. History, Cicero thought, was "the life of the memory." Cicero, quoted in Koselleck, "Historia Magistra Vitae: The Dissolution of the Topos into the Perspective of a Modernized Historical Process": 279, note 7. For Livy the past provides "lessons" embodied in monuments that Romans ought to "behold," asking how "to imitate" them. Livy, *From the Founding of the City*: 7.
57. Aristotle, *The Poetics of Aristotle*, transl. S. H. Butcher: 15.

58. By tracing the pleasure of mimesis to the artist's skill discernible in the representation of the original, Aristotle opens the gap between object and its artistic re-presentation, thus initiating the realism debates. Richard McKeon translates "precision of description that produces 'fidelity' to the original" with "the most realistic representations." McKeon, Aristotle, *POETICA (Poetics)*: 1457.
59. Aristotle, *The Poetics: 15* emphasis mine. In the translation of McKeon: "gathering the meaning of things, e.g. *that the man there is so-and-so*." Aristotle, *POETICA (Poetics)*: 1457.
60. Scenes of recognition are central plot elements.
61. Alison Cooley, *Res Gestae Divi Augusti: Text, Translation, and Commentary*: 58.
62. Augustus, *Res Gestae Divi Augusti*: 60.
63. Ibid.: 62.
64. The procession panel with Augustus adjoins the panel depicting Aeneas. On the narrative connecting past and present hero, see Diana E. E. Kleiner, "Semblance and Storytelling in the Age of Augustus": 218–225. The altar was dedicated in 9 BCE.
65. Zanker, *The Power*: 121. The panels depict "the newly constituted leading aristocracy" (123). The altar simultaneously idealizes and mobilizes the recognition effect of realism described by Plato as the result of the painter carrying "a mirror" through the city. Plato, *The Republic*: 315.
66. Elsner, *Roman Eyes*: 2.
67. Philostratus, quoted in Elsner, *Roman Eyes*: 3. Roman art pulls the viewer into the "enchanting waters of desire and illusion," and the viewer "identifies with, objectifies, and may even be seen by the image" (2). However stylized Roman images were, they remained within the register of realism and functioned within a system of repetition (spread across the empire), thus producing a vast archive of symbolic practices and their images.
68. Augustus, *Res Gestae Divi Augusti*: 86.
69. Ibid.: 90.
70. Ibid.: 92.
71. Elsner, *Roman Eyes*: 117. The *Res Gestae* seem to elaborate on a passage in Virgil's epic. Singling out Augustus in the parade of heroes, Anchises exclaims: "*hic vir, hic est*"—"*This is the man*, this one . . . Augustus" (*AFi*, 187–188). See also Galinsky's reading of the passage as announcing the return of Saturn's golden age.
72. Augustus, *Res Gestae*: 100
73. François Hartog, *Memories of Odysseus*: 19.
74. Virgil, *Aeneid*, book 1, line 198, http://data.perseus.org/citations/urn:cts:latinLit:phi0690.phi003.perseus-lat1:1.198-1.207.
75. The funerals evolved into "increasingly elaborate settings of props and participants," and the actors addressed the crowd, "acting in character for the audience." Flower, *Ancestor Masks*: 92, 104.

76. Ibid.: 91. Caesar was not represented in the train of masks because he was a god (104).
77. Freud, "The Dynamics of Transference": 100.
78. Karl Marx, "*The Eighteenth Brumaire of Louis Bonaparte*": 595.
79. Ibid.
80. Ibid.
81. Ellen O'Gorman, "Repetition and Exemplarity in Historical Thought: Ancient Rome and the Ghosts of Modernity": 272. They did so with a certain "degree of self-consciousness" (273).
82. Lupher, *Romans*: 9. Las Casas used Augustine's attacks on the Romans' treatment of their subjects as "barbarian" (256).
83. Ibid.: 31. Addressing Charles V, Cortés's secretary omitted the Romans altogether: "The greatest event since the creation of the world, apart from the Incarnation and death of its creator, is the discovery of the Indies; and that is why they called it the New World." Lupher, *Romans*: 8.
84. Ibid.
85. Ibid.
86. Ibid.: 32.
87. Phiroze Vasunia, *The Classics and Colonial India*: 147.
88. Robert Syme, *Colonial Elites: Rome, Spain, and the Americas*: 63.
89. In Cromer's view, the main question was whether the Romans' "somewhat hazardous experiment" of employing subjects from the colonies would bring the British Empire down as it had Rome. Lord Cromer, *Ancient*: 37.
90. Bhabha, "Of Mimicry and Man: The Ambivalence of Colonial Discourse": 87. It generates the "desire for a reformed, recognizable Other" (86).
91. Ibid.
92. In "Difference, Discrimination and the Discourse of Colonialism," Bhabha's reliance on Lacan's scopic scene of the dialectics of subject formation and Franz Fanon's "primal scenes" in *Black Skin White Masks* about the colonized's bodily ego "crumbling" into ruin and their core drama of "seeing/being seen" are more explicit (203).
93. Ibid.: 88.
94. Both the process of colonial subject formation and the performance of mimicry as one of its variants revolve around the historical overdeterminations of an ontological lack at the core of the subject's (imaginary) identity. Bhabha theorizes the subject formation of colonizer and colonized with the help of Lacan's account of the imaginary and its visual register, on the one hand, and Freud's model of fetishism and its scopic drive, on the other. That is, he explores the historically specific emergence of imaginary self-identity in the encounter with the image of the other, that is, the encounter of the "white" and "black" subject. Analyzed from the perspective of the colonizer, this encounter leads first to an act of nonrecognition of the self in the "black" image of the other (and an act of [mis]recognition by "returning" to the

image of the white other); second, it leads to the phobic projection of the colonial subject's own ontological lack onto the other (while withholding recognition). Both processes involve a fetish, black skin, as the signifier of (historically constituted) racial difference, and as an object that both acknowledges and denies lack (which in the register of the imaginary is difference *and* absence).

95. Ibid.: 91. Mimicry produces the colonial subject as "[a]lmost the same but not white" (89). This "visibility of mimicry" is *generated* "at the site of interdiction" (89). The categories of "whiteness"/"blackness" are a product of the process of colonial subjection.
96. That is, post-Roman mimesis as the staging of imitation on the symbolic level is always partial imitation.
97. Burke, "Presenting and Re-Presenting Charles V": 408, 410.
98. However, our access to this imaginary dimension of the public act of imitation is barred. Some post-Romans like Napoleon or Mussolini make their identifications a public matter, but here too we remain on the level of the symbolic. *The Conquest of Ruins* does not engage in the analysis of individual psyches.
99. Or, put differently, encountering lack on the level of empirical fact. That this confrontation involves more than an empirical fact is something I will discuss in chapter 23.
100. Again, this is a form of colonial subjectivity desired by the colonizer, not a model of colonial subjectivity *per se*.
101. Goldhill, "The Erotic Eye: Visual Stimulation and Cultural Conflict": 185.
102. Garcilaso de la Vega, *Sonnet to Boscan from Goleta*, in Richard Helgerson, *A Sonnet from Carthage: Gracilaso and the New Poetry of Sixteenth-Century Europe*: no page nrs.
103. And where this name "stands for all that empire destroyed." Helgerson, *A Sonnet from Carthage*: 41.
104. Ibid.: 33.
105. The imperial arts tended to occupy a space apart from imperial power: "Imperial self-making necessarily entails . . . an undoing that speaks for the victims of the empire." Ibid.: 54.
106. Where Helgerson reads the poem's intertextual chain of associations to Dido, I also read them from Garcilaso's lyric "I" to Scipio's.
107. I argued that in this death scene Virgil restages Polybios's ruin gazer scenario as a moment on the Roman stage, a moment when this stage is envisioned by its audience as the crumbling of the imperial *scaenae frons*.
108. As the imperial subject slides from one subject position to another, the sonnet hints at the possibility of the breakdown of the scenario.
109. Burke, "Presenting and Re-Presenting Charles V": 438; Wallerstein, "Charles V and the Nascent World-Economy": 374. Wallerstein refers to a 1559 peace treaty between Spain and France, both bankrupted by their world-imperial ambitions.

110. Burke, "Presenting and Re-Presenting Charles V": 425.
111. Pliny the Elder, *The Natural History*, book 35, chapter 2.
112. Freud, *Civilization and Its Discontents*: 69.
113. Ibid.: 70.
114. Ibid.
115. Ibid.
116. Ibid.
117. Ibid.
118. Ibid.

PART 3 PREFACE

1. Quoted in Brendon, *Decline*: 31.
2. Karl Marx, *Capital*, vol. 1: 915.
3. Ibid.: 925.

CHAPTER SEVEN

1. Tarnya Cooper, "Forgetting Rome and the Voice of Piranesi's 'Speaking Ruins'": 111.
2. Etienne du Pérac, for instance, juxtaposed ruins to their reconstructions, and Andrea Palladio discussed his conjectures. Margaret M. McGowan, "Unwillkürliches Gedächtnis": 25.
3. Edward Gibbon, *The History of the Decline and Fall of the Roman Empire*, vol. 3 *(hereafter DFIII)*: 1084.
4. John Wilton-Ely, "Design through Fantasy: Piranesi as Designer": 23.
5. Ibid.
6. Beacham, *The Roman Theater*: 171.
7. Ferdinando Galli Bibiena, *L'architettura* (1711): 60. Thanks to Amy Kulper.
8. Fatma Ipek Ek and Deniz Sengel, "Piranesi between Classical and Sublime": 22.
9. Irritated by Winckelmann's Hellenism, Piranesi defended "the creative legacy of ancient Rome." Giovanni Battista Piranesi, *Observations on the Letter of Monsieur Mariette*, ed. John Wilton-Ely: 33.
10. Denis Diderot, "Supplement to Bougainville's 'Voyage'": 188. Diderot executes a polemical reversal: "We respected our own image in you," the Tahitian states (ibid.).
11. Diderot, "Salon of 1767" :197.
12. Ibid.: 196–197. There is affirmation of human subjectivity against death, but the quote belies Roland Mortier's claim that for Diderot, the ruin has lost the historical character of memorial. Roland Mortier, *La Poétique des Ruines en France: Ses Origines, ses variations de la renaissance à Victor Hugo*: 92.
13. Philippe Junod, "Poétique des ruines et perception du temps: Diderot et Hubert": 323.

14. Diderot, "Salon of 1767": 197.
15. G. W. F. Hegel, *Philosophy of Right* (1820): 13.
16. In *The Philosophy of History*, lectures held in the winter of 1822–1823, Hegel, the former admirer of Napoleon, turned his backward gaze at the ruins of Rome.
17. See Todd Samuel Presner, "Hegel's Philosophy of World History via Sebald's Imaginary of Ruins"; and Susan Buck-Morss, *Hegel, Haiti, and Universal History*.
18. Johann Gottfried Herder, *Ideen zur Philosophie der Geschichte der Menschheit* (hereafter I): 384.
19. Immanuel Kant, *Anthropologie in pragmatischer Sicht*: 333.
20. On Herder's theology, his anti-universalist, anti-rationalist stadial theory, and his historicist hermeneutics, see Suzanne Marchand, *German Orientalism in the Age of Empire*: 44, 45, and 47.
21. Herder, *This Too a Philosophy of History for the Formation of Humanity: 289.*
22. Ibid.: 320. Herder thus reintroduces god's plan into the Scottish Enlightenment philosophers' stadial theories of the emergence of civilization.
23. Ibid.: 338.
24. Ibid.: 290.
25. Ibid.: 312.
26. Ibid.: 322.
27. Ibid.: 329. On the brutality of European colonialism, see 315, 325, and 328.
28. On Herder's "Imperialist hubris" *and* "anticolonial sentiment," see Suzanne Marchand, *German Orientalism:* 49.
29. Herder's notion of the "Volk" is inextricably tied to "its oral language with distinctive accents and tones." Chenxi Tang, *The Geographic Imagination: Geography, Literature, and Philosophy in German Romanticism*: 46. It is the "word of the soul" by which a people becomes a "community" (47, 46).
30. With an eye on the events in France, Herder adds that we have come to detest the "new Romans" (I, 384).
31. Pausanias is the other voice in this passage about the ruined landscape of ancient Greece.
32. Volney (1757–1820) composed *Les Ruines* as an appendix to his *Voyage en Égypte et en Syrie* (1787). On the success of *Les Ruines* in Great Britain, see Alexander Cook, "Reading Revolution: Towards a History of the Volney Vogue in England."
33. C. F. Volney, *The Ruins, or, Meditations on the Revolutions of Empire and the Law of Nature (hereafter RE): 3.*
34. Richard Stoneman, *Palmyra and Its Empire: Zenobia's Revolt against Rome*: 111.
35. Theodor Mommsen, *A History of Rome under the Emperors*: 351.
36. MacDonald, *The Architecture of the Roman Empire*: 252 and 251.
37. Longinus supposedly instigated "territorial expansion." Southern, *Zenobia*: 96. See also Stoneman, *Palmyra*: 129–131.
38. Robert Wood, *The Ruins of Palmyra, otherwise Tedmor, in the desart*: 19.

39. This is the British archeologists' text quoted verbatim in Volney's *Voyage en Égypte et en Syrie*: 325.
40. On the use of Volney's famous opening in British literature, see Katie Trumpener, *Bardic Nationalism*: 144ff.
41. The more immediate context for Volney was the publication of Louis-Sébastien Mercier's twelve-volume *Tableaux de Paris* (1781–1788). Asking what will happen to Paris, Mercier answers that it will be a ruin like Palmyra. Geimer, *Die Vergangenheit*: 203.
42. Special collections exhibition, "Unpacking Ruins: architecture from antiquity"; New Zealand; available online at http://www.library.otago.ac.nz/exhibitions/ruins/case_one.html.
43. Palmyra models became fashionable. On *The Ruins of Palmyra* and Schloss Wörlitz, see Stoneman, *Palmyra*: 193.
44. Macaulay, *Pleasure*: 70.
45. Ibid.: 42.
46. Wood, *The Ruins of Palmyra*: 36.
47. Ibid.: 44.
48. Said, *Orientalism*: 87.
49. According to Montesquieu, the empire's increasing decadence was an effect of its territorial expansion, unwisely going beyond the limits set by "Nature." Montesquieu, Considérations *sur les causes de la grandeur des Romains et de leur decadence: 57.*
50. Pocock, *Barbarism and Religion, vol. 3*: 388. I am referring to Adam Smith's *The Wealth of Nations* (1776) and Adam Ferguson's *Essay on the History of Civil Society* (1767).
51. Virgil assigned this cosmic view to Jupiter. See, for instance, AFi, 11.
52. Cicero, "The Dream of Scipio," in *The Republic*: 89.
53. Ibid.: 87.
54. Ibid.
55. Ibid.: 88.
56. Andrew J. E. Bell, "Cicero and the Spectacle of Power": 4.
57. Cicero, "Dream of Scipio": 89. "Pinprick" replaces "dot" in other translations.
58. Ibid.: 90.
59. See for instance, Augustine, *City of God*: 72.
60. Seneca alluded to Cicero's *topos* of empire as "pinprick." Seneca, quoted in Harry M. Hine, "Rome, the Cosmos, and the Emperor": 45.
61. On Columbus and Seneca, see Sabine MacCormack, *On the Wings of Time*: 248.
62. Volney's "attack on luxury" also draws on Plato and Aristotle. Goldstein, *Ruins and Empire*: 144.
63. *The Ruins* was published while France experienced its first colonial revolution in Haiti (1791). As his support for the invasion of Egypt shows, Volney was a firm believer in the civilizing mission of European colonialism.
64. Beard, *The Roman Triumph*: 123.
65. Southern, *Zenobia*: 121.

66. DF, 317.
67. Wood and Dawkins, *The Ruins*: 37.

CHAPTER EIGHT

1. See Glen W. Bowersock, "The Vanishing Paradigm of the Fall of Rome": 30–31; Gibbon published volume 1 in 1776 and volumes 2 and 3 in 1781. Volumes 4, 5, and 6 were published in 1788.
2. Bowersock, "The Vanishing Paradigm": 31.
3. He follows his classical predecessors, Thucydides and Quintillian. See Janice Hewlett Koelb, *The Poetics of Description*: 33–35.
4. On Gibbon's defense of imperialism, see Adam Rogers and Richard Hingley, "Edward Gibbon and Francis Haverfield: Traditions of Imperial Decline": 190–191.
5. Ibid.: 192.
6. Wilton-Ely, "Design through Fantasy": 24; and Wilton-Ely, "Introduction," in Piranesi, *Observations on the Letter of Monsieur Mariette*: 41.
7. Brendon, *The Decline*: 49 and 47.
8. Gibbon, "*General Observations on the Fall of the Roman Empire in the West," in The Decline and Fall of the Roman Empire, vol. 2 (hereafter DFII)*: 511.
9. On this topic, see Bell, *The Idea of Greater Britain*: 219; and Phiroze Vasunia, *The Classics and Colonial India*: 148.
10. John Adams studied Scipio's strategy against Carthage. Carl Richard, *The Founders and the Classics*: 66. At other times, they discovered Caesar in their adversaries (91).
11. Bernard Bailyn, *Ideological Origins of the American Revolution*: 137. Thanks to Gina Morantz-Sanchez.
12. Ibid.: 136 and 131.
13. Arendt, *On Revolution*: 207.
14. See Margaret Malamud, "*Translatio Imperii*: America as the New Rome, ca. 1900": 251.
15. Bailyn, *Ideological Origins*: 135–136.
16. Malamud, "*Translatio Imperii*": 252.
17. Richard, *The Founders*: 164; emphasis mine.
18. Rogers and Hingley, "Edward Gibbon": 200.
19. Brendon, *The Decline*: 9.
20. Quoted in Christopher Kelly, "A Grand Tour: Reading Gibbon's 'Decline and Fall'": 51.
21. Smith, *The Wealth of Nations, vol. 2*: 60; Sankar Muthu, *Enlightenment against Empire*: 4.
22. Smith, *The Wealth*: 60, 56.
23. Ibid.: 58.
24. Ibid.: 59.
25. Ibid.: 59–60; emphasis mine.

26. Brendon, *The Decline*: 37.
27. On the importance of Virgil for Burke's argument, see Vasunia, *The Classics and Colonial India*: 256–261.
28. Burke, quoted in Uday Singh Mehta, *Liberalism and Empire*: 138.
29. Kirsten McKenzie, "Britain: Ruling the Waves": 131.
30. Javed Majeed, "Comparativism and References to Rome": 108.
31. Quoted in Gregory Evans Dowd, "'We Are the Heir Apparent to the Romans': Imperial Myths and Indigenous Status": 54.
32. Kostas Vlassopoulos, "Imperial Encounters: Discourses on Empire and the Uses of Ancient History during the Eighteenth-Century": 37 and 40.
33. E. W. Montagu, quoted in Vlassopoulos, "Imperial Encounters": 42.
34. Rogers and Hingley, "Edward Gibbon": 199.
35. Kate Fullagar, "'Savages That Are Among Us'": 212.
36. Bernard Smith, *Imagining the Pacific in the Wake of Cook's Voyages*: 175.
37. Georg Forster, *Voyage Round the World*, vol. 1 (hereafter FE): 447.
38. Bernard Smith, *European Vision and the South Pacific*: 40–41.
39. George Steinmetz, *The Devil's Handwriting*: 268. They became the "visual archetypes of the Maori warrior." Smith, *Imagining the Pacific*: 81. This archive of tattooed warriors has another layer: in the wake of comparisons of Virginia's Native Americans to Ancient Britons, engravings of tattooed Picts became fashionable (one wielding the severed head of his Roman oppressor). See Sam Smiles, *The Image of Antiquity*: 129.
40. J. C. Beaglehole, "General Introduction": xxi.
41. Ibid.
42. Fullagar, "Savages": 225; and C. A. Bayly, *Imperial Meridian: The British Empire and the World, 1780–1830*: 191.
43. Bayly, *Imperial Meridian*: 194; Fullagar, "Savages": 230.
44. Fullagar, "Savages": 230.
45. Anthony Grafton delineates this Renaissance rediscovery of Rome and the emergence of antiquarianism as the study of ruins. Grafton, *Bring Out Your Dead*: 37.
46. G. W. Bowersock, "Gibbon on Civil War": 29.
47. On Gibbon and travel literature, see Robert Shackleton, "The Impact of French Literature on Gibbon": 42.
48. J. G. A. Pocock, *Barbarians, Savages, and Empires*, vol. 4 of *Barbarianism and Religion*: 231.
49. Bowersock, "Gibbon's Historical Imagination": 17.
50. Volume 7 was published in 1788.
51. Gibbon commented that Romans must have found the "ancient picture" intriguing (DFIII, 1062).
52. Combining interest in civic architecture with reflections on Rome's decay, Gibbon "recorded how he began to 'collect the substance of my Roman decay.'" Rogers and Hingley, "Edward Gibbon": 194.
53. Gibbon, *The Autobiographies of Edward Gibbon*: 302.

54. Catharine Edwards, *Writing Rome*: 85.
55. Patricia B. Craddock, "Edward Gibbon and the 'Ruins of the Capitol'": 67 and 66.
56. Ibid.: 79.
57. Ibid.
58. Poggio Bracciolini arrived at a perfect allegory of time broken, a Benjaminian melancholic *avant la lettre*.
59. Gibbon, quoted in Kelly, "A Grand Tour": 49.
60. Ibid.
61. Gibbon, quoted in Giuseppe Giarrizzo, "Toward the 'Decline and Fall'": 61 and 59.
62. Composed before 1774, "General Observations" was revised in 1781.
63. Friedrich Meinecke locates Gibbon between natural-law Enlightenment history and historicism. See Meinecke, *Historism*: 186–192. Gerald J. Gruman sees a multilayered argument. See Gruman, "'Balance' and 'Excess' as Gibbon's Explanation of the Decline and Fall": 75–85.
64. In volume 1, Gibbon emphasized Caracalla's extension of citizenship and the role of Romanized barbarians.
65. With this reading of the beginnings of European history as *barbarian* came the "rediscovery of the 'savage'" in the course of the Oceanic conquest, and Europeans began to see "herding peoples as both their 'others' and their ancestors." Pocock, *Barbarism and Religion*, vol. 4: 100. With Smith and Ferguson, "the 'Enlightened narrative'" becomes "the narrative of Europe as world empire." Pocock, *Barbarism and Religion*, vol. 2: 317. However, Gibbon collapsed the notion of "savages" and "barbarians." François Furet, "Civilization and Barbarism in Gibbon's History": 163.
66. On Gibbon's essays on Virgil, see Vasunia, *The Classics and Colonial India*: 254–257.
67. Quoted in Kelly, "A Grand Tour": 45.
68. Furet, "Civilization": 164.
69. On Gibbon's obsession with Britain's potential "decline and fall," see also Vasunia, *The Classics and Colonial India*: 256.
70. Vasunia, *The Classics and Colonial India*: 144–145.
71. F. Haverfield, quoted in Morley, *The Roman Empire*: 109–110.
72. In 1845 the Maori assaulted the largest settlement on New Zealand. See Marshall Sahlins, *Islands of History*: viii.
73. Brendon, *The Decline*: 55.
74. Ibid.: 56.
75. Ibid.

CHAPTER NINE

1. "Appendix A" (1804) in Porterfield and Siegfried, eds., *Staging Empire*: 190. Invoking "imperial ancestors" was part of stressing "military achievements." Siegfried, "Ingres's Napoleon I": 80.

2. Hegel, *Vorlesungen über die Philosophie der Weltgeschichte (Lectures on the Philosophy of History)*: 17.
3. Ibid.: 18.
4. Ibid.
5. See Todd Samuel Presner, "Dialectics at a Standstill": 193–211.
6. On Bertrand as the author of the Algerian colonists, see Azzedine Haddour, *Colonial Myths*: 24–27.
7. Hegel, *Vorlesungen*: 437. Inventing "the politics of power," imperial Rome "locked [all gods] into its pantheon of world domination" (393). In this state, the universal suffocated the particular.
8. Forster, "Leitfaden zu einer künftigen Geschichte der Menschheit" (1789), http://www.zeno.org/nid/20004782410, under paragraph 18.
9. *See also Reise um die Welt* (hereafter FG): 443. The text was first published in English in 1777, then in German in 1778–1790.
10. Banks, quoted in Smith, *European Vision*: 43.
11. On this topic, see Steinmetz, *The Devil's Handwriting*, chapter 4.
12. See Bougainville, *Voyage autour du monde* ([1771] 1982): 247.
13. Smith, *Imagining the South Pacific in The Wake of the Cook Voyages*: 21, 24.
14. Bougainville, *Voyage*: 231.
15. Temporarily separated from Aeneas, some Trojans encountered races living in a "primitive state" (AFi, 22–23).
16. See James E. G. Zetzel, "Rome and Its Traditions": 190–191.
17. Mentioning his founding of a French colony, Bougainville quotes lines about Augustus from Virgil's *Georgics*: "Tibi serviat ultima Thule." Bougainville, *Voyage*: 82. On this earlier French mission, see Harry Liebersohn, *The Travelers' World*: 86–87.
18. *The Journals of Captain Cook on his Voyages of Discovery*, ed. J. C. Beaglehole, vol. 2: 354.
19. Lupher, *Romans in a New World*: 252.
20. This is part of a general critique of *empires* as oppressing the defenseless (FG, 63).
21. Brendon, *The Decline*: 61. The popular performance of the "pantomime" *Omai or A Trip Round the World* in 1785 included an "Apotheosis of Captain Cook." McCormick, *Omai: Pacific Envoy*: 318.
22. O-Mai returned to Tahiti on Cook's *Resolution*.
23. Georg Forster, "Cook, der Entdecker," http://www.zeno.org/nid/20004782364, under last paragraph. Here, the Arcadia *topos* becomes a "fantasy image" guiding humanity.
24. Edmund Burke, quoted in Michael Heffernan, "Historical Geographies of the Future: Three Perspectives from France, 1750–1825": 136.
25. Ibid.
26. The Royal Society's instructions; see Bernard Smith, *Imagining the Pacific*: 43. See also Vanessa Agnew, "Dissecting the Cannibal: Comparing the Function of the Autopsy Principle in the Diaries and Narratives of Cook's Second Voyage": 50–60.

27. See Harry Liebersohn, *The Travelers' World: Europe to the Pacific*: 35.
28. David Bindman, "'Philanthropy Seems Natural to Mankind'": 22. On Forster's analogy between the maturing of societies and human beings, see Nicholas Thomas, "Hodges as Anthropologist and Historian": 28.
29. Nicholas Thomas and Oliver Berghof, "Introduction": xxxiii.
30. Jonathan Lamb understands the incident as Maori deliberately spooking the voyagers. See FE, 459, note 16.
31. On Forster's ambivalence, see Vanessa Agnew, "Ethnographic Transgressions and Confessions in Georg Forster's 'Voyage Round the World'": 304–315.
32. Kennedy, "Virgilian Epic": 148.
33. Forster's view of the inhabitants ranges from neutral descriptions to Maori as "absolutely sunk to a state of barbarism."
34. Diderot, "Supplement": 181.
35. The crew had stopped at New Zealand, where William Hodges sketched his portraits of New Zealand men (see chapter 8).
36. Beaglehole, ed., *The Journals of Captain Cook*: 359.
37. Recall Virgil's visual palimpsest: witnessing the building of Dido's *colonia*, the readers "see" the new Augustan Carthage rise while simultaneously remembering images of Carthage's fall and Dido's curse: that Rome too will be ruined.
38. C. F. von Volney, *Die Ruinen und Das natürliche Gesetz*, transl. Georg Forster (Leipzig: Philipp Reclam Jun., 1792).
39. Smith, *Imagining the Pacific*: 52.
40. Ibid.: 24. Under the political-epistemological pressures of exploratory travel, idealized landscapes gave way to landscapes meant to serve navigation, and history painting gave way to depictions of first encounters.
41. See Smith, *European Vision*: 71.
42. Piranesi connected Roman "engineering" to Etruscan monumental architecture. John Wilton-Ely, "Design through Fantasy": 27.
43. The former belongs to the *Le Antichità Romane* (1756), the latter to a series on Paestum.
44. Natasha Eaton, "Hodges' Visual Genealogy for Colonial India": 36, 35.
45. See Bindman, "'Philanthropy Seems Natural to Mankind'": 21–26.
46. Quoted in Mike Heffernan, "Historical Geographies of the Future": 136.
47. Marshall Sahlins, *Islands of History*: 56, note 27. "In deciding how to act in the present, [the Maori] examine the panorama of history spread before their eyes, and select the model." Far from "living in the past," they are "drawing on the past for guidance, bringing the past into the present and the future." Ibid.

CHAPTER TEN

1. Michelet, *La cité des vivants et des morts*: 411.
2. Ibid.: 405.

3. Ibid.
4. Michelet, *Histoire Romaine*: 6.
5. Ibid.
6. Alain Niderlinder and Marie-Pierre Demarcq, eds., *Le Voyage de L'Obélisque Luxor/Paris 1829–1836*: 4.
7. Ibid.: 22.
8. Quoted in Todd Porterfield, *The Allure of Empire: Art in the Service of French Empire 1798–1830*: 13; emphasis mine.
9. Ibid.
10. Ibid.
11. "Thus a family is made, a city common to the living and the dead." Michelet, quoted in Claude Lefort, ed., *La cité des vivants et des morts*: 63.
12. Napoleon met Volney (traveling with Louis-François Cassas). Nina Burleigh, *Mirage: Napoleon's Scientists and the Unveiling of Egypt*: 17.
13. Among Jacobins, interest in "postslavery colonialism" reawakened. Juan Cole, *Napoleon's Egypt: Invading the Middle East*: 13. Egypt was meant to replace Haiti or St. Domingo (20).
14. Savary, quoted in Jean-Joël Brégeon, *L'Égypte de Bonaparte*: 66.
15. See Brégeon, *L'Égypte*: 69.
16. See Cole, *Napoleon's Egypt*: 12ff.
17. Brégeon, *L'Égypte*: 283.
18. Vol. 2 of the *Description*, *Antiquités*, was devoted to these ancient ruins.
19. Quoted in Brian A. Curran et al., eds., *Obelisk*: 231.
20. Moiret, *Memoirs of Napoleon's Egyptian Expedition*: 36; emphasis mine.
21. Ibid. Immersed in Greek and Roman history, the officers were identifying readily with the conquests of Alexander and Augustus. Cole, *Napoleon's Egypt*: 11. On Bonaparte's ideas of a "republican empire," see 101ff.
22. On Egypt *as scene*, see Timothy Mitchell, *Colonizing Egypt*.
23. The invasion enriched the British Museum's Egyptian collection and the Louvre. Napoleon was congratulated on having replicated the Romans' appropriation of Greek art. See David Wengrow, "Forgetting the *Ancien Régime*": 183.
24. Moiret, *Memoirs*: 39.
25. Ibid.: 88.
26. Ibid.: 90.
27. Brégeon, *L'Égypte*: 72.
28. Cole, *Napoleon's Egypt*: 27.
29. Charles Norry, quoted in ibid.
30. Moiret, *Memoirs*: 46.
31. Ibid.: 47.
32. Ibid.
33. Ibid.: 64.
34. Pagden, *Worlds at War*: 366. On Volney's exalted vision of a future French Empire uniting East and West, see 396–398.

35. Edward Said, *Orientalism*: 84.
36. Fourier, quoted in Said, *Orientalism*: 86. He turned Egyptian history into world history, that is, European history (ibid.).
37. See, for instance, David Wengrow's reading in "Forgetting the *Ancien Régime*": 182–183.
38. Porterfield, *The Allure*: 114.
39. Moiret, *Memoirs*: 157.
40. Cole, *Napoleon's Egypt*: 247. The campaign was seen as a "prologue" to Algeria's conquest (245).
41. Napoleon "understood the difference between Caesar and Octavian-Augustus." Valérie Huet, "Napoleon I: A New Augustus?": 55.
42. Predating the July Monarchy, plans for the obelisk included a project by Denon. Porterfield, *The Allure*: 28.
43. Denon, quoted in Porterfield, *The Allure*: 30.
44. Ibid.
45. Siegfried, "Ingres's Napoleon I": 78.
46. Roman art was used to "assert a direct filiation from a Roman emperor, Trajan, and at the same time it marked Napoleon's difference" as "the true reincarnation of a Roman emperor." Valérie Huet, "Napoleon I": 66.
47. Denon, quoted in Siegfried, *Staging Empire*: 79.
48. Siegfried, "Ingres's Napoleon I": 80.
49. Siegfried, *Staging Empire*: 48.
50. Siegfried, "Ingres's Napoleon I": 80.
51. Ibid.: 40.
52. Huet, "Napoleon I": 67.
53. Ronald T. Ridley, *The Eagle and the Spade: The Archeology of Rome during the Napoleonic Era*: 5.
54. Ibid.
55. Susan Vandiver Nicassio, *Imperial City: Rome under Napoleon*: 25.
56. Quoted in ibid.: 31.
57. Ibid.: 21.
58. Ibid.: 177.
59. Ibid.
60. Ibid.
61. Nicassio, *Imperial City*: 31.
62. Ridley, *The Eagle*: 169.
63. Nicassio, *Imperial City*: 31.
64. Ridley, *The Eagle*: 171.
65. Tournon, quoted in ibid.: 63.
66. Tournon, quoted in ibid.
67. Tournon, quoted in Nicassio, *Imperial City*: 184.
68. Porterfield, *The Allure*: 115.
69. Fourier, "Préface historique" (hereafter FP): viii.
70. Richard Wagner, *Art and Revolution* (1849): 36.

71. The Egyptian Campaign was a "*memorable war*," a "memorable expedition" (FP, iv and viii)—these are two examples of Fourier's rhetoric of commemoration.
72. Fourier writes an imperial history of Europe, linking the expedition to the imperial desire of post-Roman Europe, and the discoveries of Columbus and Vasco da Gama (FP, xi).
73. The British abandoned Egypt to this state when they handed it back to the Ottomans.
74. The geopolitical design was a French Mediterranean (FP, ix).
75. Brian A. Curran et al., *Obelisk*: 46.
76. Porterfield, *The Allure*: 25.
77. Ibid.: 31.

CHAPTER ELEVEN

1. See Ian Warrell, *Turner Inspired: In the Light of Claude*: 44.
2. Barry Venning, *Turner*: 139.
3. Turner inherited the stagelike setting from Claude's *Seaport with the Embarkation of Saint Ursula* (1641), using the angled view in a more dramatic manner.
4. Turner, quoted in Warrell, *Turner Inspired*: 93.
5. Ibid.: 81.
6. Venning, *Turner*: 142.
7. Woolf, "Inventing Empire in Ancient Rome": 312 and 318.
8. Woolf, "World-Systems Analysis and the Roman Empire": 54.
9. Franck Laurent, *Le Voyage en Algérie*: 803. Bertrand always intended to write an epic novel like the *Aeneid*. See Bertrand, "Préface de la Nouvelle Edition," *Le Sang des Races* (1920): xii. The novel belongs to his "African cycle." Patricia Lorcin, "Decadence and Renaissance": 183.
10. Bertrand delivered his speech at the Eucharistic Congress. On the centenary events in Algeria (including the Vincennes colonial exposition), see Nabila Oulebsir, *Les usages du patrimoine. Monuments, musées et politique colonial en Algérie (1830–1930)*: 261–292. According to centenary officials, "Roman Africa [was] the true blossoming of [a] civilizing nation." Quoted in Caroline Ford, "The Inheritance of Empire and the Ruins of Rome in French Colonial Algeria": 76. The anniversary coincided with Augustine's. See Louis Bertrand, "L'Église D'Afrique" (1930): 415.
11. Bertrand used the existing anthropological concept of "Latins of Africa" for his ideological idea of African Latinity. Lorcin, "Rome and France in Africa": 312.
12. Bertrand, "Préface à la Nouvelle Édition": xiii.
13. Louis Bertrand, "Les Villes D'Or" (1921): 53.
14. French refugees from Alsace-Lorraine joined the European settler population of Spaniards, Italians, Corsicans, and Maltese.
15. Lorcin, "Rome and France": 312.

16. Ibid.: 301, note 21.
17. Ibid.: 300.
18. Ibid.: 298.
19. Oulebsir, *Les usages*: 14.
20. Between 1830 and 1880, territorial expansion significantly increased, and with it, the work of scholars and artists, "heirs to the explorations in Egypt." Oulebsir, *Les usages*: 17.
21. Ford, "The Inheritance of Empire": 62.
22. On the *Académie*'s role, see Lorcin, "Rome and France": 301.
23. Gsell directed the "musée national des antiquités algériennes" and was in charge of the twenty-six-volume history of ancient North Africa. See Oulebsir, *Les usages*: 191, 190.
24. Gsell, *Les monuments antiques de L'Algérie*, vol. 1: 113.
25. Ford, "The Inheritance of Empire": 65, 67.
26. Ibid.: 67.
27. Ibid.
28. Ibid.: 71. The Romans also failed "to change hearts and minds" (67).
29. Oulebsir, *Les usages*: 65, 68.
30. As the country's "original inhabitants," they were equivalent to the Germanic tribes; Kabyles were "primitive Romans." Lorcin, "Rome and France": 306, 307.
31. Ibid.: 307.
32. Roger Benjamin, "Colonial Panoramania": 113.
33. Tocqueville, "Second Letter on Algeria (22 August 1837)": 26.
34. Ibid.: 23.
35. Ibid.: 23–24.
36. Tocqueville, "First Report on Algeria (1847)": 144. He situates Arabs as a "barbarous" nation between the savage Kabyle and Europe's "civilized nations" (ibid.).
37. Tocqueville, "Notes on the Voyage to Algeria in 1841": 56.
38. Tocqueville, "Essay on Algeria": 61.
39. Ibid.: 59.
40. Ibid.: 61.
41. Ibid.: 60–61 and 70.
42. Gsell, *Les monuments antiques*, vol. 1: 112.
43. Bertrand, "L'Église d'Afrique": 406.
44. Ibid.: 408.
45. Lavigerie inspired "priest-archeologists." Bertrand, "Les Villes D'Or" (1920): 703.
46. They became part of Bertrand's myth of origins. Bertrand called himself a "lost Rumi in an Islamic land." Lorcin, "Rome and France": 316.
47. The history of Islam was the massacres of Christians. See Bertrand, "Massacreurs et Tortionnaires" (1911): 241–248. On the official policy toward Islam, see 225.

48. Bertrand, *Sur les Routes du Sud* (1936): 218.
49. In 1858, Flaubert saw only crumbling walls at Carthage, but by 1900, archeologists had uncovered Roman, and by 1925, Punic Carthage.
50. On Bertrand and Barrès's notion of "rootedness," see Dunwoodie, "Colonizing Space": 999–1000.
51. Barrès "coined the word *barbare* as a definition of 'the Other.'" Lorcin, *Imperial Identities: Stereotyping, Prejudice & Race in Colonial Algeria*: 199.
52. Ibid.: 203.
53. On this topic, see also Lorcin, "Decadence and Renaissance": 181–195.
54. Laurent, *Le Voyage en Algérie*: 807. Herbert Spencer published "Re-Barbarization," arguing that British imperialism's militarization constituted a relapse into barbarian forms of social organization. Spencer, "Re-Barbarization" (1902): 174 and 176.
55. Lorcin, "Rome and France": 321.
56. Arthur de Gobineau, *The Inequality of Human Races*: 2 and 1.
57. Gobineau, *Inequality*: 1 and 2. A post-Roman imperial thinker, Gobineau writes about the fate of Europe and the "blood of the civilizing race." Ibid.: 33.
58. Ibid.: 168.
59. Ibid.: 33.
60. Gobineau dismissed Montesquieu's and Polybios's explanations. See ibid.: 4, 1, 10, 11, and 12.
61. Ibid.: 33.
62. Ibid.
63. Ibid.
64. Gobineau opened with a global panoramic scenario of ruin gazing where the reader's gaze sweeps across ruinscapes that included the ancient empires of the Americas. See ibid.: 1–2.
65. Ibid.: 102.
66. Ibid.: 104.
67. Ibid.: 171.
68. Ibid.: 173.
69. Arthur de Gobineau, *Essai sur l'inégalité des races humaines* (1853), vol. 2: 347–348.
70. Bertrand, *Sur les Routes*: 63.
71. Ibid.: 78 and 79.
72. Ibid.: 78.
73. "The concept of the barbarian," Lorcin writes, "was integral to his [Bertrand's] theory." "Decadence and Renaissance": 183.
74. Bertrand, *Sur les Routes*: 54, 55.
75. Bertrand, "Le Jardin de la mort," quoted in Laurent, *Le Voyage*: 805. In 1897, Léonce Bénédicte organized an exhibit at the *Institut de Carthage,* and the Society of French Orientalist Painters formed in 1899. Roger Benjamin, "Colonial Panoramania": 112.

76. Laurent, *Le Voyage*: 805.
77. Bertrand, *Sur les Routes*: 63.
78. Ibid.
79. Ibid.: 62.
80. Ibid.: 63.
81. Ibid.: 71.
82. Ibid.; emphasis mine.
83. Ibid.: 58.
84. Ibid.: 71.
85. Ibid.: 72.
86. Ibid.: 79, 80.
87. Benjamin, "Colonial Panoramania": 113.
88. Bertrand, "Préface" (1905), *Le Jardin de la Mort: i.*
89. Ibid.: vii.
90. Chateaubriand, *Mémoires d'outre-tombe* (1848–1850), vol. 1: 276.
91. Napoleon asked him about Egypt, Arabs, and their "strange" prayer habits. Chateaubriand, *Memoires*, vol. 2: 331.
92. Chateaubriand, *Mémoires*, vol. 2: 527.
93. Ibid.: 528.
94. Bertrand, "Préface" (1905), *Le jardin de la mort*: xii.
95. Ibid.: ix.
96. Ibid. Never reconstructing, Arab invaders dwelled in Roman ruins. As a consequence, "Rome's seal" remained "visible" (viii).
97. He compared his experiences in Tipasa's ruins to those of Chateaubriand's in Rome. See Bertrand, *Sur les Routes*: 221.
98. Bertrand, "L'Église": 403.
99. Ibid.
100. Ibid.
101. Ibid. Lavigerie's motto for the congress was a quote from Leo XIV: "sive resurgat gloriosa aliquando!" (403).
102. Bertrand, "L'Église": 403.
103. Woolf, "Inventing Empire": 313.
104. Bertrand, "Préface" (1905): ix.
105. Ibid.
106. Ibid.: x.
107. Bertrand, *Sur les Routes du Sud* (1936): 218. In the spirit of Gobineau, it meant "keep[ing] the Latin race pure." Lorcin, ed., *Imperial Identities*: 203.
108. Re-barbarization means that "we can assume the qualities that make [the barbarian] strong and turn them against him so he won't crush us." Bertrand, quoted in Lorcin, *Imperial Identities*: 204.
109. Louis Bertrand, "Les Villes D'Or" (1921): 54.
110. Bertrand, "Les Villes D'Or" (1920): 699.
111. Ibid.: 698.
112. Ibid.

113. Haddour, *Colonial Myths*: 26. The "space of the colonized is desertified and presented in a state of ruins and their history as a derelict site—the Roman ruins" (ibid.).
114. Bertrand, quoted in Oulebsir, *Les usages*: 286.
115. Ibid. Translation by Caroline Ford, "The Inheritance": 77.
116. Bertrand, quoted in Oulebsir, *Les usages*: 286.
117. Bertrand, "Les Villes D'Or" (1921): 53. The epistemological ground of this view of history is Bertrand's "metaphysical" race concept. The "illusion of time vanishes" from the perspective of race as "essential . . . condition" (54).
118. Bertrand, "Préface": xi.
119. Bertrand, *Sur les Routes*: 80.
120. Bertrand, "Préface": xii.
121. Bertrand, quoted in Dunwoodie, "Colonizing Space": 1012.
122. Bertrand's North African theater of repetition is very different from the elusive Carthaginian site of Chateaubriand's theater of memory (and his resurrectional mimesis very different form the latter's Romantic aesthetics of the lost moment).
123. Bertrand, *Le Sens de L'Ennemi*: 242.
124. Ibid.
125. Lorcin, *Imperial Identities*: 200.
126. Bertrand, "L'Eglise": 408. With Tertullian, "our history" begins (ibid.).
127. Bertrand, *Sur les Routes du Sud* (1936): 80.
128. Ibid.
129. Michelet, *Histoire Romaine*: 205. This trope had a long life. According to Alfred Rosenberg, would-be-philosopher and Nazi governor of Ukraine after 1941, Carthage embodied "orientalism" and represented what he called the "near-Asiatic Semitic-Jewish command center." Rosenberg, *Der Mythus des Zwanzigsten Jahrhunderts* (1935): 55.
130. Michelet, *Histoire Romaine*: 204.
131. Bertrand, "Les Villes D'Or" (1921): 53.
132. Ibid.: 54.
133. Ibid.: 59.
134. Mobilizing the immersive technologies of dioramas, for instance, the 1900 Paris Universal Exhibition transported spectators to the shores of the Mediterranean, most spectacularly in the "Panorama du Tour du Monde." Benjamin, "Colonial Panoramania": 120. A critic of modernity, Bertrand wanted actual experience.
135. Bertrand, "Les Villes D'Or" (1921): 58.
136. Bertrand, "Les Villes D'Or" (1920): 709.
137. Ibid.: 696.
138. Ibid.
139. Ibid.: 695.
140. Bertrand, "Les Villes D'Or" (1921): 59.
141. Ibid.: 62 and 59.

142. Ibid.: 62 and 63.
143. Ibid.: 67.
144. Ibid.: 65.

CHAPTER TWELVE

1. Joseph Goebbels, "Der Insulaner und die Spanienfrage" (1941): 48–55.
2. The Protectorate of German New Guinea existed from 1884 to 1914. German Samoa was a protectorate from 1900 to 1914. The *Kolonialamt* acquired fifty of Nolde's watercolors. See Ingrid Brugger, Andreas Fluck, Christiane Lange, Manfred Reuther, and Gabriele Weiss, eds., *Emil Nolde und die Südsee*: 23. On German Samoa and the representations of Samoans, see George Steinmetz, *The Devil's Handwriting*, chapters 4 and 5.
3. Emil Nolde, *Welt und Heimat: Die Südseereise 1913–1918*: 57; see also 59.
4. In his polemic against ornament in architecture, Erich Loos discussed tattooing among "the papua" (who eat their "enemy") as the origin of art. Ornaments correspond to a state of an amoral existence. What is amoral at this stage is "degenerate" today. Loos, "Ornament und Verbrechen" (1908): 276. See https://de.wikisource.org/wiki/Ornament_und_Verbrechen.
5. The governor's attempts to disarm Samoans involved "the traditional Samoan knife dance." George Steinmetz, *The Devil's Handwriting*: 338. On the comparison of French communards to South Sea Islanders, see Alice Bullard, *Exile to Paradise: Savagery and Civilization in Paris and the South Pacific*.
6. See also Margaret W. Ferguson, "The Afflatus of Ruins": 34–35, on Edmund Spenser's *The Ruines of Time*.
7. Thomas B. Macaulay, "von Ranke": 548.
8. Macaulay, quoted in Catharine Edwards, "Translating Empire? Macaulay's Rome": 80.
9. Horace Walpole predicted that "travelers from the New World would 'visit England and give a description of the ruins of St. Paul.'" Brendon, *Decline*: 9. In an anonymous booklet published in 1875, a "triumphal arch" rises above the Parisian ruinscape, visited by explorers from the South Pacific. *Les Ruines de Paris En 4875* (1875): 43. Earlier texts about "savage" visitors from the New World include Montaigne's famous report in which he argued that they were less savage than his compatriots. Montaigne, "On Cannibals": 114.
10. Junod argues that Doré deliberately increased the spatial distance of this spectator (from "the other end of the world") toward the scene he contemplates as a critical gesture toward the modern metropolis. Philippe Junod, "Babylone-sur-Tamise: Londres vue par Gustave Doré": 77.
11. Macaulay, quoted in Sam Smiles, *The Image of Antiquity*: 147.
12. Ibid.: 148.
13. Macaulay, "Minute on Indian Education," quoted in Mehta, *Liberalism and Empire*: 15.
14. Macaulay, quoted in Mehta, *Liberalism and Empire*: 69.

15. Metcalfe, quoted in Brendon, *The Decline*: 56.
16. Ibid.
17. Ibid.
18. Ibid.
19. Macaulay, quoted in Smiles, *The Image of Antiquity*: 147. Macaulay "anticipated with approval the day when Indians would acquire sufficient knowledge of western practices for self-government." Edwards, "Translating Empire?": 83.
20. Macaulay, quoted in Smiles, *The Image of Antiquity*: 147.
21. The Maori is both the subject of the look and an object in the field of vision. See Jacques Lacan, "What Is a Picture?": 105–106. The onlooker desires the gaze, which constitutes the act of looking inscribed into this scene: looking with the subject and looking at the subject, looking.
22. Angela Miller, *The Empire of the Eye: Landscape Representations and American Cultural Politics, 1825–1875*: 39. Laurence Goldstein foregrounds Cole's "desecration-of-nature theme." Goldstein, *Ruins and Empire: The Evolution of a Theme in Augustan and Romantic Literature*: 229. As Cole traces the stages of this destruction, the stagelike setting becomes more pronounced.
23. Doré echoes the *mise-en-scène* of the colonial other at the nineteenth-century exhibits. At these world fairs, "the world became a world theater." Werner Hofmann, quoted in Alexander C. T. Geppert, "Welttheater: Die Geschichte des europäischen Ausstellungswesens im 19. und 20. Jahrhundert": 18. In Germany, the practice continued until 1932, in France until the early 1940s.
24. Ian McGibbon, *The Oxford Companion to New Zealand Military History* (2000): 310. In 1942, New Zealand's 28th Maori Battalion arrived in Italian Libya, driving through the Marble Arch erected in 1937.
25. Quoted in Patricia Lorcin, ed., *Imperial Identities*: 205.
26. Bertrand, *Le Sens de L'Ennemi*: 221.
27. Ibid. Too many Europeans still thought like Flaubert, who opined that France should send "a Voltaire" when "Turks massacred Christians," not weapons (222).
28. The original lines are quoted in Anthony Bryer, "Gibbon and the Later Byzantine Empires": 110. It seems to come directly from Tursun Beg's account, hinting at a Persian reference to Rustam's night attack on Afrasiyab's palace in Ferdowsi's Sha-Nahma (110). Thanks to Anton Shamas for this reference.
29. On the "Islamic trope of ruins," the theme of "the disintegration of empires" in the work of a sixteenth-century Mughal chronicler, see Natasha Eaton, "Between Memory and Nostalgia in Northern India": 128–133.

PART 4 PREFACE

1. Osterhammel, *Die Verwandlung der Welt: Eine Geschichte des 19. Jahrhunderts*: 104.
2. Ibid.: 575.

3. Ibid.: 581.
4. Ibid.: 106.

CHAPTER THIRTEEN

1. Heinrich Heine, *Ideas. "Buch Le Grand" of the Reisebilder of Heinrich Heine*, transl. I. B.: 58. In Theodor Fontane's anti-Napoleonic novel, *Vor dem Sturm: Roman aus dem Winter 1812 auf 13* (1878), noble marble becomes a "yellow wax-face" (31).
2. Ibid.: 58.
3. Günderrode, quoted in Kelly Barry, "*The Subject and Object of Mythology* ": 499; translation modified.
4. On the appropriations of Tacitus's portrayal of the Germanic tribes, see Christopher B. Krebs, *A Most Dangerous Book: Tacitus's Germania from the Roman Empire to the Third Reich*: 182–213.
5. On the play as guerilla theater, see Wolf Kittler, "1806. Die Hermannsschlacht." Kleist used the Germanic name for Arminius, the leader of the Germanic tribes' anti-Roman revolt in 9 CE. Germanicus was in charge of Tiberius's retaliatory campaigns (10–16 CE).
6. Rüdiger Safranski, *Romantik*: 187.
7. Sean Franzl, *Connected by the Ear: The Media, Pedagogy, and Politics of the Romantic Lecture*: 180.
8. Fichte understood this re-education as "the activity of forming images." Johann Gottlieb Fichte, *Addresses to the German Nation*: 26.
9. Ibid.: 54. On linguistic purity and its subversion, see David Martyn, "Borrowed Fatherland: Nationalism and Language in Fichte's Addresses to the German Nation": 303–315.
10. Fichte, "Addresses": 54.
11. Ibid.: 70; translation modified.
12. Ibid.
13. Ibid.
14. Ibid.
15. On Fichte and the "liberal Prussian reform movement," see Franzl, *Connected*: 175.
16. "For the second time, Rome," Novalis commented, "became a ruin." Novalis (Friedrich von Hardenberg), *Die Christenheit oder Europa* (1799), http://www.zeno.org/nid/20005447070.
17. Fichte, *Addresses*: 109.
18. Fichte's heroization of Arminius fits with the monumentalizing character of his lectures. On this latter topic, see Franzl, *Connected*: 178–179.
19. Fichte, quoted by Carl Schmitt, *Über die drei Arten des rechtswissenschaftlichen Denkens*: 37.
20. Ibid.
21. Safranski, *Romantik*: 186.

22. Fichte transformed Enlightenment universalism into *völkisch* nationalist politics (see Safranski, *Romantik*: 178)—and, I would add, particularist ideas of a German *Reich*.
23. Ibid.: 189.
24. On Fichte's ethnically based nationalism, see Arash Abizadeh, "Was Fichte an Ethic Nationalist? On Cultural Nationalism and Its Double": 334–359.
25. Herder, *Briefe zur Beförderung der Humanität*, vol. 1: 264.
26. Tacitus, *The Annals of Imperial Rome*: 67. Romans compared Arminius to Hannibal. See Mary Beard, *SPQR*: 480. The retaliatory campaign "border[ed] on attempted genocide." Mattingly, *Imperialism*: 24. It was one of three famous insurrections that included Boudicca's rebellion and the Jewish revolt. While the insurgents' voices are lost, Roman writers included speeches demonstrating that they "could imagine what it was like to be in opposition to their own imperial power" (Beard, *SPQR*: 516). That is, they knew how brutal their rule was.
27. Herder, *Briefe*, vol. 1: 265.
28. Germanicus was set on the "total destruction of the tribe." Tacitus, *Annals*: 85. Tacitus, the "realist," dutifully reported the slaughter of the Cherusci. Maier, *Among Empires*: 113.
29. Arminius pretends to enter an alliance with the Romans against another Germanic leader, but secretly the two join forces, annihilating the Roman Army in the Teutoburg Forest.
30. In 1809, Kleist published his anti-Napoleonic manifesto, "Kathechismus Der Deutschen." Gneisenau drew on Josephus's *Jewish War* for his analogies.
31. With Tacitus in mind, Kleist starts the play in the German forest. See Simon Schama, "Arminius Redivivus," in his *Landscape and Memory*: 100–120.
32. Kleist, *The Battle of Herrmann*: 122. This is Fichte's geographical space. See Niels Weber, "Kleists 'Sendung des Dritten Reiches': Zur Rezeption von Heinrich von Kleists 'Hermannsschlacht' im Nationalsozialismus": 168.
33. Kleist, "Was gilt es in diesem Kriege?": 379.
34. Ibid.
35. Kleist, *The Battle*: 118; translation modified.
36. Ibid.: 119; translation modified.
37. Here, Schiller's "national stage" becomes the world stage. Michael Neumann, "'Und Sehn, Ob Uns Der Zufall Etwas Beut': Kleists Kasuistik der Ermächtigung im Drama 'Die Hermannsschlacht'": 138.
38. Kleist, *The Battle*: 122; translation modified.
39. Ibid.: 114; translation modified.
40. Theodor Mommsen, *The History of Rome*, vol. 4: 196, 270.
41. Schmitt, *The Partisan*: 7.
42. Kleist, *The Battle*: 90.
43. First flattered by Ventidius, Thusnelda has him savagely killed. Her servant appeals to her not to take "the barbarians' revenge." Kleist, *The Battle*: 106; translation modified.

44. Arthur Moeller van den Bruck, the radical conservative, defined Germany as the "land of Europe's uncanny middle." Moeller van den Bruck, "Das unheimliche Deutschland" (1924): 107. By using the dread it evokes in its neighbors, defeated Germany will be Europe's salvation.
45. Friedrich Ratzel, *Kleine Schriften*: 309.
46. Ibid.: 133.
47. Ibid.
48. Or, as Joseph Leo Koerner argues with respect to another painting, the "experience of nature elevated to the level of a revelation, a revelation, however, whose agent and whose content have long since disappeared." Koerner, *Caspar David Friedrich and the Subject of Landscape*: 9.
49. Jost Hermand, *Sieben Arten an Deutschland zu leiden*: 22.
50. Koerner, *Caspar David Friedrich*: 133.
51. Tacitus, *Annals*: 70. See Tacitus's description of the soldiers' perception of *Germania*: "more forests, worse swamps, savage attacks" (70).
52. Tacitus, *Annals*: 69 and 65.
53. Ibid.: 67.
54. Ibid.
55. Ibid.: 67 and 57. Germanicus pursued the insurgents to the "North Sea," where his men imagined "in their terror" strange "shapes half-human and half-animal." Tacitus, *Annals*: 87 and 88.
56. Ibid.: 81.
57. Ibid.: 69.
58. Martin Steffens, *Schinkel 1781–1841: Ein Baumeister im Dienst der Schönheit*: 25.
59. Annette Dorgerloh, "Karl Friedrich Schinkels 'Triumphbogen' 1817—Programmbild und Geschichtsdenkmal": 81, 82.
60. See "The Beginnings of Rome," Mommsen, *The History of Rome*, vol. 1: 53–71.
61. Mommsen, *History*, vol. 1: 3.
62. From here, Mommsen moves to the larger picture, world history as succession of cycles of culture. World history is thus the nonsynchronous development of separate *Kulturkreise* or ethno-cultural regions following their own life cycles toward "[old] age." Mommsen, *History*, vol. 1: 4. All nations of this space experienced a "deep sense of foreignness" toward other ethno-cultural spaces, especially the space of the "Semitic stock" to which Carthage belonged. Mommsen, *History*, vol. 2: 3; translation modified. On Herder's "imaginary geography," see John Noyes, "Commerce, Colonialism, and the Globalization of Action in Late Enlightenment Germany": 84ff.
63. Mommsen, *History*, vol. 2: 3, 17. Mommsen, *Römische Geschichte*: 967.
64. Mommsen, *History*, vol. 4: 196.
65. Ibid.: 268.
66. Mommsen, *History*, vol. 4: 196.
67. Ibid.: 271; translation modified.
68. Ibid.
69. Mommsen, *Römische Geschichte*: 974.

CHAPTER FOURTEEN

1. The engineer involved in the excavation entered Berlin "like a general who has returned from the battlefield." Suzanne Marchand, *Down from Olympus: Archaeology and German Philhellenism in Germany, 1750–1970*: 96.
2. Ulrike Wulf-Rheidt, "'Die alte Herrlichkeit der Stadt des Attalos vor dem staunenden Blick hervorzaubern'—Das Pergamon-Panorama von 1886": 410.
3. Marchand, *Down from Olympus*: 95.
4. See Stephan Oettermann, "Das Pergamon-Panorama von Yadegar Asisi": 417.
5. Wulf-Rheidt, "'Die alte Herrlichkeit'": 413.
6. This was a fictional vantage point. Wulf-Rheidt, "Die alte Herrlichkeit": 413.
7. Benjamin, "Colonial Panoramania": 115. Panoramas surfaced as a popular genre depicting events of the Napoleonic Wars, such as "the 1799 Battle of the Pyramids" (117).
8. Oettermann, "Das Pergamon-Panorama": 417.
9. Wulf-Rheidt, "Die alte Herrlichkeit": 413.
10. Ibid.
11. Ibid.
12. On the colonial movement, see Hans Gründer, *Geschichte der deutschen Kolonien*: 26–33.
13. Friedrich Fabri, *Bedarf Deutschland der Kolonien? Does Germany Need Colonies?*: 60.
14. George Steinmetz, *The Devil's Handwriting*: 9.
15. Ibid.: 168. Ovahero and Khoikhoi complained about having to perform "pagan activities" (168, note 183).
16. In von Trotha's "'race war,'" the camps were "a continuation of annihilation by other means." Isabel V. Hull, *Absolute Destruction: Military Culture and the Practices of War in Imperial Germany*: 59, 90.
17. On the sharpening of nationalist consciousness in Europe as a result of imperial competition after 1870, see C. A. Bayly, *The Birth of the Modern World*: 228ff.
18. David Cannadine, *Ornamentalism: How the British Saw Their Empire*: 46ff and 111. On the royal tours, see 169–170. Queen Victoria was crowned as "Kaiser-i-Hind," a title resonating with Rome's Caesar.
19. The trip spurred debates about settler colonies versus economic and cultural imperialism. See Alexander Honold, "Nach Bagdad und Jerusalem: Die Wege des Wilhelminischen Orientalismus": 146–151.
20. Changes that German observers noticed with ironic condescension. See Honold, "Nach Bagdad und Jerusalem": 145.
21. Germany's newly founded *Oriental Society* sponsored digs with the express purpose of rivaling the museums of Paris and London. Honold, "Nach Bagdad und Jerusalem": 153.
22. Lars Petersen, "Die Orientreise des deutschen Kaisers 1898 und die Ausgrabungen in Baalbek": 403.

23. The French brought their Egyptian trophies to Paris; the British ambassador to the Ottoman Empire famously filched the so-called “Elgin Marbles.” Tong, “The Aesthetics of Imperial Ruins”: 132. Heinrich Schliemann began private excavations at Hissarlik in 1871–1872.
24. Marchand, *Down from Olympus*: 95. Prior to the acquisition of the Pergamon Altar, the Prussian Royal Museum possessed mostly Roman works.
25. This discourse about Greece replicated the Roman Empire’s appropriation of the philosophy, literature, and visual arts of its Greek colony. On this topic of the “affiliation of Greekness” as a “shared concern for the elites of the empire,” see Simon Goldhill, ed., *Being Greek under Rome: Cultural Identity, the Second Sophistic and the Development of Empire*: 13.
26. In 1937, the *limes* commission became part of the Roman-Germanic commission at the German Archeological Institute of the *Reich* (founded in 1874).
27. Marchand, *Down from Olympus*: 173.
28. See “Der Limes, das leise Welterbe,” *Monumente, Magazin für Denkmalkultur*, https://www.monumente-online.de/de/ausgaben/2006/6/der-limes-das-leise-welterbe.php#.WrMLdmrwbIU.
29. A tension was also present in 1875, when Wilhelm II, who liked to think of himself as “a new German Caesar,” attended the inauguration of the monument to Arminius. Richard H. Armstrong, *A Compulsion for Antiquity: Freud and the Ancient World*: 105. The United States celebrated the centennial of Washington’s inauguration in 1899 with “displays of classical iconography,” while Charles Chesnutt introduced Roman slavery into the American post-Roman narrative. John Levi Barnard, “Ancient History, American Time: Chesnutt’s Outsider Classicism and the Present Past”: 73.
30. Beard, *The Roman Triumph*: 109.
31. Tacitus saw this *simulacrum* of an empire as yet another sign of the “corruption of imperial rule.” Beard, *The Roman Triumph*: 109.
32. Felix Dahn, “Vorwort,” no page nrs.
33. Felix Dahn, *A Struggle for Rome*: 246.
34. Ibid.: 228 and 295; translation modified. Dahn’s Orientalist portrayals of the Byzantines’ decadent court read like *ekphrases* of paintings by Karl Wilhelm Gentz.
35. Dahn, *A Struggle*: 493.
36. Ibid.: 168.
37. Ibid.: 169.
38. Ibid.: 75; translation modified.
39. Gerald L. Weinberg, ed, *Hitler’s Table Talk 1941–1944*: 86.
40. Ibid.
41. Ibid.: 58; translation modified.
42. Oettermann, “Das Pergamon-Panorama”: 417.
43. Matthias René Hofter, “Von der Ikone zur Metapher—Der Pergamon Altar im Wilhelminischen Deutschland”: 393.
44. Oettermann, “Das Pergamon-Panorama”: 417.

CHAPTER FIFTEEN

1. Sigmund Freud, *"Delusions and Dreams in Jensen's Gradiva"*: 31.
2. Themistius, quoted in Maria Boletsi, *Barbarism and Its Discontents*: 103.
3. Elco Runia, quoted in Frank Ankersmit, *Sublime Historical Experience*: 144.
4. Friedrich Nietzsche, "The Utility and Liability of History for Life," transl. Richard T. Gray (hereafter OL): 89. I will also use Nietzsche, "On the Uses and Disadvantages of History for Life," transl. R. J. Hollingdale (hereafter OU): 70.
5. Karl Löwith, *Nietzsches Philosophie der ewigen Wiederkehr*: 15.
6. Nietzsche, "Vom Nutzen und Nachteil der Historie für das Leben," http://www.nietzschesource.org/#eKGWB/HL, page 1.
7. "Rome teaches us 'how things became what they are,'" but the "creative mimesis" of the Greece of the "Tragic Age" shows "'how totally other [things] can be.'" Hermann Siemens, "Nietzsche and the 'Classical': Traditional and Innovative Features of Nietzsche's Usage, with Special Reference to Goethe": 394, 395.
8. Nietzsche, *On the Genealogy of Morality*: 23.
9. Nietzsche, quoted in Daniel Conway, "Ecce Caesar: Nietzsche's Imperial Aspirations": 176.
10. Nietzsche, *Twilight of the Idols*, quoted in Conway, "Ecce Caesar": 176.
11. Nietzsche, *On the Genealogy of Morality*: 15 and 16.
12. Ibid.: 15.
13. Henry Morton Stanley, legendary for his brutality against the "'clothless and overtattooed'" Africans, was greeted by outrage at the conference. Adam Hochschild, *King Leopold's Ghost*: 68.
14. Nietzsche, *On the Genealogy of Morality*: 23.
15. Ibid.
16. Ibid.
17. Ibid.
18. After 1887, Nietzsche loses all interest in the topic. Miguel Skirl, "Ewige Wiederkunft": 230.
19. Wilhelm Jensen, *Gradiva: A Pompeiian Fancy (hereafter GRA): 7.*
20. The image-in-movement has such a strong effect on him that Hanold believes it drawn by the artist in the streets of Pompeii.
21. The villa's atrium is decorated with a fresco, *Dido Abandoned by Aeneas*.
22. These photographs "formed a visual stage set" for Gradiva. Mary Bergstein, *Mirrors of Memory: Freud, Photography, and the History of Art*: 189.
23. Basil Dufallo, *The Captor's Image: Greek Culture in Roman Ecphrasis*: 53. These Second-Style theatrical references in Roman villas (the *scaena frons* with masks in the Villa Oplontis or the mask in the Villa of the Mysteries) "simultaneously draw the viewer in and 'boast of their own unreality'" (52).
24. Hanold's Hellenistic Roman-ness is also the creation of social capital on the part of a member of the German *Bildungsbürgertum*. Eric Downing, *After*

Images: Photography, Archeology, and Psychoanalysis and the Tradition of Bildung: 136ff.

25. The German text conveys a stronger sense of the cityscape's details coming together to form a unified picture in Honold's imagination. See Jensen, *Gradiva: Ein pompejanisches Fantasiestück*: 131–132.
26. Downing reads *Gradiva* in the colonial context: Hanold's pure, white German-Hellenism fits with the *Kaiserreich*'s racial logic at the zenith of its colonizing ventures. See Downing, *After Images: Photography*: 143ff. Richard H. Armstrong reads this through the lens of Freud's "Imperialist Hellenism." Armstrong, *A Compulsion for Antiquity*: 105ff.
27. It is not only the archeologist's dream that expresses the desire to be "present as an eye-witness" to the past. Freud, *"Delusions and Dreams in Jensen's Gradiva"*: 93. The neo-Roman imaginary operates on this desire.

CHAPTER SIXTEEN

1. Max Nordau, *Degeneration*: 560.
2. Steven E. Aschheim, "Max Nordau, Friedrich Nietzsche and Degeneration": 643.
3. Nordau, *Degeneration*: 10.
4. A response to crisis, *Degeneration* is "structured by a violent, decisionistic logic that mandates the redemption of a new beginning." Todd Samuel Presner, *Muscular Judaism: The Jewish Body and the Politics of Regeneration*: 45.
5. On geography as a colonial science, see Jürgen Zimmerer, "Im Dienste des Imperiums: Die Geographen der Berliner Universität zwischen Kolonialwissenschaften und Ostforschung": 76.
6. Friedrich Ratzel, *Anthropo-Geographie (1882; 1891; hereafter AGI or AGII)*, vol. 1: 118. On Ratzel's support for German colonialism, see Gerhard Sandner and Mechtild Roessler, "Geography and Empire in Germany, 1871–1945": 119ff.
7. Ratzel, *Politische Geographie*: 98 and 99.
8. Ibid.: 107.
9. Ibid.: 266, 265.
10. Ibid.: 266 and 269.
11. Crediting Forster with having taken inventory of the "monuments of the distant past," Herder proposed to write a history of the earth's monuments. "On Monuments of the Distant Past": 64.
12. On the concept of border in Ratzel, see Kristin Kopp, *Germany's Wild East: Constructing Poland as Colonial Space*: 187–188.
13. Bertrand, "Le jardin de la mort": 813.
14. Touring the United States, Ratzel found modern ruins, "witnesses of a swift life," destined to an equally swift decline. Ratzel, "Ruins": 286.
15. Massimo Ferrari Zumbini, *Untergänge und Morgenröten*: 169.
16. Using Hannibal Eduard Meyer, admirer of Spengler, made the act of will the center of his methodology. See introduction to Max Weber, *The Agrarian*

Sociology of Ancient Civilizations: 16. Here, Weber theorized Caesarism after having analyzed the causes of Rome's decline in his *Habilitationsschrift*.

17. On the Weimar Republic's "cult of the heroic," see Charles Bambach, *Heidegger's Greek Roots: Nietzsche, National Socialism, and the Greeks*: 31.
18. Oswald Spengler, *The Hour of Decision*: 119.
19. I use the following translations: *Große Kultur*: Great Culture; *Kultur*: *culture*; *Zivilisation*: *civilization*.
20. Referring to "the Egyptians after the time of the Romans" (U, 760), *fellaheen* is Spengler's term for the "primitive," depoliticized masses of the first and twentieth centuries.
21. Spengler insisted that he did not read history through the lens of the natural sciences. Gilbert Merlio rightly argues that Spengler's vitalist morphological logic ultimately represents a form of "biological determinism." Merlio, "Urgefühl Angst": 93.
22. Charles Bambach points to Goethe's "principle of analogy." Bambach, "Weimar Philosophy and the Crisis in Historical Thinking": 136.
23. Ludwig Dehio, "Ranke and German Imperialism": 64. Otto Hintze distinguished Roman from Europe's "new" imperialism, advocating a more efficient coexistence of "world empires." "Imperialismus und Weltpolitik": 469. Arthur James Balfour looked back at Rome to "decipher the future of Europe." Progress did not exclude the idea that "sometime in the far future, the strength of Europe would wane." Alexander Demandt, *Der Fall Roms*: 445.
24. Ferrari Zumbini, *Untergänge*: 152.
25. John Farrenkopf, "Klio und Cäsar": 50. This world empire would eventually include the United States. Max Weber believed that American "world domination was as inevitable as that of Rome after the Punic Wars." Quoted in Farrenkopf, "Klio und Cäsar": 65. On Weber advocating the settlement of German workers in Poland, see Andrew Zimmerman, *Alabama in Africa: Booker T. Washington, the German Empire, and the Globalization of the New South*: 103.
26. Spengler now uses "the paradigm of the Roman empire" no longer exclusively "to describe and foretell the demise" but also "to announce imperialism's rise." Gilbert Merlio, "Über Spenglers Modernität": 121.
27. This is the "parallel" between the twentieth century and the time of "Roman civil wars and Caesarism." Carl Schmitt, "Die geschichtliche Struktur des heutigen Welt-Gegensatzes von Ost und West": 536.
28. Zimmerman, *Alabama in Africa*: 100–101.
29. Ferrari Zumbini makes a convincing case for Nietzsche's anti-Semitism directed against "Ostjuden." Zumbini, *Untergänge*: 17.
30. Hintze voiced the melancholic insight that our "dream of a world governed by the white race is beginning to dissolve." Hintze, quoted in Dehio, "Ranke and German Imperialism": 54.
31. See Jeffrey Herf, *Reactionary Modernism: Technology, Politics, and Culture in Weimar and the Third Reich*: 49–69.

32. The movement and its organizations emerged in the 1890s. Merlio calls Spengler the Ruhr industrialists' "quasi-official ideologue." Merlio, "Über Spengler's Modernität": 124.
33. "Conservative revolutionary" puts the accent on the voluntarism informing the concept of a dictatorial state centered on a strong leader characteristic of the anti-democratic politics of Spengler and Schmitt.
34. Spengler argued against historicism and Darwinist paradigms. On his critique of historicism, see Charles Bambach, "Weimar Philosophy and the Crisis of Historical Thinking": 135–139.
35. The other Great Cultures are Chinese and Ancient Mexican-Peruvian. Comparing the latter's development to that of Antiquity, Spengler lamented the ruination of the Mayans' "Hellenist" cities by the "bandits" of Charles V (U, 608, 607).
36. The course of Western Culture between 1800 and 2000 corresponds to the transition of Hellenism to Roman civilization; Napoleon's moment is analogous to the advent of *civilization* in Greco-Roman Antiquity.
37. Fernand Braudel, "The History of Civilizations": 187.
38. Spengler distinguished between fate and "mere contingency" or "Tyche": "that which could have happened differently without making an essential difference." Kirk Wetters, *Demonic History from Goethe to the Present*: 103.
39. These stages correspond to each other across all eight cultures. Alexandria, Baghdad, and Washington are built simultaneously.
40. Oswald Spengler, *Politische Schriften, 1919–1926*: 12.
41. It also means moving from the intense lived experience of time to the abstract "concept" of time (U, 159). In *culture*, the soul lives time; in civilization, reason measures, reifying time into a concept.
42. Despite Spengler's relativist stance, *The Decline* tilts toward a Eurocentric perspective because he grounds historiography in Faustian culture. *The Decline* is not "consequent relativierend," as Alexander C. T. Geppert argues in "Werden und Vergehen eines sprachgewaltigen Schicksalsszenarios" (121).
43. Merlio, "Urgefühl Angst": 93. During the Third Reich, imperialism's demonic force, causing the decay of sovereignty, will be a core concern of conservative revolutionaries.
44. In the sections dealing with time, Spengler distinguished between Oriental or Magic Culture's conception of history as eschatological and Faustian Culture's as teleological.
45. Braudel, "The History of Civilizations": 188.
46. Landscapes shape humans, and *soul* is particular to each *Kulturkreis*, leading to fundamental alterity.
47. Cathedral, mosque, and archaic cult spaces serve as examples.
48. The same tension of longing and fear also characterizes a culture's experience of time at the moment of its awakening.
49. And the civilized, practical Roman again differs from the "cultured men" of Hellenism (U, 310).

50. The Greeks' clear demarcations made for peaceful coexistence with the "barbarian." With Caracalla's citizenship reform, the boundaries broke down and hatred of the other emerged.
51. Reactionary and metaphysical, Spengler's *Decline* had this advantage: it put an end to historicism's ever-narrowing focus on the European nation-state. On Spengler's "relativist historicism," see Merlio, "Über Spenglers Modernität": 116–117.
52. Civilization is the age of capitalism, the market, liberal democracy, and "the machine."
53. I find the "rabble" inhabiting "our mega-cities" repugnant. Spengler, *Ich beneide jeden, der lebt: Die Aufzeichnungen "Eis heauton" aus dem Nachlaß*: 56.
54. National "Wachsein" or being-awake is equivalent to the idea of the polis in antiquity (U, 780). Spengler implicitly denies Jews the sense of nation/nationalism.
55. A cultural notion of race, it often shades into the biological. Spengler is at his most racist in his definition of *life* outside the eight Great Cultures, those who have "history only in the biological sense" (U, 613).
56. In volume 2, Spengler locates emerging forms of this "unlimited personal regiment" even earlier with the generals of the Punic Wars, including Hannibal (U, 1084).
57. Let us get the causality of Spengler's story straight. While imperialism's relentless expansion is not a mere epiphenomenon of civilization, it is also not the primary cause of civilization's trajectory toward death. The primary cause of decline is the waning of life's power, which in the economic-political sphere takes the form of imperialism-*cum*-Caesarism.
58. John Farrenkopf, *Prophet of Decline: Spengler on World History and Politics*: 35. Spengler criticized the Hellenistic concepts of *Reich* popular among the followers of Stefan George, author of *Das neue Reich* (1928).
59. Only Caesar envisioned governing by the dynastic principle, the "symbol" of "duration" (U, 174).
60. Spengler, *Ich beneide jeden, der lebt*: 55.
61. Confessing his love of Antiquity, Spengler called it our "illusion assembled from everything that we are lacking." Spengler, *Ich beneide jeden, der lebt*: 56.
62. Spengler, *Der Mensch und die Technik: Beitrag zu einer Philosophie des Lebens*: 74.
63. Theodor W. Adorno, "Spengler after the Decline": 72.
64. This scenario is a pastiche of a passage in Eduard Meyer's *Die wirtschaftliche Entwicklung des Altertums*. Ferrari Zumbini, *Untergänge*: 159.
65. Signs of the slow relapse of late *civilization* into barbarism appear early. By the end of the first century, Rome was an imperial metropolis with slums, wilderness zones breeding a new type of "primeval being," and many intellectuals sensed the coming of this exhausted "Fellaheen-world" (U, 676, 785).
66. Otto Seeck made a Darwinist argument about decline. See Seeck, *Geschichte des Untergangs der antiken Welt (1895–1920)*: 389–390. Spengler fell back on a different kind of biological determinism.

67. Not a trace is left of *The Decline*'s structural relativism, or what Ernst Bloch described as the antiquarian Spengler, lovingly tending to the world's "Culture gardens," turning millennia of history into museal spaces. Ernst Bloch, "Anhang: Spenglers Raubtiere": 320.
68. Oswald Spengler, *The Hour of Decision* (hereafter H): 204.
69. Spengler disdained the Nazis' "grotesque" race ideas (H, 219ff).
70. Oswald Spengler, *Neubau des deutschen Reiches* (1924): 103.
71. Worrying about Britain's re-barbarization, J. A. Hobson also compared modern imperialism to Rome. Barbarians remained a threat: "uncivilized Kaffirs" become dangerous when they are suddenly wrenched from their traditional existence. Hobson, *Imperialism: A Study* (1902): 275.
72. Louis Bertrand, *Sur les Routes du Sud*: 218.
73. Nordau, *Degeneration*: 18.
74. Eric Santner, *My Own Private Germany*: 113.

PART 5 PREFACE

1. Martin Heidegger, quoted in Emmanuel Faye, *Heidegger: The Introduction of Nazism into Philosophy*: 102.
2. Joachim Fest, *Albert Speer: Conversations with Hitler's Architect*: 68.
3. Jawaharlal Nehru, *Glimpses of World History*: 1065.
4. Thomas Mann, "Nietzsches Philosophie im Lichte unserer Erfahrung": 703 and 698. Mann here connects Nietzsche to Spengler.
5. Mann, "Bruder Hitler" (1938): 56–57.
6. Spengler, quoted in Stefan Breuer, *Anatomie der konservativen Revolution*: 210, note 55.
7. "Germanen," Hitler replied in the 1942 edition of *Mein Kampf (hereafter MK)*, were not "barbarians" (433).
8. Simone Weil, "The Great Beast: Some Reflections on the Origins of Hitlerism" (1940): 101.
9. Ibid.: 113.
10. Ibid.: 119.
11. Ibid.: 100.
12. Martin Heidegger, *Überlegungen VII–XI (Schwarze Hefte 1938/1939)*: 110.

CHAPTER SEVENTEEN

1. The exhibition opened after "the proclamation of empire in 1936." Simonetta Falasca-Zamponi, *Fascist Spectacle: The Aesthetics of Power in Mussolini's Italy*: 93.
2. See Alex Scobie, *Hitler's State Architecture*: 28.
3. Virgil's anniversary was celebrated in 1930, Horace's in 1936, and Livy's in 1941.
4. Joshua Arthurs, *Excavating Modernity: The Roman Past in Fascist Italy*: 107.

After the Nazi *nomenclatura* arrived, "terror" lingered over the city. Louis Gillet, "Hitler à Rome: Choses Vues" (1938): 675 and 679.

5. *Mostra Augustea della Romanità: Catalogo*: 142.
6. See ibid.: 434. "The Immortality Room" centered on a victory statue, inscribed with Mussolini's 1936 speech about the rebirth of empire. Flavia Marcello, "Mussolini and the Idealization of Empire: The Augustan Exhibition of Romanita": 240.
7. Mussolini, quoted in Arthurs, *Excavating Modernity*: 1.
8. Giglioli, quoted in Arthurs, *Excavating Modernity*: 113.
9. Mussolini, quoted in Mabel Berezin, *Making the Fascist Self*: 124; and in Arthurs, *Excavating Modernity*: 125. Declaring the king emperor, Mussolini established Italian East Africa (Ethiopia, Somaliland, and Eritrea).
10. Maria Wyke, *Projecting the Past: Ancient Rome, Cinema, and History*: 21. In 1911, archeological digs in Libya uncovered the "eternal 'Italian' presence." Arthurs, *Excavating Modernity*: 127.
11. *Mostra Augustea della Romanità: Catalogo*: 434.
12. Arthurs, *Excavating Modernity*: 2, and Emilio Gentile and Lawrence S. Rainey, "The Conquest of Modernity: From Modernist Nationalism to Fascism": 74.
13. Arthurs, *Excavating Modernity*: 114.
14. See *Mostra Augustea della Romanità: Catalogo*. 511.
15. Weil, "The Great Beast": 144. Like Michelet, Weil thought of men who "faithfully cop[ied] the Roman model" as lacking creativity (129).
16. Nehru, *Glimpses*: 112.
17. The governor inspected a plaster model in 1933. See Jeffrey T. Schnapp, *Staging Fascism: 18 BL and the Theater of Masses for Masses*: 126.
18. The model was based *on* the marble map used by Piranesi for his *Antichità Romane*. The exhibit's collection was transferred to a permanent *Museum of the Roman Empire*. Arthurs, *Excavating Modernity*: 97.
19. Giglioli, quoted in Arthurs, *Excavating Modernity*: 106.
20. Spiro Kostof, "The Emperor and the Duce: The Planning of Piazzale Augusto Imperatore in Rome": 279.
21. Cecchelli, quoted in Atkinson, "Hitler's Grand Tour": 11.
22. Kostof, "The Emperor and the Duce": 285.
23. Atkinson, "Hitler's Grand Tour": 9.
24. Kostof, "The Emperor and the Duce": 279.
25. Alex Scobie, *Hitler's State Architecture*: 27.
26. Wilhelm Weber, "ROM: Mussolinis cäsarische Vision" (1940): 137, 146.
27. Ibid.: 141.
28. Ibid.: 138.
29. Ibid.: 137.
30. Bernhard Leitner and Sophie Wilkins, "Speer, the Architect: from a Conversation of July 21, 1978": 33. Temporary decorations for triumphs are a tradition. In 1898, Fifth Avenue was decorated with a triumphal arch. See Margaret Malamud, "*Translatio Imperii*: America as the New Rome ca. 1900": 261.

31. Scobie, *Hitler's State Architecture*: 13.
32. Arthurs, *Excavating Modernity*: 63.
33. Aristotle Kallis, "The 'Third Rome' of Fascism: Demolitions and the Search for a New Urban Matrix": 78.
34. It was a "spiritual path," an archeologist observed, "open to the past" and "a greater future." Arthurs, *Excavating Modernity*: 67 and 66.
35. "[The] Pantheon must be visible from the Piazza Colonna." Mussolini, quoted in Scobie, *Hitler's State Architecture*: 9.
36. Arthurs, *Excavating Modernity*: 77.
37. Kostof, "The Emperor and the Duce": 284; and Mark Antliff, "Fascism, Modernism, and Modernity": 152. See also Orietta Osini, "From Oblivion to the Reassembly": 13–21.
38. Kostof, "The Emperor and the Duce": 304.
39. Ibid.: 285.
40. Ibid.: 289.
41. Ibid.: 271.
42. Tomb and altar were inaugurated in September 1938 at the closing of the *Mostra Augustea*.
43. Kallis, "'Framing Romanità': The Celebrations for the Bimillenario Augusteo and the Augusteo-Ara Pacis Project": 823. Drawing on Foucault's *heterotopia* and Gentile's analysis of fascism as political religion, Kallis reads this space of time-lessness as expressing the "new fascist temporality," at once "heroic and mythic" (823, 824).
44. Ibid.: 287.
45. Arthurs, *Excavating Modernity*: 80.
46. Aristotle Kallis, "The 'Third Rome' of Fascism": 55.
47. Atkinson, "*Hitler's Grand Tour*": 15. Italy conquered territories around the Eastern Mediterranean until Hitler began to claim the Eastern European areas. See Rodogno, *Fascism's European Empire*: 18–19. The Italians consequently turned toward Northern Africa.
48. Their manifestos dripped with contempt for the Romantic veneration of ruins. See Marinetti, quoted in Adrian Lyttelton, "Futurism, Politics, and Society": 59. Some Futurists celebrated themselves as "modern barbarian[s]." Gentile and Rainey, "The Conquest of Modernity": 74.
49. Scobie, *Hitler's State Architecture*: 50.
50. Ibid.
51. Ibid.
52. Sandro Scarrocchia, "Baumeister des Faschismus: Marcello Piacentini and Albert Speer": 189.
53. Aristotle Kallis, "'Framing Romanità'": 824.
54. Vale, *Architecture, Power, and National Identity*: 30. After the fair, all temporary exhibition halls would be removed, leaving administrative buildings, embassies, and so on. The fair was canceled, but by 1950 the EUR area was completed.

55. Arthurs, *Excavating Modernity*: 132–133.
56. Scarrocchia, "Baumeister des Faschismus": 189. Piacentini was ridiculed as a "jumped-up Vitruvius." Scobie, *Hitler's State Architecture*: 12.
57. Arthurs, *Excavating Modernity*: 133.
58. For a photograph of the Marble Arch, see the battalion's website: https://28maoribattalion.org.nz/photo/te-rau-aroha-libya.
59. Curzio Malaparte, *The Skin*: 290.
60. Joshua Arthurs, *Excavating Modernity*: 148.

CHAPTER EIGHTEEN

1. Frederick T. Birchall, "Gilded Rome Is Set to Dazzle Hitler" (1938): 14.
2. Christian Dietrich Grabbe's play *Die Hermannsschlacht* (1835) saw a similar revival.
3. Christopher Krebs makes the case for this "Germanic revolution." Christopher B. Krebs, *A Most Dangerous Book*: 217.
4. Rosenberg, *Der Mythus*: 55.
5. The Nazis connected empire-building and mass murder, their plans resulting in the mass killings and deportations of the subject people of the East and the extermination of European Jews. "Nazi imperialism took the ideological distinction between Germans and others to a racist extreme." Jane Burbank and Frederick Cooper, *Empires in World History*: 399.
6. Victor Klemperer, *I Will Bear Witness: 1933–1940*: 257.
7. Moeller van den Bruck, "Italia Docet": 124.
8. Gerald Weinberg, ed., *Hitler's Table Talk 1941–1944*: 81. As Alexander Demandt points out, the model of Rome at the time of the Punic Wars, not the late "decadent" empire. See Demandt, "Klassik als Klischee: Hitler und die Antike": 300.
9. Hitler's visit was "co-operation mingled with competition." Kallis, "'Framing Romanità'": 827.
10. Albert Speer, *Spandau: The Secret Diaries*: 126.
11. Germans expected their future colonies to participate in the exhibition. See Sandro Scarrocchia, "Baumeister des Faschismus": 183–186.
12. Alexander Demandt discusses Hitler's pronouncement on Greco-Roman antiquity as connected to European imperialism and to his efforts to situate himself as leader within a "universal-historical framework, in which antiquity occupied a central place." Demandt, "Klassik als Klischee": 286.
13. Weinberg, ed., *Hitler's Table Talk*: 111.
14. Ibid.: 110.
15. Ibid.: 78.
16. Ibid.: 290. Recall that the Maori became known as the "noblest of Polynesian warriors" *and* as barbarian cannibals. Steinmetz, *The Devil's Handwriting*: 257. Demandt mentions a "völkisch" author who argued that Indian Aryans populated New Zealand. Demandt, "Klassik als Klischee": 297.

17. Weinberg, ed., *Hitler's Table Talk*: 289.
18. Ibid.: 290.
19. Timothy Snyder succinctly outlines this gradual move toward the final solution in "A New Approach to the Holocaust": 54–56.
20. Anonymous, *Volk und Reich: Politische Monatshefte* 9 (1934): no page nrs.
21. See "Ostorientierung oder Ostpolitik," in MK, 726–758; or "Eastern Orientation or Eastern Policy" in Adolf Hitler, *Mein Kampf* (hereafter MKe), transl. Ralph Manheim: 641ff. I am using the 1942 edition because it appeared when the Nazi empire reached its zenith. Manheim's translation is based on the first edition (vol. 1 was published in 1925, vol. 2 in 1926).
22. Weinberg, ed., *Hitler's Table Talk*: 110.
23. Ibid.: 617.
24. Heinrich Hoffmann and A. R. Marsani, eds., *Deutscher Osten: Land der Zukunft* (1943): 38, 61.
25. Anonymous (Werner Best), "Herrenschicht oder Führungsvolk?" (1942): 123.
26. Ulrich Herbert, *Best: Biographische Studien über Radikalismus, Weltanschauung und Vernunft*: 413.
27. Farrenkopf, "Klio und Cäsar": 63.
28. Weinberg, ed., *Hitler's Table Talk*: 33.
29. Plans to re-create "a central African empire" peaked in 1940. Shelley Baranowski, *Nazi Empire: German Colonialism and Imperialism from Bismarck to Hitler*: 257–258. This included the so-called Madagascar plan.
30. Hitler, *Monologe im Führerhauptquartier 1941–1944*: 63.
31. Jürgen Zimmerer, "Im Dienste des Imperiums": 97.
32. Joachim Fest, *Hitler*: 621.
33. Shelley Baranowski, *Nazi Empire*: 270.
34. Weinberg, ed., *Hitler's Table Talk*: 33 and 34.
35. See Mark Mazower, *Hitler's Empire*: 150.
36. On the circle in Himmler's *Reichssicherheitshauptamt*, see Herbert, *Best*: 273.
37. On the long tradition of plans to conquer the East, see Geoff Eley, *Nazism as Fascism*: 134–136.
38. The text is also a "manual." Albrecht Koschorke, "Ideology in Execution: On Hitler's *Mein Kampf*": 12.
39. Repeating Rome's fate, France would descend into a "European-African mulatto state" (MKe, 644).
40. Hitler, "Warum sind wir Antisemiten?": 191.
41. Demandt, "Klassik als Klischee": 304.
42. On the protectorate he envisioned in the East, see Mazower, *Hitler's Empire*: 157.
43. Rosenberg, *Der Mythus*: 55.
44. Ibid.: 53.
45. Ibid.
46. Ibid.: 55.

47. This is the first of two speeches held at Posen/Poznań; the second one dates from October 6.
48. As armament minister, Speer oversaw an increase in war-related production. Richard J. Evans, *The Third Reich at War*: 329–330.
49. Peter Longerich, *Heinrich Himmler*: 748.
50. Mazower, *Hitler's Empire*: 146.
51. Longerich, *Heinrich Himmler*: 642.
52. Ibid.: 578. On Hegewald, see Wendy Lower, *Nazi Empire-Building and the Holocaust in Ukraine*: 162–179.
53. Longerich, *Heinrich Himmler*: 574, 263.
54. Mazower, *Hitler's Empire*: 148.
55. See Longerich, *Heinrich Himmler*: 13.
56. Himmler, quoted in Longerich, *Heinrich Himmler*: 44.
57. Ibid.: 297.
58. Ibid.: 386.
59. Herbert, *Best*: 274.
60. Werner Best, "Grundfragen einer deutschen Grossraum-Verwaltung" (hereafter GV): 50.
61. Herbert, *Best*: 317.
62. Best's four models of imperial governance ranged from indirect to direct rule.
63. Best's concept of *völkisch* encompasses "Blut, Rasse, Volk." Herbert, *Best*: 274.
64. Herbert, *Best*: 61.
65. Ibid.: 282.
66. Ibid.: 309.
67. With this essay, the man who considered himself a rational anti-Semite, not an irrational Jew-hater, becomes a "theorist of extermination." Herbert, *Best*: 283.
68. Anonymous (Best), "Herrenschicht oder Führungsvolk?" (1942): 124, note 1.
69. Heinrich Himmler, "Rede des Reichsführers SS bei der SS-Gruppenführertagung in Posen am 4. Oktober 1943" (hereafter PR): 20; online edition 1000dokumente.de, Dokumente zur deutschen Geschichte des 20. Jahrhunderts.
70. Himmler portrays SS officers as spectators at mass executions of Jews, praising them for having endured this spectacle while remaining "decent" (PR, 20). On this passage, see LaCapra, *Representing the Holocaust: History, Theory, Trauma*: 107–110.
71. Longerich, *Heinrich Himmler*: 264. Himmler presented himself as bearing the "heavy responsibility" of "extermination." Saul Friedländer, *The Years of Extermination: Nazi Germany and the Jews, 1939–1945*: 541.
72. Longerich, *Heinrich Himmler*: 695.
73. Ibid. The Nazis' obsession with ruins (what Mark Featherstone calls their "ideological necrophilia" in his "Ruin Value") is thus related in rather unmediated ways to the genocidal nature of their imperial project, generating the anticipation of retaliation.

74. By 1943, the trope of "cannibalism" was circulating, and the image of "primitive Slavs" was as thoroughly barbarized as that of the Red Army soldiers, the infamous "Asiatic hordes." Mazower, *Hitler's Empire*: 165–166 and 159. On Himmler's use of the trope, see PR, 11.
75. Michael Geyer, "Endkampf 1918 and 1945: German Nationalism, Annihilation, and Self-Destruction": 50.
76. Ibid.: 51.

CHAPTER NINETEEN

1. Haushofer, quoted in Felix Blindow, *Carl Schmitts Reichsordnung: Strategie für einen europäischen Großraum*: 69.
2. Karl Haushofer, "Kulturkreis und Kulturkreisüberschneidungen": 97.
3. Haushofer, *Weltpolitik von heute*: 259. Translation: Even if the entire globe should crumble, the ruins will hit him unafraid. *Weltpolitik* contained a chapter on "Territory—State Ruins": 89–97.
4. Quoted in Karl Christ, *Klios Wandlungen: Die deutsche Althistorie vom Neuhumanismus bis zur Gegenwart*: 222.
5. In 1919, Weber longed for a new *Reich* and the coming of "the illustrious one." Christ, *Klios Wandlungen*: 73.
6. Joseph Vogt, *Vom Reichsgedanken der Römer* (hereafter RR) (1942): 5. Vogt joined Alfred Rosenberg's *Institut zur Erforschung der Judenfrage* in 1942.
7. Vogt, quoted in Faber, *Abendland*: 177; and *RR*, 11.
8. Christ, *Klios Wandlungen*: 59. On *Aktion Ritterbusch*, see Stefan Rebenich, "Alte Geschichte in Demokratie und Diktatur: Der Fall Helmut Berve": 474–475. Vogt and Berve collaborated on Helmut Berve's collection, *Das neue Bild der Antike* (1942), and Vogt's collection, *Rom und Karthago* (1943). Distributed to Nazi elite schools, these books reflected a shift to a "radically Nazified interpretation of history." Volker Losemann, "Classics in the Second World War": 325.
9. See Ernst Kornemann, *Das Imperium Romanum: Sein Aufstieg und Niedergang* (1941).
10. Helmut Berve, *Imperium Romanum* (1942).
11. Wilhelm Weber, "Römische Geschichte bis zum Verfall des Weltreichs" (1940): 302–372.
12. Haushofer used once more the metaphorics of world history as theater. Karl Haushofer, "Einleitung: Die raumpolitischen Grundlagen der Weltgeschichte" (1935): 26. Wilhelm Weber connected "space, blood, and tradition" in his entry, "Das römische Kaiserreich und der Eintritt der Germanen in die Weltgeschichte" (1935): 280.
13. Willy Andreas, "Einleitung": 4.
14. Berve, "Die Antike und der nationalsozialistische Staat" (1934): 258, 268.
15. Wilhelm Weber, "ROM: Mussolinis cäsarische Vision" (1940): 142.
16. Quoted in Faber, *Abendland*: 26.

17. Gottfried Benn, "Dorische Welt: Eine Untersuchung über die Beziehung von Kunst und Macht" (1934): 147.
18. Scobie, *Hitler's State Architecture*: 16.
19. Berve, "Vorwort": 6.
20. Ibid.: 5, 7. Vol. 1 focused on Greece, vol. 2 on Rome as Nazi Europe's foundation.
21. Ibid.: 6.
22. Ibid.: 6, 10.
23. Ibid.: 9, 8.
24. Vogt, *Vom Reichsgedanken der Römer*: 5. Vogt revised *Vom Reichsgedanken der Römer* for vol. 2 of *Das neue Bild der Antike* under the title "Raumauffassung und Raumordnung in der römischen Politik" (100–132).
25. James Porter, *Nietzsche and the Philology of the Future*: 272.
26. Wilamowitz, quoted in Porter, *Nietzsche*: 411.
27. Ibid.
28. Berve, "Vorwort": 8.
29. Arthurs, *Excavating Modernity*: 107.
30. Cooley, *Res Gestae Divi Augusti*: 53. The *Mostra*'s façade juxtaposed AUGUSTUS and DUX.
31. Ernst Kornemann, *Augustus: Der Mann und sein Werk*: 15. On Kornemann and Spengler, see Karl Christ, *Römische Geschichte und deutsche Geschichtswissenschaft*: 134ff.
32. See Weber, "ROM: Mussolinis cäsarische Vision": 137.
33. *Die Antike*, vol. 13, no. 3 (1937): 153.
34. Augustus, quoted in Carl Weickert, "Augustus: Bild und Geschichte": 208.
35. Rodenwaldt, "Kunst um Augustus" (1937): 157, 174–175.
36. Rodenwaldt, *Kunst um Augustus* (1943): 50. This sentence was added to this 1943 republication of the article as a book.
37. Rodenwaldt, "Kunst um Augustus" (1937): 174.
38. Ibid.: 159.
39. Ibid.: 155.
40. Johannes Stroux, "Imperator" (1937): 211.
41. Ibid.
42. Weickert, "Augustus: Bild und Geschichte (1938)": 208. These texts expressed the ambivalence of conservative intellectuals who welcomed a strong leader, and yet as members of Germany's educated elite, harbored reservations about him.
43. Ibid.: 216.
44. Ibid.: 222.
45. In 1935, Weber, anti-French to the core and sounding like Fichte's ghost, was still anti-Roman, praising the Nordic Germans' struggle against Rome: we are not "barbarians," and do not care about Virgil or Augustus. Wilhelm Weber, "Vom neuen Reich der Deutschen" (1935): 11.
46. Ibid.: 6.

47. During the bimillenary, the RGDA were at the center of discussions. Christ, *Klios Wandlungen*: 71.
48. See Ines Stahlmann, *Imperator Caesar Augustus: Studien zur Geschichte des Prinzipatverständnisses in der deutschen Altertumswissenschaft bis 1945: 169*.
49. Determined to shape his "image," Augustus prescribed his funeral rituals. Weber, *Princeps*: 25.
50. Weber, *Knaurs Weltgeschichte*: 220 and 229.
51. Ibid.: 220.
52. Weber, "Der Tatsachenbericht des Augustus: 'Monumentum Ancyranum'": no page nrs.
53. Rodenwaldt, *Kunst um Augustus (1943)*: 5.
54. Ibid.
55. Weber, "ROM: Mussolinis caesarische Vision": 138.
56. Ibid.: 141.
57. Ibid.: 137.
58. *Reich* as "unity of power and spirit in a global space" was Roman (RR, 5–6).
59. Since the Punic Wars, Romans were guided by a particular way of perceiving large spaces, their "eye" first seizing the territory as a whole before securing its parts "from the outermost edge of this space" (RR, 45). In a very literal sense, Rome's elite was thus "far-seeing" (RR, 53).

CHAPTER TWENTY

1. By 1936, the *Reich* had undergone two moments of its bloody foundation: the first wave of persecutions in the wake of the *Reichstagsbrand* targeting the regime's enemies, and the second wave in 1934, annihilating the National Sozialistische Deutsche Arbeiter Partei's (NSDAP) internal opposition. The year 1936 marked another caesura in the formation of the Nazi state.
2. The play performed was a "German version of the antique model." Heinz Frank, "Das Frankfurter Würfelspiel: Eberhard Wolfgang Moellers Dichtung auf der Dietrich-Eckart-Bühne" (1938).
3. Rüdiger Hachtmann, "Reichssportfeld: das monumentale Bauwerk Berlins," *Völkischer Beobachter*.
4. See also the Greek style "Thingstätten" of the early 1930s. On this topic, see *The Third Reich Sourcebook*: 606–609.
5. Riefenstahl, in Herman Weigel, "Interview mit Leni Riefenstahl": 406.
6. Thanks to Rick Rentschler for sharing with me his shot-by-shot analysis of the prologue.
7. Shot by Willy Zielke, the prologue was re-edited by Riefenstahl, eliminating the "dreamy" quality. Cooper C. Graham, *Leni Riefenstahl and Olympia*: 157. Riefenstahl worked with Walter Hege, who collaborated with Gerhart Rodenwaldt on *Die Akropolis* (1930) and *Olympia* (1936). His photographs strove for a "monumental effect," conveying the ruins' "heroic" nature. Maren

Hobein, "Monument und Ideal: Die Griechenlandphotographien von Walter Hege": 51.

8. Riefenstahl's modernist sensibility differs from Goebbels's conventional Hellenism. On Goebbels's visit to the Akropolis in 1936, see Peter Longerich, *Joseph Goebbels*: 323.
9. One of the Berlin Museums exhibited a bronze statuette of Myron's *Disc Thrower* in 1936. Hitler acquired the Lancelotti *Discobolus* (a Roman copy) in 1938. Ian Jenkins, *The Discobolus*: 53.
10. Berve, "Vorwort," *Das Neue Bild der Antike*, vol. 1: 6.
11. There is a modernist aesthetics at work here that has "a powerful and persuasive effect." Rick Rentschler, *The Ministry of Illusion*: 22. Italian films refined the resurrectional techniques. Alternating between shots of ruined Pompeii and reconstructed film sets, one of the films about Pompeii "ris[ing] again" modeled this aesthetics of "precise recreation." Maria Wyke, *Projecting the Past*: 167. This realism by modernist means characterized the resurrectional work of the artists in this chapter.
12. Arno Breker sculpted this iconic figure of the Aryan runner for Speer's *Reich Chancellery*. See Rentschler on Breker, Speer, and their aesthetics as "state terror." *The Ministry of Illusion:* 22–23.
13. On Riefenstahl and Winckelmann, see Brigitte Peucker, *The Material Image*: 57. For Winckelmann's encounters with Greek statues as an experience of loss, see, for instance, his discussion of Hercules as "one of the last perfect works of art" before Greece became "a Roman province." Winckelmann, *The History of the Art of Antiquity* (1764): 323.
14. Lacan, quoted in Claus Dieter Rath, "Zur Einführung: Olympiade 1936": 20. Lacan reacted to Ernst Kris telling him in 1938: "One doesn't do that" (20).
15. Lacan's theory of subjectivity connects to National Socialism's cultivation of the imaginary I through the "emphasis on will and self-discipline," the *volk*'s unified body, the figure of "the great father," and the identification of Jews with the "unnatural" or *civilizational* realm of language/writing/interpretation (ibid.: 21, 24, 22).
16. Gottfried Benn, cited in Helmut Lethen, *Der Sound der Väter*: 172 and 173. Ernst Jünger also celebrated being "barbarian," meaning the heroic modern subject's readiness to kill and be killed. Lethen, *Der Sound*: 140.
17. Benn, "Lebensweg eines Intellektualisten": *197*.
18. Ibid. Benn here polemicized against Brecht's Marxism.
19. Martin Heidegger, "The Self-Determination of the German University" (1933), quoted in Victor Farias, *Heidegger and Nazism*: 101, 108.
20. See Benn, "Lebensweg": 196.
21. Benn, "Kunst und Macht" (1934; hereafter KM): 198. Nazism was revolutionary *and* "geschichtsgebunden," vital and a carrier of the "deutsch-abendländische Erbmasse" (198).
22. Benn, "Lebensweg": 196.

23. Benn, "Dorische Welt: Eine Untersuchung über die Beziehung von Kunst und Macht" (1934; hereafter DW): 135.
24. Helmut Berve, *Sparta*: 26. Berve finds one stain, "Päderastie," leading to decline (47).
25. Ibid.: 79, 60.
26. Ibid.: 79.
27. Eberhardt, "Die Antike und wir": 115.
28. Ibid.: 121.
29. Ibid.: 116.
30. Ibid.: 120. Augustus's "Latin idea of civilization" is still alive in France (123).
31. Ibid.: 123.
32. Hippolyte Taine's *Philosophie der Kunst* and Jacob Burckhardt's *Griechische Kulturgeschichte*. With a modernist gesture, Benn thus melds fragments (from other texts, but also bas-reliefs) into a whole: the story about an Athenian citizen walking through the ancient city.
33. Berve published on the Roman Empire's fall in 1942, and toured the country with lectures about the annihilation of Carthage's "Semitedom." Berve, quoted in Rebenich, "Alte Geschichte in Demokratie und Diktatur": 484.
34. "Dorische Welt" is one of the essays which allude to Benn's radically "amimetic" postwar aesthetics of autonomous "spatial" art. Neil H. Donahue, "Ecstatic Montage: Paratactic Visions in Gottfried Benn's Novella Cycle 'Brains' (1916)": 162, 164.
35. Benn's resurrectional prose is self-reflexively so: ruins are restored to their former *gestalt*, but as the presence of the artist indicates, this is the result of his artistic production, of his imagination, and a specific mode of representation. Benn's resurrection is based on Nietzsche's anti-historicist program in the service of what Benn calls "Gesundheitslehre des Lebens." Benn, "Sein und Werden": 204.
36. Benn tells the story of the Nazis' seizure of power as the reconstitution of Sparta, its state and its art. Reviving Sparta's political aesthetics, this is Benn's wager, will give form to the era of the new *Reich*.
37. For the Greeks, a slave economy was a necessary precondition of high culture.
38. This community is different from the "Orient" (Benn speaks of "Persians," but his readers will have heard "Jews"). Spartans value victory, "Persians" money. Benn, "Dorische Welt": 130, 140, and 137.
39. Ibid.: 144 and 145. Benn's essay was first published under the title "Der Krieger und die Statue." Benn shared the Nazis' fetish of firm foundations; see Benn, "Kunst und Macht": 198.
40. Ibid.: 146.
41. Recall that Thomas Mann turned Benn's trope against the new barbarians (see the preface to part 5).
42. Berve, *Sparta*: 79.
43. Ibid. This new state/style ultimately realized "the occidental" defined as the "gathering of fragments" (151).

44. However, there is a tension between this imaginary register (celebrating Sparta as a model, exhibiting Spartan bodies, reviving the Spartan artist's gaze) and a historical narrative portraying the present as late heir to Sparta, advocating complete aesthetic autonomy (DW, 150).
45. Heidegger, quoted in Charles Bambach, *Heidegger's Roots: Nietzsche, National Socialism, and the Greeks*: 301.
46. Benn, "Dorische Welt": 564; editor's notes to text.
47. Ibid.
48. Arno Breker's statues belong in this context. He also worked on reliefs for Speer's Arch and the Nuremberg tribune, relying on forced labor. Jürgen Trimborn, *Arno Breker: der Künstler und die Macht*: 278.
49. Eberhardt, "Die Antike und wir": 124.
50. Karl Stamm, "'Degenerate Art' on the Screen": 202–203.
51. Moeller van den Bruck, *Das Dritte Reich* (1923): 245.
52. Spengler, *The Hour of Decision*: 227–228.
53. Emmanuel Faye, *Heidegger: The Introduction of Nazism into Philosophy*: 102, 258.
54. Friedrich Matz argued that this axial structure conformed to "ur-Germanic principle." Altekamp, "Germanita: Archäologische Kolonialfantasien": 583.
55. Pausanias, *Guide to Greece*, vol. 1: 195.
56. Friedrich Tamms, "Das Grosse in der Baukunst" (1944): 60.

CHAPTER TWENTY-ONE

1. Wilhelm Weber, "Römische Geschichte bis zum Verfall des Weltreichs" (1935): 302.
2. Joseph Goebbels, quoted in Christoph Cornelißen, "Zur Rezeption der italienischen Architektur im 'Dritten Reich'": 381.
3. Ibid.
4. In this imperial space, Munich was supposed to function as the Reich's "Acropolis Germaniae." Stefan Schweizer, *"Unserer Weltanschauung sichtbaren Ausdruck geben": Nationalsozialistische Geschichtsbilder in historischen Festzügen*: 64.
5. Miller Lane discusses the foregrounding of "mass" and "stagelike" arrangements. Barbara Miller Lane, *Architecture and Politics in Germany 1918–1945*: 215 and 193. In *Hitler's State Architecture*, Alex Scobie emphasizes the nexus of monumentality and scenography. Léon Krier praises Speer's "colossal" architecture as "sublime." Krier, "An Architecture of Desire": 225 and 223. Dieter Bartetzko foregrounds the spectacular dimensions in *Zwischen Zucht und Ekstase: Zur Theatralik von NS-Architektur*. Joachim Fest accentuates monumental architecture's desire to master time and sees *Germania* as a "Mausoleum-world" in *Speer: Eine Biographie*: 128.
6. Walter Benjamin emphasizes discontinuity (of media/technologies of power/senses) at the expense of the continuity. While he alludes to the Reich's

"imperialistic" nature and reaches back to the Greek epic's scopic regime, his analysis of the politics of spectacle ignores the specifically imperial, post-Roman genealogy that I emphasize. Benjamin, "The Work of Art in the Age of Mechanical Reproduction": 242.

7. Karl Haushofer, "Die raumpolitischen Grundlagen der Weltgeschichte": 26.
8. Gerhard Rodenwaldt, "Kunst um Augustus" (1937): 191.
9. Rodenwaldt, "Via Dell'Impero" (1939): 264.
10. See Rodenwaldt, *Kunst um Augustus* (1943): 7–8.
11. Rodenwaldt, "Römische Staatsarchitektur" (1942): 357. Sepp Schüller discussed post-Roman architecture as the "will to safeguard the legacy of civilization" against the Western and Eastern offensive. *Das Rom Mussolinis: Rom als moderne Hauptstadt*: 11.
12. Rodenwaldt, "Via Dell'Impero" (1939): 264.
13. Dieter Bartetzko, *Illusionen im Stein: Stimmungsarchitektur im deutschen Faschismus. Ihre Vorgeschichte in Theater- und Film-Bauten*: 281.
14. Heinrich Wolff, ed., *Die neue Reichskanzlei: 60 Bilder. Die Kunst im deutschen Reich* published models of Wilhelm Kreis's restructured "island of museums." Karl Arndt, "Problematischer Ruhm: die Großaufträge in Berlin 1937–1943": 174.
15. On the speech, see Sandro Scarrocchia, *Die Untermauerung der Achse Piacentini und Speer*: 179.
16. Alan Balfour, *Berlin: The Politics of Order*: 85. *Germania*'s completion would be followed by a world's fair uniting the world "on this eternal stage." Ibid.
17. Fest, *Speer: Eine Biographie*: 107.
18. Bernhard Leitner, "Albert Speer": 19. Hitler closely inspected the *Mostra Augustea*'s Rome model, and the marble map of the ancient metropolis in the *Palazzo dei Conservatori*. Alex Scobie, *Hitler's State Architecture*: 39. Films showed Mussolini inspecting the model of E42.
19. Eric Michaud analyzes the "Artist-Führer" as one of the myths in the Nazis' eschatological politics in his *The Cult of Art in Nazi Germany*: 26ff. I privilege the lineage of Augustus's self-presentation as conqueror, ruler, and city-builder.
20. Anthony M. Tung, *Preserving the World's Great Cities*: 36–37.
21. Oswald Spengler, *The Hour of Decision*: 119.
22. Leitner and Wilkins, "Albert Speer, the Architect": 20.
23. The stand was "calculated for a long-distance effect." Léon Krier, ed. *Albert Speer, Architecture 1932–1942*: 165.
24. Speer's staff made the drawing. Fest, *Speer: Eine Biographie*: 129.
25. Nina Dubin, *Futures & Ruins: Eighteenth Century Paris and the Art of Hubert Robert*: 153. On C. D. Friedrich and Hubert, see Phillipe Junod, "Future in the Past": 55. On Gandy's *View of the Rotunda the Bank of England in Ruins* (1798), see Christopher Woodward, *In Ruins*: 161–165.
26. Looking at Speer's sketch, Hitler said that "great buildings can hold up the march of time." Hitler, quoted in Joachim Fest, *Albert Speer: Conversations*

with Hitler's Architect: 68. Speer agrees with Fest that Hitler's reaction was puzzling since he had just argued the "superior strength of time" (ibid.).

27. Speer, quoted in Fest, *Speer*: 130.
28. Hitler, quoted in Fest, *Speer*: 130. See also Hitler, quoted in *Albert Speer, Architektur*: 115.
29. Medina Lasansky, *The Renaissance Perfected*: xxvii.
30. Kallis, "Framing Romanità": 809.
31. Friedrich Tamms, "Das Grosse in der Baukunst" (1944): 60. On Tamms, see also Eric Michaud, "National Socialist Architecture as an Acceleration of Time": 231–232.
32. They are creatures of the "moloch of great capital"; and utopia is a city "without Jews." Hitler, *Reden Schriften Anordnungen*, vol. 3: 185 and 191.
33. Hitler, *Reden Schriften Anordnungen*, vol. 3: 192 and 187.
34. We admire "in the ruins and wreckage of the ancient world," Hitler wrote, "not former business palaces but temples and state structures" (MKe, 265).
35. Hitler, *Reden Schriften Anordnungen*, vol. 3: 192.
36. Rodenwaldt, "Römische Staatsarchitektur": 358.
37. August Stürzenacker, "Die deutsche Baukunst und die Antike" (1938): 624.
38. Spotts: *Hitler and the Power of Aesthetics*: 351.
39. Hitler, quoted in Brian Ladd, *Ghosts of Berlin*: 126.
40. The Berlin plans involved "aryanizing dwellings." Paul B. Jaskot, *The Architecture of Oppression: The SS, Forced Labor, and the Nazi Monumental Building Economy*: 88.
41. Weinberg, ed., *Hitler's Table Talk*: 81.
42. Ibid.: 523.
43. Ibid.: 81.
44. Ibid.: 523.
45. Rodenwaldt, "Römische Staatsarchitektur": 356.
46. Ibid.: 373.
47. Rodenwaldt, *Kunst*: 16.
48. Speer, quoted in Balfour, *Berlin*: 95.
49. According to another Nazi architect, Speer created a "*Führer*-centered architecture." Wilhelm Lotz, "Das Reichsparteitagsgelände in Nürnberg": 266. For a critique of the concept of *Führertum* as based on "an absolute equality between the Führer and his followers" (in Carl Schmitt's texts), see Giorgio Agamben, *The Kingdom and the Glory*: 76.
50. Krier, ed. *Albert Speer*: 85. On the Führer balconies, see Bernhard Leitner, "Albert Speer, the Architect": 14. On the model of the *Führer Palace*, see ibid.: 50.
51. Bernhard Leitner, "Architecture as a Weapon: Hitler's Speer": 53. Speer compared the stand to the Pergamon Altar, and Scobie saw the *Ara Pacis*. Scobie, *Hitler's State Architecture*: 91.
52. Weber, "ROM": 141.
53. Ibid.: 137.
54. Neoclassicism did of course not represent a fundamental "deviation" from

European neoclassicism. Miller Lane, *Architecture*: 215. Neoclassicist monumentality is part of a long imperial history.
55. Scobie, *Hitler's State Architecture*: 117.
56. Hitler, quoted in Brian Ladd, *The Ghosts of Berlin*: 126.
57. Granite linked Speer's architecture to the fascist slave economy. See Jaskot, *The Architecture of Oppression*: 97 and 139.
58. Scobie, *Hitler's State Architecture*: 51, note 63.
59. Winfried Nerdinger, "Wilhelm Kreis—Repräsentant der deutschen Architektur des 20. Jahrhunderts": 166.
60. Friedrich Tamms, "Die Kriegerehrenmäler von Wilhelm Kreis" (1943): 50. Gerdy Troost, quoted in Nerdinger, "Wilhelm Kreis": 163.
61. Russians would live outside the "German" cities. Hitler, quoted in Jochen Thies, "Hitler's European Building Program": 417.
62. Fest, *Speer*: 126; and Balfour, *Berlin*: 85.

CHAPTER TWENTY-TWO

1. Weinberg, ed., *Hitler's Table Talk*: 10.
2. Ralph-Miklas Dobler, "Hitler in Rome 1938": 2.
3. Atkinson, "Hitler's Grand Tour": 10.
4. Berezin, *Making the Fascist Self*: 96.
5. L. Bottazzi, quoted in Atkinson, "Hitler's Grand Tour": 11.
6. Dobler, "Hitler in Rome 1938": 2.
7. For a map of the route, see Scobie, *Hitler's State Architecture*: 25.
8. Ibid.: 24.
9. Dobler, "Hitler in Rom 1938": 2.
10. Scobie, *Hitler's State Architecture*: 24.
11. Atkinson, "Hitler's Grand Tour": 12–13.
12. Walter Pater, quoted in Kennedy, "A Sense of Place": 23.
13. Scobie, *Hitler's State Architecture*: 24.
14. Trevor Roper, ed., *Hitler's Table Talk*: 24. During the occupation of Paris, "the Nazis repeated their triumphal march along the Champs Elysées every day at noon." Vale, *Architecture*: 20.
15. Spotts, *Hitler and the Power of Aesthetics*: 317. Spotts connects Mann's "Bruder Hitler" to the state visit.
16. Walter Benjamin, "Theses on the Philosophy of History": 256.
17. Heinrich Hansen, ed., *Der Schlüssel zum Frieden*: no page nrs.
18. See Frederic Spotts, *Hitler and the Power of Aesthetics*: 3.
19. Hansen, ed., *Der Schlüssel zum Frieden*: no page nrs.
20. Ibid.
21. Ibid. Heinrich Hoffmann, ed., *Hitler in Italien: 126 Bilder* (1938), documents the military events.
22. Victor Klemperer, *I Will Bear Witness 1933–1941*: 256.

23. Quoted in Edwards, "Translating Empire?": 79.
24. On the intertextual nature of travel to Rome, see Kennedy, "A Sense of Place": 19ff.
25. Goethe traveled in 1787, publishing the travelogue later. On Goethe's Italian journey, see John Zilcosky, *Uncanny Encounters: Literature, Psychoanalysis, and the End of Alterity*.
26. This appeal to the German *Bildungsbürgertum* was part of the early years of the Nazi regime.
27. Johann Wolfgang Goethe, *Italienische Reise*: 205.
28. Ibid.: 404.
29. See ibid.: 154.
30. In Rome, Goethe met Louis-François Cassas (1756–1827), who showed him a set of drawings, depicting Palmyra's ruins. See Goethe, *Italienische Reise*: 395–396.
31. Scobie, *Hitler's State Architecture*: 30.
32. *Der Schlüssel*: no page nrs. The text reads like the voiceover for a weekly newsreel; the visit was indeed filmed by German, British, French, and American news services.
33. Thematizing the power of the leader's unmasking gaze, Goebbels argued that Jews have a "natural instinct" to "practice mimicry," thus the paradoxical nature of the Third Reich's "global enemy," at once Bolshevist and western plutocrat. Goebbels, "Mimikry" (1941): 531, 526, 531.
34. Pollock, "Empire and Imitation": 185.
35. Ibid.: 179.
36. Eric Michaud, "National Socialist Architecture as an Acceleration of Time": 230. By imitating Roman monumentalism, the Nazis aimed "to make [their community] into the past" (228). The fleeting nature of modernity's community is overcome by the acceleration toward death, "into a solid and eternal Reich" (230).
37. As Himmler's 1943 speech demonstrates, their obsession with ruins is also connected to the anticipation of retaliation (chapter 18).
38. Gerhard L. Weinberg, *A World at War*: 447.
39. Ian McGibbon, *The Oxford Companion to New Zealand Military History*: 310. See also http://www.28maoribattalion.org.nz.
40. Jérome Carcopino, "L'héritage de Rome en Tunisie" (1951): 38.
41. Goebbels was immersed in Mommsen's portrait of decadent Carthage's unproductive elite and intellectuals serving capital. See Theodor Mommsen, *The History of Rome*, vol. 1: 191.
42. Peter Longerich, *Joseph Goebbels*: 575.
43. Saul Friedländer, *The Years of Extermination*: 649 and 657.
44. Hitler, quoted in Speer, *Spandau: The Secret Diaries*: 29.

CHAPTER TWENTY-THREE

1. Saul Friedländer, *The Years of Extermination*: 658.
2. Peter Longerich, *Joseph Goebbels*: 572.
3. Goebbels responded to the mounting crisis in the east by intensifying the "anti-bolshevist and anti-Jewish propaganda campaign." Ibid.: 575.
4. Joseph Vogt, ed., *Rom und Karthago*: 5.
5. Helmut Berve, quoted in Rebenich, "Alte Geschichte": 484.
6. Goebbels, *Die Tagebücher von Joseph Goebbels*, part 2, vol. 15: 394. The *topos* of Semitic Carthage fit perfectly with Goebbels's second theme, "Jewish retaliation." Longerich, *Goebbels*: 660.
7. Goebbels, *Die Tagebücher*: 394.
8. See also Hermann Bengtson, "Scipio Africanus: Seine Persönlichkeit und weltgeschichtliche Bedeutung" (1943): 487.
9. Goebbels, *Die Tagebücher*: 394.
10. Helmut Heiber, ed., *Goebbels-Reden*: 408.
11. See Goebbels, *Die Tagebücher*: 676.
12. Anonymous, "Cannae" (April 1944): no page nrs.
13. Hugo Landgraf, "Roms Triumph über Hannibal," *Völkischer Beobachter* (April 1945): no page nrs.
14. Walter Frank, "Hannibal vor den Toren: Senat und Volk von Rom in den Punier Kriegen," *Das Reich*, April 8 and 15, 1945: no page nrs.
15. Ibid.: no page nrs.
16. Frank's triumph references two intertexts: Felix Dahn's *A Struggle for Rome* (see chapter 14) and book 6 of the *Aeneid (see chapter 3).*
17. Frank, "Hannibal": no page nrs.
18. Friedländer, *The Years of Extermination*: 658.
19. Goebbels, *Die Tagebücher*: 689. Having entered Majdanek, the Red Army continued westward through other "killing centers." Richard Evans, *The Third Reich at War*: 707.
20. Helmut Heiber, *Walter Frank und sein Reichsinstitut für Geschichte des neuen Deutschlands*: 1210. He left an unfinished biography of Carl Peters behind.
21. Hitler's "innermost ideological landscape" never changed. "[I]nternational Jewry" in the form of capitalism and Bolshevism was his "metahistorical enemy." Friedländer, *The Years of Extermination*: 657.
22. Hitler, quoted in Friedländer, *The Years of Extermination*: 659.
23. Ibid.
24. Adolf Hitler, *Mein Politisches Testament*; http://www.1000dok.digitale-sammlungen.de/dok_0228_hte.pdf.
25. Joachim Fest, *Albert Speer: Conversations with Hitler's Architect:* 61.
26. Hitler, *Mein Politisches Testament*: 5.
27. Ibid.
28. Hitler, quoted in Friedländer, *The Years of Extermination*: 659; translation modified; emphasis mine.

29. The "Political Testament" is a "scarcely veiled confession" that the genocide was an act of revenge "for the part he supposed they had played in starting the war." Evans, *The Third Reich at War*: 726.
30. Heiber, ed., *Goebbels-Reden*: 449.
31. Ibid.: 451.
32. Ibid.: 454.
33. Fest, *Hitler*: 747.
34. Hitler here returns to the "Conclusion" of *Mein Kampf*, where he argued that the racially conscious state will rule the earth (MKe, no page nrs.).
35. Michael Geyer characterizes the Nazi leadership's military strategy in the spring of 1945 as the "politics of the funeral pyre." Michael Geyer, "Endkampf 1918 und 1945: German Nationalism, Annihilation, and Self-Destruction": 51. This funeral pyre is Dido's.
36. The text articulates Mussolini's and Hitler's idea of Roman ruined monuments as a bridge across centuries to Dido's call for revenge.
37. Joachim Fest, *Albert Speer*: 61.
38. Weinberg, ed., *Hitler's Table Talk*: 125.
39. Angela Schönberger, *Die neue Reichskanzlei von Albert Speer: Zum Zusammenhang von nationalsozialistischer Ideologie und Architektur*: 147.
40. At this moment, Hitler's study was still undamaged, in contrast to the rest of the Reich Chancellery. Since we know that Hitler started composing his *Political Testament* before April 1945, it is plausible that he did so in this study, facing Romanelli's Aeneas and Dido.
41. Quoted in Geyer, "Endkampf 1918 und 1945": 51.
42. Ibid.
43. His generation's enthusiasm for Nazism, Rahn wrote in 1949, stemmed from the desire to save the "Abendland" from Bolshevism and to break the "imperial systems of domination." Rudolf Rahn, *Ruheloses Leben: Aufzeichnungen und Erinnerungen*: 197 and 297.
44. On Rahn, see Herf, *Nazi Propaganda for the Arab World*: 68–69.
45. Memmi remembers passing under the "stone arches" of Hadrian's aqueduct. Albert Memmi, *The Pillar of Salt*: 309.
46. Rahn, *Ruheloses Leben*: 216.
47. Ibid.
48. Benn, *Der Ptolemäer: Eine Berliner Novelle*: 55.
49. Ernst Jünger, *Strahlungen, vol. 1*: 409.
50. Ernst Jünger, *Heliopolis*: 153.

PART 6 PREFACE

1. Carl Schmitt, "Stellungnahme I: Untermauerung der Hitlerschen Großraumpolitik?": 78.
2. On the similarities between the conservative critique of modernity of Spengler, Schmitt, and Heidegger, see Raphael Gross, *Carl Schmitt and the Jews*: 108.

CHAPTER TWENTY-FOUR

1. Jacob Taubes, *Ad Carl Schmitt: Gegenstrebige Fügung*: 62.
2. Schmitt, "The 'Fourth' (Second) Interrogation of Carl Schmitt at Nuremberg" (April 11, 1947): 39.
3. Ibid.: 41.
4. Herman Melville, *Benito Cereno*: 46. The mutinous slaves force Cereno to act the part of sovereign commander when they encounter an American merchant ship. See also Schmitt, *Ex Captivitate Salus: Erfahrungen der Zeit 1945/47*: 21–22.
5. Ernst Jünger, *Strahlungen I*: 265.
6. Schmitt did not distance himself from the Nazis; on the contrary, "National Socialism turned away from him." Günter Meuter, *Der Katechon: Zu Carl Schmitts fundamentalistischer Kritik der Zeit*: 245. In his *Carl Schmitt and the Jews,* Raphael Gross thoroughly refutes apologetic interpretations of Schmitt.
7. Schmitt distanced himself from Best and Höhn, the SS's "new elite," in his memoranda for Kempner. Reinhard Mehring, *Carl Schmitt: Aufstieg und Fall*: 451.
8. Schmitt, *Glossarium: Aufzeichnungen der Jahre 1947–1951* (1991): 194.
9. Jerry Muller, *The Other God That Failed: Hans Freyer and the Deradicalization of German Conservativism*: 79.
10. Schmitt, quoted in Mark Neocleous, "Friend or Enemy? Reading Schmitt Politically": 18.
11. Taubes, *Ad Carl Schmitt*: 71.
12. In these pre-1933 reflections, Schmitt is interested in the "sovereign decision" arresting "history's mechanism of decay" as distinct from the "occasionalism of the merely arbitrary act." Meuter, *Der Katechon*: 254.
13. Carl Schmitt, *Political Theology*, transl. George Schwab (1985): 63; translation modified.
14. On Donoso's lack of the *katechon*, see Schmitt, *Glossarium*: 63.
15. Schmitt, *Political Theology*: 5. In other words, *only* the sovereign possesses the authority of political decision-making.
16. Recall contemporary statements like James Bryce's proclaiming that "the Roman empire was the civilized world," adding "Outside roared the wild chaos of barbarism." Bryce, quoted in Morley, *The Roman Empire*: 109–110.
17. Schmitt, *Roman Catholicism and Political Form*: 17.
18. Ibid.: 38, 8, 37.
19. Schmitt, *Der Begriff des Politischen*: 27; and *The Concept of the Political*: 27.
20. Schmitt, *The Concept*: 27; translation modified.
21. Schmitt, *Der Begriff*: 27.
22. See Schmitt, *The Concept*: 68; and *Der Begriff*: 67.
23. Ibid.
24. Schmitt, *The Concept*: 68; translation modified.
25. Schmitt, *The Concept*: 68; *Der Begriff*: 67.

26. Schmitt, *The Concept*: 67; *Der Begriff*: 67.
27. Ibid.
28. Schmitt believed in the power of images, celebrating for instance the visual power of Theodor Däubler's descriptions in *Nordlicht*. Carl Schmitt, *Nordlicht*: 36.
29. George Schwab, "Introduction," *Political Theology*: xviii.
30. Schmitt replaced the concept of "des Anderen" with "Andersgeartete" in the 1933 edition of the *Concept of the Political*. "Enemy" included the external enemy (or "Staats-Fremder") and Jews as the "Andere." Gross, *Carl Schmitt and the Jews*: 178.
31. Schmitt, quoted in Bernd Rüthers, *Carl Schmitt im Dritten Reich*: 101. Schmitt's internal enemy is a version of the wandering Jew. Reviving the trope, a Nazi geopolitician analyzed Jews' supposed "nomadic instinct" in an article about the "Neuformung des Ostens" and the "radical solution to the Jewish question." P. H. Seraphim, "Die Wanderungsbewegung des jüdischen Volkes": 9, 27, 30.
32. Schmitt, *Glossarium*: 18. On "Maskenexistenz," see Rüthers, *Carl Schmitt*: 109.
33. Words like "Rassenunrat." Goebbels, "Mimikry": 531.
34. Gross compellingly situates Schmitt's anti-Semitism as a conservative critique of capitalist modernity, analyzing Schmitt's conception of the economic sphere (in terms of "exchange and deception") and of Jews as the depoliticizing, accelerating force of secularization. *Carl Schmitt and the Jews*: 182.
35. Schmitt, "Beschleuniger wider Willen, oder: Problematik der westlichen Hemisphäre," *Das Reich* (April 1942): 436.
36. Giorgio Agamben, *The Kingdom and the Glory*: 16.
37. For a detailed discussion of *Grossraum* and empire, see Jan-Werner Müller, *A Dangerous Mind: Carl Schmitt in Postwar European Thought*: 41–46.
38. Mehring, *Carl Schmitt*: 428. The appearance of the *katechon* in Schmitt's writing in 1942 is a sign of the latter's insight that "the Reich [was] no longer a sovereign ordering power" (428; translation mine); he then moves from the concept of *Reich* to *nomos* and world-historical reflections.
39. The essays are: "Beschleuniger wider Willen, oder: Problematik der westlichen Hemisphäre," originally published in *Das Reich* in April 1942; "Die Raumrevolution: Durch den totalen Krieg zu einem totalen Frieden," originally published in *Das Reich* in September 1940; and "Raumrevolution: Vom Geist des Abendlandes," published in *Deutsche Kolonialzeitung* in 1942.
40. Carl Schmitt, *Politische Theologie II*: 90. See also Felix Blindow on the *katechon* exegesis from Paul/Tertullian to the Weimar Republic. *Carl Schmitts Rechtsordnung*: 144–160.
41. That is, when critics ask whether Schmitt proposed a structural analogy between political and theological concepts, or whether the concepts' theological shadow functions as their foundation.
42. See Ruth Groh, *Arbeit an der Heillosigkeit der Welt*: 222. That is, did he aban-

don the idea of a decisionist rupture outside the law, turning into an institutional thinker invested in maintaining the existing political order?

43. Groh, *Arbeit*: 222.
44. Koenen anchors the *katechon* in the debates among the Weimar Republic's conservative Catholic and Protestant agitators for a new *Reich*. Koenen, *Der Fall Carl Schmitt*: 42.
45. Gross eliminates the distance that Koenen established between Schmitt and the Nazis. See Koenen, *Der Fall Carl Schmitt*: 577–598.
46. Gross, *Carl Schmitt and the Jews*: 108. Gross argues that the *katechon* is tied to the figure of the assimilated Jew as the antichrist or liberal-capitalist "Beschleuniger," with whom the *katechon* as "Aufhalter" is locked in struggle. The *katechon*'s office is to unmask and combat the internal enemy.
47. The *katechon* appears in the winter of 1941–1942, when Schmitt turns from an offensive *Grossraum* politics to a defensive stance. Gross, *Carl Schmitt*: 295; see also Mehring, *Carl Schmitt*: 428.
48. Meuter, *Der Katechon*: 214.
49. Groh, *Arbeit*: 214 and 216. Peter Uwe Hohendahl argues that the *katechon* retrospectively sheds light on the Marcion theology (based on the idea of an irredeemably fallen world) informing Schmitt's earlier writings. Peter-Uwe Hohendahl, "Political Theology Revisited: Carl Schmitt's Postwar Reassessment": 24.
50. Koenen's analysis remains committed to the narrow notion of German *Reich*. See Koenen, *Der Fall Carl Schmitt*: 578–579. Richard Faber collapses Schmitt's "Völkerrechtliche Grossraumordnung" too quickly into the imperial mimesis of Rome (174–175).
51. Schmitt, *Glossarium*: 63; translation mine. Reviewing Karl Löwith's *Meaning and Time* (1949), Schmitt affirmed that "eschatological belief and historical consciousness can co-exist." "Drei Stufen historischer Sinngebung" (1950): 930.
52. Carl Schmitt, *The Nomos of the Earth*: 60.
53. Schmitt, *Political Theology II*: 59; translation modified.
54. Ibid.
55. Taubes, *Ad Carl Schmitt*: 61.
56. Schmitt's radical conservative critique of modernity, his engagement with theology and modernity's lack of foundations, thus converge in the *katechon* with his theory of empire.
57. Schmitt, *The Nomos of the Earth*: 59; emphasis mine.
58. On the conquistadors' Marian theology, see *The Nomos*: 101–125.
59. Meuter, *Der Katechon*: 256.
60. Schmitt, "Völkerrechtliche Großraumordnung mit Interventionsverbot für raumfremde Mächte" (1941; hereafter GO): 308. This is the revised edition of the 1939 edition, which did not include the section entitled "Der Raumbegriff in der Rechtswissenschaft."

61. Schmitt acknowledged his debt to Friedrich Naumann, Friedrich Ratzel, and Haushofer.
62. On Schmitt's *völkisch*-ness as a displacement from his concept of nation to that of his Sorelian myth of *volk,* see Groh, *Arbeit*: 104–114.
63. Carl Schmitt, "Die Raumrevolution: durch den totalen Krieg zu einem totalen Frieden" (1940; hereafter RII): 389.
64. The *Völker* within the borders of this new *Reich* would exchange subjection for protection and the guarantee of cultural and *völkisch* autonomy.
65. Schmitt "[gave] a constitutional status to the concept of race" when he defined the particularity of the German concept of *Führertum* as based on "an absolute equality between the Führer and his followers." Agamben, *The Kingdom and the Glory*: 76.
66. On the Monroe Doctrine, see GO, 297–298. In "*Raum* und *Rom*—Zur Phonetik des Wortes Raum" (1951), Schmitt wrote "that space [Raum] and Rome [Rom] is the same word" (491).
67. Carl Schmitt, "Raumrevolution: vom Geist des Abendlandes" (hereafter RI), *Deutsche Kolonialzeitung*, vol. 12 (1942): 219.
68. Reinhard Höhn and Best attacked Schmitt for the legal formalism of his *Großraum* concept. Herbert, *Best*: 275–276.
69. Blindow, *Carl Schmitts Reichsordnung*: 67. On the genealogy of the "Mitteleuropa-Idee," see Geoff Eley, *Nazism as Fascism*: 134–136.
70. Müller, *A Dangerous Mind*: 39.
71. Schmitt was opposed to the "war of annihilation" conducted in the east after 1941. Mehring, "'Raumrevolution' als Rechtsproblem": 108.
72. Cicero, "Scipio's Dream": 90.
73. Schmitt, "Raum und Rom: Zur Phonetik des Worters Raum": 492.
74. Schmitt, "Der neue Nomos der Erde": 518; emphasis mine. Tracing the etymology of *nomos* to the *Book of Daniel*, Schmitt reanalyzed *nomos* here as an act of seizing, distributing, and exploiting territory that founds law.
75. Recall that Schmitt's friend Joseph Vogt tied *Scipio's Dream* to the moment when Romans wondered whether they had transgressed the limits of their *völkisch* space (chapter 19).
76. Carl Schmitt, "Die deutsche Rechtswissenschaft im Kampf gegen den jüdischen Geist" (1936), quoted in Taubes, *Ad Carl Schmitt*: 8.
77. Schmitt, *Land und Meer (*1942; hereafter L): 39.
78. Emphasizing the optics of spatial imagination, Schmitt later replaced "ideology" with "iconography." "Die geschichtliche Struktur des heutigen Weltgegensatzes von Ost und West" (1953): 526. For the Spanish conquerors, Mary iconographically embodied their order's territorialization. Schmitt fully developed these ideas on the (pagan/Christian) spatio-political theology of *nomoi* in *Politische Theologie II*.
79. In 1939, Schmitt asserted that history was a history of *Reiche* (*GO,* 309). In "Raumrevolution," he claimed that "*world history is a history of land-*

appropriations" accompanied by "fratricidal wars" among land-taking conquerors (RI, 221).

80. Schmitt remained committed to his Spenglerian concept of Europe. Europe constitutes the "substance" between two orders lacking substance: "A majority of meaningful, concrete great spaces are facing the global unity of a planetary imperialism—be it of the capitalist or communist kind." Schmitt, "Die letzte globale Linie": 447.
81. Schmitt, "Beschleuniger wider Willen" (hereafter BWW): 436.
82. Mehring, *Carl Schmitt*: 428.
83. Anonymous (Werner Best), "Herrenschicht oder Führungsvolk?" (hereafter HS): 130.
84. After Stalingrad and Tunis, Weber explained empire-building as a hard, long process, arguing that empires last more than a thousand years. Replicating "life's path," Rome's rise and fall was the work of many generations. Wilhelm Weber, "Aufstieg und Untergang Roms" (1943): 14.
85. Best worked with a Fichtean conception of *volk* as organic "body" (HS, 123). As the Romans became imperial "masters," the "*völkisch*" empire lost its organic base, peasant-workers of Roman blood (HS, 125). Best described the ruinous consequences with a series of quotes from Mommsen's *History of Rome*.
86. Mommsen, quoted in HS, 128. Best's model was the Italian "Impero" (128).
87. Herbert, *Best*: 287. *Völkisch* decay generated the "eschatological fear of death," whose ultimate symptom was *De Civitate Dei* by the "African Augustine" (HS, 132).
88. Werner Kornemann made similar arguments in his "contribution to the first European Großraum-formation." Ernst Kornemann, *Das Imperium Romanum: Sein Aufstieg und Niedergang*: 27. The Spenglerian Gerhard Nebel argued that colonizing Africa would save the Occident's civilization from decline because contact with the warrior mentality of Africans would renew "echte[s] Herrentum." Nebel, "Der weisse Mann und die Tropen" (1941): 140.
89. Best's definition of Caesarism (populism-*cum*-imperialism) resembles Spengler's.
90. Carl Schmitt, *Land and Sea: A World-Historical Meditation,* transl. Samuel Garrett Zeitlin: 16 and 17. This translation is based on the revised 1981 edition of *Land und Meer*.
91. Reinhard Mehring, *Pathetisches Denken. Carl Schmitts Denkweg am Leitfaden Hegels: Katholische Grundstellung und antimarxistische Hegelstrategie*: 217.
92. The text was written between 1939 and 1945.
93. Hans Freyer, *Weltgeschichte Europas*: 377.
94. Ibid. Critical of (post)Roman empires, Freyer assigned them nonetheless the function of acting as "preserving power" (based on his reading of Paul, Tertullian, and Augustine). Freyer, *Weltgeschichte*: 379.
95. *Land and Sea* is the story of sea-, land-, and air-based empires, or *nomoi*, with a strong dose of technological determinism.

96. Carl Schmitt, *Land und Meer: Eine weltgeschichtliche Betrachtung* (1942): 10.
97. Ibid.
98. Schmitt later revised this passage, leaving out the story's "cannibalistic" side and adding a reference to Heinrich Heine. See *Land and Sea*: 13.
99. On the 1937 anniversary of Abravanel, see Gross, *Carl Schmitt and the Jews*: 276. In chapter 2 of *The Nomos*, Francisco de Vitoria is the positive counterfigure to Abravanel.
100. Melville, *Benito Cereno*: 7.
101. Ibid.: 6 and 22.
102. Ibid.: 7.
103. Ibid.
104. Ibid.: 8. Like Virgil's *Aeneid*, Melville's story constitutes yet another thread in the imperial genealogy of Schmitt's *katechon* as a scenario that gradually crystallized out of his preoccupation with empire, imperial space and its scopic dimension, and the trope of rise and fall in the early 1940s.
105. Wilhelm Weber, "Aufstieg und Untergang Roms": 41.
106. On Spain as Schmitt's "politische Heimat," see Mehring, "'Raumrevolution' als Rechtsproblem": 112; and Müller, *A Dangerous Mind*: 248.
107. Schmitt makes an ontological argument about the nature of empires as states of exception structuring the temporality of the imperial imaginary.
108. At the moment when Schmitt supposedly renounced decisionism, he wrote that for order to be restored, "it is not important *what* is decided but only *that* a decision is made." Schmitt, quoted in Groh, *Arbeit*: 217.
109. Schmitt rethought Spengler's Caesarism as *katechon*. Fascinated by Spengler's (anti-Semitic) critique of modernity and critical of his pessimism, Schmitt countered Spengler's morphological logic of history by emphasizing political action (as decisionism, *Raumrevolution*, and the founding act of *Landnahme)*. He thereby reworked the tension between Spengler's morphological determinism and his nihilist political voluntarism (embodied in the Caesarist dictator).
110. Freyer, *Weltgeschichte*: 45.
111. Meuter, *Der Katechon*: 256.
112. Gross argues that the *katechon* is in its essence anti-Semitic. The *katechon* is locked in struggle with the figure of the assimilated Jew as the internal enemy or modernity's accelerating "agent[s]," combatting *and* unmasking him. Gross, *Carl Schmitt and the Jews*: 166.
113. Reinhard Mehring, "Karl Löwith, Carl Schmitt, Jacob Taubes und das Ende der Geschichte": 234. Mehring traces the transition from an "impatient" eschatology to one of "expectation" as transition from political theology to a theology of history following Schmitt's withdrawal from politics. Mehring, *Pathetisches Denken*: 217. There was no withdrawal from politics. Mehring also claims that Schmitt distanced himself from his 1939 concept of *Reich* with *Land und Meer,* but Schmitt's text is much more ambivalent.
114. Mehring, "Karl Löwith": 234.

115. The Third Reich thus functioned as *katechon* in Schmitt's writing during the Nazi period—however ambivalently.
116. Schmitt, *The Nomos of the Earth*: 59; translation modified.
117. Ibid.: 60.
118. Ibid.
119. Ibid.: 59.
120. Schmitt, *Political Theology II*: 145, note 2.
121. Ibid. It includes the "Augustan religion of Italian-pagan piety." Schmitt, *Political Theology II*: 40.
122. Ibid.: 40; translation modified.
123. Ibid.
124. Ibid.: 41.
125. Schmitt, *Glossarium*: 61. Schmitt's notion of theology further proves that we are dealing with an impero-political and, ultimately, formalist concept. "Since there are many different religions and many different kinds and methods of politics, there are many political theologies." Schmitt, *Politische Theologie II*: 41.
126. According to Herbert, Schmitt added the *völkisch* angle in response to Best's criticism. Herbert, *Best*: 274. I see a closer affinity to Spengler's organic *culture* and his conservative critique of modernity more generally.
127. Schmitt, *"Solange das Imperium da ist"*: 45.
128. Ibid.: 49.
129. Ibid.: 50.
130. Ibid.
131. Alexander Schmitz and Marcel Lepper, eds., *Hans Blumenberg/Carl Schmitt Briefwechsel 1971–1978*: 131.
132. By justifying "the fact that the promised end did not occur," Tertullian established the Christian diaspora as a political power. Ibid. 131.
133. Blumenberg, *The Legitimacy*: 42.
134. "The time is coming," Schmitt wrote, excited about the publication of *Nomos*, "when the final battle for world-dominion will be fought." Schmitt, *Glossarium:* 309.

CHAPTER TWENTY-FIVE

1. Heidegger could imagine a *völkisch Reich*, extending into the East, but reacted with unease to the invasion of the Soviet Union.
2. Karl Haushofer, "Der Kolonialgedanke im Wandel der Zeiten" (1944): 37.
3. Ibid.; emphasis mine. In this context, Haushofer quotes Virgil ("Flectere si nequeo superos Acheronta movebo"), a quote that famously opened Freud's *Interpretation of Dreams* (ibid.).
4. Ibid.: 38.
5. Ibid.: 42 and 37. See also Heidegger on Spengler's notion of "vital energy" in Faye, *Heidegger*: 260.

6. Ibid.: 41.
7. In his thorough engagement with Heidegger's anti-Semitism in the *Black Notebooks, Heidegger & The Myth of a Jewish World Conspiracy* (2015), Peter Trawny never mentions Spengler. The authors in *Reading Heidegger: Black Notebooks 1931–1941*, ed. Ingo Farrin and Jeff Malpas, also barely mention Spengler.
8. With the publication of "Die Zeit des Weltbildes" (The Age of the World-Picture) in 1950, Heidegger made the claim that his analysis of Western metaphysics (with the nexus of technological rationality and unfettered imperialism) established his credentials as critic of National Socialism. As Sidonie Kellerer's philological scrutiny of this essay's divergences from the 1938 lecture shows, Heidegger's famous "turn" is part of his postwar "self-staging." Kellerer, "Rewording the Past: The Postwar Publication of a 1938 Lecture by Martin Heidegger": 596. I am interested in 1) how influential a text Spengler's *Decline of the West* was for Heidegger; and 2) how Heidegger fits not only into the context of the Third Reich but the long discussion about (Roman) empire and time. On Gottfried Benn's Evolian-Spenglerian vision of empire, see "Expressionismus" (1933–1934): 88–89.
9. Heidegger, quoted in Emmanuel Faye, *Heidegger: The Introduction of Nazism into Philosophy*: 210.
10. Ibid.
11. Ibid.: 203.
12. Heidegger, quoted in ibid.: 212.
13. Heidegger, *Basic Concepts (hereafter BC)*: 14.
14. Faye, *Heidegger*: 203.
15. Faye traces quotes from Spengler's *The State* (1924) about "nobility" as "strong race" bred by "discipline." Faye, *Heidegger*: 261.
16. Heidegger, quoted in ibid.: 91, 102.
17. Heidegger, quoted in ibid.: 92.
18. Ibid.: 260. Translating Spengler's "vitalistic vocabulary" into ontology, Heidegger stated that "existence is 'political' in that it affirms itself." Faye, *Heidegger*: 261.
19. Heidegger, *Überlegungen VII–XI (hereafter ÜVII)*: 138; and Heidegger, *Überlegungen XII—XV* (hereafter ÜXII): 270.
20. Heidegger put his own twist on Spengler's anti-Semitism, inventing "a highly unusual species of 'ontological-historical' [*seinsgeschichtliche*] anti-Semitism." Peter E. Gordon, "Heidegger in Black," *New York Review of Books* (October 9, 2014); http://www.nybooks.com/articles/2014/10/09/heidegger-in-black/.
21. Nietzsche thinks "in purely Roman terms," incapable of understanding "the Greek origin of Occidental thought" (*ÜXII*, 199).
22. Heidegger, quoted in Gordon, "Heidegger": 8.
23. On "Planetarismus," and machination's "unconditional power," see also ÜXII, 261.

24. Heidegger, quoted in Michael Fagenblat, "'Heidegger' and the Jews": 148.
25. Ibid.
26. Ibid.
27. Philosophy and anti-Semitism are hopelessly entangled. "The ascendancy of Jews belonged to 'the metaphysics of the West' that helped to spread both 'empty rationality'" and "'a capacity for calculation.'" With his ideas about the "worldlessness of Jewry," Heidegger recycled the trope of the wandering Jew. Gordon, "Heidegger": 4.
28. Translation in Trawny, *Heidegger*: 72.
29. "World Jewry is ungraspable everywhere and doesn't need to get involved in military action while continuing to unfurl its influence, whereas we are left to sacrifice the best blood of the best of our people." Heidegger, quoted in Gordon, "Heidegger": 9.
30. In opposition to these, Jews are not the "cause" of modernity's decline but "symptoms." Gordon, "Heidegger": 5.
31. Heidegger also spoke at the Institute of German Studies in Rome in 1935, together with Haushofer, Schmitt, and Karl Löwith. See Victor Farrias, *Heidegger and Nazism*: 235.
32. Here, Heidegger refers to Hölderlin's statement that even if he were forced to leave for "Otaheiti," he would remain German. Heidegger, "*Hölderlins Hymne 'Andenken'*": 23. Through this act of remembrance, the return to the origin or home "unfold[s] as a dialogue with the foreign." William McNeill, "The Hölderlin Lectures": 234. Heidegger thinks about the "historical vocation of the Germans in relation to the Greeks" not in terms of "appropriation" but as "'the dialogue between one's own and the foreign.'" Ibid. On the original lecture, "Hölderlin and the Essence of Poetry," see Faye, *Heidegger*: 103ff.
33. Adorno, "Spengler after the Decline" (1941): 65.
34. Faye, *Heidegger*: 210.
35. Heidegger develops his phenomenological concepts of time, temporality, and historicity in confrontation with Paul's eschatological temporality and primordial Christian religiosity. See Coyne, *Heidegger's Confessions*: 17–52. Paul's *Letters* matter to Heidegger because of the heightened state of wakefulness characterizing all acts in the expectation of the other beginning. At first glance, this reading of Paul is radically different from Schmitt's and his *katechontic* deferral of the end—and yet Schmitt too makes this ecstatic experience of time part of his *katechontic* sovereignty (as the intensity of the last, decisive battle). For Spengler's analysis of Paul as a Hellenist thinker of Roman civilization and his eschatology as an example of civilization's many attempts to master the inexorable course of time, see D2, 220ff.
36. Spengler theorized a Great Culture's end stage as the return to prehistory and biological temporality, mere duration.
37. With this Roman project, they stepped out of the heroic scene at the heart of Heidegger's commitment to National Socialism, man's willingness to put himself "at risk" (BC, 2), or, as he formulated it in 1933: Germany "*risking* its

history in the arena of world power." Heidegger, quoted in Farias, *Heidegger and Nazism*: 104.

38. Heidegger, "*Hölderlins Hymne 'Andenken'*": 53.
39. Ibid.: 114.
40. Ibid.: 87–88.
41. Ibid.: 87.
42. Ibid.
43. Ibid.: 88.
44. Ibid.
45. Ibid. The present moment, the beginning of the *Abendland*'s end, is thus merely the prehistory of authentic Greco-German being.
46. Ryan Coyne, *Heidegger's Confessions*: 80. Heidegger theorized "ruinance" as life's "collapse" in his work on Aristotle (ibid.). "Life," Coyne comments, "is dead-set on rendering itself null and void. This drive toward self-nullification on the part of life [by taking refuge in objectivity and fleeing its finitude] is so extreme, Heidegger concludes, that we cannot subsume it under the general category of emptiness, but must think of it in terms of a disastrous fall"—or "ruinance" (81, 80).
47. Heidegger, quoted in William McNeill, "Heidegger's Hölderlin Lectures": 234.
48. Heidegger, quoted in Charles Bambach, *Heidegger's Greek Roots*: 35.
49. On the significance of Paul's "question of 'how' one waits" and his concept of the *parousia* as "the other beginning," see Charles Bambach, "Weimar Philosophy and the Crisis of Historical Thinking": 145. See also n35, above.
50. Modernity makes all things past into something "immediately and cheaply available" (ÜVII, 111).
51. Classicist epochs are "historical paintings covering the condition of modern man" (ÜVII, 201).
52. Matz, "Wesen und Wirkung der Augusteischen Kunst: Ein Vortrag": 233.
53. On Heidegger's replacing historicism's "subject-object metaphysics" with the "ontological question about the meaning of historical being," see Bambach, "The Crisis of Historical Thinking": 144–147. Similarly, Spengler saw the experience of lived time and historicity as the prerogative of *Kultur*.
54. Heidegger, "*Hölderlins Hymne 'Andenken'*": 132.
55. Ibid.: 129.
56. Joseph Goebbels, "Rede im Berliner Sportpalast [Wollt Ihr den totalen Krieg], 18. Februar 1943": 6. While Schmitt's and Heidegger's texts cannot be reduced to Goebbels's cynical Spenglerian appeal to the West, they too draw on Spengler's *Decline*.

EPILOGUE

1. Carl Schmitt, "Die geschichtliche Struktur des heutigen Weltgegensatzes von Ost und West": 527.

2. Both "distanced and ironic," the photographs document "conceptual art 'actions'" inspired by Joseph Beuys. Matthew Biro, *Anselm Kiefer*: 10, 9.
3. Andreas Huyssen, "Anselm Kiefer: The Terror of History, the Temptation of Myth": 216. This was a "self conscious mise-en-scène," but the controversies around the series often mistook this "conceptual core" of the work (ibid.).
4. Transcription of the audio guide to *Chute d'Étoiles/Sternenfall*.
5. Ibid.

Bibliography

Abizadeh, Arash. 2005. "Was Fichte an Ethic Nationalist? On Cultural Nationalism and Its Double." *History of Political Thought* 26.2(Summer):334–359.

Adams, Julia, and George Steinmetz. 2015. "Sovereignty and Sociology: From State Theory to Theories of Empire." *Political Power and Social Theory* 28:269–285.

Adler, Hans, and Ernest A. Menze. 1997. "Introduction: On the Way to World History: Johann Gottfried Herder." In *On World History: An Anthology. Johann Gottfried Herder*. Armonk, NY: M. E. Sharpe, 3–19.

Adorno, Theodor W. [1941] 1981. "Spengler after the Decline." In *Prisms*. Cambridge, MA: MIT Press, 51–72.

Aeschylus. 2017. *Agamemnon*, transl. Sarah Ruben. In *The Greek Plays: Sixteen Plays by Aeschylus, Sophocles, and Euripides*, edited by Mary Lefkowitz and James Romm. New York: Modern Library.

Agamben, Giorgio. n.d. "The Time That Is Left." Available online at https://lineafuga.files.wordpress.com/2010/08/agamben_the-time-that-is-left.pdf.

———. 2005. *State of Exception*. Chicago: University of Chicago Press.

———. 2005. *The Time That Remains: A Commentary on the Letter to the Romans*. Stanford, CA: Stanford University Press.

———. 2011. *The Kingdom and the Glory: For a Theological Genealogy of Economy and Government*. Stanford, CA: Stanford University Press.

Agnew, Vanessa. 1995. "Ethnographic Transgressions and Confessions in Georg Forster's 'Voyage Round the World.'" In *Schwellen*, edited by Nicholas Saul, Daniel Steuer, Frank Möbus, and Birgit Illner. Würzburg: Königshausen and Neumann, 304–315.

———. 1999. "Dissecting the Cannibal: Comparing the Function of the Autopsy Principle in the Diaries and Narratives of Cook's Second Voyage." In *Marginal Voices, Marginal Forms: Diaries in European Literature and History*, edited by Rachel Langford and Russell West. Amsterdam: Editions Rodopi, 50–60.

Alcock, Susan E., John F. Cherry, and Jaś Elsner, eds. 2000. *Pausanias: Travel and Memory in Roman Greece*. Oxford: Oxford University Press.

Aldrich, Robert, ed. 2007. *The Age of Empires*. London: Thames & Hudson.

Alpers, Svetlana. 1983. *The Dutch Art of Describing: Dutch Art in the Seventeenth Century*. Chicago: University of Chicago Press.

Alston, Richard. 2011. "Seeing Caesar in Ruins: Towards a Radical Aesthetics of Ruins." *European Review of History—Revue européenne d'histoire* 18(5–6):697–716.

Altekamp, Stefan. 2008. "Germanità: Archäologische Kolonialfantasien." In *Das große Spiel: Archäologie und Politik 1860–1940*, edited by Charlotte Trümpler. Cologne: Dumont, 580–585.

Amer, Sarah, and Laura Doyle. 2015. "Introduction: Reframing Postcolonial and Global Studies in the *Longer Durée*." *PMLA* 130(2, March):331–335.

Ando, Clifford. 2015. *Roman Social Imaginaries: Language and Thought in Contexts of Empire*. Toronto: University of Toronto Press.

Andreas, Willy. 1940. "Einleitung." In *Die Neue Propyläen Weltgeschichte*, vol. 1, edited by Willy Andreas. Berlin: Propyläen-Verlag, 3–8.

Anonymous. *1875. Les Ruines de Paris en 4875*. Paris: Librairie Léon Willem.

———. *1934. Volk und Reich: Politische Monatshefte* 9: no page nrs.

———. 1944. "Cannae." *SS-Leitheft* 10(April): no page nrs.

Antliff, Mark. 2001. "Fascism, Modernism, and Modernity." *Art Bulletin* 84(1, March):148–169.

Appian. 1889. *The Punic Wars*, In *The Foreign Wars*, translated by Horace White. New York: Macmillan, http://data.perseus.org/texts/urn:cts:greekLit:tlg0551.tlg009.perseus-eng1

Arendt, Hannah. [1944] 2005. "Franz Kafka: A Revaluation." In *Essays in Understanding 1930–1954*, edited by Jerome Kohn. New York: Schocken, 69–80.

———. [1944] 2005. "Understanding and Politics (The Difficulty of Understanding)." In *Essays in Understanding 1930–1954*, edited by Jerome Kohn. New York: Schocken, 307–327.

———. 1976. *The Origins of Totalitarianism*. New York and London: Harcourt Brace.

———. 1978. *The Life of the Mind*. New York: Harcourt Brace and Company.

———. 1987. *On Revolution*. London and New York: Penguin Books.

Aristotle. 2001. *De Anima (On the Soul)*. In *The Basic Works of Aristotle*, edited by Richard McKeon. New York: Modern Library, 535–603.

———. 2001. *De Memoria et Reminiscentia (On Memory and Reminiscence)*. In *The Basic Works of Aristotle*, edited by Richard McKeon. New York: Modern Library, 607–617.

———. 2001. *ETHICA NICOMACHEA (Nichomachean Ethics)*. In *The Basic Works of Aristotle*, edited by Richard McKeon. New York: Modern Library, 935–1112.

———. 2001. *METAPHYSICA (Metaphysics)*. In *The Basic Works of Aristotle*, edited by Richard McKeon. New York: Modern Library, 689–934.

———. 2001. *POETICA (Poetics)*. In *The Basic Works of Aristotle*, edited by Richard MacKeon. New York: Modern Library, 1455–1487.

———. 1907. *The Poetics of Aristotle*, edited and translated by S. H. Butcher. London: Macmillan and Co.

Armstrong, Richard. *2005. A Compulsion for Antiquity: Freud and the Ancient World.* Ithaca, NY: Cornell University Press.

Arndt, Karl. 1994. "Problematischer Ruhm: die Großaufträge in Berlin 1937–1943." In *Wilhelm Kreis: Architekt zwischen Kaiserreich und Demokratie 1873–1955*, edited by Winfried Nerdinger and Ekkehard Mai. Munich: Klinkhardt & Biermann, 169–187.

Arthurs, Joshua. 2012. *Excavating Modernity: The Roman Past in Fascist Italy*. Ithaca, NY: Cornell University Press.

Aschheim, Steven E. 1993. "Max Nordau, Friedrich Nietzsche and Degeneration." *Journal of Contemporary History* 28(4):643–657.

Atkinson, David. 1997. "Hitler's Grand Tour: The Triumphant Entrance to Rome 1938." Working Paper 8, Royal Holloway University of London Geography Department, 1–25.

Augustine. 2003. *Concerning the City of God against the Pagans*, translated by Henry Bettenson and with a new introduction by G. R. Evans. London: Penguin Books.

Bailyn, Bernard. 1967. *The Ideological Origins of the American Revolution*. Cambridge, MA: Belknap Press of Harvard University Press.

Balfour, Alan. 1990. *Berlin: The Politics of Order, 1737–1989*. New York: Rizzoli International Publications.

Bambach, Charles. 2003. *Heidegger's Greek Roots: Nietzsche, National Socialism, and the Greeks*. Ithaca, NY: Cornell University Press.

———. 2013. "Weimar Philosophy and the Crisis of Historical Thinking." In *Weimar Thought: A Contested Legacy*, edited by Peter Gordon and John P. McCormick. Princeton, NJ: Princeton University Press, 131–149.

Baranowski, Shelley. 2011. *Nazi Empire: German Colonialism and Imperialism from Bismarck to Hitler*. Cambridge: Cambridge University Press.

Barnard, John Levi. 2014. "Ancient History, American Time: Chesnutt's Outsider Classicism and the Present Past." *PMLA* 129(1):71–86.

Barry, Kelly. 2004. "The Subject and Object of Mythology." In *A New History of German Literature*, edited by David E. Wellbery. Cambridge, MA: Harvard University Press, 494–500.

Bartetzko, Dieter. 1985. *Zwischen Zucht und Ekstase: Zur Theatralik von NS-Architektur* Berlin: Gebr. Mann Verlag.

———. 1985. *Illusionen im Stein: Stimmungsarchitektur im deutschen Faschismus. Ihre*

Vorgeschichte in Theater- und Film-Bauten. Reinbeck bei Hamburg: Rowohlt Verlag.

Bayly, C. A. 1989. *Imperial Meridian: The British Empire and the World, 1780–1830*: London: Longman.

———. 2004. *The Birth of the Modern World 1780–1914*. London: Blackwell.

Beacham, Richard C. 1996. *The Roman Theatre and Its Audience*. Cambridge, MA: Harvard University Press.

Beaglehole, J. C. 1955. "General Introduction." In *The Journals of Captain James Cook on His Voyages of Discovery*, vol. 1, edited by J. C. Beaglehole. Cambridge: Cambridge University Press, xxi–clxxi.

———. 1961. *The Journals of Captain Cook on His Voyages of Discovery*, vol. 2, edited by J. C. Beaglehole. Cambridge: Cambridge University Press.

Beard, Mary. 2007. *The Roman Triumph*. Cambridge, MA: Harvard University Press.

———. 2015. *SPQR: A History of Ancient Rome*. London: W. W. Norton.

Bell, Andrew J. E. 1997. "Cicero and the Spectacle of Power." *Journal of Roman Studies* 87:1–22.

Bell, Duncan. 2007. *The Idea of Greater Britain: Empire and the Future World Order, 1860–1900*. Princeton, NJ: Princeton University Press.

———. 2016. *Reordering the World: Essays on Liberalism and Empire*. Princeton, NJ: Princeton University Press.

Bengtson, Hermann. 1943. "Scipio Africanus: Seine Persönlichkeit und weltgeschichtliche Bedeutung." *Historische Zeitschrift* 168(3):487–508.

Benjamin, Roger. 2014. "Colonial Panoramania." In *Empires of Vision: A Reader*, edited by Martin Jay and Sumathi Ramaswamy. Durham, NC: Duke University Press.

Benjamin, Walter. [1938] 1978. "Theses on the Philosophy of History." In *Illuminations: Essays and Reflections*. New York: Schocken Books, 253–264.

———. [1938] 1978. "The Work of Art in the Age of Mechanical Reproduction." In *Illuminations: Essays and Reflections*. New York: Schocken Books, 217–251.

———. 1986. "On the Mimetic Faculty." *Reflections*. New York: Schocken Books, 333–336.

———. 2003. *The Origin of German Tragic Drama*. London and New York: Verso.

Benn, Gottfried. [1935] 1989. "Sein und Werden." In *Sämtliche Werke—Stuttgarter Ausgabe*, edited by Gerhard Schuster, vol. 4. Stuttgart: Klett-Cotta, 202–212.

———. [1934] 1989. "Dorische Welt: Eine Untersuchung über die Beziehung von Kunst und Macht." In *Sämtliche Werke—Stuttgarter Ausgabe*, edited by Gerhard Schuster, vol. 4. Stuttgart: Klett-Cotta, 124–153.

———. [1934] 1989. "Kunst und Macht: Vorwort." In *Sämtliche Werke—Stuttgarter Ausgabe*, edited by Gerhard Schuster, vol. 4. Stuttgart: Klett-Cotta, 198–201.

———. [1934] 1989. "Lebensweg eines Intellektualisten." In *Sämtliche Werke—Stuttgarter Ausgabe*, edited by Gerhard Schuster, vol. 4. Stuttgart: Klett-Cotta, 154–197.

———. [1933–34] 1989. "Expressionismus." In *Sämtliche Werke—Stuttgarter Ausgabe*, edited by Gerhard Schuster, vol. 4. Stuttgart: Klett-Cotta, vol. 4, 76–90.

———. 1989. *Der Ptolemäer. Berliner Novelle, 1947.* In *Sämtliche Werke—Stuttgarter Ausgabe,* edited by Gerhard Schuster, vol. 5. Stuttgart: Klett-Cotta, 8–55.

Berezin, Mabel. 1997. *Making the Fascist Self: The Political Culture of Interwar Italy.* Ithaca, NY, and London: Cornell University Press.

Bergmann, Bettina. 2001. "Meanwhile, Back in Italy . . . : Creating Landscapes of Allusion." In *Pausanias: Travel and Memory in Greece,* edited by Susan Alcock, John Cherry, and Jaś Elsner. Oxford: Oxford University Press, 154–166.

Bergstein, Mary. 2010. *Mirrors of Memory: Freud, Photography, and the History of Art.* Ithaca, NY: Cornell University Press.

Berman, Russell. 1998. *Enlightenment or Empire: Colonial Discourse in German Culture.* Lincoln: University of Nebraska Press.

Bertrand, Louis. 1917. "Massacreurs et Tortionnaires." In *Le Sens de l'Ennemi.* Paris: A. Fayard, 241–248.

———. 1917. *Le Sens de L'Ennemi.* Paris: A. Fayard.

———. [1895] 1920. "Préface de la Nouvelle Edition." *Le Sang des Races.*

———. 1920. "Les Villes D'Or." I: "De la Mer Atlantide Au Pats des Lotophages." *Revue des Deux Mondes* 6(58):695–709.

———. 1920. "Les Villes D'Or." II: "La Resurrection de Carthage." *La Revue des Deux Mondes* 6(59, September/October):52–73.

———. 1921. "Préface." *Le jardin de la mort.* Paris: Librairie Ollendorf, i–xii.

———. 1930. "L'Église d'Afrique." *Revue des deux mondes* 57(May/June):402–415.

———. 1936. *Sur les Routes du Sud.* Paris: A. Fayard.

Berve, Helmut. 1934. "Die Antike und der nationalsozialistische Staat." *Vergangenheit und Gegenwart* 24:257–272.

———. 1937. *Sparta.* Leipzig: Bibliographisches Institut.

———, ed. 1942. *Das neue Bild der Antike.* 2 vols. Leipzig: Koehler & Amelang.

———. 1942. "Vorwort." In *Das neue Bild der Antike,* vol. 1, edited by Helmut Berve. Leipzig: Kohler & Amelang, 5–12.

———. 1942. *Imperium Romanum.* Leipzig: Koehler & Amelang.

Best, Werner. 1941. "Grundfragen einer deutschen Grossraum-Verwaltung." *Festgabe für Heinrich Himmler.* Darmstadt: L. S. Wittich Verlag, 33–60.

———. 1942. Anonymous (Werner Best). "Herrenschicht oder Führungsvolk?" *Reich-Volksordnung-Lebensraum,* vol. 3, 122–141.

Bhabha, Homi. 1983. "Difference, Discrimination, and the Discourse of Colonialism." In *The Politics of Theory,* edited by Francis Barker et al. Colchester: University of Essex, 194–211.

———. 1994. "Of Mimicry and Man: The Ambivalence of Colonial Discourse." In *The Location of Culture.* London and New York: Routledge, 85–92.

Bibiena, Ferdinando Galli. 1978. *L'architettura civile* and *Direzioni.* In *The Italian Baroque Stage,* edited by Dunbar H. Ogden. Berkeley: University of California Press, 49–70.

Bilsel, Can. 2012. *Antiquity on Display: Regimes of the Authentic in Berlin's Pergamon Museum.* Oxford: Oxford University Press.

Bindman, David. 2004. "'Philanthropy Seems Natural to Mankind': Hodges and

Captain Cook's Second Voyage to the South Seas." In *William Hodges 1744–1797: The Art of Exploration*, edited by Geoff Quilley and John Bonehill. New Haven, CT: Yale University Press, 21–26.

Birchall, Frederick T. 1938. "Gilded Rome Is Set to Dazzle Hitler." *New York Times* (May 3), 14.

Biro, Matthew. 2013. *Anselm Kiefer*. London and New York: Phaidon Press.

Blindow, Felix. 1997. *Carl Schmitts Reichsordnung: Strategie für einen europäischen Großraum*. Berlin: Akademieverlag.

Bloch, Ernst. 1985. "Anhang: Spenglers Raubtiere und relative Kulturgärten." In *Erbschaft dieser Zeit*. Frankfurt: Suhrkamp, 318–329.

Blumenberg, Hans. 1983. *The Legitimacy of the Modern Age*, translated by Robert M. Wallace. Cambridge, MA: MIT Press.

Boletsi, Maria. 2013. *Barbarism and Its Discontents*. Stanford, CA: Stanford University Press.

Bollas, Christopher. 2000. *Hysteria*. London and New York: Routledge.

Bonehill, John. 2004. "Hodges and Cook's Second Voyage." In *William Hodges 1744–1797: The Art of Exploration*, edited by Geoff Quilley and John Bonehill. New Haven, CT: Yale University Press, 109–136.

Bonnett, Alastair. 2003. "From White to Western: 'Racial Decline' and the Idea of the West in Britain, 1890–1930." *Journal of Historical Sociology* 16(3, September):320–347.

Book of Daniel (Daniel 2). New International Version of the Bible. https://www.biblica.com/bible/niv/daniel/2/.

Bougainville, Louis-Antoine de. 1982. *Voyage autour du monde, par le frégate du Roi la Boudeuse et la flute L'Étoile*. Paris: Gallimard.

Bowersock, Glen W. 1996. "The Vanishing Paradigm of the Fall of Rome." *Bulletin of the American Academy of Arts and Sciences* 49(May 8):29–43.

———. 2009. "Gibbon on Civil War and Rebellion in the Decline of the Roman Empire." In *From Gibbon to Auden: Essays on the Classical Tradition*. Oxford: Oxford University Press, 20–32.

———. "Gibbon's Historical Imagination." *From Gibbon to Auden: Essays on the Classical Tradition*. Oxford: Oxford University Press, 3–19.

Bradley, Mark. 2010. "Introduction" to *Classics and Imperialism in the British Empire, edited* by Mark Bradley. Oxford: Oxford University Press, 1–25.

Braudel, Fernand. 1980. "The History of Civilizations: The Past Explains the Present." In Braudel, *On History*, translated by Sarah Matthews. Chicago: University of Chicago Press, 177–219.

Brégeon, Jean-Joël. 1991. *L'Égypte de Bonaparte*. Paris: Perrin.

Brendon, Piers. 2008. *The Decline and Fall of the British Empire, 1781–1997*. New York: Knopf.

Breuer, Stefan. 1982. *Anatomie der konservativen Revolution*. Darmstadt: Wissenschaftliche Buchgesellschaft.

Brugger, Ingrid, et al., eds. 2001. *Emil Nolde und die Südsee*. Munich: Hirmer Verlag.

Bryer, Anthony. 1997. "Gibbon and the Later Byzantine Empires." In *Edward Gib-*

bon and Empire, edited by Rosamond McKitterick and Roland Quinault. Cambridge: Cambridge University Press, 101–116.

Buck-Morss, Susan. 1991. *The Dialectics of Seeing: Walter Benjamin and the Arcades Project*. Cambridge, MA: MIT Press.

———. 2009. *Hegel, Haiti, and Universal History*. Pittsburgh: University of Pittsburgh Press.

Bullard, Alice. 2000. *Exile to Paradise: Savagery and Civilization in Paris and the South Pacific*. Stanford, CA: Stanford University Press.

Burbank, Jane, and Fred Cooper. 2010. *Empires in World History: Power and the Politics of Difference*. Princeton, NJ: Princeton University Press.

Burke, Peter. 1999. "Presenting and Re-Presenting Charles V." In *Charles V and His Time, 1500–1558*, edited by Hugo Soly. Antwerp: Mercatorfonds, 393–476.

Burleigh, Nina. 2007. *Mirage: Napoleon's Scientists and the Unveiling of Egypt*. New York: HarperCollins.

Caesar. 1996. *Seven Commentaries on The Gallic War*, translated by Carolyn Hammond. Oxford: Oxford University Press.

Calhoun, Craig, Frederick Cooper, and Kevin M. Moore, eds. 2006. *Lessons of Empire: Imperial Histories and American Power*. New York: New Press.

Cannadine, David. 2001. *Ornamentalism: How the British Saw Their Empire*. Oxford: Oxford University Press.

Caradini, Andrea, ed. 2017. *The Atlas of Ancient Rome: Biography and Portraits of the City*. Princeton, NJ: Princeton University Press.

Carcopino, Jérome. 1951. "L'héritage de Rome en Tunisie." *Cahiers Charles de Foucauld*, vol. 17: 37–50.

Cassas, Louis-François. 1799. *Voyage pittoresque de la Syrie, de la Phénicie, de la Palestine, et de la Bas-Égypte*. Paris: Imprimerie de la République.

Charle, Christophe, Julien Vincent, and Jay Winter, eds. 2007. *Anglo-French Attitudes: Comparisons and Transfers between English and French Intellectuals since the Eighteenth Century*. Manchester: Manchester University Press.

Chapoutot, Johann. 2016. *Greeks, Romans, Germans: How the Nazis Usurped Europe's Classical Past*. Berkeley: University of California Press.

Chateaubriand, François-René, vicomte de. 1910. *Mémoires d'outre-tombe*, vols. 1 and 2. Paris: Garnier.

Chevallier, Raymond. 1988. *Voyages et déplacements dans l'empire Romain*. Paris: Armand Collin.

Christ, Karl. 2006. *Klios Wandlungen: Die deutsche Althistorie vom Neuhumanismus bis zur Gegenwart*. Munich: C. H. Beck.

———. 1982. *Römische Geschichte und deutsche Geschichtswissenschaft*. Munich: C. H. Beck.

Cicero. 2008. *The Republic and The Laws*, translated by Niall Rudd. Oxford: Oxford University Press.

Clark, Katerina. 2011. *Moscow, The Fourth Rome: Stalinism, Cosmopolitanism, and the Evolution of Soviet Culture, 1931–1941*. Cambridge, MA: Harvard University Press.

Clarke, John R. 2005. "Augustan Domestic Interiors: Propaganda or Fashion." In *The Cambridge Companion to the Augustan Age.* Cambridge: Cambridge University Press, 273–274.

———. 2005. "Augustan Domestic Interiors: Propaganda or Fiction?" In *The Cambridge Companion to the Age of Augustus*, edited by Karl Galinsky. Cambridge: Cambridge University Press, 264–278.

Clendinnen, Inga. 1993. "'Fierce and Unnatural Cruelty': Cortés and the Conquest of Mexico." In *New World Encounters*, edited by Stephen Greenblatt. Berkeley: University of California Press, 12–47.

Colas, Alejandro. 2007. *Empire*. Cambridge: Polity.

Cole, Juan. 2007. *Napoleon's Egypt: Invading the Middle East.* New York: Palgrave Macmillan.

Collier, Andrew. 2005. "Critical Realism." In *The Politics of Method in the Human Sciences: Positivism and Its Epistemological Others*, edited by George Steinmetz. Durham, NC: Duke University Press, 327–345.

Collingwood, R. G. 1956. *The Idea of History*. Oxford: Oxford University Press.

Connolly, Joy. 2018. "The Promise of the Classical Canon: Hannah Arendt and the Romans." *Classical Philology* 113:6–19.

Conrad, Joseph. 2002. *Heart of Darkness*. Stuttgart: Reclam.

Conrad, Sebastian. 2012. *German Colonialism: A Short Introduction*. Cambridge: Cambridge University Press.

Conway, Daniel W. 2002. "Ecce Caesar: Nietzsche's Imperial Aspirations." In *Nietzsche, Godfather of Fascism? On the Uses and Abuses of a Philosophy*, edited by Jacob Golomb and Robert S. Wistrich. Princeton, NJ: Princeton University Press, 173–195.

Cook, Alexander. 2007. "Reading Revolution: Towards a History of the Volney Vogue in England." In *Anglo-French Attitudes: Comparisons and Transfers between English and French Intellectuals since the Eighteenth Century*, edited by Christophe Charle, Julien Vincent, and Jay Winter. Manchester: Manchester University Press, 125–146.

Cooley, Alison E. 2009. *Res Gestae Divi Augusti: Text, Translation, and Commentary*. Cambridge: Cambridge University Press.

Cooper, Tarnya. 1999. "Forgetting Rome and the Voice of Piranesi's 'Speaking Ruins.'" In *The Art of Forgetting*, edited by Adrian Forty and Susanne Kuchler. Oxford and New York: Berg, 107–125.

Cornelißen, Christoph. 2009. "Zur Rezeption der italienischen Architektur im 'Dritten Reich.'" In *Für den Faschismus bauen: Architektur und Städtebau im Italien Mussolinis*, edited by Aram Mattioli and Gerald Steinacher. Luzern: Orell Füssli Verlag, 373–395.

Coulston, Jon. 2001. "Transport and Travel on the Column of Trajan." In *Travel and Geography in the Roman Empire*, edited by Colin Adams and Ray Laurence. London and New York: Routledge, 106–137.

Coyne, Ryan. 2015. *Heidegger's Confessions: The Remains of Saint Augustine in Being and Time & Beyond*. Chicago: University of Chicago Press.

Craddock, Patricia B. 1984. "Edward Gibbon and the 'Ruins of the Capitol.'" In *Roman Images*, edited by Annabel Patterson. Baltimore and London: Johns Hopkins University Press, 63–82.

Curran, Brian A., Anthony Grafton, Pamela O. Long, and Benjamin Weiss, eds. 2009. *Obelisk: A History*. Cambridge, MA: Burndy Library Publications.

Dahn, Felix. [1876] 2005. *A Struggle for Rome*, translated by Herb Parker. London: Athena Press.

———. [1876] 1976. "Vorwort." *Ein Kampf um Rom*. Munich: Wilhelm Heyne Verlag.

Damrosh, David. 1986. "The Politics of Ethics: Freud and Rome." In *Pragmatism's Freud: The Moral Disposition of Psychoanalysis*, edited by J. H. Smith and W. Kerrigan. Baltimore: Johns Hopkins University Press, 102–125.

Davis, Creston, and Patrick Aaron Riches. 2005. "Metanoia: The Theological Praxis of Revolution." In *Theology and the Political: The New Debate*, edited by Creston Davis, John Milbank, and Slavoj Žižek. Durham, NC: Duke University Press, 22–51.

Dehio, Ludwig. 1950. "Ranke and German Imperialism." In *Germany and World Politics in the Twentieth Century*, translated by Dieter Pevsner. New York: Norton, 28–71.

de Man, Paul. 1971. "Literary History and Literary Modernity." In *Blindness and Insight: Essays in the Rhetoric of Contemporary Criticism*. Oxford: Oxford University Press, 142–165.

Demandt, Alexander. 1984. *Der Fall Roms: Die Auflösung des römischen Reiches im Urteil der Nachwelt*. Munich: Beck.

———. 2002. "Klassik als Klischee: Hitler und die Antike." *Historische Zeitschrift* 274:281–313.

Demandt, Alexander, and John Farrenkopf, eds. 1994. *Der Fall Spengler: Eine kritische Bilanz*. Cologne and Weimar: Böhlau Verlag.

Dickson, Martin Bernard, and Stuart Cary Welch. 1981. *The Houghton Shahnameh*. Cambridge, MA: Harvard University Press.

Diderot, Denis. [1796] 1956. "Supplement to Bougainville's 'Voyage.'" In *Rameau's Nephew and Other Works*, edited by Jacques Barzun and Ralph H. Bowen. New York: Bobbs-Merrill, 179–228.

———. 1995. "Salon of 1767." In *Diderot on Art*, vol. 2, edited and translated by John Goodman. New Haven, CT: Yale University Press.

Dobler, Ralph-Miklas. 2010. "Hitler in Rome 1938." Forschungsbericht 2010-Bibliotheca Hertziana-Max-Planck-Institut für Kunstgeschichte. https://www.mpg.de/376970/.

Donahue, Neil H. 1993. "Ecstatic Montage: Paratactic Visions in Gottfried Benn's Novella Cycle 'Brains' (1916)." In *Forms of Disruption: Abstraction in Modern German Prose*. Ann Arbor: University of Michigan Press, 161–183.

Dorgerloh, Annette. 2007. "Karl Friedrich Schinkels 'Triumphbogen' 1817—Programmbild und Geschichtsdenkmal." In *Klassizismus—Gothik: Karl Friedrich Schinkel und die patriotische Baukunst*, edited by Annette

Dorgerloh, Michael Niedermeier, and Horst Bredekamp. Munich: Deutscher Kunstverlag, 81–98.

Dowd, Gregory Evans. 2008. "'We Are the Heir Apparent to the Romans': Imperial Myths and Indigenous Status." In *Empire and Dissent: The United States and Latin America*, edited by Fred Rosen. Durham, NC: Duke University Press, 53–67.

Downing, Eric. 2006. *After Images: Photography, Archaeology, and Psychoanalysis and the Tradition of Bildung*. Detroit: Wayne State University Press.

Dubin, Nina. 2010. *Futures & Ruins: Eighteenth-Century Paris and the Art of Hubert Robert*. Los Angeles: Getty Research Institute.

Dufallo, Basil. 2007. *The Ghosts of the Past: Latin Literature, the Dead, and Rome's Transition to Principate*. Columbus: Ohio State University Press.

———. 2013. *The Captor's Image: Greek Culture in Roman Ecphrasis*. Oxford: Oxford University Press.

Dünne, Jörg, and Stephan Günzel, eds. 2006. *Raumtheorie*. Frankfurt: Suhrkamp Verlag.

Dunwoodie, Peter. 2010. "Colonizing Space: Louis Bertrand's Algeria in 'Le Sang des Races' and 'Sur les Routes du Sud.'" *Modern Language Review* 105(4, October):998–1014.

Eaton, Natasha. 2004. "Hodges's Visual Genealogy for Colonial India, 1780–97." In *William Hodges 1744–1797: The Art of Exploration*, edited by Geoff Quilley and John Bonehill. New Haven, CT: Yale University Press, 35–42.

———. 2013. *Mimesis across Empires: Artworks and Networks in India 1765–1860*. Durham, NC: Duke University Press.

Eberhardt, Walter. 1935. "Die Antike und wir." *Nationalsozialistische Monatshefte* 6:115–127.

Edwards, Catharine. 1996. *Writing Rome: Textual Approaches to the City*. Cambridge: Cambridge University Press.

———, ed. 1999. *Roman Presences: Receptions of Rome in European Culture, 1789–1945*. Cambridge: Cambridge University Press.

———. 1999. "Translating Empire? Macaulay's Rome." In *Roman Presences*, edited by Catharine Edwards. Cambridge: Cambridge University Press, 70–87.

———. 2011. "Imagining Ruins in Ancient Rome." *European Review of History–Revue européenne d'histoire* 18(5–6):645–661.

Ek, Fatma Ipek, and Deniz Sengel. 2007. "Piranesi between Classical and Sublime." *METU JFA* 24(1):17–34.

Eley, Geoff. 2013. *Nazism as Fascism: Violence, Ideology, and the Ground of Consent in Germany 1930–1944*. London and New York: Routledge.

———. 2014. "Empire by Land or Sea? Germany's Imperial Imaginary, 1840–1945." In *German Cultures of Colonialism: Race, Nation, and Globalization*, edited by Geoff Eley and Bradley Naranch. Durham, NC: Duke University Press.

Eliot, T. S. 1974. *What Is a Classic? An Address Delivered before the Virgil Society on the 16th of October, 1944*. New York: Haskell House Publishers.

Elliott, Anthony. 2005. "Psychoanalysis and the Theory of the Subject." In *The Poli-*

tics of Method in the Human Sciences: Positivism and Its Epistemological Others, edited by George Steinmetz. Durham, NC: Duke University Press, 427–450.

Elliott, J. H. 2007. *Empires of the Atlantic World: Britain and Spain in America*. New Haven, CT: Yale University Press.

Elliott, Neil. 1997. "The Anti-Imperial Message of the Cross." In *Paul and Empire: Religion and Power in Roman Imperial Society*, edited by Richard A. Horsley. Harrisburg, PA: Trinity Press International, 167–183.

Elsner, Jaś. 1994. "From the Pyramids to Pausanias and Piglet: Monuments, Travel, and Writing." In *Art and Text in Ancient Greek Culture*. Cambridge: Cambridge University Press, 224–254.

———. 2001. "Structuring Greece: Pausanias' *Periegesis* as a Literary Construct." In *Pausanias: Travel and Memory in Roman Greece*, edited by S. E. Alcock, J. F. Cherry, and J. Elsner. Oxford: Oxford University Press, 3–20.

———. 2007. *Roman Eyes: Visuality & Subjectivity in Art & Text*. Princeton, NJ: Princeton University Press.

Engels, Friedrich, and Karl Marx. 1956. *The Holy Family or Critique of Critical Critique*. Moscow: Foreign Languages Publishing House.

Erskine, Andrew. 2011. *The Hellenistic Stoa: Political Thought and Action*. London: Bristol Classical Press.

Evans, Richard J. 2008. *The Third Reich at War: How the Nazis Led Germany from Conquest to Disaster*. London: Penguin Books.

Faber, Richard. 2002. *Abendland, ein politischer Kampfbegriff*. Berlin/Wien: PHILO.

Fabian, Johannes. 1983. *Time and the Other: How Anthropology Makes Its Object*. Columbia University Press.

Fabri, Friedrich. [1879] 1998. *Bedarf Deutschland der Kolonien?/Does Germany Need Colonies?*, edited and translated by E. C. M. Breuning and M. E. Chamberlain. Lewiston, NY: Edwin Mellon Press.

Fagenblat, Michael. 2015. "'Heidegger' and the Jews." In *Reading Heidegger's Black Notebooks 1931–1941*, edited by Ingo Farin and Jeff Malpas. Cambridge, MA: MIT Press, 145–168.

Falasca-Zamponi, Simonetta. 1997. *Fascist Spectacle: The Aesthetics of Power in Mussolini's Italy*. Berkeley: University of California Press.

Farrenkopf, John. 1994. "Klio und Cäsar: Spenglers Philosophie im Dienste der Staatskunst." In *Der Fall Spengler: Eine kritische Bilanz*, edited by Alexander Demandt and John Farrenkopf. Cologne and Weimar: Böhlau Verlag, 45–73.

Farrias, Victor. 1989. *Heidegger and Nazism*. Philadelphia: Temple University Press

Farin, Ingo, and Jeff Malpas, eds. 2016. *Reading Heidegger: Black Notebooks 1931–1941*. Cambridge, MA: MIT Press.

Favro, Diane. 2005. "Making Rome a World City." In *The Cambridge Companion to the Age of Augustus*, edited by Karl Galinsky. Cambridge: Cambridge University Press, 234–263.

———. 2014. "Moving Events: Curating the Memory of the Roman Triumph." In *Memoria Romana: Memory in Rome and Rome in Memory*, edited by Karl Galinsky. Ann Arbor: University of Michigan Press.

Faye, Emmanuel. 2009. *Heidegger: The Introduction of Nazism into Philosophy*. New Haven, CT: Yale University Press.

Featherstone, Mark. 2005. "Ruin Value." *Journal for Cultural Research* 9(3):301–321.

Feldherr, Andrew. 1998. *Spectacle and Society in Livy's History*. Berkeley: University of California Press.

Ferrari Zumbini, Massimo. 1999. *Untergänge und Morgenröten: Nietzsche-Spengler-Antisemitismus*. Würzburg, Germany: Königshausen and Neumann.

Ferguson, Margaret W. 1984. "'The Afflatus of Ruins': Meditations on Rome by Du Bellay, Spenser, and Stevens." In *Roman Images*, edited by Annabel Patterson. Baltimore and London: Johns Hopkins Press, 23–50.

Fest, Joachim. *2005. Speer: Eine Biographie*. Frankfurt a.M.: Fischer Taschenbuch Verlag.

———. 2007. *Albert Speer: Conversations with Hitler's Architect*. Cambridge: Polity Press.

Fichte, Johann Gottlieb. 2008. *Addresses to the German Nation*, edited and translated by Gregory Moore. Cambridge: Cambridge University Press.

Flower, Harriet I. 1996. *Ancestor Masks and Aristocratic Power in Roman Society*. Oxford: Clarendon Press.

Fontane, Theodor. [1878] 1971. *Vor dem Sturm: Roman aus dem Winter 1812 auf 13*. In *Sämtliche Erzählungen, Gedichte, Nachgelassenes*, vol. 3. Munich: Carl Hanser.

Ford, Caroline. 2015. "The Inheritance of Empire and the Ruins of Rome in French Colonial Algeria." *Past and Present* 10:57–77.

Forster, Georg. [1789] 1971. "Leitfaden zu einer künftigen Geschichte der Menschheit." In *Werke in vier Bänden*, vol. 3. Leipzig: Insel, 81–89. http://www.zeno.org/nid/20004782410.

———. 1971. "Cook, der Entdecker." In *Werke in vier Bänden*, vol. 2. Leipzig: Insel, 105–114. http://www.zeno.org/nid/20004782364.

———. 1983. *Reise um die Welt*, edited by Gerhard Steiner. Frankfurt: Insel Verlag.

———. 2000. *A Voyage Round the World*. 2 vols., edited by Nicholas Thomas and Oliver Berghof; assisted by Jennifer Newell. Honolulu: University of Hawai'i Press.

Fourier, Jean-Baptiste-Joseph. 1809–1828. "Préface historique." *In Description de L'Égypte*, vol. 1. Paris: Imprimerie royale, i–clv.

Fowler, Don. 2000. "Even Better Than the Real Thing." In *Roman Constructions: Readings in Postmodern Latin*. Oxford: Oxford University Press, 86–108.

———. 2000. "The Ruin of Time: Monuments and Survival at Rome." In *Roman Constructions: Readings in Postmodern Latin*. Oxford: Oxford University Press, 193–217.

Fox, Robin Lane. 2006. *The Classical World: An Epic History from Homer to Hadrian*. New York: Basic Books.

Frank, Heinz. 1938. "Das Frankfurter Würfelspiel: Eberhard Wolfgang Moellers Dichtung auf der Dietrich-Eckart-Bühne." *Völkischer Beobachter*, August 4, no page nrs.

Frank, Walter. 1945. "Hannibal vor den Toren: Senat und Volk von Rom in den Punier Kriegen." *Das Reich*. April 8 and 15, no page nrs.

Franzl, Sean. 2013. *Connected by the Ear: The Media, Pedagogy, and Politics of the Romantic Lecture*. Evanston, IL: Northwestern University Press.

Fremeaux, Jacques. 2007. "France: Empire and the Mère-Patrie." In *The Age of Empires*, edited by Robert Aldrich. London: Thames & Hudson, 112–175.

Freud, Sigmund. 1975. *Aus der Geschichte einer infantilen Neurose [Der Wolfsmann]*. In *Studienausgabe*, edited by Alexander Mitscherlich, et al. vol. 8. Frankfurt: S. Fischer Verlag, 127–232.

———. 1975. "Bruchstück einer Hysterie-Analyse." In *Studienausgabe*, edited by Alexander Mitscherlich, et al., vol. 6. Frankfurt: S. Fischer Verlag, 83–186.

———. 1999. "Fragment of an Analysis of a Case of Hysteria." In *The Standard Edition of the Complete Psychological Works of Sigmund Freud*, translated and edited by James Strachey, vol. 7: 3–122.

———. 1999. "Delusions and Dreams in Wilhelm Jensen's Gradiva." In *The Standard Edition of the Complete Psychological Works of Sigmund Freud*, translated and edited by James Strachey, vol. 9. London: Hogarth Press: 7 - 95.

———. 1985. *The Complete Letters of Sigmund Freud to Wilhelm Fliess 1887–1904*, edited by Jeffrey Moussaieff Masson. Cambridge, MA: Harvard University Press.

———. *1999. "From the History of an Infantile Neurosis."* In *The Standard Edition of the Complete Psychological Works of Sigmund Freud*, translated and edited by James Strachey, vol. 17. London: Hogarth Press, 7–122.

———. 1999. "The Aetiology of Hysteria." In *The Standard Edition of the Complete Psychological Works of Sigmund Freud*, translated and edited by James Strachey, vol. 3: 191–221.

———. 1999. *Civilization and Its Discontents*. In *The Standard Edition of the Complete Psychological Works of Sigmund Freud*, translated and edited by James Strachey, vol. 21: 59–146.

———. 1999. "The Dynamics of Transference." In *The Standard Edition of the Complete Psychological Works of Sigmund Freud*, translated and edited by James Strachey, vol. 12: 97–108.

———. 1975. "Zur Ätiologie der Hysterie." In *Studienausgabe*, edited by Alexander Mitscherlich et al., vol. 6: 51–81.

———. 1999. "Group Psychology and the Analysis of the Ego." In *The Standard Edition of the Complete Psychological Works of Sigmund Freud*, translated and edited by James Strachey, vol. 18: 67–143.

———. 1999. "The Economic Problem of Masochism." In *The Standard Edition of the Complete Psychological Works of Sigmund Freud*, translated and edited by James Strachey, vol. 19: 157–170.

———. 1999. *An Autobiographical Study*. In *The Standard Edition of the Complete Psychological Works of Sigmund Freud*, translated and edited by James Strachey, vol. 20: 7–74.

———. 1999. "Instincts and Their Vicissitudes." In *The Standard Edition of the Com-*

plete Psychological Works of Sigmund Freud, translated and edited by James Strachey, vol. 14: 117–140.

———. 1975. “Triebe und Triebschicksale.” In *Studienausgabe*, edited by Alexander Mitscherlich et al., vol. 3: 75–102.

———. 1999. *The Interpretation of* Dreams *(First Part)*. In *The Standard Edition of the Complete Psychological Works of Sigmund Freud*, translated and edited by James Strachey, vol. 4.

Freyer, Hans. 1931. *Revolution von rechts*. Jena: Eugen Diederichs Verlag.

———. 1954. *Weltgeschichte Europas*. Stuttgart: Deutsche Verlagsanstalt.

Friedländer, Saul. 2007. *The Years of Extermination: Nazi Germany and the Jews 1939–1945*. New York: HarperCollins.

Fritzsche, Peter. 2004. *Stranded in the Present: Modern Time and the Melancholy of History*. Cambridge, MA: Harvard University Press.

———. 2008. *Life and Death in the Third Reich*. Cambridge, MA: Harvard University Press.

Fuchs, Barbara. 2001. *Mimesis and Empire: The New World, Islam, and European Identities*. Cambridge: Cambridge University Press.

———. 2003. “Imperium Studies: Theorizing Early Modern Expansion.” In *Postcolonial Moves: Medieval through Modern*, edited by Patricia Clare Ingham and Michelle R. Warren. New York: Palgrave, 71–92.

———. *2015. “Another Turn for Transnationalism*: Empire, Nation, and Imperium in Early Modern Studies.” *PMLA* 130(2, March):413–418.

Fuchs, Harald. 1964. *Der geistige Widerstand gegen Rom in der antiken Welt*. Berlin: Walter de Gruyter.

Fullagar, Kate. 2008. “‘Savages That Are Among Us’: Mai, Bennelong, and British Imperial Culture.” *Eighteenth Century* 49(3):211–237.

Furber, David, and Wendy Lower. 2009. “Colonialism and Genocide in Nazi-Occupied Poland.” In *Empire, Colony, and Genocide: Conquest, Occupation, and Subaltern Resistance in World History*, edited by A. Dirk Moses. New York and Oxford: Berghahn Books, 372–402.

Furet, François. 1977. “Civilization and Barbarism in Gibbon’s History.” In *Edward Gibbon and the Decline and Fall of the Roman Empire*, edited by Glen W. Bowersock, John Clive, Stephen R. Graubard. Cambridge, MA: Harvard University Press, 159–166.

Galinsky, Karl. 1996. *Augustan Culture: An Interpretive Introduction*. Princeton, NJ: Princeton University Press.

———. 2005. “Virgil’s *Aeneid* and Ovid’s *Metamorphoses* as World Literature.” In *The Cambridge Companion to the Age of Augustus*, edited by Karl Galinsky. Cambridge: Cambridge University Press, 340–359.

———. 2012. *Augustus: Introduction to the Life of an Emperor*. Cambridge: Cambridge University Press.

———. 2014. “Introduction.” In *Memoria Romana: Memory in Rome and Rome in Memory*, edited by Karl Galinsky. Ann Arbor: University of Michigan Press, 1–12.

Gebauer, Gunter, and Christoph Wulf. 1992. *Mimesis: Kultur, Kunst, Gesellschaft.* Reinbeck bei Hamburg: Rowohlt.

Geimer, Peter. 2002. *Die Vergangenheit der Kunst: Strategien der Nachträglichkeit im 18. Jahrhundert.* Weimar: VDG.

Gentile, Emilio, and Lawrence S. Rainey. 1994. "The Conquest of Modernity: From Modernist Nationalism to Fascism." *modernism/modernity* 1(3):55–87.

Georgi, Dieter. 1997. "God Turned Upside Down." In *Paul and Empire: Religion and Power in Roman Imperial Society*, edited by Richard A. Horsley. Harrisburg, PA: Trinity Press International, 148–157.

Geppert, Alexander C. T. 2002. "Welttheater: Die Geschichte des europäischen Ausstellungswesens im 19. und 20. Jahrhundert. Ein Forschungsbericht." *neue politische literatur. Berichte über das internationale Schrifttum* 1:10–61.

———. 2011. "Werden und Vergehen eines sprachgewaltigen Schicksalsszenarios." In *Gewalt und Gesellschaft: Klassiker modernen Denkens neu lessen*, edited by Uffa Jensen, Habbo Knoch, Daniel Morat, and Miriam Rür. Göttingen: Wallstein Verlag, 112–121.

Geyer, Michael. 2006. "Endkampf 1918 und 1945: German Nationalism, Annihilation, and Self-Destruction." In *No Man's Land of Violence*, edited by Alf Lüdtke and Bernd Weisbrod. Göttingen: Wallstein Verlag, 35–68.

Giarrizzo, Giuseppe. 1976. "Toward the 'Decline and Fall': Gibbon's Other Historical Interests." *Daedalus* 105(3, Summer):49–62.

Gibbon, Edward. 1896. *The Autobiographies of Edward Gibbon*, edited by John Murray. London: John Murray.

———. [1776–1788] 1994–2005. *The History of the Decline and Fall of the Roman Empire*, edited by David Womersley. 3 vols. London: Penguin Books.

———. 1995. "General Observations on the Fall of the Roman Empire in the West," in The History of the Decline and Fall of the Roman Empire, edited by David Womersley, vol. 2. London: Penguin Books, 508–516.

Gillet, Louis. 1938. "Hitler à Rome: Choses Vues." *Revue des deux mondes* 45(June):669–683.

Ginsberg, Robert. 2004. "The Terminology of Ruin." In *The Aesthetics of Ruins.* Amsterdam and New York: Rodopi, 285–314.

Gleason, Maud. 2001. "Mutilated Messengers: Body Language in Josephus." In *Being Greek under Rome: Cultural Identity, the Second Sophistic and the Development of Empire*, edited by Simon Goldhill. Cambridge: Cambridge University Press, 50–85.

Gobineau, Arthur, de. 1999. *The Inequality of Human Races*, translated by Adrian Collins, preface by George L. Mosse. London: William Heinemann.

Goebbels, Joseph. 1941. "Mimikry." In *Die Zeit ohne Beispiel: Reden und Aufsätze aus den Jahren 1939/40/41.* Munich: Zentralverlag der NSDAP, 526–531.

———. 1995. *Die Tagebücher von Joseph Goebbels*, pt. 2, vol. 15, edited by Elke Fröhlich. Munich: K.G. Saur.

———. [1939] 1941. "Der Insulaner und die Spanienfrage." In *Die Zeit ohne Beispiel*, 48–55.

———. "Rede im Berliner Sportpalast [Wollt Ihr den totalen Krieg], 18. Februar 1943." http://1000dok.digitale-sammlungen.de/dok_0200_goe.pdf.

Goethe, Johann Wolfgang. [1829] 2004. *Italienische Reise*, edited by Herbert von Einem. Munich: Deutscher Taschenbuch Verlag.

Goldhill, Simon. 1988. *Reading Greek Tragedy*. Cambridge: Cambridge University Press.

———. 1996. "Refracting Classical Vision: Changing Cultures of Viewing." In *Vision in Context: Historical and Contemporary Perspectives on Sight*, edited by Teresa Brennan and Martin Jay. London and New York: Routledge, 15–28.

———, ed. 2001. *Being Greek under Rome: Cultural Identity, the Second Sophistic and the Development of Empire*. Cambridge: Cambridge University Press.

———. 2001. "The Erotic Eye: Visual Stimulation and Cultural Conflict." In *Being Greek under Rome: Cultural Identity, the Second Sophistic and the Development of Empire*, edited by Goldhill, 154–194.

———. 2008. *Jerusalem: City of Longing*. Cambridge, MA: Harvard University Press.

Goldstein, Laurence. 1977. *Ruins and Empire: The Evolution of a Theme in Augustan and Romantic Literature*. Pittsburgh: University of Pittsburgh Press.

Goldsworthy, Adrian. 2006. *The Fall of Carthage: The Punic Wars 265–146 BC*. London: Phoenix.

Gordon, Peter E. 2014. "Heidegger in Black." *New York Review of Books*, October 9. http://www.nybooks.com/articles/archives/2014/oct/09/heidegger-in-black/.

Gowning, Alain M. 2005. *Empire and Memory: The Representation of the Roman Republic in Imperial Culture*. Cambridge: Cambridge University Press.

Grabbe, Lester L. 2002. "A Dan(iel) for All Seasons." In *The Book of Daniel: Composition and Reception*, vol. 1, edited by John J. Collins and Peter W. Flint. Boston: Brill Academic Publishers, 229–246.

Grafton, Anthony. 2001. *Bring Out Your Dead: The Past as Revelation*. Cambridge, MA: Harvard University Press.

Graham, Cooper C. 1986. *Leni Riefenstahl and Olympia*. London: Scarecrow Press.

Graichen, Gisela, and Horst Gründer. 2005. *Deutsche Kolonien: Traum und Trauma*. Berlin: Ullstein Verlag.

Grandsden, K. W. 2003. "Commentary." In Virgil, *Aeneid: Book VIII*, edited by K. W. Grandsden. Cambridge: Cambridge University Press, 75–187.

Groh, Ruth. 1998. *Arbeit an der Heillosigkeit der Welt: Zur politisch-theologischen Mythologie und Anthropologie Carl Schmitts*. Frankfurt: Suhrkamp Verlag.

Gross, Raphael. 2007. *Carl Schmitt and the Jews: The "Jewish Question," the Holocaust, and German Legal Theory*, translated by Joel Golb. Madison: University of Wisconsin Press.

Gruman, Gerald J. 1960. "'Balance' and 'Excess' as Gibbon's Explanation of the Decline and Fall." *History and Theory* 1(1):75–85.

Gründer, Hans. 2004. *Geschichte der deutschen Kolonien*. Paderborn: Schöningh.

Gsell, Stéphane. 1901. *Les monuments antiques de l'Algérie*, vol. 1. Paris: Albert Fontemoing.

Hachtmann, Rüdiger. 1936. "Reichssportfeld: das monumentale Bauwerk Berlins." *Völkischer Beobachter*: 28.

Haddour, Azzedine. 2000. *Colonial Myths: History and Narrative*. Manchester: Manchester University Press.

Halliwell, Stephen. 2002. *The Aesthetics of Mimesis: Ancient Texts and Modern Problems*. Princeton, NJ: Princeton University Press.

Hansen, Heinrich, ed. 1938. *Der Schlüssel zum Frieden: Führertage in Italien*. Berlin: M. A. Klieber.

Hardie, Philip. 1986. *Virgil's Aeneid: Cosmos and Imperium*. Oxford: Clarendon Press.

———. 2000. "Virgil and Tragedy." In *The Cambridge Companion to Virgil*, edited by Charles Martindale. Cambridge: Cambridge University Press, 312–326.

Hardt, Michael, and Antonio Negri. 2000. *Empire*. Cambridge, MA: Harvard University Press.

Hartog, François. 1988. *The Mirror of Herodotus: An Essay on the Representation of the Other*. Berkeley: University of California Press.

———, ed. 1999. *L'histoire d'Homère à Augustin*. Paris: Éditions du Seuil.

———. 2001. *Memories of Odysseus: Frontier Tales from Ancient Greece*. Chicago: University of Chicago Press.

———. 2005. *Anciens, modernes, sauvages*. Paris: Galaade.

———. 2010. "Polybius and the First Universal History." In *Historiae Mundi: Studies in Universal History*, edited by Peter Liddel and Andrew Fear. Manchester: Duckworth, 30–40.

———. 2015. *Regimes of Historicity: Presentism and the Experience of Time*. New York: Columbia University Press.

Haushofer, Karl. 1934. "Kulturkreis und Kulturkreisüberschneidungen." In *Raumüberwindende Mächte*, edited by Karl Haushofer. Leipzig and Berlin: B. G. Teubner, 91–109.

———. 1934. *Weltpolitik von heute*. Berlin: Zeitgeschichte Verlag.

———. 1935. "Einleitung: Die raumpolitischen Grundlagen der Weltgeschichte." In *Knaurs Weltgeschichte. Von der Urzeit bis zur Gegenwart*, edited by K. U. von Müller and P. R. Rohden. Berlin: Thomas Knaur, 11–43.

———. 1944. "Der Kolonialgedanke im Wandel der Zeiten." *Beiträge zur Kolonialforschung*, edited by Günther Wolff, vol. 6, 37–44.

Heer, Friedrich. 1996. *The Holy Roman Empire*. London: Phoenix.

Heffernan, Michael. 1999. "Historical Geographies of the Future: Three Perspectives from France, 1750–1825." In *Geography and Enlightenment*, edited by David Livingstone and Charles Withers. Chicago: University of Chicago Press, 139–164.

Hegel, G. F. W. 1967. *Hegel's Philosophy of Right*, translated by T. M. Knox. Oxford: Oxford University Press.

———. 1996. *Vorlesungen über die Philosophie der Weltgeschichte.*, edited by Ilting, Karl Heinz, Karl Brehmer, and Hoo Nam Seelmann. Hamburg: Felix Meiner Verlag.

Heiber, Helmut. 1966. *Walter Frank und sein Reichsinstitut für Geschichte des neuen Deutschlands*. Stuttgart: Deutsche Verlags-Anstalt.

———, ed. 1972. *Goebbels-Reden*, vol. 2: 1939–1945. Düsseldorf: Droste Verlag.

Heidegger, Martin. 1982. *"Hölderlins Hymne 'Andenken.'" Gesamtausgabe*, vol. 52, edited by Curd Ochwadt. Frankfurt am Main: Vittorio Klostermann.

———. 1994. *Phänomenologische Interpretationen zu Aristoteles: Einführung in die phänomenologische Forschung. Gesamtausgabe*, vol. 61, edited by Walter Bröcker and Käte Bröcker-Oltmanns. Frankfurt am Main: Vittorio Klostermann.

———. 1998. *Basic Concepts*, translated by Gary E. Aylesworth. Bloomington: Indiana University Press.

———. 2014. *Überlegungen VII–XI (Schwarze Hefte 1938/1939). Gesamtausgabe*, vol. 95, edited by Peter Trawny. Frankfurt am Main: Vittorio Klostermann.

———. 2014. *Überlegungen XII–XV (Schwarze Hefte 1939–1941). Gesamtausgabe*, edited by Peter Trawny. Frankfurt am Main: Vittorio Klostermann.

Heine, Heinrich. [1826] 1884. *Ideas. "Buch Le Grand" of the Reisebilder of Heinrich Heine*, translated by I. B. London: Macmillan and Co.

Heinz, Franz. 1938. "Das Frankfurter Würfelspiel: Eberhard Wolfgang Moellers Dichtung auf der Dietrich-Eckart-Bühne." *Völkischer Beobachter* (August 4): no page nrs.

Helgerson, Richard. 2007. *A Sonnet from Carthage: Garcilaso de la Vega and the New Poetry of Sixteenth-Century Europe*. Philadelphia: University of Pennsylvania Press.

Hell, Julia. 2008. "Ruins Travel: Orphic Journeys through 1940s Germany." In *Writing Travel*, edited by John Zilcosky. Toronto: University of Toronto Press, 123–160.

———. 2009. "The Twin Towers of Anselm Kiefer and the Trope of Imperial Decline." *Germanic Review* 84(1):84–93.

———. 2009. "Imperial Ruin Gazers, or Why Did Scipio Weep?" In *Ruins of Modernity*, edited by Julia Hell and Andreas Schönle. Durham, NC: Duke University Press, 169–192.

———. 2009. "*Katechon*: Carl Schmitt's Imperial Theology and the Ruins of the Future." *Germanic Review* 84(4):283–326.

Hell, Julia, and Andreas Schönle. 2010. "Introduction." In *Ruins of Modernity*, edited by Hell and Schönle. *Durham, NC:* Duke University Press, 1–14.

Herbert, Ulrich. 2011. *Best: Biographische Studien über Radikalismus, Weltanschauung und Vernunft 1903–1989*. Bonn: Verlag J. H. W. Dietz.

Herder, Johann Gottfried. [1774] 2002. "This Too a Philosophy of History for the Formation of Humanity." In *Johann Gottfried von Herder: Philosophical Writings*, edited and translated by Michael N. Forster. Cambridge: Cambridge University Press, 272–358.

———. [1784–91] 1985. *Ideen zur Philosophie der Geschichte der Menschheit*. Wiesbaden: Fourier Verlag.

———. [1792] 1997. "On Monuments of the Distant Past." In *On World History: An*

Anthology, edited by Hans Adler and Ernest A. Menze; translated by Ernest A. Menze with Michael Palma. Armonk, NY: M. E. Sharpe, 63–80.

Herf, Jeffrey. 1996. *Reactionary Modernism: Technology, Culture, and Politics in Weimar and the Third Reich*. Cambridge: Cambridge University Press.

———. 2009. *Nazi Propaganda for the Arab World*. New Haven, CT: Yale University Press.

Hermand, Jost. 1979. *Sieben Arten an Deutschland zu leiden*. Königstein: Athenäum.

Himmler, Heinrich. "Rede des Reichsführers SS bei der SS-Gruppenführertagung in Posen am 4. Oktober 1943." http://1000dok.digitale-sammlungen.de/dok_0008_pos.pdf

Hine, Harry M. 2006. "Rome, the Cosmos, and the Emperor in Seneca's 'Natural Questions.'" *Journal of Roman Studies* 96:42–72.

Hintze, Otto. 1970. "Imperialismus und Weltpolitik." In *Gesammelte Abhandlungen*, vol. 1. Göttingen: Vandenhoeck & Ruprecht, 457–469.

Hitler, Adolf. 1942. *Mein Kampf*. Munich: Zentralverlag der NSDAP.

———. 1971. *Mein Kampf*, translated by Ralph Manheim. Boston: Houghton Mifflin.

———. *Mein Politisches Testament*. http://www.1000dok.digitale-sammlungen.de/dok_0228_hte.pdf.

———. 1980. "Warum sind wir Antisemiten?" In *Hitler. Sämtliche Aufzeichnungen 1905–1924*, edited by Eberhard Jaeckel. Stuttgart: Deutsche Verlags-Anstalt, 184–204.

———. 1980. *Monologe im Führerhauptquartier 1941–1944*, edited by Werner Jochmann. Hamburg: Albrecht Knaus Verlag.

———. 1994. "Rede auf NSDAP-Versammlung in München, 9. April 1929." In Hitler, *Reden Schriften Anordnungen*, vol. 3, edited by Klaus Lankheit. Munich: K. G. Saur.

Hobein, Maren. 1990. "Monument und Ideal: Die Griechenlandphotographien von Walter Hege." In *Das Land der Griechen mit der Seele suchen: Photographien des 19. und 20. Jahrhunderts*. Cologne: Römisch-Germanisches Museum, 48–58.

Hobson, J. A. 1965. *Imperialism: A Study*. Ann Arbor: University of Michigan Press.

Hochschild, Adam. 1999. *King Leopold's Ghost: A Story of Greed, Terror, and Heroism in Colonial Africa*. New York: Mariner Books.

Hoffmann, Heinrich, ed. 1938. *Hitler in Italien: 126 Bilder*. Munich: Verlag Heinrich Hoffmann.

Hoffmann, Heinrich, and A. R. Marsani, eds. 1943. *Deutscher Osten: Land der Zukunft*. Munich: Heinrich Hoffmann Verlag.

Hofter, Matthias René. 2012. "Von der Ikone zur Metapher—Der Pergamon Altar im Wilhelminischen Deutschland." In *Pergamon: Panorama der antiken Metropole. Begleitbuch zur Ausstellung*, edited by Ralf Grüßinger, Volker Käster, and Andreas Scholl. Berlin: Staatliche Museen zu Berlin and Michael Imhof Verlag, 392–397.

Hohendahl, Peter-Uwe. 2008. "Political Theology Revisited: Carl Schmitt's Postwar Reassessment." *Konturen* 1:1–28.

Hölkeskamp, Karl-J. 2014. "In Defense of Concepts, Categories, and Other Abstractions: Remarks on a Theory of Memory (in the Making)." In *Memoria Romana. Memory in Rome and Rome in Memory*, edited by Karl Galinsky. Ann Arbor: University of Michigan Press, 63–70.

Hölscher, Tonio. 2004. *The Language of Images in Roman Art*. Cambridge University Press.

———. 2006. "Greek Styles and Greek Art in Augustan Rome." In *Classical Pasts: The Classical Traditions of Greece and Rome*, edited by James I. Porter. Princeton, NJ: Princeton University Press, 237–269.

Homer. 1990. *The Iliad*, translated by Robert Fagles. London: Penguin Books.

Honold, Alexander. 2002. "Nach Bagdad und Jerusalem: Die Wege des Wilhelminischen Orientalismus." In *Kolonialismus als Kultur*, edited by Alexander Honold and Oliver Simons. Tübingen und Basel: A. Francke Verlag, 143–166.

Horace. 30 BCE. *Epodon Liber.Poem 16.* http://data.perseus.org/citations/urn:cts:latinLit:phi0893.phi003.perseus-lat1:16.

Horkheimer, Max, and Theodor W. Adorno. 2002. *Dialectic of Enlightenment*. New York: Continuum.

Horn, Hendrik J. 1989. *Jan Cornelisz Vermeyen: Painter of Charles V and the Conquest of Tunis*. Netherlands: DAVACO.

Horsley, Richard A. 1997. "Paul's Counter-Imperial Gospel: Introduction." In *Paul and Empire*, edited by Richard A. Horsley. Harrisburg, PA: Trinity International, 140–147.

Huet, Valérie. 1999. "Napoleon I: A New Augustus?" In *Roman Presences: Receptions of Rome in European Culture, 1789–1945*, edited by Catharine Edwards. Cambridge University Press, 53–69.

Hull, Isabel V. 2005. *Absolute Destruction: Military Culture and the Practices of War in Imperial Germany*. Ithaca, NY, and London: Cornell University Press.

Huyssen, Andreas. 1995. "Anselm Kiefer: The Terror of History, the Temptation of Myth." In *Twilight Memories*. New York: Routledge, 209–247.

Iacopi, Irene. 2007. *La casa di augusto: le pitture*. Milano: Electa.

Itkin, Alan Joshua. 2017. *Underworlds of Memory: W. G. Sebald's Journeys*. Evanston, IL: Northwestern University Press.

Jaskot, Paul B. 2000. *The Architecture of Oppression: The SS, Forced Labor, and the Nazi Monumental Building Economy*. London: Routledge.

Jay, Martin. 1988. "Scopic Regimes of Modernity." In *Vision and Visuality*, edited by Hal Foster. New York: Bay Press, 3–27.

———. 1993. *Downcast Eyes: The Denigration of Vision in Twentieth-Century French Thought*. Berkeley: University of California Press.

———. 2011. "Scopic Regimes of Modernity Revisited." In *Essays from the Edge: Parerga & Paralipomena*. Charlottesville: University of Virginia Press, 51–63.

Jay, Martin, and Sumathi Ramaswamy, eds. 2014. *Empires of Vision: A Reader*. Durham, NC: Duke University Press.

Jeffreys, David, ed. 2003. *Views of Ancient Egypt since Napoleon Bonaparte: Imperial-*

ism, Colonialism, and Modern Appropriations. London: UCL Press, Institute of Archaeology.

Jenkins, Ian. 2012. *The Discobolus*. London: British Museum.

Jenkyns, Richard. 2013. *God, Space, & City in the Roman Imagination*. Oxford: Oxford University Press.

———. 2014. "The Memory of Rome in Rome." In *Memoria Romana: Memory in Rome and Rome in Memory*, edited by Karl Galinsky. Ann Arbor: University of Michigan Press, 15–26.

Jensen, Wilhelm. 1903. *Gradiva: ein pompejanisches Phantasiestück*. Dresden and Leipzig: C. Reissner.

———. [1903] 2003. *Gradiva: A Pompeiian Fancy*. In *Wilhelm Jensen / Sigmund Freud. Gradiva / Delusion and Dream in Jensen's Gradiva*, translated by Helen M. Downey. Los Angeles: Green Integer Series 86, 7–140.

Johnson, W. R. 1976. *Darkness Visible: A Study of Vergil's Aeneid*. Berkeley: University of California Press.

Josephus, Flavius. 1981. *The Jewish War*, translated by G. A. Williamson. London: Penguin.

———. 2006. *Jewish Antiquities*, translated by William Whiston. Hertfordshire: Wordsworth.

Jünger, Ernst. 1979. *Strahlungen I. Sämtliche Werke*, vol. 2. Stuttgart: Klett-Cotta.

———. 1980. *Heliopolis. Sämtliche Werke*, vol. 16. Stuttgart: Klett-Cotta.

Junod, Philippe. 1984. "Future in the Past." *Oppositions* 26:43–63.

———. 1985. "Poétique des ruines et perception du temps: Diderot et Hubert." *Colloque international Diderot*. 1984. Paris: Aux amateurs des livres, 321–326.

———. 1987. "Babylone-sur-Tamise: Londres vue par Gustave Doré." In *Le temps de la réflexion*, vol. 8, *La Ville inquiète*. Paris: Gallimard, 61–77.

Kahane, Ahuvia. 2011. "Antiquity and the Ruin: Introduction." *European Review of History–Revue européenne d'histoire* 18(5–6):631–644.

Kallis, Aristotle. 2011. "Framing Romanità: The Celebrations for the Bimillenario Augusteo and the Augusteo-Ara Pacis Project." *Journal of Contemporary History* 46:809–831.

———. 2012. "The 'Third Rome' of Fascism: Demolitions and the Search for a New Syntax." *Journal of Modern History* 84(March):40–79.

Kant, Immanuel. 1983. *Anthropologie in pragmatischer Sicht*. Reclam: Stuttgart.

Kantorowicz, Ernst. 1985. *The King's Two Bodies: A Study in Medieval Political Theology*. Princeton, NJ: Princeton University Press.

Karmon, David. 2011. *The Ruin of the Eternal City: Antiquity & Preservation in Renaissance Rome*. Oxford: Oxford University Press.

Kellerer, Sidonie. 2014. "Rewording the Past: The Postwar Publication of a 1938 Lecture by Martin Heidegger." *Modern Intellectual History* 11(3):575–602.

Kelly, Christopher. 1997. "A Grand Tour: Reading Gibbon's Decline and Fall." *Greece and Rome* 44(1):39–58.

Kennedy, Duncan F. 1997. "Virgilian Epic." In *The Cambridge Companion to Vir-*

gil, edited by Charles Martindale. Cambridge: Cambridge University Press, 145–154.

———. 1999. "A Sense of Place: Rome, History, and Empire Revisited." In *Roman Presences*, edited by Catharine Edwards. Cambridge: Cambridge University Press, 19–34.

Kittler, Wolf. 2004. "1806. Die Hermannsschlacht and the Concept of Guerilla Warfare." In *A New History of German Literature*, edited by David Wellbery. Cambridge, MA: Harvard University Press, 505–511.

Kleiner, Diana E. E. 2005. "Semblance and Storytelling in the Age of Augustus." In *The Cambridge Companion to the Age of Augustus*, edited by Karl Galinsky. Cambridge: Cambridge University Press, 197–233.

Kleist, Heinrich von. 1982. "Empfindungen vor Friedrichs Seelandschaft." *Sämtliche Werke und Briefe in vier Bänden*, vol. 3, edited by Helmut Sembdner. München: Carl Hanser Verlag, 327–328.

———. 1982. "Kathechismus der Deutschen. Abgefaßt nach dem Spanischen. Zum Gebrauch für Kinder und Alte." *Sämtliche Werke und Briefe in vier Bänden*, vol. 3, edited by Helmut Sembdner. München: Carl Hanser Verlag, 350–360.

———. 2008. *The Battle of Herrmann*, translated by Rachel MagShamrain. Würzburg: Königshausen & Neumann.

———. "Was gilt es in diesem Kriege?" *Sämtliche Werke und Briefe in vier Bänden*, vol. 3, edited by Helmut Sembdner. München: Carl Hanser Verlag, 377–379.

Klemperer, Victor. 1999. *I Will Bear Witness 1933–1941: A Diary of the Nazi Years*. New York: Modern Library.

Knox, Bernard. 2006. "Introduction." In Virgil, *The Aeneid*, translated by Robert Fagles. New York: Viking, 1–41.

Koelb, Janice Hewlett. 2006. *The Poetics of Description: Imagined Places in European Literature*. New York: Palgrave.

Koenen, Andreas. 1995. *Der Fall Carl Schmitt: Sein Aufstieg zum "Kronjuristen des Dritten Reiches."* Darmstadt: Wissenschaftliche Buchgesellschaft.

Koerner, Joseph Leo. 1995. *Caspar David Friedrich and the Subject of Landscape*. New Haven, CT: Yale University Press.

Koester, Helmut. 1997. "Imperial Ideology and Paul's Eschatology in 1 Thessalonians." In *Paul and Empire*, edited by Richard A. Horsley. Harrisburg, PA: Trinity Press International, 158–166.

Konuk, Kader. 2010. *East West Mimesis: Auerbach in Turkey*. Stanford, CA: Stanford University Press.

Kornemann, Ernst. 1937. *Augustus: Der Mann und sein Werk. Breslauer Historische Forschungen* 4.

———. 1941. *Das Imperium Romanum: Sein Aufstieg und Niedergang*. Vorträge der Friedrich-Wilhelms-Universität Breslau im Kriegswinter 1940/41. Breslau: Korn.

Koschorke, Albrecht. 2012. *Wahrheit und Erfindung: Grundzüge einer Allgemeinen Erzähltheorie*. Frankfurt: S. Fischer Verlag.

———. 2015. "Ideology in Execution: On Hitler's *Mein Kampf*." *New German Critique* 124(February):1–22.

Koselleck, Reinhart. 1985. "Chance as Motivational Trace in Historical Writing." In *Futures Past: On the Semantics of Historical Time*, translated by Keith Tribe. Cambridge, MA: MIT Press, 115–127.

———. 1985. "*Historia Magistra Vitae*." In *Futures Past*, 26–42.

———. 2002. "'Progress' and 'Decline': An Appendix to the History of Two Concepts." In *The Practice of Conceptual History: Timing History, Spacing Concepts*, translated by Todd Samuel Presner. Stanford, CA: Stanford University Press, 218–235.

———. 2002. "Transformations of Experience and Methodological Change: A Historical-Anthropological Essay." In *The Practice of Conceptual History*, 45–83.

Kostof, Spiro. 1980. "The Emperor and the Duce: The Planning of Piazzale Augusto Imperatore in Rome." In *Art and Architecture in the Service of Politics*, edited by Henry Millon and Linda Nochlin. Cambridge, MA: MIT Press, 270–325.

Kraut, Richard. 2017. "Aristotle's Ethics." *The Stanford Encyclopedia of Philosophy*, edited by Edward N. Zalta. Summer 2017 ed. https://plato.stanford.edu/archives/sum2017/entries/aristotle-ethics/.

Krebs, Christopher B. 2011. *A Dangerous Book: Tacitus's Germania from the Roman Empire to the Third Reich*. New York: Norton.

Krier, Léon, ed. 2013. *Albert Speer: Architecture 1932–1942. New York:* Monacelli Press.

———. 2013. "An Architecture of Desire." In *Albert Speer: Architecture 1932–1942*, edited by Léon Krier. New York: Monacelli Press, xi–xxvii.

Kundrus, Birthe. 2014. "Colonialism, Imperialism, National Socialism? How Imperial Was the Third Reich?" In *German Cultures of Colonialism: Race, Nation, and Globalization*, edited by Geoff Eley and Bradley Naranch. Durham, NC: Duke University Press.

Lacan, Jacques. 1981. "What Is a Picture?" In *The Four Fundamental Concepts of Psycho-Analysis*. New York: Norton & Company, 105–119.

LaCapra, Dominick. 1998. "History and Memory: In the Shadow of the Holocaust." *History and Memory after Auschwitz*. Ithaca, NY: Cornell University Press, 8–42.

Ladd, Brian. 1997. *The Ghosts of Berlin*. Chicago: University of Chicago Press.

Landgraf, Hugo. 1945. "Roms Triumph über Hannibal." *Völkischer Beobachter.* April. No page nrs.

Laplanche, J., and J.-B. Pontalis. 1973. *The Language of Psychoanalysis*. New York and London: Norton & Company.

Lasansky, Medina. 2004. *The Renaissance Perfected: Architecture, Spectacle, and Tourism in Fascist Italy*. University Park: Pennsylvania State University Press.

Laurent, Franck, ed. 2008. *Le Voyage en Algérie: Anthologie de voyageurs français dans l'Algérie coloniale—1830–1930*. Paris: Éditions Robert Laffont.

Lawrence, Sara E., et al., eds. 2007. *Piranesi as Designer*. New York: Smithsonian Cooper-Hewitt National Design Museum.

Leach, Eleanor Winsor. 2004. *The Social Life of Painting in Ancient Rome and on the Bay of Naples*. Cambridge: Cambridge University Press.

Leitner, Bernhard. 1970. "Architecture as a Weapon: Hitler's Speer." *Artforum* (December):51–55.

———. 1982. "Albert Speer, the Architect. From a Conversation of July 21, 1978." *October* 20(Spring):14–50.

Leonard, Miriam. 2018. "Arendt's Revolutionary Antiquity." *Classical Philology* 113:53–66.

Lethen, Helmut. 2006. *Der Sound der Väter. Gottfried Benn und seine Zeit*. Berlin: Rowohlt.

Ley, Graham. 2006. *A Short Introduction to the Ancient Greek Theater*. Chicago: University of Chicago Press.

———. 2007. *The Theatricality of Greek Tragedy: Playing Space and Chorus*. Chicago: University of Chicago Press.

Lianeri, Alexandra. 2011. *The Western Time of Ancient History: Historiographical Encounters with the Greek and Roman Past*. Cambridge: Cambridge University Press.

Liebersohn, Harry. 2006. *The Traveler's World: Europe to the Pacific*. Cambridge, MA: Harvard University Press.

Longerich, Peter. 2010. *Joseph Goebbels: Biographie*. Munich: Siedler Verlag.

———. 2012. *Heinrich Himmler*. Oxford: Oxford University Press.

Loos, Erich. [1908] 1962. "Ornament und Verbrechen." In *Sämtliche Schriften*, vol. 1, edited by Franz Glück. Vienna and Munich: Verlag Herold: 276–288. https://de.wikisource.org/wiki/Ornament_und_Verbrechen.

Lorcin, Patricia. 2000. "Decadence and Renaissance: Louis Bertrand and the Concept of Rebarbarization in Fin de Siècle Algeria." In *New Perspectives on the Fin de Siècle in Nineteenth- and Twentieth-Century France*, edited by Kay Chadwick and Timothy Unwin. Lewiston, NY: E. Mellen Press, 181–195.

———. 2002. "Rome and France in Africa: Recovering Colonial Algeria's Latin Past." *French Historical Studies* 25(2):295–329.

———. 2014. *Imperial Identities: Stereotyping, Prejudice & Race in Colonial Algeria. Lincoln:* University of Nebraska Press.

Lord Cromer, Evelyn Baring. 1910. *Ancient and Modern Imperialism*. London: J. Murray.

Losemann, Volker. 2007. "Classics in the Second World War." In *Nazi Germany and the Humanities*, edited by Wolfgang Bialas and Anson Rabinbach. London: One World Publisher, 306–340.

Lotz, Wilhelm. 1938. "Das Reichsparteitagsgelände in Nürnberg." *Kunst im deutschen Reich* 2:264–269.

Lower, Wendy. 2005. *Nazi Empire-Building and the Holocaust in Ukraine*. Chapel Hill: University of North Carolina Press.

Löwith, Karl. 1949. *Meaning in History*. Chicago: University of Chicago Press.

———. 1986. *Nietzsches Philosophie der ewigen Wiederkehr*. Hamburg: Felix Meiner Verlag.

Lucan. 65–61 BCE. *Pharsalia*. Latin version available at http://www.perseus.tufts.edu/hopper/text?doc=urn:cts:latinLit:phi0917.phi001

———. 1919. *The Pharsalia*, vol. 1, translated by Sir Edward Ridley. London: Arthur L. Humphreys. https://archive.org/stream/pharsaliatransla01lucauoft#page/4/mode/2up.

Lugard, Frederick John Dealtry. [1922] 1965. *The Dual Mandate in British Tropical Africa*. London: Frank Cass.

Lupher, David A. 2003. *Romans in a New World: Classical Models in Sixteenth-Century Spanish America*. Ann Arbor: University of Michigan Press.

Lyttelton, Adrian. 2014. "Futurism, Politics, and Society." In *Italian Futurism, 1909–1944*, edited by Vivian Greene. New York: Guggenheim, 58–76.

Macaulay, Rose. [1953] 1996. *Pleasure of Ruins*. New York: Barnes and Noble.

Macaulay, Thomas Babington. [1840] 1889. "Review of von Ranke's *The Ecclesiastical and Political History of the Popes of Rome, during the Sixteenth and Seventeenth Centuries*." In *Lord Macaulay's Essays*. London: Longmans, Green, and Co., 547–569.

MacCormack, Sabine. 2009. *On the Wings of Time: Rome, the Incas, Spain, and Peru*. Princeton, NJ: Princeton University Press.

MacDonald, William L. 1996. *The Architecture of the Roman Empire*. Vol. 2: *An Urban Appraisal*. New Haven, CT: Yale University Press.

Mackinder, H. J. 1911. "The Teaching of Geography from an Imperial Point of View, and the Use Which Could and Should Be Made of Visual Instruction." *Geographical Teacher* 6(2, Summer):79–86.

Maier, Charles S. 2007. *Among Empires: American Ascendancy and Its Predecessors*. Cambridge, MA: Harvard University Press.

Majeed, Javed. 1999. "Comparativism and References to Rome in British Imperial Attitudes to India." In *Roman Presences*, edited by Catharine Edwards. Cambridge: Cambridge University Press, 88–109.

Makarius, Michel. 2004. *Ruinen: Die gegenwärtige Vergangenheit*, translated from the French by Michael Bayer. Paris: Edition Flammarion.

Malamud, Margaret. 2010. "*Translatio Imperii*: America as the New Rome, ca. 1900." In *Classics and Imperialism in the British Empire*, edited by Mark Bradley. Oxford: Oxford University Press, 249–283.

Malaparte, Curzio. 2013. *The Skin*. New York: New York Review of Books.

Mann, Thomas. 1960. "Nietzsches Philosophie im Lichte unserer Erfahrung." *Gesammelte Werke*, vol. 9. Frankfurt: S. Fischer Verlag, 675–712.

———. 1968. "Bruder Hitler." In *Politische Schriften und Reden*, vol. 3, edited by Hans Bürgin. Frankfurt: Fischer Bücherei, 53–58.

Marcello, Flavia. 2011. "Mussolini and the Idealization of Empire: The Augustan Exhibition of Romanità." *Modern Italy* 16(3, August):223–247.

Marchand, Suzanne. 2003. *Down from Olympus: Archaeology and Philhellenism in Germany, 1750–1970*. Princeton, NJ: Princeton University Press.

———. 2009. *German Orientalism in the Age of Empire*. Cambridge: Cambridge University Press.

Marin, Louis. 1999. "Fragments of a Walk through Poussin's Ruins." In *Sublime Poussin*. Stanford, CA: Stanford University Press, 143–151.

Martyn, David. 1997. "Borrowed Fatherland: Nationalism and Language in Fichte's Addresses to the German Nation." *Germanic Review* 72(4):303–315.

Marx, Karl. [1852] 1972. "The Eighteenth Brumaire of Louis Bonaparte." In *The Marx Engels Reader*, edited by Robert C. Tucker. New York: W. W. Norton & Company, 594–617.

———. 1977. *Capital*, vol. 1. New York: Vintage Books.

Mattingly, David J. 2011. *Imperialism, Power, and Identity: Experiencing the Roman Empire*. Princeton, NJ: Princeton University Press.

Matz, Friedrich. 1938. "Wesen und Wirkung der Augusteischen Kunst: Ein Vortrag." *Die Welt als Geschichte* 4(2–3):191–233.

Mazower, Mark. 2008. *Hitler's Empire: How the Nazis Ruled Europe*. New York: Penguin Press.

McCormick, E. H. 1977. *Omai: Pacific Envoy*. Auckland and Oxford: Auckland University Press and Oxford University Press.

McGibbon, Ian, ed. 2000. *The Oxford Companion to New Zealand Military History*. Oxford: Oxford University Press.

McGing, Brian. 2010. *Polybius'* Histories. Oxford and New York: Oxford University Press.

McGowan, Margaret M. 2002. "Unwillkürliches Gedächtnis: Rom-Erfahrungen in der Spät-Renaissance." In *Ruinenbilder*, edited by Aleida Assmann, Monika Gomille, and Gabriele Rippl. Munich: Wilhelm Fink Verlag, 17–30.

McKenzie, Kirsten. 2007. "Britain: Ruling the Waves." In *The Age of Empires*, edited by Robert Aldrich. London: Thames & Hudson, 128–151.

McNeill, William. 2013. "The Hölderlin Lectures." In *The Bloomsbury Companion to Heidegger*, edited by François Raffoul and Eric S. Nelson. London and New York: Bloomsbury, 223–236.

Mehring, Reinhard. 1989. *Pathetisches Denken. Carl Schmitts Denkweg am Leitfaden Hegels: Katholische Grundstellung und antimarxistische Hegelstrategie*. Berlin: Duncker & Humblot.

———. 1996. "Karl Löwith, Carl Schmitt, Jacob Taubes und das Ende der Geschichte." *Zeitschrift für Religions-und Geistesgeschichte* 48(3):231–248.

———. 2008. "'Raumrevolution' als Rechtsproblem. Zum politischen Kontext und Wandel von Carl Schmitts Großraumdenken." *Großraum-Denken. Carl Schmitts Kategorie der Großraumordnung*, edited by Rüdiger Voigt. Stuttgart: Franz Steiner Verlag, 99–118.

———. 2009. *Carl Schmitt: Aufstieg und Fall*. Munich: C. H. Beck.

Mehta, Uday Singh. 1999. *Liberalism and Empire: A Study in Nineteenth-Century British Liberal Thought*. Chicago: University of Chicago Press.

Meinecke, Friedrich. 1972. *Historism*. New York: Herder and Herder.

Melville, Herman. 2008. *Benito Cereno*. Brooklyn, NY: Melville House Publishing.

Memmi, Albert. 1992. *The Pillar of Salt*. Boston: Beacon Press.
Merlio, Gilbert. 1994. "Über Spenglers Modernität." In *Der Fall Spengler: Eine kritische Bilanz*, edited by Alexander Demandt and John Farrenkopf. Cologne and Weimar: Böhlau Verlag, 115–128.
———. 2007. "Urgefühl Angst." In Oswald Spengler, *Ich beneide jeden, der lebt: Die Aufzeichnungen "Eis heauton" aus dem Nachlaß*. Düsseldorf: Lilienfeld Verlag.
Meuter, Günter. 1994. *Der Katechon: Zu Carl Schmitts fundamentalistischer Kritik der Zeit*. Berlin: Duncker & Humblot.
Michaud, Eric. 1993. "National Socialist Architecture as an Acceleration of Time." *Critical Inquiry* 19(2):220–233.
———. 2004. *The Cult of Art in Nazi Germany*. Stanford, CA: Stanford University Press.
Michelet, Jules. 2002. *La cité des vivants et des morts*, edited by Claude Lefort. Paris: Belin.
———. 2003. *Histoire Romaine*. Paris: Les Belles Lettres.
Miles, Richard. 2004. "Rivaling Rome: Carthage." In *Rome the Cosmopolis*, edited by Catharine Edwards and Greg Woolf. Cambridge: Cambridge University Press, 123–146.
Miller, Angela. 1993. *The Empire of the Eye: Landscape Representations and American Cultural Politics, 1825–1875*. Ithaca, NY: Cornell University Press.
Miller Lane, Barbara. 1968. *Architecture and Politics in Germany 1918–1945*. Cambridge, MA: Harvard University Press.
Mitchell, Timothy. 1988. *Colonizing Egypt*. Berkeley: University of California Press.
Moeller van den Bruck, Arthur. [1924] 1932. "Das unheimliche Deutschland." In Moeller van den Bruck, *Das Recht der jungen Völker*. Berlin: Der nahe Osten, 103–108.
———. [1922] 1932. "Italia docet." In Moeller van den Bruck, *Das Recht der jungen Völker*, 123–125.
Moiret, Captain Joseph-Marie. 2001. *Memoirs of Napoleon's Egyptian Expedition 1798–1801*, translated and edited by Rosemary Brindle. London and New York: Greenhill Books and Stackpole Books.
Momigliano, Arnaldo. 1987. *On Pagans, Jews, and Christians*. Middletown, CT: Wesleyan University Press.
———. 1994. *Essays on Ancient and Modern Judaism*, edited by Silvia Berti. Chicago: University of Chicago Press.
Mommsen, Theodor. [1854, 1855, 1856] 1932. *Römische Geschichte*, abridged edition, edited by Eduard Norden. Wien and Leipzig. Phaidon Verlag.
———. 1920–1921. *The History of Rome*. 4 vols. Translated by William Purdie Dickinson. London: J. M. Dent & Sons.
———. 1996. *A History of Rome under the Emperors*, translated by Clare Krojzl. Edited by Thomas Wiedemann. London: Routledge.
Montaigne, Michel. 1973. "On Cannibals." In *Essays*. Middlesex: Penguin Books, 105–118.

Montesquieu, Charles Secondat, baron de. 1968. *Considérations sur les causes de la grandeur des Romains et de leur décadence.* Paris: Garnier-Flammarion.

Morley, Neville. 2010. *The Roman Empire: Roots of Imperialism.* London and New York: Pluto Press.

Mortier, Roland. 1974. *La Poétique des Ruines en France: Ses Origines, ses variations de la renaissance à Victor Hugo.* Geneva: Librairie Droz.

Moses, Dirk. 2010. "Redemptive Anti-Semitism and the Imperialist Imaginary." In *Years of Persecution, Years of Extermination: Saul Friedländer and the Future of Holocaust Studies,* edited by Paul Betts and Christian Wiese. London: Continuum, 233–254.

———. "Security and the Völkisch Imagination." Unpublished conference paper.

———. 2013. "Das römische Gespräch in a New Key: Hannah Arendt, Genocide, and the Defense of Republican Civilization." *Journal of Modern History* 85(4, December):867–913.

———. 2011. "Empire and History: Reconceptualizing the Colonial Transfer Debate in National Socialism and the Holocaust." In *Wissen–Transfer–Differenz: Transnationale und interdiskursive Verflechtungen von Rassismen ab 1700,* edited by Claudia Bruns and Michaela Hampf. Göttingen: Wallenstein Verlag.

Mostra Augustea della Romanità. 1937. Catalogo. Terzio Editione. Roma: Casa Editrice C. Colombo.

Müller, Heiner. [1993] 1998. "Mommsens Block." *Die Gedichte,* edited by Frank Hörnigk. Frankfurt: Suhrkamp Verlag, 257–263.

Müller, Jan-Werner. 2009. *A Dangerous Mind: Carl Schmitt in Post-War European Thought.* New Haven, CT: Yale University Press.

Muller, Jerry. 1987. *The Other God That Failed: Hans Freyer and the Deradicalization of German Conservativism.* Princeton, NJ: Princeton University Press.

Münckler, Herfried. 2007. *Empires.* Cambridge: Polity Press.

Muthu, Sankar. 2003. *Enlightenment against Empire.* Princeton University Press.

Näf, Beat, ed. 2001. *Antike und Altertumswissenschaft in der Zeit von Faschismus und Nationalsozialismus.* Mandelbachtal/Cambridge: edition cicero.

Nebel, Gerhard. 1941. "Der weisse Mann und die Tropen." *Neue Rundschau 52(3)*:132–141.

Nehru, Jawaharlal. 2004. *Glimpses of World History.* London: Penguin Books.

Neocleous, Mark. 1996. "Friend or Enemy? Reading Schmitt Politically." *Radical Philosophy* 79(September–October):12–23.

Nerdinger, Winfried. 1994. "Wilhelm Kreis—Repräsentant der deutschen Architektur des 20. Jahrhunderts." In *Wilhelm Kreis: Architekt zwischen Kaiserreich und Demokratie 1873–1955,* edited by Winfried Nerdinger and Ekkehard Mai. Munich: Klinkhardt & Biermann, 9–27.

Neumann, Michael. 2006. "'Und Sehn, Ob Uns Der Zufall Etwas Beut': Kleists Kasuistik der Ermächtigung im Drama 'Die Hermannsschlacht.'" *Kleist Jahrbuch*: 137–156.

Nicassio, Susan Vandiver. 2005. *Imperial City: Rome under Napoleon.* Chicago: University of Chicago Press.

Nicolet, Claude. 1991. *Space, Geography, and Politics in the Early Roman Empire*. Ann Arbor: University of Michigan Press.

Niderlinder, Alain, and Marie-Pierre Demarcq, eds. 2014. *Le Voyage de L'Obelisque Luxor/Paris 1829–1836*. Paris: Musée de la Marine.

Niebuhr, Barthold G. 1874. *Römische Geschichte*, vol. 3. Berlin: Verlag von S. Calvary & Co.

Nietzsche, Friedrich. [1874]. "Vom Nutzen und Nachtheil der Historie für das Leben." Digitale Kritische Gesamtausgabe. Digital version of the German critical edition of the complete works of Nietzsche, edited by Giorgio Colli and Mazzino Montinari. Available at Nietzsche Source, http://www.nietzschesource.org/#eKGWB/HL.

———. 1995. "The Utility and Liability of History for Life." In *Unfashionable Observations*, translated and with an afterword by Richard Gray. Stanford, CA: Stanford University Press.

———. 1997. "On the Uses and Disadvantages of History for Life." In *Untimely Meditations*, edited by Daniel Breazeale and translated by R. J. Hollingdale. Cambridge: Cambridge University Press, 59–123.

———. 2007. *On the Genealogy of Morality*, edited by Keith Ansell-Pearson and translated by Carol Diethe. Cambridge: Cambridge University Press.

Nolde, Emil. 1965. *Welt und Heimat: Die Südseereise 1913–1918*. Cologne: DuMont Verlag.

Nordau, Max. 1895. *Degeneration*. New York: D. Appleton and Company. No translator mentioned.

Novalis. 1799. *Die Christenheit oder Europa*. http://www.zeno.org/nid/20005447070.

Noyes, John. 2006. "Commerce, Colonialism, and the Globalization of Action in Late Enlightenment Germany." *Postcolonial Studies* 9(1):81–98.

Oettermann, Stephan. 2012. "Das Pergamon-Panorama von Yadegar Asisi." In *Pergamon: Panorama der antiken Metropole. Begleitbuch zur Ausstellung*, edited by Ralf Grüßinger, Volker Käster, and Andreas Scholl. Berlin: Staatliche Museen zu Berlin and Michael Imhof Verlag, 416–421.

O'Gorman, Ellen. 2004. "Cato the Elder and the Destruction of Carthage." *Helios* 31(1–2):91–125.

———. 2011. "Repetition and Exemplarity in Historical Thought: Ancient Rome and the Ghosts of Modernity." In *The Western Time of Ancient History: Historiographical Encounters with the Greek and Roman Past*, edited by Alexandra Lianeri. Cambridge: Cambridge University Press, 264–279.

Oliensis, Ellen. 2009. *Freud's Rome: Psychoanalysis and Latin Poetry*. Cambridge: Cambridge University Press.

Osini, Orietta. 2015. "From Oblivion to the Reassembly." *ARA PACIS Guide*. Rome: Roma Capitale, 13–21.

Osterhammel, Jürgen. 2009. *Die Verwandlung der Welt: Eine Geschichte des 19. Jahrhunderts*. Munich: C. H. Beck.

Oulebsir, Nabila. 2004. *Les usages du patrimoine: Monuments, musées et politique colonial en Algérie (1830–1930)*. Paris: Éditions de la Maison des sciences de l'homme.

Pace, Clare. 1969. "Claude the Enchanted: Interpretations of Claude in England in the Earlier Nineteenth-Century." *Burlington Magazine* 111(801):733–740.

Pagden, Anthony. 1982. *The Fall of Natural Man: The American Indian and the Origins of Comparative Ethnology*. Cambridge: Cambridge University Press.

———. 1995. *Lords of All the World: Ideologies of Empire in Spain, Britain and France c. 1500–c. 1800*. New Haven, CT: Yale University Press.

———. 2001. *Peoples and Empires: A Short History of European Migration, Exploration, and Conquest, from Greece to the Present*. New York: Random House.

———. 2009. *Worlds at War: The 2,500-Year Struggle between East and West*. New York: Random House.

———. 2016. *The Burdens of Empire, 1539 to the Present*. Berkeley: University of California Press.

Patterson, Orlando. 2012. *An Absence of Ruins*. Leeds: Peepal Tree Press.

Paul. 2005. *First Letter to the Thessalonians* and *Second Letter to the Thessalonians*. In Giorgio Agamben, *The Time That Remains: A Commentary on the Letter to the Romans*. Stanford, CA: Stanford University Press, 183–184.

Pausanias. [Before 175 CE] 1971. *Guide to Greece*. 2 vols. Translated and with an introduction by Peter Levi. Harmondsworth: Penguin.

Petersen, Lars. 2008. "Die Orientreise des deutschen Kaisers 1898 und die Ausgrabungen in Baalbek." In *Das grosse Spiel: Archäologie und Politik 1860–1940*, edited by Charlotte Trümpler. Ruhr Museum Essen and Dumont Verlag, 398–409.

Peucker, Brigitte. 2007. *The Material Image: Art and the Real in Film*. Stanford, CA: Stanford University Press.

Picker, Henry. 1963. *Hitlers Tischgespräche im Führerhauptquartier 1941–1942*, edited by Percy Ernst Schramm. Stuttgart: Sewald Verlag.

Piranesi, Giovanni Battista. 2002. *Observations on the Letters of Monsieur Mariette*, translated by Caroline Beamish and David Britt with an introduction by John Wilton-Ely. Los Angeles: Getty Publications.

———. [1775] 2000. *Le Antichità Romane* (I–IV). In *Piranesi. The Complete Etchings*, edited by Luigi Ficacci. Cologne, London, and New York: TASCHEN, 166–320.

Pitts, Jennifer. 2001. "Introduction." In Alexis de Tocqueville, *Writings on Empire and Slavery*, edited by Jennifer Pitts. Baltimore and London: Johns Hopkins University Press, ix–xxxviii.

Plato. 2017. *The Republic*, edited by G. R. F. Ferrari and translated by Tom Griffith. Cambridge: Cambridge University Press.

Pliny the Elder. 1855. *The Natural History*, edited by John Bostock and translated by H. T. Riley. London: Taylor and Francis. Available at http://data.perseus.org/texts/urn:cts:latinLit:phi0978.phi001.perseus-eng1.

Pocock, J. G. A. 1999. *The Enlightenments of Edward Gibbon, 1737–1764*. Vol. 1 of *Barbarism and Religion*. Cambridge: Cambridge University Press.

———. 1999–2003. *Barbarism and Religion*. 4 vols. Cambridge: Cambridge University Press.

———. 2003. *The First Decline and Fall*. Vol. 3 of *Barbarism and Religion*. Cambridge: Cambridge University Press.

———. 2003. *Narratives of Civil Government*. Vol. 2 of *Barbarism and Religion*. Cambridge: Cambridge University Press.

———. 2005. *Barbarians, Savages, and Empires*. Vol. 4 of *Barbarism and Religion*. Cambridge: Cambridge University Press.

Pollock, Sheldon. 2006. "Empire and Imitation." In *Lessons of Empire: Imperial Histories and American Power*, edited by Craig Calhoun, Frederick Cooper, and Kevin M. Moore. New York: New Press, 175–188.

Polybius. [1927] 1995. *The Histories*, translated by W. R. Paton. Cambridge, MA: Harvard University Press

———. 1979. *The Rise of the Roman Empire*, translated by Ian Scott-Kilvert, selected with an introduction by F. W. Walbank. London: Penguin Books.

Porter, James I. 2000. *Nietzsche and the Philology of the Future*. Stanford, CA: Stanford University Press.

———. 2001. "Ideals and Ruins: Pausanias, Longinus, and the Second Sophistic." In *Pausanias: Travel and Memory in Roman Greece*, edited by S. E. Alcock, J. F. Cherry, and J. Elsner. Oxford: Oxford University Press, 63–92.

———. 2008. "Reception Studies: Future Prospects." In *A Companion to Classical Receptions*, edited by Lorna Hardwick and Christopher Stray. Wiley-Blackwell, 469–481.

Porterfield, Todd. 1998. *The Allure of Empire: Art in the Service of French Imperialism 1798–1936. Princeton, NJ:* Princeton University Press.

Porterfield, Todd, and Susan L. Siegfried, eds. 2006. *Staging Empire: Napoleon, Ingres, and David*. University Park: Pennsylvania State University Press.

Potter, David. 1994. *Prophets and Emperors: Human and Divine Authority from Augustus to Theodosius*. Cambridge, MA: Harvard University Press.

———. 1999. *Literary Texts and the Historian*. London and New York: Routledge.

———. 2009. *Ancient Rome: A New History*. New York: Thames & Hudson.

———. 2011. "The Greek Historians of Imperial Rome." *The Oxford History of Historical Writing*, vol. 1, edited by Andrew Feldherr and Grant Hardy. Oxford: Oxford University Press, 316–344.

———. 2009. *The Roman Empire at Bay AD 180–395*. London and New York: Routledge.

Potts, Alex. 2005. "Disparities between Part and Whole in the Description of Works of Art." In *Regimes of Description: In the Archive of the Eighteenth Century*, edited by John Bender and Michael Marrinan. Stanford, CA: Stanford University Press, 135–150.

———. 2006. "Introduction." *Winckelmann: History of the Art of Antiquity*. Los Angeles: Getty Research Institute, 1–53.

Prantner, Anton Helmut. 2013. "Imperium USA: Die aktuelle englischsprachige Argumentation." *Zeitschrift für Weltgeschichte* 14(2):135–157.

Pratt, Mary Louise. 1992. *Imperial Eyes: Travel Writing and Transculturation*. London: Routledge.

Presner, Todd, David Shepard, and Yoh Kawano, eds. 2014. *HyperCities: Thick Mapping in the Digital Humanities*. Cambridge, MA, and London: Harvard University Press.

Presner, Todd Samuel. 2010. "Hegel's Philosophy of World History via Sebald's Imaginary of Ruins: A Contrapuntal Critique of the 'New Space' of Modernity." In *Ruins of Modernity*, edited by Julia Hell and Andreas Schönle. Durham, NC: Duke University Press, 193–211.

———. 2007. *Muscular Judaism: The Jewish Body and the Politics of Regeneration*. London and New York: Routledge.

Puff, Helmut. 2014. *Miniature Monuments: Modeling German History*. Berlin/Boston: Walter de Gruyter.

Quaritsch, Helmut, ed. 1988. *Complexio Oppositorum—über Carl Schmitt*. Berlin: Duncker & Humblot.

Quint, David. *1993. Epic and Empire: Politics and Generic Form from Virgil to Milton. Princeton, NJ:* Princeton University Press.

Rabinbach, Anson, and Sander L. Gilman, eds. 2013. *The Third Reich Sourcebook*. Berkeley: University of California Press.

Rahn, Rudolf. 1949. *Ruheloses Leben: Aufzeichnungen und Erinnerungen*. Düsseldorf: Peter Diederichs Verlag.

Rasch, William. 2004. *Sovereignty and Its Discontents: On the Primacy of Conflict and the Structure of the Political*. London: Birkbeck Law Press.

Rath, Claus Dieter. 1994. "Zur Einführung: Olympiade 1936." In *Lacan und das Deutsche. Die Rückkehr der Psychoanalyse über den Rhein*, edited by Jutta Prasse and Claus-Dieter Rath. Freiburg: Kore Verlag: 11–27.

Ratzel, Friedrich. 1882–1891. *Anthropo-Geographie*. 2 vols. Stuttgart: Verlag Engelhorn.

———. 1906. *Kleine Schriften*, edited by Hans Helmolt. Munich and Berlin: R. Oldenbourg.

———. [1897] 1923. *Politische Geographie*, 3rd ed. Munich: R. Oldenbourg.

———. 1988. "Ruins." In *Sketches of Urban and Cultural Life in North America*, edited by Stewart A. Stehlin. New Brunswick, NJ: Rutgers University Press, 285–295.

Rebenich, Stefan. 2001. "Alte Geschichte in Demokratie und Diktatur: Der Fall Helmut Berve." *Chiron* 31:457–496.

Reed, J. D. 2007. *Virgil's Gaze: Nation and Poetry in the Aeneid*. Princeton, NJ: Princeton University Press.

Rentschler, Rick. 1996. *The Ministry of Illusion: Nazi Cinema and Its Afterlife*. Cambridge, MA: Harvard University Press.

Richard, Carl. 1994. *The Founders and the Classics*: *Greece, Rome, and the American Enlightenment*. Cambridge, MA: Harvard University Press.

Ridley, Ronald T. 1986. "To Be Taken with a Pinch of Salt: The Destruction of Carthage." *Classical Philology* 81(2, April):140–146.

———. 1992. *The Eagle and the Spade: The Archeology of Rome during the Napoleonic Era 1809–1814*. Cambridge: Cambridge University Press.

Rodenwaldt, Gerhart. 1937. "Kunst um Augustus." *Die Antike* 13(3):155–196.

———. 1939. "Via Dell'Impero." *Kunst im Deutschen Reich* 3(July):262–264.

———. 1942. "Römische Staatsarchitektur." In *Das neue Bild der Antike*, vol. 2, edited by Helmut Berve. Leipzig: Koehler and Amelang, 356–373.

———. *1943. Kunst um Augustus*. Berlin: de Gruyter.

Rodogno, David. 2006. *Fascism's European Empire: Italian Occupation during the Second World* War. Cambridge: Cambridge University Press.

Rogers, Adam, and Richard Hingley. 2010. "Edward Gibbon and Francis Haverfield: Traditions of Imperial Decline." In *Classics and Imperialism in the British Empire,* edited by Mark Bradley. Oxford: Oxford University Press, 190–191.

Ros, Karen E. 1996. "The Roman Theater at Carthage." *American Journal of Archaeology* 100(3, July):449–489.

Rosenberg, Alfred. *1935. Der Mythus des 20. Jahrhunderts*. Munich: Hoheneichen Verlag.

Roth, Michael, Claire Lyons, and Michael Merewether, eds. 1997. *Irresistible Decay: Ruins Reclaimed*. Los Angeles: Getty Research Institute of the History of Art and the Humanities.

Rüthers, Bernd. 1990. *Carl Schmitt im Dritten Reich*. Munich: C. H. Beck.

Safranski, Rüdiger. 2009. *Romantik: Eine deutsche Affäre*. Frankfurt: Fischer Taschenbuch Verlag.

Sahin, Kaya. 2010. "Constantinople and the End of Times: The Ottoman Conquest as a Portent of the Last Hour." *Journal of Early Modern History* 14:317–354.

Sahlins, Marshall. 1981. *Historical Metaphors and Mythical Realities: Structure in the Early History of the Sandwich Islands Kingdom*. Ann Arbor: University of Michigan Press.

———. 1985. *Islands of History*. Chicago: University of Chicago Press.

Said, Edward. 1978. *Orientalism*. New York: Vintage.

Sallust. 2007. *Catiline's War, The Jughurtine War, Histories*, translated by A. J. Woodman. London: Penguin.

Sandner, Gerhard, and Mechtild Roessler. 1994. "Geography and Empire in Germany, 1871–1945." In *Geography and Empire*, edited by Anne Godlewska and Neil Smith. London: Blackwell, 115–127.

Santner, Eric. 1996. *My Own Private Germany: Daniel Paul Schreber's Secret History of Modernity*. Princeton, NJ: Princeton University Press.

———. 1999. "Freud's *Moses* and the Ethics of Nomotropic Desire." *October* 88: 3–41.

Sauron, Gilles. 2014. "Mythe et Pouvoir: La Mystification Augustienne." In *Auguste*, edited by Eugenio La Rocca. Saint-Juste-la-Pendue: Chirat, 32–33.

Savary, Claude-Étienne. 1785–1786. *Lettres sur l'Égypte*. 3 vols. Paris: Onfroi.

Scarrocchia, Sandro. 2000. "Baumeister des Faschismus: Marcello Piacentini and Albert Speer." In *Deutsche Italomanie in Kunst, Wissenschaft und Politik*, edited by Wolfgang Lange and Norbert Schnitzler. Munich: Wilhelm Fink Verlag, 179–206.

———. 1995. *Die Untermauerung der Achse Piacentini und Speer*. Dissertation. Rheinische Friedrichs-Wilhelms-Universität Bonn.

Schama, Simon. 1995. *Landscape and Memory*. New York: Alfred A. Knopf.

Schmitt, Carl. 1916. *Theodor Däubler's Nordlicht. Drei Studien über die Elemente, den Geist und die Aktualität des Werkes*. Georg Müller: Munich.

———. 1942. *Land und Meer: Eine weltgeschichtliche Betrachtung*. Leipzig: Reclam Verlag.

———. 1942. "Raumrevolution: vom Geist des Abendlandes." *Deutsche Kolonialzeitung* 12:219–221.

———. 1950. *Ex Captivitate Salus: Erfahrungen der Zeit 1945/47*. Cologne: Greven Verlag.

———. 1950. "Drei Stufen historischer Sinngebung." *Universitas* 5:927–931.

———. [1927; 1932] 1976. *The Concept of the Political*, translated and with an introduction by George Schwab. New Brunswick, NJ: Rutgers University Press.

———. [1922] 1985. *Political Theology: Four Chapters on the Concept of Sovereignty*, translated by George Schwab. Cambridge, MA: MIT Press.

———. 1991. *Glossarium: Aufzeichnungen der Jahre 1947–1951*, edited by Eberhard Freiherr von Medem. Berlin: Duncker & Humblot.

———. [1934] 1993. *Über die drei Arten des rechstwissenschaftlichen Denkens*. Duncker & Humblot: Berlin.

———. [1921] 1994. *Die Diktatur. Von den Anfängen des modernen Souveränitätsgedankens bis zum proletarischen Klassenkampf*. Berlin: Duncker & Humblot.

———. [1939] 1994. "Neutralität und Neutralisierungen." In *Positionen und Begriffe*. Berlin: Duncker & Humblot, 309–334.

———. [1939] 1994. "Der Reichsbegriff im Völkerrecht." In *Positionen und Begriffe im Kampf um Weimar*. Berlin: Duncker & Humblot, 344–354.

———. [1929] 1994. "Das Zeitalter der Neutralisierungen und Entpolitisierungen" In *Positionen und Begriffe im Kampf um Weimar*. Berlin: Duncker & Humblot, 138–150.

———. [1942] 1995. "Beschleuniger wider Willen." In *Staat, Großraum, Nomos. Arbeiten aus den Jahren 1916–1969*, edited by Günter Maschke. Berlin: Duncker & Humblot, 431–436.

———. [1955] 1995. "Die geschichtliche Struktur des heutigen Welt-Gegensatzes von Ost und West." In *Staat, Großraum, Nomos. Arbeiten aus den Jahren 1916–1969*, edited by Günter Maschke. Berlin: Duncker & Humblot, 523–551.

———. [1943] 1995. "Die letzte globale Linie." In *Staat, Großraum, Nomos. Arbeiten aus den Jahren 1916–1969*, edited by Günter Maschke. Berlin: Duncker & Humblot, 441–448.

———. [1955] 1995. "Der neue Nomos der Erde." In *Staat, Großraum, Nomos. Arbeiten aus den Jahren 1916–1969*, edited by Günter Maschke. Berlin: Duncker & Humblot, 519–522.

———. [1951] 1995. "Raum und Rom—Zur Phonetik des Wortes Raum." In *Staat,*

Großraum, Nomos. Arbeiten aus den Jahren 1916–1969, edited by Günter Maschke. Berlin: Duncker & Humblot, 491–494.

———. [1940] 1995. "Die Raumrevolution: durch den totalen Krieg zu einem totalen Frieden." In *Staat, Großraum, Nomos. Arbeiten aus den Jahren 1916–1969*, edited by Günter Maschke. Berlin: Duncker & Humblot, 388–391.

———. 1995. *Staat, Großraum, Nomos. Arbeiten aus den Jahren 1916–1969*, edited by Günter Maschke. Berlin: Dunckler & Humblot.

———. [1939; revised 1941] 1995. "Völkerrechtliche Großraumordnung mit Interventionsverbot für raumfremde Mächte. Ein Beitrag zum Reichsbegriff im Völkerrecht.". In *Staat, Großraum, Nomos. Arbeiten aus den Jahren 1916–1969*, edited by Günter Maschke. Berlin: Duncker & Humblot, 269–320.

———. [1970] 1996. *Politische Theologie II. Die Legende von der Erledigung jeder Politischen Theologie*. Berlin: Duncker & Humblot.

———. [1923] 1996. *Roman Catholicism and Political Form*, translated by G. L. Ulmen. Westport, CT, and London: Greenwood Press.

———. 2000. "Stellungnahme I: Untermauerung der Hitlerschen Großraumpolitik?" In *Carl Schmitt: Antworten in Nürnberg*, edited by Helmut Quaritsch. Berlin: Duncker & Humblot, 68–82.

———. [1927; revised 1932] 2002. *Der Begriff des Politischen: Text von 1932 mit einem Vorwort und drei Corollarien*. Berlin: Duncker & Humblot.

———. [1950] 2003. *The Nomos of the Earth in the International Law of Jus Publicum Europaeum*, translated by G. L. Ulmen. New York: Telos Press.

———. *[1922] 2004. Politische Theologie. Vier Kapitel zur Lehre von der Souveranität.* Berlin: Duncker & Humblot.

———. 2007. "The 'Fourth' (Second) Interrogation of Carl Schmitt at Nuremberg." *Telos* 139:35–43.

——— [1963] 2007. *Theory of the Partisan: Intermediate Commentary on the Concept of the Political*, translated by G. L. Ulmen. New York: Telos Press.

———. 2008. *Political Theology II: The Myth of the Closure of Any Political Theology*. Cambridge: Polity.

———. 2009. "Donoso Cortés in gesamteuropäischer Perspektive." In *Donoso Cortés in gesamteuropäischer Perspektive*. Berlin: Dunckler & Humblot, 80–114.

———. 2010. *"Solange das Imperium da ist." Carl Schmitt im Gespräch mit Klaus Figge und Dieter Groh*, edited by Frank Hertweck. Berlin: Duncker & Humblot.

———. [1942] 2015. *Land and Sea. A World-Historical Meditation*, translated by Samuel Garrett Zeitlin. Edited and with introductions by Russell A. Berman and Samuel Garrett Zeitlin. New York: Telos Press.

Schmitz, Alexander, and Marcel Lepper, eds. 2007. *Hans Blumenberg/Carl Schmitt Briefwechsel 1971–1978*. Frankfurt: Suhrkamp Verlag.

Schnapp, Jeffrey T. 1996. *Staging Fascism: 18 BL and the Theater of Masses for Masses*. Stanford, CA: Stanford University Press.

Schönberger, Angela. 1981. *Die neue Reichskanzlei von Albert Speer: Zum Zusammenhang von nationalsozialistischer Ideologie und Architektur*. Berlin: Gebr. Mann Verlag.

Schönle, Andreas. 2011. *The Architecture of Oblivion: Ruins and Historical Consciousness in Russia*. De Kalb: Northern Illinois University Press.

Schorske, Carl E. 1980. "Freud: The Psycho-Archeology of Civilizations." *Proceedings of the Massachusetts Historical Society*. Third Series, vol. 92, 52–67.

Schramm, Percy Ernst, ed. 1963. *Hitlers Tischgespräche im Führerhauptquartier 1941–1942*. Stuttgart: Seewald Verlag.

Schüller, Sepp. *1943. Das Rom Mussolinis: Rom als moderne Hauptstadt*. Düsseldorf: Mosella-Verlag.

Schweizer, Stefan. 2007. *"Unserer Weltanschauung sichtbaren Ausdruck geben": Nationalsozialistische Geschichtsbilder in historischen Festzügen*. Göttingen: Wallstein Verlag.

Scobie, Alexander. 1990. *Hitler's State Architecture: The Impact of Classical Antiquity*. University Park: Pennsylvania State University Press.

Seeck, Otto. 1897–1921. *Geschichte des Untergangs der antiken Welt*. 4 vols. Berlin: Siemenroth & Worms.

Seider, Aaron M. 2013. *Memory in Virgil's Aeneid: Creating the Past*. Cambridge: Cambridge University Press.

Seraphim, P. H. 1939–1940. "Die Wanderungsbewegung des jüdischen Volkes." *Schriften zur Geopolitik* 16:12 and 17:5–30.

Shackleton, Robert. 1976. "The Impact of French Literature on Gibbon." *Daedalus* 105(3):37–48.

Siegfried, Susan. 2006. "Ingres's Napoleon I on His Imperial Throne." In *Staging Empire: Napoleon, Ingres, and David*, edited by Todd Porterfield and Susan L. Siegfried. University Park: Pennsylvania State University Press, 25–114.

———. 2006. "Staging an Empire." In *Staging Empire: Napoleon, Ingres, and David*, edited by Todd Porterfield and Susan L. Siegfried. University Park: Pennsylvania State University Press, 3–22.

———. 2009. *Ingres: Painting Reimagined*. New Haven, CT: Yale University Press.

Siemens, Hermann. 2004. "Nietzsche and the 'Classical': Traditional and Innovative Features of Nietzsche's Usage, with Special Reference to Goethe." In *Nietzsche and Antiquity: His Reaction and Response to the Classical Tradition*, edited by Paul Bishop. New York: Camden House, 391–410.

Simmel, Georg. 1965. "The Ruin." In *Essays on Sociology, Philosophy and Aesthetics*, edited by Kurt H. Wolff. New York: Harper and Row, 259–266.

Skirl, Miguel. 2000. "Ewige Wiederkunft." In *Nietzsche-Handbuch: Leben-Werk-Wirkung*, edited by Henning Ottmann. Stuttgart and Weimar: Verlag J. B. Metzler, 222–230.

Small, Lisa, ed. 2006. *Napoleon on the Nile*. New York: Dahesh Museum of Art.

Smiles, Sam. 1994. *The Image of Antiquity: Ancient Britain and the Romantic Imagination*. New Haven, CT: Yale University Press.

Smith, Adam. [1776] 1910. *The Wealth of Nations*, vol. 2. London: J. M. Dent.

Smith, Bernard. 1988. *European Vision and the South Pacific, 1769–1850; A Study in the History of Art and Ideas*. New Haven, CT: Yale University Press.

———. 1992. *Imagining the Pacific: In the Wake of the Cook Voyage*. New Haven, CT: Yale University Press.

Snyder, Timothy. 2011. "A New Approach to the Holocaust." *New York Review of Books* 58(11, June):54–56.

Sonnabend, Martin, and Jon Whiteley, eds. 2012. *Claude Lorrain: Die verzauberte Landschaft*. Ostfildern: HatjeCantz.

Southern, Pat. 2008. *Empress Zenobia: Palmyra's Rebel Queen*. London: Continuum.

Speer, Albert. 1941. *Neue deutsche Baukunst*. Berlin: Volk und Reich Verlag.

———. 1981. *Inside the Third Reich: Memoirs*, translated by Richard and Clara Winston. New York: Macmillan.

———. 1976. *Spandau: The Secret Diaries*, translated by Richard and Clara Winslow. New York: Macmillan.

———. 2005. *Spandauer Tagebücher*. Berlin: Ullstein Verlag..

———. 1978. *Architektur: Arbeiten 1933–1942*. Frankfurt/Berlin/Wien: Propyläen Verlag.

Spencer, Herbert. 1902. "Re-Barbarization." In *Facts and Comments*. New York: D. Appleton, 172–188.

Spengler, Oswald. 1924. *Neubau des deutschen Reiches*. Munich: C. H. Beck.

———. *1942. The Hour of Decision*, part 1: *Germany and World-Historical Evolution*, translated by Charles Francis Atkinson. New York: A. A. Knopf.

———. 1957. *The Decline of the West*, 2 vols., translated by Charles Francis Atkinson. New York: Alfred A. Knopf.

———. [1918; 1922] 2003. *Der Untergang des Abendlandes: Umrisse einer Morphologie der Weltgeschichte*. Munich: Deutscher Taschenbuchverlag.

———. 2007. *Ich beneide jeden, der lebt: Die Aufzeichnungen "Eis heauton" aus dem Nachlaß*. Düsseldorf: Lilienfeld Verlag.

———. 2009. *Politische Schriften, 1919–1926*. Waltrop and Leipzig: Manuskriptum.

Spivak, Gayatri. 1985. "The Rani of Samur: An Essay in Reading the Archives." *History and Theory* 24(3):247–272.

Spotts, Frederic. 2001. *Hitler and the Power of Aesthetics*. London: Hutchinson.

Stahlmann, Ines. 1988. *Imperator Caesar Augustus: Studien zur Geschichte des Prinzipatverständnisses in der deutschen Altertumswissenschaft bis 1945*. Darmstadt: Wissenschaftliche Verlagsbuchhandlung.

Stamm, Karl. 2014. "'Degenerate Art' On the Screen." In *Degenerate Art: The Attack on Modern Art in Nazi Germany 1937*, edited by Olaf Peters. New York: Prestel, 196–205.

Steffens, Martin. 2003. *Schinkel 1781–1841: Ein Baumeister im Dienst der Schönheit*. Cologne: Taschen.

Steinmetz, George. 2003. "The State of Emergency and the Revival of American Imperialism: Toward an Authoritarian Post-Fordism." *Public Culture* 15(2, Spring):323–346.

———. 2007. *The Devil's Handwriting: Precoloniality and the German Colonial State in Qingdao, Samoa, and Southwest Africa*. Chicago: University of Chicago Press.

Stoneman, Richard. 1994. *Palmyra and Its Empire: Zenobia's Revolt against Rome*. Ann Arbor: University of Michigan Press.

Strabo. 1923. *The Geography of Strabo*, vol. 2, edited and translated by Horace L. Jones. London: William Heinemann and New York: G. P. Putnam's Sons.

———. *The Geography*. Book 5, translated by H. L. Jones. http://penelope.uchicago.edu/Thayer/E/Roman/Texts/Strabo/home.html.

Stroux, Johannes. 1937. "Imperator." *Die Antike* 13(3):197–212.

Sturm, Hermann. 1996. "Gegenwartsformen der Vergangenheit—Zu einer Ästhetik des Diversen." In *Ruinen des Denkens: Denken in Ruinen*, edited by Norbert Bolz and Willem van Reijen. Frankfurt: Suhrkamp Verlag, 91–125.

Stürzenacker, August. 1938. "Die deutsche Baukunst und die Antike." *Baugilde* 20(19, July):623–624.

Syme, Robert. 1958. *Colonial Elites: Rome, Spain, and the Americas*. Oxford: Oxford University Press.

Tacitus. 1996. *The Annals of Imperial Rome*, translated by Michael Grant. London: Penguin Books.

Tamms, Friedrich. 1943. "Die Kriegerehrenmäler von Wilhelm Kreis." *Die Kunst im deutschen Reich*. Ausgabe B(March):43–57.

———. 1944. "Das Grosse in der Baukunst." *Die Kunst im deutschen Reich. Beilage Baukunst* 8(3):47–60.

Tang, Chenxi. 2008. *The Geographic Imagination: Geography, Literature, and Philosophy in German Romanticism*. Stanford, CA: Stanford University Press.

Taubes, Jacob. 1987. *Ad Carl Schmitt: Gegenstrebige Fügung*. Berlin: Merve Verlag.

Taussig, Michael. 1993. *Mimesis and Alterity: A Particular History of the Senses*. New York and London: Routledge.

Tertullian. Circa 197 CE. *Apology, translated by T. R. Glover. In Apology. De Spectaculis, translated by T. R. Glover and Gerald H. Rendell. Cambridge, MA: Harvard University Press, 2–227.*

Thies, Jochen. 1978. "Hitler's European Building Program." *Journal of Contemporary History* 13:413–431.

Thomas, Nicholas. 2004. "Hodges as Anthropologist and Historian." In *William Hodges 1744–1797: The Art of Exploration*, edited by Geoff Quilley and John Bonehill. New Haven, CT: Yale University Press, 27–34.

Thomas, Nicholas, and Oliver Berghof. 2000. "Introduction." In Georg Forster, *A Voyage Round the World*, vol. 1, edited by Nicholas Thomas and Oliver Berghof. Honolulu: University of Hawai'i Press, xix–xliii.

Tocqueville, Alexis de. 2001. "Second Letter on Algeria (22 August 1837)." In *Writings on Empire and Slavery*, edited by Jennifer Pitts. Baltimore: Johns Hopkins University Press: 14–26.

———. "Essay on Algeria (October 1841)." In *Writings on Empire and Slavery*, 59–116.

———. "Notes on the Voyage to Algeria 1941." In *Writings on Empire and Slavery*, 36–58.

———. "First Report on Algeria (1847)." In *Writings on Empire and Slavery*, 129–173.

Todorov, Tzvetan. 1984. *The Conquest of America: The Question of the Other*, translated by Richard Howard. New York: Harper & Row.

Tong, Q. S. 2006. "The Aesthetics of Imperial Ruins: The Elgins and John Bowring." *boundary 2* 33(1):123–150.

Trawny, Peter. 2015. *Heidegger & The Myth of a Jewish World Conspiracy*. Chicago: University of Chicago Press.

Trevor Roper, H. R., ed. 1953. *Hitler's Table Talk 1941–1944*, translated by Norman Cameron and H. R. Stevens. London: Weidenfeld and Nicolson.

Trimborn, Jürgen. 2011. *Arno Breker: der Künstler und die Macht*. Berlin: Aufbau Verlag.

Trumpener, Katie. 1997. *Bardic Nationalism: The Romantic Novel and the British Empire*. Princeton, NJ: Princeton University Press.

Tung, Anthony M. 2001. *Preserving the World's Great Cities: The Destruction and Renewal of the Historic Metropolis*. New York: Clarkson Potter.

Urban, Bernd, ed. 2003. *Sigmund Freud. Der Wahn und die Träume in W. Jensens "Gradiva." Mit dem Text der Erzählung von Wilhelm Jensen und Sigmund Freuds Randbemerkungen*. Frankfurt: Fischer Taschenbuch Verlag.

Vale, Lawrence J. 1992. *Architecture, Power, and National Identity*. New Haven, CT: Yale University Press.

Vasunia, Phiroze. 2013. *The Classics and Colonial India*. Oxford: Oxford University Press.

Venning, Barry. 2004. *Turner*. London: Phaidon Press.

Virgil. 29–9 BCE. *The Aeneid*. http://data.perseus.org/texts/urn:cts:latinLit:phi0690.phi003.perseus-lat1.

———. [37–29 BCE]. 1982. *The Georgics*, translated by L. P. Wilkinson. London: Penguin.

———. [29–19 BCE]. 1990. *The Aeneid*, translated by Robert Fitzgerald. New York: Vintage.

———. [29–19 BCE]. 2003. *Aeneid: Book VIII*, edited by K. W. Grandsden. Cambridge: Cambridge University Press.

———. [29–19 BCE]. 2006. *The Aeneid*, translated by Robert Fagles. New York: Viking.

Vitruvius, Pollio [30–15 BCE]. 1999. *Ten Books on Architecture*, edited by Ingrid W. Rowland and Thomas Noble Howe. Cambridge University Press,.

———. [30–15 BCE]. *De Architectura*, edited by Valentinus Rose. http://www.gutenberg.org/ebooks/51812.

Vittinghoff, Friedrich. 1964. "Zum geschichtlichen Selbstverständnis der Spätantike." *Historische Zeitschrift* 198(3):529–573.

Vlassopoulos, Kostas. 2010. "Imperial Encounters: Discourses on Empire and the Uses of Ancient History during the Eighteenth-Century." In *Classics and Imperialism in the British Empire*, edited by Mark Bradley. Oxford: Oxford University Press, 29–53.

Vogel, Hans. 1948. *Die Ruine in der Darstellung der abendländischen Kunst*. Kassel: Karl Winter Verlag.

Vogt, Joseph. 1929. *Orbis Romanus. Zur Terminologie des römischen Imperialismus*. Tübingen: Mohr.

———. 1942. *Vom Reichsgedanken der Römer*. Leipzig: Koehler und Amelang.

———. 1942. "Raumauffassung und Raumordnung in der römischen Politik." In *Das neue Bild der Antike*, edited by Helmut Berve, vol. 2. Leipzig: Koehler & Amelang, 100–132.

———. 1943. *Rom und Karthago*. Leipzig: Koehler and Amelang.

Volney, Constantin-François de. [1791] 1890. *The Ruins, or, Meditation on the Revolutions of Empires: and The Law of Nature*, edited by Peter Eckler. No translator. New York: Twentieth Century Publishing Company. Reprint by Baltimore: Black Classic Press, n.d. http://www.gutenberg.org/files/1397/1397-h/1397-h.htm.

———. 1959. *Voyage en Égypte et en Syrie*. Paris: Mouton.

Wagner, Richard. [1849] 1993. "*Art and Revolution*." In *The Art-Work of the Future and Other Works,* translated by William Ashton Ellis. Lincoln and London: University of Nebraska Press, 30–68.

Walbank, Frank W. 1964. "Zum geschichtlichen Selbstverständnis der Spätantike." *Historische Zeitschrift* 198:529–574.

———. 1979. "Introduction." In Polybius, *The Rise of the Roman Empire,* translated by Ian Scott-Kilvert, with an introduction by F. W. Walbank. London: Penguin Books, 9–40.

———. 1980. "The Idea of Decline in Polybius." In *Niedergang: Studien zu einem geschichtlichen Thema,* edited by Reinhart Koselleck and Paul Widmer. Stuttgart: Ernst Klett, 41–58.

———. 2002. *Polybius, Rome, and the Hellenistic World: Essays and Reflections*. Cambridge: Cambridge University Press.

Wallerstein, Immanuel. 1999. "Charles V and the Nascent Capitalist World-Economy." In *Charles V and His Time, 1500–1558,* edited by Hugo Soly. Antwerp: Mercatorfonds, 365–391.

———. *2003. Decline of American Power: The U.S. in a Chaotic World*. New York: New Press.

Walter, Marco. 2010. "Between Fascination and Deterrence: Roman Decadence and Empire." *Mediterraneo Antico* 8(1–2):17–30.

Warrell, Ian. 2012. *Turner Inspired: In the Light of Claude*. London: National Gallery and Yale University Press.

Weber, Max. 2013. *The Agrarian Sociology of Ancient Civilizations,* translated by R. I. Frank. London: Verso.

Weber, Niels. 2006. "Kleists 'Sendung des Dritten Reiches': Zur Rezeption von Heinrich von Kleists 'Hermannsschlacht' im Nationalsozialismus." *Kleist Jahrbuch*: 157–170.

Weber, Wilhelm. 1935. "Das römische Kaiserreich und der Eintritt der Germanen in die Weltgeschichte." In *Knaurs Weltgeschichte: Von der Urzeit bis zur Gegenwart,* edited by K. U. von Müller and P. R. Rohden. Berlin: Thomas Knaur, 165–280.

———. 1935. *Vom neuen Reich der Deutschen. Rede gehalten bei der Feier der Reichsgründung und der Erneuerung des Reichs durch den Führer am 30. Januar 1930.* Berlin, 3–16.

———. 1936. *Princeps: Studien zur Geschichte des Augustus.* Stuttgart: Kohlhammer.

———. 1940. "ROM: Mussolinis cäsarische Vision." *Geist der Zeit* 18:136–151.

———. 1940. "Römische Geschichte bis zum Verfall des Weltreichs." In *Die Neue Propyläen Weltgeschichte,* vol. 1, edited by Willy Andreas. Berlin: Propyläen-Verlag, 273–372.

———. 1940. "Der Tatsachenbericht des Augustus. 'Monumentum Ancyranum.'" In *Die Neue Propyläen Weltgeschichte,* vol. 1, edited by Willy Andreas. Berlin: Propyläen-Verlag; no page nos.

———. 1943. "Aufstieg und Untergang Roms." *Wille und Macht* 7(11, November/December):1–41.

Weickert, Carl. 1938. "Augustus: Bild und Geschichte." *Die Antike* 14(3):202–230.

Weigel, Hermann. 1972. "Interview mit Leni Riefenstahl." *Filmkritik* 16(8): 395–410.

Weil, Simone. [1940] 1962. "The Great Beast: Some Reflections on the Origins of Hitlerism." In *Selected Essays 1934–1943,* edited and translated by Richard Reese. Oxford: Oxford University Press, 89–144.

Weinberg, Gerhard L. 2010. *A World at War: A Global History of World War II.* Cambridge: Cambridge University Press.

———, ed. 1953. *Hitler's Table Talk 1941–1944,* translated by Norman Cameron and R. H. Stevens with an introductory essay by H. R. Trevor-Roper. London: Weidenfeld and Nicholson.

Wengrow, David. 2003. "Forgetting the *Ancien Régime*: Republican Values and the Study of the Ancient Orient." In *Views of Ancient Egypt since Napoleon Bonaparte: Imperialism, Colonialism, and Modern Appropriations,* edited by David Jeffreys. London: UCL Press, Institute of Archaeology, 179–193.

Wetters, Kirk. 2014. *Demonic History from Goethe to the Present.* Evanston, IL: Northwestern University Press.

White, L. Michael. 2005. "Herod and the Jewish Experience of Augustan Rule." In *The Cambridge Companion to the Age of Augustus,* edited by Karl Galinsky. Cambridge: Cambridge University Press, 361–388.

Whitmarsh, Tim. 2006. "Quickening the Classics: The Politics of Prose in Roman Greece." In *Classical Pasts: The Classical Traditions of Greece and Rome,* edited by James Porter. Princeton University Press, 353–374.

Wiles, David. 1997. *Tragedy in Athens: Performance Space and Theatrical Meaning.* Cambridge: Cambridge University Press.

Wilson Nightingale, Andrea. 2004. *Spectacles of Truth in Classical Greek Philosophy: Theoria in Its Classical Contexts.* Cambridge: Cambridge University Press.

Wilson Joyce, Jane. 1993. "General Introduction." In Lucan *Pharsalia,* translated by Jane Wilson Joyce. Ithaca and London: Cornell University Press, ix–xxv.

Wilton-Ely, John, ed. 2002. *Giovanni Battista Piranesi, Observations on the Letter of Monsieur Mariette.* Los Angeles: Getty Publications.

———. 2002. "Introduction" to *Giovanni Battista Piranesi, Observations on the Letter of Monsieur Mariette*, edited by John Wilton-Ely. Los Angeles: Getty Research Institute, 27.

———. 2007. "Design through Fantasy: Piranesi as Designer." In *Piranesi as Designer*, edited by Sara E. Lawrence. New York: Smithsonian Cooper-Hewitt National Design Museum, 11–90.

Winckelmann, Johann Joachim. *1756. Gedanken über die Nachahmung der griechischen Werke in der Malerei und Bildhauerkunst*. Dresden and Leipzig: Verlag der Waltherischen Handlung.

———. *2006. History of the Art of Antiquity*. Introduction by Alex Potts. Translated by Harry Francis Mallgrave. Los Angeles: Getty Research Institute.

Wiseman, T. P. 2014. "Popular Memory." In *Memoria Romana: Memory in Rome and Rome in Memory*, edited by Karl Galinsky. Ann Arbor: University of Michigan Press, 43–62.

Wolff, Heinrich, ed. n.d. *Die neue Reichskanzlei: 60 Bilder*.

Womersley, David. 2005. "Introduction." In Edward Gibbon, *The History of the Decline and Fall of the Roman Empire*, edited by David Womersley. London: Penguin Books, xi–cvi.

Wood, Robert. 1753. *The Ruins of Palmyra, Otherwise Tedmor, in the desart*. London: n.p.

Woodward, Christopher. 2001. *In Ruins*. New York: Pantheon Books.

Woolf, Greg. 1990. "World-Systems Analysis and the Roman Empire." *Journal of Roman Archaeology* 3:44–58.

———. 2001. "Inventing Empire in Ancient Rome." In *Empires: Perspectives from Archaeology and History*, edited by Gregory Woolf. Cambridge: Cambridge University Press.

———. 2011. *Tales of the Barbarians: Ethnography and Empire in the Roman West*. Oxford: Wiley-Blackwell.

———. 2012. *Rome: An Empire's Story*. Oxford: Oxford University Press.

Wulf-Rheidt, Ulrike. 2012. "'Die alte Herrlichkeit der Stadt des Attalos vor dem staunenden Blick hervorzaubern'—Das Pergamon-Panorama von 1886." In *Pergamon: Panorama der antiken Metropole. Begleitbuch zur Ausstellung*, edited by Ralf Grüßinger, Volker Käster, and Andreas Scholl. Berlin: Staatliche Museen zu Berlin and Michael Imhof Verlag, 410–415.

Wyke, Maria. 1997. *Projecting the Past: Ancient Rome, Cinema, and History*. New York: Routledge.

Young, Elizabeth. 2013. "Homer in a Nutshell: Virgilian Miniaturization and the Sublime." *PMLA* 128(1):57–72.

Zanker, Paul. 1988. *The Power of Images in the Age of Augustus*. Ann Arbor: University of Michigan Press.

———. 2010. *Roman Art*. Los Angeles: Getty Museum.

Zetzel, James E. G. 1997. "Rome and Its Traditions." In *The Cambridge Companion to Virgil*, edited by Charles Martindale. Cambridge: Cambridge University Press, 188–203.

Zilcosky, John. 2016. *Uncanny Encounters: Literature, Psychoanalysis, and the End of Alterity.* Evanston, IL: Northwestern University Press.

Ziogas, Ioannis. 2018. "Singing for Octavia: Vergil's Life, Marcellus' Death, and the End of Epic." *Harvard Studies in Classical Philology* 109(February).

Zimmerer, Jürgen. 2004. "Im Dienste des Imperiums: Die Geographen der Berliner Universität zwischen Kolonialwissenschaften und Ostforschung." *Jahrbuch für Universitätsgeschichte* 7:73–99.

———. 2005. "The Birth of the Ostland Out of the Spirit of Colonialism: A Postcolonial Perspective on the Nazi Policy of Conquest and Extermination." *Patterns of Prejudice* 39(2):197–219.

Zimmerman, Andrew. 2010. *Alabama in Africa: Booker T. Washington, the German Empire, and the Globalization of the New South.* Princeton: NJ: Princeton University Press.

Index

Page numbers in italics refer to figures.